Middle School 2-1
학교시험 완벽대비

KB100551

1학기 전과정
적중 100 plus

영어 기출문제집

중2
시사 | 송미정

Best Collection

구성과 특징

교과서의 주요 학습 내용을 중심으로 학습 영역별 특성에 맞춰 단계별로 다양한 학습 기회를 제공하여
단원별 학습능력 평가는 물론 중간 및 기말고사 시험 등에 완벽하게 대비할 수 있도록 내용을 구성

Words & Expressions

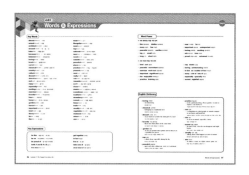

Step1　Key Words 단원별 핵심 단어 설명 및 풀이
　　　　　Key Expression 단원별 핵심 숙어 및 관용어 설명
　　　　　Word Power 반대 또는 비슷한 뜻 단어 배우기
　　　　　English Dictionary 영어로 배우는 영어 단어

Step2　실력평가 단원별 수시평가 대비 주관식, 객관식 문제풀이

Step3　서술형 대비 학업성취도 및 수행능력평가 대비 서술형 문제풀이

Conversation

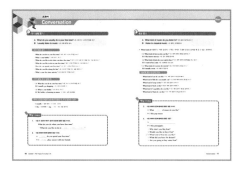

Step1　핵심 의사소통 소통에 필요한 주요 표현 방법 요약
　　　　　핵심 Check 기본적인 표현 방법 및 활용능력 확인

Step2　대화문 익히기 교과서 대화문 심층 분석 및 확인

Step3　교과서 확인학습 빈칸 채우기를 통한 문장 완성 능력 확인

Step4　기본평가 시험대비 기초 학습 능력 평가

Step5　실력평가 단원별 수시평가 대비 주관식, 객관식 문제풀이

Step6　서술형 대비 학업성취도 및 수행능력평가 대비 서술형 문제풀이

Grammar

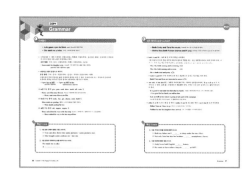

Step1　주요 문법 단원별 주요 문법 사항과 예문을 알기 쉽게 설명
　　　　　핵심 Check 기본 문법사항에 대한 이해 여부 확인

Step2　기본평가 시험대비 기초 학습 능력 평가

Step3　실력평가 단원별 수시평가 대비 주관식, 객관식 문제풀이

Step4　서술형 대비 학업성취도 및 수행능력평가 대비 서술형 문제풀이

Reading

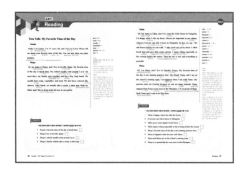

Step1　구문 분석 단원별로 제시된 문장에 대한 구문별 분석과 내용 설명
　　　　　확인문제 문장에 대한 기본적인 이해와 인지능력 확인

Step2　확인학습A 빈칸 채우기를 통한 문장 완성 능력 확인

Step3　확인학습B 제시된 우리말을 영어로 완성하여 작문 능력 키우기

Step4　실력평가 단원별 수시평가 대비 주관식, 객관식 문제풀이

Step5　서술형 대비 학업성취도 및 수행능력평가 대비 서술형 문제풀이
　　　　　교과서 구석구석 교과서에 나오는 기타 문장까지 완벽 학습

Composition

|영역별 핵심문제|

단어 및 어휘, 대화문, 문법, 독해 등 각 영역별 기출문제의 출제 유형을 분석하여 실전에 대비하고 연습할 수 있도록 문제를 배열

|단원별 예상문제|

기출문제를 분석한 후 새로운 시험 출제 경향을 더하여 새롭게 출제될 수 있는 문제를 포함하여 시험에 완벽하게 대비할 수 있도록 준비

|서술형 실전 및 창의사고력 문제|

학교 시험에서 점차 늘어나는 서술형 시험에 집중 대비하고 고득점을 취득하는데 만전을 기하기 위한 학습 코너

|단원별 모의고사|

영역별, 단계별 학습을 모두 마친 후 실전 연습을 위한 모의고사

on the textbook

교과서 파헤치기

- **단어Test1~3** 영어 단어 우리말 쓰기, 우리말을 영어 단어로 쓰기, 영영풀이에 해당하는 단어와 우리말 쓰기
- **대화문Test1~2** 대화문 빈칸 완성 및 전체 대화문 쓰기
- **본문Test1~5** 빈칸 완성, 우리말 쓰기, 문장 배열연습, 영어 작문하기 복습 등 단계별 반복 학습을 통해 교과서 지문에 대한 완벽한 습득
- **구석구석지문Test1~2** 지문 빈칸 완성 및 전문 영어로 쓰기

이책의 차례 Contents

Lesson 1

My Bucket List

 의사소통 기능

- 바람, 소망 말하기
  A: I hope I can travel to Europe this summer.
  B: That sounds great.

- 계획 묻고 답하기
  A: What are you planning to do at the school festival?
  B: I'm planning to sell snacks.

언어 형식

- 최상급
  I think the guitar has **the most beautiful** sound of all musical instruments.

- to부정사의 부사적 용법(목적)
  I will put more effort into studying math **to overcome** my weakness.

Words & Expressions

Key Words

- **adopt**[ədápt] 동 입양하다
- **band**[bænd] 명 밴드
- **book fair** 도서 박람회
- **bucket list** 버킷 리스트(달성하고 싶은 일들을 적은 목록)
- **by**[bai] 전 ~까지(는)
- **can**[kæn] 조 ~할 수 있다
- **cartoon**[kɑːrtúːn] 명 만화
- **challenging**[tʃælindʒiŋ] 형 도전적인, 힘든, 간단하지 않은
- **Chinese**[tʃàiníːz] 명 중국어 형 중국의
- **complete**[kəmpliːt] 동 완료하다, 완결하다
- **concert**[kɑ́ːnsərt] 명 콘서트
- **detective**[ditéktiv] 명 탐정, 형사
- **drama**[drɑ́ːmə] 명 드라마
- **draw**[drɔː] 동 그리다
- **Europe**[júərəp] 명 유럽, 유럽 대륙
- **exercise**[éksərsàiz] 동 운동하다 명 운동
- **experience**[ikspíəriəns] 동 경험하다 명 경험
- **famous**[féiməs] 형 유명한, 잘 알려진
- **favor**[féivər] 명 호의, 친절
- **favorite**[féivərit] 형 아주 좋아하는
- **festival**[féstəvəl] 명 축제
- **finally**[fáinəli] 부 마지막으로
- **freely**[fríːli] 부 자유롭게
- **fully**[fúlli] 부 완전히
- **goal**[goul] 명 목표
- **hope**[houp] 동 희망하다, 바라다 명 희망
- **introduce**[ìntrədjúːs] 동 소개하다
- **missing**[mísiŋ] 형 없어진, 분실한
- **most**[moust] 부 가장
- **musical instrument** 악기
- **national**[nǽʃənl] 형 국가의, 국민의
- **overcome**[òuvərkʌ́m] 동 극복하다
- **plan**[plæn] 명 계획 동 계획하다
- **pleased**[pliːzd] 형 기쁜
- **ride**[raid] 동 타다
- **right**[rait] 부 바로
- **save**[seiv] 동 구하다, 아끼다
- **sell**[sel] 동 팔다, 판매하다
- **someday**[sʌ́mdei] 부 언젠가
- **special**[spéʃəl] 형 특별한
- **spend**[spend] 동 쓰다, 소비하다
- **start**[stɑːrt] 동 시작하다
- **stay**[stei] 동 머무르다, 지내다
- **subject**[sʌ́bdʒikt] 명 과목
- **surprise**[sərpráiz] 동 놀라게 하다
- **talk**[tɔːk] 동 말하다
- **walk**[wɔːk] 동 걷게 하다, 데리고 가다
- **wash**[wɑʃ] 동 씻다
- **weak**[wiːk] 형 약한
- **weakness**[wíːknis] 명 약점
- **worry**[wʌ́ːri] 동 걱정하다
- **writer**[ráitər] 명 작가

Key Expressions

- **ask for help**: 도움을 청하다
- **be planning to** 동사원형: ~할 계획이다
- **be ready to** 동사원형: ~할 준비가 되다
- **be willing to** 동사원형: 기꺼이 ~하다
- **by the end of** ~: ~ 말까지
- **do a favor**: 호의를 베풀다
- **for a while**: 잠깐
- **get better**: (병·상황 등이) 나아지다
- **get interested in**: ~에 관심을 갖게 되다
- **get into**: ~에 흥미를 갖게 되다
- **get one's hair cut**: ~의 머리를 자르다
- **go back to** ~: ~으로 돌아가다
- **go on a tour**: 관광하다, 여행을 떠나다
- **how to** 동사원형: ~하는 방법
- **make a friend**: 친구를 사귀다
- **make an effort**: 노력하다
- **put effort into** ~: ~에 노력을 들이다, 힘들이다
- **share A with B**: A를 B와 나누다[공유하다]
- **stand in line**: 줄을 서서 기다리다
- **take a picture with**: ~와 사진을 찍다
- **take care of**: ~을 돌보다
- **throw away**: ~을 버리다, ~을 던지다
- **would like to** 동사원형: ~하고 싶다

Word Power

※ 서로 반대되는 뜻을 가진 단어
- □ **sell** (팔다) ↔ **buy** (사다)
- □ **weak** (약한) ↔ **strong** (강한)
- □ **special** (특별한) ↔ **general** (일반적인)

- □ **finish** (끝내다) ↔ **begin** (시작하다)
- □ **weakness** (약함, 약점) ↔ **strength** (힘, 강점)
- □ **hope** (희망) ↔ **despair** (절망)

※ 서로 비슷한 뜻을 가진 단어
- □ **complete** (완료하다, 완결하다) = **finish** (끝내다)
- □ **finally** (마지막으로) = **lastly** (마지막으로, 끝으로)
- □ **goal** (목표) = **aim** (목표)
- □ **pleased** (기쁜) = **glad** (기쁜)

- □ **famous** (유명한, 잘 알려진) = **well-known** (유명한, 잘 알려진)
- □ **fully** (완전히) = **completely** (완전히, 완벽하게)
- □ **missing** (없어진, 행방불명의) = **lost** (잃은, 분실한)
- □ **start** (시작하다) = **begin** (시작하다)

English Dictionary

- □ **book fair** 도서 박람회
  → an event at which people or businesses show and sell their books
  사람들이나 기업들이 그들의 책을 보여주고 파는 행사

- □ **band** 밴드
  → a group of musicians, especially a group that plays popular music
  음악가들의 그룹, 특히 대중적인 음악을 연주하는 그룹

- □ **challenging** 도전적인
  → difficult in an interesting or enjoyable way
  흥미롭거나 재미있는 방식으로 어려운

- □ **complete** 완료하다, 완결하다
  → to finish doing or making something, especially when it has taken a long time
  특히 긴 시간이 걸릴 때 무엇인가를 하거나 만드는 행위를 끝내다

- □ **detective** 탐정
  → someone whose job is to discover what has happened in a crime or other situation and to find the people involved
  범죄나 다른 상황에서 무슨 일이 일어났는지 발견하고 관련된 사람들을 찾는 것이 직업인 사람

- □ **draw** 그리다
  → to produce a picture of something using a pencil, pen, etc.
  연필이나 펜을 사용해서 어떤 것의 그림을 만들다

- □ **favor** 호의, 친절
  → something that you do for someone in order to help them or be kind to them
  누군가를 돕거나 친절하게 하기 위해서 하는 어떤 것

- □ **freely** 자유롭게
  → without anyone stopping or limiting something
  어떤 것을 멈추거나 제한하는 사람 없이

- □ **fully** 완전히
  → completely
  완전히

- □ **goal** 목표
  → something that you hope to achieve in the future
  미래에 달성하기를 바라는 어떤 것

- □ **most** 가장
  → to a greater degree or more times than anything else
  다른 어떤 것보다 더 많은 정도나 더 많은 횟수

- □ **overcome** 극복하다
  → to successfully control a feeling or problem
  감정이나 문제를 성공적으로 통제하다

- □ **right** 바로
  → exactly in a particular position or place
  정확히 특정한 위치나 장소에

- □ **save** 구하다, 살리다
  → to make someone or something safe from danger, harm, or destruction
  위험, 해 또는 파괴로부터 어떤 사람이나 사물을 안전하게 만들다

- □ **someday** 언젠가
  → at an unknown time in the future, especially a long time in the future
  미래 특히 긴 시간 후의 미래의 어떤 알지 못하는 시기에

- □ **spend** 쓰다, 소비하다
  → to use your money to pay for goods or services
  상품이나 서비스에 돈을 사용하다

01 다음 문장의 빈칸에 알맞은 것은?

> They were recommended to _____ dogs from animal shelters instead of buying them from pet stores.

① adopt
② adapt
③ accompany
④ admit
⑤ acquire

02 밑줄 친 부분의 의미가 나머지 넷과 다른 하나는?

① Mike wants to learn Chinese.
② This Chinese food matches well with chicken soup.
③ The number of schools which teach Chinese is increasing.
④ His name means "orange" in Chinese.
⑤ I study Chinese day and night.

03 다음 제시된 단어를 사용하여 자연스러운 문장을 만들 수 없는 것은?

> bucket list   band   overcome   introduce

① She can _____ herself in Spanish.
② I want to see my favorite _____ in a concert.
③ Did you complete your _____ for this year?
④ A woman _____ two cats.
⑤ I hope I can _____ my weakness.

서답형

04 다음 빈칸에 들어갈 알맞은 단어를 〈보기〉에서 찾아 쓰시오.

> ┤ 보기 ├
> in   to   for   of

(1) I talked with my friends _____ a while.
(2) People are standing _____ line to buy tickets.

중요

05 다음 중 밑줄 친 부분의 뜻풀이가 바르지 않은 것은?

① She was standing right in the middle of the room. (오른쪽에)
② The band was playing old Beatles songs. (밴드)
③ It's important to exercise regularly. (운동하다)
④ What's your favorite color? (아주 좋아하는)
⑤ Christmas is one of the famous festivals. (축제)

06 밑줄 친 부분과 의미가 가장 가까운 것은?

> Teamwork is required in order to achieve the aim.

① effort
② turn
③ cause
④ goal
⑤ result

서답형

07 다음 주어진 우리말에 맞게 빈칸을 채우시오.

(1) Could you do me _____ _____?
(부탁 좀 들어줄래?)
(2) I _____ the cake _____ _____.
(나는 케이크를 그들과 나누었다.)

01 다음 빈칸에 알맞은 단어를 〈보기〉에서 골라 쓰시오. (형태 변화 가능)

┌─── 보기 ├───
ask   get   take   make

(1) I know you don't like her, but please _____ an effort to be polite.

(2) Who's _____ care of the dog while you're away?

(3) Sheila _____ interested in starting her own business these days.

(4) Some people think it is difficult to _____ for help.

02 다음 대화의 빈칸에 우리말과 일치하도록 알맞은 말을 쓰시오.

A: What's wrong? You look worried.
B: My son is sick. He is in the hospital.
A: I _____ _____ son _____ better soon.
(나는 너의 아들이 곧 나아지기를 바라.)

03 우리말에 맞게 주어진 단어를 바르게 배열하시오.

(1) 나는 그가 하는 말을 완전히 인정한다.
(accept, he, I, says, what, fully)
➡ _____

(2) 그 집은 바로 너의 앞에 있다.
(is, right, of, the house, front, you, in)
➡ _____

(3) 그것은 오직 특별한 상황에서만 사용되었다.
(only, situations, was, special, it, on, used)
➡ _____

(4) 좋지 못한 빛은 약한 식물을 만든다.
(weak, poor, plants, produces, light)
➡ _____

[04~05] 다음 영영풀이에 해당하는 말을 주어진 철자로 시작하여 쓰시오.

04
f_____: without anyone stopping or limiting something

05
c_____: difficult in an interesting or enjoyable way

06 다음 빈칸에 공통으로 들어갈 말을 쓰시오.

• How much are they willing _____ pay?
• He was always ready _____ help us.

07 다음 〈보기〉에서 빈칸에 공통으로 들어갈 단어를 골라 쓰시오.

┌─── 보기 ├───
experience effect exercise enjoy

(1) • I _____ for half an hour in the morning.
• Most people need to do more _____.

(2) • Children need to _____ things for themselves in order to learn from them.
• I had some _____ in fashion design.

Conversation

1 바람, 소망 말하기

A   I hope I can travel to Europe this summer. 나는 이번 여름에 유럽 여행을 할 수 있기를 바라.

B   That sounds great. 거거 좋은데.

■ 'I hope (that) 주어+동사'로 소망을 표현할 수 있다. 어떤 일이 일어나기를 바랄 때, 동사 hope를 사용하여 소망을 표현할 수 있다.

바람, 소망 말하기

- I hope (that) 주어 (can) 동사 ~.
- I hope to 동사원형 ~. (나는 ~하기를 바란다.)
- I hope for 명사 ~. (나는 ~을 바란다.)
- I want to 동사원형 ~. (나는 ~하기를 원한다.)
- I want 목적어 to 동사원형 ~. (나는 목적어가 ~하기를 원한다.)

- I hope to get a good score. (나는 좋은 점수를 받기를 바라.)
- I'm hoping for good weather. (나는 좋은 날씨를 바라고 있어.)
- I want to wake up early. (나는 일찍 일어나기를 원해.)
- I want you to keep a diary every day. (나는 네가 매일 일기 쓰기를 원해.)

핵심 Check

1. 다음 우리말과 일치하도록 빈칸에 알맞은 말을 쓰시오.

   G: What's your plan for this year? (올해 뭐 할 계획이니?)

   B: I _____ that _____ many books. (나는 많은 책을 읽을 수 읽기를 바라.)

   G: _____ year. (나는 올해는 좋은 성적을 얻기를 바라.)

   B: You will. Don't worry. (그럴 거야. 걱정하지 마.)

2. 다음 주어진 단어를 이용하여 대화를 완성하시오.

   A: _____ (learn, hope, how, swim, to, can)

   B: That sounds great.

   A: I have a lot of homework.

   B: _____ (it, that, hope, soon, finish)

2 계획 묻고 답하기

A What are you planning to do at the school festival? 학교 축제에서 뭐 할 계획이니?

B I'm planning to sell snacks. 간식을 팔 계획이야.

■ 'I'm planning to 동사원형 ~.'은 '~할 계획이다'라는 뜻으로, 앞으로의 계획이나 의도에 대해 말할 때 사용하는 표현으로 to 다음에는 동사원형이 온다.

계획 말하기

• I'm planning to 동사원형 ~. (나는 ~할 계획이야.)
• I'm going to 동사원형 ~. (나는 ~할 거야.)
• I'll 동사원형 ~. (나는 ~할 거야.)

• A: I'll go to the party tonight. (나는 오늘 밤 파티에 갈 거야.)
  B: Me, too. I'm going to wear a yellow dress. (나도 그래. 나는 노란색 드레스를 입을 거야.)

계획 묻기

• Be동사 주어 planning to 동사원형 ~?
• 의문사 be동사 주어 planning to 동사원형 ~?
• Be 동사 주어 going to 동사원형 ~?
• 의문사 be동사 주어 going to 동사원형 ~?
• Will 주어 동사원형 ~?
• 의문사 will 주어 동사원형 ~?

• A: Are you planning to eat out tonight? (너 오늘 밤 외식할 거니?)
  B: Yes, I am. (응. 그래.)
• A: Where are you planning to eat out tonight? (너 오늘 밤 어디서 외식할 거니?)
  B: I am planning to go to the Italian restaurant. (나는 이탈리아 식당에 갈 거야.)

핵심 Check

3. 다음 주어진 단어를 이용하여 대화를 완성하시오.

   A: I'm going to go to the zoo this Saturday. How about you?

   B: _____ (planning, games, friends)

4. 다음 주어진 단어를 배열하여 대화를 완성하시오.

   A: _____ (meet, where, they, are, to, planning)

   B: They are planning to meet at the airport.

Listen and Speak 1-B

B: Hana, ❶it's your birthday today. Happy birthday!

G: Thank you.

B: ❷What do you want ❸for your birthday?

G: ❹I hope I get a new computer.

B: 하나야, 오늘은 너의 생일이야. 축하해!

G: 고마워.

B: 생일 선물로 뭘 원하니?

G: 새 컴퓨터를 받길 바라.

❶ it: 날짜를 나타내는 비인칭 주어 / 날씨, 시간, 요일, 날짜, 거리, 명암 등을 나타낼 때 it을 주어로 사용.

❷ What: '무엇'의 의미로 의문대명사 / want는 '원하다'라는 의미의 일반동사로, '의문사+do[does/did]+주어+동사원형 ～?'으로 의문문 형식이 사용됨

❸ for: ～을 위한

❹ I hope (that) I get a new computer. / get: 얻다, 획득하다

Check(√) True or False

(1) Today is Hana's birthday.   T ☐ F ☐

(2) She wants to get a new computer for her birthday present.   T ☐ F ☐

B: Kate, do you have any special plans for the new school year?

G: ❶I'm planning to study one new Chinese word every day.

B: I didn't know you ❷were interested in Chinese. When did you start studying Chinese?

G: Only last month. But now I can introduce ❸myself in Chinese.

B: That's amazing! How did you ❹get so into Chinese?

G: It's because I'm a big fan of Chinese dramas. I hope I can soon watch them in Chinese and understand what they're saying.

B: Well, ❺keep studying hard, and I'm sure you'll be able to do it someday.

G: I hope so. What about you? What are your plans for this year?

B: Let me think. Hmm.... Getting a good grade in every subject? As usual.

G: Hahaha.

B: Kate, 새 학년을 맞이하여 특별한 계획이 있니?

G: 나는 매일 새로운 중국어 단어 하나를 공부할 계획이야.

B: 나는 네가 중국어에 관심이 있는지 몰랐어. 언제 중국어 공부를 시작했니?

G: 겨우 지난달에. 그러나 지금은 중국어로 내 소개를 할 수 있어.

B: 놀라워! 어떻게 중국어에 그토록 관심을 가지게 되었어?

G: 중국 드라마의 열렬한 팬이기 때문이야. 나는 곧 드라마를 중국어로 보고, 무슨 말을 하는지 이해할 수 있기를 바라.

B: 음, 계속 열심히 공부하면 언젠가는 그렇게 할 수 있을 거야.

G: 그랬으면 좋겠어. 너는 언제? 올해 계획이 뭐니?

B: 생각 좀 해보고. 음.... 모든 과목에서 좋은 성적 얻기? 평소처럼.

G: 하하하.

❶ be planning to 동사원형: ～할 계획이다

❷ be interested in 명사/동명사: ～에 흥미[관심]가 있다 / Chinese: 중국어; 중국의

❸ 주어(I)와 목적어가 같기 때문에 재귀대명사 myself를 사용함.

❹ get into: ～에 관심을 갖게 되다

❺ keep Ving: ～을 계속하다, 유지하다

Check(√) True or False

(3) Kate started studying Chinese last year.   T ☐ F ☐

(4) Kate likes to see Chinese movies.   T ☐ F ☐

Listen and Speak 1

G: ❶What are you doing?

B: ❷I'm making my wish list for the new school year.

G: That ❸sounds cool! What's the first thing on your list?

B: I hope I ❹ make a lot of new friends.

❶ 무엇을 하고 있는지 묻는 표현
❷ be+동사원형ing: ∼하는 중이다
❸ sound+형용사: ∼하게 들리다
❹ make friends: 친구를 사귀다 / a lot of: 많은 (= lots of = many)

Listen and Speak 1

G: ❶How was your English class?

B: ❷It was fun! We ❸wrote down our dreams for the future.

G: Oh, did you? So tell me. What's ❹yours?

B: Well, first. ❺I hope I become a rock star someday.

❶ How was ∼?: '∼은 어땠니?'라는 의미로, 과거의 경험에 대해 느낀 점을 묻는 표현
❷ It은 앞 문장의 your English class를 받는 인칭대명사
❸ write down: ∼을 적다
❹ yours = your dream for the future
❺ I hope (that) 주어 동사: 주어가 ∼하는 것을 바라다 / become+명사: ∼가 되다 / someday: 언젠가

Listen and Speak 2

B: ❶What are you planning to do tomorrow?

G: I'm planning to go to ❷the book fair with Jimmy. ❸Would you like to join us?

B: Sure. ❹What time are you going to meet?

G: ❺At 3:00 in front of the school cafeteria.

❶ What are you planning to 동사원형 ∼?: 너는 무엇을 할 계획이니?
❷ book fair: 도서 박람회 / with: ∼와 함께
❸ would like to 동사원형: ∼하고 싶다, ∼하기를 바라다(= want to 동사원형)
❹ What time: 몇 시에 / be going to 동사원형: ∼할 것이다, ∼할 예정이다
❺ at+시간: ∼시에 / in front of+명사: ∼ 앞에서 / cafeteria: 카페테리아, 구내식당

Listen and Speak 2

G: ❶What are you planning to do tomorrow?

B: Well, I'm not ❷sure.

G: Then ❸ how about going to a movie with me?

B: That sounds wonderful.

❶ 미래의 계획을 묻는 표현 (= What are you going to do tomorrow? = What will you do tomorrow?)
❷ sure: 확실한
❸ How about 동사원형ing ∼?: '∼하는 건 어때?'라는 의미로 권유할 때 사용 (= What about 동사원형ing) ∼?/ go to a movie: 영화를 보러 가다

Listen and Speak 2

G: Jack! ❶Can you do me a favor?

B: Yes, what is ❷it?

G: ❸I'm planning to buy a new bike tomorrow. Can you ❹help me choose one?

B: Sure, I'd love to.

❶ 부탁하는 표현 / favor: 부탁
❷ it은 앞 문장의 a favor를 받는 인칭대명사
❸ be planning to 동사원형 ∼?: ∼할 계획이다(= be going to 동사원형 = will 동사원형)
❹ help 목적어 (to)동사원형: 목적어가 ∼하는 것을 돕다

Wrap Up

G: Hi, Brian.

B: Hi, Somin. It's Friday! Are you planning to do ❶anything special this weekend?

G: Well, I'm planning to ❷visit my grandmother. She is sick.

B: Oh, ❸I'm sorry to hear that. I hope she ❹gets better soon.

G: Thank you. What about you? What's your plan?

B: I'm planning to ❺wash my dog.

❶ -thing, -one, -body로 끝나는 부정대명사는 형용사가 후치 수식 / this weekend: 이번 주말에
❷ visit: 방문하다
❸ 상대방에게 유감을 나타내는 표현
❹ get better: (병·상황 등이) 나아지다
❺ wash: 씻기다

• 다음 우리말과 일치하도록 빈칸에 알맞은 말을 쓰시오.

Listen & Speak 1 A

G: I _____ I _____ good grades this year.

B: You will. Don't _____.

해석

1. G: 난 올해 좋은 성적을 얻길 바라.
   B: 그럴 거야. 걱정하지 마.

Listen & Speak 1 B

1. B: Hana, _____ your birthday today. Happy birthday!

   G: Thank you.

   B: _____ do you _____ _____ your birthday?

   G: _____ _____ _____ _____ a new computer.

2. G: _____ are you doing?

   B: _____ _____ my wish list for the new school year.

   G: That sounds cool! What's _____ _____ thing on your list?

   B: I _____ I _____ a lot of new friends.

3. G: _____ was your English class?

   B: _____ _____ fun! We _____ down our dreams _____ the future.

   G: Oh, did you? So _____ me. What's _____?

   B: Well, first, I _____ _____ become a rock star _____.

1. B: 하나야. 오늘은 너의 생일이야. 축하해!
   G: 고마워.
   B: 생일 선물로 뭘 원하니?
   G: 새 컴퓨터를 받길 바라.

2. G: 뭐 하고 있니?
   B: 나는 새 학년을 맞이하여 소원 목록을 만들고 있어.
   G: 멋지다! 목록의 첫 번째는 뭐니?
   B: 나는 새로운 친구들을 많이 사귈 수 있기를 바라.

3. G: 영어 수업은 어땠니?
   B: 재밌었어! 우리는 미래에 대한 꿈을 적었어.
   G: 오, 그랬니? 나에게 말해줘. 너의 꿈은 뭐니?
   B: 음, 우선, 나는 내가 언젠가 록 스타가 되길 바라.

Listen & Speak 1 C

1. A: I _____ _____ can travel to Europe _____ summer.

   B: That _____ great.

2. A: I hope I can see my grandmother.

   B: That _____ great.

3. A: I _____ _____ _____ _____ how _____ swim.

   B: That sounds great.

1. A: 나는 이번 여름에 유럽으로 여행을 할 수 있기를 바라.
   B: 좋은데.

2. A: 나는 할머니를 뵐 수 있기를 바라.
   B: 좋은데.

3. A: 나는 수영하는 법을 배울 수 있기를 바라.
   B: 좋은데.

Everyday English 2. A Function Practice 2

G: _____ _____ _____ _____ _____ do tomorrow?

B: I'm _____ _____ _____ my hair cut.

G: 내일 뭐 할 계획이니?
B: 이발을 할 계획이야.

Everyday English 2 – B Listening Activity

1. B: What are you _____ _____ _____ _____?

   G: _____ _____ to go to the _____ _____ _____ Jimmy. Would you _____ _____ join us?

   B: Sure. _____ _____ are you going to meet?

   G: _____ 3:00 _____ _____ _____ the school cafeteria.

2. G: What _____ _____ _____ to do tomorrow?

   B: Well, I'm _____ sure.

   G: Then how _____ _____ to a movie _____ me?

   B: That sounds wonderful.

3. G: Jack! _____ you do me _____ _____?

   B: Yes, what is it?

   G: I'm planning _____ _____ a new bike _____. Can you _____ me _____ _____ _____?

   B: Sure, I'd love to.

1. B: 내일 뭐 할 거니?
   G: 지미랑 도서 박람회에 갈 계획이야. 같이 갈래?
   B: 물론이지. 몇 시에 만날 거니?
   G: 학교 식당 앞에서 3시에.

2. G: 내일 뭐 할 계획이니?
   B: 글쎄, 잘 모르겠어.
   G: 그럼, 나랑 영화 보러 가는 게 어때?
   B: 좋아.

3. G: 잭! 부탁 좀 들어줄래?
   B: 응, 뭔데?
   G: 내일 새 자전거를 살 계획이야. 하나 고르는 걸 도와줄 수 있니?
   B: 좋아. 그러고 싶어.

Listen & Speak 2 C

1. A: What are you planning to _____ _____ the school festival?

   B: I'm planning _____ _____ snacks.

2. A: What _____ _____ _____ _____ _____ do at the school festival?

   B: I'm planning _____ _____ _____ _____ show.

3. A: _____ _____ _____ _____ to do at the school festival?

   B: I'm planning _____ _____ _____ _____ _____ _____.

1. A: 학교 축제에서 뭐 할 계획이니?
   B: 간식을 팔 계획이야.

2. A: 학교 축제에서 뭐 할 계획이니?
   B: 마술 쇼를 할 계획이야.

3. A: 학교 축제에서 뭐 할 계획이니?
   B: 그룹으로 춤 출 계획이야.

01 다음 대화의 빈칸에 공통으로 들어갈 말은?

> A: What are you _____ do at the school festival?
> B: I'm _____ sell snacks.

① planning   ② making   ③ going

④ planning to   ⑤ taking to

[02~03] 다음 대화를 읽고 물음에 답하시오.

> B: Hana, it's your birthday today. Happy birthday!
> B: Thank you.
> B: _____ do you want for your birthday?
> G: I hope I get a new computer.

02 위 대화의 빈칸에 알맞은 것을 고르시오.

① What   ② What computer   ③ When

④ How   ⑤ What time

03 위 대화의 밑줄 친 부분과 바꾸어 쓸 수 <u>없는</u> 것을 <u>모두</u> 고르시오.

① I hope that I get a new computer.

② I hope to get a new computer.

③ I hope getting a new computer.

④ I want to get a new computer.

⑤ I want you to get a new computer.

04 다음 대화의 빈칸에 알맞은 것을 고르시오.

> A: _____
> B: I'm planning to dance in a group.

① What are you doing at the school festival?

② What are you planning to do at the school festival?

③ What did you do at the school festival?

④ What can you do at the school festival?

⑤ What are you looking for at the school festival?

01 주어진 문장 다음에 이어질 문장의 순서로 알맞은 것은?

> Hi, Somin. It's Friday! Are you planning to do anything special this weekend?

> (A) Thank you. What about you? What's your plan?
> (B) Well, I'm planning to visit my grandmother. She is sick.
> (C) Oh, I'm sorry to hear that. I hope she gets better soon.

① (A) - (C) - (B) 　② (B) - (A) - (C)
③ (B) - (C) - (A) 　④ (C) - (A) - (B)
⑤ (C) - (B) - (A)

[02~03] 다음 대화를 읽고 물음에 답하시오.

G: What are you doing?
B: I (A)_____ my wish list for the new school year.
G: That sounds (B)_____! What's the first thing on your list?
B: (C)I hope making lot of new friends.

02 빈칸 (A)와 (B)에 알맞은 것으로 짝지어진 것을 고르시오.

① make – cool
② make – well
③ am making – cool
④ am making – well
⑤ was making – cool

03 밑줄 친 (C)에서 어색한 부분을 찾아 고치시오. (2개)

➡ (1) _____
　 (2) _____

04 대화의 순서를 바르게 배열하시오.

> (A) At 3:00 in front of the school cafeteria.
> (B) What are you planning to do tomorrow?
> (C) I'm planning to go to the book fair with Jimmy. Would you like to join us?
> (D) Sure. What time are you going to meet?

➡ _____

[05~07] 다음 대화를 읽고 물음에 답하시오.

G: (A)_____
B: ①It was fun! ②We wrote down our dreams for the future.
G: ③Oh, did you? ④So tell me. ⑤What's your?
B: Well, first. (B)나는 내가 언젠가 록 스타가 되길 바라. (become, hope, someday)

05 위 대화의 빈칸 (A)에 알맞은 것은?

① How was your English class?
② What do you want to be?
③ Will you write down your dream?
④ Did you make your list?
⑤ How about taking an English class?

06 위 대화의 ①~⑤ 중 어색한 부분을 찾아 번호를 쓰고 고치시오.

_____ ➡ _____

07 위 대화의 밑줄 친 우리말 (B)를 주어진 단어를 이용해 영작하시오.

➡ _____

[08~11] 다음 대화를 읽고 물음에 답하시오.

B: Kate, do you have any special plans for the new school year? (①)
G: (A)나는 매일 새로운 중국어 단어 하나를 공부할 계획이야.(every day, to, Chinese, study, one, planning)
B: I didn't know you were interested in Chinese. (②)
G: Only last month. But now I can introduce myself in Chinese. (③)
B: That's amazing! How did you get so into Chinese?
G: It's because I'm a big fan of Chinese dramas. I hope I can soon watch them in Chinese and understand (B)[that / what] they're saying. (④)
B: Well, keep (C)[studying / to study] hard, and I'm sure you'll be able to do it someday. (⑤)
G: I hope so. What about you? (D)_____
B: Let me think. Hmm.... Getting a good grade in every subject? As usual.
G: Hahaha.

08 위 대화의 ①~⑤ 중 다음 주어진 말이 들어갈 알맞은 곳은?

> When did you start studying Chinese?

①   ②   ③   ④   ⑤

09 밑줄 친 (A)의 우리말을 주어진 단어를 이용해 영작하시오.

➡ _____

10 괄호 (B)와 (C)에서 알맞은 말을 고르시오.

➡ _____

11 빈칸 (D)에 알맞은 말을 고르시오.

① Did you get a good grade?
② Are you going to make plans?
③ What was your plan for last month?
④ What are your plans for this year?
⑤ Where are you planning to go?

[12~13] 다음 대화를 읽고 물음에 답하시오.

B: Hana, it's your birthday today. Happy birthday!
G: Thank you.
B: 생일 선물로 뭘 원하니?
G: I hope I get a new computer.

12 주어진 우리말과 같도록 영작할 때 두 번째와 다섯 번째에 오는 단어를 쓰시오. (총 7단어)

➡ _____

13 위의 대화에서 알 수 없는 것을 고르시오. (2개)

① Is it Hana's birthday today?
② What does the boy want to get?
③ What did the boy plan to buy as Hana's present?
④ Whose birthday is today?
⑤ What does the girl hope to get?

01 다음 그림을 보고 주어진 단어를 이용하여 답하시오.

(1) What are you planning to do at the school festival? (in, planning, to, a group)

➡ _____

(2) What's your dream for this year? (summer, hope, travel, to, can, Europe)

➡ _____

[02~03] 다음 대화를 읽고 물음에 답하시오.

A: Do you have any special plans for this year?
B: I hope I can take pictures with my favorite singer.
A: How do you plan to (A)do that?
B: I'm planning go to one of his concert.

02 (A)가 가리키고 있는 내용을 본문에서 찾아 영어로 쓰시오.

➡ _____

03 밑줄 친 문장에서 어색한 부분을 찾아 고치시오. (2개)

➡ _____ , _____

[04~06] 다음 대화를 읽고 물음에 답하시오.

B: ①Kate, did you have any special plans for the new school year?
G: ②I'm planning to study one new Chinese words every day.
B: 나는 네가 중국어에 관심이 있는지 몰랐어. (in, didn't, interested) ③When did you start studying Chinese?
G: ④Only last month. ⑤But now I can introduce myself in Chinese.

04 위 대화의 ①~⑤ 중 어색한 부분을 찾아 쓰고 고치시오.

_____ ➡ _____

05 밑줄 친 우리말을 주어진 단어를 이용해 영작하시오. (8 words)

➡ _____

06 위 대화의 내용과 일치하도록 빈칸을 채우시오.

Kate _____ _____ to study one new Chinese _____ every day. She started _____ _____ Chinese _____ month. She can _____ introduce _____ _____ Chinese.

Grammar

① 최상급

This is **the largest** room in the house. 이것이 그 집에서 가장 큰 방이다.

Harry is **the tallest** player in my team. Harry는 내 팀에서 가장 키가 큰 선수이다.

■ 최상급

- 비교급은 서로 다른 두 대상이 가진 공통된 특징을 비교하는 표현인데 반하여 최상급은 여러 비교 대상 중에서 (셋 이상을 비교) 어떤 성질이 가장 뛰어나다는 것을 나타낸다.
- '최상급+명사'의 형태로 '~중 가장 …한'으로 해석하며 일반적으로 '~에서'라고 범위를 나타내는 말을 함께 쓴다.
- 형용사의 최상급은 정관사 the를 사용하지만, 부사의 최상급에서는 정관사 the를 생략하는 것이 일반적이며 범위를 나타낼 때에는 보통 'of+비교 대상의 복수 명사' 또는 'in+장소, 단체 등의 단수 명사'를 사용한다.

• 비교급 · 최상급 만드는 법

조건	비교급	최상급	예시
대부분의 1음절, 2음절 형용사 / 부사	원급 + -er	원급 + -est	long - longer- longest tall - taller - tallest
'-e'로 끝나는 단어	원급 + -r	원급 + -st	large - larger - largest
'자음+y'로 끝나는 2음절 단어	y → i + -er	y → i + -est	busy - busier - busiest early - earlier - earliest
'단모음+단자음'으로 끝나는 1음절 단어	마지막 자음을 한 번 더 쓰고 -er	마지막 자음을 한 번 더 쓰고 -est	big - bigger - biggest hot - hotter - hottest
3음절 이상의 단어 및 '-ing, -ous, -ful' 등으로 끝나는 단어	more + 원급	most + 원급	famous - more famous – most famous
불규칙하게 변하는 단어 (불규칙 변화형)	many - more - most　　little - less - least good - better - best　　bad - worse - worst well - better - best		

Anne is **the cleverest** daughter. (Anne이 가장 영리한 딸이다.)

It was **the best** movie. (그것은 최고의 영화였다.)

핵심 Check

1. 괄호 안에서 알맞은 단어를 고르시오.

　(1) He is (the tallest / tallest) student in his class.

　(2) It's the (longer / longest) bridge in the world.

　(3) Olivia wants to have (the coolest / the most cool) smartphone.

② to부정사의 부사적 용법 (목적)

Jack went to the library **to borrow** some books.

Jack은 책을 몇 권 빌리러 도서관에 갔다.

He went to the gym **to exercise**. 그는 운동하기 위해 체육관에 갔다.

- 'to+동사원형' 형태의 to부정사가 부사처럼 쓰여, 목적의 의미를 나타내며 '~하기 위해서, ~하러'라는 의미를 갖는다. 이외에도 부사적 용법의 to부정사는 '(감정의) 원인', '조건', '결과', '이유나 판단의 근거' 등을 나타내며 형용사를 수식한다.

- 목적의 뜻을 보다 분명하게 하기 위하여 to부정사 앞에 in order나 so as를 쓰기도 한다.

- **to부정사의 부사적 용법**

  (1) 원인

  Harry was happy **to win** the contest. (Harry는 그 대회에서 우승을 해서 기뻤다.) (to win the contest가 was happy의 원인을 나타낸다.)

  (2) 이유나 판단의 근거

  Mike must be foolish **to do** such a thing. (그런 짓을 하다니 Mike는 멍청함에 틀림없다.) (to do such a thing 이 be foolish로 판단하는 근거를 나타낸다.)

  (3) 결과

  Her grandmother lived **to be** 100. (그녀의 할머니는 100세까지 사셨다.) (to be 100이 동사 lived의 결과를 나타낸다.)

  (4) 형용사 수식

  Advertisements should be easy **to understand**. (광고는 이해하기 쉬워야 한다.) (to understand가 형용사 easy를 수식한다.)

핵심 Check

2. 괄호 안에서 알맞은 것을 고르시오.

   (1) She waved her hand (to say / say) good bye.

   (2) Lindsey turned on her computer (doing / to do) her homework.

   (3) John visited Korea (to write / writes) a report on K-pop.

3. 다음 우리말에 맞게 괄호 안의 단어를 바르게 배열하시오.

   • 그는 과학자가 되기 위해 과학을 열심히 공부한다.

   (he, to, very, a scientist, hard, science, be, studies)

   ➡ _____

01 다음 문장에서 어법상 <u>어색한</u> 부분을 찾아 바르게 고쳐 쓰시오.

(1) Mt. Halla is highest mountain in South Korea.

_____ ➡ _____

(2) This sparrow is the most small bird at this park.

_____ ➡ _____

(3) You have to be diligent being a cook.

_____ ➡ _____

(4) She exercises hard in order to not gain weight.

_____ ➡ _____

02 다음 〈보기〉의 단어를 이용하여 문장을 완성하시오.

┌─ 보기 ┤

order　cheap　boring　meet　thin　healthy

(1) This is _____ _____ wallet of all.

(2) It is _____ _____ _____ book I've read.

(3) How much is _____ _____ laptop here?

(4) My mother went to the school _____ _____ my English teacher.

(5) We need to relax _____ _____ _____ _____ healthy.

03 다음 우리말에 맞게 주어진 단어를 바르게 배열하시오. (필요하면 어형을 바꿀 것)

(1) 세 자매 중에서 Alice가 가장 예쁘다. (pretty / three / Alice / the / sisters / of / the / is)

➡ _____

(2) 일 년 중에 가장 바쁜 날이 언제인가요? (year / when / day / of / busy / the / the / is)

➡ _____

(3) 그는 한국 TV 드라마를 보기 위해 한국어를 열심히 공부한다. (Korean / Korean / as / he / TV dramas / so / hard / watch / study / to)

➡ _____

(4) 나는 첫 기차를 놓치지 않으려고 일찍 일어났다. (early / train / I / to / not / get up / the / in / miss / first / order)

➡ _____

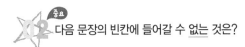

01 다음 빈칸에 알맞은 것은?

> This is _____ one of my blouses.

① expensive
② expensiver
③ more expensive
④ most expensive
⑤ the most expensive

02 다음 문장의 빈칸에 들어갈 수 <u>없는</u> 것은?

> This hamburger is _____ one of all the hamburgers.

① the cheapest
② the thickest
③ the most special
④ the most largest
⑤ the most delicious

03 다음 빈칸에 알맞은 말이 바르게 짝지어진 것은?

> • That is _____ one of the programs.
> • He was _____ player in this team.

① the most silliest - the most valuable
② the silliest – the most valuable
③ the silliest – the valuablest
④ silliest – valuablest
⑤ silly – valuable

서답형
04 다음 문장에서 어법상 틀린 부분을 바르게 고쳐 다시 쓰시오.

> He is a fastest swimmer in my team.

➡ _____

서답형
05 괄호 안에서 알맞은 것을 고르시오.

(1) This is going to be (the most / most) interesting event today.
(2) He was one of the greatest men (in / of) the world.
(3) What can we do (to celebrate / celebrate) her?
(4) We met yesterday (to go / going) shopping together.
(5) His father lived (be / to be) 90.
(6) Einstein grew up (be / to be) a world famous scientist.

06 다음 〈보기〉의 밑줄 친 부분과 용법이 <u>다른</u> 하나는?

> ┤ 보기 ├
> Mom went to the department store <u>to buy</u> holiday gifts.

① Mom has enough time <u>to make</u> chocolate cake for me.
② He studied very hard not <u>to fail</u> the exam.
③ She bought hiking boots <u>to climb</u> the mountain.
④ I dropped by the bank <u>to save</u> my money.
⑤ Mom had a party <u>to celebrate</u> my middle school graduation.

07 다음 빈칸에 공통으로 알맞은 말은?

> • He turned on his computer _____
>   check his email.
> • She bought a fishbowl _____ raise
>   some gold fish.

① in order that   ② in order to
③ so as that   ④ so long as
⑤ as long as

08 다음 대화의 빈칸에 들어갈 알맞은 말을 쓰시오.

> A: Do you like this red dress?
> B: Yes. It is _____ _____ dress that
>   I've ever seen.

09 다음 우리말에 맞게 영작한 것을 고르시오.

> Stephanie는 나를 깨우기 위해서 아침 일찍 전
> 화했다.

① Stephanie called me waking me up early
  in the morning.
② Stephanie called me to wake me up early
  in the morning.
③ Stephanie called me woke me up early
  in the morning.
④ Stephanie called me wakes me up early
  in the morning.
⑤ Stephanie called me to waking me up
  early in the morning.

10 주어진 단어를 이용하여 빈칸에 들어갈 알맞은 말을 쓰시오.

> She was _____(sad) woman in
> this village when she heard of his death.

11 다음 중 밑줄 친 부분의 쓰임이 다른 두 개는?

① I don't have enough time to do my
  homework.
② She flew to Korea to meet her father.
③ Her grandfather lived to be 90 years old.
④ My mother allowed us to stay up late
  tonight.
⑤ He was happy to help the children in
  need.

12 다음 우리말을 영작했을 때 빈칸에 적절하지 않은 것은?(2개)

> • 그는 교실을 청소하기 위해 이 빗자루를 샀다.
> = He bought this broom _____ our
>   classroom.

① so as to clean   ② cleaning
③ to cleaning   ④ to clean
⑤ in order to clean

13 다음 문장에서 어법상 어색한 부분을 바르게 고쳐 다시 쓰시오.

(1) I want to win first prize surprising my
  mom.
➡ _____

(2) Jack used a compass found the right
  direction.
➡ _____

(3) I visited the museum to seeing the
  works of Gogh.
➡ _____

(4) Tom and Judy went to the restaurant so
  that to have lunch.
➡ _____

14 다음 중 어법상 올바른 문장을 <u>모두</u> 고르시오.

① Biggest fruit in this shop is that watermelon.
② The light bulb is one of the famousest inventions of the 19th century.
③ This is the thinnest laptop that the store has.
④ The most wisest man in the world was Gandhi.
⑤ One of the most beautiful mountains in Korea is Mt. Seorak.

15 다음 우리말과 일치하도록 주어진 단어를 이용하여 빈칸에 알맞은 말을 쓰시오.

(1) George는 친구들과 농구를 하기 위해 공원으로 갔다.
➡ George went to the park _____ _____ _____ with his friends. (play)

(2) Bella는 공부하기 위해서 영어 책을 펼쳤다.
➡ Bella _____ the English book _____ _____. (open, study)

(3) Clint는 어젯밤에 축구 경기를 보기 위해 TV를 켰다.
➡ Clint _____ _____ the TV _____ _____ the soccer game last night. (turn, watch)

(4) 어제는 이번 겨울 들어 가장 추운 날이었다.
➡ Yesterday was _____ _____ day of this winter. (cold)

(5) 네 친구들 중에서 누가 가장 똑똑한 학생이니?
➡ Who is _____ _____ student among your friends? (clever)

(6) 이 영화는 금년의 모든 영화 중에서 최악이다.
➡ This movie is _____ _____ _____ all the movies of this year. (bad)

16 다음 표의 내용에 맞게 설명한 것을 고르시오.

	age	height	weight
giraffe	5	350cm	520kg
kangaroo	9	212cm	110kg
flamingo	7	120cm	4kg

① The giraffe is not the youngest of all.
② The kangaroo is not the oldest of all.
③ The flamingo is the tallest of all.
④ The kangaroo is the heaviest of all.
⑤ The flamingo is the smallest of all.

17 다음 주어진 두 문장을 한 문장으로 만들 때, 빈칸에 알맞은 말을 쓰시오.

(1) • Steve studies math very hard.
 • He wishes to be a math teacher.
➡ Steve studies math very hard _____ _____ _____ _____.

(2) • Vivian visited the shopping mall.
 • She wanted to buy a dress.
➡ Vivian visited the shopping mall _____ _____ _____ _____.

(3) • Lincoln took a taxi in a hurry.
 • He didn't want to be late for the meeting.
➡ Lincoln took a taxi in a hurry _____ _____ _____ for the meeting.

18 다음 문장에서 어법상 바르지 <u>못한</u> 것을 찾아 고쳐 쓰시오.

We don't know which star is truly the most brightest. Some scientists say Deneb may be the most brightest star but some other bright stars have been seen in the night sky.

_____ ➡ _____

01 다음 글에서 문맥이나 어법상 잘못 쓰인 것을 찾아 알맞게 고치시오.

> Do you want to be a fast runner? These shoes are a great pick for you. These are the best running shoes when you run long distance. You should wear heaviest shoes when you run a marathon.

_____ ➡ _____

02 주어진 문장과 같은 뜻이 되도록 다음 빈칸에 알맞은 말을 쓰시오.

• Sue went to the library to return the books.
(1) Sue went to the library _____ _____ _____ return the books.
(2) Sue went to the library _____ _____ _____ return the books.
(3) Sue went to the library _____ _____ _____ she _____ return the books.

03 주어진 다음 문장과 같은 뜻이 되도록 빈칸에 알맞은 말을 쓰시오.

• This is the heaviest bag in this shop.
(1) This is _____ _____ any other _____ in this shop.
(2) _____ other bag in this shop is _____ _____ this.
(3) _____ other bag in this shop is _____ _____ as this.

04 다음 두 문장을 한 문장으로 만드시오.

(1) • Arthur was pleased.
  • He got a good grade in science.
  ➡ _____
(2) • Sue went out at night.
  • She had to buy some water.
  ➡ _____
(3) • Brenda went to Paris.
  • She wanted to study art.
  ➡ _____

05 다음 중 어법상 잘못된 것을 고쳐 문장을 다시 쓰시오.

(1) This is the most largest room in my house.
  ➡ _____
(2) John is the taller of the boys in his class.
  ➡ _____
(3) Marilyn studies English hard got good grades.
  ➡ _____
(4) I want to use my computer finding the information on the Internet.
  ➡ _____
(5) The most famous scientist, Isaac Newton, lived to being 74.
  ➡ _____

06 다음 문장을 to부정사를 이용하여 바꿔 쓸 때 빈칸에 알맞은 말을 쓰시오.

(1) Brian went to the bakery for some loaves of bread.

= Brian went to the bakery _____ _____ some loaves of bread.

(2) They set the table for dinner.

= They set the table _____ _____ dinner.

(3) Rob took a taxi to the restaurant because he didn't want to be late for dinner.

= Rob took a taxi to the restaurant _____ _____ _____ _____ for dinner.

07 다음 우리말을 괄호 안에 주어진 어휘를 이용하여 영작하시오.

(1) 엄마는 내 옷을 사기 위하여 그 가게에 가셨다. (mom, the store, dress)

➡ _____

(2) 그녀는 딸의 머리를 빗기기 위해 머리빗을 사용했다. (use, a hairbrush, brush)

➡ _____

(3) Tom은 그녀가 Mike를 사랑하는 것을 알고 실망했다. (disappointed, find, that, love)

➡ _____

(4) Solomon은 세상에서 가장 현명한 사람들 중의 하나였다. (one, of, wise)

➡ _____

(5) 이 책은 내가 갖고 있는 모든 책들 중에서 가장 유용하다. (this book, useful, that, of)

➡ _____

08 다음 그림을 보고 주어진 어휘를 이용하여 빈칸에 알맞은 말을 쓰시오.

(1) Nick _____ _____ _____ shirt of the three. (wear, bright)

(2) Alex is _____ _____ person of the three. (heavy)

(3) Jay _____ _____ _____ hair of the three. (have, dark)

09 다음 〈보기〉의 어휘 중에서 골라 어법에 맞게 빈칸을 채우시오.

보기
get   make   give
nice   pretty   long

(1) Laura bought _____ _____ dress in the shop _____ _____ it to her daughter.

(2) Hamilton used _____ _____ computer in his office _____ _____ the video.

(3) She spent _____ _____ night in her life _____ _____ the ticket.

10 다음 물음의 답에 있는 빈칸을 채워 자신의 답을 쓰시오.

(1) Q: Why did you buy the books?

A: I bought them _____.

(2) Q: Why do you want a new computer?

A: I want it _____.

Reading

My "Bucket List" for the New School Year

Hi, everyone. Today is the first day of our new school year.
<u>first</u> one의 서수

I want to hear your <u>plans</u> and <u>hopes</u> for this year.
계획　　　희망

What do you want to do <u>most</u>? Think about three <u>things</u> you want to
가장　　　　　　　　　선행사　목적격 관계대명사 생략

<u>do</u>. And then, make a <u>bucket list</u> and <u>share</u> it with your friends.
죽기 전에 꼭 해야 할 일이나 달성하고 싶은 목표 리스트, 공유하다

bucket list 버킷 리스트
share 함께 쓰다, 공유하다
freely 자유롭게
musical instrument 악기
weakness 약함
subject 과목
overcome 극복하다
put effort into ~에 노력을 들이다

확인문제

● 다음 문장이 본문의 내용과 일치하면 T, 일치하지 <u>않으면</u> F를 쓰시오.

1　Today is the first day of the new school year. ☐

2　The writer wants to hear the plans and hopes for next year. ☐

3　You should think about four things you want to do. ☐

4　After making a bucket list, share it with your friends. ☐

Jinsu

Hi! I'm Jinsu. This is my bucket list for this year.

First, I want to <u>go on a bike tour</u> of Jejudo this summer.
자전거 여행을 떠나다

I've <u>been there before</u>, but I want to <u>experience</u> the <u>island</u> <u>more freely</u>
현재완료 'have[has]+p.p.' 경험 '~한 적이 있다'　　　경험하다　　섬　　freely의 비교급

on my bike <u>this time</u>. My second <u>goal</u> is to learn <u>how to</u> play the
이번에는　　　　　　목표　　　　how+to부정사 '~하는 방법'

guitar. I think the guitar has <u>the most</u> beautiful sound of all <u>musical</u>
형용사의 최상급. 3음절 이상의 단어는 앞에 'the most'를 써서 최상급을 만듦

<u>instruments</u>. I hope I can play my <u>favorite</u> song on my guitar <u>by the</u>
악기　　　　　　　　　　아주 좋아하는

<u>end of this year</u>. <u>Finally</u>, I want to get a good <u>grade</u> in <u>math</u>. Math is
올해 말쯤에　　마지막으로　　　　　　성적　　수학

my <u>weakest</u> <u>subject</u>. This year, I'll <u>put</u> more <u>effort into</u> studying math
최상급. '원급+est'. 과목　　　　　　~에 노력을 기울이다

to <u>overcome</u> my <u>weakness</u>.
to부정사의 부사적 용법. 극복하다　약점

확인문제

● 다음 문장이 본문의 내용과 일치하면 T, 일치하지 <u>않으면</u> F를 쓰시오.

1 Jinsu wants to go on a bike tour of Jejudo this summer. ☐

2 Jinsu has never been to Jejudo before. ☐

3 Math is Jinsu's weakest subject. ☐

4 Jinsu will put more effort into teaching math. ☐

Somi

Hi! My name is Somi. First, I want to see a concert of my favorite
band right in front of the stage. I'm willing to stand in line all night to
enter the front area. Second, I want to adopt a puppy.
I've always wanted a puppy. I think I'm fully ready to take care of a
pet now. My last goal is a little more challenging. I'd like to read all of
the Sherlock Holmes stories. I became a big fan of this detective series
last year, so I don't want to miss a single one.

band (가수를 중심으로 한) 밴드
in front of ~ 앞에서
be ready to ~할 준비가 되다
adopt 입양하다
puppy 강아지
challenging 도전적인
detective 탐정, 형사
miss 놓치다
single 단일의, 하나의

 확인문제

● 다음 문장이 본문의 내용과 일치하면 T, 일치하지 <u>않으면</u> F를 쓰시오.

1 Somi wants to see a concert of her favorite band right in front of the stage. ☐

2 Somi will not stand in line all night to enter the front area. ☐

3 Somi doesn't think she is fully ready to take care of a pet now. ☐

4 Somi became a big fan of the Sherlock Holmes stories last year. ☐

● 우리말을 참고하여 빈칸에 알맞은 말을 쓰시오.

1 My "Bucket List" _____ _____ _____ _____ _____

2 _____, everyone.

3 Today is _____ _____ _____ of our new school year.

4 I want to hear your plans and hopes _____ _____ _____.

5 What do you want to do _____?

6 Think about three things _____ _____ _____.

7 And then, _____ _____ _____ _____ and _____ it _____ your friends.

8 Hi! _____ Jinsu.

9 _____ _____ my bucket list for this year.

10 First, I want to _____ _____ _____ _____ _____ of Jejudo this summer.

11 _____ _____ _____ _____, but I want to experience the island more freely _____ _____ _____ this time.

12 My second goal is to learn _____ _____ _____ the guitar.

13 I think the guitar has _____ _____ _____ _____ of all musical instruments.

14 I hope I can play my favorite song _____ my guitar _____ _____ _____ _____ this year.

15 _____, I want to get a good grade in math.

16 Math is my _____ _____.

1 나의 새 학년 버킷 리스트

2 모두들, 안녕.

3 오늘은 우리 새 학년의 첫날이에요.

4 저는 여러분들의 올해 계획과 희망을 듣고 싶어요.

5 여러분이 가장 원하는 것은 무엇인가요?

6 여러분이 원하는 것 세 가지를 생각해 보세요.

7 그리고 나서 버킷 리스트를 만들어 친구들과 공유해 봐요.

8 안녕하세요! 저는 진수예요.

9 이것은 올해 제 버킷 리스트예요.

10 우선, 저는 이번 여름에 제주도로 자전거 여행을 가고 싶어요.

11 저는 그곳을 전에 가 본 적이 있지만 이번에는 제 자전거를 타고 좀 더 자유롭게 그 섬을 경험해 보고 싶어요.

12 제 두 번째 목표는 기타 연주하는 법을 배우는 거예요.

13 저는 기타가 모든 악기 중에 가장 아름다운 소리를 낸다고 생각해요.

14 올해 말쯤에는 제가 가장 좋아하는 곡을 제 기타로 연주할 수 있으면 좋겠어요.

15 마지막으로 수학에서 좋은 점수를 받고 싶어요.

16 수학은 제가 가장 약한 과목이에요.

17 This year, I'll _____ more effort _____ studying math _____ _____ my weakness.

18 Hi! _____ _____ _____ Somi.

19 First, I want to see a concert of my favorite band _____ _____ _____ _____ the stage.

20 I'm _____ to _____ _____ _____ all night to enter the front area.

21 Second, I want to _____ _____ _____ .

22 _____ always _____ a puppy.

23 I think _____ fully _____ _____ take care of a pet now.

24 My last goal is _____ _____ _____ _____ .

25 _____ _____ _____ read all of the Sherlock Holmes stories.

26 I became _____ _____ _____ of this detective series last year, so I don't want to miss _____ _____ _____ .

17 올해는 제 약점을 극복하기 위해 수학 공부에 좀 더 노력을 기울일 거예요.

18 안녕하세요! 제 이름은 소미예요.

19 우선, 저는 제가 가장 좋아하는 밴드의 공연을 무대 바로 앞에서 보고 싶어요.

20 앞자리에 들어가기 위해 저는 기꺼이 밤새 줄을 서서 기다릴 거예요.

21 두 번째로, 강아지를 입양하고 싶어요.

22 저는 항상 강아지를 원해 왔어요.

23 이제는 제가 애완동물을 돌볼 준비가 완벽히 되었다고 생각해요.

24 제 마지막 목표는 좀 더 도전적이에요.

25 저는 셜록 홈스 이야기들을 모두 읽고 싶어요.

26 저는 작년에 이 탐정 시리즈의 열성 팬이 되었어요. 그래서 저는 단 하나도 놓치고 싶지 않아요.

우리말을 참고하여 본문을 영작하시오.

1 나의 새 학년 버킷 리스트

➡ _____

2 모두들, 안녕.

➡ _____

3 오늘은 우리 새 학년의 첫날이에요.

➡ _____

4 저는 여러분들의 올해 계획과 희망을 듣고 싶어요.

➡ _____

5 여러분이 가장 원하는 것은 무엇인가요?

➡ _____

6 여러분이 원하는 것 세 가지를 생각해 보세요.

➡ _____

7 그러고 나서 버킷 리스트를 만들어 친구들과 공유해 봐요.

➡ _____

8 안녕하세요! 저는 진수예요.

➡ _____

9 이것은 올해 제 버킷 리스트예요.

➡ _____

10 우선, 저는 이번 여름에 제주도로 자전거 여행을 가고 싶어요.

➡ _____

11 저는 그곳을 전에 가 본 적이 있지만 이번에는 제 자전거를 타고 좀 더 자유롭게 그 섬을 경험해 보고 싶어요.

➡ _____

12 제 두 번째 목표는 기타 연주하는 법을 배우는 거예요.

➡ _____

13 저는 기타가 모든 악기 중에 가장 아름다운 소리를 낸다고 생각해요.

➡ _____

14 올해 말쯤에는 제가 가장 좋아하는 곡을 제 기타로 연주할 수 있으면 좋겠어요.

➡ _____

15 마지막으로 수학에서 좋은 점수를 받고 싶어요.

➡ _____

16 수학은 제가 가장 약한 과목이에요.

➡ _____

17 올해는 제 약점을 극복하기 위해 수학 공부에 좀 더 노력을 기울일 거예요.

➡ _____

18 안녕하세요! 제 이름은 소미예요.

➡ _____

19 우선, 저는 제가 가장 좋아하는 밴드의 공연을 무대 바로 앞에서 보고 싶어요.

➡ _____

20 앞자리에 들어가기 위해 저는 기꺼이 밤새 줄을 서서 기다릴 거예요.

➡ _____

21 두 번째로, 강아지를 입양하고 싶어요.

➡ _____

22 저는 항상 강아지를 원해 왔어요.

➡ _____

23 이제는 제가 애완동물을 돌볼 준비가 완벽히 되었다고 생각해요.

➡ _____

24 제 마지막 목표는 좀 더 도전적이에요.

➡ _____

25 저는 셜록 홈스 이야기들을 모두 읽고 싶어요.

➡ _____

26 저는 작년에 이 탐정 시리즈의 열성 팬이 되었어요. 그래서 저는 단 하나도 놓치고 싶지 않아요.

➡ _____

[01~03] 다음 글을 읽고 물음에 답하시오.

Hi, everyone. (①) Today is the first day of our new school year. (②) I want to hear your plans and hopes for this year. (③) What do you want ⓐto do most? (④) And then, make a bucket list and share ⓑit with your friends. (⑤)

01 위 글의 흐름으로 보아, 주어진 문장이 들어가기에 가장 적절한 곳은?

Think about three things you want to do.

①   ②   ③   ④   ⑤

02 위 글의 밑줄 친 ⓐto do와 to부정사의 용법이 다른 것을 모두 고르시오.

① He has many friends to play with.
② My hope is to go to England.
③ He grew up to be a great doctor.
④ To get up early is good for the health.
⑤ I found it difficult to do so.

03 위 글의 밑줄 친 ⓑit이 가리키는 것을 본문에서 찾아 쓰시오.

➡ _____

[04~07] 다음 글을 읽고 물음에 답하시오.

Hi! I'm Jinsu. This is my bucket list for (A)[this / last] year. First, I want to go on a bike tour of Jejudo this summer. ⓐI've been there before, but I want to experience the island more freely on my bike this time. My second goal is to learn how to play the guitar. I think the guitar has the most beautiful sound of all musical instruments. I hope I can play my favorite song on my guitar ⓑ올해 말쯤에는. Finally, I want to get a good grade in math. Math is my (B)[strongest / weakest] subject. This year, I'll put more effort into studying math to overcome my (C)[strength / weakness].

04 위 글의 밑줄 친 ⓐ에 쓰인 현재완료와 용법이 같은 것을 모두 고르시오.

① She has been in Seoul since 2000.
② She has never eaten spaghetti.
③ I have lost my bag.
④ He has played baseball for two hours.
⑤ How many times have you seen it?

05 위 글의 괄호 (A)~(C)에서 문맥상 알맞은 낱말을 골라 쓰시오.

➡ (A)_____ (B)_____ (C)_____

06 위 글의 밑줄 친 ⓑ의 우리말을 6 단어로 쓰시오.

➡ _____

07 위 글의 내용과 일치하지 않는 것은?

① 진수는 이번 여름에 제주도로 자전거 여행을 가고 싶어 한다.
② 진수는 전에 제주도에 가 본 적이 없다.
③ 진수는 올해 기타 연주하는 법을 배우고 싶어 한다.
④ 수학은 진수가 가장 약한 과목이다.
⑤ 진수는 수학 공부에 좀 더 노력을 기울일 것이다.

[08~10] 다음 글을 읽고 물음에 답하시오.

Hi! My name is Somi. First, I want to see a concert of my favorite band right in front of the stage. I'm willing to ⓐ줄을 서서 기다리다 all night to enter the front area. Second, I want to adopt a puppy. I've always wanted a puppy. I think I'm fully ready to take care of a pet now. My last goal is a little more challenging. I'd like to read all of the Sherlock Holmes stories. I became a big fan of this detective series last year, so I don't want to miss a single ⓑone.

서답형

08 위 글의 밑줄 친 ⓐ의 우리말에 맞게 3 단어로 영작하시오.

➡ _____

09 위 글의 밑줄 친 ⓑ와 문법적 쓰임이 같은 것을 고르시오.

① There's only one room for one person.
② I don't like this bag. Can you show me a cheaper one?
③ He's the one person I can trust.
④ One man's meat is another man's poison.
⑤ One must observe the rules.

중요

위 글의 주제로 알맞은 것을 고르시오.

① the difficulty of seeing a band's concert
② the reason Somi stands in line all night
③ the way Somi adopts a puppy
④ a challenging goal of reading all of the Sherlock Holmes stories
⑤ what Somi wants to do this year

[11~13] 다음 글을 읽고 물음에 답하시오.

My "Bucket List" for This Year

Here is my bucket list. First, I want to learn how to make cookies. I want to make (A)[it / them] to surprise my mom. Second, I want to ⓐlive a simple life. I will throw away things ⓑthat I do not need. The (B)[last / latest] thing is to study online English lessons (C)[everyday / every day]. At the end of this year, I will overcome my problems with my weakest subject, English.

서답형

11 위 글의 괄호 (A)~(C)에서 문맥이나 어법상 알맞은 낱말을 골라 쓰시오.

➡ (A)_____ (B)_____ (C)_____

12 위 글의 밑줄 친 ⓐlive와 바꿔 쓸 수 있는 말을 고르시오.

① take   ② put
③ leave   ④ have
⑤ bring

중요

위 글의 밑줄 친 ⓑthat과 문법적 쓰임이 다른 것을 고르시오.

① Where's the letter that came yesterday?
② The watch that you gave me keeps perfect time.
③ This is the book that I bought yesterday.
④ It's the best novel that I've ever read.
⑤ She said that the story was true.

[14~16] 다음 글을 읽고 물음에 답하시오.

Hi! I'm Jinsu. This is my bucket list for this year. First, I want to go on a bike tour of Jejudo this summer. I've been there before, but I want to experience the island more freely on my bike this time. My second goal is to learn how to play the guitar. I think the guitar has the most beautiful sound of all musical instruments. I hope I can play my favorite song on my guitar by the end of this year. ___ⓐ___, I want to get a good grade in math. Math is my weakest subject. This year, I'll put more effort into studying math ⓑto overcome my weakness.

14 위 글의 제목으로 알맞은 것을 고르시오.

① Jinsu's Bucket List for This Year
② To Go on a Bike Tour of Jejudo
③ How to Experience Jejudo More Freely
④ Guitar Has the Most Beautiful Sound!
⑤ How to Get a Good Grade in Math

15 위 글의 빈칸 ⓐ에 들어갈 말을 모두 고르시오.

① After all   ② In addition
③ Finally   ④ Therefore
⑤ Lastly

16 아래 보기에서 위 글의 밑줄 친 ⓑto overcome과 to부정사의 용법이 다른 것의 개수를 고르시오.

┌─────── 보기 ───────┐
① I want a pen to write this letter with.
② We go to school to learn many things.
③ You have no need to go there.
④ It is wrong to tell a lie.
⑤ I went to the airport to see her off.
└──────────────────┘

① 1개   ② 2개   ③ 3개   ④ 4개   ⑤ 5개

[17~19] 다음 글을 읽고 물음에 답하시오.

Hi! My name is Somi. First, I want to see a concert of my favorite band ⓐright in front of the stage. I'm ___ⓑ___ to stand in line all night to enter the front area. Second, I want to adopt a puppy. I've always wanted a puppy. I think I'm fully ready to take care of a pet now. My last goal is a little more challenging. I'd like to read all of the Sherlock Holmes stories. I became a big fan of this detective series last year, so I don't want to miss a single one.

17 위 글의 밑줄 친 ⓐright와 같은 의미로 쓰인 것을 고르시오.

① Mary was standing right behind Ted.
② I hope we're doing the right thing.
③ Is this the right way to the beach?
④ What gives you the right to do that?
⑤ Keep on the right side of the road.

서답형
18 주어진 영영풀이를 참고하여 빈칸 ⓑ에 철자 w로 시작하는 단어를 쓰시오.

┌──────────────────────────────┐
│ doing something fairly hard because one │
│ wants to do it rather than because one is │
│ forced to do it   │
└──────────────────────────────┘

➡ _____

19 위 글을 읽고 대답할 수 없는 질문은?

① What does Somi want to see?
② What does Somi want to adopt?
③ How was Somi able to be fully ready to take care of a pet?
④ What is Somi's last goal?
⑤ When did Somi become a big fan of Sherlock Holmes?

[20~21] 다음 글을 읽고 물음에 답하시오.

This is the bucket list we bought.
____Ⓐ____, I hope I can meet my favorite actor.
____Ⓑ____, I hope I can have dinner with my role model. ___Ⓒ___, I hope I can travel to ⓐ another countries. We spent ninety dollars to buy these items.

서답형
20 위 글의 빈칸 Ⓐ~Ⓒ에 들어갈 알맞은 말을 쓰시오.

➡ (A)_____ (B)_____ (C)_____

서답형
21 위 글의 밑줄 친 ⓐ를 어법에 맞게 고치시오.

➡ _____

[22~24] 다음 글을 읽고 물음에 답하시오.

I hope I can visit Bangkok. It is the __ⓐ__ city __ⓑ__ delicious food. I want to go there ⓒto take a cooking class.

서답형
22 위 글의 빈칸 ⓐ에 famous의 최상급을 쓰시오.

➡ _____

23 위 글의 빈칸 ⓑ에 들어갈 알맞은 전치사를 고르시오.

① to   ② by   ③ for
④ about   ⑤ in

 위 글의 밑줄 친 ⓒ와 의미가 다른 것을 고르시오.

① so as to take a cooking class
② in order that I can take a cooking class
③ so that I may take a cooking class
④ that I might not take a cooking class
⑤ in order to take a cooking class

[25~26] 다음 대화를 읽고 물음에 답하시오.

Jinsu: Did you complete your bucket list for this year?
Somi: Yes, I did.
Jinsu: What is the first thing on your list?
Somi: I want to see my favorite band in a concert, standing in front of the stage. ⓐWhat about you?
Jinsu: The top thing on my list is a bike tour of Jejudo.

25 위 대화를 읽고 알 수 없는 것을 고르시오.

① Did Somi finish writing her bucket list for this year?
② Will Somi's bucket list come true?
③ What is Somi's first bucket list?
④ Does Somi want to see her favorite band sitting on the chair?
⑤ What is Jinsu's first bucket list?

서답형
26 위 대화의 밑줄 친 ⓐ가 물어보는 내용을 본문에서 찾아 쓰시오.

➡ _____

[01~03] 다음 글을 읽고 물음에 답하시오.

Hi, everyone. ⓐ오늘은 우리 새 학년의 첫날이에요. I want to hear your plans and hopes for this year. What do you want to do most? Think about three things you want to do. ⓑ And then, make a ⓒ_____ _____ and share it with your friends.

01 위 글의 밑줄 친 ⓐ의 우리말에 맞게 주어진 어휘를 이용하여 10 단어로 영작하시오.

> first, school year

➡ _____

02 위 글의 밑줄 친 ⓑAnd then이 가리키는 내용을 주어진 단어로 시작하여 쓰시오. (8 단어, 동명사를 사용할 것.)

➡And after _____

_____

03 주어진 영영풀이를 참고하여 빈칸 ⓒ에 철자 b로 시작하는 단어를 쓰시오.

> a list of things that people want to experience or achieve before they die

➡ _____

[04~06] 다음 글을 읽고 물음에 답하시오.

Hi! I'm Jinsu. This is my bucket list for this year. First, I want to go on a bike tour of Jejudo this summer. I've been there before, but I want to experience the island more freely on my bike this time. ⓐMy second

goal is to learn how to play guitar. ⓑ저는 기타가 모든 악기 중에 가장 아름다운 소리를 낸다고 생각해요. I hope I can play my favorite song on my guitar by the end of this year. Finally, I want to get a good grade in math. Math is my weakest subject. This year, I'll put more effort into studying math to overcome my weakness.

04 위 글의 밑줄 친 ⓐ에서 어법상 틀린 부분을 찾아 고치시오.

➡ _____

05 위 글의 밑줄 친 ⓑ의 우리말에 맞게 한 단어를 보충하여, 주어진 어휘를 알맞게 배열하시오.

> musical instruments / most / sound / I / has / all / the guitar / beautiful / of / think

➡ _____

_____

06 본문의 내용과 일치하도록 다음 빈칸 (A)와 (B)에 알맞은 말을 쓰시오.

> Jinsu's last goal is (A) _____ _____ in math because math is his (B) _____ .

[07~09] 다음 글을 읽고 물음에 답하시오.

Hi! My name is Somi. First, I want to see a concert of my favorite band right in front of the stage. I'm willing to stand in line all night to enter the front area. Second, I want to adopt a puppy. I've always wanted a puppy. I think I'm fully ready to ⓐtake care of a pet now. My last goal is a little more challenging. I'd like to read all of the Sherlock Holmes stories. I became a big fan of this detective series last year, so I don't want to miss a single ⓑ .

07 다음 문장에서 위 글의 내용과 <u>다른</u> 부분을 찾아서 고치시오.

> • Somi wants to see a concert of her favorite band right in front of the stage, so she is unwilling to stand in line all night to enter the front area.

➡ _____

8 중요 위 글의 밑줄 친 ⓐ와 바꿔 쓸 수 있는 말을 쓰시오.

➡ _____

09 위 글의 빈칸 ⓑ에 들어갈 알맞은 말을 쓰시오.

➡ _____

[10~12] 다음 글을 읽고 물음에 답하시오.

Hi! I'm Jinsu. This is my bucket list for this year. First, I want to go on a bike tour of Jejudo this summer. ⓐ나는 그곳을 전에 가 본 적이 있다, but I want to experience the island more freely on my bike this time. My second goal is to learn ⓑhow to play the guitar. I think ⓒthe guitar has the most beautiful sound of all musical instruments. I hope I can play my favorite song on my guitar by the end of this year. Finally, I want to get a good grade in math. Math is my weakest subject. This year, I'll put more effort into studying math to overcome my weakness.

10 위 글의 밑줄 친 ⓐ의 우리말에 맞게 4 단어로 영작하시오.

➡ _____

11 위 글의 밑줄 친 ⓑhow to play와 같은 뜻이 되도록 빈칸에 들어갈 알맞은 말을 쓰시오. (2 단어)

➡ how _____ play

12 중요 위 글의 밑줄 친 ⓒ를 비교급을 사용하여 고칠 때 빈칸에 알맞은 말을 쓰시오.

➡ the guitar has a more beautiful sound than any other _____ _____ does.

[13~15] 다음 글을 읽고 물음에 답하시오.

Hi! My name is Somi. First, I want to see a concert of my favorite band right in front of the stage. I'm willing to stand in line all (A)[night / nights] to enter the front area. Second, I want to adopt a puppy. I've always wanted a puppy. I think I'm fully ready (B)[taking / to take] care of a pet now. My last goal is a little more challenging. I'd like (C)[reading / to read] all of the Sherlock Holmes stories. I became a big fan of this detective series last year, so I don't want to miss a single one.

13 위 글의 괄호 (A)~(C)에서 어법상 알맞은 낱말을 골라 쓰시오.

➡ (A)_____ (B)_____ (C)_____

14 중요 다음 질문에 대한 알맞은 대답을 주어진 단어로 시작하여 쓰시오. (5 단어)

> Q: Why does Somi want to read all of the Sherlock Holmes stories without missing a single one?
> A: Because _____ .

➡ _____

15 소미의 버킷 리스트 세 가지를 우리말로 쓰시오.

➡ (1) _____
   (2) _____
   (3) _____

구석구석

Work Together Step 3

This is the bucket list we bought.
목적격 관계대명사 which나 that이 생략되어 있다.

First, I hope I can meet my favorite actor.
hope가 목적어로 that절을 받았다. hope 뒤에 that이 생략되어 있다.

Second, I hope I can have dinner with my role model.
식사하다

Third, I hope I can travel to other countries.

We spent ninety dollars to buy these items.
spend의 과거형   ～하기 위해서(부사적 용법의 목적)

구문해설 • role model: 역할 모델

해석

이것은 우리가 산 버킷 리스트이다.
첫째. 나는 내가 좋아하는 배우를 만나기를 바란다.
둘째. 나는 나의 역할 모델과 식사할 수 있기를 바란다.
셋째. 나는 다른 나라들을 여행할 수 있기를 바란다.
이것들을 사기 위해 나는 90달러를 사용했다.

Writing Workshop

My "Bucket List" for This Year

Here is my bucket list. First, I want to learn how to make cookies. I want to
～이 있다   = I should

make them to surprise my mom.
= cookies   부사적 용법(목적)

Second, I want to live a simple life. I will throw away things that I do not
동족목적어   목적격 관계대명사

need. The last thing is to study online English lessons every day. At the end of
명사적 용법(보어)

this year, I will overcome my problems with my weakest subject, English.
동격을 나타내는 콤마

구문해설 • simple 간소한 • throw away: 버리다 • overcome: 극복하다 • weakest: 가장 약한

올해의 나의 "버킷 리스트"

여기에 나의 버킷 리스트가 있어. 먼저, 나는 쿠키 만드는 법을 배우고 싶어. 나는 엄마를 놀라게 하기 위해 그것들을 만들고 싶어. 두 번째로, 나는 간소한 삶을 살고 싶어. 나는 필요하지 않은 물건들을 버릴 거야. 마지막 것은 매일 온라인으로 영어 공부를 하는 거야. 올해 말에는 나는 가장 약한 과목인 영어에서의 문제를 극복할 거야.

Solve the Problem

Hi, I am Gijun. I hope I get good grades this year, but I sleep too much. Could
좋은 성적을 받다

you give me some advice?
'다소의, 약간(조금)의'

Why don't you go to bed on time and wake up early?
～하는 게 어때?   잠자리에 들다.

→ I think you need to go to bed early and sleep on a regular schedule to get

better grades.

구문해설 • give advice: 조언을 하다 • on time: 시간을 어기지 않고, 정해진 시간에
• regular: 규칙적인, 정기적인 • schedule: 일정

안녕. 나는 기준이야. 나는 올해 좋은 성적을 받길 바라, 하지만 나는 너무 많이 자. 나에게 조언을 좀 해주겠니?
정해진 시간에 자고 일찍 일어나는 게 어떠니?
나는 좋은 성적을 받기 위해서 네가 일찍 자고 규칙적으로 잘 필요가 있다고 생각해.

영역별 핵심문제

01 다음 〈보기〉와 같은 관계가 되도록 주어진 빈칸에 알맞은 말을 쓰시오.

┤ 보기 ├
outside – inside

strength – _____

02 다음 중 밑줄 친 부분의 쓰임이 어색한 것은?

① Teaching young children is a challenging and rewarding job.
② They are looking for the missing child.
③ The restaurant is full booked this weekend.
④ The building took two years to complete.
⑤ I hope you made a really nice bucket list.

[03~05] 다음 빈칸에 공통으로 들어갈 말을 쓰시오.

03
• I want to _____ a good friend.
• I will _____ an effort to become a good person.

04
• I have to _____ back to Seoul this month.
• I want to _____ on a tour with friends.

05
• The cookies were made _____ me.
• It'll be on your desk _____ the end of this week.

06 다음 영영풀이에 해당하는 단어를 〈보기〉에서 골라 쓰시오.

┤ 보기 ├
overcome   challenge   detective   goal

(1) something that you hope to achieve in the future
➡ _____
(2) to successfully control a feeling or problem
➡ _____

07 다음 우리말과 일치하도록 괄호 안의 단어를 바르게 배열하시오.

(1) 그 개들은 사람들을 구하기 위해 더 빨리 달릴 수 있다.
(dogs, quickly, people, more, the, run, save, can, to)
➡ _____
(2) 이번이 나의 첫 유럽 방문이다.
(my, Europe, first, visit, to, this, is)
➡ _____
(3) 그 서점은 나의 회사 바로 옆에 있다.
(my, the, right, to, bookstore, next, is, company)
➡ _____

Conversation

08 다음 대화의 빈칸에 알맞은 것은?

G: I hope I get good grades this year.
B: _____

① I'm sorry to hear that.
② What about you? What's your plan?
③ Well, I'm not sure.
④ You will. Don't worry.
⑤ Yes, what is it?

[09~12] 다음 대화를 읽고 물음에 답하시오.

G: Hi, Brian.
B: Hi, Somin. It's Friday! (①) Are you (A)
_____(plan) to do anything special this
weekend?
G: Well, I'm (B)_____(plan) to visit my
grandmother. She is sick. (②)
B: Oh, I'm happy to hear that. I hope she got
better soon. (③)
G: Thank you. (④)
B: I'm planning to wash my dog. (⑤)

09 위 대화의 ①~⑤ 중 다음 주어진 말이 들어갈 알맞은 곳은?

What about you? What's your plan?

①   ②   ③   ④   ⑤

10 (A)와 (B) 빈칸에 공통으로 들어갈 말을 주어진 단어를 이용
해 쓰시오.

➡ _____

11 밑줄 친 부분에서 어색한 부분을 찾아 고치시오. (2개)

➡ (1) _____ (B) _____

12 위 대화의 내용과 일치하지 않는 것을 고르시오.

① Brian is going to wash his dog this
weekend.
② Somin's grandmother is sick.
③ Brian is sorry to hear that Somin's
grandmother is sick.
④ Somin will visit her grandmother this
Friday.
⑤ They are talking about the plan of this
weekend.

[13~14] 다음 대화를 읽고 물음에 답하시오.

B: What are you planning to do tomorrow?
G: Jimmy랑 도서 박람회에 갈 계획이야.(plan,
book fair) Would you like to join us?
B: Sure. What time are you going to meet?
G: At 3:00 in front of the school cafeteria.

13 밑줄 친 우리말을 주어진 단어를 이용해 영작하시오.

➡ _____

14 위 대화의 내용과 일치하도록 빈칸을 채우시오.

The girl is planning _____ _____
to _____ _____ _____
Jimmy _____. She suggests _____
_____ to the boy. They _____ meet
_____ 3 o'clock _____ _____
_____ the school cafeteria.

Grammar

15 형용사의 최상급 형태가 틀린 것은?

① brave – bravest
② happy – most happy
③ weak – weakest
④ hot – hottest
⑤ active – most active

16 보기의 밑줄 친 부분과 같은 용법으로 쓰인 것은?

┌─ 보기 ─┐

I took the subway to arrive there on time.

① I want to learn how to make cookies.
② I want to experience the island more freely on my bike this time.
③ Nancy studied very hard to become a scientist.
④ The last thing is to study online English lessons every day.
⑤ I want something cold to drink.

17 다음 빈칸에 알맞은 말이 바르게 짝지어진 것은?

• Which fruit is _____ in this grocery store?
• Turkey is not _____ country in the world.

① large – smallest
② largest – small
③ largest – the smallest
④ the largest – smallest
⑤ the largest – the smallest

18 다음 중 어법상 옳은 것은?

① I want getting a good grade in math.
② I'll put more effort into studying math overcome my weakness.
③ Arnold saved plenty of money bought a car.
④ She went to the theater to watch a movie with her friends.
⑤ William Shakespeare lived being fifty two.

19 다음 중 밑줄 친 부분의 쓰임이 어색한 것은?

① Garry is the busiest man in his company.
② Edga studies hardest in my school.
③ Emma is kindest girl in her school.
④ Math was the most difficult in the final exam.
⑤ Amanda is the smartest in her family.

20 괄호 안에 주어진 단어를 이용하여 다음을 영작하시오.

(1) Brian은 어제 Scarlet을 만나서 기뻤다. (pleased, 7 단어)

➡ _____

(2) Emily는 첫 기차를 타기 위해서 일찍 잠자리에 들었다. (go, bed, take, 10 단어)

➡ _____

(3) Audrey는 자라서 배우가 되었다. (grow up, be, actress, 7 단어)

➡ _____

(4) Wendy는 서울로 가서 결코 돌아오지 못했다. (go, never, return, 7 단어)

➡ _____

21 다음 두 문장의 의미가 같도록 빈칸에 들어갈 알맞은 말을 쓰시오.

> Nothing is more important than health in the world.
> = Health is _____ thing in the world.

22 다음 문장을 to부정사를 이용한 문장으로 바꿔 쓰시오.

(1) • Ann wants to go to Korea.

　• She wants to learn the Korean language.

　➡ _____

(2) • Jane is planning to dance at the school festival.

　• She wants to show her friends how well she dances.

　➡ _____

_____

Reading

[23~24] 다음 글을 읽고 물음에 답하시오.

Hi, everyone. ①Today is the first day of our new school year. ②I want to hear your plans and hopes ___ⓐ___ this year. ③When students move to a higher grade, they spend much more time studying. ④What do you want to do most? ⑤Think about three things you want to do. And then, make a bucket list and share it ___ⓑ___ your friends.

23 위 글의 ①~⑤ 중에서 전체 흐름과 관계 없는 문장은?

① ② ③ ④ ⑤

24 위 글의 빈칸 ⓐ와 ⓑ에 들어갈 전치사가 바르게 짝지어진 것은?

① for - with ② to - by
③ on - from ④ for - to
⑤ at - with

[25~27] 다음 글을 읽고 물음에 답하시오.

Hi! I'm Jinsu. This is my bucket list for this year. First, I want to go on a bike tour of Jejudo this summer. I've been there before, but I want to experience the island more (A)[free / freely] on my bike this time. My ⓐ___ goal is to learn (B)[how / what] to play the guitar. I think the guitar has ⓑ___ ___ ___ ___ of all musical instruments. I hope I can play my favorite song on my guitar by the end of this year. Finally, I want to get a good grade in math. Math is my weakest subject. This year, I'll put more effort into (C)[study / studying] math to overcome my weakness.

25 위 글의 괄호 (A)~(C)에서 어법상 알맞은 낱말을 골라 쓰시오.

➡ (A)_____ (B)_____ (C)_____

26 위 글의 빈칸 ⓐ에 들어갈 알맞은 말을 쓰시오.

➡ _____

27 다음 문장과 같은 뜻이 되도록 위 글의 빈칸 ⓑ에 알맞은 말을 쓰시오.

> I think no other musical instrument has a more beautiful sound than the guitar does.

➡ _____

[28~30] 다음 글을 읽고 물음에 답하시오.

Hi! My name is Somi. First, I want to see a concert of my favorite band right in front of the stage. I'm willing to stand in line all night to enter the front area. Second, I want to adopt a puppy. I've always wanted a puppy. I think I'm fully ready ⓐto take care of a pet now. My last goal is a little more challenging. I'd like to read all of the Sherlock Holmes stories. I became a big fan of ⓑthis detective series last year, so I don't want to miss a single one.

28 위 글의 밑줄 친 ⓐto take와 to부정사의 용법이 같은 것을 고르시오.

① He went abroad to study economics.
② I am sorry to hear that.
③ He lived to be one hundred years old.
④ He must be foolish to say so.
⑤ This book is easy to read.

29 위 글의 밑줄 친 ⓑ가 가리키는 것을 본문에서 찾아 쓰시오.

➡ _____

30 위 글의 내용과 일치하지 <u>않는</u> 것은?

① 소미는 자신이 가장 좋아하는 밴드의 공연을 무대 바로 앞에서 보고 싶어 한다.
② 소미는 강아지를 입양하고 싶어 한다.
③ 소미는 아직 애완동물을 돌볼 준비가 완전히 되어 있지는 않다.
④ 소미는 셜록 홈스 이야기를 모두 읽고 싶어 한다.
⑤ 소미는 작년에 셜록 홈스 시리즈의 열성 팬이 되었다.

[31~32] 다음 대화를 읽고 물음에 답하시오.

Jinsu: Did you complete your bucket list for this year?
Somi: Yes, I did.
Jinsu: What is the first thing on your list?
Somi: I want to see my favorite band in a concert, __ⓐ__ in front of the stage. What about you?
Jinsu: The ⓑtop thing on my list is a bike tour of Jejudo.

31 위 글의 빈칸 ⓐ에 stand를 알맞은 형태로 쓰시오.

➡ _____

32 위 대화의 밑줄 친 ⓑ와 바꿔 쓸 수 있는 단어를 본문에서 찾아 쓰시오.

➡ _____

[33~34] 다음 글을 읽고 물음에 답하시오.

My "Bucket List" for This Year
Here is my bucket list. First, I want to learn how to make cookies. I want to make them to surprise my mom. Second, I want to live a simple life. I will throw away things __ⓐ__ I do not need. The last thing is to study online English lessons every day. At the end of this year, I will overcome my problems with my weakest subject, English.

33 위 글의 빈칸 ⓐ에 들어갈 알맞은 말을 <u>모두</u> 고르시오.

① which   ② what   ③ who
④ that   ⑤ whom

34 다음 질문에 대한 알맞은 대답을 영어로 쓰시오. (1 단어)

Q: Is the writer good at English?
A: _____

출제율 90%

01 다음 짝지어진 두 단어의 관계가 같도록 주어진 철자로 시작하여 알맞은 말을 쓰시오.

(1) start : begin = finish : c_____

(2) initial : first = well-known : f_____

(3) in : out = before : a_____

(4) bright : smart = lost : m_____

출제율 100%

02 다음 빈칸에 알맞은 형태로 바르게 짝지어진 것은?

> • He is willing _____ your proposal.
> • I'll be ready _____ in about five minutes.

① accept – go

② accept – to go

③ to accept – go

④ to accept – to go

⑤ to accept – going

출제율 90%

03 다음 대화의 빈칸에 알맞은 것은?

> A: What do you want for your birthday?
> B: _____

① You will. Don't worry.

② That sounds great.

③ I'm planning to sell a new computer.

④ I hope I get a new computer.

⑤ I hope you get a new computer.

출제율 95%

04 다음 〈보기〉의 단어를 사용하여 자연스러운 문장을 만들 수 없는 것은?

> ─┤ 보기 ├─
> learn   plan   ride   surprise   walk

① I hope that you'll _____ your difficulties.

② What's the best way to _____ a language?

③ What they are saying doesn't _____ me.

④ He has never learned to _____ a bicycle.

⑤ We _____ to open a new office near the downtown area.

[05~06] 다음 대화의 순서를 바르게 배열하시오.

출제율 90%

05

> (A) I'm planning to buy a new bike tomorrow. Can you help me choose one?
> (B) Sure, I'd love to.
> (C) Yes, what is it?
> (D) Jack! Can you do me a favor?

➡ _____

출제율 85%

06

> (A) What are you planning to do tomorrow?
> (B) Then how about going to a movie with me?
> (C) Well, I'm not sure.
> (D) That sounds wonderful.

➡ _____

[07~10] 다음 대화를 읽고 물음에 답하시오.

B: Kate, do you have any special plans for the new school year?

G: ①I'm planning to study one new Chinese word every day.

B: ②I didn't know you were interested in Chinese. (A)_____

G: Only last month. ③But now I can introduce me in Chinese.

B: That's amazing! (B)_____

G: It's because I'm a big fan of Chinese dramas. 나는 곧 그것들을 중국어로 보고, 무슨 말을 하는지 이해할 수 있기를 바라.

B: Well, ④keep studying hard, and I'm sure you'll be able to do it someday.

G: I hope so. ⑤What about you? What are your plans for this year?

B: Let me think. Hmm.... Getting a good grade in every subject? As usual.

G: Hahaha.

출제율 95%

07 What are they talking about?

① the way of learning Chinese
② the importance of studying hard
③ the way of making special plans
④ getting good grades for the new school year
⑤ the plans for the new school year

출제율 90%

08 빈칸 (A)와 (B)에 어울리는 질문을 보기에서 골라 쓰시오.

┌─ 보기 ┐
• Do you like studying Chinese?
• When did you start studying Chinese?
• How many times did you visit China?
• How did you get so into Chinese?
• When are you going to start studying Chinese?

➡ (A) _____
(B) _____

출제율 100%

09 위 대화의 밑줄 친 ①~⑤ 중 어법상 틀린 것은?

①   ②   ③   ④   ⑤

출제율 80%

10 밑줄 친 우리말에 맞게 주어진 단어를 알맞게 배열하시오.

hope, them, Chinese, saying, understand, I, I, and, they, what, are, soon, can, in, watch

➡ _____
_____

출제율 90%

11 다음 중 어법상 올바른 문장은?

① Sumi is the tallest of my class.
② Today is the hottest day this summer.
③ A rabbit is one of fastest animal.
④ Bill is most hungry boy in this restaurant.
⑤ Steve is richest of the three gentlemen.

출제율 90%

12 밑줄 친 부분의 쓰임이 다른 하나를 고르시오.

① David went to the library to borrow some books.
② She went to the bus stop to take a bus.
③ To read in the plane, Morris took a book with him.
④ Sharon was very pleased to get the ticket at last.
⑤ Bruce lay on the sofa to take some sleep.

출제율 90%

13 다음 괄호 안의 단어를 빈칸에 알맞은 형태로 쓰시오.

(1) Who is the _____ girl in her class? (healthy)

(2) He is the _____ soccer player in his school. (good)

출제율 85%

14 다음 우리말과 같도록 주어진 단어를 바르게 배열하여 문장을 완성하시오.

> 비에 젖지 않게 우산을 가져가렴.
> (so / wet / to / get / as / not)

➡ Take your umbrella _____.

출제율 95%

15 어법상 잘못된 부분을 바르게 고쳐 문장을 다시 쓰시오.

(1) He is the better student in my class.

➡ _____

(2) Naomi is the most smartest girl of them all.

➡ _____

출제율 95%

16 다음 우리말을 주어진 어휘를 이용하여 영작하시오.

(1) 나는 Melanie에게 스마트폰을 사용해 전화를 했다. (use, my smartphone, call, 7 단어)

➡ _____

(2) Karen은 오늘 밤 그를 다시 보게 되어서 기뻤다. (glad, see, 8 단어)

➡ _____

[17~19] 다음 글을 읽고 물음에 답하시오.

Hi! I'm Jinsu. This is my bucket list for this year. First, ⓐ저는 자전거 여행을 가고 싶어요 this summer.(bike tour) I've been there before, but I want to experience the island more freely on my bike this time. My second ⓑgoal is to learn how to play the guitar. I think the guitar has the most beautiful sound of all musical instruments. I hope I can play my favorite song on my guitar by the end of this year. Finally, I want to get a good grade in math. Math is my ⓒ _____ subject. This year, I'll put more effort into studying math to overcome my weakness.

출제율 100%

17 위 글의 밑줄 친 ⓐ의 우리말을 주어진 어구를 써서 영어로 옮기시오.

➡ _____

출제율 95%

18 위 글의 밑줄 친 ⓑ와 뜻이 다른 말을 고르시오.

① target   ② object
③ end   ④ aim
⑤ subject

출제율 95%

19 위 글의 빈칸 ⓒ에 weak의 최상급을 쓰시오.

➡ _____

[20~22] 다음 글을 읽고 물음에 답하시오.

Hi! My name is Somi. First, I want to see a concert of my favorite band right in front of the stage. I'm (A)[willing / unwilling] to stand in line all night to enter the front area. Second, I want to (B)[adapt / adopt] a puppy. I've always wanted a puppy. I think I'm fully ready to take care of a pet now. My last goal is a little more (C)[challenging / relaxing]. I'd like to read all of the Sherlock Holmes stories. I became a big fan of this detective series last year, so I don't want to ⓐmiss a single one.

20 위 글의 괄호 (A)~(C)에서 문맥상 알맞은 낱말을 골라 쓰시오.

➡ (A)_____ (B)_____ (C)_____

21 위 글을 읽고 소미에 대해 알 수 <u>없는</u> 것을 고르시오.

① Where does she want to see a concert of her favorite band?
② Which does she want to adopt, a cat or a puppy?
③ Is she fully ready to take care of a pet now?
④ How many Sherlock Holmes stories did she read last year?
⑤ Why does she want to read all of the Sherlock Holmes stories?

22 위 글의 밑줄 친 ⓐmiss와 같은 의미로 쓰인 것을 고르시오.

① How did the train <u>miss</u> the accident?
② Don't <u>miss</u> next week's issue!
③ When you leave, I'll <u>miss</u> you.
④ When did you first <u>miss</u> the necklace?
⑤ A <u>miss</u> is as good as a mile.

[23~25] 다음 글을 읽고 물음에 답하시오.

My "Bucket List" for This Year
Here is my bucket list. First, I want to learn how to make cookies. I want to make ⓐthem to surprise my mom. Second, I want to live a simple life. I will throw away things that I do not need. The last thing is to study online English lessons every day. At the end of this year, I will overcome my problems with my weakest subject, English.

23 위 글의 밑줄 친 ⓐthem이 가리키는 것을 본문에서 찾아 쓰시오.

➡ _____

24 다음 질문에 대한 알맞은 대답을 빈칸에 쓰시오.

Q: Why does the writer want to make cookies?
A: In order to _____ his or her mom.

25 다음 중 글쓴이에 대한 내용으로 일치하지 <u>않는</u> 것을 고르시오.

① 쿠키 만드는 법을 배우고 싶어 한다.
② 간소한 삶을 살고 싶어 한다.
③ 필요하지 않은 물건들은 따로 보관할 것이다.
④ 매일 온라인으로 영어 공부를 할 것이다.
⑤ 영어가 가장 약한 과목이다.

01 다음 대화의 밑줄 친 부분과 의미가 같도록 주어진 단어를 이용하여 영작하시오.

> A: What are you planning to do tomorrow?
> B: I'm planning to go to a movie with Toby.

➡ _____ (will)

➡ _____ (going)

02 괄호 안의 단어를 이용하여 우리말을 바르게 영작하시오.

(1) 나는 내년에 일본을 여행할 수 있기를 바란다.
(can, next, to, travel, 9단어)

➡ _____

(2) 내년에는, 나는 승자가 될 수 있기를 바란다.
(the winner, become, 9단어)

➡ _____

(3) 좋은 성적을 얻기 위해서, 나는 하루 종일 공부할 계획이다. (get, all day, planning, good, grades, 10단어)

➡ _____

03 다음 대화의 밑줄 친 부분에서 어색한 것을 모두 찾아 고치시오. (3개)

> B: ①Hi, Somin. Its Friday! ②Are you planning to do special anything this weekend?
> G: Well, I'm planning to visit my grandmother. She is sick.
> B: ③Oh, I'm sorry to hear that. I hope she gets better soon.
> G: Thank you. ④What about you? ⑤How is your plan?
> B: I'm planning to wash my dog.

➡ _____
_____

04 주어진 두 문장을 한 문장으로 만들 때, 빈칸에 알맞은 말을 쓰시오.

(1) • Johanna called Greg.
  • Because she wanted to play tennis with him.
  ➡ Johanna called Greg _____ tennis with him.

(2) • Bob uses his computer.
  • He sends emails to his friends.
  ➡ Bob uses his computer _____ emails to his friends.

05 다음 중 어법상 어색한 부분을 바르게 고치시오.

(1) The Golden Gate Bridge is one of the most famous bridge in the world.

➡ _____

(2) Dogs are popularest pet in America.

➡ _____

(3) I went to the store buying glasses.

➡ _____

(4) Natalie used to jog in the morning stayed healthy.

➡ _____

06 다음 두 문장의 의미가 같도록 빈칸 하나에 한 단어씩 쓰시오.

(1) Mt. Baekdu is the highest mountain in Korea.

= Mt. Baekdu is _____ _____ _____ _____ _____ in Korea.

(2) The Eiffel Tower is the most beautiful tower in the world.

= _____ other tower is _____ _____ than the Eiffel Tower in the world.

[07~09] 다음 글을 읽고, 물음에 답하시오.

Hi! I'm Jinsu. This is my bucket list for this year. First, I want to go on a bike tour of Jejudo this summer. I've been there before, but I want to experience the island more freely on my bike this time. ⓐMy second goal is to learn how to play the guitar. I think the guitar has the most beautiful sound of all musical instruments. I hope I can play my favorite song on my guitar by the end of this year. Finally, I want to get a good grade in math. Math is my weakest subject. ⓑThis year, I'll put more effort into studying math to greet my weakness.

07 위 글의 밑줄 친 ⓐ를 다음과 같이 바꿔 쓸 때 빈칸에 알맞은 말을 쓰시오.

➡ My second goal is _____ how to play the guitar.

08 위 글의 밑줄 친 ⓑ에서 흐름상 어색한 부분을 찾아 고치시오.

➡ _____

09 진수의 버킷 리스트 세 가지를 우리말로 쓰시오.

➡ (1) _____

(2) _____

(3) _____

[10~12] 다음 글을 읽고 물음에 답하시오.

Hi! My name is Somi. First, I want to see a concert of my favorite band right in front of the stage. I'm willing to stand in line all night to enter the front area. Second, I want to adopt a puppy. I've always wanted a puppy. I think I'm fully ready to take care of a pet now. ⓐMy last goal is a little more challenged. I'd like _ⓑ_ all of the Sherlock Holmes stories. I became a big fan of this detective series last year, so I don't want to miss a single one.

10 위 글의 밑줄 친 ⓐ에서 어법상 틀린 부분을 찾아 고치시오.

➡ _____

11 위 글의 빈칸 ⓑ에 read를 알맞은 형태로 쓰시오.

➡ _____

12 본문의 내용과 일치하도록 다음 빈칸 (A)와 (B)에 알맞은 단어를 쓰시오.

Somi's (A)_____ bucket list is to adopt a puppy. Actually she has always wanted a puppy and she thinks she's fully (B)_____ for taking care of a pet now.

01 다음 표에 제시된 정보를 보고, 계획을 묻고 대답하는 대화를 완성해 봅시다.

A

	Mon.	Tue.	Wed.	Thur.	Fri.	Sat.	Sun.
afternoon	go swimming	.	go swimming		go swimming.	read a book	play volleyball
evening			visit grandma	do exercise			

B

	Mon.	Tue.	Wed.	Thur.	Fri.	Sat.	Sun.
afternoon	read a book	.		draw cartoons	do exercise		go shopping
evening		walk the dog	visit the museum			draw cartoons	

A: What are you _____ on Wednesday evening?

B: I'm going _____. _____ going to do on Wednesday afternoon?

A: I'm planning _____.

02 자신이 열심히 하고 있는 것과 그 이유를 to부정사를 이용하여 두 문장 이상 쓰시오.

(1) _____

(2) _____

03 다음 버킷 리스트 경매에 관한 내용을 바탕으로 자신의 모둠에서 구매한 세 개의 버킷 리스트를 모아서 발표하는 글을 쓰시오.

A: I hope I can meet my favorite actor. How much will you pay for this bucket list? It starts at ten dollars.

B: Twenty dollars!

C: Thirty dollars!

A: Going once. Going twice. Sold.

<경매에 나온 버킷 리스트>

I hope I can meet my favorite actor.

I hope I can have dinner with my role model.

I hope I can travel to other countries.

This is the bucket list we (A)_____. First, I hope I can meet (B)_____.
Second, I hope I can have dinner with (C)_____. Third, I hope I (D)_____ to other countries. We spent ninety dollars (E)_____ these items.

단원별 모의고사

01 다음 대화의 빈칸에 알맞은 단어를 고르시오.

> G: What are you planning to do tomorrow?
> B: I'm planning _____ my hair cut.

① do   ② to do   ③ to get
④ have   ⑤ got

02 〈보기〉의 단어를 사용하여 문장을 완성하시오.

> ┤ 보기 ├
> away at on into of to for

(1) The children are old enough to take care _____ themselves.
(2) Frank put a lot of effort _____ the exam.
(3) This could be used again. Don't throw it _____!
(4) My parents are going _____ a hiking tour.

03 다음 빈칸에 공통으로 들어갈 단어를 고르시오.

> • His _____ is to read two books a month.
> • When do you _____ to go to Europe?

① need   ② plan   ③ decide
④ ask   ⑤ get

04 빈칸에 공통으로 들어갈 단어를 주어진 철자로 시작하여 쓰시오.

> • This i_____ is used for cleaning and polishing teeth.
> • Are you learning a musical i_____ these days?

[05~08] 다음 대화를 읽고 물음에 답하시오.

> Jinsu: Did you ⓐ_____ your bucket list for this year?
> Somi: Yes, I did.
> Jinsu: What is the first thing on your list?
> Somi: I want ⓑ(see) my favorite band in a concert, ⓒ(stand) in front of the stage. What about you?
> Jinsu: 목록의 제일 위의 것은 제주도로 자전거 여행을 하는 거야.

05 위 대화의 빈칸 ⓐ에 다음 영영풀이에 해당하는 단어를 주어진 철자로 시작하여 쓰시오.

> to finish doing or making something, especially when it has taken a long time

➡ c_____

06 ⓑ와 ⓒ에 알맞은 말을 괄호 안에 주어진 단어를 이용하여 쓰시오.

➡ ⓑ: _____   ⓒ: _____

07 밑줄 친 우리말과 의미가 같도록 주어진 단어를 이용해 문장을 완성하시오.

➡ _____
(Jejudo, a bike tour, top)

08 위 대화를 읽고, 알 수 <u>없는</u> 것을 고르시오.

① Does Somi have her favorite band?
② What does Jinsu want to do this year?
③ What are they talking about?
④ What is Somi's favorite band?
⑤ Where does Somi want to see the band in the concert?

[09~12] 다음 대화를 읽고 물음에 답하시오.

B: Kate, 새 학년을 맞이하여 특별한 계획이 있니?

G: ①I'm planning to study one new Chinese word every day.

B: I didn't know you were interested ⓐ_____ Chinese. When did you start studying Chinese?

G: Only last month. But now I can introduce myself ⓑ_____ Chinese.

B: That's amazing! How did you get so ⓒ_____ Chinese?

G: ②It's because I'm a big fan of Chinese dramas. I hope I can soon watch them in Chinese and understand what they're saying.

B: ③Well, keep studying hard, and I'm not sure you'll be able to do it someday.

G: ④I hope so. ⑤What about you? What are your plans for this year?

B: Let me think. Hmm.... Getting a good grade in every subject? As usual.

G: Hahaha.

09 밑줄 친 우리말과 의미가 같도록 주어진 단어를 이용해 문장을 완성하시오.

➡ _____

_____

(any, for, school, plans, have)

10 ⓐ~ⓒ에 알맞은 단어를 〈보기〉에서 찾아 쓰시오.

┌─── 보기 ───┐
at   for   in   into   to
└──────────────┘

➡ ⓐ: _____   ⓑ: _____   ⓒ: _____

11 ①~⑤ 중 흐름상 어색한 문장을 고르시오.

①   ②   ③   ④   ⑤

12 위 대화의 내용과 일치하는 것을 모두 고르시오.

① The boy usually gets a good grade.

② Kate isn't able to introduce herself in Chinese.

③ Kate has been studying Chinese since last month.

④ Kate doesn't have any plans for this year.

⑤ The boy likes to see Chinese dramas.

[13~14] 다음 대화를 읽고 물음에 답하시오.

A: 이번 주말에 뭐 할 계획이니? (plan, are, do, this, what, weekend)

B: I'm planning to _____ my hair cut.

13 괄호 안의 단어를 이용하여 우리말을 바르게 영작하시오. (형태 변형 가능)

➡ _____

14 빈칸에 알맞은 단어를 고르시오. (2개)

① have   ② make

③ take   ④ get

⑤ keep

[15~16] 다음 대화를 읽고 물음에 답하시오.

A: Jack! Can you do me a ⓐ_____?

B: Yes, what is it?

A: I'm planning to buy a new bike tomorrow. Can you help me choose one?

B: Sure, ⓑI'd love to.

15 위 대화의 빈칸 ⓐ에 다음 영영풀이에 해당하는 단어를 주어진 철자로 시작하여 쓰시오.

> something that you do for someone in order to help them or be kind to them

➡ f_____

16 밑줄 친 ⓑ의 문장 뒤에 생략된 부분을 대화에서 찾아 쓰시오. (4 단어)

➡ _____

17 다음 괄호 안의 단어의 형태로 알맞은 것끼리 바르게 짝지어진 것은?

> • That is the (dirty) pig we have ever seen.
> • The island is the (wet) one in the world.

① dirtyest – wetest
② dirtiest – wettest
③ most dirty – most wet
④ most dirtest – most wetest
⑤ most dirtiest – most wettest

18 다음 중 어법상 <u>어색한</u> 것을 고르시오.

① Tim is wearing the darkest shirt of the three.
② Diana was at a restaurant to has lunch.
③ I will overcome my problems with my weakest subject, English.
④ I want to learn how to make cookies.
⑤ I went to the hospital to meet my friend.

19 다음 두 문장의 의미가 같도록 빈칸 하나에 한 단어씩 쓰시오.

> • Mt. Everest is the highest mountain in the world.
> = _____ other mountain is _____ _____ as Mt. Everest in the world.

20 우리말과 일치하도록 괄호 안의 단어를 바르게 배열하시오.

(1) Sarah는 학교에 가기 위해 지하철을 탔다. (Sarah, the subway, school, took, go, to, to)

➡ _____

(2) 나는 쉬기 위해 나무 아래에 앉았다. (I, tree, rest, sat, take, a, a, under, to)

➡ _____

(3) Amy는 일어나서 그녀의 휴대폰이 침대 위에 있는 것을 발견했다. (Amy, her, bed, cellphone, woke, find, the, up, on, to)

➡ _____

[21~23] 다음 글을 읽고 물음에 답하시오.

Hi! I'm Jinsu. This is my bucket list for this year. First, I want to go ①<u>on</u> a bike tour of Jejudo this summer. I've been there before, but I want to experience the island more freely ②<u>on</u> my bike this time. My second goal is to learn how to play the guitar. I think the guitar has the most beautiful sound ③<u>in</u> all musical instruments. I hope I can play my favorite song ④<u>on</u> my guitar by the end of this year. Finally, I want to get a good grade in math. Math is my weakest ⓐ<u>subject</u>. This year, I'll put more effort ⑤<u>into</u> studying math to ⓑ <u>overcome</u> my weakness.

21 위 글의 밑줄 친 ①~⑤에서 전치사의 쓰임이 적절하지 <u>않</u>은 것을 찾아 알맞게 고치시오.

➡ _____

22 위 글의 밑줄 친 ⓐsubject와 같은 의미로 쓰인 것을 고르시오.

① We are all subject to the laws of nature.
② What subject do you teach at school?
③ Let's stop this unpleasant subject of conversation.
④ Focus the camera on the subject.
⑤ We need a male subject between the ages of 18 and 25 for the experiment.

23 위 글의 밑줄 친 ⓑovercome을 바꿔 쓸 때 빈칸에 알맞은 말을 쓰시오.

➡ _____ _____ my weakness

[24~26] 다음 글을 읽고 물음에 답하시오.

Hi! My name is Somi. First, I want to see a concert of my favorite band right in front of the stage. (①) I'm willing to stand in line all night ⓐto enter the front area. (②) Second, I want to adopt a puppy. I've always wanted a puppy. (③) ⓑI think I'm fully ready to take care of a pet now. (④) I'd like to read all of the Sherlock Holmes stories. (⑤) I became a big fan of this detective series last year, so I don't want to miss a single one.

24 위 글의 흐름으로 보아, 주어진 문장이 들어가기에 가장 적절한 곳은?

> My last goal is a little more challenging.

①   ②   ③   ④   ⑤

25 위 글의 밑줄 친 ⓐ와 의미가 다른 것을 고르시오.

① so that I may enter the front area
② in order to enter the front area
③ that I may not enter the front area
④ in order that I can enter the front area
⑤ so as to enter the front area

26 위 글의 밑줄 친 ⓑ를 다음과 같이 바꿔 쓸 때 빈칸에 들어갈 알맞은 말을 쓰시오.

➡ I think I'm fully ready _____ taking care of a pet now.

[27~28] 다음 대화를 읽고, 물음에 답하시오.

Jinsu: Did you complete your bucket list for this year?
Somi: Yes, I ⓐdid.
Jinsu: What is the first thing on your list?
Somi: I want to see my favorite band in a concert, standing in front of the stage. ⓑWhat about you?
Jinsu: The top thing on my list is a bike tour of Jejudo.

27 위 대화의 밑줄 친 대동사 ⓐ가 가리키는 것을 영어로 쓰시오.

➡ _____

28 위 대화의 밑줄 친 ⓑ와 바꿔 쓸 수 있는 말을 쓰시오.

➡ _____

Let's Be Smart Smartphone Users

 의사소통 기능

- 충고하기

  A: I'm always late for school. What should I do?

  B: You should set an alarm on your smartphone.

- 당부하기

  A: Can I eat this pizza?

  B: Sure. Just make sure you wash your hands first.

 언어 형식

- to부정사의 형용사적 용법

  Here are some tips **to protect** your health.

- 사역동사

  It **makes your eyes feel** tired and dry to read small letters on a smartphone for a long time.

Words & Expressions

교과서

Key Words

- **advice**[ədváis] 명 충고
- **avoid**[əvɔ́id] 동 피하다
- **back**[bæk] 명 등
- **bend**[bend] 동 구부리다
- **blink**[bliŋk] 동 (눈을) 깜빡이다
- **break**[breik] 명 휴식
- **cause**[kɔːz] 동 초래하다, 야기하다
- **check**[tʃek] 동 확인하다
- **crack**[kræk] 명 금, 깨진 틈
- **deserted**[dizə́ːrtid] 형 버려진
- **drop**[drɑp] 동 떨어뜨리다
- **hall**[hɔːl] 명 복도
- **historical**[histɔ́ːrikəl] 형 역사적인
- **hold**[hould] 동 잡다
- **hurt**[həːrt] 동 다치게 하다, 아프다
- **increase**[inkríːs] 동 증가하다
- **lean**[liːn] 동 기대다
- **letter**[létər] 명 문자, 글자
- **life jacket** 구명 조끼

- **lower**[lóuər] 동 낮추다
- **novel**[nável] 명 소설
- **pain**[pein] 명 고통
- **pose**[pouz] 명 자세
- **pressure**[préʃər] 명 압력
- **prevent**[privént] 동 예방하다, 막다
- **protect**[prətékt] 동 보호하다
- **pull**[pul] 동 당기다
- **reduce**[ridjúːs] 동 줄이다, 감소시키다
- **rule**[ruːl] 명 규칙
- **service center** 서비스 센터, 수리소
- **text**[tekst] 동 (휴대 전화로) 문자를 보내다
- **tip**[tip] 명 조언, 비법
- **uncomfortable**[ənkʌ́mfərbəl] 형 불편한
- **under**[ʌ́ndər] 전 ~ 아래에
- **upset**[ʌ́pset] 형 화난
- **weather**[wéðər] 명 날씨
- **worse**[wəːrs] 형 나쁜
- **wrist**[rist] 명 손목

Key Expressions

- **a lot of** 많은
- **at least** 적어도
- **away from** ~에서 떨어져서
- **be good for** ~에 좋다
- **be late for** ~에 늦다
- **cut down on** ~을 줄이다
- **depend on** ~에 의존하다
- **do warm up exercise** 준비운동을 하다
- **from time to time** 가끔, 이따금
- **get in touch with** ~와 연락[접촉]하다
- **give back** 돌려주다
- **in front of** ~ 앞에
- **instead of** ~ 대신에
- **keep A from B** A를 B로부터 막다

- **keep in mind** 명심하다
- **make sure**+주어+동사 반드시 ~하도록 하다, ~을 확실히 하다
- **pay attention to** ~에 주의를 기울이다
- **put on** ~을 늘리다, 더하다
- **ride on** ~을 타다
- **right away** 당장
- **set an alarm** 자명종 시계를 맞추다
- **sleep over at** (남의 집에) 묵다
- **spend** 시간[돈] **Ving** 시간[돈]을 ~하는 데 소비하다
- **take a walk** 산책하다
- **turn off** (불 · 라디오 · 텔레비전 등을) 끄다
- **turn on** (불 · 라디오 · 텔레비전 등을) 켜다
- **watch out (for)** (~을) 조심하다

Word Power

※ 서로 반대되는 뜻을 가진 단어

□ **in front of**(~ 앞에) ↔ **behind**(~ 뒤에)

□ **lower**(낮추다) ↔ **raise**(올리다)

□ **turn on**([불 · 라디오 · 텔레비전 등을] 켜다) ↔ **turn off**([불 · 라디오 · 텔레비전 등을] 끄다)

□ **under**(~ 아래에) ↔ **over**(~ 위에)

□ **increase**(증가하다) ↔ **decrease**(감소하다), **reduce**(줄이다)

□ **pull**(당기다) ↔ **push**(밀다)

□ **worse**(더 나쁜) ↔ **better**(더 좋은)

※ 서로 비슷한 뜻을 가진 단어

□ **rule**(규칙) : **law**(법, 규율), **regulation**(규정, 규제)

□ **depend on**(~에 의존하다) : **rely on**(~에 의지[의존]하다)

□ **turn on**([불 · 라디오 · 텔레비전 등을] 켜다) : **switch on**((전등 따위의) 스위치를 켜다)

□ **reduce**(줄이다, 감소시키다) : **cut**(줄이다)

English Dictionary

□ **advice** 충고
→ an opinion you give someone about what they should do
누군가에게 그들이 해야 하는 것에 대해 당신이 주는 의견

□ **avoid** 피하다
→ to prevent something bad from happening
나쁜 일이 발생하지 않도록 막다

□ **blink** (눈을) 깜빡이다
→ to shut and open your eyes quickly
눈을 재빨리 감고 뜨다

□ **break** 휴식
→ a period of time when you stop working in order to rest, eat, etc.
쉬거나 먹기 위해서 일을 멈추는 일정한 시간

□ **cause** 초래하다, 야기하다
→ to make something happen, especially something bad
어떤 것, 특히 나쁜 것이 발생하도록 만들다

□ **crack** 금, 깨진 틈
→ a thin line on the surface of something when it is broken but has not actually come apart
어떤 것이 깨졌지만 실제로 분리되지는 않았을 때 표면에 생긴 얇은 선

□ **deserted** 버려진
→ empty and quiet because no people are there
사람들이 없어 비어 있고 조용한

□ **drop** 떨어지다
→ to fall suddenly onto the ground or into something
갑자기 땅 위로나 어떤 것 안으로 떨어지다

□ **hall** 복도
→ the area just inside the door of a house or other building, that leads to other rooms
집이나 다른 건물의 문 바로 안쪽에 있는, 다른 방으로 이어지는 지역

□ **lower** 낮추다
→ to move something down from higher up
더 높은 데서 무언가를 아래로 움직이다

□ **novel** 소설
→ a long written story in which the characters and events are usually imaginary
등장인물이나 사건이 보통 가상인 쓰여진 긴 이야기

□ **prevent** 예방하다, 막다
→ to stop something from happening, or stop someone from doing something
무엇인가가 발생하는 것을 막거나 누군가가 무엇을 하는 것을 막다

□ **protect** 보호하다
→ to keep someone or something safe from harm, damage, or illness
누군가 또는 무엇인가를 해, 손상, 질병으로부터 안전하게 유지시키다

□ **reduce** 줄이다, 감소시키다
→ to make something smaller or less in size, amount, or price
어떤 것을 크기, 양 또는 가격에서 작게 또는 보다 덜하게 만들다

□ **text** (휴대 전화로) 문자를 보내다
→ to send someone a written message on a mobile phone
휴대 전화로 쓰여진 메시지를 누군가에게 보내다

□ **tip** 조언, 비법
→ a helpful piece of advice 도움이 되는 충고

□ **uncomfortable** 불편한
→ not feeling physically comfortable, or not making you feel comfortable
신체적으로 편하게 느끼지 못하거나 또는 당신이 편하게 느끼지 못하게 하는

□ **upset** 화난
→ unhappy and worried because something unpleasant or disappointing has happened
불쾌하거나 실망시키는 무엇인가가 발생해서 불행하거나 걱정스러워하는

서답형
01 다음 짝지어진 두 단어의 관계가 같도록 빈칸에 알맞은 단어를 쓰시오.

> pull : push – _____ : decrease

02 다음 빈칸에 공통으로 들어갈 말은?

> • He walked along in front _____ me, holding the lantern.
> • Could I have tuna instead _____ ham?

① to   ② with   ③ at
④ of   ⑤ from

[03~04] 다음 빈칸에 들어갈 말로 적절한 것은?

03
> There were several small ____ in the glass.

① tips   ② cracks   ③ halls
④ lines   ⑤ pains

04
> There's lots of _____ on baby care in the book.

① advice   ② center   ③ country
④ result   ⑤ level

05 다음 대화의 빈칸에 들어갈 말로 적절한 것은?

> **A:** My phone doesn't work. What should I do?
> **B:** You should take it to the _____.

① garage   ② service center
③ gallery   ④ factory   ⑤ bank

[06~07] 다음 밑줄 친 부분과 의미가 가장 가까운 것을 고르시오.

06
> New York is planning to <u>cut</u> salt intake by at least 20 percent in 5 years.

① increase   ② lean   ③ hold
④ pull   ⑤ reduce

07
> The old <u>regulations</u> were replaced by the new ones.

① tips   ② advices   ③ conditions
④ operations   ⑤ rules

08 밑줄 친 부분의 의미가 잘못된 것은?

① It is important to look at the novel in its <u>historical</u> background. (역사적인)
② Don't say anything, you'll only make matters <u>worse</u>. (더 나쁜)
③ To avoid <u>back</u> problems, always bend your knees when you lift heavy objects. (뒤로)
④ A first rule in solving a mystery is to <u>check</u> the facts. (확인하다)
⑤ Let's take a ten-minute <u>break</u>. (휴식 시간)

서답형
09 다음 영영 풀이에 해당하는 단어를 주어진 철자로 시작하여 쓰시오.

> to stop something from happening, or stop someone from doing something

➡ p_____

01 다음 〈보기〉와 같은 관계가 되도록 빈칸에 알맞은 말을 쓰시오.

┌─ 보기 ┐
small – big
└─────────┘

(1) better – _____
(2) in front of – _____

02 다음 대화의 우리말과 일치하도록 빈칸에 알맞을 말을 쓰시오.

A: I'm _____ _____ _____ school.
(나는 항상 학교에 늦어.) What should I do?
B: You should set an alarm on your smartphone.

03 다음 빈칸에 공통으로 들어갈 말을 쓰시오.

• The play was so boring that I couldn't keep myself _____ falling asleep.
• You need to relax _____ time to time.

04 다음 빈칸에 알맞은 단어를 〈보기〉에서 골라 쓰시오. (형태 변화 가능)

┌─ 보기 ┐
bend hurt lean lower
└─────────┘

(1) He was _____ on the bridge, watching the boats go by.
(2) Would you kindly _____ your voice a bit?
(3) Be careful you don't fall and _____ yourself.
(4) _____ your knees, but keep your back straight.

05 다음 주어진 우리말에 맞게 빈칸을 채우시오. (철자가 수어진 것도 있음)

(1) 내가 너에게 연락을 취할 경우를 대비해, 전화 번호를 알려줄래?
➡ Can I have your phone number in case I need to g_____ with you?

(2) 이것은 너의 돈이 아니야, 너는 그것을 돌려줘야만 해.
➡ This isn't your money and you must _____.

(3) 물속으로 뛰어들기 전에 준비운동을 하세요.
➡ Before you dive into the water, _____.

(4) 나는 네가 말하는 것에 집중하지 않고 있었어.
➡ I wasn't _____ what you were saying.

06 다음 〈보기〉에서 빈칸에 공통으로 들어갈 단어를 골라 쓰시오.

┌─ 보기 ┐
at in on from to
└─────────┘

(1) • There's a train leaving for Seattle _____ 7 o'clock.
• _____ least once a week, he cleans his house at night.
(2) • The driver put _____ full speed to get to the station on time.
• Can I have a ride _____ your bike?

Conversation

1 충고하기

A I'm always late for school. What should I do? 나는 항상 학교에 늦어. 어떻게 해야 할까?

B You should set an alarm on your smartphone. 너는 스마트폰 알람을 맞춰야 해.

- 'What should I do?'는 '어떻게 해야 할까?'의 의미인데, 이에 대한 대답으로, 'You should + 동사원형' 이나 'You had better + 동사원형'을 이용하여 충고나 조언을 할 수 있다.

- 'I think you should 동사원형 ~.'에서 think 다음에 접속사 that이 생략되어 있다. should는 도덕적 의 무를 이야기할 때 사용하는 조동사로 must, have to에 비해 일상 회화 표현에서 자주 사용한다.

충고하기

- (I think) You should 동사원형 ~. 너는 ~해야 한다.
- Maybe you should 동사원형 ~. 아마 너는 ~해야 한다.
- You'd better + 동사원형. ~하는 것이 좋겠다.
- I advise you to 동사원형 ~. 네가 ~할 것을 충고한다.

충고의 말에 답하기

- That's a good idea. 그거 좋은 생각이다.
- I guess I should. 그래야 할 것 같아.
- OK, I will. Thanks. 그렇게 할게. 고마워.

핵심 Check

1. 괄호 안의 단어를 순서대로 배열하여 충고하는 말을 완성하시오.

A: I have a test tomorrow. I'm not fully prepared it. What should I do?

B: _____ (tonight, should, you, study)

A: My dog doesn't eat anything and doesn't sleep well. What should I do?

B: _____ (warm, you'd, better, him, keep)

2. 다음 우리말과 일치하도록 빈칸에 알맞은 말을 쓰시오.

A: Let's eat hamburgers.

B: You'd _____ _____ some vegetables. (너는 야채를 먹는 것이 좋겠다.)

A: I got a poor grade.

B: _____ harder. (너는 더 열심히 공부하는 편이 좋겠다.)

② 당부하기

A **Can I eat this pizza?** 이 피자를 먹어도 되나요?

B **Sure. Just make sure you wash your hands first.** 물론이죠. 반드시 손을 먼저 씻도록 하세요.

■ 'Make sure ~'는 '반드시 ~하도록 해라, ~을 확실히 해라'의 의미로, 상대방에게 당부할 때 사용하는 표현이다. 'make sure' 다음에 접속사 that을 생략할 수 있고 당부하고자 하는 내용을 주어와 동사를 갖춘 문장으로 쓴다.

• A: I think I caught a cold. (나 감기에 걸린 것 같아.)
  B: That's too bad. Make sure you take medicine and relax. (안됐구나. 꼭 약을 먹고 쉬도록 해.)

당부하기

• Make sure ~. (반드시 ~하도록 하세요.)
• You had better ~. (~하는 것이 좋겠다.)
• Don't forget to ~. (~할 것을 잊지 마.)
• Remember to ~. (~할 것을 기억해라.)

■ 'Make sure ~'에 대해서 응답을 할 때, 'Make sure ~' 다음에 대해 긍정이면 'OK. I will.'로 답하고, 부정이면 'OK. I won't.'로 답한다.

• A: Make sure you lock the door. (문을 꼭 잠그도록 해.)
  B: OK. I will. (알겠어요. 그럴게요.)
• A: Make sure you don't get wet. (꼭 젖지 않도록 해.)
  B: OK. I won't. (알겠어요. 젖지 않을게요.)

핵심 Check

3. 다음 우리말과 일치하도록 빈칸에 알맞은 말을 쓰시오.

   A: Can I have the cookies on the table?

   B: Sure. _____ leave some _____ your sister. (꼭 네 여동생 것을 좀 남기도록 하렴.)

   A: _____ the artwork in the museum. (반드시 박물관에서 미술품을 만지지 않도록 하렴.)

   B: OK. _____ touch the artwork. (알겠어요. 미술품을 만지지 않을게요.)

4. 다음 주어진 단어를 배열하여 대화를 완성하시오.

   A: I'm not feeling well. I think I'm catching a cold. What should I do?

   B: _____ (of, make, water, warm, you, sure, drink, a, lot)

Listen & Speak 1 A

G: Oh, no! I have dark circles ❶under my eyes.

M: ❷You should ❸get more sleep.

G: 오, 이런! 눈 밑에 다크서클이 있어요.
M: 너는 잠을 더 자야 한단다.

❶ under: ~ 아래에
❷ 상대방에게 조언을 할 때 '~해야 한다'라는 의미의 조동사 should를 이용하여 'You should 동사원형 ~.'의 형태로 표현할 수 있다. 좀 더 부드럽게 말하고 싶을 때에는 'I think (that) you should ~.'라고 말한다.
❸ get more sleep: 더 자다

Check(√) True or False

(1) The girl got too much sleep.　　　　　　　　　　T☐ F☐

(2) The girl has dark circles under her eyes.　　　　T☐ F☐

Listen & Speak 1 B-1

G: I ❶forgot Jenny's birthday!

B: Isn't she your best friend?

G: ❷Yes, she is. ❸What should I do?

B: ❹I think you should tell her you're very sorry.

G: 제니의 생일을 잊어버렸어!
B: 그녀는 너의 가장 친한 친구 아니니?
G: 응, 맞아. 어떻게 해야 할까?
B: 나는 네가 그녀에게 정말 미안하다고 말해야 한다고 생각해.

❶ forgot은 forget(잊다)의 과거형이다.
❷ 부정의문문의 질문에 대답할 때, 대답하는 내용이 긍정(그녀가 가장 친한 친구)이면 Yes로 대답한다.
❸ What should I do?: 어떻게 해야 할까?
❹ think와 you 사이에 접속사 that이 생략되어 있다. you should는 '너는 ~해야 한다'의 의미로 should가 조동사이므로 다음에는 동사원형이 온다는 점에 유의해야 한다.

Check(√) True or False

(3) The boy doesn't know Jenny.　　　　　　　　　　T☐ F☐

(4) The girl feels sorry for forgetting Jenny's birthday.　T☐ F☐

Listen & Speak 1 B-2

B: I ❶feel down.

G: Why? What's the matter?

B: I ❷put on 5kg this winter. What should I do?

G: I think you should ❸cut down on snacks.

B: 기분이 우울해.
G: 왜? 무슨 일이니?
B: 이번 겨울에 5kg이 늘었어. 어떻게 해야 할까?
G: 나는 네가 간식을 줄여야 한다고 생각해.

❶ feel down: 기분이 우울하다 = feel depressed
❷ put on: ~을 늘리다, 더하다
❸ cut down on: ~을 줄이다

Check(√) True or False

(5) The boy is happy now.　　　　　　　　　　　　　T☐ F☐

(6) The boy is too heavy now.　　　　　　　　　　　T☐ F☐

Listen & Speak 2 A

W: ❶Make sure you ❷are home ❸by 12:00.

G: ❹Okay, I will.

❶ Make sure ~.는 '반드시 ~해라, ~을 확실히 해라.'라는 뜻으로 상대방에게 당부를 할 때 사용하는 표현이다.

❷ home은 명사 또는 부사로 사용될 수 있는데, 여기서는 부사로 사용되어 are가 '있다'의 의미로 해석된다. you are home 너는 '집에 있다'

❸ by+시간: ~까지

❹ Make sure 다음에 대해 긍정이면 OK. I will. '알겠어요, 그럴게요.'로 대답한다.

Listen & Speak 2 B-1

B: Mom, ❶may I ❷sleep over at Jinsu's house?

W: Did Jinsu's mom say it was okay?

B: Yes. ❸Jinsu said she would make pizza for us.

W: Okay. Make sure you ❹text me ❺when you get to Jinsu's house.

❶ May I ~?는 '~해도 될까요?'의 의미로, 상대방에게 허락을 구하는 표현이다. May 대신에 Can을 쓸 수도 있다.

❷ sleep over at ~: (남의 집에) 묵다

❸ said 뒤에 명사절을 이끄는 접속사 that이 생략되었다.

❹ text: (휴대전화로) 문자를 보내다

❺ when은 접속사로 '~할 때'의 의미로 사용되었다. get to + 장소: ~에 도착하다

Listen & Speak 2 B-2

G: Daniel, ❶what are you doing?

B: I'm reading a ❷novel on my smartphone.

G: Make sure you don't read ❸in the dark. ❹It's not good for your eyes.

B: Okay. I'll ❺turn the light on.

❶ 현재 무엇을 하고 있는지 물어보는 표현으로 'be동사의 현재형+동사ing'인 현재진행형을 사용하여 질문한다.

❷ novel: 소설

❸ in the dark: 어둠 속에서

❹ be good for: ~에 좋다

❺ turn on: [불 · 라디오 · 텔레비전 등을] 켜다

Listen & Speak 2 B-3

B: Oh, no! I didn't ❶bring my science book!

G: Ms. Lee ❷won't be happy about ❸that.

B: I know. Umm, can I ❹borrow your science book?

G: Okay. Just ❺make sure you give it back when you're done.

❶ bring: 가져오다

❷ won't는 will not의 줄임말이다.

❸ that의 내용은 과학책을 가져오지 않았다는 사실을 의미한다.

❹ borrow: 빌리다

❺ make sure 다음에 접속사 that이 생략되어 있다. give back: 돌려주다 give back은 이어동사인데, 이어동사의 목적가 대명사인 경우는 그 목적어를 반드시 두 낱말 사이에 써야 한다.

Real-Life Zone A

G: What does your shirt say?

B: Oh, this? It says "No Cellphone ❶for 24 Hours."

G: No Cellphone? Why?

B: We ❷depend on our phones ❸too much these days.

G: That's true. ❹How often will you do this?

B: ❺I'm planning on doing it ❻once a month, but I'm not sure.

G: Try it first. Then, decide how often you should do it.

B: Okay. I'm going to ❼keep a diary of what I did without my phone for 24 hours. You should try it, too.

G: I'll think about it. Make sure you keep up with it.

B: I plan to. After I do it, I'll talk about my experience in class.

❶ for+숫자+시간 단위: ~ 동안 (during+기간 명사: ~ 동안, during summer vacation: 여름 방학 동안)

❷ depend on: ~에 의존하다, ~에 의지하다 (=rely on)

❸ too는 '너무'의 의미로 부정적인 의미를 가지고 있다.

❹ How often: 얼마나 자주

❺ be planning on ~ing: ~할 계획이다

❻ once[twice, three times, four times]+a+시간 단위[day, week, month] 여기서 a는 per(~당, ~에)의 의미로 사용된다. once a month: 한 달에 한 번

❼ keep a diary: 일기를 쓰다

● 다음 우리말과 일치하도록 빈칸에 알맞은 말을 쓰시오.

Listen & Speak 1 A

G: Oh, no! I have dark circles _____ my eyes.

M: You _____ _____ _____ _____.

Listen & Speak 1 B

1. G: I _____ Jenny's birthday!

   B: Isn't she your best friend?

   G: _____, she is. _____ _____ _____ _____?

   B: _____ _____ _____ _____ _____ her you're very sorry.

2. B: I feel _____.

   G: Why? What's the matter?

   B: I _____ _____ 5 kg _____ winter. _____ _____ I do?

   G: I think you _____ _____ _____ _____ snacks.

Listen & Speak 1 C

1. A: I'm _____ _____ _____ school. What _____ _____ do?

   B: You should _____ _____ _____ on your smartphone.

2. A: I have a headache. _____ _____ _____ do?

   B: You _____ _____ _____ _____ _____.

3. A: My phone doesn't work. _____ _____ _____ _____ _____?

   B: You should _____ it to _____ _____ _____.

Listen & Speak 2 A

W: _____ _____ you are home _____ 12:00.

G: Okay, I will.

Listen & Speak 2 B

1. **B:** Mom, may I _____ _____ _____ Jinsu's house?

   W: Did Jinsu's mom say it was okay?

   B: Yes. Jinsu said she would _____ pizza for us.

   W: Okay. _____ _____ _____ _____ me when you _____ _____ Jinsu's house.

2. **G:** Daniel, _____ are you doing?

   B: I'm _____ a novel on my smartphone.

   G: Make sure you _____ _____ _____ _____ _____. It's not _____ _____ your eyes.

   B: Okay. I'll _____ the light _____.

3. **B:** Oh, no! I didn't _____ my science book!

   G: Ms. Lee _____ be happy about that.

   B: I know. Umm, can I _____ your science book?

   G: Okay. Just _____ _____ you _____ _____ _____ when you're done.

해석

1. B: 엄마, 진수네 집에서 자고 와도 돼요?
   W: 진수 엄마가 괜찮다고 하셨니?
   B: 네. 진수는 그녀가 우리를 위해 피자를 만들 것이라고 말했어요.
   W: 알겠어. 진수네 집에 도착하면 반드시 나에게 문자 하렴.
2. G: 다니엘, 뭐 하고 있니?
   B: 스마트폰에서 소설을 읽고 있어.
   G: 반드시 어두운 곳에서 읽지 않도록 해. 너의 눈에 좋지 않아.
   B: 알겠어. 불을 켤게.
3. B: 오, 이런! 과학 책을 가져오지 않았어!
   G: 이 선생님께서 좋아하지 않으실 거야.
   B: 알아. 음, 네 과학 책을 빌릴 수 있을까?
   G: 좋아. 다 사용하면 반드시 다시 돌려주도록 해.

Listen & Speak 2 C

1. **A:** Can I eat this pizza?

   B: Sure. Just _____ _____ _____ wash your hands _____.

2. **A:** _____ _____ use this computer?

   B: Sure. Just make sure you _____ _____ _____ _____ _____ _____.

3. **A:** _____ _____ _____ _____ this boat?

   B: Sure. Just make sure you wear _____ _____ _____.

1. A: 이 피자를 먹어도 되나요?
   B: 물론이죠. 반드시 손을 먼저 씻도록 하세요.
2. A: 이 컴퓨터를 사용해도 되나요?
   B: 물론이죠. 사용 후에는 반드시 전원을 끄도록 하세요.
3. A: 이 보트를 타도 되나요?
   B: 물론이죠. 구명조끼를 반드시 입도록 하세요.

[01~02] 다음 대화의 빈칸에 알맞은 말은?

01

G: Oh, no! I have dark circles under my eyes.

M: You _____ get more sleep.

① make　　② should　　③ can　　④ will　　⑤ do

02

W: Make sure you are home by 12:00.

G: _____

① Yes, I do.　　② Yes, I am.　　③ That's too bad.

④ OK. I will.　　⑤ Okay. I won't.

03 자연스러운 대화가 되도록 순서대로 배열하시오.

(A) Did Jinsu's mom say it was okay?

(B) Yes. Jinsu said she would make pizza for us.

(C) Mom, may I sleep over at Jinsu's house?

(D) Okay. Make sure you text me when you get to Jinsu's house.

➡ _____

[04~05] 다음 대화를 읽고 물음에 답하시오.

G: ①I forgot Jenny's birthday!

B: ②Isn't she your best friend?

G: ③No, she is. ④What should I do?

B: ⑤I think you should tell her you're very sorry.

04 위 대화의 밑줄 친 ①~⑤ 중 어법상 어색한 것은?

①　　　②　　　③　　　④　　　⑤

05 위 대화를 읽고 답할 수 없는 질문은?

① Does the boy know Jenny?

② What advice does the boy give to the girl?

③ Is Jenny the girl's best friend?

④ Did the girl forget Jenny's birthday?

⑤ When is Jenny's birthday?

[01~02] 다음 대화를 읽고 물음에 답하시오.

B: I feel (A)down.

G: Why? What's the matter?

B: I put (B)_____ 5kg this winter. What should I do?

G: I think you should cut down (C)_____ snacks.

01 (A)와 바꿔 쓸 수 있는 말을 고르시오.

① disappointed   ② excited

③ depressed   ④ nervous

⑤ embarrassed

02 빈칸 (B)와 (C)에 공통으로 들어갈 말을 고르시오.

① in   ② on   ③ off

④ to   ⑤ from

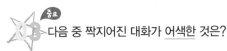

03 다음 중 짝지어진 대화가 어색한 것은?

① A: I have a headache.

   B: I think you should go see a doctor.

② A: Can I borrow your science book?

   B: Of course not. Just make sure you give it back when you're done.

③ A: I forgot the test tomorrow. What should I do?

   B: You should start studying right away.

④ A: I think my dog has a stomachache. What should I do?

   B: You should take the dog to the animal hospital.

⑤ A: Can I ride on this boat?

   B: Sure. Just make sure you wear a life jacket.

04 다음 대화의 빈칸에 알맞은 말은?

> A: Can I eat this pizza?
>
> B: Sure. _____.

① You should get more ice cream.

② Just make sure you don't read in the dark.

③ Just make sure you wash your hands first.

④ I think you should get some rest.

⑤ Make sure you turn it off after using it.

[05~06] 다음 대화를 읽고 물음에 답하시오.

> A: (A)_____ Can you give me some advice?
>
> B: You should drink warm milk before bed. And (you, about, make, minutes, sure, take, for, a, walk, 30).

05 빈칸 (A)에 알맞은 말을 고르시오.

① I can't sleep well at night.

② We have a test tomorrow.

③ I didn't bring my science book.

④ I should practice more.

⑤ I should be home by 12:00.

 서답형

06 괄호 안의 단어를 바르게 배열하시오.

➡ _____

07 밑줄 친 부분과 바꾸어 쓸 수 있는 문장을 <u>모두</u> 고르시오.

> **A:** Can I ride on this boat?
>
> **B:** Sure. <u>Just make sure you wear a life jacket.</u>

① I guess I should wear a life jacket.

② Don't forget to wear a life jacket.

③ Why don't we wear a life jacket?

④ You had better wear a life jacket.

⑤ Don't remember to wear a life jacket.

[08~09] 다음 대화를 읽고 물음에 답하시오.

> **B:** Oh, no! I (A)_____ my science book!
>
> **G:** Ms. Lee won't be happy about that.
>
> **B:** I know. Umm, can I (B)_____ your science book?
>
> **G:** Okay. <u>다 사용하면 반드시 다시 돌려주도록 해.</u>

08 빈칸 (A)와 (B)에 알맞은 것끼리 짝지어진 것을 고르시오.

	(A)	(B)
①	bring	borrow
②	bring	lend
③	didn't bring	lend
④	didn't bring	borrow
⑤	didn't bring	rent

서답형

09 밑줄 친 우리말과 같도록 주어진 단어를 이용해 영작하시오.

➡ _____

(back, just, do, give, make, when, sure)

[10~12] 다음 대화를 읽고, 물음에 답하시오.

> **G:** What's the matter, Henry?
>
> **B:** Look at my new cellphone. (①)
>
> **G:** Oh, your phone screen has a crack. (②) Did you drop it?
>
> **B:** Yes. (③) I'm so upset!
>
> **G:** I think you should get a phone case. (④) It will protect your phone.
>
> **B:** Okay. (⑤) I'll get one.

10 위 대화의 ①~⑤ 중 다음 주어진 말이 들어갈 알맞은 곳은?

> I dropped it on the way here.

①   ②   ③   ④   ⑤

서답형

11 다음 영영풀이에 해당하는 단어를 대화에서 찾아 쓰시오.

> a thin line on the surface of something when it is broken but has not actually come apart

➡ _____

12 위 대화의 내용과 일치하지 <u>않는</u> 것을 고르시오.

① A phone case can protect a phone.

② Henry is unhappy because his phone's screen has a crack.

③ Henry will buy a phone case.

④ Henry doesn't know how to use a new cellphone.

⑤ Henry bought a cellphone recently.

Conversation 서술형 시험대비

01 대화 속 괄호 안의 단어를 바르게 배열하시오.

> A: I have a headache. What should I do?
> B: (get, rest, you, some, should)

➡ _____

[02~03] 다음 대화를 읽고 물음에 답하시오.

> A: (A)무엇을 명심해야 하죠? (should, in mind)
> B: (B) _____ (the door, make, lean)

02 (A)에 주어진 어구를 이용하여 우리말을 영작하시오. (6 단어)

➡ _____

03 주어진 그림을 보고 빈칸 (B)를 괄호 안에 주어진 어구를 이용하여 채우시오.

➡ _____

04 대화의 ①~⑤ 중 어색한 부분을 찾아 바르게 고치시오.

> G: Daniel, ①what are you doing?
> B: ②I'm reading a novel on my smartphone.
> G: ③Make sure you don't read in the dark. ④It's not good for your eyes.
> B: Okay. ⑤I'll turn the light off.

➡ _____

05 자연스러운 대화가 되도록 순서대로 배열하시오.

> (A) I know. Umm, can I borrow your science book?
> (B) Oh, no! I didn't bring my science book!
> (C) Okay. Just make sure you give it back when you're done.
> (D) Ms. Lee won't be happy about that.

➡ _____

06 주어진 문장 다음에 이어질 대화의 순서를 바르게 배열하시오.

> What's the matter, Henry?

> (A) Yes. I dropped it on the way here. I'm so upset!
> (B) Okay. I'll get one.
> (C) I think you should get a phone case. It will protect your phone.
> (D) Oh, your phone screen has a crack. Did you drop it?
> (E) Look at my new cellphone.

➡ _____

07 대화의 흐름상 어색한 부분을 찾아 바르게 고치시오.

> G: Oh, no! I have dark circles under my eyes.
> M: You should get less sleep.

➡ _____

교과서
Grammar

① to부정사의 형용사적 용법

Here are some tips **to protect** your health. 여기 여러분의 건강을 지켜줄 몇 가지 조언이 있습니다.
I needed a book **to read**. 나는 읽을 책이 필요했다.

■ to부정사는 'to+동사원형'의 형태로 명사, 형용사, 부사로 사용될 수 있다.
• **To visit** Rome is his dream. 〈명사〉 로마를 방문하는 것은 그의 꿈이다.
• I want something **to drink**. 〈형용사〉 나는 마실 것을 원해.
• The problem was difficult **to solve**. 〈부사〉 그 문제는 풀기에 어려웠다.

■ to부정사가 명사(구)나 대명사(구) 뒤에 놓여서 앞의 명사(구)나 대명사(구)를 수식하는 형용사와 같은 역할을 한다. 이때 보통 바로 앞에 위치한 명사를 꾸며준다.
• She had nothing **to wear**. 그녀는 입을 것이 없었다.

■ to부정사가 형용사 역할을 할 때 전치사를 동반한 경우 수식받는 명사가 전치사의 목적어로 사용되었으면 전치사를 생략하면 안 된다.
• I need a chair **to sit on**. 나는 앉을 의자가 필요해.

■ 수식받는 명사를 전치사 다음에 넣어 전치사의 목적어인지 아닌지 확인하는 것이 좋다.
• Mike needs a friend **to play with**.
  (play with a friend (○)) Mike는 함께 놀 친구가 필요하다.
  Mike needs a friend to play. (play a friend (×))

■ to부정사가 -thing, -body, -one으로 끝나는 부정대명사를 형용사와 함께 수식할 때는 '대명사+형용사 +to부정사'의 어순임에 유의한다.
• I want something **cold to drink**. 나는 마실 차가운 것을 원해.
• We have somebody **new to meet**. 우리는 만나볼 새로 온 사람이 있어.

핵심 Check

1. 괄호 안에서 알맞은 것을 고르시오.
   (1) Dan wanted something (drink / to drink).
   (2) They need several teachers (to teach / teaching) Korean.
   (3) There was no spoon (to eat / to eat with).
   (4) I don't have anything (curious to ask / to ask curious).

② 사역동사

> My mom **made** me **clean** my room. 엄마는 내가 내 방을 청소하도록 시켰다.
>
> Susan **made** her daughter **play** the piano. Susan은 그녀의 딸이 피아노를 치도록 시켰다.

■ 사역동사는 '사역동사+목적어+목적격보어'의 형태로 '~을 하게 하다(하라고 시키다)'의 뜻을 가지며 사역동사에는 make, let, have가 있다.

• Mom **made** me **do** my homework. 엄마는 내게 숙제를 하라고 시켰다.

• **Let** me **introduce** myself. 제 소개를 하겠습니다.

■ 목적격보어로 동사원형이 오면 능동의 의미로 '~(목적어)가 …(목적격보어)을 하게 하다'의 뜻을 가지며, 과거분사가 오면 수동의 의미로 '~(목적어)가 …(목적격보어)을 당하게[되게] 하다'의 뜻을 갖는다.

• I **had** him **call** her. 〈능동〉 나는 그가 그녀에게 전화를 걸도록 시켰다. (전화를 거는 것으로 능동)

• I **had** my hair **cut**. 〈수동〉 나는 머리를 깎았다. (머리가 깎이는 것으로 수동)

■ help는 목적격보어로 동사원형이나 to부정사가 오며 뜻의 차이는 없다.

• Natalie **helped** her mom **prepare** dinner. Natalie는 엄마가 저녁 준비하는 것을 도왔다.
  = Natalie **helped** her mom **to prepare** dinner.

■ get도 '~하게 하다'라는 의미로 쓰일 수 있지만 목적격보어로 to부정사가 온다. 수동의 의미일 때는 사역동사와 마찬가지로 과거분사가 온다.

• Mom **got** me **to do** my homework. 〈능동〉 엄마는 내게 숙제를 하라고 시켰다.

• I **got** my hair **cut**. <수동> 나는 머리를 깎았다.

핵심 Check

2. 괄호 안에서 알맞은 것을 고르시오.

(1) Cartoons make me (laugh / to laugh).

(2) Nari had her computer (repairing / repaired).

(3) She helped me (to do / doing) my homework.

(4) I got him (paint / to paint) the wall.

Grammar 시험대비 기본평가

01 다음 문장에서 어법상 어색한 부분을 바르게 고쳐 쓰시오.

(1) Give me a sheet of paper to write.

‗‗‗‗‗‗‗‗‗‗ ➡ ‗‗‗‗‗‗‗‗‗‗

(2) I want to make myself looking better in photos.

‗‗‗‗‗‗‗‗‗‗ ➡ ‗‗‗‗‗‗‗‗‗‗

(3) Do you have time play soccer?

‗‗‗‗‗‗‗‗‗‗ ➡ ‗‗‗‗‗‗‗‗‗‗

(4) He helped his brother doing his homework.

‗‗‗‗‗‗‗‗‗‗ ➡ ‗‗‗‗‗‗‗‗‗‗

02 다음 중 어법상 틀린 문장은?

① She didn't have any socks to wear.
② Mom made me do the dishes.
③ I have some pictures to show you.
④ Edan got me set the table.
⑤ What is the best way to learn Korean?

03 다음 우리말에 맞게 주어진 단어를 바르게 배열하시오. (필요하면 어형을 바꿀 것)

(1) 그는 모두가 늦게까지 일하게 시켰다.

(he / work / everyone / made / late)

➡ ‗‗‗‗‗‗‗‗‗‗‗‗‗‗‗‗‗‗‗‗‗‗‗‗‗‗‗‗

(2) 가을은 수확의 계절이다.

(is / harvest / season / autumn / the / to)

➡ ‗‗‗‗‗‗‗‗‗‗‗‗‗‗‗‗‗‗‗‗‗‗‗‗‗‗‗‗

(3) 그는 내가 무거운 상자를 옮기는 것을 도와주었다.

(he / me / box / carry / helped / the / heavy)

➡ ‗‗‗‗‗‗‗‗‗‗‗‗‗‗‗‗‗‗‗‗‗‗‗‗‗‗‗‗

(4) 나는 어젯밤에 할 일이 많았다.

(I / night / work / lot / do / had / a / last / to / of)

➡ ‗‗‗‗‗‗‗‗‗‗‗‗‗‗‗‗‗‗‗‗‗‗‗‗‗‗‗‗

01 다음 빈칸에 알맞은 것은?

I need gloves _____.

① put
② to put
③ putting
④ to put in
⑤ to put on

02 다음 문장의 빈칸에 들어갈 알맞은 것은?

She made him _____ for her.

① wait
② waits
③ waited
④ waiting
⑤ to wait

03 다음 빈칸에 알맞은 말이 바르게 짝지어진 것은?

• She had him _____ the boxes. (carry)
• Jessica wants something _____ . (eat)

① carrying - eat
② carried - eating
③ carried - to eat
④ carry - eating
⑤ carry - to eat

서답형 04 다음 문장에서 어법상 틀린 부분을 찾아 바르게 고쳐 쓰시오.

I want to buy something to wear nice.

_____ ➡ _____

서답형 05 괄호 안에서 알맞은 것을 고르시오.

(1) His jokes always make me (smile / to smile).
(2) Jake had the wall (paint / painted).
(3) Anna helped me (finding / to find) the way to the station.
(4) Nicole got her son (walk / to walk) the dog.
(5) It's time (checking / to check) the e-mails.
(6) Emily has two daughters (to take care / to take care of).
(7) Is there something (to correct wrong / wrong to correct)?

06 다음 〈보기〉의 밑줄 친 부분과 성격이 다른 하나는?

┤ 보기 ├
You must bring something to eat.

① She will buy a pretty dress to wear to the party.
② He woke up to find himself famous.
③ We didn't have enough time to make cookies for them.
④ I had many files to copy.
⑤ Now it's my turn to take out the trash.

07 다음 중 밑줄 친 부분의 쓰임이 나머지 셋과 <u>다른</u> 두 개는?

① Do you have a book <u>to read</u>?
② I don't have enough money <u>to buy</u> the dress.
③ He was so surprised <u>to run</u> into a friend of his in New York.
④ My mother encouraged me <u>to study</u> history hard.
⑤ Nick needs a friend <u>to talk</u> with.

08 다음 중 어법상 <u>어색한</u> 것은?

① Can you help me to carry the boxes?
② He let the children cross the road.
③ I will have him call you back.
④ Mom let me go to the party.
⑤ My teacher made me to solve the difficult math problems.

09 다음 빈칸에 공통으로 알맞은 말은?

| • She helped me _____ the email. |
| • She had a lot of emails _____ . |

① sending   ② to send   ③ sent
④ send   ⑤ sends

10 다음 문장의 빈칸에 알맞지 <u>않은</u> 것은?

| My brother _____ me do exercise every day. |

① allowed   ② made   ③ let
④ helped   ⑤ had

11 다음 우리말에 맞게 영작한 것을 고르시오.

| 나의 부모님은 내가 밤늦게까지 밖에 있도록 하지 않으셨다. |

① My parents didn't let me to stay out late at night.
② My parents didn't let me staying out late at night.
③ My parents didn't let me stay out late at night.
④ My parents didn't let me stayed out late at night.
⑤ My parents didn't let me to staying out late at night.

서답형

12 다음 문장에서 어법상 <u>어색한</u> 부분을 바르게 고쳐 다시 쓰시오.

(1) I want to make it happening during the school festival.
➡ _____

(2) Is there anyone funny bring to the party?
➡ _____

(3) I'll have all the files copy for the meeting.
➡ _____

(4) Dominick bought his daughter a doll to play.
➡ _____

(5) Amy got her sister do her homework by herself.
➡ _____

다음 빈칸에 적절하지 <u>않은</u> 것을 고르시오.

> Her parents did not _____ her go to the concert.

① get   ② have   ③ let
④ make   ⑤ help

14 다음 우리말을 영어로 바르게 옮긴 것은?

> Anna는 지난주에 살 집을 샀다.

① Anna bought a house lived last week.
② Anna bought a house lives last week.
③ Anna bought a house living last week.
④ Anna bought a house to live last week.
⑤ Anna bought a house to live in last week.

15 다음 밑줄 친 단어의 쓰임이 주어진 문장과 같은 것은?

> Using a smartphone too much <u>makes</u> my eyes feel dry and tired.

① You will <u>make</u> a lot of friends there.
② Ann often <u>makes</u> cookies for me.
③ The springshower <u>makes</u> the grass grow.
④ Mom <u>made</u> me a cheese cake.
⑤ Flowers <u>make</u> our rooms cheerful.

서답형
16 주어진 어구를 바르게 배열하여 문장을 완성하시오. (한 단어를 보충할 것.)

> Susan / T-shirt / the hiking / wants / wear / comfortable / during / a

➡ _____

_____

서답형
17 다음 우리말에 맞게 주어진 단어를 바르게 배열하시오.

> 저는 제가 잘생겨 보이게 해줄 어떤 멋진 것을 찾고 있어요.
> (I / me / something / looking / look / am / make / nice / good / for / to)

➡ _____

_____

서답형
18 다음 우리말과 일치하도록 주어진 단어를 이용하여 빈칸에 알맞은 말을 쓰시오.

(1) Chris는 진짜 가수가 될 기회를 얻었다.
  ➡ Chris got a chance _____ _____ a real singer. (become)
(2) 무엇이 Bella로 하여금 아침 전철에서 그 일을 하게 만들었을까?
  ➡ What made Bella _____ the work in a morning subway? (do)
(3) Ken은 Nicole을 기쁘게 하기 위하여 그녀에게 줄 선물을 샀다.
  ➡ Ken bought a present _____ _____ to Nicole _____ _____ her pleased. (give, make)
(4) 나는 그 보고서를 제시간에 끝내도록 하기 위해 최선을 다했다.
  ➡ I did my best to have the report _____ on time. (finish)
(5) 대화하기에 즐거운 사람은 항상 있다.
  ➡ There is always someone interesting _____ _____ _____. (talk, with)
(6) 선생님은 우리가 잠시 동안 함께 일하도록 하셨다.
  ➡ Our teacher got us _____ _____ together for a while. (work)

01 다음 글에서 어법상 잘못 쓰인 것을 찾아 알맞게 고치시오.

> If you don't wake up energized every morning to make your day an amazing one, you probably don't have life goals achieving.

_____ ➡ _____

02 다음 문장을 to부정사를 이용하여 한 문장으로 바꿔 쓰시오.

(1) • Angie has twin sisters.
  • She has to take care of them.
  ➡ _____

(2) • Allen knows many silly jokes.
  • The jokes make us laugh.
  ➡ _____

 03 다음 중 어법상 잘못된 것을 고쳐 문장을 다시 쓰시오.

(1) Marilyn won't let her daughter to sleep over at her friend's.
  ➡ _____

(2) I don't know how she got him say yes.
  ➡ _____

(3) I asked him to have my computer repair.
  ➡ _____

(4) He helped her carrying her things.
  ➡ _____

04 주어진 어휘와 to부정사를 이용하여 자신의 문장을 쓰시오.

(1) want, ability, speak
  ➡ _____

(2) take, chance, become
  ➡ _____

(3) there, way, solve
  ➡ _____

05 다음 그림을 보고 주어진 어휘를 이용하여 빈칸에 알맞은 말을 쓰시오.

> A: My dog is sick.
> B: You should have him _____ to the animal hospital. (take)

 06 다음 〈보기〉에 주어진 단어를 이용하여 문맥에 맞게 문장을 완성하시오.

┌─ 보기 ┐
remember   decide   talk
└─────────┘

(1) It is time _____ _____ our plan.
(2) We selected some interesting topics _____ _____ _____.
(3) Harry received a list of names _____ _____.

07 다음 글에서 어법상 **틀린** 부분을 **모두** 찾아 바르게 고쳐 쓰시오.

> When I got a cold, my mom had me to eat chicken soup. It helped me feeling better.

➡ _____

08 다음 중 어법상 어색한 것을 바르게 고치시오.

(1) Here are some tips to protecting your health.

_____ ➡ _____

(2) Silvia needs someone to look her dog while she is away.

_____ ➡ _____

(3) Will you bring me a sheet of paper to write?

_____ ➡ _____

(4) Do you have important something to tell?

_____ ➡ _____

09 다음 문장을 make를 이용하여 비슷한 의미의 문장으로 바꿔 쓰시오.

(1) Our teacher told us to hand in our report by tomorrow.

➡ _____

(2) The police officer ordered them to leave immediately.

➡ _____

(3) My mom asked me to come home early today.

➡ _____

10 다음 우리말을 괄호 안에 주어진 어휘를 이용하여 영작하시오.

(1) 우리 선생님은 우리에게 수업에서 영어만 사용하도록 시키셨다. (make, only, in class)

➡ _____

(2) 그가 파리에 갔을 때 그가 의지할 사람은 아무도 없었다. (Paris, nobody, when, there, depend)

➡ _____

(3) Simon은 그의 컴퓨터를 검사받도록 했다. (have, check)

➡ _____

(4) 그들은 그들에게 영어를 가르칠 선생님이 필요했다. (need, a teacher, 8 단어)

➡ _____

(5) 나는 어제 저녁에 엄마가 식사를 준비하는 것을 도와드렸다. (Mom, prepare, dinner, 8 단어)

➡ _____

11 다음 두 문장의 뜻이 같도록 빈칸에 알맞은 말을 쓰시오.

(1) Neil got the car cleaned by the mechanic.

= Neil got the mechanic _____ the car.

(2) Sharon had Tom repair her bike.

= Sharon had her bike _____ by Tom.

Reading

Health Tips for Smartphone Users

Seongmin spends a lot of time using his smartphone.
　　　　　spend time + ～ing: ～하는 데 시간을 쓰다

He checks the news and weather.

He plays smartphone games.

He texts his friends.
　　　문자를 보내다

He finds information on the Internet.
　　　　　정보

He reads online comic books.
　　　　　　만화책

He watches movies.

Seongmin cannot take his hands off his smartphone all day long.
　　　cannot + 동사원형: ～할 수 없다　　take ～ off: ～을 떼어 놓다　　　　　온종일

He does not know that using a smartphone too much can cause health
　　　　　　　접속사 that (know의 목적어)　　　　　　　　　　　건강 문제

problems. Are you a heavy user of your smartphone like Seongmin? If
　　　　　　심한　　　　　　　　　　　　～처럼(전치사)　　만일 그렇다면

so, here are some tips to protect your health.
여기 있다　　　　　to부정사의 형용사적 용법. tips를 수식

 확인문제

● 다음 문장이 본문의 내용과 일치하면 T, 일치하지 않으면 F를 쓰시오.

1　Seongmin finds information on the Internet.　☐

2　Seongmin watches TV dramas on the Internet.　☐

3　Seongmin knows that using a smartphone too much can cause health problems.　☐

4.　Seongmin is a heavy user of his smartphone.　☐

Watch your neck and back. When you read on your smartphone, you
　　　　　목　　　　등. 시간의 접속사: ～할 때

usually bend your neck. This "text neck" pose increases the pressure
빈도 부사(동사 앞에 위치)　　　　　　　　　　증가시키다　　　　입력

on your neck and back. The best way to prevent this pressure is to
～에 대한　　　　　　　　　　to부정사의 형용사적 용법. way를 수식

bring the phone up to the level of your eyes. Another way is to lower
to부정사의 명사적 용법 (보어 역할) ～까지　　　　　　to부정사의 명사적 용법 (보어 역할)

your eyes instead of bending your neck.
　　　～하는 대신에　동명사 (전치사 of의 목적어)

Give your eyes a break. It makes your eyes feel tired and dry to read
휴식　가주어　사역동사 + 목적어 + 동사원형: ～이 …하게 하다　진주어

small letters on a smartphone for a long time. Using a smartphone in
동명사: 동사원형 + ～ing

the dark or in a moving car makes this problem worse. To avoid this,
어둠 속에서　동명사 주어는 단수 취급　bad-worse-worst.　to부정사의 부사적 용법 (목적)

give your eyes a break from time to time.
때때로

Follow the 20-20-20 rules: Every 20 minutes, take a 20-second break
따르다　콜론: 앞 문장을 보충 설명　20분마다

and look at something at least 20 feet away. Also, blink your eyes
등위접속사 (순접)　적어도　떨어져 있는　눈을 깜박이다

often. This will keep your eyes from becoming dry.
앞문장의 내용을 받는 지시대명사　～가 …하는 것을 막다

dry 마른, 건조한
letter 글자, 문자
worse 너 나쁜
avoid 피하다
rule 규칙
blink 눈을 깜박이다

확인문제

● 다음 문장이 본문의 내용과 일치하면 T, 일치하지 않으면 F를 쓰시오.

1 This "text neck" pose increases the pressure on your neck and back. ☐

2 The best way to prevent the pressure on your neck and back is to lower your neck. ☐

3 You should give your eyes a break from time to time. ☐

4 You should follow the 20-20-20 rules. ☐

5 To blink your eyes often will make your eyes dry. ☐

Do you text a lot on your smartphone? Texting for a long time can hurt
문자를 보내다　동명사 주어　가능성

your fingers and wrists. Try these exercises. They will help reduce the
손가락　손목　해보다　운동　=These exercises 준사역동사　= to reduce

pain in your fingers and wrists.
통증

Pull on each finger of each hand.
잡아당기다　each+단수명사

Put the backs of your hands together with your arms out in front of you.
손등　팔을 벌린 채로　～ 앞에

But remember. The best tip to prevent these health problems is to use
기억하다　to부정사의 형용사적 용법. tip을 수식　to부정사의 명사적 용법 (보어 역할)

your smartphone less. Give yourself some rest from your smartphone.
little의 비교급　재귀대명사

a lot 많이
wrist 손목
reduce 줄이다
pain 아픔, 통증
pull 당기다

확인문제

● 다음 문장이 본문의 내용과 일치하면 T, 일치하지 않으면 F를 쓰시오.

1 Texting for a long time can hurt your fingers and wrists. ☐

2 Pull on each wrist of each hand. ☐

3 Put the palms of your hands together. ☐

4 Take some rest from your smartphone. ☐

● 우리말을 참고하여 빈칸에 알맞은 말을 쓰시오.

1 _____ _____ for Smartphone Users

2 Seongmin _____ a lot of time _____ his smartphone.

3 He _____ the news and weather.

4 He _____ smartphone _____.

5 He _____ his friends.

6 He _____ _____ on the Internet.

7 He reads _____ _____ _____.

8 He _____ movies.

9 Seongmin cannot _____ his hands _____ his smartphone all day long.

10 He does not know that using a smartphone too much can _____ _____ _____.

11 Are you _____ _____ _____ of your smartphone like Seongmin?

12 _____ _____, here are some tips _____ _____ your health.

13 _____ your neck and back.

14 When you read on your smartphone, you _____ _____ your neck.

15 This "_____ _____" _____ increases the pressure on your neck and back.

16 The best way _____ _____ this pressure is to bring the phone _____ _____ the level of your eyes.

1 스마트폰 사용자들을 위한 건강 조언

2 성민이는 스마트폰을 사용하는 데 많은 시간을 보냅니다.

3 그는 뉴스와 날씨를 확인합니다.

4 그는 스마트폰 게임을 합니다.

5 그는 친구들에게 문자 메시지를 보냅니다.

6 그는 인터넷에서 정보를 찾습니다.

7 그는 온라인 만화책을 읽습니다.

8 그는 영화를 봅니다.

9 성민이는 하루 종일 스마트폰에서 손을 뗄 수가 없습니다.

10 그는 스마트폰을 너무 많이 사용하는 것이 건강 문제를 일으킬 수 있다는 것을 모릅니다.

11 여러분은 성민이와 같은 스마트폰 과다 사용자인가요?

12 그렇다면, 여기 여러분의 건강을 지켜 줄 몇 가지 조언이 있습니다.

13 여러분의 목과 척추를 조심하세요.

14 스마트폰을 볼 때, 여러분은 보통 목을 구부립니다.

15 이 "거북목" 자세는 여러분의 목과 척추에 가해지는 압력을 증가시킵니다.

16 이러한 압력을 예방하는 가장 좋은 방법은 휴대 전화를 여러분의 눈높이까지 올리는 것입니다.

17 _____ _____ is to lower your eyes _____ _____ _____ your neck.

18 Give your eyes _____ _____ .

19 It makes your eyes _____ _____ and dry to read small letters on a smartphone _____ _____ _____ _____ .

20 Using a smartphone _____ _____ _____ or in a moving car makes this problem _____ .

21 _____ _____ this, give your eyes a break _____ _____ _____ _____ .

22 Follow the 20-20-20 rules: _____ 20 minutes, take _____ _____ _____ and look at something at least 20 _____ _____ .

23 Also, _____ your eyes _____ .

24 This will _____ your eyes _____ _____ dry.

25 Do you text a lot _____ _____ _____ ?

26 _____ for a long time can _____ your fingers and wrists.

27 _____ these exercises.

28 They will _____ _____ the pain in your fingers and wrists.

29 _____ _____ each finger of each hand.

30 _____ the backs of your hands _____ _____ _____ _____ out in front of you.

31 But _____ .

32 _____ _____ _____ to prevent these health problems is _____ _____ your smartphone _____ .

33 Give yourself _____ _____ _____ your smartphone.

17 또 다른 방법은 여러분의 목을 구부리는 대신에 시선을 낮추는 것입니다.

18 눈을 쉬게 하세요.

19 오랫동안 스마트폰의 작은 글자를 읽는 것은 눈이 피곤해지고 건조하게 느끼도록 만듭니다.

20 어두운 곳이나 움직이는 차에서 스마트폰을 사용하는 것은 이러한 문제를 더욱 악화시킵니다.

21 이것을 피하려면, 눈을 때때로 쉬게 하세요.

22 20-20-20 규칙을 따르세요. 20분마다 20초의 휴식을 취하고 적어도 20피트 이상 떨어져 있는 사물을 바라보세요.

23 또한, 눈을 자주 깜박이세요.

24 이것은 여러분의 눈이 건조해지는 것을 막아 줄 것입니다.

25 스마트폰으로 문자 메시지를 많이 보내나요?

26 오랫동안 문자 메시지를 보내는 것은 여러분의 손가락과 손목을 상하게 할 수 있습니다.

27 이런 운동을 해 보세요.

28 그것은 여러분의 손가락과 손목의 통증을 줄이는 것을 도와줄 것입니다.

29 각 손의 각 손가락을 당기세요.

30 팔을 여러분 앞에서 벌린 채로 손등을 마주 놓으세요.

31 그러나 기억하세요.

32 이러한 건강 문제를 예방하는 가장 좋은 방법은 스마트폰을 덜 사용하는 것입니다.

33 여러분 자신에게 스마트폰으로부터 휴식을 주세요.

우리말을 참고하여 본문을 영작하시오.

1 스마트폰 사용자들을 위한 건강 조언

➡ _____

2 성민이는 스마트폰을 사용하는 데 많은 시간을 보냅니다.

➡ _____

3 그는 뉴스와 날씨를 확인합니다.

➡ _____

4 그는 스마트폰 게임을 합니다.

➡ _____

5 그는 친구들에게 문자 메시지를 보냅니다.

➡ _____

6 그는 인터넷에서 정보를 찾습니다.

➡ _____

7 그는 온라인 만화책을 읽습니다.

➡ _____

8 그는 영화를 봅니다.

➡ _____

9 성민이는 하루 종일 스마트폰에서 손을 뗄 수가 없습니다.

➡ _____

10 그는 스마트폰을 너무 많이 사용하는 것이 건강 문제를 일으킬 수 있다는 것을 모릅니다.

➡ _____

11 여러분은 성민이와 같은 스마트폰 과다 사용자인가요?

➡ _____

12 그렇다면, 여기 여러분의 건강을 지켜 줄 몇 가지 조언이 있습니다.

➡ _____

13 여러분의 목과 척추를 조심하세요.

➡ _____

14 스마트폰을 볼 때, 여러분은 보통 목을 구부립니다.

➡ _____

15 이 "거북목" 자세는 여러분의 목과 척추에 가해지는 압력을 증가시킵니다.

➡ _____

16 이러한 압력을 예방하는 가장 좋은 방법은 휴대 전화를 여러분의 눈높이까지 올리는 것입니다.

➡ _____

17 또 다른 방법은 여러분의 목을 구부리는 대신에 시선을 낮추는 것입니다.

➡ _____

18 눈을 쉬게 하세요.

➡ _____

19 오랫동안 스마트폰의 작은 글자를 읽는 것은 눈이 피곤해지고 건조하게 느끼도록 만듭니다.

➡ _____

20 어두운 곳이나 움직이는 차에서 스마트폰을 사용하는 것은 이러한 문제를 더욱 악화시킵니다.

➡ _____

21 이것을 피하려면, 눈을 때때로 쉬게 하세요.

➡ _____

22 20-20-20 규칙을 따르세요. 20분마다 20초의 휴식을 취하고 적어도 20피트 이상 떨어져 있는 사물을 바라보세요.

➡ _____

23 또한, 눈을 자주 깜박이세요.

➡ _____

24 이것은 여러분의 눈이 건조해지는 것을 막아 줄 것입니다.

➡ _____

25 스마트폰으로 문자 메시지를 많이 보내나요?

➡ _____

26 오랫동안 문자 메시지를 보내는 것은 여러분의 손가락과 손목을 상하게 할 수 있습니다.

➡ _____

27 이런 운동을 해 보세요.

➡ _____

28 그것은 여러분의 손가락과 손목의 통증을 줄이는 것을 도와줄 것입니다.

➡ _____

29 각 손의 각 손가락을 당기세요.

➡ _____

30 팔을 여러분 앞에서 벌린 채로 손등을 마주 놓으세요.

➡ _____

31 그러나 기억하세요.

➡ _____

32 이러한 건강 문제를 예방하는 가장 좋은 방법은 스마트폰을 덜 사용하는 것입니다.

➡ _____

33 여러분 자신에게 스마트폰으로부터 휴식을 주세요.

➡ _____

[01~03] 다음 글을 읽고 물음에 답하시오.

Seongmin cannot take his hands off his smartphone all day long. He does not know that using a smartphone too much can cause ⓐ____ problems. ⓑ여러분은 성민이와 같은 스마트폰 과다 사용자인가요? If so, here are some tips to protect your health.

01 위 글의 빈칸 ⓐ에 들어갈 알맞은 말을 고르시오.

① money　　② health
③ friend　　④ posture
⑤ grade

서답형
02 위 글의 밑줄 친 ⓑ의 우리말에 맞게 주어진 어휘를 이용하여 10 단어로 영작하시오.

heavy, like

➡ _____

_____

03 위 글의 뒤에 올 내용으로 가장 알맞은 것을 고르시오.

① 스마트폰 사용 시 당신의 건강을 해치는 여러 자세들
② 스마트폰 사용이 가져오는 여러 가지 장점들
③ 스마트폰 사용으로 인해 변하게 된 사람들의 일상
④ 스마트폰 사용 시 주의해야 할 내용들
⑤ 스마트폰 사용 시 여러분의 건강을 지켜 줄 몇 가지 조언

[04~06] 다음 글을 읽고 물음에 답하시오.

Watch your neck and back. When you read ⓐ____ your smartphone, you usually bend your neck. This "ⓑ____ ____" pose (A)[decreases / increases] the (B)[pleasure / pressure] ⓒ____ your neck and back. The best way to (C)[prevent / protect] this pressure is to bring the phone up to the level of your eyes. Another way is to lower your eyes instead of bending your neck.

04 위 글의 빈칸 ⓐ와 ⓒ에 공통으로 들어갈 알맞은 전치사를 고르시오.

① on　　② about
③ in　　④ for
⑤ from

서답형
05 주어진 영영풀이를 참고하여 빈칸 ⓑ에 철자 t로 시작하는 단어를 쓰시오.

the word to describe repeated stress, injury and pain in the neck resulting from excessive watching or texting on hand-held devices. It is also often known as turtle neck posture.

➡ _____

서답형
06 위 글의 괄호 (A)~(C)에서 문맥상 알맞은 낱말을 골라 쓰시오.

➡ (A)_____　(B)_____　(C)_____

[07~09] 다음 글을 읽고 물음에 답하시오.

Give your eyes a break. (①) Using a smartphone in the dark or in a moving car makes this problem worse. (②) To avoid this, give your eyes a break ⓐfrom time to time. (③) Follow the 20-20-20 rules: Every 20 minutes, take a 20-second break and look at something at least 20 feet away. (④) Also, blink your eyes often. (⑤) ⓑThis will keep your eyes from becoming dry.

07 위 글의 흐름으로 보아, 주어진 문장이 들어가기에 가장 적절한 곳은?

> It makes your eyes feel tired and dry to read small letters on a smartphone for a long time.

①   ②   ③   ④   ⑤

08 위 글의 밑줄 친 ⓐfrom time to time과 바꿔 쓸 수 없는 말을 고르시오.

① sometimes   ② rarely
③ now and then   ④ at times
⑤ once in a while

09 위 글의 밑줄 친 ⓑThis가 가리키는 것을 본문에서 찾아 영어로 쓰시오.

➡ _____

[10~12] 다음 글을 읽고 물음에 답하시오.

Seongmin spends ⓐa lot of time ⓑ his smartphone.
He checks the news and weather.
He plays smartphone games.
He texts his friends.
He finds information on the Internet.
He reads online comic books.
He watches movies.

10 위 글의 밑줄 친 ⓐa lot of와 바꿔 쓸 수 없는 말을 고르시오.

① much   ② plenty of
③ lots of   ④ many
⑤ a great deal of

11 위 글의 빈칸 ⓑ에 use를 알맞은 형태로 쓰시오.

➡ _____

12 위 글의 성민이의 스마트폰 사용에 관한 내용으로 일치하지 않는 것은?

① 스마트폰 사용에 많은 시간을 보낸다.
② 뉴스와 날씨를 확인한다.
③ 친구들에게 메일을 보낸다.
④ 인터넷에서 정보를 찾는다.
⑤ 온라인 만화책을 읽는다.

[13~15] 다음 글을 읽고 물음에 답하시오.

Do you text a lot on your smartphone? Texting for a long time can hurt your fingers and wrists. Try ⓐthese exercises. ⓑThey will help reduce the pain in your fingers and wrists.
Pull on each finger of each hand.
Put the backs of your hands together with your arms out in front of you.

13 다음 문장에서 위 글의 내용과 다른 부분을 찾아서 고치시오.

> • To text for a long time can do harm to your eyes.

➡ _____

14 위 글의 밑줄 친 ⓐthese exercises를 하는 방법을 우리말로 설명하시오.

➡ (1) _____
   (2) _____

서답형

15 위 글의 밑줄 친 ⓑ를 다음과 같이 바꿔 쓸 때 빈칸에 알맞은 말을 쓰시오.

➡ They will help _____ _____ the pain in your fingers and wrists.

[16~18] 다음 글을 읽고 물음에 답하시오.

There are both good things and bad things about using a smartphone. First, I can get in touch with my friends right away. Also, I can easily get information I need. That is useful when I have a lot of homework to do. ⓐ , ⓑ스마트폰을 너무 많이 사용하는 것은 눈이 건조하고 피곤하게 만듭니다. Also, text messages and ads keep me from paying attention to my studies. So I need to use my smartphone intelligently.

 16 위 글의 제목으로 알맞은 것을 고르시오.

① Merits of Using a Smartphone
② Weakness of Using a Smartphone
③ How to Get Information Easily
④ Pay Attention to Your Studies
⑤ Merits and Demerits of a Smartphone

17 위 글의 빈칸 ⓐ에 들어갈 알맞은 말을 고르시오.

① In addition   ② On the other hand
③ Therefore   ④ For example
⑤ Similarly

서답형

18 위 글의 밑줄 친 ⓑ의 우리말에 맞게 한 단어를 보충하여, 주어진 어휘를 알맞게 배열하시오.

> my eyes / too much / dry and tired / makes / a smartphone / feel

➡ _____

_____

[19~21] 다음 글을 읽고 물음에 답하시오.

Give your eyes a break. ⓐIt makes your eyes feel tired and dry to read small letters on a smartphone for a long time. Using a smartphone in the dark or in a moving car makes this problem worse. To avoid this, give your eyes a break from time to time. Follow the 20-20-20 rules: Every 20 minutes, take a 20-second break and look at something at least 20 feet away. Also, blink your eyes often. This will keep your eyes ⓑ becoming dry.

19 위 글의 주제로 알맞은 것을 고르시오.

① the effective way to read small letters on a smartphone
② how to use a smartphone in the dark or in a moving car
③ the difficulty of following the 20-20-20 rules
④ how to prevent the eye problems when using a smartphone
⑤ the tips for keeping your eyes clean and moist

20 위 글의 밑줄 친 ⓐIt과 문법적 쓰임이 같은 것을 고르시오.

① It is two miles from here to the beach.
② He took a stone and threw it.
③ It is impossible to get there in time.
④ Hello, Peter, it's Mike here.
⑤ I make it a rule to get up early.

서답형

21 위 글의 빈칸 ⓑ에 들어갈 알맞은 전치사를 쓰시오.

➡ _____

[22~24] 다음 스마트폰 사용 지수를 나타내는 표를 보고 물음에 답하시오.

	Always (2 points)	Sometimes (1 point)	Never (no point)
1. I use my smartphone when I eat breakfast.	✓		
2. I use my smartphone in a car.		✓	
3. I use my smartphone when I am walking.		✓	
4. I feel uncomfortable when I do not have my smartphone with me.	✓		
5. I use my smartphone in bed.	✓		

My score

0-3 Smart!   4-6 Be careful!   7-10 Danger!

서답형

22 위 표의 내용과 일치하도록 다음 빈칸에 알맞은 숫자를 쓰시오.

The writer's score is _____ .

➡ _____

서답형

23 위 표의 결과를 보고 다음 빈칸에 들어갈 알맞은 단어를 쓰시오.

➡ The writer is in the _____ situation in using the smartphone.

24 다음 글쓴이에 관한 설명 중 위 표의 내용과 일치하지 <u>않는</u> 것은?

① 아침을 먹으면서 항상 스마트폰을 사용한다.
② 차에서는 스마트폰을 사용하지 않는다.
③ 걸으면서 때때로 스마트폰을 사용한다.
④ 수중에 스마트폰이 없으면 항상 불편함을 느낀다.
⑤ 잠자리에서 항상 스마트폰을 사용한다.

[25~27] 다음 글을 읽고 물음에 답하시오.

A Smartphone & Me

There are both good things and bad things about using a smartphone. First, I can get in touch with my friends @right away. Also, I can easily get information I need. ⓑThat is useful when I have a lot of homework to do. On the other hand, using a smartphone too much makes my eyes feel dry and tired. Also, text messages and ads keep me from paying attention to my studies. So I need to use my smartphone intelligently.

25 위 글의 밑줄 친 @right away와 바꿔 쓸 수 <u>없는</u> 말을 <u>모두</u> 고르시오.

① for a moment   ② immediately
③ from time to time   ④ right now
⑤ at once

서답형

26 위 글의 밑줄 친 ⓑThat이 가리키는 것을 본문에서 찾아 영어로 쓰시오.

➡ _____

중요

27 위 글에서 설명하고 있는 스마트폰 사용의 장점을 <u>모두</u> 고르시오.

① 친구들과 즉시 연락할 수 있다.
② SNS로 친구 관계를 잘 유지할 수 있다.
③ 전 세계에 이메일을 바로 보낼 수 있다.
④ 필요로 하는 정보를 쉽게 얻을 수 있다.
⑤ 많은 광고들을 쉽게 접할 수 있다.

[01~02] 다음 글을 읽고 물음에 답하시오.

Seongmin cannot take his hands off his smartphone all day long. ⓐHe does not know that using a smartphone too much can cause health problems. Are you a heavy user of your smartphone like Seongmin? ⓑIf so, here are some tips to protect your health.

01 위 글의 밑줄 친 문장 ⓐ를 다음과 같이 바꿔 쓸 때 빈칸에 알맞은 말을 쓰시오.

➡ He does not know that _____ _____ a smartphone too much can cause health problems.

02 위 글의 밑줄 친 ⓑIf so가 가리키는 내용을 본문의 단어를 사용하여 풀어쓰시오.

➡ _____

_____

[03~05] 다음 글을 읽고 물음에 답하시오.

Watch your neck and back. When you read on your smartphone, you usually ___ⓐ___ your neck. This "text neck" pose increases the pressure on your neck and back. The best way to prevent ⓑthis pressure is to bring the phone up to the level of your eyes. ⓒAnother way is to lift your eyes instead of bending your neck.

03 다음 그림을 참조하여 위 글의 빈칸 ⓐ에 들어갈 알맞은 말을 쓰시오.

 ➡ _____

04 위 글의 밑줄 친 ⓑ가 가리키는 것을 25자 내외의 우리말로 설명하시오.

➡ _____

05 위 글의 밑줄 친 ⓒ에서 흐름상 어색한 부분을 찾아 고치시오.

➡ _____

[06~08] 다음 글을 읽고 물음에 답하시오.

ⓐGive your eyes a break. It makes your eyes feel (A)[tired / tiring] and dry to read small letters on a smartphone for a long time. Using a smartphone in the dark or in a moving car makes this problem worse. To avoid this, give your eyes a break from time to time. Follow ⓑthe 20-20-20 rules: Every 20 (B)[minute / minutes], take a (C)[20-second / 20-seconds] break and look at something at least 20 feet away. Also, blink your eyes often. This will keep your eyes from becoming dry.

06 위 글의 밑줄 친 ⓐ를 3형식으로 고치시오.

➡ _____

07 위 글의 괄호 (A)~(C)에서 어법상 알맞은 낱말을 골라 쓰시오.

➡ (A)_____ (B)_____ (C)_____

08 위 글의 밑줄 친 ⓑthe 20-20-20 rules의 내용을 우리말로 설명하시오.

➡ _____

_____

[09~11] 다음 글을 읽고 물음에 답하시오.

Do you text a lot on your smartphone? Texting for a long time can hurt your fingers and wrists. Try these exercises. They will help reduce the pain in your fingers and wrists.

(1)   (2)

But remember. ⓐThe best tip to prevent these health problems are to use your smartphone less. Give yourself some rest from your smartphone.

09 다음 문장에서 그림 (1)에 대한 설명으로 <u>틀린</u> 부분을 고치시오.

Pull on each wrist of each hand.

➡ _____

10 다음 빈칸 (A)와 (B)에 알맞은 단어를 넣어 그림 (2)에 대한 설명을 완성하시오.

Put the (A) _____ of your hands together with your arms out (B)_____ _____ _____ you.

11 위 글의 밑줄 친 ⓐ에서 어법상 <u>틀린</u> 부분을 찾아 고치시오.

➡ _____

[12~14] 스마트폰 사용으로 생긴 건강 문제를 나타내는 다음 그림을 보고 물음에 답하시오.

12 다음 빈칸 ⓐ~ⓒ에 알맞은 단어를 넣어 위 그림의 문제 A를 해결하는 알맞은 방법을 완성하시오.

The best way to prevent the ⓐ_____ from bending your neck is to bring the phone ⓑ_____ to the level of your eyes and to lower your eyes instead of ⓒ _____ your neck.

13 다음 빈칸 ⓐ~ⓒ에 들어갈 알맞은 단어를 보기에서 골라 넣어 위 그림의 문제 B를 해결하는 방법을 완성하시오.

To avoid making your ⓐ_____ feel tired and dry, give your eyes a ⓑ _____ from time to time by following the 20-20-20 rules and ⓒ_____ your eyes often.

┤ 보기 ├

wrists, open, blow, blink, break, eyes

14 다음 빈칸 ⓐ~ⓒ에 알맞은 단어를 넣어 위 그림의 문제 C를 해결하는 알맞은 방법을 완성하시오.

To reduce the pain in your ⓐ_____ and ⓑ_____, pull on each finger of each hand and put the backs of your hands together ⓒ_____ your arms out in front of you.

구석구석

Before You Read A

1. I use my smartphone when I eat breakfast.
   ~할 때(접속사)

2. I use my smartphone in a car.
   차 안에서

3. I use my smartphone when I am walking.
   현재분사

4. I feel uncomfortable when I do not have my smartphone with me.
   감각동사 feel의 보어로 형용사를 써야 함. uncomfortably(×)   ~와 함께

5. I use my smartphone in bed.
   a bed(×)

구문해설 • uncomfortable: 불편한, • in bed: 잠자리에서

해석

1. 나는 아침을 먹을 때 스마트폰을 사용한다.
2. 나는 차에서 스마트폰을 사용한다.
3. 나는 걸으면서 스마트폰을 사용한다.
4. 나는 수중에 스마트폰이 없으면 불편함을 느낀다.
5. 나는 잠자리에서 스마트폰을 사용한다.

Before You Read B

Watch Out!
= Be careful!

Yesterday, Sejin walked into a tree while texting and hurt her head. She needs
                                   └she was 생략.   hurt–hurt–hurt

to avoid using her phone while walking. Also, she should reduce the time she
avoid는 목적어로 동명사를 씀.   목적격 관계대명사 that[which] 생략

spends using it.
spend+시간+~ing

구문해설 • watch out: 조심하다, • avoid: 피하다, • reduce: 줄이다

조심해!

어제, 세진이는 문자를 보내다가 나무에 부딪쳐서 머리를 다쳤다. 그녀는 걷는 도중에 전화기를 사용하는 것을 피할 필요가 있다. 또한, 그녀는 그것을 사용하는 데 보내는 시간을 줄여야 한다.

Writing Workshop

A Smartphone & Me

There are both good things and bad things about using a smartphone. First, I
There are ~: ~가 있다   both A and B: A와 B 둘 다   동명사(전치사 about의 목적어)

can get in touch with my friends right away.
~와 연락[접촉]하다   즉시 (= immediately)

Also, I can easily get information I need. That is useful when I have a lot of
동사를 수식하는 부사   앞에 목적격 관계대명사 생략 앞 문장을 가리킨다. ~할 때   많은 = much

homework to do. On the other hand, using a smartphone too much makes my
앞의 명사 수식(형용사적 용법)   한편, 반면에   동명사 주어   동명사 주어이므로 단수 동사

eyes feel dry and tired.
make+목적어+목적격보어(동사원형)

Also, text messages and ads keep me from paying attention to my studies. So I
                         keep … from ~ing: …이 ~하는 것을 막다

need to use my smartphone intelligently.
~할 필요가 있다

구문해설 • get in touch with: ~와 연락[접촉]하다, • right away: 즉시, • easily: 쉽게,
• on the other hand: 한편, 반면에, • pay attention to: ~에 유의하다, ~에 주목하다,
• intelligently: 현명하게

스마트폰과 나

스마트폰을 사용하는 것에 대해서 좋은 것과 나쁜 것 둘 다 있다. 첫째, 내 친구들과 즉시 연락할 수 있다. 또한, 나는 내가 필요한 정보를 쉽게 얻을 수 있다. 그것은 내가 해야 할 숙제가 많을 때 유용하다. 반면에, 스마트폰을 너무 많이 사용하는 것은 나의 눈을 건조하고 피곤하게 만든다. 또한 메시지를 보내는 것과 광고들은 공부에 집중하는 것을 막는다. 그래서 나는 휴대 전화를 똑똑하게 사용할 필요가 있다.

Words & Expressions

01 다음 제시된 단어를 사용하여 자연스러운 문장을 만들 수 없는 것은? (형태 변화 가능)

┌─ 보기 ─────────────────────────┐
│   drop give reduce pay   │
└───────────────────────────────┘

① Your button has _____ off.

② Small businesses will need to _____ costs in order to survive.

③ We have to _____ down on expenses this month.

④ If you _____ more attention in class, you may actually learn something!

⑤ I'll _____ the keys back to you tomorrow morning.

02 다음 대화의 빈칸 (A)와 (B)에 들어갈 알맞은 단어를 골라 쓰시오.

┌───────────────────────────────┐
│ A: I'm always late (A)[in / for / of / to] │
│   school. What should I do?   │
│ B: You should (B)[do / have / get / set] │
│   an alarm on your smartphone.   │
└───────────────────────────────┘

➡ _____

03 다음 밑줄 친 부분의 뜻이 잘못된 것은?

① The people are in the hall. (구멍)

② Road safety is taught to young children to avoid road accidents. (피하다)

③ Could you give me some advice about buying a car? (조언)

④ Could you hold my bag for me? (들다)

⑤ I blinked as I came out into the sunlight. ((눈을) 깜빡였다)

04 다음 대화의 밑줄 친 text와 같은 의미를 지닌 문장을 고르시오.

┌───────────────────────────────┐
│ B: Mom, may I sleep over at Jinsu's │
│   house?   │
│ W: Okay. Make sure you text me when │
│   you get to Jinsu's house.   │
└───────────────────────────────┘

① The text of the song may sing well.

② These books contain fewer pictures and a lot more texts.

③ Type the message text you wish to send.

④ I'll text you the final score.

⑤ She sent me a lot of text messages late last night.

[05~06] 다음 빈칸에 공통으로 들어갈 말을 쓰시오.

05
┌───────────────────────────────┐
│ • Try to _____ a diary every day. │
│ • It's a good idea. I'll _____ it in │
│   mind.   │
└───────────────────────────────┘

06
┌───────────────────────────────┐
│ • You should _____ it to the service │
│   center.   │
│ • I think you should _____ a walk for │
│   about 30 minutes.   │
└───────────────────────────────┘

07 밑줄 친 단어와 의미가 같은 단어를 모두 고르시오.

┌───────────────────────────────┐
│ The helmet law will reduce injuries in │
│ motorcycle accidents.   │
└───────────────────────────────┘

① cut   ② protect   ③ decrease

④ increase   ⑤ avoid

Conversation

08 다음 대화의 빈칸에 알맞은 것을 모두 고르시오.

> G: Oh, no! I have dark circles under my eyes.
> B: _____

① I will get more sleep.
② You should get more sleep.
③ I guess I should get more sleep.
④ I think you should get more sleep.
⑤ You'd better get more sleep.

[09~12] 다음 대화를 읽고 물음에 답하시오.

G: What's the matter, Henry? (①)
B: Look at my new cellphone.
G: (②) Did you drop it?
B: Yes. I dropped it on the way here. (③) I'm so upset!
G: (④) I think you should get a phone case. It will (A)_____ your phone.
B: Okay. (⑤) I'll get one.

09 위 대화의 ①~⑤ 중 다음 주어진 말이 들어갈 알맞은 곳은?

> Oh, your phone screen has a crack.

①   ②   ③   ④   ⑤

10 빈칸 (A)에 들어갈 알맞은 말은?

① protect   ② prevent   ③ increase
④ avoid   ⑤ produce

11 다음 영영풀이에 해당하는 단어를 대화에서 찾아 쓰시오.

> to fall suddenly onto the ground or into something

➡ _____

12 위 대화를 읽고 답할 수 있는 질문을 고르시오.

① Why did Henry drop his cellphone?
② Where will Henry get a phone case?
③ Where did Henry buy a new cellphone?
④ How does the phone have a crack?
⑤ Does the girl have a phone case?

13 다음 중 짝지어진 대화가 어색한 것은?

① A: There are no fish in the river.
   B: I think it's because of the trash. We should pick up the trash in the river.
② A: What should I keep in mind?
   B: Make sure you don't run in the hall.
③ A: I'm worried about gaining weight.
   B: I think you should do exercise every day.
④ A: You should turn off the light.
   B: OK. I will.
⑤ A: Can you give me some advice for water activity?
   B: You should not wear your life jacket.

Grammar

14 괄호 안에 주어진 단어를 이용하여 빈칸에 알맞은 말을 어법에 맞게 쓰시오.

> (1) There are many dresses _____ in the store. (sell)
> (2) There are many sights _____ in Seoul. (see)

15 〈보기〉의 밑줄 친 부분과 같은 용법으로 쓰인 것은?

> ┌─ 보기 ─┐
>
> I want to have some time to take a rest.

① He is the last man to tell a lie.
② The book is not difficult to read.
③ The thing I want to do is to play online soccer games.
④ Lucy studies very hard to become a teacher.
⑤ Isaac grew up to be a famous scientist.

16 다음 빈칸에 알맞은 말을 쓰시오.

> 그녀의 부모님은 그녀가 그 콘서트에 가게 하지 않으셨다.
> = Her parents did not _____ her go to the concert.

➡ _____

17 다음 두 문장을 to부정사를 이용하여 바꿔 쓸 때 빈칸에 알맞은 말을 쓰시오.

(1) • Kay bought a pen.
　　• She will write letters with it.
　　= Kay bought a pen _____ .
(2) • Sonya is looking for a camera.
　　• She will take pictures with it.
　　= Sonya is looking for a camera _____ .
(3) • Angelina bought a house.
　　• She wants to live in the house.
　　= Angelina bought a house _____ .

18 밑줄 친 부분의 쓰임이 나머지 넷과 다른 것은?

① He had me help him.
② He had his students submit their report the next day.
③ Melanie had her pictures taken at the amusement park.
④ He had no time to meet her.
⑤ Did she have him fix her new computer?

19 다음 빈칸에 알맞은 것은?

> Larry's car is not clean. I'll have it _____ .

① wash　　　② washes
③ washed　　④ washing
⑤ to wash

20 다음 빈칸에 들어갈 수 없는 것은?

> Mom _____ me study all day long.

① lets　　② gets　　③ has
④ makes　⑤ helps

21 다음 중 어법상 어색한 문장은?

① The president didn't have anything to say about the accident.
② Sadly it's time to say good-bye.
③ The reporters had many questions to ask of the K-pop singer.
④ Would you give me anything hot to drink?
⑤ Linda doesn't have any patients to take care.

22 다음 문장 중 어법상 자연스러운 것은?

① My sister often helps me doing my homework.
② They had many options choose about the experiment.
③ I'll have your health check.
④ Please let me go to the concert next weekend.
⑤ He spends a lot of time use his smartphone.

23 다음 〈보기〉의 어휘 중에서 골라 어법에 맞게 빈칸을 채우시오.

┌─── 보기 ───┐
build   turn down   put   produce
└─────────────┘

(1) They made the company _____ a factory _____ electricity.
(2) John had me _____ the TV volume because he had his younger brother _____ to bed.

24 다음 답을 보고 물음에 있는 빈칸을 알맞게 채우시오.

Q: What is your topic _____?
A: I want to talk about the environment.

Reading

[25~27] 다음 글을 읽고 물음에 답하시오.

Give your eyes a ⓐbreak. It makes your eyes feel tired and dry to read small letters on a smartphone for a long time. ⓑUsing a smartphone in the dark or in a ⓒmoving car makes this problem worse. To avoid this, give your eyes a break from time to time. Follow the 20-20-20 rules: Every 20 minutes, take a 20-second break and look at something at least 20 feet away. Also, blink your eyes often. This will keep your eyes from becoming dry.

25 위 글의 밑줄 친 ⓐbreak와 같은 의미로 쓰인 것을 고르시오.

① Don't break the law.
② Who will break the news to her?
③ She worked all day without a break.
④ Be careful not to break a window.
⑤ Waves break against the rocks.

26 아래 보기에서 위 글의 밑줄 친 ⓑUsing이나 ⓒmoving과 문법적 쓰임이 같은 것을 각각 고르시오.

┌─── 보기 ───┐
① My dad is watching TV now.
② He is good at playing tennis.
③ I saw her entering the room.
④ The girl helping her mom is pretty.
⑤ Did you finish doing your homework?
└─────────────┘

➡ ⓑ와 같은 것: _____
ⓒ와 같은 것: _____

27 다음 질문에 대한 알맞은 대답을 본문에서 찾아 쓰시오.

Q: According to the paragraph, what makes your eyes feel more tired and drier?
A: _____

[28~29] 다음 글을 읽고 물음에 답하시오.

Watch your neck and back. When you read on your smartphone, you usually bend your neck. This "text neck" pose increases the pressure on your neck and back. The best way to prevent this pressure is to bring the phone up to the level of your eyes. Another way is to lower your eyes instead of ___ⓐ___ your neck.

28 위 글의 빈칸 ⓐ에 bend를 알맞은 형태로 쓰시오.

➡ _____

29 위 글의 내용과 일치하지 <u>않는</u> 것은?

① 스마트폰을 볼 때, 여러분은 보통 목을 구부린다.
② 목을 구부리는 자세를 "거북목" 자세라고 한다.
③ "거북목" 자세는 여러분의 목과 척추에 가해지는 압력을 증가시킨다.
④ 이러한 압력을 예방하는 가장 좋은 방법은 당신의 목을 전화기 쪽으로 숙이는 것이다.
⑤ 또 다른 방법은 목을 구부리는 대신에 시선을 낮추는 것이다.

[30~32] 다음 글을 읽고 물음에 답하시오.

A Smartphone & Me

There are both good things and bad things about using a smartphone. (①) First, ⓐ나는 친구들과 바로 연락할 수 있다. (②) Also, I can easily get information I need. (③) On the other hand, using a smartphone too much makes my eyes feel dry and tired. (④) Also, text messages and ads keep me from paying attention to my studies. (⑤) So I need to use my smartphone ___ⓑ___ .

30 위 글의 흐름으로 보아, 주어진 문장이 들어가기에 가장 적절한 곳은?

> That is useful when I have a lot of homework to do.

① ② ③ ④ ⑤

31 위 글의 밑줄 친 ⓐ의 우리말에 맞게 주어진 어휘를 이용하여 10 단어로 영작하시오.

> get in touch, right away

➡ _____

32 위 글의 빈칸 ⓑ에 들어갈 알맞은 말을 고르시오.

① all the time ② intelligently
③ slowly ④ immediately
⑤ again and again

[33~34] 다음 글을 읽고 물음에 답하시오.

Seongmin cannot take his hands (A)[on / off] his smartphone all (B)[day / days] long. He does not know that using a smartphone too much can cause health problems. Are you a (C)[heavy / proper] user of your smartphone like Seongmin? If so, here are some ___ⓐ___ to protect your health.

33 위 글의 괄호 (A)~(C)에서 문맥이나 어법상 알맞은 낱말을 골라 쓰시오.

➡ (A)_____ (B)_____ (C)_____

34 주어진 영영풀이를 참고하여 빈칸 ⓐ에 철자 t로 시작하는 단어를 쓰시오.

> useful pieces of advice

➡ _____

01 출제율90%

다음 보기에 짝지어진 두 단어의 관계와 같도록 빈칸에 알맞은 말을 쓰시오.

┌─ 보기 ─┐
happen : occur
└────────┘

(1) rely on : _____ _____
(2) tip : _____

02 출제율95%

다음 〈보기〉의 단어를 사용하여 자연스러운 문장을 만들 수 없는 것은?

┌─ 보기 ─┐
on   from   for
└────────┘

① Stay away _____ the fire.
② Do you still get in touch _____ John ?
③ Fresh fruit and vegetables are good _____ you.
④ They eat lunch in the park _____ time to time.
⑤ Cut down _____ fatty food if you want to lose weight.

03 출제율90%

다음 밑줄 친 부분의 뜻이 잘못된 것은?

① The rules of the game are quite simple. (규칙)
② The weather was a lot worse this year. (더 나쁜)
③ Debbie was upset that he didn't spend more time with her. (화난)
④ We worked for ten hours without a break. (깨뜨리다)
⑤ Keep your head up and your back straight. (등)

04 출제율90%

다음 우리말에 맞게 빈칸을 완성하시오.

(1) His _____ injury may _____ _____ _____ in tomorrow's game. (등 부상이 그가 내일 경기를 못하게 할지 모른다.)
(2) What problems _____ I _____ _____ _____ when buying an old house? (오래된 집을 살 때 무슨 문제를 주의해야 하나요?)
(3) _____ _____ _____ _____ school. (나는 학교에 지각했다.)
(4) You probably picked up my keys _____ _____ yours. (네가 아마 네 열쇠 대신에 내 것을 가져갔을 거야.)

[05~06] 다음 대화의 순서를 바르게 배열하시오.

05 출제율90%

┌──────────────────────────────────┐
(A) Yes, she is. What should I do?
(B) Isn't she your best friend?
(C) I forgot Jenny's birthday!
(D) I think you should tell her you're very sorry.
└──────────────────────────────────┘

➡ _____

06 출제율85%

┌──────────────────────────────────┐
(A) I think you should cut down on snacks.
(B) I feel down.
(C) I put on 5kg this winter. What should I do?
(D) Why? What's the matter?
└──────────────────────────────────┘

➡ _____

[07~08] 다음 대화를 읽고 물음에 답하시오.

B: Oh, no! I didn't bring my science book!
G: Ms. Lee ①won't be happy about that.
B: I know. Umm, ②can I borrow your science book?
G: Okay. Just ③make sure you ④give back it ⑤when you're done.

07 위 대화의 어법상 어색한 문장을 고르시오.

①   ②   ③   ④   ⑤

08 위 대화를 읽고 답할 수 없는 질문을 모두 고르시오.

① What book didn't the boy bring?
② How long is the science class?
③ Who can lend the science book to the boy?
④ What subject does Ms. Lee teach?
⑤ Why didn't the boy bring the science book?

[09~11] 다음 대화를 읽고 물음에 답하시오.

G: What does your shirt say?
B: Oh, this? (①)
G: No Cellphone? Why?
B: We depend on our phones too much these days. (②)
G: That's true. How often will you do this?
B: 한 달에 한 번 할 계획이야, but I'm not sure. (③)
G: Try it first. Then, decide how often you should do it. (④)
B: (⑤) Okay. I'm going to keep a diary of what I did without my phone for 24 hours. You should try it, too.
G: I'll think about it. Make sure you keep up with it.
B: I plan to. After I do it, I'll talk about my experience in class.

09 위 대화의 ①~⑤ 중 주어진 말이 들어갈 알맞은 곳은?

It says "No Cellphone for 24 Hours."

①   ②   ③   ④   ⑤

10 밑줄 친 우리말과 의미가 같도록 주어진 단어를 이용해 문장을 완성하시오.

➡ _____

(on, a, planning, month)

11 위 대화의 내용과 일치하지 않는 것을 고르시오.

① The girl will do what the boy said.
② The boy is going to talk about his one-day experience of not using his cellphone.
③ The girl agrees with his view that people rely on cellphones too much.
④ The boy thinks we use cellphones a lot these days.
⑤ The boy is wearing a shirt with letters.

12 다음 대화의 흐름상 어색한 문장을 고르시오.

G: ①Daniel, what are you doing?
B: ②I'm reading a novel on my smartphone.
G: ③Make sure you don't read in the dark. ④It's good for your eyes.
B: ⑤Okay. I'll turn the light on.

①   ②   ③   ④   ⑤

13 다음 중 어법상 올바른 문장은?

① The best way to preventing this pressure is to bring the phone up to the level of your eyes.

② I had my computer fixed yesterday.

③ Some were really beautiful, but others made me to feel scared.

④ I have something to tell important you.

⑤ I'll get him do the work.

14 어법상 <u>잘못된</u> 부분을 바르게 고쳐 문장을 다시 쓰시오.

(1) My dad didn't let me to go camping.

➡ _____

(2) Emily had her new dress make last week.

➡ _____

(3) There's wrong nothing to correct in this report.

➡ _____

(4) I bought my parents a house to live.

➡ _____

[15~16] 다음 글을 읽고 물음에 답하시오.

ⓐSeongmin cannot take his hands off his smartphone every day long. He does not know that using a smartphone too much can cause health problems. Are you a heavy user of your smartphone ⓑlike Seongmin? If so, here are some tips to protect your health.

15 위 글의 밑줄 친 ⓐ에서 어법상 어색한 것을 고치시오.

➡ _____

16 위 글의 밑줄 친 ⓑlike와 같은 의미로 쓰인 것을 고르시오.

① Which season do you <u>like</u> best?

② He has hobbies <u>like</u> reading and painting.

③ I <u>like</u> playing tennis.

④ He ran <u>like</u> the wind.

⑤ Do you <u>like</u> vegetables?

[17~19] 다음 글을 읽고 물음에 답하시오.

Watch your neck and back. When you read on your smartphone, you usually bend your neck. This "text neck" pose increases the pressure on your neck and back. The best way ⓐto prevent this pressure is to bring the phone up to the level of your eyes. Another way is to lower your eyes ⓑ_____ bending your neck.

17 위 글의 밑줄 친 ⓐto prevent와 to부정사의 용법이 같은 것을 <u>모두</u> 고르시오.

① She was happy <u>to get</u> the present.

② I want something <u>to write</u> on.

③ He awoke <u>to find</u> himself famous.

④ He decided <u>to buy</u> new shoes.

⑤ There is no water <u>to drink</u>.

18 위 글의 빈칸 ⓑ에 들어갈 알맞은 말을 고르시오.

① in spite of   ② according to

③ because of   ④ instead of

⑤ together with

19 위 글의 요지로 알맞은 것을 고르시오.

① 여러분의 목과 척추를 조심해야 한다.

② 스마트폰을 볼 때 목을 구부리는 것이 편하다.

③ 스마트폰을 사용할 때 "거북목" 자세를 방지해야 한다.

④ "거북목" 자세를 방지하기 위해 스마트폰을 사용하지 말아야 한다.

⑤ 스마트폰을 사용할 때 목을 구부리는 것이 시선을 낮추는 것보다 더 좋다.

22 위 글의 내용과 일치하지 <u>않는</u> 것은?

① 오랫동안 스마트폰의 작은 글자를 읽는 것은 당신의 머리를 피곤하게 만든다.

② 어두운 곳이나 움직이는 차에서 스마트폰을 사용하는 것은 눈을 더 건조하게 느끼도록 만든다.

③ 눈이 피로해지는 것을 피하기 위해서는 눈을 때때로 쉬게 해야 한다.

④ 20-20-20 규칙을 따라야 한다.

⑤ 눈을 자주 깜빡이는 것은 눈이 건조해지는 것을 막아 준다.

[20~22] 다음 글을 읽고 물음에 답하시오.

Give your eyes a break. It makes your eyes feel tired and dry to read small letters on a smartphone for a long time. Using a smartphone in the dark or in a moving car makes this problem worse. To avoid this, give your eyes a break from time to time. Follow the 20-20-20 rules: Every 20 ⓐ , take a 20-second ⓑ and look at something at least 20 feet ⓒ . Also, blink your eyes often. This will ⓓ<u>keep</u> your eyes from becoming dry.

[23~24] 다음 글을 읽고 물음에 답하시오.

Do you text (A)[a lot / a lot of] on your smartphone? Texting for a long time can hurt your fingers and wrists. Try these exercises. ⓐ<u>They</u> will help reduce the pain in your fingers and wrists.

Pull on each finger of each hand.

Put the backs of your hands together with your arms out in front of you.

But remember. The best tip to prevent these health problems is to use your smartphone (B)[more / less]. Give (C)[you / yourself] some rest from your smartphone.

20 다음 그림을 참조하여 위 글의 빈칸 ⓐ~ⓒ에 들어갈 알맞은 말을 쓰시오.

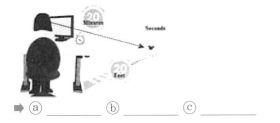

➡ ⓐ _____ ⓑ _____ ⓒ _____

23 위 글의 괄호 (A)~(C)에서 문맥이나 어법상 알맞은 낱말을 골라 쓰시오.

➡ (A)_____ (B)_____ (C)_____

21 위 글의 밑줄 친 ⓓ<u>keep</u>과 바꿔 쓸 수 있는 말을 <u>모두</u> 고르시오.

① stop   ② avoid

③ allow   ④ prevent

⑤ provide

24 위 글의 밑줄 친 ⓐ<u>They</u>가 가리키는 것을 본문에서 찾아 쓰시오.

➡ _____

01 다음 대화의 밑줄 친 부분과 의미가 같도록 주어진 단어를 이용하여 영작하시오.

> A: Can I eat this pizza?
> B: Sure. Just make sure you wash your hands first.

➡ (1) _____ (better)

➡ (2) _____ (forget)

➡ (3) _____
   (remember)

02 괄호 안의 단어를 이용하여 우리말을 바르게 영작하시오.

> B: I put on 5kg this winter. What should I do?
> G: 나는 네가 간식을 줄여야 한다고 생각해.

➡ _____

   (think, cut)

03 다음 대화의 밑줄 친 부분에서 어색한 것을 찾아 고치시오.

> G: ①I forgot Jenny's birthday!
> B: ②Isn't she your best friend?
> G: ③Yes, she is. ④What should I to do?
> B: ⑤I think you should tell her you're very sorry.

➡ _____

04 괄호 안에 주어진 단어를 이용하여 다음을 영작하시오.

(1) Brian은 오늘 해야 할 숙제가 많다. (a lot of, do, 9 단어)

➡ _____

(2) 이름들을 쓸 종이 한 장을 내게 가져다줄래? (will, bring, piece, 12 단어)

➡ _____

(3) 따로 보관할 중요한 어떤 것이 있나요? (there, valuable, keep separately, 7 단어)

➡ _____

(4) 맛있는 식사는 그에게 군침을 흘리게 하였다. (make, delicious, meal, water, 7 단어)

➡ _____

(5) 그들은 그로 하여금 새로운 계약에 서명하도록 했다. (get, sign, contract, 8 단어)

➡ _____

05 〈보기〉와 같이 주어진 두 문장을 한 문장으로 쓰시오.

> ┤ 보기 ├
> • Sharon made.
> • I waited for her.
> → Sharon made me wait for her.

(1) • Julia made.
   • I did my homework.

➡ _____

(2) • Her mom had Jenny.
   • Jenny prepared dinner.

➡ _____

(3) • Sam helped me.
   • I repaired my computer.

➡ _____

[06~08] 다음 글을 읽고 물음에 답하시오.

Watch your neck and back. When you read on your smartphone, you usually bend your neck. This "text neck" pose increases the pressure on your neck and back. The best way to prevent this pressure is to bring the phone ⓐ_____ _____ the level of your eyes. Another way is to lower your eyes instead of bending your neck.

06 본문의 내용과 일치하도록 다음 빈칸 (A)와 (B)에 알맞은 단어를 쓰시오.

> If you bend your neck when reading on your smartphone, the pressure on your (A)_____ and (B)_____ increases because of this posture.

07 다음 그림을 참조하여 위 글의 빈칸 ⓐ에 들어갈 알맞은 말을 쓰시오.

 ➡ _____

08 위 글을 읽고 "거북목" 자세로 인한 압력을 예방할 수 있는 좋은 방법 두 가지를 우리말로 설명하시오.

➡ (1) _____
(2) _____

[09~11] 다음 글을 읽고 물음에 답하시오.

Give your eyes a break. ⓐIt makes your eyes to feel tired and dry to read small letters on a smartphone for a long time. Using a smartphone in the dark or in a moving car makes this problem (A)[better / worse]. To avoid this, give your eyes a break from time to time. Follow the 20-20-20 rules: (B)[All / Every] 20 minutes, take a 20-second break and look at something (C)[at last / at least] 20 feet away. Also, blink your eyes often. ⓑ이것은 눈이 건조해지는 것을 막을 것이다.

09 위 글의 밑줄 친 ⓐ에서 어법상 틀린 부분을 찾아 고치시오.

➡ _____

10 위 글의 괄호 (A)~(C)에서 문맥상 알맞은 낱말을 골라 쓰시오.

➡ (A)_____ (B)_____ (C)_____

11 위 글의 밑줄 친 ⓑ의 우리말에 맞게 주어진 어휘를 이용하여 8 단어로 영작하시오.

> keep, becoming

➡ _____

창의사고력 서술형 문제

01 친구의 고민에 should를 이용하여 충고하는 말을 3 문장 이상 쓰시오.

> A: I am worried about gaining weight.
> B: _____
> A: I guess I should.

02 주어진 어구를 이용하여 3 문장 이상을 쓰시오.

> make   have   let
> prepare dinner   clean the room   go to the movies   play soccer

(1) _____
(2) _____
(3) _____
(4) _____

03 다음 스마트폰의 장점과 단점을 바탕으로 '스마트폰과 나'를 주제로 말하기 발표 대본을 쓰시오.

> 장점:
> (1) I can get in touch with my friends right away.
> (2) I can easily get information I need.
> 단점:
> (1) My eyes feel dry and tired.
> (2) Text messages and ads keep me from paying attention to my studies.

> A Smartphone & Me
>   There are both good things and bad things about using a smartphone. First, I can get in touch with my friends (A)_____. Also, I can easily get (B)_____ I need. That is useful when I have a lot of homework to do. On the other hand, using a smartphone too much makes my eyes feel (C)_____. Also, text messages and ads (D)_____ me from paying attention to my studies. So I need to use my smartphone (E)_____ .

단원별 모의고사

[01~03] 다음 대화의 빈칸에 알맞은 것을 고르시오.

01

> M: You forgot to turn _____ your radio again today.
> B: Oh, I'm sorry, Mom.

① over ② into ③ off
④ to ⑤ for

02

> W: Jake, you should pay attention _____ the person who talks to you.
> M: Okay, I will.

① by ② with ③ for
④ to ⑤ on

03

> A: Can I _____ this boat?
> B: Sure. Just make sure you wear a life jacket.

① ride on ② go on ③ get to
④ come on ⑤ take on

04 다음 빈칸에 공통으로 들어갈 단어를 쓰시오.

> • I live far _____ from the station.
> • I'll phone him right _____.

[05~06] 다음 대화를 읽고 물음에 답하시오.

> B: Mom, 진수네 집에서 자도 돼요?
> W: Did Jinsu's mom say it was okay?
> B: Yes. Jinsu said she would (A)_____ pizza for us.
> W: Okay. (B)_____ sure you text me when you get to Jinsu's house.

05 위 대화의 밑줄 친 우리말에 맞게 주어진 단어를 이용하여 영어로 쓰시오.

➡ _____

(over, at, may)

06 위 대화의 빈칸 (A)와 (B)에 공통으로 들어갈 알맞은 말을 쓰시오.

➡ _____

07 다음 대화의 괄호 안에 주어진 단어를 알맞게 배열하시오.

> W: _____
> (by, sure, are, 12:00, make, you, home)
> G: Okay, I will.

[08~09] 다음 대화를 읽고 물음에 답하시오.

> G: What's the matter, Henry?
> B: Look at my new cellphone.
> G: Oh, your phone screen has a crack. Did you drop it?
> B: Yes. I dropped it on the way here. I'm so upset!
> G: I think you should get a phone case. It will protect your phone.
> B: Okay. I'll (A)_____ one.

08 다음 영영풀이에 해당하는 단어를 대화에서 찾아 쓰시오.

> to keep someone or something safe from harm, damage, or illness

➡ _____

09 빈칸 (A)에 알맞은 단어를 대화에서 찾아 쓰시오.

➡ _____

[10~13] 다음 대화를 읽고 물음에 답하시오.

G: What does your shirt say?
B: Oh, this? (①) It says "No Cellphone (A) [during / for] 24 Hours."
G: No Cellphone? Why? (②)
B: We (B)[depend on / don't depend on] our phones too much these days.
G: That's true. (③) How ⓐ_____ will you do this?
B: I'm planning on doing it once a month, but I'm not sure.
G: (④) Then, decide how ⓑ_____ you should do it.
B: Okay. (⑤) I'm going to keep a diary of what I did (C)[without / with] my phone for 24 hours. You should try it, too.
G: I'll think about it. (you, with, make, it, sure, keep, up)
B: I plan to. After I do it, I'll talk about my experience in class.

10 위 대화의 ①~⑤ 중 주어진 문장이 들어갈 알맞은 곳은?

┌─────────────────────────────┐
│   Try it first.   │
└─────────────────────────────┘

① ② ③ ④ ⑤

11 위 대화의 (A)~(C)에 적절한 말을 골라 쓰시오.

➡ _____ _____ _____

12 위 대화의 ⓐ와 ⓑ에 공통으로 들어갈 단어를 쓰시오.

➡ _____

13 위 대화의 괄호 안에 주어진 단어를 알맞게 배열하시오.

➡ _____

14 다음 대화의 빈칸에 들어갈 말로 알맞은 것은?

┌─────────────────────────────┐
│ M: What do you need?   │
│ W: I need a chair _____. │
└─────────────────────────────┘

① sit   ② sitting
③ to sit   ④ to sit on
⑤ to sitting

15 다음 빈칸에 들어갈 말로 알맞은 것은?

┌─────────────────────────────┐
│ Margaret had her son _____ his room. │
└─────────────────────────────┘

① clean   ② cleans
③ cleaned   ④ to clean
⑤ cleaning

16 다음 중 어법상 <u>어색한</u> 부분을 바르게 고쳐 다시 쓰시오.

(1) It makes your eyes to feel tired and dry to read small letters.

➡ _____

(2) They had a big factory build at the top of the hill.

➡ _____

(3) There was somebody to meet important there.

➡ _____

(4) Olivia has few friends to play.

➡ _____

(5) Mike had his computer steal.

➡ _____

17 다음 중 어법상 어색한 것을 고르시오.

① My mom made me wash the dishes.
② There is a small pool to swim.
③ I want to bring some books to read.
④ My dad wouldn't let me swim in the lake.
⑤ I want to have something spicy to eat.

[18~19] 다음 글을 읽고 물음에 답하시오.

Seongmin cannot take his hands ___ⓐ___ his smartphone all day long. He does not know that using a smartphone too much can cause health problems. Are you a heavy user ___ⓑ___ your smartphone like Seongmin? ⓒ<u>만약 그렇다면</u>, here are some tips to protect your health.

18 위 글의 빈칸 ⓐ와 ⓑ에 들어갈 알맞은 말을 쓰시오.

➡ ⓐ _____ ⓑ _____

19 위 글의 밑줄 친 ⓒ의 우리말을 두 단어로 쓰시오.

➡ _____

[20~21] 다음 글을 읽고 물음에 답하시오.

Watch your neck and back. When you read on your smartphone, you usually bend your neck. This "text neck" pose increases the pressure on your neck and back. The best way to prevent this pressure is ⓐ<u>to bring</u> the phone up to the level of your eyes.

20 다음 그림을 참조하여 빈칸 (A)와 (B)에 알맞은 단어를 넣어, 본문의 마지막 부분을 완성하시오.

Another way is to lower your (A)_____ instead of bending your (B)_____.

21 아래 보기에서 위 글의 밑줄 친 ⓐto bring과 to부정사의 용법이 같은 것의 개수를 고르시오.

┌─── 보기 ───┐
① It is difficult <u>to know</u> oneself.
② I have no house <u>to live</u> in.
③ I got up early <u>to catch</u> the train.
④ This water is not good <u>to drink</u>.
⑤ He began <u>to read</u> the book.
└────────────┘

① 1개　② 2개　③ 3개　④ 4개　⑤ 5개

[22~23] 다음 글을 읽고 물음에 답하시오.

Give your eyes a break. It makes your eyes feel tired and dry to read small letters on a smartphone for a long time. ⓐUsing a smartphone in the dark or in a moving car makes this problem worse. To avoid this, give your eyes a break from time to time. Follow the 20-20-20 rules: Every 20 minutes, take a 20-second break and look at something at least 20 feet away. Also, blink your eyes often. This will keep your eyes from becoming dry.

22 위 글의 제목으로 알맞은 것을 고르시오.

① How about Giving Your Eyes a Break?
② Read Small Letters on a Smartphone!
③ Don't Use a Smartphone in the Car
④ The Difficulty of Following 20-20-20 Rules
⑤ How to Blink Your Eyes Effectively

23 위 글의 밑줄 친 ⓐ와 문장의 형식이 다른 것을 고르시오.

① She found the box empty.
② You should keep your room clean.
③ The news made her happy.
④ I found this book easily.
⑤ Please leave the door open.

[24~25] 다음 글을 읽고 물음에 답하시오.

Do you text a lot ①on your smartphone? Texting ②for a long time can hurt your fingers and wrists. Try these exercises. They will help reduce the pain ③in your fingers and wrists.
Pull on each finger of each hand.
Put the backs of your hands together ④by your arms out in front of you.

But remember. The best tip to prevent these health problems is to use your smartphone less. Give yourself some rest ⑤from your smartphone.

24 위 글의 밑줄 친 ①~⑤ 중 쓰임이 어색한 전치사를 찾아 고치시오.

➡ _____

25 위 글의 내용과 일치하지 않는 것은?

① 오랫동안 문자 메시지를 보내는 것은 손가락과 손목을 상하게 할 수 있다.
② 손가락과 손목의 통증을 줄이는 데 도움을 주는 운동이 있다.
③ 팔을 여러분 앞에서 벌린 채로 손바닥을 마주 놓아야 한다.
④ 스마트폰으로 인한 건강 문제를 예방하는 가장 좋은 방법은 스마트폰을 덜 사용하는 것이다.
⑤ 자신에게 스마트폰으로부터 약간의 휴식을 주어야 한다.

Lesson 3

The School Club Activity Day

🎤 의사소통 기능

- 능력 여부 묻기
  A: I don't know how to swim. Do you know how to?
  B: Yes, I can teach you.
- 좋아하는 것 표현하기
  A: What do you enjoy doing when you have free time?
  B: I enjoy painting pictures of people in the park.

🔧 언어 형식

- 의문사 + to부정사
  We also teach children **how to play** musical instruments as a service to our community.

- 주격 관계대명사
  Anyone **who** likes to paint can join.

Words & Expressions

Key Words

- **activity** [æktívəti] 명 활동
- **actually** [ǽktʃuəli] 부 실제로, 사실은
- **bake** [beik] 동 (빵 등을) 굽다
- **bit** [bit] 명 조금, 한 조각[가지], 부분
- **bright** [brait] 형 밝은, 똑똑한
- **clothes** [klouz] 명 옷, 의상
- **club** [klʌb] 명 동아리, 클럽
- **concert** [kάːnsərt] 명 연주회
- **cook** [kuk] 동 요리하다 명 요리사
- **cooking** [kúkiŋ] 명 요리, 음식
- **dolphin** [dάlfin] 명 돌고래
- **doughnut** [dóunət] 명 도넛
- **drone** [droun] 명 무인 비행기
- **easy** [íːzi] 형 쉬운
- **elementary school** 초등학교
- **experience** [ikspíəriəns] 명 경험, 경력
- **fly** [flai] 동 (항공기, 우주선, 인공위성 등을) 조종하다, 날게 하다
- **free time** 여가 시간
- **garden** [gάːrdn] 명 정원
- **get** [get] 동 사다, 획득하다
- **grow** [grou] 동 (동식물을) 기르다, 자라다
- **hold** [hould] 동 (모임, 식 등을) 개최하다
- **however** [hauévər] 부 그러나, 하지만

- **interest** [íntərəst] 명 관심 동 ~의 관심[흥미]을 끌다
- **introduce** [ìntrədjúːs] 동 소개하다
- **join** [dʒɔin] 동 참여하다, 가입하다
- **leader** [líːdər] 명 지도자, 대표
- **library** [láibrèri] 도서관
- **main gate** 정문
- **musical instrument** 악기
- **neighbor** [néibər] 명 이웃
- **neighborhood** [néibərhùd] 명 동네, (도시 내의 한 단위) 지역
- **note** [nout] 명 음, 음표
- **opportunity** [ὰpərtjúːnəti] 명 기회
- **orchestra** [ɔ́ːrkəstrə] 명 오케스트라, 교향악단
- **own** [oun] 형 (소유격 다음에서 강조어로 쓰여) 자기 자신의
- **practice** [prǽktis] 명 연습 동 연습하다
- **present** [préznt] 명 선물 형 참석한
- **project** [prάdʒekt] 명 사업, 계획
- **service** [sə́ːrvis] 명 봉사, 유익한[전문적인] 활동
- **several** [sévərəl] 형 몇몇의
- **Spanish** [spǽniʃ] 명 스페인어 형 스페인의
- **vegetable** [védʒətəbl] 명 채소
- **volunteer** [vὰləntíər] 동 봉사하다
- **walk** [wɔːk] 동 (사람·동물을) 걷게 하다

Key Expressions

- **a bit**: 조금
- **a little bit**: 아주 조금
- **as a result**: 결과적으로
- **ask for help**: 도움을 청하다
- **at first**: 처음에
- **at night**: 밤에
- **be good at**: ~을 잘하다
- **change into**: ~로 변화시키다[바꾸다]
- **enjoy+-ing**: ~하는 것을 즐기다
- **fall into**: ~에 빠지다

- **get better**: (병·상황 등이) 나아지다
- **have a great time**: 좋은 시간을 보내다
- **how to**+동사원형: ~하는 방법
- **let**+목적어+동사원형: …가 ~하게 하다
- **look at**: ~을 보다
- **look for**: ~을 찾다
- **participate in**: ~에 참여하다
- **thank for**: ~에 대해 감사하다
- **watch out (for)**: (~에 대해서) 조심하다
- **would like to** +동사원형: ~하고 싶다

Word Power

※ 서로 반대되는 뜻을 가진 단어

□ **bright**(밝은) ↔ **dark**(어두운)

□ **easy**(쉬운) ↔ **difficult**(어려운)

※ 서로 비슷한 뜻을 가진 단어

□ **actually**(실제로, 사실은) : **really**(정말로, 실제로)

□ **bright**(총명한) : **clever**(영리한)

□ **get**(사다, 획득하다) : **obtain**(획득하다), **gain**(얻다, 입수하다)

□ **grow**((식물을) 재배하다) : **farm**(경작하다)

□ **leader**(지도자, 대표) : **chief**(장, 우두머리)

□ **practice**(연습) : **training**(훈련), **exercise**(연습)

□ **project**(사업, 계획) : **plan**(계획)

□ **several**(몇몇의) : **a few**(약간의), **some**(조금의)

□ **foolish**(어리석은) : **stupid**(어리석은)

□ **join**(참여하다, 가입하다) : **enter**(~에 들어가다)

□ **opportunity**(기회) : **chance**(기회)

□ **present**(선물) : **gift**(선물)

English Dictionary

□ **a bit** 조금, 약간
→ slightly or to a small degree(= a little)
약간, 적은 정도로

□ **bake** (빵 등을) 굽다
→ to cook something using dry heat, in an oven
오븐 안에서 건조한 열을 사용하여 무언가를 요리하다

□ **bright** 밝은
→ strong and easy to see
강렬하며 쉽게 보이는

□ **club** 동아리
→ organization for people who share a particular interest or enjoy similar activities, or a group of people who meet together to do something they are interested in
특정한 흥미를 공유하거나 비슷한 활동을 즐기는 사람들을 위한 단체 또는 그들이 관심 있는 무언가를 위해서 같이 만나는 사람들의 모임

□ **drone** 무인 비행기
→ aircraft that does not have a pilot, but is operated by radio
조종사가 없지만 무선으로 작동되는 비행기

□ **garden** 정원
→ a part of the area next to a house, which has plants and flowers in it
집 옆에 식물과 꽃이 있는 지역의 일부

□ **grow** 자라다
→ to develop or increase in size or length
크기나 길이가 발달하거나 증가하다

□ **hold** (모임·식 등을) 개최하다
→ to have a meeting, party, election etc in a particular place or at a particular time
회의, 파티, 선거 등을 특정한 장소 또는 특정한 시간에 가지다

□ **join** 참여하다, 가입하다
→ 1. to become a member of an organization, society, or group
조직, 사회 또는 그룹의 구성원이 되다
2. to begin to take part in an activity that other people are involved in
다른 사람들이 관련된 활동에 참여하기 시작하다

□ **leader** 지도자, 대표
→ the person who directs or controls a group, organization, country, etc.
그룹, 조직, 국가 등을 총괄하거나 통제하는 사람

□ **musical instrument** 악기
→ something that you use for playing music, such as a piano or guitar
피아노나 기타와 같은 음악을 연주하기 위해 사용하는 어떤 것

□ **neighbor** 이웃
→ someone who lives next to you or near you
당신의 옆이나 근처에 사는 어떤 사람

□ **neighborhood** 인근, 이웃 사람들, 동네
→ the area around you or around a particular place, or the people who live there
당신 또는 특정한 장소 주변의 지역 또는 거기에 사는 사람들

□ **opportunity** 기회
→ a chance to do something or an occasion when it is easy for you to do something
무엇인가를 할 기회 또는 당신이 무엇인가 하는 것이 쉬운 때

□ **orchestra** 오케스트라, 교향악단
→ a large group of musicians playing many different kinds of instruments and led by a conductor
많은 여러 종류의 악기를 연주하는 음악가들과 지휘자에 의해 지휘되는 큰 규모의 집단

□ **practice** 연습하다
→ to do something regularly in order to do it better
어떤 것을 더 잘하기 위해서 규칙적으로 그것을 하다

□ **walk** (동물을) 걷게 하다
→ to take a dog for a walk for exercise
개를 운동시키기 위해 산책시키다

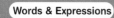
01 다음 짝지어진 두 단어의 관계가 같도록 빈칸에 알맞은 단어를 쓰시오.

> increase : decrease – difficult : _____

① easy   ② hard   ③ different
④ bright   ⑤ early

[02~03] 다음 빈칸에 들어갈 말로 적절한 것은?

02
> I'm _____ some bread in an oven.

① baking   ② eating   ③ biting
④ breaking   ⑤ buying

03
> They use organic methods of _____ vegetables.

① growing   ② flying
③ forgetting   ④ repairing
⑤ falling

중요
04 다음 밑줄 친 부분과 의미가 가장 가까운 것을 고르시오.

> It was a valuable opportunity to see how rich people lived.

① chance   ② experience   ③ effort
④ effect   ⑤ situation

서답형
05 다음 영영 풀이에 해당하는 단어를 주어진 철자로 시작하여 쓰시오.

> someone who lives next to you or near you

➡ n_____

서답형
06 다음 괄호 안의 단어를 문맥에 맞게 알맞은 형태로 고쳐 쓰시오.

> She is the _____ of the most powerful country in Europe. (lead)

07 다음 대화의 빈칸에 들어갈 말로 적절한 것은?

> A: What festival is the most famous in New York?
> B: It is Halloween festival. New York City _____ the largest Halloween parade in the U.S. every year.

① grows   ② finds   ③ falls
④ takes   ⑤ holds

08 다음 중 밑줄 친 부분의 뜻풀이가 바르지 않은 것은?

① What's the most popular free time activity for teenagers? (활동)
② I really miss your cooking. (요리)
③ She doesn't like bright colors. (밝은)
④ He plays the piano perfectly even though he cannot read a single note. (메모)
⑤ Korea has already won several medals. (몇 개의)

서답형
09 다음 우리말에 맞게 빈칸에 알맞은 말을 쓰시오.

> Anyone _____ loves books _____ _____ our event! (책을 좋아하는 사람은 누구라도 우리의 행사에 참여할 수 있어요!)

01 다음 〈보기〉와 같은 관계가 되도록 빈칸에 주어진 철자로 알맞은 말을 쓰시오.

> 보기
> happy – pleased

(1) gain – g_____
(2) gift – p_____

[02~03] 다음 빈칸에 공통으로 들어갈 말을 쓰시오. (대·소문자 무시)

02
> • The more you _____, the more you want.
> • _____ a great time before the new semester begins!

03
> • _____ can I join this club?
> • I want to learn _____ to do that.

04 다음 빈칸에 알맞은 어구를 〈보기〉에서 골라 쓰시오. (형태 변화 가능)

> 보기
> introduce / concert / doughnut / dolphin

(1) Let me _____ my friend Caden to you.
(2) I saw many _____ swimming in the sea.
(3) You should fry a _____ for 1 or 2 minutes.
(4) The orchestra held a _____ at Seoul Arts Center to help children in North Korea.

05 다음 괄호 안의 단어를 문맥에 맞게 알맞은 형태로 고쳐 쓰시오.

(1) What kind of club _____ do you like? (act)
(2) This _____ is great for shopping. (neighbor)

06 다음 주어진 우리말에 맞게 빈칸을 채우시오. (철자가 주어진 것도 있음)

(1) 나는 항상 싼 옷을 산다.
➡ I always buy cheap c_____.
(2) 어떻게 하면 우리의 제품을 많은 사람들에게 소개할 수 있을까요?
➡ How can we _____ our products to a lot of people?
(3) 나는 당신의 기사를 많은 흥미를 가지고 읽었다.
➡ I read your article with great _____.
(4) 너는 많은 신선한 과일과 야채를 먹어야 한다.
➡ You must eat a lot of fresh fruit and _____.

07 다음 우리말과 같은 뜻이 되도록 주어진 단어를 알맞은 순서로 배열하시오.

> 내가 이 동아리에 가입한다면, 나는 매우 열심히 연습할 것이다. (if, club, very, join, I, I, this, practice, will, hard)

➡ _____

Conversation

교과서

1 능력 여부 묻기

A I don't know how to swim. Do you know how to? 나는 수영하는 법을 알지 못해. 너는 방법을 알고 있니?

B Yes, I can teach you. 응, 내가 가르쳐 줄 수 있어.

■ 'how to+동사원형'은 '~하는 방법, 어떻게 ~하는지'의 의미로, 'Do you know how to + 동사원형 ~?' 을 이용해 상대방의 능력이나 무언가를 하는 방법에 대해 물을 수 있다.

능력 여부 묻기

· Do you know how to + 동사원형 ~?
· Can you + 동사원형 ~?

능력 여부 대답하기

· 긍정: Yes, I do[can]./ Of course I do[can].
· 부정: No, I don't./ No, I can't.

■ '의문사+to부정사'는 명사구로 문장에서 주어, 목적어, 보어로 쓰일 수 있다. 여기에 사용될 수 있는 의 문사는 what, when, where, how, which, whom 등이 있다.

의문사+to부정사

· what to부정사: 무엇을 ~할지
· where to부정사: 어디에서 ~할지
· how to부정사: 어떻게 ~할지, ~하는 방법

· when to부정사: 언제 ~할지
· which to부정사: 어느 것을 ~할지
· whom to부정사: 누구를 ~할지

■ '의문사+to부정사'는 '의문사+주어+should 동사원형'으로 바꾸어 쓸 수 있다.
Tell me how to do it. (내가 그것을 어떻게 해야 할지 말해 주세요.)
= Tell me how I should do it.

핵심 Check

1. 우리말과 일치하도록 빈칸에 알맞은 말을 쓰시오.

   He taught me _____ _____ _____ my new cellphone.

   (그는 나에게 새 휴대 전화를 사용하는 법을 가르쳐 주었다.)

2. 우리말과 일치하도록 주어진 단어를 배열하여 문장을 완성하시오.

   _____ (learn, pictures, I, to, good, want,

   how, take, to) (나는 좋은 사진을 찍는 법을 배우고 싶다.)

② 좋아하는 것 표현하기

A What do you enjoy doing when you have free time? 너는 여가 시간에 뭐 하는 것을 즐기니?

B I enjoy painting pictures of people in the park. 나는 공원에서 사람들을 그리는 것을 즐겨.

- 'I enjoy 동명사'는 '나는 ~하는 것을 즐긴다.'는 의미로 자신이 좋아하는 것을 나타내는 표현이다. 주로 취미 등을 묻는 'What do you enjoy doing when you have free time?', 'What do you usually do in your free time?' 등에 대한 응답으로 쓰인다.

좋아하는 것 표현하기

- I enjoy 동명사 ~.
- I like 동명사/to부정사 ~.
- I love 동명사/to부정사 ~.

- 동사를 주어, 목적어, 보어의 자리에 쓰기 위해서 동명사 또는 to부정사를 사용할 수 있다. 하지만, 특정한 동사의 목적어로 동명사나 to부정사가 사용될 때는 그 동사의 종류에 따라 동명사를 사용할지, 아니면 to부정사를 사용할지 잘 선택해야 한다.

- enjoy는 동명사를 목적어로 사용할 수 있고, want는 to부정사를 목적어로 사용한다. like와 love는 동명사와 to부정사 둘 다 목적어로 사용할 수 있다.

핵심 Check

3. 다음 대화의 우리말과 일치하도록 빈칸에 알맞은 말을 쓰시오.

A: _____ enjoy _____ when you have _____ ?
(너는 여가 시간에 뭐 하는 것을 즐기니?)

B: _____. (나는 음악을 듣는 것을 즐겨.)

4. 다음 그림을 보고, 주어진 단어를 사용하여 빈칸을 완성하시오.

A: What do you like to do on weekends?

B: _____. (enjoy)

Listen & Speak 1 A

G: ❶Do you know ❷how to make a paper cat?

B: Of course. ❸It's easy.

G: 종이 고양이 만드는 법을 알고 있니?
B: 물론이지. 그건 쉬워.

❶ 'Do you know ~?'는 어떤 것을 아는지 질문할 때 사용한다. 비슷한 의미로 'Can you tell me ~?'를 대신 사용할 수 있다.
❷ how to부정사: 어떻게 ~할지, ~하는 방법   ❸ 인칭대명사 It은 how to make a paper cat을 가리킨다.

Check(√) True or False

(1) The boy knows how to make a paper cat.   T ☐ F ☐

(2) The way to make a paper cat is not difficult.   T ☐ F ☐

Listen & Speak 1 B-1

G: I heard ❶you went to Yuna's violin concert yesterday. ❷How was it?

B: It was great. ❸I hope I can play the violin ❹like her someday.

G: I didn't know ❺you knew how to play the violin.

B: I can, but ❻I'm not good at it yet.

G: 어제 유나의 바이올린 콘서트에 갔다고 들었어. 어땠니?
B: 좋았어. 나도 언젠가 그녀처럼 바이올린을 연주할 수 있기를 바라.
G: 나는 네가 바이올린 연주하는 법을 아는지 몰랐어.
B: 할 수 있어. 그러나 아직 잘하지는 못해.

❶ heard와 you 사이에 명사절을 이끄는 접속사 that이 생략되어 있다. 'you went to Yuna's violin concert yesterday'는 heard의 목적어로 사용되었다.
❷ 과거의 경험에 대해 묻고자 할 때 'How was ~?' 표현을 사용한다. 과거의 경험에 대한 답변이 되어야 하므로 대답의 동사도 과거형을 사용한다. 여기서 it은 Yuna's violin concert를 가리킨다.
❸ 'I hope I can 동사원형 ~.'은 자신이 어떤 것을 할 수 있기를 희망하거나 기대를 한다는 표현이다.
❹ like: (전치사) ~처럼, ~와 같이
❺ know와 you 사이에 명사절을 이끄는 접속사 that이 생략되어 있다. how to부정사: 어떻게 ~할지, ~하는 방법
❻ be good at: ~을 잘하다

Check(√) True or False

(3) Yuna is good at playing the violin.   T ☐ F ☐

(4) The girl knew that the boy knew how to play the violin.   T ☐ F ☐

Listen & Speak 1 B-2

G: ❶Look at these pictures. I ❷grew these vegetables ❸myself. I have my ❹own garden.

B: Cool! Do you know how to cook the vegetables you grow, too?

G: Yes, my grandmother ❺taught me.

G: 이 사진들 좀 봐. 나는 이 채소들을 직접 길렀어. 나는 내 정원이 있어.
B: 멋지다! 네가 재배한 채소로 요리하는 법도 아니?
G: 응. 할머니께서 내게 가르쳐 주셨어.

❶ look at: ~을 보다 pictures가 복수형이므로, this가 아닌 these를 사용한다.
❷ grew는 grow의 과거형이다. grow: [식물을] 재배하다
❸ 재귀대명사의 강조 용법으로 주어 'I'를 강조하고 있다.
❹ own은 소유격 다음에서 강조어로 사용한다. own: 자기 자신의, 직접 ~한
❺ taught는 teach의 과거형 동사이다.

Check(√) True or False

(5) In the pictures, there are vegetables.   T ☐ F ☐

(6) The girl doesn't know how to cook the vegetables.   T ☐ F ☐

Listen & Speak 2 A

A: Do you enjoy ❶looking at the stars at night?
G: Yes, I ❷love doing that.

❶ enjoy는 동명사를 목적어로 취하는 동사이다. look at: ~을 보다 at night: 밤에
❷ love는 목적어로 동명사와 to부정사를 취할 수 있다. love doing it = love to do it / doing that=looking at the stars

Listen & Speak 2 B-1

B: Do you ❶enjoy reading books, Yumi?
G: Yes, I love reading science books. ❷How about you?
B: I love reading books, too.
G: Then, ❸let's go to the library ❹after school today.

❶ enjoy(~을 즐기다)를 사용해서 좋아하는 것을 말할 수 있다. enjoy는 목적어로 동명사를 취하는 동사로 reading을 사용해야 한다.
❷ 'How about you?'는 '너는 어때?'라고 묻는 내용이다. 'What about you?'로 바꿔 쓸 수 있다.
❸ 'Let's+동사원형'은 '~하자'라는 의미로, 제안하는 말을 할 때 쓴다. go to 장소: ~에 가다
❹ after school: 방과 후에

Listen & Speak 2 B-2

G: ❶What did you do on the weekend, Minsu?
B: ❷I made breakfast ❸for my family.
G: Do you enjoy cooking?
B: Yes, I'm a good ❹cook! My family loves my ❺cooking.

❶ 과거에 무엇을 했는지 묻고 싶을 때에는 What did you do?라고 묻는다. 특정한 때를 넣어 어떤 날에 무엇을 했냐고 물을 수도 있다.
❷ 과거에 무엇을 했는지 묻는 질문에 대한 대답이므로, 과거형 동사를 사용해야 한다.
❸ make는 간접목적어를 직접목적어 뒤로 보낼 때 for를 붙인다.
❹ cook: (동) 요리하다 (명) 요리사 / 이 문장에서는 명사로 쓰였다.
❺ cooking: 요리, 음식

Listen & Speak 2 B-3

B: Jiyun, that's a pretty backpack! Where did you ❶get it?
G: My sister made ❷it for me.
B: Wow! She's a really good designer.
G: Yes, she is. And she enjoys making ❸clothes, too.

❶ get: 얻다, 사다
❷ it은 앞에 나온 a backpack을 가리킨다.
❸ clothes: 옷, 의상 cloth: 천, 옷감 cloths: 옷감들

Real-Life Zone A

B: Hello, Kate. I'm Hamin, the ❶leader of the Nanum Orchestra. ❷Thank you for your interest in our club.
G: Hi. Nice to meet you.
B: You play the violin? ❸When did you start playing the violin?
G: I started learning ❹how to play the violin when I was ten.
B: ❺Do you have any experience playing in a group?
G: Yes. Actually, I was a member of an orchestra ❻when I was in elementary school.
B: Great. We also ❼volunteer to teach children. Do you enjoy teaching others?
G: I have no experience teaching others. But I enjoy working with people, so ❽I'd like to try.
B: Good. I think we'll have a great time playing together. Welcome to the Nanum Orchestra.

❶ leader: 지도자, 대표
❷ 'Thank you for ~.'는 감사를 표현하는 말로 for 다음에 감사의 이유나 원인이 나온다. interest: 관심
❸ 'When did you 동사원형 ~?'은 '너 언제 ~했니?'의 의미로, 과거에 언제 어떠한 일을 했는지 묻는 질문이다.
❹ how to부정사: 어떻게 ~할지, ~하는 방법
❺ Do you have any experience~?는 어떤 일을 한 경험이 있는지 물을 때 쓰인다.
❻ when: (접) ~할 때
❼ volunteer: 자원봉사하다
❽ 'I'd'는 'I would'를 줄여서 표현한 것이다. would like to 동사원형: ~하고 싶다

● 다음 우리말과 일치하도록 빈칸에 알맞은 말을 쓰시오.

Listen & Speak 1 A

A: Do you _____ _____ _____ make a paper cat?

B: Of course. It's easy.

해석

G: 종이 고양이 만드는 법을 알고 있니?
B: 물론이지. 그건 쉬워.

Listen & Speak 1 B

1. G: I _____ _____ _____ _____ Yuna's violin concert
   yesterday. _____ was it?

   B: It was great. _____ _____ _____ _____ the
   violin like her someday.

   G: I didn't know you _____ _____ _____ _____
   _____ _____.

   B: I can, but I'm not _____ _____ it yet.

2. G: Look _____ these pictures. I _____ these vegetables
   _____. I have my _____ garden.

   B: Cool! Do you know _____ _____ _____ the vegetables
   you grow, too?

   G: Yes, my grandmother _____ me.

1. G: 어제 유나의 바이올린 콘서트에 갔
   다고 들었어. 어땠니?
   B: 좋았어. 나도 언젠가 그녀처럼 바
   이올린을 연주할 수 있기를 바라.
   G: 나는 네가 바이올린 연주하는 법을
   아는지 몰랐어.
   B: 할 수 있어, 그러나 아직 잘하지는
   못해.
2. G: 이 사진들 좀 봐. 나는 이 채소를
   직접 길렀어. 나는 내 자신의 정원
   이 있어.
   B: 멋지다! 네가 기르는 채소로 요리
   하는 법도 아니?
   G: 응, 할머니께서 내게 가르쳐 주셨
   어.

Listen & Speak 2 A

A: Do you enjoy _____ _____ the stars _____ _____?

G: Yes, I love doing that.

B: 너는 밤에 별을 보는 것을 즐기니?
G: 응, 나는 별을 보는 것을 아주 좋아
   해.

Listen & Speak 2 B

1. B: _____ _____ _____ reading books, Yumi?

   G: Yes, I _____ _____ science books. How _____ you?

   B: I love _____ books, too.

   G: Then, let's _____ to _____ _____ after school today.

2. G: _____ _____ _____ _____ on the weekend, Minsu?

   B: I _____ breakfast for my family.

   G: _____ _____ _____ _____ _____?

   B: Yes, I'm a good _____! My family loves my _____.

1. B: 유미야, 너는 책 읽는 것을 즐기
   니?
   G: 응, 나는 과학 책을 읽는 것을
   좋아해. 너는 어때?
   B: 나도 책 읽는 것을 좋아해.
   G: 그럼 오늘 방과 후에 도서관 가
   자.
2. G: 민수야, 주말에 뭐 했니?
   B: 가족을 위해 아침을 만들었어.
   G: 너는 요리를 즐기니?
   B: 응, 나는 훌륭한 요리사야! 우리
   가족은 내 요리를 좋아해.

3. **B:** Jiyun, that's a pretty backpack! _____ did you _____ it?

G: My sister _____ _____ _____ _____.

B: Wow! She's a really good _____.

G: Yes, she is. And she _____ _____ _____, too.

Real-Life Zone A

B: Hello, Kate. I'm Hamin, _____ _____ of the Nanum Orchestra. Thank you for your _____ in our club.

G: Hi. Nice to meet you.

B: You play the violin? _____ _____ _____ _____ _____ the violin?

G: I started learning _____ _____ _____ _____ _____ I was ten.

B: Do you have any _____ _____ in a group?

G: Yes. Actually, I was a member of _____ _____ _____ I was in _____ school.

B: Great. We also _____ _____ _____ children. _____ _____ _____ _____ others?

G: I have no _____ teaching others. But I _____ _____ _____ people, so I'd like to try.

B: Good. I think we'll _____ a great time playing together. Welcome to the Nanum Orchestra.

Wrap Up

B: These cookies _____ so _____. Did you make them?

G: Yes. I _____ _____ _____ yesterday. I enjoy _____. I'm _____ _____ make doughnuts this Saturday.

B: Oh, I _____ _____ _____ _____ _____ _____ doughnuts. Is it difficult?

G: Not _____ all. You can come to my house and join me if you want.

B: Thanks, Bora. What _____ should I come?

G: At 2:00.

B: _____ good. _____ you then.

해석

3. B: 지윤아, 그거 예쁜 배낭이네! 어디
서 샀어?
   G: 언니가 내게 만들어 준 거야.
   B: 와! 그녀는 정말 훌륭한 디자이너
구나.
   G: 응, 그래. 그리고 그녀는 옷 만드
는 것도 즐겨.

B: 안녕, 케이트. 나는 나눔 오케스트라
의 대표 하민이야. 우리 동아리에 관
심을 가져줘서 고마워.
G: 안녕. 만나서 반가워.
B: 너는 바이올린을 연주하니? 언제 바
이올린 연주를 시작했니?
G: 10살 때 바이올린을 연주하는 법을
배우기 시작했어.
B: 그룹에서 연주해 본 경험이 있니?
G: 응. 사실 나는 초등학교 때 오케스트
라 단원이었어.
B: 좋아. 우리는 자원봉사로 아이들도
가르쳐. 다른 사람들을 가르치는 것을
즐기니?
G: 나는 다른 사람들을 가르친 경험이
없어. 그러나 나는 사람들과 일하는
것을 즐겨. 그래서 나는 해보고 싶어.
B: 좋아. 나는 우리가 함께 연주하며 좋
은 시간을 보낼 것이라고 생각해. 나
눔 오케스트라에 온 걸 환영해.

B: 이 쿠키들은 정말 맛있어 보여. 네가
만들었니?
G: 응. 어제 내가 직접 만들었어. 나는
제빵을 즐겨. 이번 주 토요일에 도넛
을 만들 예정이야.
B: 오, 나는 도넛 만드는 법을 배우고 싶
어. 그건 어렵니?
G: 전혀 아니야. 네가 원한다면 우리 집
에 와서 같이 해도 돼.
B: 고마워, 보라야. 내가 몇 시에 가야
해?
G: 2시에.
B: 좋아. 그때 보자.

[01~02] 다음 대화의 빈칸에 알맞은 말은?

01

> A: What do you enjoy doing when you have free time?
> B: _____

① I went shopping.
② I want to have free time.
③ I will go to the movie with my friends.
④ I enjoy painting pictures of people in the park.
⑤ I don't like to play computer games.

02

> A: Do you know _____ ?
> B: Of course. It's easy.

① how to make a paper cat
② what to make a paper cat
③ making a paper cat
④ how making a paper cat
⑤ that I can make a paper cat

03 다음 주어진 문장과 의미하는 것이 같은 문장을 고르시오.

> Do you know how to make doughnuts?

① Do you want to make doughnuts?
② Are you practicing making doughnuts?
③ Do you mind making doughnuts?
④ Can you make doughnuts?
⑤ Why don't you make doughnuts?

04 다음 문장의 빈칸에 알맞은 것을 모두 고르시오.

> G: Look at these pictures. I grew these vegetables myself. I have my own garden.
> B: Cool! Do you know how to cook the vegetables you grow, too?
> G: (A)_____ . My grandmother taught me.

① Yes, I do   ② No, I can't   ③ Of course
④ Not at all   ⑤ Yes, I am

[01~03] 다음 대화를 읽고 물음에 답하시오.

G: I heard you went to Yuna's violin concert yesterday. (①)

B: It was great. (②) I hope I can play the violin (A)like her someday. (③)

G: I didn't know you knew how to play the violin. (④)

B: I can, but I'm not good at it yet. (⑤)

01 위 대화의 ①~⑤ 중 다음 주어진 말이 들어갈 알맞은 곳은?

> How was it?

①   ②   ③   ④   ⑤

 밑줄 친 (A)like와 같은 의미로 쓴 문장을 고르시오.

① I don't know why he doesn't like me.

② I don't like to study English.

③ I could dance like that!

④ Why do you like to climb the mountain?

⑤ She likes to watch TV all day.

03 위 대화의 내용과 일치하지 <u>않는</u> 것은?

① The boy thinks that Yuna's violin concert was great.

② The boy thinks he is good at playing the violin.

③ The boy went to Yuna's violin concert.

④ Yuna's violin concert was held yesterday.

⑤ The boy knows how to play the violin.

04 다음 대화의 빈칸에 알맞은 말은?

> A: I don't know how to speak Spanish.
>
> _____
>
> B: Yes, I can teach you.

① Do you know how to?

② Why don't we learn to speak Spanish?

③ What are you going to speak?

④ How do you say this in Spanish?

⑤ What are you good at?

05 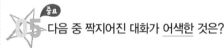 다음 중 짝지어진 대화가 <u>어색한</u> 것은?

① A: Do you know how to use the washing machine?
   B: Yes. I do.

② A: Do you know how to play the guitar?
   B: No, I don't.

③ A: What do you do after school?
   B: I enjoy drawing cartoons.

④ A: What do you like to do in your free time?
   B: I enjoy reading books. How about you?

⑤ A: Do you know how to take pictures?
   B: Of course I am.

서답형

06 (A)와 (B)에 주어진 단어를 이용해 빈칸에 들어갈 수 있는 말을 쓰시오.

> A: Do you enjoy (A)_____(look) at the stars at night?
>
> G: Yes, I love (B)_____(do) that.

[07~09] 다음 대화를 읽고 물음에 답하시오.

B: Jiyun, that's a pretty backpack! (①)
G: (②) My sister made it for me. (③)
B: Wow! She's a really good designer. (④)
G: (A)_____ (⑤) And she enjoys making clothes, too.

07 위 대화의 ①~⑤ 중 다음 주어진 말이 들어갈 알맞은 곳은?

> Where did you get it?

①   ②   ③   ④   ⑤

08 빈칸 (A)에 알맞은 말을 고르시오.

① Yes, she does.   ② Yes, she can.
③ No, she isn't.   ④ No, she doesn't.
⑤ Yes, she is.

09 위 대화의 내용과 일치하지 않는 것은?

① Jiyun's sister made her a backpack.
② Jiyun knows how to make a backpack.
③ Jiyun's sister is a good designer.
④ Jiyun's sister enjoys making clothes.
⑤ Jiyun has a sister.

[10~13] 다음 대화를 읽고 물음에 답하시오.

B: Hello, Kate. I'm Hamin, the leader of the Nanum Orchestra. Thank you for your interest in our club.
G: Hi. Nice to meet you.
B: You play the violin? When did you start playing the violin? (①)
G: (the, I, I, ten, started, when, how, learning, was, play, violin, to)

B: Do you have any experience playing (A) [alone / in a group]? (②)
G: Yes. Actually, I was a member of an orchestra when I was in elementary school.
B: Great. (③) Do you enjoy teaching others?
G: I have (B)[no experience / many experiences] teaching others. (④) But I enjoy working with people, so I'd like to try.
B: (⑤) Good. I think we'll have a great time playing together. Welcome to the Nanum Orchestra.

10 위 대화의 ①~⑤ 중 다음 주어진 말이 들어갈 알맞은 곳은?

> We also volunteer to teach children.

①   ②   ③   ④   ⑤

서답형
11 (A)~(B)에 들어갈 말로 적절한 것을 고르시오.

➡ (A) _____ (B) _____

서답형
12 괄호 안에 주어진 어휘를 바르게 배열하여 문장을 완성하시오. (I로 시작할 것)

➡ _____

13 위 대화의 내용과 일치하지 않는 것을 고르시오.

① Kate will join the Nanum Orchestra after this conversation.
② Kate is a member of an orchestra now.
③ Kate knows how to play the violin.
④ Hamin is the leader of the Nanum Orchestra.
⑤ Kate and Hamin meet for the first time.

[01~02] 주어진 문장 다음에 이어질 대화의 순서를 바르게 배열하시오.

01

| Mina, do you enjoy cooking? |

| (A) Then why don't you join the cooking club?
(B) Hmm, let me think about it.
(C) Sometimes. I know how to make a pizza. |

➡ _____

02

| Did you buy that drone? |

| (A) No, I got it as a present from my parents, but I don't know how to use it. Do you know how to?
(B) Then, I will ask her for help.
(C) No, maybe Jina knows how to do it. She enjoys flying drones. |

➡ _____

[03~05] 다음 대화를 읽고 물음에 답하시오.

G: Look   (A)   these pictures. (B)I grew these vegetables me. I have my own garden.
B: Cool! (C)네가 기르는 채소를 요리하는 법을 아니, too?
G: Yes, my grandmother taught me.

03 빈칸 (A)에 알맞는 전치사를 쓰시오.

➡ _____

04 밑줄 친 (B)에서 어색한 것을 찾아 고치시오.

➡ _____

05 (C)의 밑줄 친 우리말을 주어진 단어를 이용해 영작하시오.

➡ _____

(how, vegetables)

06 밑줄 친 부분에서 어색한 것을 찾아 고치시오. (2개)

| A: Do you enjoy looking at the stars at night?
B: Yes, I enjoyed do that. |

➡ _____

[07~08] 다음 대화를 읽고 물음에 답하시오.

G: I heard you went to Yuna's violin concert yesterday. How was it?
B: It was great. I hope I can play the violin like her someday.
G: (A)나는 네가 바이올린 연주하는 법을 아는지 몰랐어.
B: I can, but (B)(not, at, yet, I'm, good, it).

07 (A)에 주어진 우리말을 영작하시오. (10 단어)

➡ _____

08 괄호 (B) 안에 주어진 어휘를 알맞게 배열하여 문장을 완성하시오.

➡ _____

Grammar

교과서

1 의문사 + to부정사

> We also teach children **how to play** musical instruments as a service to our community. 우리는 지역 사회를 위한 봉사로 아이들에게 악기를 연주하는 법도 가르칩니다.
> I don't know **what to do.** 나는 무엇을 해야 할지 모르겠어.

- '의문사+to부정사'는 문장 속에서 주어, 목적어, 보어 역할을 하는 명사구로 사용되어 '~해야 할지, ~하는 것이 좋을지'라는 뜻을 나타낸다.
- Please tell me **when to go.** (언제 가야 할지 나에게 말해 줘.)

- what, which, who, whom, how, when, where 등의 의문사가 사용되지만 why는 쓰지 않는다는 점에 주의한다.

형태	의미	예문
how + to부정사	어떻게 ~할지	He doesn't know how to talk politely.
what + to부정사	무엇을 ~할지	Please tell me what to do next.
when + to부정사	언제 ~할지	I also don't know when to ask him.
where + to부정사	어디에 ~할지	I am not sure where to put the key.

- '의문사+to부정사'는 '의문사+주어+should/can+동사원형'으로 바꾸어 쓸 수 있다.
- She asked me **whom to meet.** (그녀는 내게 누구를 만나야 할지 물었다.)
  = She asked me whom she should meet.

- 의문사가 의문형용사로 쓰여 to부정사와의 사이에 명사가 올 수 있다.
- The host usually tells the guests **what time to leave.** (주인은 대개 손님들에게 몇 시에 떠나야 하는지를 말해 준다.)

핵심 Check

1. 다음 우리말과 일치하도록 빈칸에 알맞은 말을 쓰시오.

(1) 나는 그녀에게 무슨 말을 해야 할지 모르겠어.

➡ I don't know _____ _____ say to her.

= I don't know _____ _____ _____ say to her.

(2) 이번 주말에 그를 어디서 만날지 내게 말해줘.

➡ Tell me _____ _____ _____ him this weekend.

= Tell me _____ _____ _____ _____ him this weekend.

---

2 주격 관계대명사

Anyone **who** likes to paint can join. 그림 그리는 것을 좋아하는 사람은 누구나 가입할 수 있습니다.

She has a cat **which** has brown hair. 그녀는 갈색 털을 가진 고양이를 갖고 있다.

■ 관계대명사는 접속사와 대명사의 역할을 한다. 관계대명사절은 명사를 수식해 주는 절의 한 종류로 관계대명사절이 꾸며 주는 말을 선행사라고 하고 관계대명사는 앞의 선행사와 같은 대상을 가리킨다. 관계대명사절이 되기 전의 문장에서 주어로 쓰였으면 주격 관계대명사로, 소유격으로 쓰였으면 소유격 관계대명사로, 목적격으로 쓰였으면 목적격 관계대명사가 된다. 주격 관계대명사는 관계대명사절에서 주어 역할을 하므로 그 다음에는 동사가 온다.

• Mr. Kim is a farmer. He(=Mr. Kim) grows apples.

= Mr. Kim is a farmer **who**[**that**] grows apples. (주격)

• This is the smartphone. She bought it(=the smartphone) at the shop.

= This is the smartphone **which**[**that**] she bought at the shop. (목적격)

• This is the dress. Its color is blue.

= This is the dress **whose** color is blue. (소유격)

■ 관계대명사는 선행사에 따라 다음과 같이 사용되며, 목적격 관계대명사는 생략할 수 있다.

	주격	소유격	목적격
사람	who/that	whose	whom[who]/that
동물, 사물	which/that	whose/of which	which/that

■ 주격 관계대명사절의 동사는 선행사의 인칭과 수에 일치시킨다.

• I have a friend **who**[**that**] helps me a lot. (나를 많이 도와주는 친구가 있다.)

■ 관계대명사 that은 who, whom과 which 대신 사용할 수 있으며 소유격은 없다. 또한 선행사가 '사람+동물[사물]'인 경우에는 반드시 that을 써야 한다.

• There are a boy and his dog **that** are running in the park. 공원에서 뛰고 있는 소년과 그의 개가 있다.

■ '주격 관계대명사 + be동사'는 생략이 가능하다.

• The boy (**who is**) singing on the stage is my brother. (무대에서 노래하고 있는 소년은 내 동생이다.)

핵심 Check

2. 다음 우리말과 일치하도록 빈칸에 알맞은 말을 쓰시오.

(1) 나는 서울에 살고 있는 친구가 있다.

➡ I have a friend _____ lives in Seoul.

(2) 매우 멋있어 보이는 저 옷 좀 봐.

➡ Look at that dress _____ looks very nice.

01 다음 문장에서 어법상 <u>어색한</u> 부분을 바르게 고쳐 쓰시오.

(1) I can't decide what eating.

_____ ➡ _____

(2) Do you know when go?

_____ ➡ _____

(3) There is a man which is waiting for his bag.

_____ ➡ _____

(4) This is the movie who made me laugh a lot.

_____ ➡ _____

02 다음 중 어법상 <u>어색한</u> 문장을 <u>모두</u> 고르시오.

① Marie Curie is the person who first found radium.
② I lost the watch which my father had given to me.
③ I want to show you some pictures who I took a few days ago.
④ Please show me how do it.
⑤ Will you tell me where to stay in Seoul?

03 다음 우리말에 맞게 주어진 단어를 바르게 배열하시오. (필요하면 어형을 바꿀 것)

(1) 그녀는 내게 무엇을 해야 할지 묻지 않았다.
   (she / me / what / do / ask / didn't / to)

   ➡ _____

(2) Mariel은 어디로 가야 할지 몰랐다.
   (where / Mariel / go / know / didn't / to)

   ➡ _____

(3) Degas는 춤추고 있는 무용수를 그리는 것을 좋아했다.
   (Degas / dancers / who / liked / dancing / paint / were / to)

   ➡ _____

(4) 그는 어제 그 소녀에게 짖은 개를 갖고 있다.
   (he / that / dog / girl / yesterday / the / the / barked / has / at)

   ➡ _____

01 다음 빈칸에 알맞은 것은?

> I don't know _____ to do it.

① how   ② what
③ that   ④ whom
⑤ why

02 다음 문장의 빈칸에 들어갈 알맞은 것은?

> Look at the boy _____ is dancing.

① which   ② who
③ whose   ④ whom
⑤ what

03 다음 빈칸에 알맞은 말이 바르게 짝지어진 것은?

> • She knows _____ to solve the problem.
> • Molly is reading the message from Kate _____ arrived yesterday.

① what – which   ② what – who
③ how – which   ④ how – who
⑤ that – that

서답형
04 다음 문장에서 어법상 틀린 부분을 찾아 바르게 고쳐 쓰시오.

> The painting is about a party who took place in a small town.

_____ ➡ _____

05 다음 중 어법상 어색한 것은?

① I don't know how to make a paper doll.
② Can you tell me whom to wait for here?
③ We asked him when to start.
④ Morri told us where to go after we finished the work.
⑤ I wanted to know what to do it.

06 다음 중 어법상 올바른 것은?

① This is the book who has many exciting stories.
② Anyone which loves books can join our event!
③ I saw a tree who looked like a big elephant.
④ He is the man that lived next door five years ago.
⑤ Amy likes movies who have sad endings.

07 다음 중 어법상 올바른 것은?

① They went to the restaurant who was famous for its traditional Korean food.
② I know a girl who name is Karen.
③ Please let me know how way I should go.
④ Tom has a painting who was drawn by a famous artist.
⑤ The two brothers always argue about how to share their presents.

서답형

08 괄호 안에서 알맞은 것을 고르시오.

(1) This is a sea horse (which / who) lives in the sea.

(2) There lived a girl and her dog (that / which) would play on the grass together.

(3) They enjoyed samgyupsal (that / who) tasted yummy last night.

(4) Let's look at some paintings that (was / were) painted by my aunt.

(5) He is a great novelist (who / which) writes many interesting novels.

(6) This is the boy (who / whom) helped me yesterday.

(7) Paul gave her a bag (which / which was) made in Korea.

서답형

09 다음 우리말을 두 가지로 영작하시오.

> 나는 무엇을 입을지 결정하지 못하겠어.

➡ _____

➡ _____

서답형

10 다음 중 관계대명사가 들어갈 곳을 고르고 알맞게 쓰시오.

(1) I can't ① remember ② the lady ③ visited ④ me ⑤ last night.

(2) There ① was ② a big house ③ has ④ a beautiful garden ⑤ over there.

➡ (1) _____ (2) _____

서답형

11 괄호 안에서 알맞은 것을 고르시오.

(1) Let me tell you (how / what) to use the machine.

(2) I don't know where (spending / to spend) the holidays.

(3) Jennifer didn't know (what / why) to do, so she just waited for him.

(4) I'm not sure what (I should / I) do after graduation.

(5) At first, he did not know (how he read / how to read) a note.

중요

12 다음 〈보기〉의 밑줄 친 부분과 쓰임이 같은 것은?

> ┤ 보기 ├
>
> These are the animals <u>which</u> live both on the land and in the water.

① <u>Which</u> do you like better, this one or that one?

② That is the dog <u>which</u> barked at me the other day.

③ Can you tell me <u>which</u> one will be good for Harry?

④ The scarf <u>which</u> she is wearing around her neck looks beautiful.

⑤ Let's decide <u>which</u> way to take.

13 다음 빈칸에 적절하지 <u>않은</u> 것을 모두 고르시오.

> He didn't tell us _____ to go.

① what   ② where   ③ when

④ how   ⑤ why

14 다음 중 주어진 문장의 밑줄 친 that과 용법이 같은 것은?

> The girl that is talking to Jack over there is very kind.

① Yuna has a cat that likes to hide in boxes.
② Don't forget that small efforts can make big differences.
③ I didn't know that.
④ Look at that big bird.
⑤ I can't understand you when you speak that fast.

서답형
15 두 문장의 의미가 같아지도록 빈칸에 알맞은 말을 쓰시오.

(1) We are going to teach them how to do magic.
= We are going to teach them _____ _____ _____ magic.
(2) I can't decide where to put this computer.
= I can't decide _____ _____ _____ _____ this computer.
(3) Please inform me what to do next.
= Please inform me _____ _____ _____ _____ next.

16 다음 빈칸에 공통으로 알맞은 말은?

> • The boy _____ gave me a present is my boyfriend.
> • She has a dog _____ has a short tail.

① who
② whose
③ whom
④ which
⑤ that

[17~18] 다음 우리말에 맞게 영작한 것을 고르시오.

17
> 아버지는 그 기계를 어떻게 사용해야 하는지 배우셨다.

① My father learned when to use the machine.
② My father learned where to use the machine.
③ My father learned how to use the machine.
④ My father learned what to use the machine.
⑤ My father learned that to use the machine.

18
> 기린은 긴 목을 가진 동물이다.

① A giraffe is an animal who has a long neck.
② A giraffe is an animal whose has a long neck.
③ A giraffe is an animal whom has a long neck.
④ A giraffe is an animal which has a long neck.
⑤ A giraffe is an animal that it has a long neck.

서답형
19 우리말과 일치하도록 주어진 어휘를 이용하여 빈칸에 알맞은 말을 쓰시오.

(1) 그는 그것을 어디서 살지 모른다. (buy)
➡ He doesn't know _____ _____ _____ it.
(2) 나는 사진이 많이 들어간 여행 책을 좋아한다. (have)
➡ I like travel books _____ _____ lots of pictures.

01 다음 글에서 어법상 <u>잘못</u> 쓰인 것을 찾아 알맞게 고치시오. (3개)

> I volunteered at a computer school for old people. I met several old people which want to know about computers. I helped the teacher taught them how using a computer.

➡ _____

02 다음 중 어법상 어색한 것을 바르게 고치시오.

(1) I want to have a toy who can speak.

_____ ➡ _____

(2) The dog is running after the girl has long ears.

_____ ➡ _____

(3) Angie likes to take pictures of old ladies whom are working.

_____ ➡ _____

(4) Look at the people who is standing in line.

_____ ➡ _____

(5) She is the teacher who she teaches us English.

_____ ➡ _____

03 다음 빈칸에 알맞은 것을 쓰시오.

(1) Do you know how to swim?
= Do you know _____ _____ _____ _____?

(2) Which movie to watch is hard for us to decide.
= _____ _____ _____ _____ _____ is hard for us to decide.

(3) I did not know whom to thank for the gift.
= I did not know _____ _____ _____ _____ for the gift.

04 주어진 두 문장을 한 문장으로 바꿔 쓰시오.

(1) • Here are two club leaders.
    • They want students to join their clubs.

➡ _____
_____

(2) • This is the tea.
    • It is good for your health.

➡ _____

(3) • The movie was interesting.
    • It was directed by James Cameron.

➡ _____
_____

(4) • There are a boy and his dog.
    • They are running at the playground.

➡ _____
_____

(5) • Do you know the girl?
    • She is dancing on the stage.

➡ _____

05 다음 중 어법상 잘못된 것을 고쳐 문장을 다시 쓰시오.

(1) You need to know how play an instrument to join our club.

➡ _____

_____

(2) The old man didn't know what to use the smartphone.

➡ _____

(3) When I to visit London has to be decided.

➡ _____

(4) I don't know why to go there.

➡ _____

06 다음 중 생략할 수 있는 것을 찾아 쓰시오.

(1) The man who is dancing there lives next door.

➡ _____

(2) These are the pictures which were taken at our field trip in spring.

➡ _____

07 주어진 어구와 to부정사를 이용하여 자신의 문장을 쓰시오.

(1) how, speak

➡ _____

(2) what, say to

➡ _____

(3) where, park

➡ _____

[08~09] 다음 그림을 보고 주어진 어휘를 이용하여 빈칸에 알맞은 말을 쓰시오.

08
A: Do you know the girl _____ _____? (be, read)
B: Oh, she is Sumi.

09
A: Does Minsu know _____ the piano? (play)
B: Of course. He plays the piano very well.

10 다음 우리말을 괄호 안에 주어진 어구를 이용하여 영작하시오.

(1) 어떻게 영어로 이메일을 쓸 수 있는지 나에게 말해 줄 수 있니? (tell, write, an email, in English, 12 단어)

➡ _____

(2) 나는 무엇을 먼저 해야 할지 모르겠어. (know, do, first, 8 단어)

➡ _____

(3) 너는 강을 따라 뛰고 있는 저 남자를 알고 있니? (that, run, along the river, 11 단어)

➡ _____

_____

Reading

Why Don't You Join Our Club?

Participating in club activities is a great way to enjoy your school
life. How about joining a club? Here are two club leaders who want
students to join their clubs. Let's listen to what they say.

The Picasso Art Club

   Hi! I am Sora Kang from the Picasso Art Club. As you can guess
from the name of our club, we paint. We also do volunteer work from
time to time. Last summer, our club members participated in the
"Change Our Neighborhood" project. On the dirty old walls of the
buildings in our neighborhood, we painted birds flying high in the sky
and dolphins jumping over blue waves.
As a result, the old neighborhood changed into a bright and beautiful
place. The neighbors were happy to see our work and thanked us. You
don't have to be a good painter. Anyone who likes to paint can join.
Come and be a member of the Picasso Art Club.

join 가입하다
club 동아리
participate in ～에 참여하다
leader 대표, 회장
volunteer 자원봉사자
neighborhood 동네, 이웃
dolphin 돌고래
bright 밝은
as a result 결과적으로

확인문제

● 다음 문장이 본문의 내용과 일치하면 T, 일치하지 않으면 F를 쓰시오.

1 The Picasso Art Club is a painting club. ☐

2 The Picasso Art Club has no interest in volunteer work. ☐

3 This summer, the club members of the Picasso Art Club joined the "Change Our
   Neighborhood" project. ☐

4 The old neighborhood changed into a bright and beautiful place. ☐

5 If you aren't a skillful painter, you can't join the Picasso Art Club. ☐

6 If you like to paint, you can join the Picasso Art Club. ☐

The Boram Orchestra

Hi! I am Minsu Jang, the leader of the Boram Orchestra. Did you see
several students playing music at the main gate when you came to
school today? We were those students. We play music for our friends
every morning. You need to know how to play an instrument a little
bit to join our club. But don't worry if you don't play well. We will
practice hard and get better together. We also teach children how to
play musical instruments as a service to our community. I am teaching
an eleven-year-old boy to play the violin. At first, he did not know
how to read a note. Now he can play a simple song. Hearing him play
the violin makes me very happy. By joining our club, you can have an
opportunity to help others. Come and join our club. We are waiting for
you.

orchestra 관현악단, 오케스트라
several 몇몇의
a littel bit 조금, 약간
service 서비스, 봉사
practice 연습하다
community 지역 사회
note 음표
opportunity 기회
wait for ~을 기다리다

 확인문제

● 다음 문장이 본문의 내용과 일치하면 T, 일치하지 않으면 F를 쓰시오.

1   Minsu Jang is the leader of the Boram Orchestra. ☐

2   The members of the Boram Orchestra play music for their friends after school. ☐

3   If you can't play an instrument, you can't join the Boram Orchestra. ☐

4   The members of the Boram Orchestra teach children how to play musical
    instruments. ☐

5   Minsu is teaching an eleven-year-old boy to play the violin. ☐

6   Hearing the boy play the violin makes Minsu very upset. ☐

● 우리말을 참고하여 빈칸에 알맞은 말을 쓰시오.

1 _____ _____ _____ Join Our Club?

2 _____ _____ club activities is a great way _____ _____ your school life.

3 _____ _____ joining a club?

4 Here are two club leaders _____ _____ students _____ _____ their clubs.

5 Let's listen to _____ they say.

6 The Picasso _____ _____

7 Hi! I am Sora Kang _____ the Picasso Art Club.

8 _____ you can _____ _____ the name of our club, we paint.

9 We also _____ _____ _____ from time to time.

10 Last summer, our club members _____ _____ the "Change Our Neighborhood" project.

11 _____ _____ _____ _____ _____ of the buildings in our neighborhood, we painted birds _____ high in the sky and dolphins _____ over blue waves.

12 _____ _____ _____, the old neighborhood changed _____ a bright and beautiful place.

13 The neighbors were happy _____ _____ our work and _____ us.

14 You _____ _____ _____ be a good painter.

15 _____ _____ likes to paint can join.

---

1 우리 동아리에 가입하는 게 어때?

2 동아리 활동에 참여하는 것은 학교생활을 즐기는 좋은 방법이에요.

3 동아리에 가입하는 게 어떤가요?

4 여기 학생들이 그들의 동아리에 가입하기를 원하는 두 명의 동아리 대표가 있어요.

5 그들이 하는 말을 들어 봅시다.

6 피카소 미술 동아리

7 안녕하세요! 저는 피카소 미술 동아리의 강소라입니다.

8 우리 동아리의 이름에서 추측할 수 있듯이, 우리는 그림을 그립니다.

9 우리는 가끔 자원봉사도 합니다.

10 지난여름, 우리 동아리 회원들은 "우리 마을 바꾸기" 프로젝트에 참여했습니다.

11 우리 마을에 있는 건물의 더럽고 오래된 벽에 하늘 높이 나는 새들과 푸른 파도 위로 점프하는 돌고래들을 그렸습니다.

12 결과적으로, 오래된 마을은 밝고 아름다운 곳으로 바뀌었습니다.

13 이웃들은 우리의 작품을 보고 행복해 했고 고마워했습니다.

14 여러분은 그림을 잘 그릴 필요는 없습니다.

15 그림 그리는 것을 좋아하는 사람은 누구나 가입할 수 있습니다.

16 _____ _____ _____ a member of the Picasso Art Club.

17 The Boram _____

18 Hi! I am Minsu Jang, _____ _____ of the Boram Orchestra.

19 Did you see several students _____ _____ at the main gate when you _____ _____ _____ today?

20 We were _____ students.

21 We _____ _____ _____ our friends every morning.

22 You need to know _____ _____ _____ an instrument _____ _____ _____ to join our club.

23 But _____ _____ if you don't play well.

24 We will _____ and _____ together.

25 We _____ children how to play musical instruments _____ _____ _____ our community.

26 I am teaching _____ _____ _____ to play the violin.

27 _____ _____, he did not know how to _____ _____ _____.

28 Now he can play _____ _____ _____.

29 _____ _____ _____ the violin _____ me very happy.

30 _____ _____ our club, you can _____ _____ _____ to help others.

31 _____ _____ _____ our club.

32 We are waiting _____ you.

16 와서 피카소 미술 동아리의 회원이 되세요.

17 보람 오케스트라

18 안녕하세요! 저는 보람 오케스트라의 회장 장민수입니다.

19 오늘 학교에 왔을 때 정문에서 음악을 연주하는 몇 명의 학생들을 보았습니까?

20 우리가 그 학생들이었습니다.

21 우리는 매일 아침 친구들을 위해 음악을 연주합니다.

22 우리 동아리에 가입하기 위해서는 악기 연주하는 법을 조금 알아야 합니다.

23 그러나 여러분이 연주를 잘 못한다고 해서 걱정하지 마세요.

24 우리는 열심히 연습하고 함께 좋아질 것입니다.

25 우리는 지역 사회에 대한 봉사로 아이들에게 악기를 연주하는 법도 가르칩니다.

26 저는 열한 살 소년에게 바이올린을 가르치고 있습니다.

27 처음에 그는 음표를 읽는 법을 알지 못했습니다.

28 이제는 간단한 노래도 연주할 수 있습니다.

29 그가 바이올린을 연주하는 걸 듣는 것은 저를 매우 행복하게 합니다.

30 우리 동아리에 가입함으로써, 여러분은 다른 사람들을 도울 수 있는 기회를 가질 수 있습니다.

31 와서 우리 동아리에 가입하세요.

32 우리는 여러분을 기다리고 있습니다.

● 우리말을 참고하여 본문을 영작하시오.

1 우리 동아리에 가입하는 게 어때?

➡ _____

2 동아리 활동에 참여하는 것은 학교생활을 즐기는 좋은 방법이에요.

➡ _____

3 동아리에 가입하는 게 어떤가요?

➡ _____

4 여기 학생들이 그들의 동아리에 가입하기를 원하는 두 명의 동아리 대표가 있어요.

➡ _____

5 그들이 하는 말을 들어 봅시다.

➡ _____

6 피카소 미술 동아리

➡ _____

7 안녕하세요! 저는 피카소 미술 동아리의 강소라입니다.

➡ _____

8 우리 동아리의 이름에서 추측할 수 있듯이, 우리는 그림을 그립니다.

➡ _____

9 우리는 가끔 자원봉사도 합니다.

➡ _____

10 지난여름, 우리 동아리 회원들은 "우리 마을 바꾸기" 프로젝트에 참여했습니다.

➡ _____

11 우리 마을에 있는 건물의 더럽고 오래된 벽에 하늘 높이 나는 새들과 푸른 파도 위로 점프하는 돌고래들을 그렸습니다.

➡ _____
_____

12 결과적으로, 오래된 마을은 밝고 아름다운 곳으로 바뀌었습니다.

➡ _____

13 이웃들은 우리의 작품을 보고 행복해 했고 고마워했습니다.

➡ _____

14 여러분은 그림을 잘 그릴 필요는 없습니다.

➡ _____

15 그림 그리는 것을 좋아하는 사람은 누구나 가입할 수 있습니다.

➡ _____

16 와서 피카소 미술 동아리의 회원이 되세요.

➡ _____

17 보람 오케스트라

➡ _____

18 안녕하세요! 저는 보람 오케스트라의 회장 장민수입니다.

➡ _____

19 오늘 학교에 왔을 때 정문에서 음악을 연주하는 몇 명의 학생들을 보았습니까?

➡ _____

20 우리가 그 학생들이었습니다.

➡ _____

21 우리는 매일 아침 친구들을 위해 음악을 연주합니다.

➡ _____

22 우리 동아리에 가입하기 위해서는 악기 연주하는 법을 조금 알아야 합니다.

➡ _____

23 그러나 여러분이 연주를 잘 못한다고 해서 걱정하지 마세요.

➡ _____

24 우리는 열심히 연습하고 함께 좋아질 것입니다.

➡ _____

25 우리는 지역 사회에 대한 봉사로 아이들에게 악기를 연주하는 법도 가르칩니다.

➡ _____

26 저는 열한 살 소년에게 바이올린을 가르치고 있습니다.

➡ _____

27 처음에 그는 음표를 읽는 법을 알지 못했습니다.

➡ _____

28 이제는 간단한 노래도 연주할 수 있습니다.

➡ _____

29 그가 바이올린을 연주하는 걸 듣는 것은 저를 매우 행복하게 합니다.

➡ _____

30 우리 동아리에 가입함으로써, 여러분은 다른 사람들을 도울 수 있는 기회를 가질 수 있습니다.

➡ _____

31 와서 우리 동아리에 가입하세요.

➡ _____

32 우리는 여러분을 기다리고 있습니다.

➡ _____

[01~03] 다음 글을 읽고 물음에 답하시오.

Participating in club activities (A)[is / are] a great way to enjoy your school life. ⓐ How about joining a club? Here are two club leaders who (B)[want / wants] students (C) [joining / to join] their clubs. Let's listen to what ⓑthey say.

서답형
01 위 글의 괄호 (A)~(C)에서 어법상 알맞은 것을 골라 쓰시오.

➡ (A)_____ (B)_____ (C)_____

중요
02 위 글의 밑줄 친 ⓐHow about joining과 바꿔 쓸 수 있는 말을 모두 고르시오.

① What about joining
② How do you join
③ Why don't you join
④ Which about joining
⑤ Why do you join

서답형
03 위 글의 밑줄 친 ⓑthey가 가리키는 것을 본문에서 찾아 쓰시오.

➡ _____

[04~06] 다음 글을 읽고 물음에 답하시오.

The Picasso Art Club
Hi! I am Sora Kang from the Picasso Art Club. ⓐAs you can guess from the name of our club, we paint. We also do volunteer work from time to time. (①) Last summer, our club members participated in the "Change Our Neighborhood" project. (②) On the dirty old walls of the buildings in our

neighborhood, we painted birds flying high in the sky and dolphins jumping over blue waves. (③) The neighbors were happy to see our work and thanked us. (④) You don't have to be a good painter. (⑤) Anyone who likes to paint can join. Come and be a member of the Picasso Art Club.

04 위 글의 흐름으로 보아, 주어진 문장이 들어가기에 가장 적절한 곳은?

> As a result, the old neighborhood changed into a bright and beautiful place.

①   ②   ③   ④   ⑤

중요
05 위 글의 밑줄 친 ⓐAs와 같은 의미로 쓰인 것을 고르시오.

① As he often lies, I don't like him.
② As she grew older, she became wiser.
③ She respects him as a mentor.
④ As you know, Julia is leaving soon.
⑤ He told it to me as we went along.

06 위 글의 피카소 미술 동아리에 대한 설명으로 옳지 않은 것은?

① 그림 동아리이다.
② 가끔 자원봉사도 한다.
③ 지난여름, 동아리 회원들은 "우리 마을 바꾸기" 프로젝트에 참여했다.
④ 이웃 마을에 있는 건물의 더럽고 오래된 벽에 그림을 그렸다.
⑤ 동아리 회원이 되려면 그림을 잘 그려야 한다.

[07~09] 다음 글을 읽고 물음에 답하시오.

The Boram Orchestra
Hi! I am Minsu Jang, the leader of the Boram

Orchestra. ⓐDid you see several students to play music at the main gate when you came to school today? We were those students. We play music for our friends every morning. You need to know ⓑ_____ to play an instrument a little bit to join our club. But don't worry if you don't play well. We will practice hard and get better together. We also teach children how to play musical instruments as a service to our community. I am teaching an eleven-year-old boy to play the violin. At first, he did not know how to read a note. Now he can play a simple song. Hearing him play the violin makes me very happy. By joining our club, you can have an opportunity to help others. Come and join our club. We are waiting for you.

서답형

07 위 글의 밑줄 친 ⓐ에서 어법상 틀린 부분을 찾아 고치시오.

➡ _____

08 위 글의 빈칸 ⓑ에 들어갈 알맞은 말을 고르시오.

① what　　② whom　　③ how
④ when　　⑤ whether

서답형

09 다음 중 보람 오케스트라 동아리에 가입할 수 있는 사람을 고르시오.

> 지혜: I'm interested in doing volunteer work.
> 보람: I don't know how to play an instrument at all, but I like music.
> 선미: I like painting pictures and helping others.
> 준호: I'm not a skillful pianist, but I practice playing the piano hard.
> 혜영: I know how to read a note, but I can't play any instrument.

➡ _____

[10~12] 다음 글을 읽고 물음에 답하시오.

Boram Middle School
Club Membership Form
• **Name of Club**: FC Boram
• **Student Name**: Sunho Park
• **Why You Want to Join the Club**: I love soccer and would like to join FC Boram. I am good at passing the ball and running fast. ⓐ_____, I don't know how to head the ball, so I want to learn how to do that. I want to become a soccer player who can make wonderful heading goals.
• **Your Goals**: ⓑIf I will join this club, I will practice very hard and become a good team player!

10 위 글의 빈칸 ⓐ에 들어갈 알맞은 말을 고르시오.

① Moreover　　② However
③ Therefore　　④ Similarly
⑤ For instance

서답형

11 위 글을 읽고 순호가 잘하는 것과 못하는 것을 우리말로 쓰시오.

➡ 잘하는 것: _____
➡ 못하는 것: _____

서답형

12 위 글의 밑줄 친 ⓑ에서 어법상 틀린 부분을 찾아 고치시오.

➡ _____

[13~15] 다음 글을 읽고 물음에 답하시오.

Participating in club activities is a great way ⓐto enjoy your school life. How about ⓑ joining a club? Here are two club leaders ⓒ_____ want students to join their clubs. Let's listen to what they say.

★ 13 위 글의 밑줄 친 ⓐto enjoy와 to부정사의 용법이 다른 것을 <u>모두</u> 고르시오.

① I have much work to do today.

② He is rich enough to buy the car.

③ I have nothing particular to do today.

④ I don't know what to do next.

⑤ Give me a chair to sit on.

서답형
14 위 글의 밑줄 친 ⓑjoining과 바꿔 쓸 수 있는 말을 본문에서 찾아 쓰시오.

➡ _____

서답형
15 위 글의 빈칸 ⓒ에 들어갈 알맞은 말을 쓰시오.

➡ _____

[16~18] 다음 글을 읽고 물음에 답하시오.

The Picasso Art Club

Hi! I am Sora Kang from the Picasso Art Club. As you can guess ⓐ the name of our club, we paint. We also do volunteer work from time to time. Last summer, our club members participated in the "Change Our Neighborhood" project. On the dirty old walls of the buildings in our neighborhood, we painted birds flying high in the sky and dolphins jumping over blue waves. ⓑ , the old neighborhood changed ⓒ a bright and beautiful place. The neighbors were happy ⓓto see our work and thanked us. You don't have to be a good painter. Anyone who likes to paint can join. Come and be a member of the Picasso Art Club.

16 위 글의 빈칸 ⓐ와 ⓒ에 들어갈 전치사가 바르게 짝지어진 것은?

① from – into   ② by – for

③ in – from   ④ from – on

⑤ for – into

17 위 글의 빈칸 ⓑ에 들어갈 알맞은 말을 고르시오.

① However   ② In addition

③ For example   ④ As a result

⑤ In other words

★ 18 아래 보기에서 위 글의 밑줄 친 ⓓto see와 to부정사의 용법이 같은 것의 개수를 고르시오.

┌─── 보기 ───
① He promised not to do it.
② English is difficult to learn.
③ She has many children to take care of.
④ What a fool he is to say such a thing!
⑤ She worked hard to pass the exam.
└─────────

① 1개   ② 2개   ③ 3개   ④ 4개   ⑤ 5개

[19~21] 다음 글을 읽고 물음에 답하시오.

The Boram Orchestra

Hi! I am Minsu Jang, the leader of the Boram Orchestra. Did you see several students playing music at the main gate when you came to school today? We were those students. We play music for our friends every morning. You need to know how to play an instrument a little bit to join our club. But don't worry if you don't play well. We will practice hard and get better together. We also teach children ⓐ musical instruments as a service to our community. I am teaching an eleven-year-old boy to play the violin. At first, he did not know how to read a ⓑnote. Now he can play a simple song. Hearing him play the violin makes me very happy. By joining our club, you can have an opportunity to help others. Come and join our club. We are waiting for you.

서답형

19 위 글의 빈칸 ⓐ에 play를 알맞은 형태로 쓰시오.

➡ _____

20 위 글의 밑줄 친 ⓑnote와 같은 의미로 쓰인 것을 고르시오.

① Please make a <u>note</u> of what I'm saying.
② He is striking a <u>note</u> on a piano.
③ She left a <u>note</u> for Ben on the table.
④ Can I borrow your lecture <u>note</u>?
⑤ You must <u>note</u> that this is essential.

서답형

21 위 글을 읽고 보람 오케스트라 동아리의 활동 두 가지를 우리말로 쓰시오.

➡ (1) _____
   (2) _____

[22~24] 다음 글을 읽고 물음에 답하시오.

Boram Middle School
Club Membership Form

• **Name of Club**: FC Boram
• **Student Name**: Sunho Park
• **Why You Want to Join the Club**: I love soccer and would like ①joining FC Boram. I am good at ②passing the ball and ③running fast. However, I don't know ④how to head the ball, so I want to learn how to do that. I want to become a soccer player ⑤who can make wonderful heading ⓐgoals.
• **Your** ⓑ**Goals**: If I join this club, I will practice very hard and become a good team player!

서답형

22 위 글의 밑줄 친 ①~⑤ 중 어법상 틀린 것을 찾아 고치시오.

➡ _____

23 위 글의 박 순호에 대한 설명으로 옳지 않은 것은?

① FC Boram에 가입하고 싶어 한다.
② 공을 패스하는 것을 잘한다.
③ 빨리 달린다.
④ 공을 헤딩하는 것을 잘한다.
⑤ 멋진 헤딩 골을 만들 수 있는 축구 선수가 되기를 원한다.

서답형

24 위 글의 밑줄 친 ⓐgoals와 ⓑGoals의 뜻을 쓰시오.

➡ ⓐ_____, ⓑ_____

[25~27] 다음 글을 읽고 물음에 답하시오.

Looking For Volunteers

We will ⓐ____ a book fair at Nanum Middle School on May 5. We are looking for volunteers who can introduce and sell books to people. Anyone who loves books can join our event! If you are interested, please let us know!

중요

25 위 글의 빈칸 ⓐ에 들어갈 알맞은 말을 고르시오.

① take   ② turn
③ hold   ④ bring
⑤ grow

서답형

26 다음 질문에 대한 알맞은 대답을 영어로 쓰시오. (8 단어)

Q: What will volunteers do at the event?

A: _____

27 위 글을 읽고 전시회에 대해 알 수 <u>없는</u> 것을 고르시오.

① 전시회의 종류   ② 개최 장소
③ 전시회의 규모   ④ 개최일
⑤ 전시회 참가 자격

[01~03] 다음 글을 읽고 물음에 답하시오.

The Picasso Art Club

Hi! I am Sora Kang from the Picasso Art Club. As you can guess from the name of our club, we paint. We also do volunteer work from time to time. Last summer, our club members participated in the "Change Our Neighborhood" project. On the dirty old walls of the buildings in our neighborhood, we painted birds ⓐ high in the sky and dolphins ⓑ over blue waves. As a result, the old neighborhood changed into a bright and beautiful place. The neighbors were happy to see our work and thanked us. You ⓒdon't have to be a good painter. Anyone who likes to paint can join. Come and be a member of the Picasso Art Club.

01 다음 빈칸 (A)~(C)에 알맞은 단어를 넣어 Picasso Art Club 에 대한 소개를 완성하시오. 단, (B)와 (C)에는 같은 단어를 쓰시오.

> The Picasso Art Club is an art club and sometimes does (A)_____ _____, too. Anyone who likes (B)_____ can join it and don't have to be good at (C)_____.

02 위 글의 빈칸 ⓐ와 ⓑ에 fly와 jump를 각각 알맞은 형태로 쓰시오.

➡ ⓐ_____, ⓑ_____

03 위 글의 밑줄 친 ⓒdon't have to와 바꿔 쓸 수 있는 어구를 쓰시오.

➡ _____

[04~06] 다음 글을 읽고 물음에 답하시오.

The Boram Orchestra

Hi! I am Minsu Jang, the leader of the Boram Orchestra. Did you see several students playing music at the main gate when you came to school today? We were those students. We play music for our friends every morning. You need to know how to play an instrument (A)[a few / a little] bit to join our club. But don't worry ⓐif you don't play well. We will practice hard and get better together. ⓑ우리는 지역 사회에 대한 봉사로 아이들에게 악기를 연주하는 법도 가르칩니다(musical instruments / teach / a service / children / to our community / we / how to play / also). I am teaching an (B) [eleven-year-old / eleven-years-old] boy to play the violin. At first, he did not know how to read a note. Now he can play a simple song. Hearing him play the violin makes me very (C)[happy / happily]. By joining our club, you can have an opportunity to help others. Come and join our club. We are waiting for you.

04 위 글의 괄호 (A)~(C)에서 어법상 알맞은 것을 골라 쓰시오.

➡ (A)_____ (B)_____ (C)_____

05 위 글의 밑줄 친 ⓐ를 다음과 같이 바꿔 쓸 때 빈칸에 들어갈 알맞은 말을 쓰시오.

➡ _____ you play well

06 위 글의 밑줄 친 ⓑ의 우리말에 맞게 한 단어를 보충하여, 괄호 안에 주어진 어휘를 알맞게 배열하시오.

➡ _____
_____

[07~09] 다음 글을 읽고 물음에 답하시오.

The Picasso Art Club

Hi! I am Sora Kang from the Picasso Art Club. As you can guess from the name of our club, we paint. We also do volunteer work from time to time. Last summer, our club members participated in the "Change Our Neighborhood" project. On the dirty old walls of the buildings in our neighborhood, we painted birds flying high in the sky and dolphins jumping over blue waves. As a result, the old neighborhood changed into a bright and beautiful place. The neighbors were happy to see our work and thanked us. ⓐYou must not be a good painter. ⓑ그림 그리는 것을 좋아하는 사람은 누구나 가입할 수 있습니다. Come and be a member of the Picasso Art Club.

07 다음 질문에 대한 알맞은 대답을 영어로 쓰시오.

Q: How did Sora Kang's neighborhood change after the "Change Our Neighborhood" project?

A: _____

08 위 글의 밑줄 친 ⓐ에서 흐름상 어색한 부분을 찾아 고치시오.

➡ _____

09 위 글의 밑줄 친 ⓑ의 우리말에 맞게 주어진 어휘를 이용하여 7 단어로 영작하시오.

anyone, who

➡ _____

[10~12] 다음 글을 읽고 물음에 답하시오.

The Boram Orchestra

Hi! I am Minsu Jang, the leader of the Boram Orchestra. Did you see several students playing music at the main gate when you came to school today? We were those students. We play music for our friends every morning. You need to know how to play an instrument a little bit to join our club. But don't worry if you don't play well. We will practice hard and get better together. We also teach children how to play musical instruments as a service to our community. I am teaching an eleven-year-old boy to play the violin. At first, he did not know how to read a note. Now he can play a simple song. ⓐHearing him play the violin make me very happy. By joining our club, you can have an opportunity to help others. Come and join our club. We are waiting for you.

10 위 글을 읽고 보람 오케스트라 동아리의 가입 자격을 우리말로 쓰시오.

➡ _____

11 본문의 내용과 일치하도록 다음 빈칸 (A)와 (B)에 들어갈 알맞은 단어를 본문에서 찾아 쓰시오.

Minsu tells the students not to (A)_____ even though they don't play a musical instrument well because they will practice hard and (B)_____ _____ together.

12 위 글의 밑줄 친 ⓐ에서 어법상 틀린 부분을 찾아 고치시오.

➡ _____

After You Read

April 30

Today, Minsu, the leader of the Boram Orchestra, came to community center.
Minsu와 the leader of the Boram Orchestra는 동격이다.

He started teaching me how to play the violin last month. At first, I didn't
start는 동명사와 to부정사를 목적어로 취한다.　how to+동사원형: ~하는 방법　　　　　　처음에는

know how to read a note.
음, 음표

I hope to join the Boram Orchestra and play the violin at the main gate when I
hope는 to부정사를 목적어로 취한다. join: 가입하다　　　　　　　　　　　　　(접) ~할 때

become a middle school student.

구문해설　• commnunity: 지역 사회　• the main gate: 정문

해석

오늘, 보람 오케스트라의 대표인 민수가 지역 주민 회관에 왔다. 그는 지난달에 바이올린을 연주하는 법을 나에게 가르쳐 주기 시작했다. 처음에는 나는 하나의 음표도 읽는 법을 알지 못했다. 나는 보람 오케스트라에 가입하여, 내가 중학생이 될 때 정문에서 바이올린을 연주하기를 희망한다.

Writing Workshop

Boram Middle School
Club Membership Form

• Name of Club: FC Boram

• Student Name: Sunho Park

• Why You Want to Join the Club: I love soccer and would like to join FC
= The reason　　　　　　　　　　　　　　　　　　　　　　~하고 싶다. ~하는 것을 바라다

Boram. I am good at passing the ball and running fast. However, I don't know
be good at: ~을 잘하다. 동명사　　　　　　　동명사

how to head the ball, so I want to learn how to do that. I want to become a
= how I should head　그래서　　　　　　　　　　　　=head the ball

soccer player who can make wonderful heading goals.
주격 관계대명사(= that)

• Your Goals: If I join this club, I will practice very hard and become a good
조건의 부사절에서 현재시제가 미래시제를 대신함.　　　　열심히

team player!

구문해설　• be good at: ~을 잘하다.　• however: 그러나.　• wonderful: 아주 멋진.　• goal: 득점, 목표,
• practice: 연습하다

보람중학교 동아리 지원서

동아리 이름: FC Boram

학생 이름: 박순호

가입을 원하는 이유: 나는 축구를 사랑하고 FC Boram에 가입하고 싶다. 나는 공을 패스하는 것을 잘하고 빨리 달린다. 그러나, 나는 공을 헤딩하는 법을 모르기 때문에 그것을 하는 법을 배우고 싶다. 나는 멋진 헤딩 골을 만들 수 있는 축구 선수가 되기를 원한다.

당신의 목표: 만약 내가 이 동아리에 가입하면, 나는 매우 열심히 연습해서 좋은 팀 플레이어가 될 것이다.

Real Life Zone

I would like to introduce our new orchestra member, Kate. She knows how
= want to　　　　　　　　　　동격(콤마로 연결)

to play the violin. She also has lots of experience playing in a group. And she
의문사+to부정사: ~하는 법　　　= much(양과 수 모두에 쓰임)　동명사앞에 전치사 in이 생략된 것으로 볼 수 있음)

said she enjoys working with people.
enjoys의 목적어로 쓰인 동명사

Let's all welcome her to the Nanum Orchestra.
모두　　　= Kate

구문해설　• introduce: 소개하다, experience: 경험

나는 우리의 새로운 오케스트라 회원인 케이트를 소개하고 싶어. 그녀는 바이올린을 연주하는 법을 알아. 그녀는 또한 그룹에서 연주해 본 경험이 많아. 그리고 그녀는 사람들과 일하는 것을 즐긴다고 말했어. 모두 그녀가 나눔 오케스트라에 온 걸 환영하자.

Words & Expressions

01 다음 짝지어진 낱말의 관계가 나머지 넷과 <u>다른</u> 것은?

① gift – present　　② dark – bright

③ activity – action　④ actually – really

⑤ enter – join

02 다음 빈칸에 알맞은 말이 순서대로 바르게 나열된 것은?

> • Are you pretty _____ at using computers?
> • We are _____ for volunteers who can introduce books to people.
> • I will _____ in the event next time!

① well – starting – participate

② well – looking – enter

③ good – looking – participate

④ good – starting – enter

⑤ good – looking – enter

03 밑줄 친 단어와 의미가 같은 단어를 고르시오.

> What should I <u>get</u> them for their wedding gift?

① keep　　　② bring　　　③ carry

④ buy　　　⑤ find

04 다음 빈칸에 공통으로 들어갈 말을 쓰시오.

> • You can ask _____ help when you need it.
> • Thank you _____ showing your interest.

05 다음 우리말에 맞게 빈칸을 완성하시오. (철자가 주어진 경우, 그 철자로 시작할 것)

(1) 사실 오늘 밤에 나는 나가고 싶지 않다.

➡ A_____, I don't think I want to go out tonight.

(2) 너는 어디서 요리하는 것을 배웠니?

➡ _____ did you learn _____ _____?

(3) 이것은 돈을 절약할 기회이다.

➡ This is an o_____ to save money.

Conversation

[06~07] 다음 대화를 읽고 물음에 답하시오.

> B: Do you enjoy ⓐto read books, Yumi?
> G: Yes, I love ⓑreading science books. ⓒ<u>What</u> about you?
> B: I love ⓓto read books, too.
> G: Then, let's ⓔ<u>to go</u> to the library after school today.

06 위 대화의 밑줄 친 ⓐ~ⓔ 중 어법상 틀린 개수를 고르시오.

① 1개　② 2개　③ 3개　④ 4개　⑤ 5개

07 위 대화를 읽고 답할 수 <u>없는</u> 질문을 고르시오.

① What is the boy's hobby?

② What kinds of books does Yumi love reading?

③ Where are they going to go after school?

④ Does Yumi love reading?

⑤ Does the boy love reading?

[08~09] 다음 대화를 읽고 물음에 답하시오.

G: (A)_____, Minsu?
B: I made breakfast for my family.
G: Do you enjoy ⓐ_____?
B: Yes, I'm a good ⓑ_____! My family loves my ⓒ_____.

08 빈칸 (A)에 들어갈 알맞은 말을 고르시오.

① Where did you go on the weekend
② Where did you get it
③ What are you going to do on the weekend
④ What are you making for your family
⑤ What did you do on the weekend

09 빈칸 ⓐ~ⓒ에 들어갈 알맞은 말을 보기에서 골라 쓰시오.

┌─── 보기 ───┐
cook   cooking   to cook   cooked
└──────────────┘

➡ ⓐ_____ ⓑ_____ ⓒ_____

[10~12] 다음 대화를 읽고 물음에 답하시오.

B: Hello, Kate. I'm Hamin, the leader of the Nanum Orchestra. Thank you for your (A)_____ in our club. (①)
G: Hi. Nice to meet you.
B: You play ⓐthe violin? ⓑWhen did you start playing the violin?
G: I started learning how to play the violin ⓒthat I was ten. (②)
B: Do you have any experience playing in a group?
G: Yes. Actually, I was a member of an orchestra ⓓwhen I was in elementary school. (③)
B: Great. We also volunteer ⓔto teach children. Do you enjoy teaching others? (④)
G: I have no experience teaching others. (⑤)
B: Good. I think we'll have a great time playing together. Welcome to the Nanum Orchestra.

10 위 대화의 ①~⑤ 중 다음 주어진 말이 들어갈 알맞은 곳은?

┌──────────────────────────────┐
│ But I enjoy working with people, so I'd │
│ like to try. │
└──────────────────────────────┘

①   ②   ③   ④   ⑤

11 빈칸 (A)에 들어갈 알맞은 말을 고르시오.

① interest   ② surprise   ③ event
④ attention   ⑤ effort

12 위 글의 밑줄 친 ⓐ~ⓔ 중 어법상 틀린 것을 고르시오.

① ⓐ   ② ⓑ   ③ ⓒ   ④ ⓓ   ⑤ ⓔ

[13~14] 다음 대화를 읽고 물음에 답하시오.

A: Do you enioy ⓐlook at the stars at night?
B: Yes, I love ⓑdoing that.

13 위 대화의 밑줄 친 ⓐ를 알맞은 형으로 고치시오.

➡ _____

14 위 대화의 밑줄 친 ⓑ가 가리키는 것을 영어로 쓰시오.

➡ _____

Grammar

15 다음 빈칸에 알맞은 것을 모두 고르시오.

┌──────────────────────────────┐
│ Jin is a girl _____ likes to play the piano. │
└──────────────────────────────┘

① who   ② whose   ③ whom
④ which   ⑤ that

16 다음 주어진 단어를 이용하여 빈칸에 알맞은 말을 쓰시오.

> 지수는 엄마에게 어디에 가방을 둬야 할지 물어
> 봤다.
> = Jisu asked her mother _____
>   the bag. (put)

17 밑줄 친 that의 쓰임이 나머지 넷과 다른 것은?

① A baker is a person that bakes bread.

② She told me that I should be more careful.

③ I walked to my school that is three stops away.

④ I know the very person that will do the job quickly.

⑤ The girl that is talking on the phone is my sister, Susan.

18 다음 괄호 안에 주어진 단어를 어법에 맞게 빈칸에 쓰시오.

(1) Do you know how _____ _____ _____ to the National Museum? (get)

(2) I don't know where _____ _____ the bus. (take)

(3) I told him who _____ _____ for. (look)

(4) You should choose _____ dress _____ _____ to the party. (wear)

19 빈칸에 알맞은 말을 어법에 맞게 쓰시오. (that은 쓰지 말 것)

> (1) Look at the boy _____ is playing the piano on the street.
> (2) The coat _____ is black is mine.

20 다음 중 어법상 어색한 문장은?

① I want to become a soccer player who can make wonderful heading goals.

② Would you tell me where to park the car?

③ I have a smartphone that was made in Korea.

④ Her mother taught her how to make delicious spaghetti.

⑤ The writer couldn't decide what to write the story.

21 다음은 두 문장을 관계대명사를 사용하여 한 문장으로 쓴 것이다. 빈칸에 다른 한 문장을 쓰시오.

(1) • _____
   • They can introduce and sell books to people.
   → We are looking for volunteers who[that] can introduce and sell books to people.

(2) • My class has some students.
   • _____
   → My class has some students who[that] are good at English.

(3) • I have a friend.
   • _____
   → I have a friend who[that] lives in New Zealand.

(4) • Angelina loved the present.
   • _____
   → Angelina loved the present that[which] Chuck gave to her on her birthday.

22 다음 밑줄 친 부분의 쓰임이 나머지 넷과 다른 것은?

① I want to learn how to do that.

② Do you know when to start the performance?

③ He couldn't decide what to do.

④ Julia bought a book to read on the train.

⑤ She asked me where to find the ladies' room.

23 두 문장을 관계대명사를 사용하여 한 문장으로 쓰시오.
(that은 사용하지 말 것)

(1) • She wants to see a movie.
  • The movie is interesting.
  ➡ _____

(2) • Rose is Jake's best friend.
  • She works for a bank.
  ➡ _____

(3) • James bought a new computer.
  • The computer is really nice
  ➡ _____

Reading

[24~26] 다음 글을 읽고 물음에 답하시오.

The Boram Orchestra
Hi! I am Minsu Jang, the leader of the Boram Orchestra. Did you see several students playing music at the main gate when you came to school today? We were ⓐthose students. We play music for our friends every morning. You need to know how to play an instrument a little bit to join our club. But don't worry if you don't play well. We will practice hard and get better together. We also teach children how to play musical instruments as a service to our community. I am teaching an eleven-year-old boy to play the violin. At first, he did not know how to read a note. Now he can play a simple song. ⓑHearing him play the violin

makes me very happy. By joining our club, you can have an opportunity to help others. Come and join our club. We are waiting for you.

24 위 글의 밑줄 친 ⓐthose students가 가리키는 것을 본문에서 찾아 쓰시오.

➡ _____
_____

25 위 글의 밑줄 친 ⓑHearing과 문법적 쓰임이 다른 것을 모두 고르시오.

① Look at the man hearing the lecture.

② He is interested in hearing the lecture.

③ My dream is hearing the lecture.

④ Are they hearing the lecture now?

⑤ I enjoyed hearing the lecture.

26 위 글의 내용과 일치하지 않는 것은?

① 민수는 매일 방과 후에 친구들을 위해 음악을 연주한다.

② 보람 오케스트라 동아리에 가입하려면 악기를 연주하는 법을 조금 알아야 한다.

③ 보람 오케스트라 동아리는 아이들에게 악기를 연주하는 법도 가르친다.

④ 민수는 열한 살 난 소년에게 바이올린을 가르치고 있다.

⑤ 보람 오케스트라 동아리에 가입함으로써 다른 사람들을 도울 수 있는 기회를 가질 수 있다.

[27~29] 다음 글을 읽고 물음에 답하시오.

The Picasso Art Club
Hi! I am Sora Kang from the Picasso Art Club. As you can guess from the name of our club, we paint. We also do volunteer work ⓐfrom time to time. (A)[Last summer / In last summer], our club members participated

in the "Change Our Neighborhood" project. On the dirty old walls of the buildings in our neighborhood, we painted birds flying (B)[high / highly] in the sky and dolphins jumping over blue waves. As a result, the old neighborhood changed into a bright and beautiful place. The neighbors were happy to see our work and (C)[to thank / thanked] us. You don't have to be a good painter. Anyone who likes ___ⓑ___ can join. Come and be a member of the Picasso Art Club.

27 위 글의 밑줄 친 ⓐfrom time to time과 의미가 다른 것을 모두 고르시오.

① once in a while ② always
③ now and then ④ sometimes
⑤ rarely

28 위 글의 괄호 (A)~(C)에서 문맥이나 어법상 알맞은 낱말을 골라 쓰시오.

➡ (A)_____ (B)_____ (C)_____

29 위 글의 빈칸 ⓑ에 들어갈 알맞은 말을 고르시오.

① to change the neighborhood
② to play music
③ to paint
④ to help others
⑤ to play sports

[30~31] 다음 글을 읽고 물음에 답하시오.

Hello, everyone. I'm Jason, the leader of the Abracadabra Club. On May 5, our club members will go to Hanguk Hospital to visit sick children. We are going to show them magic and teach ⓐthem how to do magic.

30 위 글의 밑줄 친 ⓐthem이 가리키는 것을 본문에서 찾아 쓰시오.

➡ _____

31 Abracadabra 동아리에 대한 소개를 완성하도록 다음 빈칸에 공통으로 들어갈 단어를 쓰시오.

The Abracadabra Club is a _____ club. On May 5, its members will go to Hanguk Hospital and show _____ to sick children and teach them how to do _____.

[32~33] 다음 글을 읽고 물음에 답하시오.

We will hold a book ⓐfair at Nanum Middle School on May 5. We are looking ⓑ_____ volunteers who can introduce and sell books ⓒ_____ people. Anyone who loves books can join our event! If you are interested, please let us know!

32 위 글의 밑줄 친 ⓐfair와 같은 의미로 쓰인 것을 고르시오.

① We have to be fair to both players.
② Let's take the kids to the fair.
③ She has long fair hair.
④ A fair number of people came along.
⑤ It was a fair and breezy day.

33 위 글의 빈칸 ⓑ와 ⓒ에 들어갈 전치사가 바르게 짝지어진 것은?

① at – to ② for – of
③ in – on ④ at – or
⑤ for – to

출제율 85%

01 다음 짝지어진 두 단어의 관계가 같도록 주어진 철자로 시작해 빈칸에 쓰시오.

chief : leader – training : p_____

출제율 95%

02 다음 〈보기〉의 단어를 사용하여 자연스러운 문장을 만들 수 없는 것은?

보기
drone   garden   interest   leader

① He is the _____ of the music club.
② Do you have any _____ in the opera?
③ The house has a _____ with trees and flowers.
④ You can come a little _____ later.
⑤ A _____ is a small remote-controlled helicopter.

[03~06] 다음 대화를 읽고 물음에 답하시오.

B: ⓐThese cookies look so delicious. Did you make ⓑthem?
G: Yes. I made ⓒthem myself yesterday. I enjoy baking. I'm going to make doughnuts this Saturday.
B: Oh, I want to learn how to make ⓓthem. Is it difficult?
G: Not at all. You can come to my house and join me if you want.
B: Thanks, Bora. (A)_____ should I come?
G: At 2:00.
B: Sounds good. See you then.

출제율 90%

03 밑줄 친 ⓐ～ⓓ 중 가리키는 것이 같은 것끼리 짝지어진 것을 고르시오.

① ⓐ, ⓓ   ② ⓑ, ⓓ
③ ⓒ, ⓓ   ④ ⓐ, ⓑ, ⓒ
⑤ ⓐ, ⓑ, ⓒ, ⓓ

출제율 95%

04 빈칸 (A)에 들어갈 말을 쓰시오. (2 단어)

➡ _____

출제율 90%

05 다음 영영풀이에 해당하는 단어를 대화에서 찾아 쓰시오.

1. to become a member of an organization, society, or group
2. to begin to take part in an activity that other people are involved in

➡ _____

출제율 100%

06 대화를 읽고 답할 수 없는 질문을 고르시오.

① Who made the cookies?
② Where are they going to meet this Saturday?
③ What kinds of food does the boy know how to make?
④ When did the girl make the cookies?
⑤ What will the girl make this Saturday?

07 다음 빈칸에 공통으로 들어갈 말을 쓰시오.

> • I'd like _____ _____ soccer.
>
> • I don't know how _____ _____ the piano or violin.

08 다음 우리말 해석에 맞게 빈칸을 완성하시오.

(1) _____ _____ _____, my team lost. (결과적으로, 우리 팀은 졌다.)

(2) _____ _____, I was very _____ in acting. (처음에, 나는 연기에 아주 관심이 많았다.)

(3) It can _____ _____ different types of chair. (그것은 다른 종류들의 의자로 변할 수 있다.)

(4) Please _____ _____ _____ _____ _____ do it. (그것을 어떻게 해야 하는지 우리에게 알려주세요.)

[09~10] 주어진 문장 다음에 이어질 대화의 순서를 바르게 배열하시오.

09

> What did you do on the weekend, Minsu?

> (A) Yes, I'm a good cook! My family loves my cooking.
>
> (B) I made breakfast for my family.
>
> (C) Do you enjoy cooking?

➡ _____

10

> Jiyun, that's a pretty backpack! Where did you get it?

> (A) Wow! She's a really good designer.
>
> (B) My sister made it for me.
>
> (C) Yes, she is. And she enjoys making clothes, too.

➡ _____

11 대화의 밑줄 친 우리말을 주어진 단어를 이용해 영작하시오.

> A: 너는 여가 시간에 뭐 하는 것을 즐기니?
>
> B: I enjoy taking pictures of people in the park.

➡ _____

(free, enjoy, have, when)

12 다음 우리말을 주어진 어휘를 이용하여 영작하시오.

(1) Jisu는 그녀의 엄마에게 어디에 가방을 둬야 할지 물어봤다. (where, the bag, put, to)

➡ _____

(2) 너는 다음에 우리가 무엇을 해야 할지 아니? (what, should, next)

➡ _____

(3) 나는 무엇을 요리할지 결정할 수 없었다. (decide, cook, to)

➡ _____

(4) 운동장에서 농구를 하고 있는 소녀들이 몇 명 있다. (there, a few girls, playing, the playground.)

➡ _____

(5) Janet은 재미있는 그림이 많은 책을 아주 좋아한다. (pictures, funny, have, love, many)

➡ _____

(6) 길을 건너던 Linda와 그녀의 개가 부상을 입었다. (crossing the street, injured)

➡ _____

_____

출제율 100%

13 다음 중 어법상 올바른 문장은?

① I know a girl which is good at English.

② I want to buy a bag who is expensive.

③ When to use the model has to be decided.

④ I asked her where putting the baggage.

⑤ We also teach children how play musical instruments as a service to our community.

출제율 90%

14 다음 중 어법상 잘못된 것을 바르게 고치시오.

(1) Can you tell me how get to the subway station?

➡ _____

(2) There are some tips for what to lose weight.

➡ _____

(3) What he to eat is important to him.

➡ _____

(4) I have a friend which likes soccer.

➡ _____

(5) The girl is standing under the tree is waiting for you.

➡ _____

(6) Christel sent a letter to her mom whom missed her a lot.

➡ _____

(7) Mike is wearing shoes that is too small for him.

➡ _____

(8) Peter Pan was a boy who he liked to fly.

➡ _____

[15~16] 다음 글을 읽고 물음에 답하시오.

ⓐParticipating in club activities is a great way to enjoy your school life. How about joining a club? Here are two club leaders who want students ⓑ their clubs. Let's listen to what they say.

출제율 95%

15 위 글의 밑줄 친 ⓐParticipating과 문법적 쓰임이 같은 것을 모두 고르시오.

① She isn't playing tennis.

② My hobby is taking pictures.

③ I saw him walking with his friends.

④ Look at the man sitting on the bench.

⑤ He is proud of being Korean.

출제율 85%

16 위 글의 빈칸 ⓑ에 join을 알맞은 형태로 쓰시오.

➡ _____

[17~19] 다음 글을 읽고 물음에 답하시오.

The Picasso Art Club

Hi! I am Sora Kang from the Picasso Art Club. As you can guess from the name of our club, we paint. We also do ⓐ work from time to time. Last summer, our club members participated in the "Change Our Neighborhood" project. On the dirty old walls of the buildings in our neighborhood, ⓑ하늘 높이 나는 새들과 푸른 파도 위로 점프하는 돌고래들을 그렸습니다. As a result, the old neighborhood changed into a bright and beautiful place. The neighbors were happy to see our work and thanked us. You don't have to be a good painter. ⓒAnyone who likes to paint can join. Come and be a member of the Picasso Art Club.

17 주어진 영영풀이를 참고하여 빈칸 ⓐ에 철자 v로 시작하는 단어를 쓰시오.

출제율 90%

someone who does work without being paid for it, because they want to do it

➡ _____

18 위 글의 밑줄 친 ⓑ의 우리말에 맞게 한 단어를 보충하여, 주어진 어휘를 알맞게 배열하시오.

출제율 90%

dolphins / in the sky / and / painted / over blue waves / birds / jumping / flying / we

➡ _____
_____

19 위 글의 밑줄 친 ⓒAnyone who와 바꿔 쓸 수 있는 말을 고르시오.

출제율 95%

① Whoever ② Whichever
③ Whatever ④ However
⑤ Whomever

[20~22] 다음 글을 읽고 물음에 답하시오.

The Boram Orchestra
Hi! I am Minsu Jang, the leader of the Boram Orchestra. (①) Did you see several students playing music at the main gate when you came to school today? (②) We play music for our friends every morning. (③) You need to know how to play an instrument a little bit to join our club. (④) But don't worry if you don't play well. (⑤) We will practice hard and get better together. We also teach children how to play musical instruments ⓐas a service to our community. I am teaching an eleven-year-old

boy to play the violin. ___ⓑ___, he did not know how to read a note. Now he can play a simple song. Hearing him play the violin makes me very happy. By joining our club, you can have an opportunity to help others. Come and join our club. We are waiting for you.

20 위 글의 흐름으로 보아, 주어진 문장이 들어가기에 가장 적절한 곳은?

출제율 90%

We were those students.

① ② ③ ④ ⑤

21 위 글의 밑줄 친 ⓐas와 같은 의미로 쓰인 것을 고르시오.

출제율 100%

① As she was tired, she soon fell asleep.
② Do as you like.
③ I love you as much as I love her.
④ This box can be used as a chair.
⑤ Her anger grew as she talked.

22 위 글의 빈칸 ⓑ에 들어갈 알맞은 말을 고르시오.

출제율 90%

① Finally ② At first
③ At last ④ Therefore
⑤ As a result

01 다음 대화의 순서를 바르게 배열하시오.

(A) Yes, I love reading science books. How about you?

(B) I love reading books, too.

(C) Then, let's go to the library after school today.

(D) Do you enjoy reading books, Yumi?

➡ _____

02 다음 대화의 밑줄 친 부분과 의미가 같도록 조동사를 이용하여 영작하시오.

A: Do you know how to make a paper cat?

B: Of course. It's easy.

➡ _____

[03~04] 다음 대화를 읽고 물음에 답하시오.

G: Did you buy that drone?

B: No, I got it as a present from my parents, but I don't know how to use it. 어떻게 하는지 아니?

G: No, maybe Jina knows how to do it. She enjoys flying drones.

B: Then, (ask, help, will, I, her, for)

03 괄호 안의 단어를 이용하여 밑줄 친 우리말을 바르게 영작하시오. (5 단어)

➡ _____ (how)

04 괄호 안의 단어를 배열하여 문장을 만드시오.

➡ _____

05 다음 두 문장의 의미가 같도록 빈칸을 완성하시오.

(1) Do you know how I can get to the National Museum?

= Do you know _____ _____ _____ to the National Museum?

(2) Brigette taught us how we should make a paper cat.

= Brigette taught us _____ _____ _____ a paper cat.

(3) Tell me when I should wake you up.

= Tell me _____ _____ _____ you up.

(4) Tell the driver where he should stop.

= Tell the driver _____ _____ _____.

(5) I do not know what I should do.

= I do not know _____ _____ _____.

(6) Whom I should meet became the most important to me.

= _____ _____ _____ became the most important to me.

06 두 문장을 관계대명사를 사용하여 한 문장으로 쓰시오. (that은 사용하지 말 것)

(1) • Kay lives in a house.
• The house has a beautiful garden.

➡ _____

(2) • Naomi is standing over there.
• She is very beautiful.

➡ _____

[07~09] 다음 글을 읽고 물음에 답하시오.

The Picasso Art Club

Hi! I am Sora Kang from the Picasso Art Club. As you can guess from the name of our club, we paint. We also do volunteer work from time to time. Last summer, our club members participated in the "Change Our Neighborhood" project. On the dirty old walls of the buildings in our neighborhood, we painted birds flying high in the sky and dolphins jumping over blue waves. ⓐ a result, the old neighborhood changed into a bright and beautiful place. The neighbors were happy to see our work and thanked us. You don't have to be a good painter. Anyone ⓑwho likes to paint can join. Come and be a member of the Picasso Art Club.

07 다음 질문에 대한 알맞은 대답을 영어로 쓰시오. (8 단어)

Q: What did the members of the Picasso Art Club do last summer?

A: _____

08 위 글의 빈칸 ⓐ에 알맞은 단어를 쓰시오.

➡ _____

09 위 글의 밑줄 친 ⓑwho와 바꿔 쓸 수 있는 단어를 쓰시오.

➡ _____

[10~12] 다음 글을 읽고 물음에 답하시오.

The Boram Orchestra

Hi! I am Minsu Jang, the leader of the Boram Orchestra. Did you see several students playing music at the main gate when you came to school today? We were (A)[that / those] students. We play music for our friends every morning. You need to know how to play an instrument a little bit to join our club. But don't worry if you don't play well. We will practice (B)[hard / hardly] and get better together. We also teach children ⓐhow to play musical instruments as a service to our community. I am teaching an eleven-year-old boy to play the violin. At first, he did not know how to read a note. Now he can play a simple song. Hearing him (C)[play / to play] the violin makes me very happy. By joining our club, you can have an opportunity to help others. Come and join our club. We are waiting for you.

10 위 글의 괄호 (A)~(C)에서 문맥이나 어법상 알맞은 낱말을 골라 쓰시오.

➡ (A)_____ (B)_____ (C)_____

11 위 글의 밑줄 친 ⓐ를 다음과 같이 바꿔 쓸 때 빈칸에 들어갈 알맞은 말을 쓰시오.

➡ how _____ _____ play

12 위 글의 내용을 다음과 같이 정리하고자 한다. 빈칸 (A)와 (B)에 들어갈 알맞은 단어를 본문에서 찾아 쓰시오.

Minsu Jang is the (A)_____ of the Boram Orchestra and he introduces the activities of his club and tells students to (B)_____ his club.

창의사고력 서술형 문제

01 다음 그림을 보고 주어진 〈조건〉에 맞게 문장을 완성하시오.

주어진 단어를 사용하고 필요하면 단어의 형태를 변화시킬 것

(1)

➡ I _____. (enjoy, fly)

(2)

➡ We _____. (a pizza, make, want)

02 다음 가입하고 싶은 동아리와 그 이유를 바탕으로 동아리 지원서를 작성하시오.

Club	FC Boram
What I Am Good at	• pass the ball
	• run fast
What I Want to Learn	• head the ball
My Goals	• practice hard
	• become a good team player

Boram Middle School
Club Membership Form
• (A)_____ of Club: FC Boram
• Student Name: Sunho Park
• Why You Want to Join the Club: I love soccer and would like to join (B)_____. I am good at (C)_____ the ball and (D)_____ fast. However, I don't know how to head the ball, so I want to learn how to do that. I want to become a soccer player who can make wonderful (E)_____ goals.
• Your Goals: If I join this club, I will practice very hard and become (F)_____!

03 주어진 어휘와 표현을 이용하여 3 문장 이상을 쓰시오.

what	how	when	where	whom
go	start	play	find	say

(1) _____
(2) _____
(3) _____
(4) _____
(5) _____

단원별 모의고사

[01~02] 다음 대화의 빈칸에 알맞은 단어를 고르시오.

01

> A: What do you enjoy doing when you have free time?
> B: I enjoy _____ my dog in the park.

① making　② getting　③ walking
④ climbing　⑤ knowing

02

> B: Jiyun, that's a pretty backpack! Where did you _____ it?
> G: My sister made it for me.

① get　② see　③ bake
④ grow　⑤ join

03 다음 빈칸에 들어갈 말을 〈보기〉에서 찾아 쓰시오. (형태 변화 가능)

> ┌─ 보기 ─┐
> join　own　neighbor　interest

(1) Ben shows much _____ in learning French.
(2) I decided to _____ the army.
(3) One of the _____ complained about the noise from the party.
(4) Bring your _____ book.

04 다음 영영풀이에 해당하는 단어를 주어진 철자로 시작하여 쓰고, (1), (2), (3)에 알맞는 단어를 쓰시오. (형태 변화 가능)

> • p_____ : to do something regularly in order to do it better
> • h_____ : to have a meeting, party, election, etc in a particular place or at a particular time
> • n_____ : the area around you or around a particular place, or the people who live there

(1) The meeting will be _____ at this hotel.
(2) Is there a good Chinese restaurant in the _____?
(3) I need to _____ playing the guitar.

[05~07] 다음 대화를 읽고 물음에 답하시오.

> B: These cookies look so delicious. Did you make (A)[it / them]? (①)
> G: Yes. I made them myself yesterday. (②) I enjoy baking. (B)[I went / I'm going] to make doughnuts this Saturday.
> B: Oh, I want to learn how to make doughnuts. (③) Is it difficult?
> G: Not at all. (④)
> B: Thanks, Bora. (⑤) What time should I (C)[come / to come]?
> G: At 2:00.
> B: Sounds good. See you then.

05 위 대화의 ①~⑤ 중 다음 주어진 말이 들어갈 알맞은 곳은?

> You can come to my house and join me if you want.

①　　②　　③　　④　　⑤

06 (A), (B), (C)에 적절한 말을 골라 쓰시오.

➡ (A)_____　(B)_____　(C)_____

07 위 대화의 내용과 일치하지 <u>않는</u> 것을 <u>모두</u> 고르시오.

① The boy wants to learn how to make doughnuts.

② The boy went to her house at 2:00.

③ The girl thinks that making doughnuts is not difficult.

④ The boy wants to go to the girl's house to learn how to make cookies.

⑤ The girl enjoys baking.

[08~10] 다음 대화를 읽고 물음에 답하시오.

G: Did you buy that drone? (①)

B: No, I got it as a present from my parents, but I don't know (A)_____ use it. (②) Do you know how to? (③)

G: (④) No, maybe Jina knows (B)_____ do it. (⑤)

B: Then, I will ask her for help.

08 위 대화의 ①~⑤ 중 다음 주어진 말이 들어갈 알맞은 곳은?

She enjoys flying drones.

①　　　②　　　③　　　④　　　⑤

09 다음 영영풀이에 해당하는 단어를 대화에서 찾아 쓰시오.

an aircraft that does not have a pilot, but is operated by radio

➡ _____

10 (A)와 (B)에 공통으로 들어갈 말을 대화에서 찾아 쓰시오.

➡ _____

11 다음 대화에서 <u>어색한</u> 부분을 찾아 고치시오.

A: ①Do you know ②how to ③make a paper cat?

B: ④Of course not. ⑤It's easy.

➡ _____

[12~14] 다음 대화를 읽고 물음에 답하시오.

B: Hello, Kate. I'm Hamin, the leader of the Nanum Orchestra. 우리 동아리에 관심을 가져줘서 고마워.

G: Hi. Nice to meet you.

B: You play the violin? (A)_____?

G: I started learning how to play the violin when I was ten.

B: (B)_____?

G: Yes. Actually, I was a member of an orchestra when I was in elementary school.

B: Great. We also volunteer to teach children. (C)_____?

G: I have no experience teaching others. But I enjoy working with people, so I'd like to try.

B: Good. I think we'll have a great time playing together. Welcome to the Nanum Orchestra.

12 다음 영영풀이에 해당하는 단어를 대화에서 찾아 쓰시오.

(1)

the person who directs or controls a group, organization, country, etc.

➡ _____

(2)

a large group of musicians playing many different kinds of instruments and led by a conductor

➡ _____

13 밑줄 친 우리말과 의미가 같도록 주어진 단어를 이용해 문장을 완성하시오.

➡ _____

(in, you, your, our)

14 (A)~(C)에 알맞은 질문을 〈보기〉에서 골라 쓰시오.

┌─ 보기 ├─
- Do you know how to play the violin?
- Do you enjoy teaching others?
- What do you enjoy doing when you have free time?
- When did you start playing the violin?
- Do you have any experience playing in a group?

➡ (A) _____
(B) _____
(C) _____

15 다음 빈칸에 들어갈 말로 알맞지 <u>않은</u> 것은? (2개)

| He let me know _____ to do it. |

① what   ② how   ③ when
④ why   ⑤ where

16 다음 중 어법상 어색한 것을 고르시오.

① I don't know when to start.
② Where are the pictures that it was taken by Gibson?
③ Can you teach me how to play the guitar?
④ Anyone who likes to paint can join our club.
⑤ This is the key which was lost yesterday.

17 다음 중 어법상 <u>어색한</u> 것을 바르게 고쳐 다시 쓰시오.

(1) Tell me how use this computer.

➡ _____

(2) He didn't know what to go.

➡ _____

(3) Do you know how should you to swim?

➡ _____

(4) The doctors are working in this hospital are very kind.

➡ _____
_____

(5) Did you meet the girl that she is wearing sunglasses?

➡ _____

(6) Mary has a cousin which live in Seoul.

➡ _____

(7) Melina took some pictures of her friends whom were on a hiking trip.

➡ _____
_____

[18~20] 다음 글을 읽고 물음에 답하시오.

The Picasso Art Club
Hi! I am Sora Kang from the Picasso Art Club. As you can guess from the name of our club, we paint. We also do volunteer work from time to time. Last summer, our club members ⓐparticipated in the "Change Our Neighborhood" project. On the dirty old walls of the buildings in our neighborhood,

we painted birds ⓑflying high in the sky and dolphins jumping over blue waves. As a result, the old neighborhood changed into a bright and beautiful place. The neighbors were happy to see our work and thanked us. You don't have to be a good painter. Anyone who likes to paint can join. Come and be a member of the Picasso Art Club.

18 위 글의 밑줄 친 ⓐparticipated in과 바꿔 쓸 수 있는 것을 모두 고르시오.

① joined
② made a plan for
③ prepared for
④ took part in
⑤ took care of

19 아래 보기에서 위 글의 밑줄 친 ⓑflying과 문법적 쓰임이 다른 것의 개수를 고르시오.

┌─── 보기 ───┐
① She was watching TV in the living room.
② Thank you for visiting our house.
③ Talking behind others' back is not good.
④ He enjoyed listening to her stories.
⑤ Is your hobby playing tennis?
└──────────┘

① 1개   ② 2개   ③ 3개   ④ 4개   ⑤ 5개

20 다음 빈칸 (A)와 (B)에 알맞은 단어를 넣어 피카소 미술 동아리의 가입 조건을 완성하시오.

┌────────────────────────────┐
You can be a member of the Picasso Art Club if you like (A)_____ _____ but there is no need for you to be (B)_____ _____ _____.
└────────────────────────────┘

[21~23] 다음 글을 읽고 물음에 답하시오.

The Boram Orchestra

Hi! I am Minsu Jang, the leader of the Boram Orchestra. Did you see several students playing music at the main gate when you came to school today? We were those students. We play music for our friends every morning. You need to know how to play an instrument a little bit to join our club. But don't worry if you don't play well. We will practice hard and get better together. We also teach children how to play musical instruments __ⓐ__ a service to our community. I am teaching an eleven-year-old boy to play the violin. At first, he did not know ⓑhow to read a note. Now he can play a simple song. ⓒ그가 바이올린을 연주하는 걸 듣는 것은 저를 매우 행복하게 합니다. __ⓓ__ joining our club, you can have an opportunity to help others. Come and join our club. We are waiting for you.

21 위 글의 빈칸 ⓐ와 ⓓ에 들어갈 전치사가 바르게 짝지어진 것은?

① to – By
② as – To
③ as – By
④ at – In
⑤ on – For

22 위 글의 밑줄 친 ⓑhow to read와 to부정사의 용법이 다른 것을 모두 고르시오.

① It is interesting to play tennis.
② Tell me the way to play tennis well.
③ I think it interesting to play tennis.
④ He got up early to play tennis.
⑤ I'm healthy enough to play tennis.

23 위 글의 밑줄 친 ⓒ의 우리말에 맞게 주어진 어휘를 이용하여 9 단어로 영작하시오.

┌────────────────────────────┐
hearing
└────────────────────────────┘

➡ _____

4

The Two Roads

 의사소통 기능

- 걱정 표현하기와 안심시키기
  A: I'm worried about your health.
  B: Don't worry. I'm going to the doctor tomorrow.
- 의견 묻기
  A: What do you think of my bike?
  B: It looks light and fast.

 언어 형식

- 현재완료
  I **have lived** quietly and well.
- 접속사 'if'
  How can we know **if** we don't try?

Words & Expressions

Key Words

- **besides** [bisáidz] 부 게다가
- **character** [kǽriktər] 명 등장인물
- **comfortable** [kʌ́mfərtəbl] 형 편안한
- **correct** [kərékt] 형 올바른
- **cub** [kʌb] 명 (곰, 사자 등의) 새끼
- **disappointed** [dìsəpɔ́intid] 형 실망한, 기대에 어긋난
- **ever** [évər] 부 언제든, 한 번이라도
- **foreign** [fɔ́:rən] 형 외국의
- **foreigner** [fɔ́:rənər] 명 외국인
- **friendly** [fréndli] 형 친절한
- **happiness** [hǽpinis] 명 행복
- **item** [áitəm] 명 품목
- **join** [dʒɔin] 동 함께 하다
- **journey** [dʒə́:rni] 명 여행
- **nearby** [níərbài] 부 근처에
- **nervous** [nə́:rvəs] 형 불안한
- **noisy** [nɔ́izi] 형 시끄러운

- **opinion** [əpínjən] 명 의견
- **regret** [rigrét] 동 후회하다
- **reply** [riplái] 동 대답하다
- **review** [rivjú:] 명 감상문, 논평
- **rule** [ru:l] 동 지배하다
- **scary** [skɛ́əri] 형 무서운
- **scene** [si:n] 명 장면
- **school cafeteria** 학교 식당
- **seagull** [sí:gʌl] 명 갈매기
- **separate** [sépəreit] 동 헤어지다
- **such** [sʌtʃ] 형 그러한, 너무나 ~한
- **support** [səpɔ́:rt] 명 지지 동 지지하다
- **teenager** [tínèidʒər] 명 십 대
- **throne** [θroun] 명 왕좌, 왕위
- **title** [táitl] 명 제목
- **weather** [wéðər] 명 날씨
- **wide** [waid] 형 넓은

Key Expressions

- **be good at**: ~을 잘하다
- **be scared of**: ~을 두려워하다
- **be worried about**: ~에 대해 걱정하다
- **break out**: 발발하다
- **by the way**: 그런데(대화에서 화제를 바꿀 때 씀)
- **get**+형용사: ~하게 되다
- **get better**: (병·상황 등이) 나아지다
- **go into**: ~에 들어가다
- **go to the doctor**: 병원에 가다
- **have a good time**: 좋은 시간을 보내다

- **look for**: ~을 찾다
- **look good (on** 사람): (~에게) 잘 어울리다
- **look like**+명사: ~처럼 보이다
- **not anymore**: 더 이상 ~ 않다
- **take away**: ~을 빼앗다
- **take ~ for a walk**: ~을 산책하러 데리고 가다
- **try to**+동사원형: ~하는 것을 노력하다
- **What do you think of/about** ~?: ~에 대해 어떻게 생각해?
- **What if** 주어 동사 ~?: 만약 ~이라면 어떻게 될까?
- 비교급 **and** 비교급: 점점 더 ~한[하게]

Word Power

※ 서로 비슷한 뜻을 가진 단어

☐ **correct**(올바른) : **right**(바른, 옳은)

☐ **happiness**(행복) : **pleasure**(즐거움, 기쁨)

☐ **nervous**(불안한) : **worried**(걱정되는), **concerned**(우려하는)

☐ **journey**(여행) : **trip**(여행)

☐ **rule**(지배하다) : **control**(통제하다)

☐ **reply**(대답하다) : **answer**(답하다)

※ 서로 반대의 뜻을 가진 단어

☐ **correct**(올바른) ↔ **incorrect**(올바르지 않은)

☐ **happiness**(행복) ↔ **unhappiness**(불운, 불행)

☐ **separate**(헤어지다) ↔ **unite**(통합하다)

☐ **friendly**(친절한) ↔ **unfriendly**(불친절한, 쌀쌀맞은)

☐ **noisy**(시끄러운) ↔ **quiet**(조용한)

☐ **wide**(넓은) ↔ **narrow**(좁은)

※ 형용사에 -ness를 붙여 명사가 되는 단어

☐ **happy**(행복한) ↔ **happiness**(행복)

☐ **dark**(어두운) ↔ **darkness**(어두움)

☐ **sad**(슬픈) ↔ **sadness**(슬픔)

☐ **kind**(친절한) ↔ **kindness**(친절)

English Dictionary

☐ **besides** 게다가
→ used to give an additional reason for something
무언가에 대해 추가적인 이유를 제시할 때 사용되는 말

☐ **character** 등장인물
→ a person in a film, book, or play
영화, 책 또는 연극에 있는 인물

☐ **correct** 올바른
→ having no errors 잘못을 가지고 있지 않은

☐ **cub** (곰, 사자 등의) 새끼
→ the young of a bear, lion or other mammals
곰, 사자 또는 다른 포유류의 어린 새끼

☐ **ever** 언제든, 한 번이라도
→ at any time 언제든지

☐ **foreign** 외국의
→ from a country other than one's own
자기 나라 이외의 다른 나라로부터

☐ **happiness** 행복
→ the feeling of pleasure 기쁨의 감정

☐ **journey** 여행
→ a trip from one place to another
한 장소에서 다른 장소로 가는 여행

☐ **nervous** 불안한
→ worried and anxious about something that is happening or might happen
일어나고 있는 일 또는 일어날 수도 있는 일에 대해서 걱정하고 염려하는

☐ **noisy** 시끄러운
→ making a lot of loud noise
많은 시끄러운 소음을 만드는

☐ **opinion** 의견
→ a thought or belief about something
어떤 것에 대한 생각이나 믿음

☐ **reply** 대답하다
→ to say or write something in response to something
어떤 것에 응답하여 무언가를 말하거나 쓰다

☐ **review** 감상문, 논평
→ a critical comment in a newspaper that gives an opinion about a new book or film
새로운 책이나 영화에 대해 의견을 내는 신문의 비평적인 언급

☐ **rule** 지배하다
→ to be in control of an area and its people
한 지역과 그곳의 사람들을 제어하다

☐ **seagull** 갈매기
→ a bird with white or gray feathers that lives near the sea
바다 근처에서 사는 하얗거나 회색의 깃털을 가진 새

☐ **separate** 헤어지다
→ to move apart 따로 이동하다

☐ **such** 너무나 ~한
→ so great (often used to emphasize a quality)
너무 엄청난(보통 질을 강조하기 위해 사용됨)

☐ **support** 지지, 후원
→ help, encouragement, or comfort given to someone during a difficult or unhappy time
어렵거나 불행한 시기 동안 누군가에게 주어지는 도움, 격려 또는 위로

☐ **teenager** 십대
→ a person between the ages of thirteen and nineteen
13살에서 19살 사이의 사람

☐ **throne** 왕좌, 왕위
→ a decorative chair that a king, queen, or emperor sits on 왕, 여왕 또는 황제가 앉는 장식용 의자

☐ **title** 제목
→ the name of a book, film, or other artistic works
책, 영화 또는 다른 예술 작품의 이름

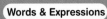

01 주어진 단어 뒤에 ness를 붙여 명사를 만들 수 <u>없는</u> 것을 고르시오.

① happy   ② silent   ③ sad
④ kind   ⑤ dark

[02~03] 밑줄 친 부분과 의미가 가장 가까운 것을 고르시오.

02

> <u>Besides</u>, it's very cold outside.

① Next   ② Despite
③ Likewise   ④ In addition
⑤ However

03

> I didn't know how to <u>reply</u>.

① react   ② answer
③ explain   ④ consider
⑤ understand

[04~05] 다음 빈칸에 알맞은 단어를 고르시오.

04

> You look _____ a totally new person in that suit.

① as   ② so   ③ with   ④ in   ⑤ like

05

> Some people are worried that a war could break _____.

① out   ② away   ③ into
④ up   ⑤ off

06 다음 밑줄 친 부분의 의미로 알맞지 <u>않은</u> 것은?

① It was a long <u>journey</u>. (여행)
② Would you mind giving me your <u>opinion</u> about that? (의견)
③ Most <u>teenagers</u> are under a lot of stress. (십대)
④ The <u>seagulls</u> are flying above my head. (갈매기)
⑤ Your uncle looks like a <u>foreigner</u>. (외국의)

07 다음 주어진 우리말에 맞게 빈칸을 채우시오. (철자가 주어진 것도 있음)

(1) 너무나 아름다운 날씨예요!
➡ It is _____ a beautiful day!

(2) 이 홀은 백 명을 수용할 정도로 충분히 넓다.
➡ This hall is _____ enough to accommodate one hundred.

(3) 아이에게서 가위를 빼앗아라.
➡ T_____ the scissors _____ from the child.

(4) 나는 드디어 병원에 가기로 결정했어.
➡ I finally decided to _____ _____ the doctor.

(5) 어렸을 때, 난 어둠이 무서웠다.
➡ As a child, I _____ s_____ _____ the dark.

(6) 만약 그 애가 한 말들이 사실이 아니라면 어떻게 될까?
➡ _____ _____ the things she said are not true?

01 다음 짝지어진 단어의 관계가 같도록 주어진 철자로 시작하여 빈칸에 알맞은 말을 쓰시오.

> beautiful : beauty – dark : d_____

[02~03] 다음 빈칸에 공통으로 들어갈 말을 쓰시오.

02
> • I _____ nervous every time I stand on stage to sing.
> • I heard the weather was going to _____ better today.

03
> • He likes to _____ his dogs for a walk along the coast.
> • They _____ bad things away from the air.

04 다음 영영풀이에 해당하는 말을 주어진 철자로 시작하여 쓰고, 알맞은 것을 골라 문장을 완성하시오. (형태 변화 가능)

> • c_____ : the young of a bear, lion or other mammal
> • o_____ : a thought or belief about something
> • t_____ : a decorative chair that a king, queen, or emperor sits on

(1) Who will succeed to the _____?
(2) The _____ are taken care of by a zookeeper.
(3) We have a different _____ about adopting a cat.

05 다음 빈칸에 들어갈 말을 〈보기〉에서 찾아 쓰시오.

> ┤ 보기 ├
> good   foreign   scared   worried

(1) What is the most effective way to learn a _____ language?
(2) Do you think those people were _____ of the dentist, too?
(3) His family are _____ about him because of his unhealthy diet.
(4) He is _____ at solving difficult math problems.

06 다음 우리말에 맞게 주어진 단어를 바르게 배열하시오.

(1) 이 영화에서 네가 가장 좋아하는 등장인물이 누구니?
(this, who, favorite, character, movie, is, your, in, ?)
➡ _____

(2) 넌 전에 인도에 가본 적이 있니?
(ever, before, have, India, to, you, been, ?)
➡ _____

(3) 나는 저 드라마의 마지막 장면이 마음에 들었다.
(last, in, I, that, the, liked, scene, drama)
➡ _____

Conversation

1 걱정 표현하기와 안심시키기

A I'm worried about your health. 나는 네 건강이 걱정돼.

B Don't worry. I'm going to the doctor tomorrow. 걱정하지 마. 내일 진찰받으러 병원에 갈 거야.

- 걱정 표현하기(I'm worried about ~.)에서 'be worried about'은 걱정을 나타내는 표현으로, '~에 대해 걱정하다'라는 뜻을 지닌다. 걱정의 정도를 강조할 때에는, be so[very] worried about과 같이 worried 앞에 so 또는 very를 사용할 수 있다.

- 걱정을 표현하는 다른 것으로 'I'm worried (that)+주어+동사'가 있다. 이것은 '나는 (주어)가 ~인 것이 걱정돼'라는 의미로 that절 이하에 걱정하는 내용이 온다. 그 외에 '~에 대해 걱정하다'라는 의미의 표현으로 be anxious about, be concerned about 등이 있다.

걱정 표현하기

- be worried about (동)명사 ~.
- be concerned about (동)명사 ~.
- be anxious about (동)명사 ~.
- be worried that 주어 동사 ~.

걱정에 관련한 표현

- I'm worried about ~. (나는 ~에 대해 걱정하고 있어.)
- I'm not worried about ~. (나는 ~을 걱정하지 않아.)
- I never worry about ~. (나는 ~을 전혀 걱정 안 해.)

안심시키기

- Don't worry. (걱정하지 마.)
- Try not to get worried. You'll do fine[great]. (걱정하지 않도록 해 봐. 넌 잘할 거야.)
- I'm sure everything will be OK. (분명히 모든 일이 잘될 거야.)
- Take it easy. Everything will be all right. (마음 편히 가져. 모든 일이 좋아질 거야.)

핵심 Check

1. 다음 우리말과 일치하도록 빈칸에 알맞은 말을 쓰시오.

   A: _____ worried _____ the English test tomorrow. (나는 내일 영어 시험이 걱정 돼.)

   B: Don't _____. You _____ _____ it. (걱정 마. 넌 합격할 수 있어.)

2. 다음 대화의 순서를 바르게 배열하시오.

   Try not to worry about it too much. You can do well.

   I'm worried about the speech contest.

   You don't look good. Is something wrong?

   ➡ _____

2 의견 묻기

A What do you think of my bike? 내 자전거에 대해 어떻게 생각해?

B It looks light and fast. 가볍고 빨라 보여.

■ 'What do you think of ~?'는 '~에 대해 어떻게 생각해?'의 의미로, 무언가에 대하여 상대방의 의견을 물을 때 사용할 수 있다. 'of' 대신에 'about'을 쓸 수도 있다.

■ 의견을 묻는 말에 대한 대답은 'I like it.'이나 'I don't like it.' 등을 말하고 그 이유를 제시할 수 있다.

의견 묻기

- What do you think of[about] ~?
- What's your opinion of[about/on] ~?
- What's your view on ~?
- How do you feel about ~?
- How do you like ~?

의견 답하기

- In my opinion[viewpoint], ~. 내 생각[관점]에는, ~.
- I (don't) like ~. 나는 ~을 (안) 좋아해.
- It's terrific[wonderful/excellent/great]. 그것 좋다.
- It is so touching[impressive]. 아주 감동적이야.
- I recommend it. 나는 그것을 추천해.
- It is not bad. 나쁘지 않아.
- It is terrible. 끔찍해.

핵심 Check

3. 다음 대화의 우리말과 일치하도록 빈칸에 알맞은 말을 쓰시오.

(1) **A:** What do _____ online shopping? (너는 온라인 쇼핑에 대해 어떻게 생각하니?)

   B: In my opinion, it saves time. (내 생각에 그것은 시간을 절약해 줘.)

(2) **A:** How _____ about that movie? (너는 저 영화에 대해 어떻게 생각하니?)

   B: I like it a lot. (아주 좋아.)

4. 다음 대화의 순서를 바르게 배열하시오.

(A) How did you like it?

(B) I ate a hamburger.

(C) What did you eat yesterday, Jisu?

(D) I liked it a lot. It was delicious.

➡ _____

Conversation 교과서 대화문 익히기

Listen & Speak 1 B-1

B: ❶Do you have any special plans for tomorrow?

G: I'm going to Jejudo in the morning. But ❷I'm worried about the weather.

B: ❸Don't worry. ❹It won't rain on Jejudo tomorrow.

G: Oh, ❺that's good to hear.

B: 내일 특별한 계획 있니?
G: 아침에 제주도에 갈 거야. 그런데 날씨가 걱정돼.
B: 걱정하지 마. 내일 제주도에는 비가 내리지 않을 거야.
G: 오, 반가운 소리네.

❶ 'Do you have any special plans for ~?'는 상대방에게 무엇을 할 계획인지(또는 어떤 계획이 있는지) 물어볼 때 사용하는 표현이다. 'What are you planning to do tomorrow?', 'What are you going to do tomorrow?', 'What are your plans for tomorrow?' 등으로 바꾸어 쓸 수 있다. weather: 날씨

❷ 'be worried about'은 걱정을 나타내는 표현으로, '~에 대해 걱정하다'라는 뜻을 지닌다. 걱정의 정도를 강조할 때에는, be so[very] worried about과 같이 worried 앞에 so 또는 very를 사용할 수 있다.

❸ 'Don't worry.'는 '걱정하지 마.'의 의미로 걱정이나 두려움을 표현한 상대를 안심시키는 표현이다. 비슷한 표현으로 'Try not to get worried. You'll do fine.', 'Everything will be OK.' 등이 있다.

❹ 시간, 거리, 계절, 요일, 명암, 날씨, 날짜 등을 이야기할 때 비인칭 주어 it을 사용한다. won't = will not(~하지 않을 것이다)

❺ 'that's good to hear.'는 안도감을 나타내는 표현이다. 여기서 to hear는 앞의 good을 수식하는 to부정사의 '부사적 용법'에 해당된다.

Check(√) True or False

(1) It is not going to rain on Jejudo tomorrow.   T ☐ F ☐

(2) The boy is going to Jejudo tomorrow morning.   T ☐ F ☐

(3) The girl is worried about the weather of Jejudo.   T ☐ F ☐

Listen & Speak 2 B-1

G: Did you watch ❶the movie, *The Daughter*?

B: ❷Yes, I saw it last Saturday.

G: ❸What did you think of it?

B: I was ❹disappointed. It wasn't very good.

G: 너 영화 '딸' 봤니?
B: 응, 지난 토요일에 봤어.
G: 어떻게 생각했어?
B: 나는 실망했어. 별로 좋지 않았어.

❶ the movie와 The Daughter는 동격이다.

❷ 'Did you 동사원형 ~?'이 질문이므로, see의 과거형 동사 saw를 사용하여 대답한다. 여기서 it은 the movie, The Daughter를 의미한다. last Saturday: 지난 토요일

❸ 'What do you think of+명사?'는 '~에 대해 어떻게 생각해?'의 의미로, 무언가에 대하여 상대방의 의견을 물을 때 사용할 수 있다.

❹ disappointed: 실망한, 기대에 어긋난

Check(√) True or False

(4) The boy saw the movie last Saturday.   T ☐ F ☐

(5) The boy thinks the movie was very good.   T ☐ F ☐

(6) The boy was disappointed that the movie wasn't very good.   T ☐ F ☐

Listen & Speak 1 B-2

B: Jina, can you ❶go into your house first?

G: Why? ❷What's wrong?

B: ❸I'm scared of your dog.

G: ❹Don't worry. He's a ❺friendly dog. ❻He just looks scary because he's so big.

❶ go into: ~에 들어가다

❷ 상대방이 뭔가에 불만족하거나 실망하고 있는 것을 보고 그 원인을 물을 때 'What's wrong?'이라고 물을 수 있다. 비슷한 표현으로 'What's the matter?', 혹은 'What's the problem?'이 있다.

❸ be scared of: ~을 두려워하다

❹ 걱정하는 상대방을 안심시키는 표현이다.

❺ friendly: 친절한

❻ 어떤 일에 대하여 이유를 말할 때는 'because'를 사용한다. 즉 '결과 +because+이유'로 말하면 되는데 보통 여기에서의 결과와 이유는 문장으로 말한다. look+형용사: ~하게 보이다 scary: 무서운

Listen & Speak 2 B-2

B: ❶What do you think of our school cafeteria food?

G: ❷I think the cafeteria food is delicious.

B: ❸What do you think is the best item?

G: I like the Gimbap the best.

❶ 'What do you think of+명사?'는 '~에 대해 어떻게 생각해?'의 의미로, 무언가에 대하여 상대방의 의견을 물을 때 사용할 수 있다. 'of' 대신에 'about'을 쓸 수도 있다. school cafeteria: 학교 식당

❷ think와 the cafeteria 사이에 접속사 that이 생략되어 있다. delicious: 맛있는

❸ What do you think is the best item?: 최고의 품목이 뭐라고 생각하니? best: 최고의

Listen & Speak 2 B-3

G: ❶What do you think of this painting?

B: It looks great. I like the colors.

G: ❷I'm happy that you like it. I painted it ❸ myself.

❶ What do you think of+명사?: ~에 대해 어떻게 생각해? (= What's your opinion of[about/on] ~? = What's your view on ~? = How do you feel about ~? = How do you like ~?)

❷ 'I'm happy that ~.'은 '~해서 나는 기쁘다'라는 뜻으로, that은 생략하기도 한다. that절 이하에는 기쁜 이유가 제시된다.

❸ 주어를 강조하기 위해 재귀대명사를 사용하였다.

Real-Life Zone

G: I saw you with someone ❶who ❷looked like a foreigner yesterday.

B: Yes. We ❸had lunch together.

G: You looked like you were ❹having a good time.

B: ❺We were. We try to meet twice a month for lunch.

G: ❻I wish I could feel more comfortable talking with a foreigner.

B: I ❼was worried about speaking in English before, but not anymore.

G: I ❽get really nervous when I try to speak in English.

B: Well, the first time is ❾the hardest. After that, it gets easier and easier.

G: ❿What do you think about me ⓫joining both of you for lunch?

B: That's a great idea.

❶ 주격 관계대명사로 선행사 someone을 수식한다.

❷ look like 명사: ~처럼 보이다

❸ had는 have(먹다)의 과거형이다. ate으로 바꾸어 쓸 수 있다.

❹ have a good time: 좋은 시간을 보내다

❺ We were 다음에 having a good time이 생략되어 있다.

❻ 현재 사실과 반대되는 일에 대한 소망이나 유감을 나타낼 때 'I wish+주어 +could+동사원형 ~.'으로 쓰며 '~라면 좋을 텐데'라고 해석한다. 'I wish+ 주어+동사의 과거형 ~.'으로도 나타내며 be동사는 were를 쓴다.

❼ 'be worried about'은 걱정을 나타내는 표현으로, '~에 대해 걱정하다'라는 뜻을 지닌다. about은 전치사이므로 뒤에 명사나 동명사가 올 수 있다.

❽ get+감정형용사: ~해지다

❾ the hardest(가장 힘든)는 hard(힘든)의 최상급이다.

'What do you think about+명사?'는 '~에 대해 어떻게 생각해?'의 의미로, 무언가에 대하여 상대방의 의견을 물을 때 사용할 수 있다.

⓫ 동명사로 전치사 about의 목적어이다. 앞에 있는 me는 joining의 의미상의 주어이다.

● 다음 우리말과 일치하도록 빈칸에 알맞은 말을 쓰시오.

Listen & Speak 1 A

B: I'm w_____ _____ the math test.

W: _____ worry. You'll do fine.

B: 저는 수학 시험이 걱정돼요.
W: 걱정하지 마. 넌 잘할 거야.

Listen & Speak 1 B

1. B: _____ _____ _____ any special _____ for tomorrow?

   G: I'm going _____ Jejudo in the morning. But I'm w_____ _____ the weather.

   B: Don't _____. It _____ rain on Jejudo tomorrow.

   G: Oh, that's good to hear.

2. B: Jina, can you _____ into your house first?

   G: Why? What's _____?

   B: I'm _____ _____ your dog.

   G: Don't worry. He's a f_____ dog. He just _____ _____ _____ he's so big.

1. B: 내일 특별한 계획 있니?
   G: 아침에 제주도에 갈 거야. 그런데 날씨가 걱정돼.
   B: 걱정하지 마. 내일 제주도에는 비가 내리지 않을 거야.
   G: 오, 반가운 소리네.

2. B: 진아야, 네가 먼저 집에 들어갈 수 있어?
   G: 왜? 무슨 일 있니?
   B: 난 네 개가 무서워.
   G: 걱정하지 마. 친절한 개야. 너무 커서 무섭게 보일 뿐이야.

Listen & Speak 1 C

1. A: _____ _____ _____ your health.

   B: _____ _____. I'm going to the doctor tomorrow.

2. A: _____ _____ _____ the speech contest.

   B: Don't worry. _____ _____ _____.

3. A: _____ _____ _____ _____ _____ _____.

   B: Don't _____. You'll _____ _____ you like to do.

1. A: 나는 네 건강이 걱정돼.
   B: 걱정하지 마. 내일 진찰받으러 병원에 갈 거야.

2. A: 나는 말하기 대회가 걱정돼.
   B: 걱정하지 마. 넌 잘할 거야.

3. A: 나는 내 미래가 걱정돼.
   B: 걱정하지 마. 네가 하고 싶은 것을 발견할 거야.

Listen & Speak 2 A

B: _____ _____ _____ think _____ these sunglasses?

G: They're cool! You look _____ a movie star.

B: 이 선글라스에 대해 어떻게 생각해?
G: 멋져! 너는 영화배우 같아.

Listen & Speak 2 B

1. **G:** Did you watch the movie, *The Daughter*?

   B: Yes, I _____ it last Saturday.

   G: _____ _____ _____ _____ _____ _____?

   B: I was d_____. It wasn't very good.

2. **B:** _____ _____ _____ _____ _____ our school cafeteria food?

   G: I _____ the cafeteria food is d_____.

   B: _____ do you think is the best item?

   G: I like the Gimbap the best.

3. **G:** What _____ _____ _____ _____ this painting?

   B: It looks great. I like the colors.

   G: I'm _____ _____ you like it. I painted it _____.

Listen & Speak 2 C

1. **A:** What do you _____ _____ my bike?

   B: It _____ _____ and fast.

2. **A:** _____ _____ _____ _____ of these shoes?

   B: They look _____ _____ _____.

Real-Life Zone

G: I saw you with someone _____ _____ _____ a foreigner yesterday.

B: Yes. We h_____ lunch together.

G: You _____ like you were having a good time.

B: We _____. We try _____ _____ twice a month for lunch.

G: I wish I could feel more _____ talking with a foreigner.

B: I _____ _____ _____ _____ in English before, but not _____.

G: I get really nervous when I try to speak in English.

B: Well, the first time is _____ _____. After that, it gets easier and easier.

G: _____ _____ _____ think a_____ me joining both of you for lunch?

B: That's a great idea.

해석

1. G: 너 영화 '딸' 봤니?
   B: 응, 지난 토요일에 봤어.
   G: 어떻게 생각했어?
   B: 나는 실망했어. 별로 좋지 않았어.

2. B: 학교 식당 음식에 대해 어떻게 생각해?
   G: 식당 음식이 맛있다고 생각해.
   B: 최고의 품목이 뭐라고 생각하니?
   G: 나는 김밥을 제일 좋아해.

3. G: 이 그림에 대해 어떻게 생각해?
   B: 아주 멋있어. 나는 색이 마음에 들어.
   G: 네가 좋아하니 기뻐. 내가 직접 그렸어.

1. A: 내 자전거에 대해 어떻게 생각해?
   B: 가볍고 빨라 보여.

2. A: 이 신발에 대해 어떻게 생각해?
   B: 너에게 잘 어울려.

G: 나는 어제 네가 외국인처럼 보이는 누군가와 있는 것을 봤어.
B: 응. 우리는 점심을 같이 먹었어.
G: 너희들은 좋은 시간을 보내고 있는 것처럼 보였어.
B: 그랬어. 우리는 한 달에 두 번 만나서 점심을 먹으려고 해.
G: 나는 외국인과 더 편하게 이야기할 수 있으면 좋을 텐데.
B: 나는 전에는 영어로 말하는 것에 대해 걱정했었지만, 더 이상은 아니야.
G: 영어로 말하려고 할 때 정말 불안해.
B: 음, 처음이 가장 힘들지. 그 후에 점점 쉬워져.
G: 내가 너희 둘과 함께 점심 먹는 거 어떻게 생각해?
B: 좋은 생각이야.

[01~03] 다음 대화의 빈칸에 알맞은 것을 고르시오.

01

> B: I'm worried about the math test.
> W: _____ You'll do fine.

① I'm happy about that.　　② What an amazing test!
③ Never mind.　　④ Don't worry.
⑤ I think I should study more.

02

> B: Do you have any special plans for tomorrow?
> G: I'm going to Jejudo in the morning. But _____
> B: Don't worry. It won't rain on Jejudo tomorrow.
> G: Oh, that's good to hear.

① I'm worried about the weather.
② the weather was nice.
③ don't worry about the weather.
④ I was concerned about you.
⑤ I'm happy with today's weather.

03

> A: What do you think of our history class?
> B: _____

① It's difficult for me.　　② It looks good on you.
③ It looks light and fast.　　④ It looks great.
⑤ You'll do great.

04 다음 대화의 순서를 바르게 배열하시오.

> (A) Yes, I saw it last Saturday.
> (B) What did you think of it?
> (C) Did you watch the movie, *The Daughter*?
> (D) I was disappointed. It wasn't very good.

➡ _____

01 다음 대화의 빈칸에 알맞은 것을 고르시오.

> A: I'm worried about my smartphone.
> B: Don't worry. _____

① It won't rain.
② You are good at science.
③ Let me teach you how to draw.
④ There is a service center nearby.
⑤ I'm not good at math.

[02~04] 다음 대화를 읽고 물음에 답하시오.

> B: (A)_____
> G: I'm going to Jejudo in the morning. But I'm worried about the (B)_____.
> B: Don't worry. It won't rain on Jejudo tomorrow.
> G: Oh, that's good to hear.

02 빈칸 (A)에 알맞은 말을 고르시오.

① What do you think of Jejudo?
② What did you do in the morning?
③ Do you have any special plans for tomorrow?
④ Have you been to Jejudo?
⑤ Where did you go last Sunday?

03 빈칸 (B)에 알맞은 말을 고르시오.

① season   ② weather
③ experience   ④ pollution
⑤ climate

04 위 대화의 내용과 일치하지 <u>않는</u> 것을 고르시오.

① The girl has a plan to do tomorrow morning.
② The girl is worried about the weather of Jejudo.
③ The boy knows whether it will rain or not on Jejudo tomorrow.
④ The boy is going to Jejudo tomorrow morning.
⑤ It will not rain on Jejudo tomorrow.

05 다음 중 짝지어진 대화가 <u>어색한</u> 것은?

① A: What do you think of Van Gogh?
   B: I think he is a great artist.
② A: What do you think of Jihun?
   B: I think he's smart and handsome.
③ A: It looks like rain.
   B: Don't worry. It will be fine in the afternoon.
④ A: I'm worried about losing my things.
   B: Why don't you write your name on your things?
⑤ A: What do you think of comic books?
   B: I think you're great.

06 다음 대화의 빈칸에 알맞은 말을 고르시오.

> A: I'm worried _____ my English test.
> B: Don't worry. You'll do great.

① for   ② at
③ about   ④ by
⑤ in

[07~08] 다음 대화를 읽고 물음에 답하시오.

B: What do you think (A)_____ these sunglasses?

G: They're cool! You look (B)_____ a movie star.

07 빈칸 (A)에 알맞은 말을 <u>모두</u> 고르시오.

① of   ② from   ③ into
④ with   ⑤ about

서답형
08 빈칸 (B)에 알맞은 말을 쓰시오.

➡ _____

[09~10] 다음 대화를 읽고 물음에 답하시오.

G: I saw you with someone (A)[which / who] looked like a foreigner yesterday.

B: Yes. We had lunch together.

G: You looked like you were having a good time.

B: We were. We try to meet twice a month for lunch.

G: I wish I could feel more comfortable talking with a foreigner.

B: I was worried about speaking in English before, (B)[but / and] not anymore.

G: I get really nervous (C)[that / when] I try to speak in English.

B: Well, the first time is the hardest. After that, it gets easier and easier.

G: What do you think about me joining both of you for lunch?

B: That's a great idea.

서답형
09 (A)~(C)에 알맞은 말을 골라 쓰시오.

➡ (A)_____ (B)_____ (C)_____

10 위 대화를 읽고 대답할 수 <u>없는</u> 질문을 고르시오.

① How does the girl feel when she speaks in English?

② What did the boy do with the foreigner yesterday?

③ What is the boy worried about now?

④ When did the girl see the boy?

⑤ How often does the boy meet the foreigner?

[11~12] 다음 대화를 읽고 물음에 답하시오.

W: Jimin, you look worried. What's wrong?

G: Mom, I can't find the book that I borrowed from the library. (①)

W: What book are you looking (A)_____? (②) *Jonathan Livingston Seagull*? I think I saw it in the living room. (③)

G: Yes, that's it. Thank you, Mom. (④)

W: By the way, have you read the book? What did you think (B)_____ it? (⑤)

G: I've read it two times already. It was really interesting. I loved the character of Jonathan a lot.

중요
11 ①~⑤ 중 주어진 문장이 들어갈 곳은?

Have you seen it?

①   ②   ③   ④   ⑤

서답형
12 빈칸 (A)와 (B)에 알맞은 전치사를 쓰시오.

➡ (A) _____ (B) _____

[01~02] 다음 대화에서 어법상 또는 흐름상 어색한 부분을 찾아
고치시오. (1개)

01

B: Do you have any special plans for tomorrow?
G: I'm going to Jejudo in the morning. But I'm worried about the weather.
B: Don't worry. It will rain on Jejudo tomorrow.
G: Oh, that's good to hear.

➡ _____

02

B: What do you think of these sunglasses?
G: It's cool! You look like a movie star.

➡ _____

[03~04] 다음 대화를 읽고 물음에 답하시오.

G: I saw you with someone who looked like a foreigner yesterday.
B: Yes. We had lunch together.
G: You looked like you were having a good time.
B: We were. We try to meet twice a month for lunch.
G: I wish I could feel more comfortable talking with a foreigner.
B: I was worried about speaking in English before, but not anymore.
G: I get really nervous when I try to speak in English.
B: Well, the first time is the hardest. After that, (A)점점 쉬워져.
G: (B)내가 너희 둘과 함께 점심 먹는 거 어떻게 생각해?(for, do, joining, you, both, about, lunch, what, you, me, of, think, ?)
B: That's a great idea.

03 (A)의 밑줄 친 우리말을 주어진 단어를 이용해 영작하시오.

➡ _____ (it, easy, get, and)

04 괄호 안의 주어진 단어를 알맞게 배열하여 밑줄 친 (B)의 우리말을 영작하시오.

➡ _____

[05~06] 주어진 문장 다음에 이어질 문장의 순서를 바르게 배열하시오.

05

What do you think of our school cafeteria food?

(A) What do you think is the best item?
(B) I think the cafeteria food is delicious.
(C) I like the Gimbap the best.

➡ _____

06

Jimin, you look worried. What's wrong?

(A) Mom, I can't find the book that I borrowed from the library. Have you seen it?
(B) Yes, that's it. Thank you, Mom.
(C) What book are you looking for? *Jonathan Livingston Seagull*? I think I saw it in the living room.

➡ _____

Grammar

교과서

1 현재완료

> I **have lived** quietly and well. 나는 조용히 잘 살아 왔어.
> **Have** you ever **written** a diary in English? 영어로 일기를 써 본 적 있니?

- 현재완료는 'have[has] + 과거분사'의 형태로 과거의 일이 현재까지 영향을 주는 동작·상태의 의미를 나타낸다.
- 부정형은 'have[has] + not[never] + 과거분사'이며, 의문형은 'Have[Has] +주어 + 과거분사 ~?'로 나타낸다.
- I **haven't cleaned** my room yet. 나는 아직 내 방 청소를 안했다.
- **Have** you **read** The Little Prince already? 너는 '어린 왕자'를 벌써 읽었니?

- 현재완료는 '완료(최근에[막] …했다), 경험(…해 본 적이 있다), 계속((지금까지) 계속 …해 왔다), 결과 (…해서 (그 결과) 지금 ~하다)'의 네 가지 용법으로 쓰인다.

  완료 용법은 보통 'just, already, yet'과 같은 부사와 함께 쓰이며, 경험은 'ever, never, once, before' 등과 같은 부사와 함께 쓰인다. 계속적 용법은 보통 'for+기간'이나 'since+기준이 되는 때'와 함께 쓰이며 결과적 용법은 과거에 발생한 사건이 현재 미치고 있는 결과를 포함한다.
- Tom **has** already **finished** his homework. 〈완료〉 Tom은 이미 그의 숙제를 끝마쳤다.
- I **have** never **been** to Vietnam. 〈경험〉 저는 베트남에 가 본 적이 없습니다.
- He **has studied** English for 10 years. <계속> 그는 10년 동안 영어를 공부해 오고 있다.
- She **has lost** her pen in the park. <결과> 그녀는 공원에서 펜을 잃어버렸다. (그 결과 (펜이) 지금 없다.)

***have[has] been to와 have[has] gone to**

have[has] been to는 '~에 가 본 적이 있다'는 경험을 나타내고, have[has] gone to는 '~에 가고 없다'는 결과를 나타낸다. 그러므로 have[has] gone to는 3인칭만 주어로 쓸 수 있다.

- 현재완료는 과거의 일이 현재까지 영향을 주는 동작·상태를 나타내므로 과거를 나타내는 어구와 함께 쓸 수 없다.
- He went to London last month.　　(○)
- He has gone to London last month. (×)

핵심 Check

1. 주어진 동사를 어법에 맞게 쓰시오.
   (1) Christine _____ _____ to England. So you cannot meet her now. (go)
   (2) Hannah _____ _____ the piano for 10 years. (play)
   (3) _____ you ever _____ Alita? (watch).

② 접속사 if

> How can we know **if** we don't try? 우리가 시도하지 않으면 어떻게 알 수 있어?
>
> **If** it is sunny, I will go shopping. 만약 날씨가 좋으면, 나는 쇼핑하러 갈 거야.

■ if는 '만약 ~한다면'이라는 뜻의 접속사로 종속절 앞에 쓰여 그것을 주절에 연결해 준다. if절은 조건을 나타내는 부사절이다. 접속사가 사용된 문장에서 접속사가 붙은 절을 종속절, 접속사가 붙지 않은 나머지 절을 주절이라고 하는데, 주절이 먼저 나올 수도 있고 종속절이 먼저 나올 수도 있다.

• You can catch the next train **if** you leave now. 너는 지금 출발하면 다음 기차를 탈 수 있어.

■ 접속사 **unless**

'만약 ~하지 않는다면'의 뜻으로 'if ~ not'과 같은 의미이다.

• **If** it doesn't rain, I will go swimming.
  = **Unless** it rains, I will go swimming. 비가 안 오면 나는 수영하러 갈 거야.

■ 시간이나 조건의 부사절에서는 미래의 의미를 갖더라도 will을 쓰지 않고 현재 시제를 쓴다.

• **If** it **snows** tomorrow, I will go skiing. 내일 눈이 오면 나는 스키를 타러 갈 거야.

• Mina will watch TV **after** she **finishes** doing her homework. Mina는 숙제를 끝낸 후에 TV를 볼 거야.

■ 'if절이 명사 역할을 하는 경우도 있으며 (이때 if는 whether와 같은 의미이다.) 이때는 '~인지 아닌지'로 해석하며 미래를 나타낼 때에는 미래 시제를 써야 한다.

• Please ask Ben **if** he is able to attend the meeting. Ben이 그 모임에 참석할 수 있는지 그에게 물어 보세요.

핵심 Check

2. 다음 우리말과 일치하도록 빈칸에 알맞은 말을 쓰시오.

(1) 내 추측이 맞는다면 그는 틀림없이 40세 정도 되었다.

➡ _____ my guess is right, he must be about forty.

(2) 지금 출발하면 늦지 않을 거야.

➡ If you _____ right now, you _____ _____ late.

(3) 나는 그녀가 내일 집에 있을지 궁금하다.

➡ I wonder _____ she _____ _____ at home tomorrow.

01 다음 중 어법상 <u>어색한</u> 문장은?

① Marie has studied Chinese for three years.
② The train has just arrived.
③ We have gone to Seoul.
④ Have you ever been to a K-pop concert?
⑤ Jane met her sister yesterday.

02 다음 우리말에 맞게 괄호 안에 주어진 단어를 빈칸에 바르게 배열하시오. (필요하면 어형을 바꿀 것)

(1) 만약 학교가 일찍 끝난다면, 나는 영화를 볼 거야. (school, early, end, if)
➡ _____, I will watch the movie.
(2) Audrey는 초대받지 않으면 그 파티에 참석하지 않을 것이다.
(she, the party, is, attend, won't, invited, not, if)
➡ Audrey _____.

03 다음 문장에서 어법상 <u>어색한</u> 부분을 바르게 고치시오.

(1) I have play the piano for two years.
_____ ➡ _____
(2) She has met John last Saturday.
_____ ➡ _____
(3) Does he have written his report?
_____ ➡ _____
(4) Kate has worn the dress for 2000.
_____ ➡ _____
(5) If it will rain tomorrow, I will stay at home.
_____ ➡ _____
(6) I can't hear you unless you don't turn down the radio.
_____ ➡ _____

01 다음 중 어법상 바르지 않은 것은?

① I have been to San Francisco three times.
② I have lived in this house since I was born.
③ I've never heard that kind of strange story.
④ Marianne has not cleaned her house yet.
⑤ When have you bought your new computer?

02 다음 문장의 빈칸에 알맞은 것은?

_____ you study hard, you will pass the exam.

① If
② Unless
③ That
④ Although
⑤ What

03 다음 빈칸에 알맞은 말이 바르게 짝지어진 것은?

• How long _____ you been employed here?
• The children have _____ to play with their friends.

① were – gone
② were – been
③ have – gone
④ have – been
⑤ did – being

04 다음 중 문맥이나 어법상 바르지 않은 것은?

① I forget things unless I take notes.
② If we don't have homework tomorrow, I will go to see a movie.
③ You should visit the museum if you have some free time.
④ If we arrive on time, she will get angry.
⑤ If you miss the class, you will have to hand in a long report instead.

05 다음 대화의 빈칸에 들어갈 말로 알맞은 것은?

M: Have you been to Vietnam before?
W: Yes, I have _____.

① just
② already
③ yet
④ for
⑤ since

서답형
06 다음 괄호 안에서 알맞은 말을 고르시오.

(1) Emma (have / has) gone to Germany.
(2) We have (visited / visit) Angkor Wat, Cambodia once.
(3) Lingling is not here now. She has (been / gone) to China.
(4) Melanie (has been / went) to Paris last year.
(5) I will go hiking, (if / unless) it's fine.
(6) If you (will call / call) her, you will know why she left the party so early.

07 다음 중 어법상 옳은 것은?

① Jenny has raised a dog last year.
② Karen have been to Malaysia three times.
③ Susan and I have gone to Paris.
④ Tom has studied English since ten years.
⑤ Have you ever watched the movie?

서답형

08 주어진 어휘를 이용하여 다음 우리말을 두 가지로 영작하시오.
(You로 시작할 것)

> 더 빨리 걷지 않으면 버스를 놓칠 거야. (the bus, miss, quickly)

➡ _____
➡ _____

09 다음 질문에 대한 응답으로 알맞은 것은?

> Has she ever been in such a serious situation?

① No, she hasn't.
② No, she isn't.
③ No, she doesn't.
④ Yes, she is.
⑤ Yes, she does.

10 다음 밑줄 친 부분의 의미가 <u>다른</u> 하나는?

① <u>If</u> you exercise regularly, you can lose weight.
② I'm not sure <u>if</u> I can do it.
③ <u>If</u> you study hard, you will pass the exam.
④ She can stay with us <u>if</u> she wants.
⑤ <u>If</u> it's fine tomorrow, I'll go swimming.

11 다음 두 문장을 한 문장으로 바르게 연결한 것은?

> • Julia went back to Ukraine.
> • And she is there now.

① Julia went to Ukraine.
② Julia went to Ukraine already.
③ Julia hasn't been to Ukraine.
④ Julia has gone to Ukraine.
⑤ Julia hasn't come back yet.

12 다음 우리말과 일치하도록 빈칸에 알맞은 단어로 묶은 것은?

> • 수지를 만나면 그녀에게 이 편지를 줄 것이다.
> • If I _____ Suji, I _____ her this letter.

① will meet – will give
② will meet – give
③ meet – will give
④ have met – will give
⑤ meet – give

13 다음 중 밑줄 친 부분의 용법이 <u>다른</u> 것을 <u>두 개</u> 고르시오.

① The train for Busan <u>has</u> just <u>left</u> the station.
② Harry and Jenny <u>have</u> just <u>finished</u> their project.
③ I <u>have known</u> Emily since I was 8 years old.
④ We <u>have</u> already <u>cleaned</u> our classroom.
⑤ <u>Have</u> you <u>heard</u> about the K-pop singer before?

서답형

14 다음 문장을 어법에 맞게 고쳐 쓰시오.

(1) If my friend will move near my house, I can see her more often.

➡ _____

_____

(2) You will be late unless you don't hurry up.

➡ _____

_____

(3) Please let us know if you come to the party tomorrow.

➡ _____

_____

서답형

15 다음 두 문장을 비슷한 뜻을 가진 한 문장으로 고쳐 쓰시오.

(1) Anna fell in love with Sam when she met him first. And she still loves him.

➡ _____

(2) Mariel started to live in Tallinn seven years ago. And she still lives there.

➡ _____

16 다음 문장의 빈칸에 들어가기에 의미상 자연스러운 것은? (2개)

• It is about 5 km to the meeting place. So, _____, you will be late for the meeting.

① unless you go there on foot
② unless you leave right now
③ if you leave immediately
④ if you don't take the subway
⑤ if you don't take time

중요

17 다음 〈보기〉의 밑줄 친 부분과 용법이 같은 것은?

┌─ 보기 ─┐
I <u>have been</u> to Budapest four times.
└──────┘

① Joseph <u>has visited</u> the museum three times.
② Linda <u>has lost</u> her cell phone.
③ I <u>have known</u> the girl since she was a baby.
④ I <u>have finished</u> washing my car.
⑤ She <u>has gone</u> to Thailand.

[18~19] 다음 우리말에 맞게 영작한 것을 고르시오.

18

이 버튼을 누르면 벨이 울릴 것이다.

① If you don't push the button, the bell will ring.
② If you will push the button, the bell will ring.
③ If you push the button, the bell will ring.
④ Unless you push the button, the bell will ring.
⑤ Unless you don't push the button, the bell will ring.

19

너는 일본에 가 본 적 있니?

① Did you go to Japan?
② Do you have visited Japan?
③ Do you have gone to Japan?
④ Have you gone to Japan?
⑤ Have you been to Japan?

01 다음 우리말에 맞게 주어진 어구를 바르게 배열하시오.

(1) 찰리와 초콜릿 공장을 벌써 읽었니?

(you / *Charlie and the Chocolate Factory* / already / have / read)

➡ _____

(2) Jina는 여행을 하면서 많은 것을 경험했다.

(Jina / traveling / while / experienced / lot / has / a)

➡ _____

(3) 웃는 법을 모르면, 가게를 열지 마라.

(you / a shop / how / don't / know / open / smile / unless / to)

➡ _____

(4) 배고프면 간식을 먹는 것이 어떠니?

(why / some snacks / you / you / eat / are / don't / if / hungry)

➡ _____

02 다음 글에서 어법상 잘못 쓰인 것을 찾아 알맞게 고치시오. (3곳)

> This story is about a trumpeter naming Louis. When he was born, he was unable to speak, so he tried lots of things to get over it. I like this story because it has help me learn about the way to overcome my weakness. The book says that I can overcome my weakness unless I work hard.

➡ _____

03 다음 그림을 보고, 주어진 동사를 이용하여 자신의 경험에 대해 쓰시오. (현재완료 시제로 주어와 동사를 갖춘 완전한 문장으로 쓸 것.)

(1) (cook, ramyeon)

➡ _____

(2) (experience, ski)

➡ _____

04 주어진 두 문장을 한 문장으로 바꿔 쓰시오.

(1) • Sophia lost her cap.

• So, she doesn't have it now.

➡ _____

(2) • I visited Paris again.

• It was my second visit.

➡ _____

05 다음 중 어법상 <u>어색한</u> 것을 바르게 고치시오.

(1) You have had a lot of trouble then.

　➡ ＿＿＿＿＿＿＿＿＿＿＿＿＿＿

(2) Mariel has lived in Seoul since 10 years.

　➡ ＿＿＿＿＿＿＿＿＿＿＿＿＿＿

(3) Grace has been to Greece and she is there now.

　➡ ＿＿＿＿＿＿＿＿＿＿＿＿＿＿

(4) If I will go to Paris, I will visit the Louvre museum.

　➡ ＿＿＿＿＿＿＿＿＿＿＿＿＿＿

(5) Unless you are tired, you should have a rest.

　➡ ＿＿＿＿＿＿＿＿＿＿＿＿＿＿

06 다음 우리말을 괄호 안에 주어진 어휘를 이용하여 영작하시오.

(1) Jason은 한국 음식을 먹어 본 적이 있다. (eat, Korean food, 5 단어)

　➡ ＿＿＿＿＿＿＿＿＿＿＿＿＿＿

(2) 인류는 수 천 년 동안 존재해 왔다. (mankind, exist, thousands of years, 7 단어)

　➡ ＿＿＿＿＿＿＿＿＿＿＿＿＿＿

(3) 비가 내린다면 나는 우산을 가져갈 것이다. (rain, take, an umbrella, with, 10 단어)

　➡ ＿＿＿＿＿＿＿＿＿＿＿＿＿＿

(4) 그것이 아주 중요한 일이 아니면 수업에 빠지지 마라. (don't, miss, your classes, it, really, 9 단어)

　➡ ＿＿＿＿＿＿＿＿＿＿＿＿＿＿

07 다음 문장을 부정문과 의문문으로 각각 바꿔 쓰시오.

(1) Stephanie has used her computer for 3 years.

부정문: ＿＿＿＿＿＿＿＿＿＿＿＿

의문문: ＿＿＿＿＿＿＿＿＿＿＿＿

(2) You have seen it before.

부정문: ＿＿＿＿＿＿＿＿＿＿＿＿

　　　　＿＿＿＿＿＿＿＿＿＿＿＿

의문문: ＿＿＿＿＿＿＿＿＿＿＿＿

08 다음 두 문장의 뜻이 같도록 빈칸에 알맞은 말을 쓰시오.

(1) Exercise regularly, and you can stay healthy.

　➡ ＿＿＿＿＿ you exercise regularly, you can stay healthy.

(2) Get up early tomorrow morning, or you'll miss the first train.

　➡ ＿＿＿＿＿ you get up early tomorrow morning, you'll miss the first train.

09 두 문장의 의미가 같도록 빈칸에 알맞은 말을 쓰시오.

(1) It started to rain two days ago. It still rains.

= It ＿＿＿＿＿＿ for two days.

(2) Miranda went to her country. She is in her country now.

= Miranda ＿＿＿＿＿＿ to her country.

(3) My smartphone broke down. And it still doesn't work.

= My smartphone ＿＿＿＿＿＿ down.

 Reading

The Two Brothers

Two brothers went on a journey. They found a rock in front of a
　　　　　　　　여행을 떠났다　　　　　　　　　　　　　　　　　　　　　　　　　～ 앞에서
forest. It said, "Go into the forest and swim across the river. There
　　　　　　　　　　　　　　　　　　　　　　　　　　　　～ 건너서, ～을 가로질러
you will find a bear and her cubs. Take the bear cubs and run up the
　　　　　　　　　　　　　　　(곰, 사자 등의) 새끼　　　　　　　　　등위접속사 ～ 위로 달리다
mountain. There you will find happiness."
　　　　　　　앞 문장의 'the mountain'을 가리킴　　　행복

The younger brother said, "Let's go and find happiness together."
　　　　　　　　　　　　　　　　　　병렬 구문

"No," said the older brother, "How can we know this is true? What
　　　　　　　　　　　　　　　　　　　　　　　　　　앞에 접속사 'that' 생략~하면 어쩌지?
if the river is too wide? Besides, will it be easy to take the cubs away
　　　　　　　　넓은　　　　　게다가　　　　가주어　　　　진주어　　take away: 빼앗다
from their mother? Instead of finding happiness, we can be killed!"
　　　　　　　　　　　～하는 대신에　　　　　　　　　　　수동태(be동사+과거분사): 죽임을 당하다

The younger brother replied, "How can we know if we don't try?"
　　　　　　　　　　　대답하다　　　　　　　　　　　조건의 접속사: 만약 ～한다면

They separated, and they both went their own way.
　　　떨어지다, 헤어지다　　　　　　　go one's own way: 자신의 길을 가다

The younger brother went into the forest and swam across the river.
　　　형용사의 비교급: 원급+er　　　　　　　숲

There was the bear. She was sleeping. He took her cubs and ran up the
　　　　　　　　　　　　　과거진행형(was/were+～ing): ～하고 있었다

mountain.

journey 여행
cub (곰, 사자 등의) 새끼
happiness 행복
wide 넓은
besides 게다가
reply 대답하다
separate 헤어지다
take away 빼앗다

확인문제

- 다음 문장이 본문의 내용과 일치하면 T, 일치하지 <u>않으면</u> F를 쓰시오.

1　Two brothers found a rock in front of a forest. ☐

2　The rock said, "Go into the village and swim across the river." ☐

3　The older brother said, "Let's go and find happiness together." ☐

4　The older brother said, "What if the river is too wide?" ☐

5　The younger brother replied, "How can we know if we don't try?" ☐

6　Two brothers went into the forest and swam across the river. ☐

When he reached the top, some people took him to their city and
시간의 접속사: ~할 때　~에 도착했다　　　　　　　　그를 ~으로 데려갔다

made him their king. There he lived as a king for five years. Then a
5형식(make+목적어+목적격보어): ~을 ~이 되게 하다　　전치사: ~로(서)

war broke out, and he lost his throne. He was on the road again.
발발했다　　　　　　　왕위

　　One day, the two brothers met again and talked about their lives
어느 날　　　　　　　　　　　　　　　　　　　　　　　　life의 복수

for the last five years. The older brother said, "I was right. I have
~ 동안

lived quietly and well. You were once a king, but you have had a
현재완료(have/has+p.p.): ~해 왔다　　　　　　　현재완료(have/has + p.p.): ~해 왔다

lot of trouble." The younger brother answered, "I don't regret my
　　　　　　　　　　　　　　　　　　　　　　　후회하다

choice. I may have nothing now, but I will always have something to
선택　　　추측의 조동사: ~일지도 모른다　　　　　　　　　to부정사의

remember."
형용사적 용법: ~할, ~하는

- reach ~에 도착하다
- lose 잃다, 지다
- throne 왕위, 왕좌
- road 길, 도로
- regret 후회하다
- break out 발발하다
- choice 선택

확인문제

● 다음 문장이 본문의 내용과 일치하면 T, 일치하지 <u>않으면</u> F를 쓰시오.

1　Some people took the younger brother to their city and made him their king. ☐

2　After ten years, the younger brother lost his throne. ☐

3　The older brother had a lot of trouble. ☐

4　The younger brother didn't regret his choice. ☐

● 우리말을 참고하여 빈칸에 알맞은 말을 쓰시오.

1 The Two Brothers

2 Two brothers _____ _____ a journey.

3 They found a rock _____ _____ _____ a forest.

4 It _____, "Go _____ the forest and swim _____ the river.

5 There you will find a bear and _____ _____.

6 _____ the bear cubs and _____ _____ the mountain.

7 There you will _____ _____."

8 The younger brother said, "Let's _____ _____ _____ happiness together."

9 "No," said the older brother, "_____ _____ _____ _____ this is true?

10 _____ _____ the river is too wide?

11 _____, will it be easy to take the cubs _____ _____ their mother?

12 _____ _____ finding happiness, we can be killed!"

13 The younger brother replied, "_____ can we know _____ we don't try?"

14 They separated, and they both _____ _____ _____ _____.

15 The younger brother _____ _____ the forest and _____ _____ the river.

16 _____ _____ the bear.

---

1 두 형제

2 두 형제는 여정을 떠났다.

3 그들은 숲 앞에서 바위를 발견했다.

4 거기에 쓰여 있었다. "숲에 들어가 강을 헤엄쳐 건너시오.

5 당신은 거기에서 곰과 새끼들을 발견할 것입니다.

6 곰 새끼들을 데리고 산 위로 뛰어 올라가시오.

7 거기에서 당신은 행복을 찾을 수 있을 것입니다."

8 동생이 말했다. "함께 가서 행복을 찾자."

9 "싫어." 형은 말했다. "이것이 사실인지 우리가 어떻게 알 수 있어?

10 강이 너무 넓으면 어쩌지?

11 게다가, 곰 새끼들을 엄마에게서 빼앗는 것이 쉬울까?

12 행복을 찾는 대신에, 우리는 죽을 수 있어!"

13 동생은 대답했다. "우리가 시도하지 않으면 어떻게 알 수 있어?"

14 그들은 헤어졌고, 둘 다 자신의 길을 갔다.

15 동생은 숲에 들어가서 강을 헤엄쳐 건넜다.

16 곰이 있었다.

17 She was _____.

18 He _____ _____ _____ and ran up the mountain.

19 When he reached the top, some people _____ _____ _____ their city and _____ him their king.

20 There he lived _____ _____ _____ for five years.

21 Then a war _____ _____, and he _____ _____ _____.

22 He was _____ _____ _____ again.

23 One day, the two brothers met again and _____ _____ their lives _____ _____ _____ five years.

24 The older brother said, "_____ _____ _____.

25 I _____ _____ quietly and well.

26 You were once a king, but you _____ _____ a lot of trouble."

27 The younger brother answered, "I don't _____ _____ _____.

28 I may have _____ now, but I will always have _____ _____ _____."

17 그녀는 자고 있었다.

18 그는 새끼들을 데리고 산을 뛰어 올라갔다.

19 그가 정상에 도착했을 때, 어떤 사람들이 그를 자기들 도시로 데려가서 그들의 왕으로 만들었다.

20 그곳에서 그는 5년간 왕으로 살았다.

21 그런 다음 전쟁이 일어났고, 그는 왕좌를 잃었다.

22 그는 다시 길바닥에 나앉았다.

23 어느 날, 두 형제는 다시 만났고 지난 5년 동안의 그들의 삶에 대해 이야기했다.

24 형은 말했다. "내가 옳았어.

25 나는 조용히 잘 살았어.

26 너는 한때 왕이었지만 많은 어려움을 겪었지."

27 동생은 대답했다. "나는 내 선택을 후회하지 않아.

28 나는 지금 아무것도 없지만 언제까지나 기억할 어떤 것이 있어."

우리말을 참고하여 본문을 영작하시오.

1 두 형제

⇒ _____

2 두 형제는 여정을 떠났다.

⇒ _____

3 그들은 숲 앞에서 바위를 발견했다.

⇒ _____

4 거기에 쓰여 있었다. "숲에 들어가 강을 헤엄쳐 건너시오.

⇒ _____

5 당신은 거기에서 곰과 새끼들을 발견할 것입니다.

⇒ _____

6 곰 새끼들을 데리고 산 위로 뛰어 올라가시오.

⇒ _____

7 거기에서 당신은 행복을 찾을 수 있을 것입니다."

⇒ _____

8 동생이 말했다. "함께 가서 행복을 찾자."

⇒ _____

9 "싫어." 형은 말했다. "이것이 사실인지 우리가 어떻게 알 수 있어?

⇒ _____

10 강이 너무 넓으면 어쩌지?

⇒ _____

11 게다가, 곰 새끼들을 엄마에게서 빼앗는 것이 쉬울까?

⇒ _____

12 행복을 찾는 대신에, 우리는 죽을 수 있어!"

⇒ _____

13 동생은 대답했다. "우리가 시도하지 않으면 어떻게 알 수 있어?"

⇒ _____

14 그들은 헤어졌고, 둘 다 자신의 길을 갔다.

⇒ _____

15 동생은 숲에 들어가서 강을 헤엄쳐 건넜다.

⇒ _____

16 곰이 있었다.

⇒ _____

17 그녀는 자고 있었다.

➡ _____

18 그는 새끼들을 데리고 산을 뛰어 올라갔다.

➡ _____

19 그가 정상에 도착했을 때, 어떤 사람들이 그를 자기들 도시로 데려가서 그들의 왕으로 만들었다.

➡ _____

20 그곳에서 그는 5년간 왕으로 살았다.

➡ _____

21 그런 다음 전쟁이 일어났고, 그는 왕좌를 잃었다.

➡ _____

22 그는 다시 길바닥에 나앉았다.

➡ _____

23 어느 날, 두 형제는 다시 만났고 지난 5년 동안의 그들의 삶에 대해 이야기했다.

➡ _____

24 형은 말했다. "내가 옳았어.

➡ _____

25 나는 조용히 잘 살았어.

➡ _____

26 너는 한때 왕이었지만 많은 어려움을 겪었지."

➡ _____

27 동생은 대답했다. "나는 내 선택을 후회하지 않아.

➡ _____

28 나는 지금 아무것도 없지만 언제까지나 기억할 어떤 것이 있어."

➡ _____

[01~03] 다음 글을 읽고 물음에 답하시오.

Two brothers went ___ⓐ___ a journey. They found a rock in front of a forest. ⓑIt said, "Go into the forest and swim ___ⓒ___ the river. There you will find a bear and her cubs. Take the bear cubs and run up the mountain. There you will find happiness."

01 위 글의 빈칸 ⓐ와 ⓒ에 들어갈 전치사가 바르게 짝지어진 것은?

① for - by
② in - across
③ on - across
④ on - over
⑤ in - by

서답형

02 위 글의 밑줄 친 ⓑIt이 가리키는 것을 본문에서 찾아 쓰시오.

➡ _____

중요

03 위 글의 바위에 쓰여 있는 내용이 <u>아닌</u> 것은?

① 숲에 들어가라.
② 강을 헤엄쳐 건너라.
③ 곰과 새끼들을 발견할 것이다.
④ 곰과 새끼들을 데리고 산 위로 뛰어 올라가라.
⑤ 산 위에서 행복을 찾을 수 있을 것이다.

[04~06] 다음 글을 읽고 물음에 답하시오.

The younger brother said, "Let's go and find happiness together." (①) "No," said the older brother, "How can we know this is true? (②) What if the river is too wide? (③) Besides, will it be easy to take the cubs away from their mother? (④) Instead of ⓐfinding happiness, we can be killed!" (⑤) They separated, and they both went their own way.

The younger brother went into the forest and swam across the river. There was the bear. She was sleeping. He took her cubs and ran up the mountain.

중요

04 위 글의 흐름으로 보아, 주어진 문장이 들어가기에 가장 적절한 곳은?

> The younger brother replied, "How can we know if we don't try?"

①　　②　　③　　④　　⑤

05 아래 보기에서 위 글의 밑줄 친 ⓐfinding과 문법적 쓰임이 같은 것의 개수를 고르시오.

┌─ 보기 ─┐
① He gave up finding happiness.
② Finding happiness is not difficult.
③ My goal is finding happiness.
④ She continued finding happiness.
⑤ There are many people finding happiness.
└────────┘

① 1개　② 2개　③ 3개　④ 4개　⑤ 5개

06 위 글의 내용과 일치하지 <u>않는</u> 것은?

① 형은 행복을 찾는 대신에 죽을 수 있다고 말했다.
② 동생은 위험하므로 시도하지 말자고 말했다.
③ 형과 동생은 헤어져서 자신의 길을 갔다.
④ 동생은 숲에 들어가서 강을 헤엄쳐 건넜다.
⑤ 어미 곰은 자고 있었다.

[07~09] 다음 글을 읽고 물음에 답하시오.

When he reached the top, some people took ①him to their city and made him their king. There he lived as a king for five years. Then a war broke out, and he lost his throne. ②He was on the road again.

One day, the two brothers met again and talked about their lives for the last five years. The older brother said, "I was right. ③I have lived quietly and well. ④You were once a king, but you have had a lot of trouble." The younger brother answered, "⑤I don't regret my choice. I may have nothing now, but I will always have something ⓐto remember."

07 위 글의 밑줄 친 ①~⑤ 중에서 가리키는 대상이 나머지 넷과 다른 것은?

①   ②   ③   ④   ⑤

08 위 글의 밑줄 친 ⓐto remember와 to부정사의 용법이 다른 것을 모두 고르시오.

① She has a few friends to play with.

② The book is too difficult to read.

③ It isn't easy to write good English.

④ I have something to tell you.

⑤ Give me a chance to go abroad.

09 위 글을 읽고 대답할 수 없는 질문은?

① Why did some people make the younger brother their king?

② Why did the younger brother lose his throne?

③ How has the older brother lived for the last five years?

④ What did they talk about when they met again?

⑤ Did the younger brother regret his choice?

[10~12] 다음 글을 읽고 물음에 답하시오.

The younger brother said, "Let's go and find happiness together." "No," said the older brother, "How can we know this is true? What if the river is too wide? Besides, will it be easy ⓐto take the cubs away from their mother? Instead of finding happiness, we can be killed!" The younger brother replied, "ⓑ How can we know if we don't try?" They separated, and they both went their own way.

The younger brother went into the forest and swam across the river. There was the bear. She was sleeping. He took her cubs and ran up the mountain.

10 위 글의 제목으로 알맞은 것을 고르시오.

① Let's Find Happiness Together

② Two Choices toward Happiness

③ What If This Is Not True?

④ The Older Brother's Doubtful Response

⑤ Put It Into Practice

11 위 글의 밑줄 친 ⓐto take와 to부정사의 용법이 다른 것을 모두 고르시오.

① She chose to go there by train.

② There is nothing to see.

③ My desire is to see you again.

④ He grew up to be a great musician.

⑤ To know oneself is difficult.

12 위 글의 밑줄 친 ⓑ에서 알 수 있는 동생의 성격으로 가장 알맞은 것을 고르시오.

① negative   ② selfish   ③ generous

④ passive   ⑤ challenging

[13~15] 다음 글을 읽고 물음에 답하시오.

A Book Review
Title: Jonathan Livingston Seagull: a story
Writer: Richard Bach
This story is about a seagull named Jonathan Livingston. He dreams of flying better than others. To reach ⓐhis goal, he works hard and practices flying. I like this story because it has helped me learn about the power of my own beliefs. The book says ⓑthat I can do anything ⓒthat I want if I do not give up.

서답형
13 위 글의 밑줄 친 ⓐhis goal이 가리키는 것을 본문에서 찾아 쓰시오.

➡ _____

중요
14 아래 보기에서 위 글의 밑줄 친 ⓑthat, ⓒthat과 문법적 쓰임이 같은 것을 각각 모두 고르시오.

┌─── 보기 ├───
① It's true that he was a little hungry.
② This is the house that we live in.
③ It's the best novel that I've ever read.
④ I believe that you'll pass the exam.
⑤ He is the first man that came here.
└─────────────

➡ ⓑ와 같은 것: _____ ,
  ⓒ와 같은 것: _____

서답형
15 다음 질문에 대한 알맞은 대답을 빈칸에 쓰시오. (2 단어)

Q: Why does the reviewer like this book?
A: Because it has helped the reviewer learn about the power of his/her _____ _____.

[16~18] 다음 글을 읽고 물음에 답하시오.

When he reached the top, some people took him to their city and made him their king. There he lived as a king for five years. Then a war broke out, and he lost his throne. ⓐ그는 다시 길바닥에 나앉았다.
One day, the two brothers met again and talked about their lives for the last five years. The older brother said, "I was right. I ⓑhave lived quietly and well. You were once a king, but you have had a lot of trouble." The younger brother answered, "I don't regret my choice. ⓒI may have something now, but I will always have nothing to remember."

서답형
16 밑줄 친 ⓐ의 우리말에 맞게 주어진 어휘를 이용하여 6단어로 영작하시오.

┌─────────────────────┐
│   on, road   │
└─────────────────────┘

➡ _____

17 위 글의 밑줄 친 ⓑhave lived와 현재완료의 용법이 같은 것을 모두 고르시오.

① She hasn't cleaned her room yet.
② I have studied English for two hours.
③ He has lost his car key.
④ Have you ever seen a lion?
⑤ She has been ill since last year.

서답형
18 밑줄 친 ⓒ에서 흐름상 어색한 부분 두 군데를 본문의 단어를 사용하여 고치시오.

➡ _____

[19~21] 다음 글을 읽고 물음에 답하시오.

Title: Jonathan Livingston Seagull: a story
Writer: Richard Bach

This story is about a seagull ⓐ Jonathan Livingston. He dreams of flying better than (A)[the other / others]. To reach his goal, he works (B)[hard / hardly] and practices flying. I like this story because it has helped me (C)[learn / learning] about the power of my own beliefs. The book says that I can do anything that I want if I do not give up.

서답형
19 위 글의 빈칸 ⓐ에 name을 알맞은 형태로 쓰시오.

➡ _____

서답형
20 위 글의 괄호 (A)~(C)에서 문맥이나 어법상 알맞은 낱말을 골라 쓰시오.

➡ (A)_____ (B)_____ (C)_____

21 위 글의 종류로 알맞은 것을 고르시오.

① essay　　　　② biography
③ book review　　④ diary
⑤ article

[22~25] 다음 글을 읽고 물음에 답하시오.

[Scene #4]
One day, the two brothers met again and talked about their lives for the last five years.
OB: Brother, we ⓐhaven't seen each other for a long time.
YB: Yes, it's been several years. ⓑHow have you been?
OB: I have lived quietly and well. And you?
YB: ⓒActually I became a king.

OB: Well.... You look like a traveler, not a king now.
YB: ⓓThat's true. I lost my throne after a war.
OB: So, I was right. I don't think you found happiness because you have had a lot of trouble.
YB: Well, I may have nothing now, but I will always have something to remember. I don't regret my choice.

중요
22 아래 보기에서 위 글의 밑줄 친 ⓐhaven't seen과 현재완료의 용법이 <u>다른</u> 것의 개수를 고르시오.

┌─ 보기 ─┐
① I have already seen the boy.
② How many times have you read it?
③ He has gone to Paris.
④ I have lived in Seoul since 2010.
⑤ How long has she been sick?
└────────┘

① 1개　② 2개　③ 3개　④ 4개　⑤ 5개

23 위 글의 밑줄 친 ⓑ와 바꿔 쓸 수 <u>없는</u> 말을 <u>모두</u> 고르시오.

① What have you been up to?
② What have you been doing?
③ How do you do?
④ How have you been getting along?
⑤ How are you feeling?

서답형
24 위 글의 밑줄 친 ⓒActually와 바꿔 쓸 수 있는 말을 쓰시오. (in과 as를 이용할 것) (두 개)

➡ _____

서답형
25 위 글의 밑줄 친 ⓓThat이 가리키는 것을 본문에서 찾아 쓰시오.

➡ _____

[01~03] 다음 글을 읽고 물음에 답하시오.

The younger brother said, "Let's go and find happiness together." "No," said the older brother, "How can we know this is true? ⓐ강이 너무 넓으면 어떡해? Besides, will it be easy to take the cubs away from their mother? Instead of finding happiness, we can be killed!" The younger brother replied, "How can we know if we don't try?" ⓑThey united, and they both went their own way.

The younger brother went into the forest and swam across the river. There was the bear. She was sleeping. He took her cubs and ran up the mountain.

01 위 글의 밑줄 친 ⓐ의 우리말에 맞게 다음 빈칸에 들어갈 알맞은 말을 쓰시오.

_____ _____ the river is too wide?

02 다음 빈칸 (A)~(D)에 알맞은 단어를 넣어 형과 동생이 선택한 것을 완성하시오.

The (A)_____ brother chose (B)_____ to go with his brother, and the (C)_____ brother alone went into the forest, swam across the river, took the cubs and (D)_____ up the mountain.

03 위 글의 밑줄 친 ⓑ에서 흐름상 어색한 부분을 찾아 고치시오.

➡ _____

[04~05] 다음 글을 읽고 물음에 답하시오.

When he (A)[reached / reached to] the top, some people took him to their city and made him their king. There he lived as a king for five years. Then a war (B)[broke / was broken] out, and he lost his ⓐ . He was on the road again.

One day, the two brothers met again and talked about their lives for the last five years. The older brother said, "I was right. I have lived (C)[quiet / quietly] and well. You were once a king, but you have had a lot of trouble." The younger brother answered, "I don't regret my choice. I may have nothing now, but I will always have something to remember."

04 위 글의 괄호 (A)~(C)에서 어법상 알맞은 낱말을 골라 쓰시오.

➡ (A)_____ (B)_____ (C)_____

05 주어진 영영풀이를 참고하여 빈칸 ⓐ에 철자 t로 시작하는 단어를 쓰시오.

the position of being king, queen, or emperor

➡ _____

[06~08] 다음 글을 읽고 물음에 답하시오.

The younger brother said, "Let's go and find happiness together." "No," said the older brother, "How can we know this is true? What if the river is too wide? Besides, will it be easy to take the cubs away from their mother? ⓐ Instead of finding happiness, we can kill!" The younger brother replied, "How can we know

ⓑif we don't try?" They separated, and they both went their own way.

The younger brother went into the forest and swam across the river. There was the bear. She was sleeping. He took her cubs and ran up the mountain.

06 위 글의 밑줄 친 ⓐ에서 어법상 **틀린** 부분을 찾아 고치시오.

➡ _____

07 형이 동생의 제안에 반대하는 이유 네 가지를 우리말로 쓰시오.

➡ (1) _____
(2) _____
(3) _____
(4) _____

08 위 글의 밑줄 친 ⓑ를 unless를 사용하여 고치시오.

➡ _____

[09~11] 다음 글을 읽고 물음에 답하시오.

When he reached the top, some people took him to their city and made him their king. There he lived as a king for five years. Then a war broke out, and he lost his throne. He was on the road again.

One day, the two brothers met again and talked about their lives ____ⓐ____ the last five years. The older brother said, "I was right. I have lived quietly and well. You were once a king, but you have had a lot of trouble." The younger brother answered, "I don't regret my choice. ⓑ나는 지금 아무것도 없지만 늘 기억할 어떤 것이 있을 거야."

09 위 글의 빈칸 ⓐ에 들어갈 알맞은 전치사를 쓰시오.

➡ _____

10 위 글의 밑줄 친 ⓑ의 우리말에 맞게 한 단어를 보충하여, 주어진 어휘를 알맞게 배열하시오.

something / will / I / have / remember / but / always / I / to / have / may / now / ,

➡ _____
_____

11 다음 빈칸 (A)와 (B)에 알맞은 단어를 넣어 지난 5년 동안 두 형제가 각자 어떻게 살았는지를 완성하시오.

The older brother has lived (A)_____ _____ _____ and the younger brother lived (B)_____ _____ _____ for the last five years.

[12~13] 다음 글을 읽고 물음에 답하시오.

A Book Review
Title: Jonathan Livingston Seagull: a story
Writer: Richard Bach

This story is about a seagull named Jonathan Livingston. He dreams of flying better than others. To reach his goal, he works hard and practices ____ⓐ____. I like this story because it has helped me learn about the power of my own beliefs. The book says that I can do anything that I want if I do not give up.

12 위 글의 빈칸 ⓐ에 fly를 알맞은 형태로 쓰시오.

➡ _____

13 본문의 내용과 일치하도록 다음 빈칸에 알맞은 단어를 쓰시오.

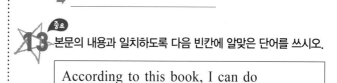

According to this book, I can do _____ that I want if I do not stop trying to do it.

Before You Read

A

There is a box filled with gold behind a tree across the river.
there is ~: ~가 있다   filled with: ~로 가득 찬

But watch out! Dangerous animals are in the river.
'주어+be 동사+부사구 ~.'에서 be동사는 '있다'로 해석한다.

B

Mr. Allen chose to go on journey to the city for his vacation.
choose는 to부정사를 목적어로 취한다. go on journey to ~: ~로 여행가다

Sadly the city streets were dirty and noisy. A car even almost hit him. He had
슬프게도(문장 전체 수식)   have trouble: 어려움을 겪다

lots of trouble there. After a few days in the city, he regretted his choice and
= in[at] the city

went back to his hometown.
접속사 and로 regretted와 went는 병렬 관계를 이룬다.

구문해설 • regret: 후회하다

Writing Workshop

A Book Review

Title: *Jonathan Livingston Seagull*: a story

Writer: Richard Bach

This story is about a seagull named Jonathan Livingston. He dreams of
~라는 이름을 가진

flying better than others. To reach his goal, he works hard and practices flying.
동명사 비교급 than: ~보다 더 잘 to부정사의 부사적 용법(목적)   practice는 목적어로 동명사를 취한다.

I like this story because it has helped me learn about the power of my own
help+목적어+동사원형[to부정사]

beliefs. The book says that I can do anything that I want if I do not give up.
접속사   관계대명사   = unless I

구문해설 • A named[called] B: B라는 이름을 가진[B라고 불리는] A • reach: ~에 도달하다
• goal: 목표 • practice: 연습하다 • belief: 믿음 • give up: 포기하다

Into the World

Happiness is when what you think, what you say, and what you do are in
접속사   복수 동사(주어는 3개의 what ~. what ~. and what ~)

harmony.   – Mahatma Gandhi

When one door of happiness closes, another opens. – Helen Keller
또 다른 하나(= another door)

Happiness is not something ready-made. It comes from your own actions.
-thing으로 끝나는 부정대명사는 형용사가 뒤에서 수식 = Happiness   자신의(소유격 강조)
                                                                – Dalai Lama XIV

구문해설 • harmony: 조화 • ready-made: 이미 만들어져 나오는[다 만들어서 파는], 기성품의, 준비된

해석

A

강 건너 나무 뒤에 황금으로 가득 찬 상자가 있다. 하지만 조심해! 위험한 동물들이 강에 있어.

B

Allen씨는 휴가를 보내기 위해 도시로 여행을 가기로 결정했다. 슬프게도 도시의 거리는 더럽고 시끄러웠다. 심지어 차가 그를 칠 뻔 했다. 그는 거기서 많은 어려움을 겪었다. 도시에서의 며칠 후, 그는 그의 선택을 후회하고 고향으로 다시 돌아갔다.

독서 감상문

제목: *Jonathan Livingston Seagull*(갈매기의 꿈): 이야기

작가: Richard Bach

이 이야기는 Jonathan Livingston이라는 이름의 갈매기에 대한 것이다. 그는 다른 갈매기들보다 더 잘 나는 것을 꿈꾼다. 그의 목표에 도달하기 위해 그는 열심히 노력하고 비행을 연습한다. 이 이야기가 내 자신의 믿음의 힘에 대해 배우도록 도와주었기 때문에 나는 이 이야기를 좋아한다. 이 책은 내가 포기하지 않으면 내가 원하는 어떤 것이라도 할 수 있다고 말한다.

행복은 생각, 말, 행동이 조화를 이룰 때 찾아온다.

– Mahatma Gandhi

행복의 한쪽 문이 닫히면 다른 쪽 문이 열리게 된다.

– Helen Keller

행복은 준비된 것이 아니다. 행복은 당신 자신의 행동에서 비롯된다.

– Dalai Lama XIV

Words & Expressions

01 다음 짝지어진 두 단어의 관계가 같도록 빈칸에 알맞은 말을 쓰시오.

(1) noisy : quiet – friendly : _____

(2) popular : popularity – happy : _____

02 다음 중 밑줄 친 부분의 뜻풀이가 바르지 <u>않은</u> 것은?

① Every <u>item</u> in the store is on sale! (품목)

② I made a <u>review</u> of his work in the paper. (논평)

③ At first, she wanted the role of Cinderella, the most important <u>character</u>. (성격)

④ What is the <u>title</u> of the bestseller? (제목)

⑤ They <u>separated</u> last month. (헤어졌다)

03 다음 영영풀이가 나타내는 말을 고르시오.

> having no errors

① correct   ② complete

③ wrong   ④ natural

⑤ entire

04 우리말에 맞게 주어진 단어를 알맞게 배열하시오.

(1) 왕은 오랫동안 자기 나라를 다스렸다. (for, the, his, long, a, ruled, king, time, country)

➡ _____

(2) 당신의 지지에 감사드려요. (thank, support, for, your, you)

➡ _____

Conversation

05 다음 중 의도하는 바가 나머지 넷과 <u>다른</u> 하나는?

① What's your opinion of that?

② How do you feel about that?

③ What do you think of that?

④ What do you feel like doing?

⑤ How do you feel about that?

06 다음 중 짝지어진 대화가 <u>어색한</u> 것은?

① A: I'm worried that I'm getting fat.
   B: Try not to worry about it too much.

② A: Make sure to come back before dark.
   B: Don't worry. We'll be back soon.

③ A: What do you think about the movie?
   B: It is good. I really enjoyed it.

④ A: The more we have, the more we want.
   B: I'm worried about you.

⑤ A: What do you think of my new shoes?
   B: I like them. They look great.

07 다음 대화의 빈칸에 알맞은 말을 고르시오.

> A: What do you think of our history class?
>
> B: _____

① It's difficult for me.

② It looks good on you.

③ I'm happy that you like it.

④ That's a great idea.

⑤ It looks light and fast.

[08~09] 다음 대화를 읽고 물음에 답하시오.

G: What do you think of this painting?
B: It looks (A)[great / greatly]. I like the colors.
G: I'm happy (B)[about / that] you like it. I painted it myself.

08 (A)와 (B)에서 알맞은 것을 골라 쓰시오.

➡ (A)＿＿＿＿＿ (B)＿＿＿＿＿

09 위 대화의 내용과 일치하도록 빈칸을 채우시오.

> They are talking ＿＿＿＿＿ which the girl ＿＿＿＿＿. The boy likes ＿＿＿＿＿ of the painting.

10 (A)와 (B)에 알맞은 것을 〈보기〉에서 골라 쓰시오

> ┤ 보기 ├
> Who   What   How   Why   Where

> B: (A)＿＿＿ do you think of our school cafeteria food?
> G: I think the cafeteria food is delicious.
> B: (B)＿＿＿ do you think is the best item?
> G: I like the Gimbap the best.

[11~12] 다음 대화를 읽고 물음에 답하시오.

G: I saw you with someone who looked like a foreigner yesterday.
B: ＿＿＿＿＿＿＿＿＿＿＿＿
G: ＿＿＿＿＿＿＿＿＿＿＿＿
B: ＿＿＿＿＿＿＿＿＿＿＿＿
G: ＿＿＿＿＿＿＿＿＿＿＿＿
B: 나는 전에는 영어로 말하는 것에 대해 걱정했었지만, 더 이상은 아니야.
G: I get really nervous when I try to speak in English.
B: Well, the first time is the hardest. After that, it gets easier and easier.
G: What do you think about me joining both of you for lunch?
B: That's a great idea.

> ┤ 보기 ├
> (A) We were. We try to meet twice a month for lunch.
> (B) You looked like you were having a good time.
> (C) Yes. We had lunch together.
> (D) I wish I could feel more comfortable talking with a foreigner.

11 위 대화의 빈칸에 들어갈 말을 〈보기〉에서 골라 순서대로 옳게 배열한 것은?

① (B)-(A)-(C)-(D)   ② (B)-(C)-(D)-(A)
③ (C)-(A)-(B)-(D)   ④ (C)-(B)-(A)-(D)
⑤ (C)-(D)-(B)-(A)

12 주어진 단어를 이용해 밑줄 친 우리말을 영작하시오. (총 11 단어)

➡ ＿＿＿＿＿＿＿＿＿＿＿＿

＿＿＿＿＿＿＿＿＿＿＿＿

(speak, anymore, be, about, in, worried)

Grammar

13 다음 빈칸에 들어갈 표현이 순서대로 바르게 짝지어진 것을 고르시오.

> Three years _____ since he _____ his home.

① have passed – left　② passed – left

③ passed – has left　④ have passed – has left

⑤ have passed – had left

14 다음 표를 보고 괄호 안에 주어진 어휘를 이용하여 빈칸을 알맞게 채우시오.

Spring people	friendly, talkative
Summer people	quiet, thoughtful
Fall people	energetic, active
Winter people	faithful, honest

➡ _____, you must be friendly and talkative. (if)

15 밑줄 친 부분의 쓰임이 나머지 넷과 다른 것은?

① Emily has studied math for 6 hours.

② How long have you played soccer?

③ Sean has lived in Korea for 4 years.

④ We have known Jerry since he was a little boy.

⑤ Someone has stolen my wallet.

16 빈칸에 공통으로 들어갈 접속사를 고르시오.

> • Mike, _____ you're finished, may I use the phone?
> • Let me know _____ you need my advice.

① if　　② because　　③ as

④ though　⑤ unless

17 다음 ⓐ~ⓔ 중 옳은 것을 모두 고르면?

> ⓐ I have met Mariel two years ago.
> ⓑ I have lost my cell phone.
> ⓒ How long have you been in Korea?
> ⓓ I have gone to Hong Kong.
> ⓔ I like this story because it has helped me learn about the power of my own beliefs.

① ⓐ, ⓒ　　　　② ⓐ, ⓓ

③ ⓑ, ⓒ　　　　④ ⓑ, ⓒ, ⓔ

⑤ ⓒ, ⓓ, ⓔ

18 다음 밑줄 친 부분의 쓰임이 나머지 넷과 다른 것은?

① If you leave now, you can catch the next train.

② I will be happy if I have a house someday.

③ I don't know if Sarah will like the idea.

④ If you're free tomorrow, let's go see a movie.

⑤ We will stay home if it rains tomorrow.

19 다음 중 어법상 어색한 문장은?

① If I wear warm clothes, I won't be cold.

② You will be late for school if you don't get up now.

③ The news of the war has caused great sadness around the world.

④ It's been several years since we met after graduation.

⑤ The writer has finished his new novel last week.

Reading

[20~22] 다음 글을 읽고 물음에 답하시오.

Two brothers went on a journey. ⓐ They founded a rock in front of a forest. It said, "Go into the forest and swim across the river. There you will find a bear and her __ⓑ__ . Take the bear __ⓑ__ and run up the mountain. ⓒThere you will find happiness."

20 위 글의 밑줄 친 ⓐ에서 흐름상 어색한 부분을 찾아 고치시오.

➡ _____

21 주어진 영영풀이를 참고하여 빈칸 ⓑ에 철자 c로 시작하는 단어를 쓰시오. (복수형으로 쓸 것)

the young of certain wild animals such as the bear or wolf or lion

➡ _____

22 위 글의 밑줄 친 ⓒThere가 가리키는 것을 본문에서 찾아 영어로 쓰시오.

➡ _____

[23~24] 다음 글을 읽고 물음에 답하시오.

The younger brother said, "Let's go and find happiness together." "No," said the older brother, "How can we know this is true? What if the river is too wide? ⓐBesides, will it be easy to take the cubs away from their mother? Instead of finding happiness, we can be killed!" The younger brother replied, "ⓑHow can we know if we don't try?" They separated, and they both went their own way.

The younger brother went into the forest and swam across the river. There was the bear. She was sleeping. He took her cubs and ran up the mountain.

23 위 글의 밑줄 친 ⓐBesides와 바꿔 쓸 수 있는 어휘를 쓰시오. (in을 이용할 것)

➡ _____

24 위 글의 밑줄 친 ⓑ와 어울리는 속담을 고르시오.

① Look before you leap.
② Nothing ventured, nothing gained.
③ Don't cry over spilt milk.
④ Easier said than done.
⑤ Every dog has his day.

[25~27] 다음 글을 읽고 물음에 답하시오.

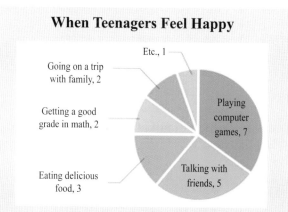

When Teenagers Feel Happy

We have asked our classmates ①when they are happy. Seven students say they are happy ②when they play computer games. Five students are happy ③when they talk with friends. Three students say they are happy ④ when they eat delicious food. There are two students who are happy ⑤when they get a good grade in math. And there are also two students who are happy when they go on a trip with family.

25 다음 빈칸에 들어갈 알맞은 말을 쓰시오.

_____ percent of the students are happy when they talk with friends.

26 밑줄 친 ①~⑤ 중에서 문법적 쓰임이 나머지 넷과 다른 것은?

①   ②   ③   ④   ⑤

27 위 글의 내용과 일치하지 <u>않는</u> 것은?

① 위 도표는 십대들이 언제 행복하다고 느끼는지를 조사한 표이다.

② 7명의 학생들은 컴퓨터 게임을 할 때 행복하다고 답했다.

③ 친구와 이야기할 때 행복한 학생이 맛있는 음식을 먹을 때 행복한 학생보다 더 많다.

④ 맛있는 음식을 먹을 때 행복한 학생이 수학에서 좋은 점수를 받을 때 행복한 학생보다 더 적다.

⑤ 가족과 여행갈 때 행복한 학생과 수학에서 좋은 점수를 받을 때 행복한 학생의 수는 같다.

[28~29] 다음 글을 읽고 물음에 답하시오.

A Book Review

Title: Jonathan Livingston Seagull: a story
Writer: Richard Bach

This story is about a seagull named Jonathan Livingston. He dreams of flying better than others. ⓐTo reach his goal, he works hard and practices flying. I like this story because it has helped me learn about the power of my own beliefs. The book says that I can do anything that I want if I do not give up.

28 아래 보기에서 위 글의 밑줄 친 ⓐTo reach와 to부정사의 용법이 같은 것의 개수를 고르시오.

┌─ 보기 ─
① It wasn't easy to reach his goal.
② He studied hard to reach his goal.
③ He went abroad to reach his goal.
④ He knew the best way to reach his goal.
⑤ He really wants to reach his goal.
└─

① 1개   ② 2개   ③ 3개   ④ 4개   ⑤ 5개

29 위 글을 읽고 대답할 수 <u>없는</u> 질문은?

① What's the title of this book?
② Who wrote this book?
③ Who is the main character?
④ What's the dream of Jonathan?
⑤ When does Jonathan practice flying?

[30~31] 다음 글을 읽고 물음에 답하시오.

Mr. Allen chose to go on a journey to the city for his vacation. Sadly, the city streets were dirty and noisy. A car even almost hit him. He had lots of trouble there. After a few days in the city, he ⓐ his choice and went back to his hometown.

30 위 글의 빈칸 ⓐ에 들어갈 알맞은 말을 고르시오.

① accepted   ② regretted
③ improved   ④ achieved
⑤ refused

31 위 글을 읽고 Mr. Allen의 심경 변화로 가장 알맞은 것을 고르시오.

① bored → disappointed
② expectant → pleased
③ frightened → satisfied
④ expectant → disappointed
⑤ satisfied → bored

출제율 95%

01 다음 제시된 단어를 사용하여 자연스러운 문장을 만들 수 없는 것은? (어형 변화 가능)

┌─ 보기 ─┐
regret   reply   rule   support
└───────┘

① Did you _____ a good time on your vacation?

② Rome _____ the world for more than 500 years.

③ I asked her what she does, but she didn't _____.

④ You should respect her choice and _____ her.

⑤ I _____ having been so careless.

[02~03] 다음 대화의 빈칸에 알맞은 말을 쓰시오.

출제율 90%

02

A: What do you think of these shoes?

B: They _____ good _____ you.

출제율 100%

03

A: I'm worried _____ the science project.

B: Don't worry. You _____ good _____ science.

출제율 90%

04 다음 주어진 우리말에 맞게 빈칸을 채우시오. (주어진 철자가 있으면 그 철자로 시작할 것)

(1) 만약 문제를 고치지 않으면, 그것은 점점 더 커질 거예요.

➡ If you don't get your problem fixed, it will get _____. (3 words)

(2) 행복은 돈보다 더 중요하다.

➡ H_____ is more important than money.

출제율 90%

05 다음 글의 빈칸에 알맞은 말을 고르시오.

I'm worried about my math test. I'm not good at math. I think I should _____.

① find the book that I borrowed from the library

② study harder to get good grades

③ speak in English

④ have a good time with friends

⑤ take my dog for a walk in the evening

출제율 95%

06 다음 대화의 순서를 바르게 배열하시오.

(A) Don't worry. It won't rain on Jejudo tomorrow.

(B) Oh, that's good to hear.

(C) Do you have any special plans for tomorrow?

(D) I'm going to Jejudo in the morning. But I'm worried about the weather.

➡ _____

출제율 85%

07 다음 대화의 빈칸 ⓐ~ⓔ에 들어갈 수 없는 표현을 고르시오.

B: Jina, can you go into your house ⓐ _____?

G: Why? What's ⓑ _____?

B: I'm scared of your dog.

G: Don't worry. He's a ⓒ _____ dog. He just looks ⓓ _____ because he's so ⓔ _____.

① friendly   ② big   ③ last

④ wrong   ⑤ scary

[08~11] 다음 대화를 물음에 답하시오.

W: Jimin, you look worried. What's wrong?

G: Mom, I can't find the book that I borrowed from the library. (①) Have you seen it? (②)

W: What book are you looking for? *Jonathan Livingston Seagull*? (③) I think I saw it in the living room.

G: Yes, that's it. Thank you, Mom. (④)

W: (A)_____, have you read the book? What did you think of it?

G: (⑤) It was really interesting. I loved the character of Jonathan a lot.

출제율 100%

08 ①~⑤ 중 주어진 문장이 들어갈 곳은?

I've read it two times already.

①   ②   ③   ④   ⑤

출제율 90%

09 위 대화에서 다음 영영풀이에 해당하는 단어를 찾아 쓰시오.

a person in a film, book, or play

➡ _____

출제율 95%

10 빈칸 (A)에 알맞은 말을 고르시오.

① Finally   ② On the other hand

③ Eventually   ④ By the way

⑤ On the contrary

출제율 100%

11 위 내화를 읽고 알 수 **없는** 것을 고르시오.

① How many times has the girl read *Jonathan Livingston Seagul*?

② What relationship are they?

③ What character does the woman like in *Jonathan Livingston Seagul*?

④ At first, why did the girl look worried?

⑤ What book did the girl borrow from the library?

출제율 90%

12 밑줄 친 우리말을 주어진 단어를 이용해 영작하시오.

B: 학교 식당 음식에 대해 어떻게 생각해?

G: I think the cafeteria food is delicious.

B: What do you think is the best item?

G: I like the Gimbap the best.

➡ _____

(think, what, of)

출제율 90%

13 다음 우리말을 주어진 어구를 이용하여 영작하시오.

(1) 그들은 모든 책을 다 팔았다. (그래서 남아 있는 책이 없다.) (sell, all the books)

➡ _____

(2) Mina는 벼룩시장에 한 번 가 본 적이 있다. (once, the flea market)

➡ _____

(3) 나는 태어난 이후로 Paris에서 살고 있다. (live, Paris, was born)

➡ _____

(4) 열차는 이미 역을 떠났다. (have, the station, depart, already)

➡ _____

(5) 내일 날씨가 화창하면, 우리는 해변에 갈 거야. (sunny, the beach)

➡ _____

(6) 그 옷이 너한테 잘 어울릴지 궁금해. (the dress, wonder, look, good, if, on)

➡ _____

출제율 90%

14 다음 중 어법상 **잘못된** 것을 바르게 고치시오.

(1) I have gone to the British Museum before.

➡ _____

(2) When has the technology become available on the market?

➡ _____

(3) Dr. Lee has studied animal diseases for 2002.

➡ _____

(4) Abigail lived in London until now.

➡ _____

(5) If you will push the button, the bell will ring.

➡ _____

[15~17] 다음 글을 읽고 물음에 답하시오.

The younger brother said, "Let's go and find happiness together." "No," said the older brother, "How can we know this is true? What if the river is too wide? Besides, @곰 새끼들을 엄마에게서 빼앗는 것이 쉬울까? ⓑ_____ finding happiness, we can be killed!" The younger brother replied, "How can we know ⓒif we don't try?" They separated, and they both went their own way.

The younger brother went into the forest and swam across the river. There was the bear. She was sleeping. He took her cubs and ran up the mountain.

출제율 95%

15 위 글의 밑줄 친 @의 우리말에 맞게 한 단어를 보충하여, 주어진 어구를 알맞게 배열하시오.

> their mother / easy / from / to take / will / away / the cubs / be

➡ _____
_____

출제율 95%

16 위 글의 빈칸 ⓑ에 들어갈 알맞은 말을 고르시오.

① In addition to ② Along with
③ Because of ④ Instead of
⑤ As well as

출제율 100%

17 위 글의 밑줄 친 ⓒif와 의미가 **다른** 것을 고르시오.

① I wonder if I should wear a coat.
② If you see him, give him this note.
③ If necessary, I can come at once.
④ You can stay for a week if you like.
⑤ If you work hard, you will succeed.

[18~20] 다음 글을 읽고 물음에 답하시오.

When he @reached the top, some people took him to their city and made him their king. There he lived as a king for five years. Then a war broke out, and he lost his throne. He was on the road again.

One day, the two brothers met again and talked about their lives for the last five years. (①) The older brother said, "I was right. (②) I have lived quietly and well. (③) You were once a king, but you have had a lot of trouble." (④) The younger brother answered, "(⑤) I may have nothing now, but I will always have something to remember."

18 위 글의 흐름으로 보아, 주어진 문장이 들어가기에 가장 적절한 곳은?

> I don't regret my choice.

①   ②   ③   ④   ⑤

19 위 글의 밑줄 친 ⓐreached와 바꿔 쓸 수 있는 말을 <u>모두</u> 고르시오.

① started from   ② left for
③ arrived at   ④ contacted
⑤ got to

20 위 글의 제목으로 알맞은 것을 고르시오.

① The Younger Brother Lived as a King!
② I'm Satisfied with My Choice!
③ Get along with Your Brother
④ The Quarrel between Two Brothers
⑤ How to Keep Harmonious Relations

[21~23] 다음 글을 읽고 물음에 답하시오.

When he reached the top, some people took him to their city and made him their king. There he lived as a king for five years. Then ⓐ전쟁이 일어났고, and he lost his throne. He was on the road again.

One day, the two brothers met again and talked about their lives for the last five years. The older brother said, "I was right. I have lived quietly and well. You were once a king, but you have had a lot of trouble." The younger brother answered, "I don't regret my choice. I ⓑmay have nothing now, ⓒbut I will always have something to remember."

21 위 글의 밑줄 친 ⓐ의 우리말을 네 단어로 쓰시오.

➡ _____

22 위 글의 밑줄 친 ⓑmay와 같은 의미로 쓰인 것을 고르시오.

① May I come in?
② He works hard so that he may succeed.
③ May she rest in peace.
④ The rumor may be true.
⑤ You may go there at any moment.

23 위 글의 밑줄 친 ⓒ를 읽고, 자신의 선택에 대한 'I'의 심경을 나타내는 가장 알맞은 말을 고르시오.

① bored   ② regretful
③ satisfied   ④ disappointed
⑤ anxious

[24~25] 다음 글을 읽고 물음에 답하시오.

> **Have You Ever Read *The Little Prince*?**
> It is a story about a prince who takes a trip to the stars. ⓐThe main character, the Little Prince, understands how important is his friend to him after his trip. It is such an interesting book. ⓑ Why don't you read it?

24 위 글의 밑줄 친 ⓐ에서 어법상 <u>틀린</u> 부분을 찾아 고치시오.

➡ _____

25 위 글의 밑줄 친 ⓑ와 같은 뜻이 되도록 How를 사용하여 바꿔 쓰시오.

➡ _____

[01~02] 대화의 ①~⑤ 중 흐름상이나 어법상 어색한 곳을 고치시오.

01

> G: ①Did you watch the movie, *The Daughter*?
> B: Yes, ②I saw it ③last Saturday.
> G: ④What did you think of it?
> B: ⑤I was excited. It wasn't very good.

➡ _____

02 (2개)

> G: ①What do you think with this painting?
> B: ②It looks great. ③I like the colors.
> G: ④I'm happy that you like it. ⑤I painted it mine.

➡ _____

_____

03 중요 대화의 밑줄 친 부분과 같은 뜻이 되도록 빈칸을 완성하시오.

> A: I'm worried about my math test.
> B: Don't worry. You'll do great.

➡ (1) _____ a_____ about my math test.

(2) _____ c_____ about my math test.

04 다음 빈칸에 알맞은 단어를 〈보기〉에서 골라 쓰시오.

> ┤ 보기 ├
> ago   before   for   since

(1) I met Juliet 5 years ago. We have known each other _____ five years.

(2) Yesterday I went to the zoo and saw a tiger. I have never seen it _____.

(3) I have taken piano lessons _____ I was young.

05 중요 다음 두 문장의 의미가 같도록 문장의 빈칸을 완성하시오.

(1) Eunji began to live in Kwangju 5 years ago, and she still lives there.
= Eunji _____ _____ in Kwangju for 5 years.

(2) Brian went to New York, so he isn't here now.
= Brian _____ _____ _____ New York.

(3) I visited the museum and it was my third visit.
= I _____ _____ the museum _____ _____ .

06 두 문장을 한 문장으로 쓰시오.

(1) Finish your report by 6, and you can play the computer games.
➡ _____

_____

(2) Work hard, or you won't overcome your weakness.
➡ _____

_____

07 다음 중 어법상 어색한 문장을 찾아 바르게 고쳐 쓰시오.

① We have asked our classmates when they are happy.

② If I will meet Suji, I will give her this letter.

③ Jim will go hiking if it is sunny tomorrow.

④ Work hard if you aim for the sky.

⑤ I like this story because it has helped me learn about the way to overcome my weakness.

➡ _____

[08~10] 다음 글을 읽고 물음에 답하시오.

When he reached the top, some people took him to their city and made him their king. There he lived as a king for five years. Then a war broke out, and he lost his throne. He was on the road again.

One day, the two brothers met again and talked about their lives for the last five years. The older brother said, "I was right. I have lived quietly and well. You were once a king, but you have had a lot of trouble." The younger brother answered, "I don't regret my ⓐ . I may have nothing now, but I will always have something to remember."

08 다음 문장에서 위 글의 내용과 다른 부분을 찾아서 고치시오.

> • When a war broke out, the older brother lost his throne and was on the road again.

➡ _____

09 위 글의 빈칸 ⓐ에 choose를 알맞은 형태로 쓰시오.

➡ _____

10 위 글을 읽고 자신들이 내렸던 선택에 대한 두 형제의 생각을 각각 우리말로 쓰시오.

➡ 형의 생각: " _____ "
  동생의 생각: " _____ "

[11~13] 다음 글을 읽고 물음에 답하시오.

The younger brother said, "Let's go and find happiness together." "No," said the older brother, "(A)[How / What] can we know this is true? What if the river is too wide? (B) [Beside / Besides], will it be easy to take the cubs away from their mother? ⓐ행복을 찾는 대신에, 우리는 죽을 수 있어!" The younger brother replied, "How can we know (C)[if / that] we don't try?" They separated, and they both went their own way.

The younger brother went into the forest and swam across the river. There was the bear. ⓑ She was sleeping. ⓒHe took her cubs and ran up the mountain.

11 위 글의 괄호 (A)~(C)에서 문맥과 어법상 알맞은 낱말을 골라 쓰시오.

➡ (A)_____ (B)_____ (C)_____

12 위 글의 밑줄 친 ⓐ의 우리말에 맞게 주어진 어휘를 이용하여 8 단어로 영작하시오.

> killed

➡ _____

13 위 글의 밑줄 친 ⓑShe와 ⓒHe가 가리키는 것을 본문에서 찾아 쓰시오.

➡ ⓑ_____ ⓒ_____

창의사고력 서술형 문제

01 주어진 정보와 그림을 이용해 빈칸에 알맞은 말을 쓰시오..

<조건>
- 걱정을 나타내는 표현을 사용할 것
- worry, read, finish를 이용할 것
- 접속사 that을 꼭 넣을 것

A: _____

B: Don't worry. I know you'll do great.

02 주어진 어구와 조건의 부사절을 이용하여 3 문장 이상을 쓰시오.

sunny	go to Jejudo	know the result	exercise hard
go hiking	swim in the sea	let me know	become healthy

(1) _____

(2) _____

(3) _____

(4) _____

03 자신이 좋아하는 책의 주인공을 소개하는 글을 완성하시오.

Have You Ever Read *the Little Prince*?

It is a story about a prince (A)_____ takes a trip to the stars. The main (B)_____, *the Little Prince*, understands (C)_____ important his friend is to him after his trip. It is (D)_____ an interesting book. (E)_____ read it?

단원별 모의고사

01 다음 짝지어진 단어의 관계가 나머지 넷과 <u>다른</u> 하나를 고르시오.

① separate – unite
② disappointed – discouraged
③ character – role
④ happiness – pleasure
⑤ correct – right

02 빈칸에 알맞은 말을 〈보기〉에서 골라 쓰시오.

> ┤ 보기 ├
> at for to about in as

> I'm worried _____ my dog. She has _____ stay alone during the day. I think I should take her _____ a walk _____ night.

03 다음 제시된 단어를 사용하여 자연스러운 문장을 만들 수 <u>없는</u> 것은?

> ┤ 보기 ├
> comfortable scary nervous noisy

① It's _____ to be all alone in this big house.
② I feel very _____ before an exam.
③ Select the _____ date and time.
④ I can't concentrate on my work in _____ places.
⑤ It helps people feel happier and more _____.

04 단어와 영영풀이의 연결이 <u>잘못된</u> 것을 고르시오.

① support: help, encouragement, or comfort given to someone during a difficult or unhappy time
② reply: to say or write something in response to something
③ teenager: a person between the ages of thirteen and nineteen
④ ever: at no time in the past or at no time in the future
⑤ separate: to move apart

05 다음 대화의 빈칸에 알맞은 말을 고르시오.

> A: _____
> B: Don't worry. You'll find something you like to do

① I never worry about your grades.
② I'm concerned about my dog.
③ I'm worried about speaking English.
④ I'm anxious about my speech test.
⑤ I'm worried about my future.

06 다음 괄호 안의 단어를 알맞게 배열하여 문장을 만드시오.

> A: (think, this, painting, what, of, do, you, ?)
> B: It's wonderful.

➡ _____

[07~08] 다음 대화를 읽고 물음에 답하시오.

B: Do you have any special plans for tomorrow?

G: I'm going to Jejudo in the morning. But I'm (A)_____ about the weather.

B: Don't worry. It (B)_____ rain on Jejudo tomorrow.

G: Oh, (C)_____

07 대화의 단어를 이용해 빈칸 (A)를 채우시오.

➡ _____

08 빈칸 (B)와 (C)에 들어갈 말로 알맞게 연결된 것을 고르시오.

(B)	(C)
① will	you'll do fine.
② will	that's good to hear.
③ won't	you'll do fine.
④ won't	that's good to hear.
⑤ won't	I'm sorry to hear that.

[09~10] 다음 대화를 읽고 물음에 답하시오.

B: Jina, can you go into your house first?

G: Why? What's wrong?

B: 난 네 개가 무서워.

G: Don't worry. He's a friendly dog. He just looks scary (A)_____ he's so big.

09 밑줄 친 우리말을 주어진 단어를 이용하여 영작하시오.

➡ _____ (scare)

10 빈칸 (A)에 알맞은 말을 고르시오.

① when   ② while
③ although   ④ which
⑤ because

[11~12] 다음 대화를 읽고 물음에 답하시오.

G: I saw you with someone who looked like a foreigner yesterday.

B: Yes. We had lunch together. (①)

G: You looked like you were having a good time. (②)

B: We were. We try to meet twice a month for lunch.

G: I wish I could feel more comfortable talking with a foreigner. (③)

B: I was worried about speaking in English before, but not anymore. (④)

G: I get really nervous when I try to speak in English.

B: Well, the first time is the hardest. (⑤)

G: What do you think about me joining both of you for lunch?

B: That's a great idea.

11 ①~⑤ 중 주어진 문장이 들어갈 곳은?

After that, it gets easier and easier.

①   ②   ③   ④   ⑤

12 대화에서 다음 영영풀이에 해당하는 단어를 찾아 쓰시오.

worried and anxious about something that is happening or might happen

➡ _____

13 대화의 빈칸 ⓐ~ⓔ에 들어갈 수 없는 표현을 고르시오. (대·소문자 무시)

W: Jimin, you ⓐ_____. What's wrong?

G: Mom, I can't find the book ⓑ_____ from the library. ⓒ_____ it?

W: What book are you looking for? *Jonathan Livingston Seagull*? I think I saw it in the living room.

G: Yes, that's it. Thank you, Mom.

W: By the way, ⓓ _____ the book? ⓔ _____ of it?

G: I've read it two times already. It was really interesting. I loved the character of Jonathan a lot.

① that I borrowed
② have you seen
③ look interested
④ what did you think
⑤ have you read

14 다음 주어진 문장의 밑줄 친 부분과 쓰임이 같은 것은?

· If you have any problems, I will help you.

① I don't know <u>if</u> Sarah will like the idea.
② The woman was not sure <u>if</u> the thief was a man or a woman.
③ You can go out and play <u>if</u> you finish your homework by three.
④ Please see <u>if</u> the children are dressed for school.
⑤ Only time will tell <u>if</u> I was wrong or not.

15 다음 중 어법상 어색한 것을 고르시오.

① I have never seen Minho since he moved to Yongin.
② I have already had lunch an hour ago.
③ If I can stand the cold, I will help the prince more.
④ You will get wet if you go out now.
⑤ I was ill yesterday and don't feel any better today.

16 다음 문장에서 어법상 <u>어색한</u> 것을 바르게 고치시오.

(1) When have you started working at the company?

➡ _____

(2) Today is July 10, and I arrived here on July 1. So, I was here for 10 days.

➡ _____

(3) She has taught them English since two years.

➡ _____

(4) If you will sleep in class, your teacher will be angry.

➡ _____

(5) Unless she doesn't wear a muffler, she will be cold.

➡ _____

_____

17 주어진 두 문장을 현재완료를 이용해 한 문장으로 만드시오.

(1) Judy arrived at her friend's house two hours ago. She is still in her friend's house.

➡ _____

(2) Someone took away my umbrella. So, I don't have my umbrella now.

➡ _____

[18~20] 다음 글을 읽고 물음에 답하시오.

The younger brother said, "Let's go and find happiness together." "No," said the older brother, "How can we know this is true? What if the river is too wide? ⓐ , will ⓑ it be easy to take the cubs away from their mother? Instead of finding happiness, we can be killed!" The younger brother replied, "How can we know if we don't try?" They separated, and they both went their own way.

The younger brother went into the forest and swam across the river. There was the bear. She was sleeping. He took her cubs and ran up the mountain.

18 위 글에서 알 수 있는 형의 성격으로 가장 알맞은 것을 고르시오.

① positive
② doubtful
③ active
④ confident
⑤ diligent

19 위 글의 빈칸 ⓐ에 들어갈 알맞은 말을 고르시오.

① However
② Therefore
③ Besides
④ For example
⑤ In other words

20 위 글의 밑줄 친 ⓑit과 문법적 쓰임이 같은 것을 고르시오.

① Did you make it?
② It was raining this morning.
③ I make it a rule to get up early.
④ It is 2 miles from here to the airport.
⑤ It is impossible to get there in time.

[21~24] 다음 글을 읽고 물음에 답하시오.

When he reached the top, some people took him ___ⓐ___ their city and made him their king. There he lived ⓑas a king for five years. Then a war broke out, and he lost his throne. He was on the road again.

One day, the two brothers met again and talked ___ⓒ___ their lives for the last five years. The older brother said, "I was right. I have lived quietly and well. You were once a king, but you have had a lot of trouble." The younger brother answered, "I don't regret my choice. I may have nothing now, but I will always have something to remember."

21 위 글의 빈칸 ⓐ와 ⓒ에 들어갈 전치사가 바르게 짝지어진 것은?

① to - for
② for - about
③ for - to
④ to - about
⑤ on - to

22 위 글의 밑줄 친 ⓑas와 같은 의미로 쓰인 것을 고르시오.

① As we go up, the air grows colder.
② He is famous as a statesman.
③ As I was tired, I soon fell asleep.
④ Do in Rome as the Romans do.
⑤ Take as much as you want.

23 다음 질문에 대한 알맞은 대답을 빈칸에 쓰시오.

Q: Why did the younger brother answer that he didn't regret his choice?
A: Because maybe he didn't have anything then, but there would always be something that he could _____.

24 위 글의 내용과 일치하지 않는 것은?

① 동생이 도시에 도착했을 때, 어떤 사람들이 그를 그들의 왕으로 만들었다.
② 동생은 5년간 왕으로 살았다.
③ 지난 5년 동안 형은 조용히 잘 살았다.
④ 동생은 자신의 선택을 후회하지 않는다고 말했다.
⑤ 동생은 지금 아무것도 없지만 언제까지나 기억할 거리가 있다고 말했다.

Lesson 5

We Love Baseball

 의사소통 기능

- 선호하는 것 묻고 답하기
  A: Which story book do you like? *Peter Pan* or
  The Last Leaf?
  B: I like *Peter Pan*.

- 희망, 기대 표현하기
  A: What are you going to do on your vacation?
  B: I'm going to take a boat ride. I can't wait.

언어 형식

- 부가의문문
  Jian, this is your first time to come to the
  baseball stadium, **isn't it**?

- 수동태
  The numbers **were determined** by the players'
  batting order.

Words & Expressions
교과서

Key Words

- **anxious** [ǽŋkʃəs] 형 불안한
- **base** [beis] 명 (야구의) 루, 베이스
- **batter** [bǽtər] 명 타자
- **better** [bétər] 형 더 좋은, 더 나은(**good**의 비교급)
- **competition** [kàmpətíʃən] 명 대회
- **crack** [kræk] 명 찢어지는 듯한[날카로운] 소리
- **decide** [disáid] 동 결정하다
- **determine** [ditə́ːrmin] 동 결정하다
- **dirt** [dəːrt] 명 먼지, 때
- **either** [íːðər] 부 (부정문에서) ~도
- **fit** [fit] 동 맞다
- **forget** [fərgét] 동 잊다
- **get** [get] 동 획득하다, 사다
- **hide** [haid] 동 감추다, 숨기다
- **home run** 홈런
- **home team** 홈팀
- **international** [ìntərnǽʃənəl] 형 국제적인
- **match** [mætʃ] 명 경기, 성냥
- **mean** [miːn] 동 의미하다
- **miss** [mis] 동 놓치다, 그리워하다
- **order** [ɔ́ːrdər] 명 순서, 명령
- **past** [pæst] 명 과거
- **pet** [pet] 명 애완동물
- **pitch** [pitʃ] 명 투구
- **rock climbing** 암벽 등반
- **rule** [ruːl] 명 규칙
- **shorts** [ʃɔːrts] 명 반바지
- **sometime** [sʌ́mtàim] 부 언젠가
- **stadium** [stéidiəm] 명 경기장
- **support** [səpɔ́ːrt] 동 (특정 스포츠 팀을) 응원하다, 지원하다
- **team** [tiːm] 명 팀
- **then** [ðen] 부 (시간적·공간적으로) 그 뒤에, 그런 다음
- **thunder** [θʌ́ndər] 명 천둥
- **ticket** [tíkit] 명 티켓
- **vacation** [veikéiʃən] 명 휴가
- **visit** [vízit] 동 방문하다
- **visiting team** 원정 팀

Key Expressions

- **at bat** 타석에 서서
- **be a big fan of** ~의 열렬한 팬이다
- **be about to** 동사원형 막 ~하려고 하다
- **be excited about** ~에 신나다, ~에 들뜨다
- **between A and B** A와 B 사이에
- **can't wait to** 동사원형 ~을 몹시 기대하다
- **come back to** ~로 돌아오다
- **come out** 나오다
- **hurry up** 서둘러 ~하다
- **I can't wait** 너무 기다려져
- **in a hurry** 서둘러
- **in the past** 과거에
- **live in** ~에서 살다
- **look at** ~을 보다
- **look forward to** (동)명사 ~을 기대하다
- **over there** 저기, 저쪽에
- **think about** ~에 대해 생각하다
- **twice a week** 일주일에 두 번
- **wait for** ~을 기다리다
- **warm up** (스포츠나 활동 전에) 몸을 천천히 풀다, 준비 운동을 하다
- **Which** 명사 **do you like** (**better/more**), **A or B**? A나 B 중 어느 것이 (더) 좋습니까?
- **which** 명사 어느 명사
- **while**+동사**ing** ~하는 동안
- **Why don't you** ~? ~하는 게 어때?
- **Why not**? 좋아, 왜 아니겠어?
- **would like to** 동사원형 ~하고 싶다

Word Power

※ 동작 동사에 'er'을 붙여 동작의 행위자가 되는 단어 (어미가 e로 끝나면 r만 붙임)

- □ **bake**(굽다) – **baker**(제빵사)
- □ **bat**(공을 치다) – **batter**(타자)
- □ **drive**(운전하다) – **driver**(운전자)
- □ **lead**(지휘하다, 이끌다) – **leader**(지도자)
- □ **manage**(경영하다) – **manager**(경영자)

- □ **play**(경기를 하다) – **player**(선수)
- □ **run**(달리다) – **runner**((달리기) 주자)
- □ **sing**(노래하다) – **singer**(가수)
- □ **teach**(가르치다) – **teacher**(교사)
- □ **write**(쓰다) – **writer**(작가)

※ 'go' vs 'play'

- □ **go skiing** 스키 타러 가다
- □ **go surfing** 서핑하러 가다
- □ **go swimming** 수영하러 가다

- □ **play baseball** 야구를 하다
- □ **play soccer** 축구를 하다
- □ **play tennis** 테니스를 치다

English Dictionary

- □ **anxious** 불안한
  → very nervous or worried about something
  매우 긴장하거나 어떤 것에 대해 걱정을 하는

- □ **base** (야구의) 루, 베이스
  → each corner of the square that makes a baseball diamond
  (야구) 내야를 만드는 사각형의 각 모퉁이

- □ **competition** 대회
  → an event or contest in which people try to win something by defeating others
  사람들이 다른 사람들을 물리침으로써 어떤 것을 얻으려고 하는 행사나 경기

- □ **crack** 찢어지는 듯한[날카로운] 소리
  → the sudden loud explosive sound of something when it falls or bumps into itself or something else
  어떤 것이 떨어지거나 자체로 또는 다른 것과 부딪칠 때 나는 갑작스러운 큰 폭발음

- □ **determine** 결정하다
  → to decide or establish something conclusively
  최종적으로 어떤 것을 결정하거나 수립하다

- □ **either** (부정문에서) ~도
  → used in a negative sentence to indicate a similarity with a statement just made
  부정문에서 방금 언급된 진술에 대해 비슷함을 보여주기 위해 사용되는 것

- □ **fit** 맞다
  → to be the right size and shape for someone or something
  어떤 사람이나 사물에 알맞은 크기나 모양이 되다

- □ **hide** 감추다, 숨기다
  → to put something out of sight
  보이지 않는 곳에 무언가를 두다

- □ **home team** 홈팀
  → a sports team playing on its own ground
  홈그라운드에서 경기를 하는 스포츠 팀

- □ **international** 국제적인
  → relating to or involving different countries
  다른 나라들을 포함하거나 관련된

- □ **order** 순서
  → the arrangement or disposition of people or things in a list from first to last
  어떤 목록에서 처음부터 끝까지 사람이나 사물의 배열이나 배치

- □ **past** 과거
  → the time before the moment of speaking or writing
  말하거나 쓰는 순간 이전의 시간

- □ **pitch** 투구
  → a throw of the ball for the batter to hit it
  타자가 치도록 공을 던지는 것

- □ **stadium** 경기장
  → an athletic or sports ground used for playing and watching sports with rows of seats
  운동 경기를 하고 그 경기를 보기 위해 사용되는 여러 줄의 의자가 있는 육상경기나 운동경기장

- □ **team** 팀
  → a group of people who play a sport or game together against other groups of people
  다른 모임의 사람들에 대항해서 운동이나 경기를 함께 하는 사람들의 모임

- □ **thunder** 천둥
  → the loud noise in the sky heard after a lightning flash during a storm
  폭풍우 동안 번개가 번쩍인 후에 들리는 하늘에서 나는 큰 소리

- □ **ticket** 티켓
  → an official piece of paper or card that shows you have paid to enter a place or do something
  어느 장소에 들어가기 위해 또는 어떤 것을 하기 위해 당신이 돈을 지불했다는 것을 보여 주는 공식적인 종이나 카드

- □ **visiting team** 원정 팀
  → a sports team playing on the competing team's field or court
  경쟁하는 팀의 경기장이나 코트에서 경기를 하는 스포츠 팀

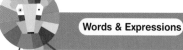

01 다음 중 낱말의 관계가 나머지와 다른 하나는?

① lead – leader   ② bake – baker
③ sing – singer   ④ teach – teacher
⑤ cook – cooker

서답형
02 다음 우리말을 주어진 어휘를 알맞게 배열하여 영작하시오.

내가 네게 막 전화를 걸려던 참인데 네가 전화했어.
(I, me, you, you, was, call, called, when, to, about) (I로 시작할 것)

➡ _____

03 다음 빈칸에 들어갈 말로 알맞은 것은?

Let's take the problems in a different
_____.

① order   ② class
③ lesson   ④ kind
⑤ nature

서답형
04 다음 빈칸에 공통으로 들어갈 말을 쓰고 그 뜻을 쓰시오.

(1) Is there a particular baseball team that you _____?
(2) His parents wanted to _____ the community center.
(3) Without the _____ of your friends you will not succeed.

(1) _____ (2) _____ (3) _____

중요
05 다음 빈칸에 공통으로 알맞은 말을 고르시오. (대·소문자 무시)

• You can go slow because this work is not _____ a hurry.
• _____ the past, doctors didn't know the reason.

① at   ② from   ③ to
④ in   ⑤ as

06 다음 중 밑줄 친 'miss'의 뜻이 〈보기〉와 다른 것을 고르시오.

┤ 보기 ├
Hurry up, or you'll <u>miss</u> the school bus.

① I hate to <u>miss</u> the beginning of a movie.
② Do not <u>miss</u> this exciting festival next year.
③ I'm sure you will <u>miss</u> your school days.
④ Don't <u>miss</u> this chance to learn and experience science!
⑤ It's a pity to <u>miss</u> the match.

07 다음 영영 풀이에 해당하는 단어를 고르시오.

the loud noise in the sky heard after a lightning flash during a storm

① earthquake   ② wave
③ hurricane   ④ thunder
⑤ typhoon

01 다음 〈보기〉와 같은 관계가 되도록 빈칸에 알맞은 말을 쓰시오.

┌─ 보기 ─┐
act – actor

(1) bat – _____ (2) write – _____

02 다음 주어진 두 문장이 비슷한 의미가 되도록 빈칸을 알맞게 채우시오.

I'm looking forward to the New Year's Eve party.
➡ I _____ _____ for the New Year's Eve party.

03 다음 빈칸에 알맞은 단어를 〈보기〉에서 골라 쓰시오.

┌─ 보기 ─┐
home team   match   stadium   thunder

(1) This _____ is so huge, isn't it?
(2) The _____ beat the visiting team 3 to 0.
(3) The alarm sounds like _____.
(4) The Spanish team is leading the soccer _____.

04 다음 대화의 빈칸에 공통으로 들어갈 말을 쓰시오.

A: _____ don't we go skiing together this afternoon?
B: _____ not?

[05~06] 다음 빈칸에 공통으로 들어갈 말을 쓰시오.

05
• He wanted to _____ back to Paris.
• New novels _____ out almost every day.

06
• Can you hurry _____? I don't have much time.
• Warm _____ before lifting heavy weights.

07 다음 주어진 우리말에 맞게 빈칸을 채우시오. (철자가 주어진 것도 있음)

(1) 나는 비틀즈의 열렬한 팬이다.
➡ I am _____ _____ _____ _____ the Beatles.
(2) 내가 가장 좋아하는 선수가 타석에 선다.
➡ My favorite player is _____ _____.
(3) 조용히 해 주세요. 영화가 곧 시작합니다.
➡ Be quiet, please. The movie _____ _____ start.
(4) 저기 검정색 재킷을 입은 여자는 누구인가요?
➡ Who is that woman _____ _____ in the black jacket?
(5) 나는 일주일에 두 번 요가를 한다.
➡ I do yoga _____ _____ _____.
(6) 음악 클럽에 가입하고 싶어요.
➡ I would _____ _____ join a music club.

교과서

Conversation

1 선호하는 것 묻고 답하기

A Which story book do you like? *Peter Pan* or *The Last Leaf*?

너는 어느 이야기책을 좋아하니? "피터팬" 아니면 "마지막 잎새?"

B I like *Peter Pan*. "피터팬"을 좋아해.

■ 주어진 대상 가운데 어느 것을 더 좋아하는지를 물을 때는 'Which do you like better[more], A or B?' 또는 'Which do you prefer, A or B?' 등으로 표현한다. which는 뒤에 나오는 명사를 수식하는 의문형용사로 쓰일 수 있다.

· Which (sport) do you like more[better], baseball or soccer?

· Which do you prefer, baseball or soccer?

■ 더 좋아하는 것에 대해 말할 때는 'I like A.', 'I like A better[more] than B.' 또는 'I prefer A to B.'로 표현한다. 이때 비교 대상이 되는 'than B'나 'to B'는 생략할 수 있다. 'prefer A to B'에서 to가 전치사이므로 뒤에 (동)명사가 오는 것에 유의해야 한다.

· A: Which color do you prefer, red or blue?

B: I prefer red (to blue). / I love red (more than blue). / I like red (more than blue).

선호 묻기

· Which (명사) do[would] you like better[more], A or B?

· Which (명사) do you prefer?

· Which (명사) do you prefer, A or B?

선호 대답하기

· I like A.　　· I like A better[more] than B.　　· I prefer A (to B).

핵심 Check

1. 다음 우리말과 일치하도록 빈칸에 알맞은 말을 쓰시오.

A: _____ do you like better, meat _____ _____? (너는 어느 것을 더 좋아하니? 고기 아니면 생선?)

B: I prefer _____ to fish. (나는 생선보다 고기를 더 좋아해.)

2. 다음 우리말과 일치하도록 주어진 단어를 배열하여 문장을 완성하시오.

A: _____ _____ _____ _____ _____, _____ _____ _____?

(cats, do, dogs, which, you, or, better, like)

(너는 어느 것을 더 좋아하니, 개 아니면 고양이?)

B: I like dogs. (나는 개를 좋아해.)

② 희망, 기대 표현하기

A What are you going to do on your vacation? 휴가 때 무엇을 할 예정이니?

B I'm going to take a boat ride. I can't wait. 나는 보트를 타러 갈 거야. 너무 기다려져.

- 'I can't wait.'는 '너무 기다려져.' 또는 '나는 빨리 ~했으면 좋겠다.'라는 의미로 희망이나 기대를 나타내는 표현이다. 'I can't wait.' 뒤에는 'for+명사'나 'to+동사원형'을 덧붙여 쓸 수 있다. 'I'm going to take a boat ride. I can't wait.'에서 'I can't wait'를 'I can't wait for a boat ride.'나 'I can't wait to take a boat ride.'로 쓸 수 있다.

- 유사한 표현으로는 'I'm looking forward to+(동)명사'가 있다. 'I can't wait' 다음의 to 다음에는 동사원형이 오는 것과 달리, 'I'm looking forward to'의 to는 전치사이므로, 뒤에는 (동)명사가 오는 것에 주의해야 한다.

희망, 기대 표현하기

- I can't wait. 너무 기다려져.
- I can't wait for 명사.
- I can't wait to 동사원형.
- I'm looking forward to (동)명사.

핵심 Check

3. 다음 대화의 순서를 바르게 배열하시오.

   (A) That sounds great.

   (B) What are your plans for this weekend?

   (C) Yes. I'm looking forward to it.

   (D) I'm going to go to the party this Saturday.

   ➡ _____

4. 다음 주어진 단어를 이용하여 대화의 밑줄 친 부분과 같은 의미의 문장을 쓰시오.

   A: I heard that you are going to take the trip this summer.

   B: Yeah! I'm looking forward to taking the trip.

   ➡ _____ (for, wait)

   _____ (to, wait)

5. 다음 대화의 우리말과 일치하도록 빈칸에 알맞은 말을 쓰시오.

   A: Do you want to watch *Harry Potter* with me this weekend? (나와 이번 주말에 해리 포터 볼래?)

   B: Sure, I'd love to. I _____ wait _____ watch it. (물론, 그리고 싶어. 그것을 정말 보고 싶어.)

Listen & Speak 1 B-2

G: I'm ❶thinking about getting a pet. Do you have a pet?

B: Yes, I do. I have a dog and a cat.

G: ❷What do you think? ❸Which pet is better for me? A cat or a dog?

B: ❹Why don't you come to my house someday and play with my pets? ❺Then you can decide.

G: 나는 애완동물을 기르는 것에 대해 생각 중이야. 넌 애완동물을 기르니?

B: 응, 길러. 개와 고양이가 있어.

G: 어떻게 생각해? 어떤 애완동물이 나에게 더 나아? 고양이 아니면 개?

B: 어느 날 우리 집에 와서 내 애완동물과 놀아 보는 게 어때? 그런 다음 너는 결정할 수 있을 거야.

❶ think about: ~에 대해서 생각하다 (= think of)

❷ What do you think?: 어떻게 생각해? (의견을 묻는 표현) 대화의 흐름상 애완동물을 기르는 것에 대해 어떻게 생각하는지 상대방의 의견을 묻고 있다. (= What do you think about[of] getting a pet?)

❸ better는 good의 비교급으로 '더 좋은'의 의미를 가진다.

❹ Why don't you ~?: ~하는 게 어때? (상대방에게 권유) come과 play는 접속사 and로 연결되어 있다.

❺ then: (시간적·공간적으로) 그 뒤에, 그런 다음 decide 다음에 내용상 'which pet is better for you(어떤 동물이 더 나을지)'가 생략되어 있다.

Check(√) True or False

(1) The girl has a dog and a cat.　　　　　　　　　　　　　　T ☐ F ☐

(2) The boy advises the girl to come to his house and play with his pets.　　　T ☐ F ☐

Listen & Speak 2 B-1

G: Do you ❶want to see my new mountain bike?

B: Sure. ❷When did you get it?

G: ❸Yesterday my father bought it for me. Can you come to my house this afternoon?

B: Of course. ❹I can't wait to see it.

G: 내 새 산악 자전거를 보고 싶니?

B: 물론이지. 언제 생긴 거야?

G: 어제 아빠가 나에게 사 주셨어. 오늘 오후에 우리 집에 올래?

B: 당연하지. 나는 그것을 빨리 보고 싶어.

❶ mountain bike: 산악 자전거 want는 to부정사를 목적어로 갖는다.

❷ when: 언제 get: 얻다, 사다

❸ bought는 buy(사다)의 과거형이다. it은 my new mountain bike를 받는 대명사이다. buy+간접목적어(~에게)+직접목적어(~을, 를)[4형식] = buy+직접목적어+for+간접목적어[3형식]

❹ 'I can't wait.'는 '너무 기다려져.' 또는 '나는 빨리 ~했으면 좋겠다.'라는 의미로, 희망이나 기대를 표현할 때 사용한다. I can't wait to see it. = I'm looking forward to seeing it.

Check(√) True or False

(3) The girl bought a new mountain bike yesterday.　　　　　　　T ☐ F ☐

(4) The boy is going to go to the girl's house this afternoon.　　　T ☐ F ☐

Listen & Speak 1 A

> M: ❶Which sport do you like? Soccer or basketball?
>
> G: ❷I like soccer more. I play soccer ❸twice a week.

❶ Which 명사 do you like (better/more), A or B?: 어떤 ~가 더 좋아? A 아니면 B?

❷ 더 좋아하는 것에 대해 말할 때는 'I like A.', 'I like A better[more] than B.' 또는 'I prefer A to B.'로 표현한다. 이때 비교 대상이 되는 'than B'나 'to B'는 생략할 수 있다.

❸ twice a week: 일주일에 두 번

 Listen & Speak 1 B-1

> G: ❶What are you doing?
>
> B: ❷I'm looking at a world map.
>
> G: You checked two countries. ❸Which country would you like to visit first? The U.S. or Mexico?
>
> B: I want to visit the U.S. I'd like to see a basketball game there.

❶ What are you doing?: 뭐 하고 있어?

❷ 대상의 동작이나 현재의 상태를 묘사할 때 현재진행형을 사용할 수 있다. look at: ~을 보다

❸ would like to 동사원형: ~하고 싶다 visit: 방문하다

 Listen & Speak 2 A

> G: Did you ❶get the tickets?
>
> B: ❷Yes! ❸I can't wait to watch the game.

❶ get: 얻다, 사다

❷ Yes! 다음에 'I did.'가 생략되어 있다.

❸ can't wait to 동사원형: ~하기를 몹시 기대하다(희망, 기대 표현하기) 'can't wait for+명사'나 'can't wait to+동사원형'의 형태를 취할 수 있다. I can't wait to watch the game. = I'm looking forward to watching the game.)

 Listen & Speak 2 B-2

> B: ❶Don't forget that we're going rock climbing this weekend!
>
> G: ❷Don't worry. ❸I won't forget.
>
> B: I'm excited about going. I can't wait.

❶ 상대방에게 어떠한 일을 할 것을 상기시켜 줄 때는 'Don't forget that 주어+동사 ~.' 또는 'Don't forget to+동사원형 ~.'으로 말할 수 있다. 의미는 '~할 것을 잊지 마' 정도로 볼 수 있다.

❷ 'Don't worry.'는 '걱정 마.'의 의미로 상대방을 안심시킬 때 사용한다.

❸ won't는 will not을 줄여 쓴 말이다. forget 다음에 'that we're going rock climbing this weekend'가 생략되어 있다.

 Listen & Speak 2 B-3

> G: Did you hear about Jisu?
>
> B: What about her? She ❶lives in Canada.
>
> G: She ❷came back to Korea last month. She wants to see you.
>
> B: Oh, ❸I can't wait to see her.

❶ live in: ~에서 살다

❷ come back to: ~로 돌아오다

❸ I can't wait: 너무 기다려져

 Real-Life Zone A

> B1: Jiho, why are you ❶in such a hurry?
>
> B2: Hi, Alex! I ❷have to be home before 6:00. The game ❸between the Thunders and the Cobras starts at 6:00.
>
> B1: Oh, are you a baseball fan? ❹Which team do you support? The Cobras or the Thunders?
>
> B2: The Cobras.
>
> B1: Me, too! ❺I don't want to miss the game either.
>
> B2: ❻Hurry up! We only have thirty minutes ❼left.
>
> B1: Okay. Maybe we can watch a game together ❽sometime.
>
> B2: That's a great idea! ❾How about going to the next Cobras home game together?
>
> B1: Okay. They have a game next Saturday. We can eat fried chicken ❿while watching the game!
>
> B2: That sounds great. I can't wait!

❶ in a hurry: 서둘러

❷ have to 동사원형: ~해야 한다

❸ between A and B: A와 B 사이의

❹ support: (특정 스포츠 팀을) 응원하다

❺ miss: 놓치다 either: (부정문에서) ~도

❻ hurry up: 서두르다

❼ leave: 남아 있다 → left: 남겨진

❽ sometime: 언젠가

❾ How about (동)명사 ~?: ~하는 게 어때?, ~하지 않을래?(제안하기)

❿ while+동사ing: ~하는 동안

● 다음 우리말과 일치하도록 빈칸에 알맞은 말을 쓰시오.

Listen & Speak 1 A

M: _____ _____ do you like? Soccer _____ basketball?

G: I like soccer _____. I play soccer _____ a _____.

Listen & Speak 1 B

1. G: What are you _____?

   B: _____ looking _____ a world map.

   G: You checked two countries. _____ _____ would you like to visit first? The U.S. _____ Mexico?

   B: I want _____ _____ the U.S. I'd _____ _____ see a basketball game there.

2. G: _____ _____ about _____ a pet. Do you _____ a pet?

   B: Yes, I do. I have a dog and a cat.

   G: _____ do you think? _____ pet is _____ for me? A cat _____ a dog?

   B: _____ _____ you come to my house someday and _____ _____ my pets? Then you _____ _____.

Listen & Speak 2 A

G: _____ you get the tickets?

B: Yes! I _____ _____ _____ _____ the game.

Listen & Speak 2 B

1. G: Do you _____ _____ _____ my new mountain bike?

   B: Sure. _____ _____ you get it?

   G: Yesterday my father _____ _____ _____ _____. Can you _____ to my house this afternoon?

   B: Of course. I _____ _____ _____ _____ it.

해석

M: 너는 어떤 운동을 좋아하니? 축구 아니면 농구?

G: 축구를 더 좋아해요. 저는 일주일에 두 번 축구를 해요.

1. G: 뭐 하고 있어?

   B: 세계 지도를 보고 있어.

   G: 두 나라에 표시를 했네. 어떤 나라를 먼저 방문하고 싶어? 미국 아니면 멕시코?

   B: 미국을 방문하고 싶어. 거기서 농구 경기를 보고 싶어.

2. G: 나는 애완동물을 기르는 것에 대해 생각 중이야. 넌 애완동물을 기르니?

   B: 응, 길러. 개와 고양이가 있어.

   G: 어떻게 생각해? 어떤 애완동물이 나에게 더 나아? 고양이 아니면 개?

   B: 어느 날 우리 집에 와서 내 애완동물과 놀아 보는 게 어때? 그런 다음 너는 결정할 수 있을 거야.

W: 너 티켓 구했니?

B: 응! 나는 경기를 빨리 보고 싶어.

G: 내 새 산악 자전거를 보고 싶니?

B: 물론이지. 언제 생긴 거야?

G: 어제 아빠가 나에게 사 주셨어. 오늘 오후에 우리 집에 올래?

B: 당연하지. 나는 그것을 빨리 보고 싶어.

2. **B:** Don't _____ _____ we're going rock climbing this weekend!

   G: Don't worry. I _____ _____.

   B: I'm _____ about going. _____ _____ _____.

3. **G:** Did you hear about Jisu?

   B: What _____ her? She lives _____ Canada.

   G: She _____ back to Korea last month. She _____ _____ _____ you.

   B: Oh, I _____ _____ _____ _____ her.

Real-Life Zone A

B1: Jiho, why are you in _____ a hurry?

B2: Hi, Alex! I have to be home _____ 6:00. The game _____ the Thunders and the Cobras _____ at 6:00.

B1: Oh, are you a baseball fan? _____ _____ do you _____? The Cobras or the Thunders?

B2: The Cobras.

B1: Me, too! I don't want to _____ the game _____.

B2: _____ up! We only have thirty minutes _____.

B1: Okay. Maybe we can watch a game together _____.

B2: That's a great idea! How _____ _____ _____ the next Cobras home game together?

B1: Okay. They have a game next Saturday. We can eat fried chicken _____ _____ the game!

B2: That sounds great. _____ _____ _____!

Wrap Up

B: Jimin, _____ _____ _____ _____ _____? Soccer _____ table tennis?

G: I love table tennis. How _____ you, Yunho?

B: I like soccer. I'm a _____ _____ _____ James Hood. He's a great soccer player.

G: Oh, really? There's a soccer match this weekend _____ Korea and Turkey. _____ you heard about it?

B: Of course. I already have a ticket. _____ _____ _____ the game on Saturday. I _____ _____.

G: That's _____.

---

2. **B:** 이번 주말에 암벽 등반하러 가기로 한 거 잊지 마.
   G: 걱정 마. 잊지 않을게.
   B: 등반하러 가는 거 너무 신난다. 너무 기다려져.

3. **G:** 너 지수에 대해 들었니?
   B: 그녀에 대한 거 뭐? 그녀는 캐나다에 살고 있잖아.
   G: 지난달에 그녀는 한국에 돌아왔어. 너를 보고 싶어해.
   B: 오, 그녀를 빨리 보고 싶어.

B1: 지호야, 너 왜 그렇게 서두르니?
B2: 안녕, 알렉스! 나는 6시 전에 집에 있어야 해. 천둥 대 코브라의 경기가 6시에 시작돼.
B1: 오, 너 야구 팬이니? 어느 팀을 응원해? 코브라 아니면 천둥?
B2: 코브라.
B1: 나도야! 나도 이 경기를 놓치고 싶지 않아.
B2: 서둘러! 우리는 30분밖에 안 남았어.
B1: 알겠어. 언젠가 함께 경기를 볼 수도 있겠다.
B2: 좋은 생각이야! 다음 코브라 홈 경기를 함께 보러 가지 않을래?
B1: 좋아. 다음 주 토요일에 경기가 있어. 우리는 경기를 보면서 프라이드 치킨을 먹을 수 있어!
B1: 굉장해. 너무 기다려져!

B: 지민아, 너는 어떤 운동을 좋아하니? 축구 아니면 탁구?
G: 탁구를 좋아해. 윤호야, 너는 어때?
B: 축구가 좋아. 나는 제임스 후드의 열렬한 팬이야. 그는 위대한 축구 선수야.
G: 오, 정말? 이번 주말에 한국 대 터키의 축구 경기가 있어. 그것에 대해 들었니?
B: 물론이지. 나는 이미 표가 있어. 토요일에 경기를 보러 갈 거야. 너무 기다려져.
G: 환상적이다.

01 다음 대화의 밑줄 친 부분의 의도로 알맞은 것은?

A: What are you going to do on your vacation?
B: I'm going to take a boat ride. <u>I can't wait.</u>

① 관심 표현하기　② 확신 표현하기　③ 기대 표현하기
④ 거절 표현하기　⑤ 불가능 표현하기

02 다음 대화의 빈칸에 알맞은 말은?

A: Which sport do you like? Soccer or basketball?
B: _____ I play soccer twice a week.

① I like basketball better.　② I like soccer more.
③ I don't like sports.　④ I like basketball more than baseball.
⑤ I prefer basketball.

03 다음 대화의 빈칸에 알맞은 말을 <u>모두</u> 고르시오.

A: _____ *Peter Pan* or *The Last Leaf*?
B: I like *Peter Pan*.

① Which shorts do you like?
② Which do you prefer?
③ Why don't we read a story book?
④ Which story book do you like?
⑤ How did you like the story book?

04 다음 대화의 밑줄 친 문장 대신 쓸 수 있는 것을 고르시오.

A: Which sport do you like? Bowling or tennis?
B: <u>I like tennis.</u> I'm going to play it with my friends this weekend.
　 I can't wait.

① I prefer bowling to tennis.
② I like bowling more than tennis.
③ I prefer tennis and bowling.
④ I like tennis more.
⑤ I like tennis and bowling.

[01~03] 다음 대화를 읽고 물음에 답하시오.

G: ⓐI'm thinking about getting a pet. Do you have a pet? (①)

B: Yes, I do. (②)

G: ⓑWhat do you think? (③) ⓒWhich pet is better for me? A cat or a dog? (④) ⓓI can't wait to play with your pets.

B: ⓔWhy don't you come to my house someday and play with my pets? (⑤) Then you can decide.

01 위 대화의 ①~⑤ 중 다음 주어진 말이 들어갈 알맞은 곳은?

I have a dog and a cat.

①   ②   ③   ④   ⑤

02 위 대화의 문장 ⓐ~ⓔ 중 흐름상 어색한 것을 고르시오.

① ⓐ   ② ⓑ   ③ ⓒ   ④ ⓓ   ⑤ ⓔ

03 위 대화를 읽고 알 수 없는 것을 고르시오.

① Does the boy have a pet?
② Why does the boy suggest that the girl come to his house someday?
③ Which animal does the girl like more? A dog or a cat?
④ How many dogs does the boy have?
⑤ What kind of pet does the boy have?

04 주어진 문장 이후에 이어질 대화의 순서가 바르게 배열된 것을 고르시오.

What are you doing?

(A) You checked two countries. Which country would you like to visit first? The U.S. or Mexico?
(B) I want to visit the U.S. I'd like to see a basketball game there.
(C) I'm looking at a world map.

① (A) – (C) – (B)   ② (B) – (A) – (C)
③ (B) – (C) – (A)   ④ (C) – (A) – (B)
⑤ (C) – (B) – (A)

05 다음 중 짝지어진 대화가 어색한 것은?

① A: Which do you like more, hotdogs or waffles?
   B: I like waffles more.
② A: Which do you prefer, dogs or cats?
   B: I prefer dogs to cats.
③ A: Which do you like more, to buy the books or to borrow them from the library?
   B: I like to borrow the books from the library more.
④ A: Which do you prefer, hiking or swimming?
   B: Of course I do.
⑤ A: Which shirt do you prefer, the red one or the yellow one?
   B: I think the red one is better.

[06~07] 다음 대화를 읽고 물음에 답하시오.

G: Do you want to see my new mountain bike? (①)

B: Sure. (②) When did you get it? (③)

G: Yesterday my father bought it for me. (④)

B: (⑤) Of course. 나는 그것을 빨리 보고 싶어. (wait, it, see, I, can't, to)

06 위 대화의 ①~⑤ 중 다음 주어진 말이 들어갈 알맞은 곳은?

Can you come to my house this afternoon?

①   ②   ③   ④   ⑤

서답형

07 위 대화의 밑줄 친 우리말 해석에 맞게 괄호 안의 단어를 배열하여 영작하시오.

➡ _____

[08~09] 다음 대화를 읽고 물음에 답하시오.

B1: Jiho, why are you in such a hurry?

B2: _____

B1: _____

B2: _____

B1: _____

B2: Hurry up! We only have thirty minutes left.

B1: Okay. Maybe we can watch a game together sometime.

B2: That's a great idea! How about going to the next Cobras home game together?

B1: Okay. They have a game next Saturday. We can eat fried chicken while watching the game!

B2: That sounds great. I can't wait!

08 위 대화의 빈 부분에 들어갈 순서가 올바른 것을 고르시오.

(A) The Cobras.

(B) Hi, Alex! I have to be home before 6:00. The game between the Thunders and the Cobras starts at 6:00.

(C) Oh, are you a baseball fan? Which team do you support? The Cobras or the Thunders?

(D) Me, too! I don't want to miss the game either.

① (B)–(A)–(C)–(D)   ② (B)–(C)–(A)–(D)

③ (B)–(D)–(A)–(C)   ④ (C)–(A)–(B)–(D)

⑤ (C)–(D)–(B)–(A)

09 위 대화를 읽고 질문에 답할 수 <u>없는</u> 것은?

① What time will the next Cobras home game start?

② What can they eat while watching the game?

③ When will the next Cobras home game be held?

④ Which team do they like more, the Cobras or the Thunders?

⑤ What time is it now?

서답형

10 다음 대화의 빈칸에 알맞은 말을 쓰시오.

A: What are you going to do on your vacation?

B: _____ I can't wait to go surfing.

➡ _____

Conversation 서술형 시험대비

[01~03] 다음 대화를 읽고 물음에 답하시오.

B: Don't forget (A)[to / that] we're going rock climbing this weekend!
G: Don't worry. I won't _____ⓐ_____.
B: I'm excited (B)[about / to] going. I can't wait.

01 (A)와 (B)에 알맞은 말을 골라 쓰시오.

(A) _____ (B) _____

02 위 대화의 빈칸 ⓐ에 알맞은 말을 대화에서 찾아 쓰시오.

➡ _____

03 위 대화의 내용과 일치하도록 주어진 질문에 대한 대답을 영어로 쓰시오. (9 단어, 주어진 단어를 이용할 것)

What is the boy looking forward to?

➡ _____
(wait, to)

[04~05] 주어진 문장 다음에 이어질 대화의 순서를 바르게 배열 하시오.

04
Did you hear about Jisu?

(A) She came back to Korea last month. She wants to see you.
(B) Oh, I can't wait to see her.
(C) What about her? She lives in Canada.

➡ _____

05
Which sport do you like to play? Tennis or baseball?

(A) I like to play tennis.
(B) Why not?
(C) Why don't we play tennis together this afternoon?

➡ _____

[06~07] 다음 대화를 읽고 물음에 답하시오.

B: Jimin, which sport do you like? Soccer or table tennis?
G: I love table tennis. How about you, Yunho?
B: I like soccer. I'm a big fan of James Hood. He's a great soccer player.
G: Oh, really? There's a soccer match this weekend between Korea and Turkey. __(A)__ you heard about it?
B: Of course. I already __(B)__ a ticket. I'm going to see the game on Saturday. (C)I can't wait.
G: That's fantastic.

06 위 대화의 빈칸 (A)와 (B)에 공통으로 들어갈 말을 쓰시오.

(A) _____ (B) _____

07 밑줄 친 (C)의 뒤에 생략된 부분을 주어진 단어를 넣어 쓰시 오. (6 단어)

➡ _____ (see)

Grammar

1 부가의문문

- Jian, this is your first time to come to the baseball stadium, **isn't it**?
  지안아, 네가 야구 경기장에 온 건 이번이 처음이야, 그렇지 않니?

- You don't like English, **do you**? 너 영어를 싫어하지, 그렇지?

■ 문장의 끝에 붙은 의문문으로, 상대방의 동의를 구하거나 사실을 확인하기 위해 사용된다.

- The post office is a few blocks from your office, **isn't it**?
  우체국은 네 사무실에서 몇 블록 떨어져 있잖아, 그렇지 않니?

- She didn't tell a lie, **did she**? 그녀는 거짓말을 하지 않았어, 그렇지?

부가의문문을 만드는 법은 다음과 같다.

1. 앞 문장에 be동사나 조동사가 사용되었으면 be동사나 조동사를 사용하며 일반 동사가 사용된 경우에는 'do/does/did'를 사용한다.

2. 앞 문장이 긍정이면 부정, 부정이면 긍정으로 쓴다.

3. 주어는 반드시 인칭대명사로 받는다.

4. 부정형의 경우 반드시 축약형을 쓴다.

- You aren't tired, **are you**? 너 피곤하지 않지, 그렇지?

- You want to go to the amusement park, **don't you**? 너 놀이 공원에 가고 싶지, 그렇지 않니?

■ 명령문의 부가의문문은 will you?나 won't you?를 쓰고 권유문(Let's ~)의 경우에는 shall we?를 쓴다.

- Clean your room, **won't you**? 네 방을 청소해, 그러지 않을래?

- Let's work together, **shall we**? 함께 일하자, 그럴래?

핵심 Check

1. 다음 괄호 안에서 알맞은 말을 고르시오.

(1) People usually buy presents to celebrate, (don't / aren't) they?

(2) Ted wasn't at home yesterday, was (he / Ted)?

(3) Your cellphone looks nice, (does / doesn't) it?

(4) Mary felt happy, (did / didn't) she?

② 수동태

> • Jake **made** this table. 〈능동태〉 Jake가 이 탁자를 만들었다.
> • This table **was made** by Jake. 〈수동태〉 이 탁자는 Jake에 의해 만들어졌다.

■ 수동태는 '주어+be동사+동사의 과거분사+by+행위자'의 형식을 가지며 '…에 의해 ~되다[당하다]'라는 의미로 주어가 동작의 영향을 받거나 행위를 당할 때 사용한다.

능동태를 수동태로 만드는 법

1. 능동태의 목적어를 문장의 주어로 둔다.
2. 동사를 'be동사+과거분사'로 쓴다. 이때 be동사의 시제는 능동태 문장에 맞추고 수와 인칭은 수동태 문장의 주어에 맞춘다.
3. 능동태의 주어는 'by+행위자(목적격)'의 형태로 문장 끝에 쓴다. 이때 행위자가 중요치 않거나 확실하지 않은 경우 'by+행위자'는 생략한다. • The chair **was broken** by Jerry. 그 의자는 Jerry에 의해 부서졌다.

■ 4형식 문장의 수동태는 간접목적어와 직접목적어 각각을 주어로 하는 수동태가 가능하다. 직접목적어를 주어로 한 수동태에서는 간접목적어 앞에 특정한 전치사를 써야 한다. 전치사 to를 쓰는 동사는 'give, send, tell, teach, show, bring' 등이고, 전치사 for를 쓰는 동사는 'buy, make, choose, cook, get' 등이며, 전치사 of를 쓰는 동사에는 'ask' 등이 있다. 또한 make, buy, read, write 등은 직접목적어를 주어로 하는 수동태만 가능하다.

> • Mom **bought** Jane a book. 엄마가 Jane에게 책을 사주셨다.
> • A book **was bought** for Jane by Mom. 책이 엄마에 의해 Jane에게 사 주어졌다.

■ 조동사가 있는 문장의 수동태는 '조동사+be+p.p.' 형식을 갖는다.

> • The work **will be finished** by me. 그 일은 나에 의해 끝내질 것이다.

■ 목적격보어가 원형부정사인 경우, 수동태 문장에서는 to부정사로 바뀐다.

> • Harry **was made** to do the dishes by her. Harry는 그녀에 의해 설거지하도록 시켜졌다.

■ by 이외의 전치사를 사용하는 수동태에 유의한다.

> • be interested in: ~에 흥미가 있다　　be surprised at: ~에 놀라다
> • be covered with: ~로 덮여 있다　　be filled with: ~로 가득 차다
> • be pleased with: ~로 기뻐하다　　be satisfied with: ~에 만족하다
> • be made of: ~로 만들어지다(물리적 변화)　be made from: ~로 만들어지다(화학적 변화)

핵심 Check

2. 다음 괄호 안에서 알맞은 말을 고르시오.

(1) Some nice presents were given (for / to) her by her friends.

(2) She is interested (in / with) working indoors.

01 다음 빈칸에 알맞은 것은?

> My cousin played the violin.
> ➡ The violin _____ by my cousin.

① plays ② played ③ is played
④ was played ⑤ has played

02 다음 빈칸에 들어갈 말로 적절한 것은?

> Visiting teams wear dark uniforms, _____?

① aren't they ② are they ③ don't they
④ do they ⑤ aren't them

03 다음 우리말에 맞게 빈칸에 알맞은 말을 쓰시오.

(1) 그 방은 Harold에 의해 청소되었다.
  ➡ The room _____ _____ by Harold.

(2) *Romeo and Juliet*은 William Shakespeare에 의해 쓰여졌다.
  ➡ *Romeo and Juliet* _____ _____ by William Shakespeare.

(3) 그녀는 그와 친구가 되고 싶어 해, 그렇지 않니?
  ➡ She wants to be friends with him, _____ _____?

(4) Sam은 운전할 수 없어, 그렇지?
  ➡ Sam cannot drive, _____ _____?

04 다음 문장에서 어법상 어색한 부분을 바르게 고쳐 쓰시오.

(1) The Golden Gate Bridge built in 1937.

  _____ ➡ _____

(2) Dorothy has a book, doesn't Dorothy?

  _____ ➡ _____

01 다음 빈칸에 알맞은 것은?

> The dirt _____ by the dark colors of the uniforms.

① hides　　② hid　　③ to hide

④ is hiding　　⑤ is hidden

02 다음 중 밑줄 친 부분의 쓰임이 올바른 것은?

① You can speak Japanese very well, <u>can you</u>?

② Yuna looks kind, <u>doesn't she</u>?

③ Yollanda gave the book to Petric, <u>doesn't she</u>?

④ Sophie bought a cell phone, <u>wasn't she</u>?

⑤ Mike isn't diligent, <u>doesn't he</u>?

03 다음 괄호 안에서 알맞은 것을 고르시오.

(1) Some flowers were given (to / for) her by Tim.

(2) The spaghetti was made (to / for) me by my mom.

(3) No questions were asked (to / of) us by the teacher.

(4) Laura likes roses, (does / is / doesn't / isn't) she?

(5) It is a kind of Korean traditional food, (does / is / doesn't / isn't) it?

04 다음 중 수동태로의 전환이 <u>어색한</u> 것은?

① Auguste Rodin made *the Thinker* in 1902.

→ *The Thinker* was made by Auguste Rodin in 1902.

② Harriot chose Grace a beautiful song.

→ A beautiful song was chosen for Grace by Harriot.

③ They built the Namdaemoon in 1398.

→ The Namdaemoon was built in 1398.

④ Emily gave me a nice pen.

→ A nice pen was given for me by Emily.

⑤ My teacher asked me to come to the library.

→ I was asked to come to the library by my teacher.

05 다음 중 어법상 옳은 것을 고르시오.

① Dorothy is wearing black shoes, doesn't she?

② My mom is going to make *gimbap* tonight, is she?

③ The children didn't play the violin, did they?

④ Angelina was kind to others last night, was not she?

⑤ Samanda bought a cute pink dress, didn't Samanda?

06 다음 우리말을 바르게 영작한 것은?

> 이 가방은 내 동생을 위해 엄마에 의해 만들어졌다.

① This bag was made for my sister by my mom.
② This bag was made to my sister by my mom.
③ This bag was made of my sister by my mom.
④ This bag was made to my mom by my sister.
⑤ My sister was made for this bag by my mom.

07 다음 문장의 빈칸에 알맞은 말은?

> You had dinner at the hotel last night, _____ you?

① hadn't   ② haven't   ③ have
④ didn't   ⑤ did

08 다음 문장을 수동태로 바르게 바꾼 것은?

> In the past, they determined the numbers by the players' batting order.

① In the past, the numbers determined the players' batting order.
② In the past, the numbers were determined the players' batting order.
③ In the past, the players' batting order was determined by the numbers.
④ In the past, the numbers was determined by the players' batting order.
⑤ In the past, the numbers were determined by the players' batting order.

09 다음 빈칸에 알맞은 것은?

> Kate looks friendly, _____?

① isn't she   ② does she
③ doesn't she ④ does Kate
⑤ doesn't Kate

10 다음 중 어법상 틀린 것을 고르시오.

① In the early 1800s, soccer was invented in Newgate Prison in London by the prisoners.
② The article was wrote for the school newspaper by Harry.
③ A mouse was caught by a cat.
④ Is English spoken in many countries around the world?
⑤ A nice gift was given to Stephanie on her birthday by her dad.

11 다음 중 빈칸에 들어갈 말이 다른 하나는?

① A man was waiting for Jane outside, _____?
② Jim worked at the bank, _____?
③ He made Ann do the work, _____?
④ Chris went on a vacation, _____?
⑤ A boy played the piano, _____?

12 다음 빈칸에 공통으로 들어갈 알맞은 것은?

> • His heart was filled _____ pride at that time.
> • Does that mean that you're pleased _____ the present?

① at   ② with   ③ from
④ in   ⑤ of

서답형

13 주어진 어구를 이용하여 다음 우리말을 영어로 쓰시오.

(1) 이 편지가 David에 의해 배달되었나요?
(deliver)

➡ _____

(2) 나의 삼촌 집이 홍수에 의해 무너졌다.
(the flood, destroy)

➡ _____

(3) 그 탁자는 나무로 만들어졌다.
(wood, make)

➡ _____

(4) 그 십대들은 유럽에 여행갈 거야, 그렇지 않니?
(the teenagers, travel)

➡ _____

(5) 테니스 치러 가자, 그럴래? (let, to play)

➡ _____

서답형

14 다음 빈칸에 알맞은 부가의문문을 쓰시오.

(1) Sharon studies English very hard, _____ _____?

(2) You played computer games last night, _____ _____?

(3) Marylin can't play the guitar, _____ _____?

(4) Alex wasn't angry, _____ _____?

(5) Always do the dishes after each meal, _____ _____?

(6) Let's take a walk after dinner, _____ _____?

서답형

15 다음 문장에서 어법상 어색한 부분을 찾아 바르게 고치시오.

(1) The dress was chosen to her daughter for the party by Eveline.
_____ ➡ _____

(2) Playing tennis is reduced my stress.
_____ ➡ _____

(3) The changes will not be appeared immediately.
_____ ➡ _____

(4) Mina finished washing the dishes, didn't Mina?
_____ ➡ _____

(5) You will leave a message, will you?
_____ ➡ _____

(6) She isn't going to go hiking tomorrow, does she?
_____ ➡ _____

16 다음 밑줄 친 부분 중 어법상 어색한 것은?

He ①was known as a marathon winner at the Rome and Tokyo international sports competitions. When he ②was prepared to run the marathon in Rome, he found out that his shoes did not fit well, so he decided ③to run the race without shoes. He felt pain during the race, but he finished the race as the winner. He was ④one of the greatest runners in the world, ⑤wasn't he?

① ② ③ ④ ⑤

서답형

17 주어진 단어의 형태를 알맞게 바꿔 문장을 완성하시오.

Hana Middle School Sports Day _____ (hold) on the school playing field next week.

01 다음 문장을 수동태는 능동태로, 능동태는 수동태로 고치시오.

(1) Tino cleans the big house on Sundays.

➡ _____

(2) Sarang Middle School Sports Day will be held on the school playing field on Wednesday, June 15.

➡ _____

_____

_____

(3) Jonathan made Judy delicious spaghetti.

➡ _____

_____

(4) Does your job as a tour guide satisfy you?

➡ _____

(5) Who painted *Water Lilies* in 1906?

➡ _____

(6) Cathy will make him take part in the science camp.

➡ _____

_____

(7) They are looking after the animals.

➡ _____

02 다음 빈칸에 공통으로 들어갈 말을 쓰시오.

• Mike studied hard, _____ _____?

• Joseph did his best at all times, _____ _____?

➡ _____

03 다음 빈칸에 알맞은 부가의문문을 쓰시오.

(1) These cars are really expensive, _____ _____?

(2) Her little son can't read the book, _____ _____?

(3) Matt didn't make his daughter a doll, _____ _____?

(4) Jenny isn't watching TV, _____ _____?

(5) The rock looks like a rabbit, _____ _____?

(6) Be careful when you drive a car at night, _____ _____?

(7) Let's go to the shop at which you bought your skirt, _____ _____?

04 다음 괄호 안에 주어진 어휘를 어법에 맞게 빈칸에 쓰시오.

(1) The computer _____ _____ by my father yesterday. (repair)

(2) The book _____ _____ _____ me by my father yesterday. (buy)

(3) Many smartphones _____ _____ in Korea. (make)

(4) Kathy _____ _____ _____ finish the report by her teacher. (make)

05 다음 그림을 보고 대화의 빈칸에 알맞은 말을 쓰시오.

A: She plays the game really well, _____ _____?

B: Yes, she does.

06 다음 그림을 보고 주어진 단어를 이용하여 빈칸을 알맞게 채우시오.

I and the Village _____ _____ by Marc Chagall in 1911. (paint)

07 다음 문장에서 어법상 <u>어색한</u> 부분을 바르게 고쳐 다시 쓰시오.

(1) The boy was bought the pens.

➡ _____

_____

(2) Soy sauce is made of soy beans and salt.

➡ _____

(3) Cloe was written a letter by Jack.

➡ _____

(4) Vivian was heard open the window by her son.

➡ _____

(5) *Samgyupsal* is cooked to Emma by her husband next weekend.

➡ _____

_____

(6) Whom this table was made?

➡ _____

08 다음 우리말을 괄호 안에 주어진 어휘를 이용하여 영작하시오.

(1) 내 자전거는 지난 금요일에 도둑맞았다.
(bike, steal)

➡ _____

(2) 이 과자들은 나의 엄마에 의해 만들어졌다.
(these cookies, make, my mom)

➡ _____

(3) 그의 집은 책으로 가득 차 있다. (fill)

➡ _____

(4) Jenny는 어젯밤에 파티에 없었어, 그렇지?
(at the party)

➡ _____

(5) 좋아하는 운동에 대해서 말해 보자, 그럴래?
(let's, our favorite sport, about)

➡ _____

Reading

A Day at the Baseball Stadium

Today the Thunders and the Cobras have a game. Jihun's family is at
~에 있다
the baseball stadium.

Jihun: Jian, this is your first time to come to the baseball stadium, isn't it?
to부정사의 형용사적 용법   부가의문문

Jian: Yes, I'm so excited. I can't wait for the game to start.
신이 난, 흥분된   무엇인가를 너무나 하고 싶을 때 쓸 수 있는 표현

Dad: Look, the players are coming out now!
현재진행형 be+~ing

Jian: Which team is the Thunders?
의문형용사 which: 어느 ~

Jihun: Over there, behind third base. They are wearing dark gray

uniforms because they are the visiting team.
~이기 때문에   원정 팀

Jian: Does the visiting team always wear a dark color?
빈도부사: 일반동사 앞에 위치

Jihun: Yes, that's the rule. Home teams have bright uniforms and
= the visiting team always wear a dark color
visiting teams have dark uniforms.

Jian: Why is that?
앞 문장의 내용을 받음

Mom: There is an interesting story about that. In the past, visiting
~이 있다
teams could not wash their uniforms after every game. So they

started wearing dark colors to hide the dirt.
start+-ing: ~하기 시작하다   to부정사의 부사적 용법(~하기 위해)

Jian: Hahaha! That was a good idea!
wearing dark colors to hide the dirt

base (야구의) 루, 베이스
visiting team 원정 팀
come out 나오다
dark 어두운
dirt 먼지, 때
hide 숨다, 숨기다
rule 규칙, 법칙

확인문제

● 다음 문장이 본문의 내용과 일치하면 T, 일치하지 않으면 F를 쓰시오.

1   Jihun's family is at the baseball stadium. ☐

2   This is Jihun's first time to come to the baseball stadium. ☐

3   Jian is so excited that she can't wait for the game to start. ☐

4   The Cobras are the visiting team. ☐

5   Home teams have bright uniforms and visiting teams have dark uniforms. ☐

6   In the past, visiting teams could wash their uniforms after every game. ☐

The players are warming up.

Jian: Who's your favorite player?
<u>Who is의 줄임말</u>

Jihun: Number 77.

Jian: What does the number mean?

Jihun: Hmm…. Players choose a number they like.
관계대명사 which나 that 생략

Dad: You know what? In the past, the numbers were determined by
저 있잖아, 그거 알아?   수동태: be동사+과거분사

the players' batting order.

Jihun: That means there were no players with number 77!
앞 문장의 내용을 받는 지시대명사

Now, Jihun's favorite player is about to bat. Jihun looks anxious.
막 ~하려는 참이다   ~처럼 보이다

Jian: Your favorite player is at bat.
타석에 서서

Jihun: Yes. He has hit 21 home runs already this year. If he hits one
현재완료(완료)   접속사 if: ~라면   조건 부사절에서
현재시제가 미래를 나타냄.

more today, he will be the home run leader this season.

The batter misses several balls. Now he has a full count. He is
놓치다   야구에서 스트라이크가 둘이고 볼이 셋인 상태

waiting for the next pitch.

Jihun: HOME RUN! HOME RUN!

Crack!

The ball flies fast. It is going, going, going, gone!

Glossary
warm up 준비 운동을 하다, 몸을 풀다
determine 결정하다
order 순서
anxious 불안해하는
be about to 막 ~하려고 하다
pitch 투구
wait for ~을 기다리다
crack 찢어지는 듯한 [날카로운] 소리
at bat 타석에 서서

📎 **확인문제**

- 다음 문장이 본문의 내용과 일치하면 T, 일치하지 <u>않으면</u> F를 쓰시오.

1 The players are warming up. ☐

2 In the past, players chose a number they liked. ☐

3 Jihun's favorite player is at bat. ☐

4 Jihun's favorite player has hit 20 home runs already this year. ☐

5 Jihun's favorite player misses several balls. ☐

6 Jihun's favorite player has a full count and he is out on a fly ball. ☐

● 우리말을 참고하여 빈칸에 알맞은 말을 쓰시오.

1 A Day at the _____ _____

2 Today the Thunders and the Cobras _____ _____ _____ .

3 Jihun's family _____ _____ the baseball stadium.

4 Jihun: Jian, this is _____ _____ _____ to come to the baseball stadium, _____ _____ ?

5 Jian: Yes, I'm so excited. I _____ _____ _____ the game to start.

6 Dad: Look, the players _____ _____ _____ now!

7 Jian: _____ _____ is the Thunders?

8 Jihun: Over there, _____ _____ _____ .

9 They are wearing dark gray uniforms because they are the _____ _____ .

10 Jian: Does the visiting team always _____ _____ _____ _____ ?

11 Jihun: Yes, that's the _____ .

12 Home teams _____ _____ _____ and visiting teams have dark uniforms.

13 Jian: _____ is that?

14 Mom: There is an _____ _____ about that.

15 In the past, visiting teams could not _____ _____ _____ after every game.

16 So they started wearing dark colors _____ _____ _____ .

17 Jian: Hahaha! That was _____ _____ _____ !

1 야구 경기장에서의 하루

2 오늘 천둥 대 코브라 게임이 있다.

3 지훈이네 가족은 야구 경기장에 있다.

4 지훈: 지안아, 네가 야구 경기장에 온 건 이번이 처음이야, 그렇지 않니?

5 지안: 응, 나 아주 흥분돼. 나는 경기가 빨리 시작했으면 좋겠어.

6 아빠: 봐, 선수들이 지금 나오고 있어!

7 지안: 어떤 팀이 천둥이야?

8 지훈: 저기, 3루 뒤.

9 그들은 원정 팀이기 때문에 어두운 회색 유니폼을 입고 있어.

10 지안: 원정 팀은 항상 어두운 색을 입어?

11 지훈: 응, 그게 규칙이야.

12 홈팀은 밝은 유니폼을 입고 원정팀은 어두운 유니폼을 입어.

13 지안: 왜?

14 엄마: 그것에 대한 흥미로운 이야기가 있단다.

15 과거에는 원정 팀이 매 경기 후 유니폼을 세탁할 수가 없었어.

16 그래서 그들은 때를 숨기기 위해 어두운 색을 입기 시작했지.

17 지안: 하하하! 좋은 생각이었네요!

18 The players are _____ _____.

19 Jian: Who's your _____ _____?

20 Jihun: _____ 77.

21 Jian: _____ does the number _____?

22 Jihun: Hmm.... Players _____ a number _____ _____.

23 Dad: You know _____?

24 In the past, the numbers were determined _____ _____ _____ _____ _____.

25 Jihun: That means there were _____ players _____ number 77!

26 Now, Jihun's favorite player _____ _____ _____ bat.

27 Jihun looks _____.

28 Jian: Your favorite player is _____ _____.

29 Jihun: Yes. He _____ _____ 21 home runs already this year.

30 If he _____ _____ _____ today, he will be the home run leader this season.

31 The batter _____ several balls.

32 Now he has _____ _____ _____.

33 He is waiting for the _____ _____.

34 Jihun: HOME RUN! HOME RUN!

35 _____! The ball _____ fast.

36 It is going, going, going, _____!

18 선수들이 몸을 풀고 있다.

19 지안: 가장 좋아하는 선수가 누구야?

20 지훈: 77번.

21 지안: 그 숫자는 무엇을 의미해?

22 지훈: 음... 선수들이 원하는 번호를 선택해.

23 아빠: 그거 알아?

24 과거에는 번호가 선수들의 타순에 의해 결정되었단다.

25 지훈: 77번 선수가 없었다는 뜻이네요!

26 이제 지훈이의 가장 좋아하는 선수가 막 공을 치려고 한다.

27 지훈이는 불안해 보인다.

28 지안: 오빠가 가장 좋아하는 선수가 타석에 서네.

29 지훈: 응. 그는 올해 이미 21개의 홈런을 쳤어.

30 그가 오늘 하나를 더 치면, 그는 이번 시즌 홈런 리더가 될 거야.

31 타자는 여러 개의 공을 놓친다.

32 이제 그는 풀카운트가 되었다.

33 그는 다음 투구를 기다리고 있다.

34 지훈: 홈런! 홈런!

35 땅! 공은 빠르게 날아간다.

36 그것은 가고, 가고, 가고, 사라져 버렸다!

● 우리말을 참고하여 본문을 영작하시오.

1 야구 경기장에서의 하루

➡ _____

2 오늘 천둥 대 코브라 게임이 있다.

➡ _____

3 지훈이네 가족은 야구 경기장에 있다.

➡ _____

4 지훈: 지안아, 네가 야구 경기장에 온 건 이번이 처음이야, 그렇지 않니?

➡ _____

5 지안: 응, 나 아주 흥분돼. 나는 경기가 빨리 시작했으면 좋겠어.

➡ _____

6 아빠: 봐, 선수들이 지금 나오고 있어!

➡ _____

7 지안: 어떤 팀이 천둥이야?

➡ _____

8 지훈: 저기, 3루 뒤.

➡ _____

9 그들은 원정 팀이기 때문에 어두운 회색 유니폼을 입고 있어.

➡ _____

10 지안: 원정 팀은 항상 어두운 색을 입어?

➡ _____

11 지훈: 응, 그게 규칙이야.

➡ _____

12 홈팀은 밝은 유니폼을 입고 원정팀은 어두운 유니폼을 입어.

➡ _____

13 지안: 왜?

➡ _____

14 엄마: 그것에 대한 흥미로운 이야기가 있단다.

➡ _____

15 과거에는 원정 팀이 매 경기 후 유니폼을 세탁할 수가 없었어.

➡ _____

16 그래서 그들은 때를 숨기기 위해 어두운 색을 입기 시작했지.

➡ _____

17 지안: 하하하! 좋은 생각이었네요!

➡ _____

18 선수들이 몸을 풀고 있다.

➡ _____

19 지안: 가장 좋아하는 선수가 누구야?

➡ _____

20 지훈: 77번.

➡ _____

21 지안: 그 숫자는 무엇을 의미해?

➡ _____

22 지훈: 음... 선수들이 원하는 번호를 선택해.

➡ _____

23 아빠: 그거 알아?

➡ _____

24 과거에는 번호가 선수들의 타순에 의해 결정되었단다.

➡ _____

25 지훈: 77번 선수가 없었다는 뜻이네요!

➡ _____

26 이제 지훈이의 가장 좋아하는 선수가 막 공을 치려고 한다.

➡ _____

27 지훈이는 불안해 보인다.

➡ _____

28 지안: 오빠가 가장 좋아하는 선수가 타석에 서네.

➡ _____

29 지훈: 응. 그는 올해 이미 21개의 홈런을 쳤어.

➡ _____

30 그가 오늘 하나를 더 치면, 그는 이번 시즌 홈런 리더가 될 거야.

➡ _____

31 타자는 여러 개의 공을 놓친다.

➡ _____

32 이제 그는 풀카운트가 되었다.

➡ _____

33 그는 다음 투구를 기다리고 있다.

➡ _____

34 지훈: 홈런! 홈런!

➡ _____

35 땅! 공은 빠르게 날아간다.

➡ _____

36 그것은 가고, 가고, 가고, 사라져 버렸다!

➡ _____

[01~03] 다음 글을 읽고 물음에 답하시오.

Today the Thunders and the Cobras have a game. Jihun's family is at the baseball stadium.

Jihun: Jian, this is your first time ⓐto come to the baseball stadium, ____(A)____ ?

Jian: Yes, I'm so excited. I can't wait for the game to start.

Dad: Look, the players are coming out now!

Jian: Which team is the Thunders?

Jihun: Over there, behind third base. They are wearing dark gray uniforms because they are the visiting team.

01 위 글의 빈칸 (A)에 들어갈 알맞은 부가의문문을 고르시오.

① isn't this
② is it
③ doesn't it
④ isn't it
⑤ is this

02 위 글의 밑줄 친 ⓐto come과 to부정사의 용법이 같은 것을 모두 고르시오.

① He couldn't decide what to eat.
② It's time for you to finish your work.
③ She went there to meet her friend.
④ It's good for your health to jog every day.
⑤ She wanted to buy a book to read on the train.

03 위 글의 내용과 일치하지 않는 것은?

① 오늘 천둥 대 코브라 게임이 있다.
② 지훈이네 가족은 야구 경기장에 있다.
③ 지안이가 야구 경기장에 온 건 이번이 처음이 아니다.
④ 지안이는 경기가 빨리 시작하기를 바란다.
⑤ 천둥 팀은 어두운 회색 유니폼을 입고 있다.

[04~06] 다음 글을 읽고 물음에 답하시오.

Jian: Does the visiting team always wear a dark color?

Jihun: Yes, that's the rule. Home teams have ____(A)____ uniforms and visiting teams have dark uniforms.

Jian: Why is (B)that?

Mom: There is an interesting story about that. In the past, visiting teams could not wash their uniforms after every game. So they started wearing dark colors to hide the ____(C)____ .

Jian: Hahaha! That was a good idea!

서답형

04 위 글의 빈칸 (A)에 문맥상 알맞은 말을 쓰시오.

➡ _____

서답형

05 위 글의 밑줄 친 (B)that이 가리키는 것을 본문에서 찾아 쓰시오.

➡ _____
_____

06 위 글의 빈칸 (C)에 들어갈 알맞은 말을 고르시오.

① pattern
② dirt
③ hole
④ shape
⑤ design

[07~10] 다음 글을 읽고 물음에 답하시오.

Abebe Bikila
Marathon Runner
Born: August 7, 1932
Nationality: Ethiopia
Speciality: He was known ___ⓐ___ a marathon winner at the Rome and Tokyo international sports competitions. When he was preparing (A)[to run / running] the marathon in Rome, he found out that his shoes did not fit well, so he decided (B)[to run / running] the race ___ⓑ___ shoes. He felt pain (C)[during / while] the race, but he finished the race ___ⓒ___ the winner. He was one of the greatest runners in the world, wasn't he?

07 위 글의 빈칸 ⓐ와 ⓒ에 공통으로 들어갈 알맞은 말을 고르시오.

① as   ② to   ③ for
④ by   ⑤ in

서답형

08 위 글의 빈칸 ⓑ에 들어갈 알맞은 말을 쓰시오.

➡ _____

서답형

09 위 글의 괄호 (A)~(C)에서 문맥이나 어법상 알맞은 낱말을 골라 쓰시오.

(A) _____ (B) _____ (C) _____

10 Abebe Bikila에 대한 내용과 일치하지 <u>않는</u> 것을 고르시오.

① 에티오피아 출신의 마라톤 선수였다.
② 로마 국제 스포츠 대회의 마라톤 우승자로 알려졌다.
③ 도쿄 국제 스포츠 대회의 마라톤 우승자로 알려졌다.
④ 도쿄 국제 스포츠 대회에서 신발을 신지 않고 달렸다.
⑤ 경주 도중에 통증을 느꼈지만 우승자로 경주를 끝마쳤다.

[11~13] 다음 글을 읽고 물음에 답하시오.

(A)선수들이 몸을 풀고 있다.

Jian: Who's your favorite player?
Jihun: Number 77.
Jian: What does the number mean?
Jihun: Hmm.... Players choose a number they like.
Dad: You know what? In the past, the numbers were determined ___ⓐ___ the players' batting order.
Jihun: That means there were no players ___ⓑ___ number 77!

중요

11 위 글의 빈칸 ⓐ와 ⓑ에 들어갈 전치사가 바르게 짝지어진 것은?

① for – with   ② by – in
③ in – from   ④ for – in
⑤ by – with

서답형

12 위 글의 밑줄 친 (A)의 우리말에 맞게 주어진 어휘를 변형하여 5 단어로 영작하시오.

warm

➡ _____

서답형

13 등번호 7번의 과거와 현재의 의미를 우리말로 쓰시오.

과거: _____

현재: _____

[14~16] 다음 글을 읽고 물음에 답하시오.

Now, Jihun's favorite player is about to bat. Jihun looks anxious.

Jian: Your favorite player is at bat.

Jihun: Yes. He ⓐhas hit 21 home runs already this year. If he hits one more today, he will be the home run leader this season.

The batter misses several balls. Now he has a full count. He is waiting for the next pitch.

Jihun: HOME RUN! HOME RUN!

Crack!

The ball flies fast. It is going, going, going, gone!

14 아래 〈보기〉에서 위 글의 밑줄 친 ⓐhas hit과 현재완료의 용법이 다른 것의 개수는?

┌── 보기 ──┐

① Tom has just eaten breakfast.

② Have you solved it yet?

③ I have worked for this company for two years.

④ He has already read the book.

⑤ She has lost her pen.

└─────────┘

① 1개   ② 2개   ③ 3개   ④ 4개   ⑤ 5개

서답형

15 본문의 내용과 일치하도록 다음 빈칸에 알맞은 단어를 쓰시오.

It is likely that Jihun's favorite player will be the _____ _____ _____ this season because he finally hit a home run.

중요

16 위 글을 읽고 대답할 수 없는 질문은?

① Now, who is about to bat?

② How many home runs has Jihun's favorite player hit already this year?

③ Does Jihun's favorite player miss several balls?

④ How many foul balls has Jihun's favorite player hit today?

⑤ Does Jihun's favorite player hit a home run in this inning?

[17~19] 다음 글을 읽고 물음에 답하시오.

Seri Park

Professional golfer

Born: September 8, 1977

Nationality: South Korea

Speciality: She was the school's best ___(A)___ golfer when she was young. She turned ___(B)___ golfer in 1996. She played on the LPGA Tours from 1998 to 2016. She was inducted into the World Golf Hall of Fame in November 2007. She was great, ___(C)___?

17 위 글의 빈칸 (A)와 (B)에 들어갈 알맞은 말을 고르시오.

① professional – amateur

② mature – immature

③ amateur – professional

④ professional – expert

⑤ immature – mature

서답형

18 위 글의 빈칸 (C)에 들어갈 알맞은 부가의문문을 쓰시오.

➡ _____

위 글을 읽고 박세리에 대해 알 수 <u>없는</u> 것을 고르시오.

① 직업
② 골프를 시작한 나이
③ 프로 골프 선수가 된 시기
④ LPGA Tours에 참가한 시기
⑤ 세계 골프 영예의 전당에 가입한 시기

[20~22] 다음 글을 읽고 물음에 답하시오.

> A: Today the Thunders and the Cobras have a big game.
> B: Now, it is the Thunders' ⓐturn to hit the ball.
> A: The batter with number 77 is coming out to the field. He has hit 21 home runs this year.
> B: He is at bat. The Thunders' fans look very anxious. ⓑ누가 이길 것이라고 생각하시나요? (think, win, do, who, will, you, ?)
> A: Home run! Home run!
> B: ⓒHe will be the home run leader this year!

20 위 글의 밑줄 친 ⓐturn과 같은 의미로 쓰인 것을 고르시오.

① The wheels of the car began to turn.
② Please wait for your turn.
③ Turn the sweater inside out before you wash it.
④ Make a left turn into West Street.
⑤ The weather will turn cold.

서답형
21 위 글의 밑줄 친 ⓑ의 우리말에 맞게 주어진 어휘를 알맞게 배열하시오.

➡ _____

서답형
22 위 글의 밑줄 친 ⓒ와 같은 의미가 되도록 빈칸에 들어갈 알맞은 말을 서수로 쓰시오.

> The batter with number 77 succeeds in hitting his _____ home run.

[23~27] 다음 글을 읽고 물음에 답하시오.

> A: On today's show we are going to talk about fun facts in sports! We have here with us, sports reporter Dasom. Welcome, Dasom!
> B: Hi, I'm going to talk about baseball. Do you think catchers in the old days played the same role as catchers ____ⓐ____ these days? ⓑHow do you think?
> A: Well.... I guess so.
> B: No. In the past, catchers stood about one meter behind home base and stopped the ball.
> A: ⓒThat's interesting!

서답형
23 위 글의 빈칸 ⓐ에 들어갈 알맞은 대동사를 쓰시오.

➡ _____

 위 글의 A와 B의 관계로 알맞은 것을 고르시오.

① announcer – newscaster
② newscaster – sports reporter
③ sports reporter – show host
④ newscaster – announcer
⑤ sports reporter – newscaster

25 위 글의 종류로 알맞은 것을 고르시오.

① summary ② article ③ essay
④ review ⑤ sports news script

서답형
26 위 글의 밑줄 친 ⓑ에서 어법상 <u>틀린</u> 부분을 찾아 고치시오.

_____ ➡ _____

서답형
27 위 글의 밑줄 친 ⓒ가 가리키는 것을 본문에서 찾아 쓰시오.

➡ _____
_____

[01~03] 다음 글을 읽고 물음에 답하시오.

Today the Thunders and the Cobras have a game. Jihun's family is at the baseball stadium.

Jihun: Jian, this is your first time to come to the baseball stadium, isn't it?

Jian: Yes, I'm so excited. @I can't wait for the game to start.

Dad: Look, the players are coming out now!

Jian: Which team is the Thunders?

Jihun: Over there, behind third base. ⓑ그들은 원정 팀이기 때문에 어두운 회색 유니폼을 입고 있어.

01 위 글의 밑줄 친 @를 다음과 같이 바꿔 쓸 때 빈칸에 들어갈 알맞은 말을 쓰시오.

(1) I can't _____ to watch the game start.

(2) I'm _____ to watch the game start.

02 위 글의 밑줄 친 ⓑ의 우리말에 맞게 한 단어를 보충하여, 주어진 어휘를 배열하시오.

the / wearing / because / uniforms / gray / are / dark / they / they / team / are

➡ _____

_____

03 본문의 내용과 일치하도록 다음 빈칸 (A)와 (B)에 알맞은 단어를 쓰시오.

Jian has (A)_____ come to the baseball stadium before, so she is very (B)_____.

[04~06] 다음 글을 읽고 물음에 답하시오.

Jian: Does the visiting team always wear a dark color?

Jihun: Yes, that's @the rule. Home teams have bright uniforms and visiting teams have dark uniforms.

Jian: Why is that?

Mom: There is an interesting story about that. In the past, visiting teams could not wash their uniforms after every game. So they started wearing dark colors ⓑ to hide the dirt.

Jian: Hahaha! That was a good idea!

04 위 글의 밑줄 친 @the rule의 내용을 우리말로 쓰시오.

➡ _____

05 위 글의 밑줄 친 ⓑ를 다음과 같이 바꿔 쓸 때 빈칸에 들어갈 알맞은 말을 쓰시오.

= _____ _____ to hide the dirt
= _____ _____ to hide the dirt
= _____ _____ they _____ hide the dirt
= _____ _____ they _____ hide the dirt

06 다음 문장에서 위 글의 내용과 <u>다른</u> 부분을 찾아서 고치시오.

In the past, as visiting teams could not take a shower after every game, they started wearing dark colors to hide the dirt.

_____ ➡ _____

[07~09] 다음 글을 읽고 물음에 답하시오.

The players are warming up.

Jian: Who's your favorite player?

Jihun: Number 77.

Jian: What does the number mean?

Jihun: Hmm.... ⓐPlayers choose a number they like.

Dad: You know what? In the past, the numbers were determined by the players' batting order.

Jihun: ⓑThat means there were no players with number 77!

07 위 글의 밑줄 친 문장 ⓐ에 생략된 말을 넣어 문장을 다시 쓰시오.

➡ _____

08 본문의 내용과 일치하도록 다음 빈칸에 알맞은 숫자를 쓰시오.

> In the past, if a player was the fourth batter in the lineup, his uniform number was _____.
>
> *lineup: 타순

09 위 글의 밑줄 친 ⓑ의 이유를 우리말로 쓰시오.

➡ _____
_____

[10~12] 다음 글을 읽고 물음에 답하시오.

Now, Jihun's favorite player is about to bat. Jihun looks anxious.

Jian: ⓐ오빠가 가장 좋아하는 선수가 타석에 서네.

Jihun: Yes. He ___(A)___ 21 home runs already this year. If he ___(B)___ one more today, he will be the home run leader this season.

ⓑThe batter misses several balls. Now he has a full count. He is waiting for the next pitch.

Jihun: HOME RUN! HOME RUN!

Crack!

The ball flies fast. It is going, going, going, gone!

10 위 글의 빈칸 (A)와 (B)에 hit을 알맞은 형태로 각각 쓰시오.

(A) _____ (B) _____

11 위 글의 밑줄 친 ⓐ의 우리말에 맞게 주어진 어휘를 이용하여 6단어로 영작하시오.

> your, at

➡ _____

12 위 글의 밑줄 친 ⓑThe batter가 가리키는 것을 본문에서 찾아 쓰시오.

➡ _____

구석구석

Real-Life Zone B

A: Which sport do you like? Basketball or soccer?
어떤 ~을 좋아하니? A 아니면 B? Which는 의문형용사로 sport를 수식하며 '어느, 어떤'으로 해석한다
B: I like basketball. I'm going to play it with my friends this weekend. I can't wait.
= basketball   너무 기다려져(기대를 나타내는 표현)

구문해설 • be going to 동사원형: ~할 것이다

A: 너는 어떤 운동을 좋아하니? 농구 아니면 축구?
B: 농구를 좋아해. 이번 주말에 친구들이랑 농구를 할 거야. 너무 기다려져.

Writing Workshop

Abebe Bikila

Marathon Runner

Born: August 7, 1932

Nationality: Ethiopia

Speciality: He was known as a marathon winner at the Rome and Tokyo
be known as: ~로 알려져 있다
international sports competitions. When he was preparing to run the marathon
prepare는 목적어로 to부정사를 취한다.
in Rome, he found out that his shoes did not fit well, so he decided to run the
명사절을 이끄는 접속사   decide는 목적어로 to부정사를 취한다.
race without shoes. He felt pain during the race, but he finished the race as the
신발을 신지 않고, 신발 없이   ~ 중에   우승자로서
winner. He was one of the greatest runners in the world, wasn't he?
부가의문문은 앞 문장이 긍정이면 부정으로 만든다.

구문해설 • nationality: 국적 • speciality: 전문 (분야), 특별 사항 • competition: 경쟁, 대회, 시합
• prepare: 준비하다 • find out: 알아내다, 발견하다

Abebe Bikila
마라톤 선수
생일: 1932년 8월 7일
국적: 에티오피아
특별 사항: 그는 로마 국제 스포츠 대회와 도쿄 국제 스포츠 대회의 마라톤 우승자로 알려졌다. 그가 로마에서 달리기를 준비하던 도중에 자신의 신발이 잘 맞지 않는다는 것을 알고 그는 신발을 신지 않고 달리기로 결심했다. 그는 경주 도중에 통증을 느꼈지만 우승자로 경주를 끝마쳤다. 그는 세계에서 가장 위대한 달리기 선수들 중의 한 명이었다, 그렇지 않은가?

Wrap Up

Sarang Middle School Sports Day

Sarang Middle School Sports Day will be held on the school playing field on
조동사(will)+be+pp: 미래시제 수동태   요일 앞에 전치사 on
Wednesday, June 15. There will be various games such as baseball and soccer.
~ 와 같은(= like)
There will also be table tennis. It sounds like fun, doesn't it?
sound like+명사   부가의문문

구문해설 • various: 다양한, 여러 가지의

사랑 중학교 운동회
사랑 중학교 운동회가 학교 운동장에서 6월 15일 수요일에 열립니다. 야구와 축구 같은 여러 가지 게임이 있을 것입니다. 또한 탁구도 있을 것입니다. 재미있게 들리지요, 그렇지 않나요?

Words & Expressions

01 다음 중 밑줄 친 부분의 뜻풀이가 바르지 <u>않은</u> 것은?

① After the party Tommy will clean the living room and <u>then</u> do his homework. (그런 다음)

② There are some tips for making the perfect <u>pitch</u>. (투구)

③ I heard a <u>crack</u> when the vase fell over. (날카로운 소리)

④ It's important that you follow the <u>order</u> when adding liquids. (주문)

⑤ Do you think it will <u>fit</u> me? (맞다)

02 다음 밑줄 친 부분과 의미가 가장 가까운 것을 고르시오.

> She seemed <u>anxious</u> about the interview.

① excited　② pleased　③ bored
④ nervous　⑤ interested

03 다음 빈칸에 공통으로 들어갈 말을 쓰시오.

> • The batter _____ed several balls.
> • I don't want to _____ the game.

04 다음 빈칸에 들어갈 말로 적절한 것은?

> He was covered with dust _____ walking along the road.

① for　② when　③ unless
④ while　⑤ therefore

Conversation

[05~07] 다음 대화를 읽고 물음에 답하시오.

B: Jimin, _____(A)_____ (①)
G: I love table tennis. (②)
B: I like soccer. I'm a big fan of James Hood. He's a great soccer player. (③)
G: Oh, really? There's a soccer match this weekend between Korea and Turkey. Have you heard about it? (④)
B: Of course. I already have a ticket. I'm going to see the game on Saturday. I can't wait. (⑤)
G: That's fantastic.

05 위 대화의 ①~⑤ 중 다음 주어진 말이 들어갈 알맞은 곳은?

> How about you?

①　　②　　③　　④　　⑤

06 그림을 참고하여 빈칸 (A) 들어갈 말을 다음 조건에 맞게 쓰시오.

┌─ 조건 ─
│ • 대화에 나온 단어를 이용할 것
│ • 선호하는 것을 물을 것
│ • 두 문장으로 쓸 것
│ • 총 9 단어
└

➡ _____

07 다음 영영풀이에 해당하는 단어를 대화에서 찾아 쓰시오.

> an official piece of paper or card that shows you have paid to enter a place or do something

➡ _____

08 다음 대화의 밑줄 친 ⓐ~ⓔ 중 어법상 틀린 개수를 고르시오.

> G: What are you doing?
> B: ⓐI looked at a world map.
> G: You checked two countries. ⓑWhat country ⓒwould you like to visiting first? The U.S. ⓓor Mexico?
> B: I want to visit the U.S. ⓔI'd like to seeing a basketball game there.

① 1개 ② 2개 ③ 3개 ④ 4개 ⑤ 5개

[09~10] 다음 대화를 읽고 물음에 답하시오.

> A: 너는 어느 야구 선수를 좋아하니? Mike Hans or Daniel Parker?
> B: (A)I like Mike Hans.

09 위 대화의 밑줄 친 우리말을 영작하시오. (6 words)

➡ _____

10 위 대화의 밑줄 친 (A)의 문장 뒤에 생략된 말을 쓰시오. (4 words)

➡ _____

[11~12] 다음 대화를 읽고 물음에 답하시오.

> G: ⓐDo you want to see my new mountain bike?
> B: ⓑSure. When did you get it?
> G: ⓒMy father bought it for me. ⓓCan you come to my house this afternoon?
> B: ⓔOf course. (A)I can't wait to see it.

11 문장 ⓐ~ⓔ 중에서 대화의 흐름상 어색한 것을 고르시오.

① ⓐ ② ⓑ ③ ⓒ ④ ⓓ ⑤ ⓔ

12 밑줄 친 (A)를 주어진 단어를 이용해 같은 뜻이 되도록 영작하시오.

➡ _____ (looking)

Grammar

13 다음 중 어법상 올바른 것은?

① James teaches math, isn't he?
② She was great, didn't she?
③ The door was open by Tom.
④ A cake was made for him by his mom.
⑤ The wall is painted by the painters tomorrow.

14 다음 빈칸에 들어갈 말을 바르게 짝지은 것을 고르시오.

> • Our house _____ by Mrs. Green every Thursday.
> • Jejudo has some beautiful scenery, _____?

① are cleaned – does it
② is cleaned – isn't it
③ is cleaned – doesn't it
④ are cleaning – doesn't it
⑤ is cleaning – isn't it

15 다음 문장에서 틀린 것을 고쳐 다시 쓰시오.

(1) At last the thief caught the police last Saturday.

➡ _____

_____

(2) We don't know exactly when the accident was happened.

➡ _____

_____

(3) Delicious *galbitang* is being made to him by Anna.

➡ _____

_____

(4) Your love can show to your partner by saying "I love you."

➡ _____

_____

(5) Mariel was seen go out with her friend by Andy.

➡ _____

_____

(6) The festival put off by the city on account of the bad weather.

➡ _____

_____

(7) She didn't say good-bye, was she?

➡ _____

(8) She can play soccer very well, doesn't she?

➡ _____

(9) Tino is wearing a blue shirt, doesn't Tino?

➡ _____

(10) The hotel where we stayed was near the city hall, didn't there?

➡ _____

_____

16 다음 두 문장을 부가의문문을 써서 한 문장으로 바꿔 쓰시오.

(1) Tino likes eating ice cream. Doesn't he like eating ice cream?

➡ _____

(2) It was an interesting movie. Wasn't it an interesting movie?

➡ _____

17 다음 빈칸에 들어갈 전치사가 나머지와 다른 것은?

① He was covered _____ dust while walking along the road.

② I'm interested _____ Switzerland.

③ You should be satisfied _____ what you have.

④ The president was pleased _____ the news.

⑤ The boxes were filled _____ chocolate bars for the children.

18 다음 우리말을 괄호 안에 주어진 어휘를 이용하여 영작하시오.

(1) 네 개는 어제 어디에서 발견되었니?
(your dog, find, 6단어)

➡ _____

(2) 프랑스어는 아프리카에 있는 많은 국가들에서 말해진다. (Africa, speak , 8단어)

➡ _____

(3) 박씨는 매주 일요일마다 쇼핑을 해, 그렇지 않니?
(Mr. Park, go, every, 8단어)

➡ _____

Reading

[19~21] 다음 글을 읽고 물음에 답하시오.

　Today the Thunders and the Cobras have a game. Jihun's family is at the baseball stadium.

Jihun: Jian, this is your first time ⓐto come to the baseball stadium, isn't it?

Jian: Yes, I'm so excited. I (A)[can / can't] wait for the game to start.

Dad: Look, the players are coming out now!

Jian: Which team (B)[is / are] the Thunders?

Jihun: Over there, behind third base. ⓑThey are wearing dark gray uniforms because they are the (C)[visiting / visited] team.

19 위 글의 괄호 (A)~(C)에서 문맥이나 어법상 알맞은 낱말을 골라 쓰시오.

(A) _____ (B) _____ (C) _____

20 위 글의 밑줄 친 ⓐto come과 to부정사의 용법이 같은 것을 고르시오.

① He stopped his car to check the engine.
② She needs someone to talk with.
③ They hope to visit us next year.
④ He grew up to be a famous singer.
⑤ It is difficult to solve this problem.

21 위 글의 밑줄 친 ⓑThey가 가리키는 것을 영어로 쓰시오.

➡ _____

[22~24] 다음 글을 읽고 물음에 답하시오.

Jian: Does the visiting team always wear a dark color?

Jihun: Yes, that's the rule. Home teams have _____ⓐ_____ uniforms and visiting teams have _____ⓑ_____ uniforms.

Jian: Why is that?

Mom: There is an interesting story about that. In the past, visiting teams could not wash their uniforms after every game. So they started ⓒwearing dark colors to hide the dirt.

Jian: Hahaha! That was a good idea!

22 위 글의 빈칸 ⓐ와 ⓑ에 들어갈 알맞은 말을 고르시오.

① dark – bright　　② bright – light
③ bright – dark　　④ strong – dark
⑤ light – strong

23 아래 〈보기〉에서 위 글의 밑줄 친 ⓒwearing과 문법적 쓰임이 같은 것의 개수를 고르시오.

> ① I'm fond of wearing a pink dress.
> ② She is wearing a pink dress today.
> ③ Do you know the girl wearing a pink dress?
> ④ Wearing a pink dress makes me happy.
> ⑤ She came to the party wearing a pink dress.

① 1개　② 2개　③ 3개　④ 4개　⑤ 5개

24 위 글의 내용과 일치하지 <u>않는</u> 것은?

① 홈팀은 밝은 유니폼을 입는다.
② 원정 팀은 어두운 유니폼을 입는다.
③ 과거에는 원정 팀이 매 경기 후 유니폼을 세탁할 수가 없었다.
④ 원정 팀은 때를 숨기기 위해 어두운 색을 입기 시작했다.
⑤ 원정 팀의 유니폼은 더러웠을 것이라고 지안이는 말한다.

[25~26] 다음 글을 읽고 물음에 답하시오.

> The players are warming up.
> Jian: Who's your favorite player?
> Jihun: Number 77.
> Jian: What does the number mean?
> Jihun: Hmm.... Players choose a number they like.
> Dad: You know what? In the past, the numbers were determined by the players' batting ⓐorder.
> Jihun: That means there were no players with number 77!

25 위 글의 밑줄 친 ⓐorder와 같은 의미로 쓰인 것을 고르시오.

① I would like to place an <u>order</u> for ten copies of this book.
② The names are listed in alphabetical <u>order</u>.
③ When did the officer <u>order</u> them to fire?
④ The house was kept in good <u>order</u>.
⑤ He will <u>order</u> a new suit for his son.

26 위 글을 읽고 대답할 수 <u>없는</u> 질문은?

① What are the players doing now?
② Who's Jihun's favorite player?
③ Why does Jihun like the player?
④ What does the number 77 mean?
⑤ In the past, by what were the players' numbers determined?

[27~30] 다음 글을 읽고 물음에 답하시오.

> Now, Jihun's favorite player ⓐis about to bat. Jihun looks anxious.
> Jian: Your favorite player is ___(A)___ bat.
> Jihun: Yes. He has hit 21 home runs already this year. If he hits one more today, he will be the home run leader this season.
> The batter misses several balls. Now he has a full count. He is waiting ___(B)___ the next pitch.
> Jihun: HOME RUN! HOME RUN!
> Crack!
> The ball flies fast. It is going, going, going, ___(C)___ !

27 위 글의 빈칸 (A)와 (B)에 들어갈 전치사가 바르게 짝지어진 것은?

① on – for ② at – by ③ in – to
④ on – to ⑤ at – for

28 다음과 같은 뜻이 되도록 위 글의 빈칸 (C)에 go를 알맞은 형태로 쓰시오.

> Jihun's favorite player hits a home run.

➡ _____

29 위 글의 밑줄 친 ⓐ를 다음과 같이 바꿔 쓸 때 빈칸에 들어갈 알맞은 말을 쓰시오.

> is on the point of _____

30 다음 문장에서 위 글의 내용과 <u>다른</u> 부분을 찾아서 고치시오.

> When Jihun's favorite player hits a ball, it falls to the ground.

_____ ➡ _____

출제율 95%

01 다음 빈칸에 알맞은 말이 순서대로 바르게 나열된 것은?

> • My favorite player is _____ bat.
> • The film is about _____ .
> • He also takes English lessons _____ a week.

① on – to begin – two

② on – to beginning – twice

③ at – to begin – twice

④ at – to beginning – twice

⑤ at – beginning – two

출제율 95%

02 우리말 해석에 맞게 빈칸을 완성하시오.

(1) 선수는 1루로 걸어갔다.
  ➡ The player walked to _____ _____ .

(2) 그는 대회에서 우승하기 위해 열심히 노력했다.
  ➡ He tried hard to win the _____ .

(3) 나도 초콜릿을 좋아하지 않는다.
  ➡ I don't like chocolate, _____ .

(4) 반드시 순서를 지켜 주세요.
  ➡ Be sure to follow the _____ .

출제율 90%

03 〈보기〉에 주어진 단어를 이용해 빈칸 (A)와 (B)를 채우시오.

> A: What are you going to do on your vacation?
> B: I'm going _(A)_ a boat ride. I can't _(B)_ .

┌─ 보기 ─┐
go play take wait

(A) _____ (B) _____

출제율 100%

04 다음 중 밑줄 친 부분의 뜻풀이가 바르지 않은 것을 모두 고르시오.

① My daughter hid the ring under her bed. (숨겼다)

② Don't forget to check that your helmet fits properly. (맞다)

③ He can't go and I can't, either. (둘 중 하나)

④ It's not easy to decide what to eat. (결정하다)

⑤ Which team do you support? (지원하다)

출제율 90%

05 다음 단어와 영영풀이의 연결이 잘못된 것을 고르시오.

① pitch: a throw of the ball for the batter to hit it

② anxious: very nervous or worried about something

③ fit: to be the right size and shape for someone or something

④ home team: a sports team playing on the competing team's field or court

⑤ base: each corner of the square that makes a baseball diamond

[06~08] 다음 대화를 읽고 물음에 답하시오.

B1: Jiho, why are you _____ⓐ_____ such a hurry?

B2: Hi, Alex! I have to be home before 6:00. (①) The game between the Thunders _____ⓑ_____ the Cobras starts at 6:00.

B1: Oh, are you a baseball fan? Which team do you _(A)_ ? The Cobras or the Thunders?

B2: The Cobras. (②)

B1: Me, too! (③)

B2: Hurry ___©___! We only have thirty minutes left. (④)

B1: Okay. Maybe we can watch a game together sometime. (⑤)

B2: That's a great idea! How about going to the next Cobras home game together?

B1: Okay. They have a game next Saturday. We can eat fried chicken while watching the game!

B2: That sounds great. I can't wait!

출제율 90%

06 위 대화의 ①~⑤ 중 다음 주어진 말이 들어갈 알맞은 곳은?

> I don't want to miss the game either.

①　　　②　　　③　　　④　　　⑤

출제율 95%

07 위 대화의 빈칸 (A)에 들어갈 알맞은 단어를 고르시오.

① provide　　② support　　③ make
④ enjoy　　⑤ play

출제율 100%

08 위 대화의 빈칸 ⓐ~ⓒ에 알맞은 말을 〈보기〉에서 골라 쓰시오.

┌─ 보기 ─┐
and　at　for　in　or　to　up

ⓐ _____　ⓑ _____　ⓒ _____

[09~10] 다음 대화를 읽고 물음에 답하시오.

G: What are you doing?

B: I'm looking at a world map.

G: You checked two countries. 어느 나라에 먼저 방문하고 싶어? 미국 아니면 멕시코?

B: I want to visit the U.S. I'd like to see a basketball game there.

출제율 85%

09 밑줄 친 우리말을 주어진 단어를 이용하여 영작하시오.

> (Mexico, would, country, like, The U.S.)

➡ _____
_____

출제율 95%

10 위 대화를 읽고 답할 수 없는 질문을 고르시오.

① What countries did the boy check on a world map?

② What does the boy want to do in Mexico?

③ What is the boy doing now?

④ Which country does the boy want to go first? Mexico or the U.S.?

⑤ What would the boy like to do when he visits the U.S.?

[11~12] 다음 대화를 읽고 물음에 답하시오.

B: Jimin, which sport do you like? Soccer or table tennis?

G: I love table tennis. How about you, Yunho?

B: I like soccer. I'm a big fan of James Hood. He's a great soccer player.

G: Oh, really? 이번 주말에 한국 대 터키의 축구 경기가 있어. (Korea, between, a, match, Turkey, soccer, there's, weekend, and, this) Have you heard about it?

B: Of course. I already have a ticket. I'm going to see the game on Saturday. I can't wait.

G: That's fantastic.

출제율 90%

11 위 대화의 밑줄 친 우리말에 맞게 괄호 안의 단어를 알맞게 배열하여 영작하시오.

➡ _____

_____

출제율 95%

12 위 대화의 내용과 일치하는 것을 고르시오.

① Jimin does not like soccer.

② Jimin and Yunho like table tennis.

③ Yunho has heard about the soccer match this weekend.

④ Yunho is going to see the final baseball game.

⑤ Jimin already has a soccer match ticket.

출제율 90%

13 다음 밑줄 친 부분을 생략할 수 있는 것은?

① A lot of waste is thrown away in big cities by people.

② This picture was drawn by Lio.

③ The photos were not taken by my brother.

④ Math was taught to us by Mr. Lee.

⑤ This report was written by the student.

출제율 90%

14 다음 주어진 문장과 같은 뜻이 되도록 빈칸을 채우시오.

(1) Simon will read his son the book tonight.

➡ The book _____

_____ .

(2) Peter fixed the car this morning.

➡ The car _____ .

출제율 100%

15 다음 빈칸을 두 단어로 채워 상대방의 동의를 구하는 문장으로 완성하시오.

(1) She had her hair cut, _____ _____ ?

(2) The boys can play the violin, _____

_____ ?

(3) The movie wasn't interesting at all,

_____ _____ ?

[16~18] 다음 글을 읽고 물음에 답하시오.

Today the Thunders and the Cobras have a game. Jihun's family is at the baseball stadium.

Jihun: Jian, this is your first time to come to the baseball stadium, ___ⓐ___ ?

Jian: Yes, I'm so (A)[exciting / excited]. I can't wait for the game (B)[starting / to start].

Dad: Look, the players are coming out now!

Jian: Which team is the Thunders?

Jihun: Over there, behind (C)[three bases / third base]. They are wearing dark gray uniforms because they are the visiting team.

출제율 95%

16 위 글의 빈칸 ⓐ에 들어갈 알맞은 부가의문문을 쓰시오.

➡ _____

출제율 90%

17 위 글의 괄호 (A)~(C)에서 문맥이나 어법상 알맞은 것을 골라 쓰시오.

(A) _____ (B) _____ (C) _____

출제율 100%

18 위 글을 읽고 대답할 수 없는 질문은?

① What teams have a game today?

② Where is Jihun's family now?

③ Has Jian come to the baseball stadium before?

④ How does Jian feel to be in the baseball stadium?

⑤ Why are the players of the visiting team wearing dark gray uniforms?

[19~21] 다음 글을 읽고 물음에 답하시오.

Jian: Does the visiting team always wear a dark color?

Jihun: Yes, that's the rule. Home teams have bright uniforms and visiting teams have dark uniforms.

Jian: Why is that?

Mom: There is an interesting story about that. In the past, visiting teams could not wash their uniforms after every game. So they started wearing dark colors ⓐto hide the dirt.

Jian: Hahaha! That was a good idea!

19 위 글의 주제로 알맞은 것을 고르시오.

① the reason why home teams like bright uniforms
② the reason why visiting teams wear dark uniforms
③ the difficulties that visiting teams experienced
④ the strong points of bright uniforms
⑤ the weak points of dark uniforms

20 Why did visiting teams start wearing dark colors? Fill in the blanks with suitable words.

Because visiting teams could not _____ _____ _____ after every game in the past, they started wearing dark colors _____ _____ the dirt.

21 위 글의 밑줄 친 ⓐto hide와 to부정사의 용법이 다른 것을 모두 고르시오.

① He studied hard to pass the exam.
② I didn't expect to see you here.
③ Tom needed someone to help him.
④ It's fun to teach the students.
⑤ I have come here to learn English.

[22~24] 다음 글을 읽고 물음에 답하시오.

The players are warming up.

Jian: Who's your favorite player?

Jihun: Number 77.

Jian: What does the number mean?

Jihun: Hmm.... Players choose a number they like.

Dad: ⓐYou know what? In the past, the numbers were determined by the players' batting order.

Jihun: That means there were no players with number 77!

22 What is the number that Jihun's favorite player likes? Answer in English in a full sentence. (3 words)

➡ _____

23 위 글의 밑줄 친 ⓐYou know what?과 바꿔 쓸 수 있는 말을 모두 고르시오.

① You know something?
② How do you feel about it?
③ How would you like it?
④ Guess what!
⑤ What do you think about it?

24 위 글의 내용과 일치하지 않는 것은?

① 선수들이 몸을 풀고 있다.
② 지안이가 가장 좋아하는 선수는 77번 선수이다.
③ 지훈이는 선수들이 원하는 번호를 선택한다고 말한다.
④ 과거에는 번호가 선수들의 타순에 의해 결정되었다.
⑤ 과거에는 77번 선수가 없었다.

[01~02] 다음 대화의 흐름상 어색한 부분을 찾아 고치시오.

01

> B: Don't forget that we're going rock climbing this weekend!
> G: Don't worry. I will forget.
> B: I'm excited about going. I can't wait.

_____ ➡ _____

02

> A: Which sport do you like? Bowling or baseball?
> B: I like baseball. I'm going to play it with my friends this weekend. I can wait.

_____ ➡ _____

03 대화의 밑줄 친 부분과 같은 의미가 되도록 주어진 단어를 이용하여 문장을 완성하시오.

> G: Did you get the tickets?
> B: Yes! I can't wait to watch the game.

➡ _____ (forward)

04 다음 주어진 문장을 능동태는 수동태로, 수동태는 능동태로 바꾸시오.

(1) What did she cook for her family last night?

➡ _____

(2) Dabotap was built in the eighth century by Kimdaesung.

➡ _____

(3) The plants are watered by Kevin every morning.

➡ _____

(4) My friend gave me some flowers two days ago.

➡ _____
_____
_____

05 다음 문장에서 틀린 것을 고쳐 다시 쓰시오.

(1) The light bulb invented Edison.

➡ _____
_____

(2) Sue was made a dress by her mom.

➡ _____

(3) You aren't paying attention, do you?

➡ _____

(4) You forgot to bring your umbrella, were not you?

➡ _____

Today the Thunders and the Cobras have a game. Jihun's family is at the baseball stadium.

Jihun: Jian, this is your first time to come to the baseball stadium, isn't it?

Jian: Yes, I'm so ___(A)___ . ⓐ나는 경기가 빨리 시작했으면 좋겠어.

Dad: Look, the players are coming out now!

Jian: Which team is the Thunders?

Jihun: Over there, behind third base. They are ___(B)___ dark gray uniforms because they are the visiting team.

06 위 글의 빈칸 (A), (B)에 알맞은 말을 주어진 어휘를 이용하여 쓰시오.

> (A) excite, (B) wear

(A) _____ (B) _____

07 위 글의 밑줄 친 ⓐ의 우리말에 맞게 주어진 어구를 이용하여 8단어로 영작하시오.

> can't wait, start

➡ _____

08 Why are the Thunders wearing dark gray uniforms? Fill in the blank with suitable words.

➡ Because _____ .

09 다음 문장에서 위 글의 내용과 <u>다른</u> 부분을 찾아서 고치시오.

> Jian has come to the baseball stadium before.

_____ ➡ _____

The players are (A)[warming / warmed] up.

Jian: (B)[Whose / Who's] your favorite player?

Jihun: Number 77.

Jian: What does the number mean?

Jihun: Hmm.... ⓐPlayers choose a number they like.

Dad: You know (C)[how / what]? In the past, ⓑthe numbers were determined by the players' batting order.

Jihun: ⓒThat means there were no players with number 77!

10 위 글의 괄호 (A)~(C)에서 문맥이나 어법상 알맞은 낱말을 골라 쓰시오.

(A) _____ (B) _____ (C) _____

11 위 글의 밑줄 친 ⓐ를 수동태로 고치시오.

➡ _____

_____

12 위 글의 밑줄 친 ⓑ를 능동태로 고치시오.

➡ _____

_____

13 위 글의 밑줄 친 ⓒThat이 가리키는 것을 본문에서 찾아 쓰시오.

➡ _____

_____

01 주어진 동사의 수동태를 사용하여 다양한 문장을 쓰시오.

> 보기
>
> choose,　donate,　turn off,　make,　write

(1) _____

(2) _____

(3) _____

(4) _____

(5) _____

02 다음 내용을 바탕으로 선수의 프로필을 작성하시오.

Seri Park

Professional golfer

Born: September 8, 1977

Nationality: South Korea

Speciality: • When young: the best amateur golfer

• in 1996: turned professional golfer

• from 1998 to 2016: played on the LPGA Tours

• in November 2007: inducted into the World Golf Hall of Fame

*induct: (조직에) 가입시키다

Seri Park

Professional golfer

Born: September 8, 1977

Nationality: South Korea

Speciality: She was the best (A)_____ golfer when she was young. She turned (B)_____ golfer in 1996. She played on the (C)_____ from 1998 to 2016. She was inducted into the (D)_____ in November 2007. She was great, wasn't she?

단원별 모의고사

01 다음 밑줄 친 부분과 의미가 가까운 것을 고르시오.

The price is <u>determined</u> by supply and demand.

① decided   ② got
③ agreed   ④ made
⑤ discussed

02 다음 제시된 의미에 맞는 단어를 주어진 철자로 시작하여 빈 칸에 쓰고 알맞은 것을 골라 문장을 완성하시오. (필요하면 어형 변화를 할 것)

- c_____: an event or contest in which people try to win something by defeating others
- c_____: the sudden loud explosive sound of something when it falls or bumps into itself or something else
- p_____: the time before the moment of speaking or writing
- h_____: to put something out of sight

(1) The dog _____ the bone in the ground yesterday.
(2) There were huge _____ of thunders all night long.
(3) The _____ is heating up.
(4) In the _____, people traveled on horseback.

03 다음 우리말에 맞게 빈칸에 알맞은 말을 쓰시오.

(1) 제 차는 저기 주차장에 주차되어 있습니다.
➡ My car is in the parking lot _____ _____.

(2) 그녀는 급해서 빨간 불을 무시하고 지나갔다.
➡ She was _____ _____ _____ and drove through a red light.

(3) 언제 그의 새로운 소설이 나오나요?
➡ When will his new novel _____ _____?

(4) 남자는 수하물을 기다리고 있다.
➡ The man is _____ _____ his luggage.

04 다음 중 동사와의 연결이 <u>어색한</u> 것을 고르시오.

① go surfing   ② play soccer
③ go swimming   ④ go tennis
⑤ play baseball

[05~06] 다음 대화를 읽고 물음에 답하시오.

A: Which shorts do you like? The green ones or the red ones?
B: (A)<u>I like the green ones.</u>

05 위 대화의 밑줄 친 문장 (A)에서 생략된 부분을 쓰시오.

➡ _____

06 밑줄 친 문장 (A)와 같은 의미가 되도록 주어진 단어를 이용해 문장을 완성하시오.

➡ _____ (to, 9단어)

[07~11] 다음 대화를 읽고 물음에 답하시오.

> B1: Jiho, why are you in such a hurry?
> B2: Hi, Alex! I have to be home before 6:00. The game between the Thunders and the Cobras (A)[start / starts] at 6:00. (①)
> B1: Oh, are you a baseball fan? ___ⓐ___ The Cobras or the Thunders?
> B2: The Cobras. (②)
> B1: Me, too! I don't want to miss the game (B)[either / too]. (③)
> B2: Hurry up! We only have thirty minutes (C)[left / leaving].
> B1: Okay. Maybe we can watch a game together sometime. (④)
> B2: That's a great idea! (⑤)
> B1: Okay. They have a game next Saturday. We can eat fried chicken while watching the game!
> B2: That sounds great. I can't wait!

07 위 대화의 ①~⑤ 중 다음 주어진 문장이 들어갈 알맞은 곳은?

> How about going to the next Cobras home game together?

①   ②   ③   ④   ⑤

08 위 대화의 빈칸 ⓐ에 들어갈 알맞은 표현을 고르시오.

① Where can we watch the game?
② Which team do you support?
③ Do you like baseball?
④ What are they going to do at 6:00?
⑤ What do you want to eat while watching TV?

09 위 대화의 (A)~(C)에서 알맞은 말을 골라 쓰시오.

(A) _____ (B) _____ (C) _____

10 다음 영영풀이에 해당하는 단어를 대화에서 찾아 쓰시오.

> a group of people who play a sport or game together against other groups of people

➡ _____

11 위 대화의 내용과 일치하지 <u>않는</u> 것을 고르시오.

① It is five-thirty now.
② They watched the Cobras home game together.
③ Jiho is a baseball fan.
④ There is a baseball game at 6:00.
⑤ Jiho is in a hurry to watch a baseball game.

12 다음 대화의 흐름상 어색한 부분을 찾아 고치시오. (밑줄 친 부분에서 고를 것)

> G: I'm thinking about getting a pet. Do you have a pet?
> B: Yes, I do. I have a dog and a cat.
> G: <u>What do you think?</u> <u>Which pet is more for me?</u> <u>A cat or a dog?</u>
> B: <u>Why don't you come to my house someday and play with my pets?</u> <u>Then you can decide.</u>

_____ ➡ _____

13 다음 중 어법상 바른 것은?

① Cheesecake bakes for Scott every day.
② Mr. Lee was written a letter.
③ My computer was fixed my brother.
④ Mastering English in a year or two is really difficult, isn't it?
⑤ You have a pen, do you?

14 다음 중 능동태를 수동태로 잘못 바꾼 것은?

① People living near the river have eaten fish.

= Fish have been eaten by people living near the river.

② His teacher made him study English every day.

= He was made to study English every day by his teacher.

③ They gave up the plan because of the heavy costs.

= The plan was given because of the heavy costs.

④ Sam gave Alicia a present.

= A present was given to Alicia by Sam.

⑤ Amedeo Modigliani painted *Woman with Blue Eyes* in 1918.

= *Woman with Blue Eyes* was painted by Amedeo Modigliani in 1918.

15 다음 문장에서 틀린 것을 고치시오.

(1) This house is made from stone.

_____ ➡ _____

(2) William was bought a new computer by her mother.

_____ ➡

_____

(3) The Olympic Games are taken place every four years.

_____ ➡ _____

(4) They are doctors, don't they?

_____ ➡ _____

(5) Come home by 8 o'clock tonight, can't you?

_____ ➡ _____

16 다음 밑줄 친 부분의 쓰임이 나머지 넷과 다른 것은?

① The station was <u>built</u> in 1894.

② His words often <u>made</u> no sense.

③ The roof of my house was <u>covered</u> with snow.

④ These cookies were <u>cooked</u> for him by Joanna.

⑤ The greetings are <u>used</u> to welcome people.

17 다음 빈칸에 알맞은 부가의문문을 쓰시오.

(1) You like dogs, _____ _____?

(2) Emily is tired, _____ _____?

(3) He was one of the greatest runners in the world, _____ _____?

(4) The man always parks his car on the street, _____ _____?

(5) You will go there, _____ _____?

(6) You looked so busy, _____ _____?

(7) Be good to yourself, _____ _____?

(8) Let's help that child, _____ _____?

[18~19] 다음 글을 읽고 물음에 답하시오.

Today the Thunders and the Cobras have a game. Jihun's family is at the baseball stadium.

Jihun: Jian, this is your first time to come to the baseball stadium, isn't it?

Jian: Yes, I'm so excited. I can't wait for the game to start.

Dad: Look, the players are coming out now!

Jian: Which team is the Thunders?

Jihun: Over there, behind third base. They are wearing dark gray uniforms because they are the ⓐ<u>visiting</u> team.

18 아래 〈보기〉에서 위 글의 밑줄 친 ⓐvisiting과 문법적 쓰임이 다른 것의 개수를 고르시오.

> ① I came home running all the way from school.
> ② He enjoyed studying with his friends.
> ③ Mastering foreign languages is not easy.
> ④ The boy sitting under the tree is my brother.
> ⑤ Thank you for showing me the way to the subway station.

① 1개　② 2개　③ 3개　④ 4개　⑤ 5개

19 Which team is the home team, the Thunders or the Cobras? Answer in English. (2 words)

➡ _____

[20~21] 다음 글을 읽고 물음에 답하시오.

Jian: Does the visiting team always wear a dark color?

Jihun: Yes, that's the rule. Home teams have bright uniforms and visiting teams have dark uniforms.

Jian: Why is that?

Mom: There is an interesting story about that. In the past, visiting teams could not wash their uniforms after every game. So they started wearing dark colors to hide the dirt.

Jian: Hahaha! ⓐThat was a good idea!

20 위 글의 밑줄 친 ⓐThat이 가리키는 것을 본문에서 찾아 쓰시오.

➡ _____

21 위 글을 읽고 대답할 수 없는 질문은?

① Does the home team always wear a bright color?
② What's the rule about the color of the uniforms?
③ Why did visiting teams have dark uniforms in the past?
④ What team started wearing dark colors for the first time?
⑤ What does Jian think about the origin of dark uniforms?

[22~23] 다음 글을 읽고 물음에 답하시오.

The players are warming up.

Jian: Who's your favorite player?

Jihun: Number 77.

Jian: What does the number mean?

Jihun: Hmm.... Players choose a number they like.

Dad: You know what? In the past, ⓐ번호가 선수들의 타순에 의해 결정되었단다.

Jihun: That means there were no players with number 77!

22 위 글의 밑줄 친 ⓐ의 우리말에 맞게 한 단어를 보충하여, 주어진 어휘를 알맞게 배열하시오.

> order / were / the numbers / batting / determined / the players'

➡ _____

_____

23 다음 빈칸 (A)와 (B)에 알맞은 단어를 넣어 현재 등번호가 결정되는 방법에 대한 설명을 완성하시오.

> At present, the number is chosen by (A)_____ themselves, which is a number they (B)_____.

중간 + 기말
plus
적중100
영어 기출문제집

영어 중 2
시사 | 송미정

Best Collection

내용문의 중등영어발전소 적중100 편집부 TEL 070-7707-0457

INSIGHT
on the textbook

교과서 파헤치기

영어 기출 문제집

적중 100 plus
1학기 전과정

영어 중 2

시사 | 송미정

INSIGHT
on the textbook

교과서 파헤치기

※ 다음 영어를 우리말로 쓰시오.

01 favor _____

02 overcome _____

03 detective _____

04 weak _____

05 complete _____

06 worry _____

07 Europe _____

08 experience _____

09 start _____

10 by _____

11 stay _____

12 right _____

13 adopt _____

14 freely _____

15 cartoon _____

16 writer _____

17 goal _____

18 hope _____

19 introduce _____

20 challenging _____

21 draw _____

22 wash _____

23 surprise _____

24 save _____

25 book fair _____

26 Chinese _____

27 walk _____

28 weakness _____

29 missing _____

30 someday _____

31 pleased _____

32 fully _____

33 finally _____

34 spend _____

35 take care of _____

36 be willing to 동사원형 _____

37 for a while _____

38 share A with B _____

39 ask for help _____

40 get into _____

41 be ready to 동사원형 _____

42 make an effort _____

43 throw away _____

※ 다음 우리말을 영어로 쓰시오.

01 국가의, 국민의

02 콘서트

03 달성하고 싶은 일들을 적은 목록

04 드라마

05 악기

06 구하다, 아끼다

07 놀라게 하다

08 씻다

09 탐정, 형사

10 도전적인, 힘든

11 좋아하는

12 쓰다, 소비하다

13 밴드

14 약점

15 축제

16 완전히

17 과목

18 언젠가

19 특별한

20 없어진, 분실한

21 계획; 계획하다

22 기쁜

23 타다

24 마지막으로

25 팔다, 판매하다

26 말하다

27 입양하다

28 걱정하다

29 호의, 친절

30 머무르다, 지내다

31 극복하다

32 경험하다; 경험

33 약한

34 완료하다, 완결하다

35 ~말까지

36 (병·상황 등이) 나아지다

37 ~할 준비가 되다

38 ~을 버리다, ~을 던지다

39 도움을 청하다

40 노력하다

41 잠깐

42 기꺼이 ~하다

43 친구를 사귀다

※ 다음 영영풀이에 알맞은 단어를 <보기>에서 골라 쓴 후, 우리말 뜻을 쓰시오.

1 _____ : completely: _____

2 _____ : exactly in a particular position or place _____

3 _____ : difficult in an interesting or enjoyable way: _____

4 _____ : group of musicians, especially a group that plays popular music: _____

5 _____ : without anyone stopping or limiting something: _____

6 _____ : something that you hope to achieve in the future: _____

7 _____ : to a greater degree or more times than anything else: _____

8 _____ : to successfully control a feeling or problem: _____

9 _____ : to use your money to pay for goods or services: _____

10 _____ : to produce a picture of something using a pencil, pen, etc.: _____

11 _____ : an event at which people or businesses show and sell their books: _____

12 _____ : to make someone or something safe from danger, harm, or destruction: _____

13 _____ : at an unknown time in the future, especially a long time in the future: _____

14 _____ : to finish doing or making something, especially when it has taken a long time: _____

15 _____ : something that you do for someone in order to help them or be kind to them: _____

16 _____ : someone whose job is to discover what has happened in a crime or other situation and to find the people involved: _____

보기			
right	save	freely	draw
band	complete	challenging	someday
most	favor	goal	fully
spend	detective	overcome	book fair

※ 다음 우리말과 일치하도록 빈칸에 알맞은 말을 쓰시오.

해석

Listen & Speak 1 A

G: I _____ I _____ _____ _____ this year.

B: You will. _____ _____ .

1. G: 난 올해 좋은 성적을 얻길 바라.
   B: 그럴 거야. 걱정하지 마.

Listen & Speak 1 B

1. B: Hana, _____ _____ _____ today. Happy birthday!

   G: Thank you.

   B: _____ do you _____ _____ your birthday?

   G: _____ _____ _____ _____ a new computer.

2. G: _____ are you _____ ?

   B: _____ _____ my _____ _____ for the new school year.

   G: That sounds _____ ! What's _____ _____ thing on your list?

   B: I _____ I _____ _____ _____ _____ new friends.

3. G: _____ was your _____ _____ ?

   B: _____ _____ fun! We _____ _____ our dreams _____ the future.

   G: Oh, did _____ ? So _____ me. What's _____ ?

   B: Well, first, I _____ _____ become a rock star _____ .

1. B: 하나야, 오늘은 너의 생일이야. 축하해!
   G: 고마워.
   B: 생일 선물로 뭘 원하니?
   G: 새 컴퓨터를 받길 바라.

2. G: 뭐 하고 있니?
   B: 나는 새 학년을 맞이하여 소원 목록을 만들고 있어.
   G: 멋지다! 목록의 첫 번째는 뭐니?
   B: 나는 새로운 친구들을 많이 사귈 수 있기를 바라.

3. G: 영어 수업은 어땠니?
   B: 재밌었어! 우리는 미래에 대한 꿈을 적었어.
   G: 오, 그랬니? 나에게 말해줘. 너의 꿈은 뭐니?
   B: 음, 우선, 나는 내가 언젠가 록 스타가 되길 바라.

Listen & Speak 1 C

1. A: I _____ _____ _____ _____ to Europe _____ summer.

   B: That _____ great.

2. A: I _____ I _____ _____ my grandmother.

   B: That _____ great.

3. A: I _____ _____ _____ _____ how _____ swim.

   B: That _____ _____ .

1. A: 나는 이번 여름에 유럽으로 여행을 할 수 있기를 바라.
   B: 좋은데.

2. A: 나는 할머니를 뵐 수 있기를 바라.
   B: 좋은데.

3. A: 나는 수영하는 법을 배울 수 있기를 바라.
   B: 좋은데.

Everyday English 2. A Function Practice 2

G: _____ _____ _____ _____ _____ do tomorrow?

B: I'm _____ _____ _____ my hair _____ .

Everyday English 2 – B Listening Activity

1. B: What are you _____ _____ _____ _____ ?

    G: _____ _____ to go to the _____ _____ _____ Jimmy. Would you _____ _____ _____ us?

    B: Sure. _____ _____ are you _____ _____ _____ ?

    G: _____ 3:00 _____ _____ _____ the school cafeteria.

2. G: What _____ _____ _____ to do tomorrow?

    B: Well, I'm _____ _____ .

    G: Then _____ _____ _____ to a movie _____ me?

    B: That _____ wonderful.

3. G: Jack! _____ you do me _____ _____ ?

    B: Yes, _____ is it?

    G: I'm planning _____ _____ a new bike _____ . Can you _____ me _____ _____ ?

    B: Sure, I'd _____ _____ .

Listen & Speak 2 C

1. A: What are you planning to _____ _____ the school festival?

    B: I'm _____ _____ _____ snacks.

2. A: What _____ _____ _____ _____ do at the school festival?

    B: I'm _____ _____ _____ _____ _____ _____ show.

3. A: _____ _____ _____ _____ _____ to do at the school festival?

    B: I'm planning _____ _____ _____ _____ _____ .

※ 다음 우리말에 맞도록 대화를 영이로 쓰시오.

| Listen & Speak 1 A |

G: _____

B: _____

1. G: 난 올해 좋은 성적을 얻길 바라.
   B: 그럴 거야. 걱정하지 마.

| Listen & Speak 1 B |

1. B: _____
   G: _____
   B: _____
   G: _____

2. G: _____
   B: _____
   G: _____
   B: _____

3. G: _____
   B: _____
   G: _____
   B: _____

1. B: 하나야, 오늘은 너의 생일이야. 축하해!
   G: 고마워.
   B: 생일 선물로 뭘 원하니?
   G: 새 컴퓨터를 받길 바라.

2. G: 뭐 하고 있니?
   B: 나는 새 학년을 맞이하여 소원 목록을 만들고 있어.
   G: 멋지다! 목록의 첫 번째는 뭐니?
   B: 나는 새로운 친구들을 많이 사귈 수 있기를 바라.

3. G: 영어 수업은 어땠니?
   B: 재밌었어! 우리는 미래에 대한 꿈을 적었어.
   G: 오, 그랬니? 나에게 말해줘. 너의 꿈은 뭐니?
   B: 음, 우선, 나는 내가 언젠가 록 스타가 되길 바라.

| Listen & Speak 1 C |

1. A: _____
   B: _____

2. A: _____
   B: _____

3. A: _____
   B: _____

1. A: 나는 이번 여름에 유럽으로 여행을 할 수 있기를 바라.
   B: 좋은데.

2. A: 나는 할머니를 뵐 수 있기를 바라.
   B: 좋은데.

3. A: 나는 수영하는 법을 배울 수 있기를 바라.
   B: 좋은데.

Everyday English 2. A Function Practice 2

G: _____

B: _____

Everyday English 2 – B Listening Activity

1. B: _____
   G: _____
   B: _____
   G: _____

2. G: _____
   B: _____
   G: _____
   B: _____

3. G: _____
   B: _____
   G: _____
   B: _____

1. B: 내일 뭐 할 거니?
   G: 지미랑 도서 박람회에 갈 계획이야. 같이 갈래?
   B: 물론이지. 몇 시에 만날 거니?
   G: 학교 식당 앞에서 3시에.

2. G: 내일 뭐 할 계획이니?
   B: 글쎄, 잘 모르겠어.
   G: 그럼, 나랑 영화 보러 가는 게 어때?
   B: 좋아.

3. G: 잭! 부탁 좀 들어줄래?
   B: 응, 뭔데?
   G: 내일 새 자전거를 살 계획이야. 하나 고르는 걸 도와줄 수 있니?
   B: 좋아. 그러고 싶어.

Listen & Speak 2 C

1. A: _____
   B: _____

2. A: _____
   B: _____

3. A: _____
   B: _____

1. A: 학교 축제에서 뭐 할 계획이니?
   B: 간식을 팔 계획이야.

2. A: 학교 축제에서 뭐 할 계획이니?
   B: 마술 쇼를 할 계획이야.

3. A: 학교 축제에서 뭐 할 계획이니?
   B: 그룹으로 춤 출 계획이야.

※ 다음 우리말과 일치하도록 빈칸에 알맞은 것을 골라 쓰시오.

1 _____ "Bucket List" for the New _____ _____
A. Year   B. School   C. my

2 _____, _____.
A. everyone   B. hi

3 Today is the _____ day of _____ new school _____.
A. year   B. our   C. first

4 I want to _____ your _____ and hopes for _____ year.
A. this   B. plans   C. hear

5 _____ do you _____ to do _____?
A. most   B. want   C. what

6 _____ _____ three _____ you want to do.
A. things   B. about   C. think

7 And _____, _____ a bucket list and _____ it _____ your friends.
A. with   B. share   C. make   D. then

8 Hi! _____ _____.
A. Jinsu   B. I'm

9 This is _____ bucket _____ for _____ _____.
A. year   B. this   C. list   D. my

10 _____, I want to go _____ a bike _____ of Jejudo this summer.
A. tour   B. on   C. first

11 I've _____ there before, but I want to _____ the island more _____ _____ my bike this time.
A. on   B. freely   C. experience   D. been

12 My _____ goal is _____ learn _____ to play the guitar.
A. how   B. to   C. second

13 I _____ the guitar has the _____ beautiful _____ of all musical _____.
A. instruments   B. sound   C. most   D. think

1 나의 새 학년 버킷 리스트

2 모두들, 안녕.

3 오늘은 우리 새 학년의 첫날이에요.

4 저는 여러분들의 올해 계획과 희망을 듣고 싶어요.

5 여러분이 가장 원하는 것은 무엇인가요?

6 여러분이 원하는 것 세 가지를 생각해 보세요.

7 그리고 나서 버킷 리스트를 만들어 친구들과 공유해 봐요.

8 안녕하세요! 저는 진수예요.

9 이것은 올해 제 버킷 리스트예요.

10 우선, 저는 이번 여름에 제주도로 자전거 여행을 가고 싶어요.

11 저는 그곳을 전에 가 본 적이 있지만 이번에는 제 자전거를 타고 좀 더 자유롭게 그 섬을 경험해 보고 싶어요.

12 제 두 번째 목표는 기타 연주하는 법을 배우는 거예요.

13 저는 기타가 모든 악기 중에 가장 아름다운 소리를 낸다고 생각해요.

14 I hope I can _____ my favorite song _____ my guitar _____ the _____ of this year.

    A. end   B. by   C. on   D. play

15 _____, I want to _____ a good _____ _____ math.

    A. in   B. grade   C. get   D. finally

16 Math is my _____ _____.

    A. subject   B. weakest

17 This year, I'll _____ more effort _____ studying math to _____ my _____.

    A. weakness   B. overcome   C. into   D. put

18 Hi! _____ _____ _____ Somi.

    A. is   B. name   C. my

19 First, I want to see a concert of my _____ band _____ in _____ of the _____.

    A. stage   B. front   C. right   D. favorite

20 I'm _____ to stand in _____ all night to _____ the front area.

    A. enter   B. line   C. willing

21 _____, I want to _____ a _____.

    A. puppy   B. adopt   C. second

22 I've _____ _____ a puppy.

    A. wanted   B. always

23 I think I'm _____ _____ to take _____ of a pet now.

    A. care   B. ready   C. fully

24 My _____ goal is a _____ more _____.

    A. challenging   B. little   C. last

25 I'd _____ to read _____ of the Sherlock Holmes _____.

    A. stories   B. all   C. like

26 I became a _____ fan of this _____ series last year, _____ I don't want to _____ a single one.

    A. miss   B. so   C. detective   D. big

---

14 올해 말쯤에는 제가 가장 좋아하는 곡을 제 기타로 연주할 수 있으면 좋겠어요.

15 마지막으로 수학에서 좋은 점수를 받고 싶어요.

16 수학은 제가 가장 약한 과목이에요.

17 올해는 제 약점을 극복하기 위해 수학 공부에 좀 더 노력을 기울일 거예요.

18 안녕하세요! 제 이름은 소미예요.

19 우선, 저는 제가 가장 좋아하는 밴드의 공연을 무대 바로 앞에서 보고 싶어요.

20 앞자리에 들어가기 위해 저는 기꺼이 밤새 줄을 서서 기다릴 거예요.

21 두 번째로, 강아지를 입양하고 싶어요.

22 저는 항상 강아지를 원해 왔어요.

23 이제는 제가 애완동물을 돌볼 준비가 완벽히 되었다고 생각해요.

24 제 마지막 목표는 좀 더 도전적이에요.

25 저는 셜록 홈스 이야기들을 모두 읽고 싶어요.

26 저는 작년에 이 탐정 시리즈의 열성 팬이 되었어요. 그래서 저는 단 하나도 놓치고 싶지 않아요.

※ 다음 우리말과 일치하도록 빈칸에 알맞은 말을 쓰시오.

1 My "Bucket List" _____ _____ _____ _____ _____

2 _____, _____.

3 Today is _____ _____ _____ of our _____ _____ _____.

4 I _____ _____ _____ your plans and hopes _____ _____ _____.

5 _____ do you _____ to do _____?

6 _____ _____ three things _____ _____ _____ _____.

7 And then, _____ _____ _____ _____ and _____ it _____ your friends.

8 Hi! _____ Jinsu.

9 _____ _____ my bucket list for _____ _____.

10 First, I want to _____ _____ _____ _____ _____ of Jejudo _____ _____.

11 _____ _____ _____ _____, but I want to experience the island more _____ _____ _____ _____ this time.

12 My _____ _____ is to learn _____ _____ _____ the guitar.

13 I think the guitar has _____ _____ _____ _____ of all _____ _____.

1 나의 새 학년 버킷 리스트

2 모두들, 안녕.

3 오늘은 우리 새 학년의 첫날이에요.

4 저는 여러분들의 올해 계획과 희망을 듣고 싶어요.

5 여러분이 가장 원하는 것은 무엇인가요?

6 여러분이 원하는 것 세 가지를 생각해 보세요.

7 그러고 나서 버킷 리스트를 만들어 친구들과 공유해 봐요.

8 안녕하세요! 저는 진수예요.

9 이것은 올해 제 버킷 리스트예요.

10 우선, 저는 이번 여름에 제주도로 자전거 여행을 가고 싶어요.

11 저는 그곳을 전에 가 본 적이 있지만 이번에는 제 자전거를 타고 좀 더 자유롭게 그 섬을 경험해 보고 싶어요.

12 제 두 번째 목표는 기타 연주하는 법을 배우는 거예요.

13 저는 기타가 모든 악기 중에 가장 아름다운 소리를 낸다고 생각해요.

14 I _____ I _____ _____ my favorite song _____ my guitar _____ _____ _____ _____ _____ this year.

15 _____, I want to _____ _____ _____ _____ in math.

16 Math is my _____ _____.

17 This year, I'll _____ more effort _____ studying math _____ _____ _____ _____.

18 Hi! _____ _____ _____ Somi.

19 First, I _____ _____ _____ a concert of my favorite band _____ _____ _____ _____ _____ the stage.

20 I'm _____ to _____ _____ _____ all night to enter the _____ _____.

21 _____, I want to _____ _____ _____.

22 _____ always _____ a puppy.

23 I think _____ fully _____ _____ _____ _____ _____ a pet now.

24 My _____ _____ is _____ _____ _____ _____ _____.

25 _____ _____ _____ _____ read _____ _____ the Sherlock Holmes stories.

26 I became _____ _____ _____ of this _____ _____ last year, so I don't want to _____ _____ _____ _____.

14 올해 말쯤에는 제가 가장 좋아하는 곡을 제 기타로 연주할 수 있으면 좋겠어요.

15 마지막으로 수학에서 좋은 점수를 받고 싶어요.

16 수학은 제가 가장 약한 과목이에요.

17 올해는 제 약점을 극복하기 위해 수학 공부에 좀 더 노력을 기울일 거예요.

18 안녕하세요! 제 이름은 소미예요.

19 우선, 저는 제가 가장 좋아하는 밴드의 공연을 무대 바로 앞에서 보고 싶어요.

20 앞자리에 들어가기 위해 저는 기꺼이 밤새 줄을 서서 기다릴 거예요.

21 두 번째로, 강아지를 입양하고 싶어요.

22 저는 항상 강아지를 원해 왔어요.

23 이제는 제가 애완동물을 돌볼 준비가 완벽히 되었다고 생각해요.

24 제 마지막 목표는 좀 더 도전적이에요.

25 저는 셜록 홈스 이야기들을 모두 읽고 싶어요.

26 저는 작년에 이 탐정 시리즈의 열성 팬이 되었어요. 그래서 저는 단 하나도 놓치고 싶지 않아요.

※ 다음 문장을 우리말로 쓰시오.

1 My "Bucket List" for the New School Year

➡ _____

2 Hi, everyone.

➡ _____

3 Today is the first day of our new school year.

➡ _____

4 I want to hear your plans and hopes for this year.

➡ _____

5 What do you want to do most?

➡ _____

6 Think about three things you want to do.

➡ _____

7 And then, make a bucket list and share it with your friends.

➡ _____

8 Hi! I'm Jinsu.

➡ _____

9 This is my bucket list for this year.

➡ _____

10 First, I want to go on a bike tour of Jejudo this summer.

➡ _____

11 I've been there before, but I want to experience the island more freely on my bike this time.

➡ _____

12 My second goal is to learn how to play the guitar.

➡ _____

13 I think the guitar has the most beautiful sound of all musical instruments.

➡ _____

14 I hope I can play my favorite song on my guitar by the end of this year.

➡ _____

15 Finally, I want to get a good grade in math.

➡ _____

16 Math is my weakest subject.

➡ _____

17 This year, I'll put more effort into studying math to overcome my weakness.

➡ _____

18 Hi! My name is Somi.

➡ _____

19 First, I want to see a concert of my favorite band right in front of the stage.

➡ _____

20 I'm willing to stand in line all night to enter the front area.

➡ _____

21 Second, I want to adopt a puppy.

➡ _____

22 I've always wanted a puppy.

➡ _____

23 I think I'm fully ready to take care of a pet now.

➡ _____

24 My last goal is a little more challenging.

➡ _____

25 I'd like to read all of the Sherlock Holmes stories.

➡ _____

26 I became a big fan of this detective series last year, so I don't want to miss a single one.

➡ _____

※ 다음 괄호 안의 단어들을 우리말에 맞도록 바르게 배열하시오.

1 ("Bucket / My / List" / for / New / Year / the / School)

➡ _____

2 (everyone. / hi,)

➡ _____

3 (is / today / first / the / day / of / new / our / year. / school)

➡ _____

4 (want / I / hear / to / plans / your / and / hopes / year. / this / for)

➡ _____

5 (do / you / what / want / to / most? / do)

➡ _____

6 (about / think / things / three / want / do. / you / to)

➡ _____

7 (then, / and / a / make / list / bucket / and / share / with / it / friends. / your)

➡ _____

8 (I'm / Hi! / Jinsu.)

➡ _____

9 (is / this / bucket / my / for / list / year. / this)

➡ _____

10 (I / first, / to / want / on / go / a / tour / bike / Jejudo / of / summer. / this)

➡ _____

11 (been / I've / before, / there / but / want / I / experience / to / the / more / island / freely / my / on / bike / time. / this)

➡ _____

12 (second / my / goal / is / to / how / learn / play / to / guitar. / the)

➡ _____

13 (think / I / guitar / the / has / most / the / sound / beautiful / of / all / instruments. / musical)

➡ _____

1	나의 새 학년 버킷 리스트
2	모두들, 안녕.
3	오늘은 우리 새 학년의 첫날이에요.
4	저는 여러분들의 올해 계획과 희망을 듣고 싶어요.
5	여러분이 가장 원하는 것은 무엇인가요?
6	여러분이 원하는 것 세 가지를 생각해 보세요.
7	그리고 나서 버킷 리스트를 만들어 친구들과 공유해 봐요.
8	안녕하세요! 저는 진수예요.
9	이것은 올해 제 버킷 리스트예요.
10	우선, 저는 이번 여름에 제주도로 자전거 여행을 가고 싶어요.
11	저는 그곳을 전에 가 본 적이 있지만 이번에는 제 자전거를 타고 좀 더 자유롭게 그 섬을 경험해 보고 싶어요.
12	제 두 번째 목표는 기타 연주하는 법을 배우는 거예요.
13	저는 기타가 모든 악기 중에 가장 아름다운 소리를 낸다고 생각해요.

14 (hope / I / can / I / play / favorite / my / song / my / on / guitar / by / end / the / of / year. / this)

➡ _____

15 (I / finally, / to / want / a / get / grade / good / math. / in)

➡ _____

16 (is / math / subject. / weakest / my)

➡ _____

17 (year, / this / put / I'll / effort / more / studying / into / math / overcome / to / weakness. / my)

➡ _____

18 (my / hi! / is / Somi. / name)

➡ _____

19 (I / first, / to / want / a / see / concert / of / favorite / my / right / band / of / front / in / stage. / the)

➡ _____

20 (willing / I'm / stand / to / line / in / night / all / enter / to / area. / front / the)

➡ _____

21 (I / second, / to / want / puppy. / a / adopt)

➡ _____

22 (always / I've / a / wanted / puppy.)

➡ _____

23 (think / I / fully / I'm / to / ready / care / take / now. / of / pet / a)

➡ _____

24 (last / my / goal / is / little / a / challenging. / more)

➡ _____

25 (like / I'd / read / to / of / all / the / Holmes / Sherlock / stories.)

➡ _____

26 (became / I / big / a / fan / detective / of / this / series / year, / last / so / don't / I / want / miss / to / one. / single / a)

➡ _____

14 올해 말쯤에는 제가 가장 좋아하는 곡을 제 기타로 연주할 수 있으면 좋겠어요.

15 마지막으로 수학에서 좋은 점수를 받고 싶어요.

16 수학은 제가 가장 약한 과목이에요.

17 올해는 제 약점을 극복하기 위해 수학 공부에 좀 더 노력을 기울일 거예요.

18 안녕하세요! 제 이름은 소미예요.

19 우선, 저는 제가 가장 좋아하는 밴드의 공연을 무대 바로 앞에서 보고 싶어요.

20 앞자리에 들어가기 위해 저는 기꺼이 밤새 줄을 서서 기다릴 거예요.

21 두 번째로, 강아지를 입양하고 싶어요.

22 저는 항상 강아지를 원해 왔어요.

23 이제는 제가 애완동물을 돌볼 준비가 완벽히 되었다고 생각해요.

24 제 마지막 목표는 좀 더 도전적이에요.

25 저는 셜록 홈스 이야기들을 모두 읽고 싶어요.

26 저는 작년에 이 탐정 시리즈의 열성 팬이 되었어요. 그래서 저는 단 하나도 놓치고 싶지 않아요.

※ 다음 우리말을 영어로 쓰시오.

1 나의 새 학년 버킷 리스트

➡ _____

2 모두들, 안녕.

➡ _____

3 오늘은 우리 새 학년의 첫날이에요.

➡ _____

4 저는 여러분들의 올해 계획과 희망을 듣고 싶어요.

➡ _____

5 여러분이 가장 원하는 것은 무엇인가요?

➡ _____

6 여러분이 원하는 것 세 가지를 생각해 보세요.

➡ _____

7 그러고 나서 버킷 리스트를 만들어 친구들과 공유해 봐요.

➡ _____

8 안녕하세요! 저는 진수예요.

➡ _____

9 이것은 올해 제 버킷 리스트예요.

➡ _____

10 우선, 저는 이번 여름에 제주도로 자전거 여행을 가고 싶어요.

➡ _____

11 저는 그곳을 전에 가 본 적이 있지만 이번에는 제 자전거를 타고 좀 더 자유롭게 그 섬을 경험해 보고 싶어요.

➡ _____

12 제 두 번째 목표는 기타 연주하는 법을 배우는 거예요.

➡ _____

13 저는 기타가 모든 악기 중에 가장 아름다운 소리를 낸다고 생각해요.

➡ _____

14 ▶ 올해 말쯤에는 제가 가장 좋아하는 곡을 제 기타로 연주할 수 있으면 좋겠어요.

➡ _____

15 ▶ 마지막으로 수학에서 좋은 점수를 받고 싶어요.

➡ _____

16 ▶ 수학은 제가 가장 약한 과목이에요.

➡ _____

17 ▶ 올해는 제 약점을 극복하기 위해 수학 공부에 좀 더 노력을 기울일 거예요.

➡ _____

18 ▶ 안녕하세요! 제 이름은 소미예요.

➡ _____

19 ▶ 우선, 저는 제가 가장 좋아하는 밴드의 공연을 무대 바로 앞에서 보고 싶어요.

➡ _____

20 ▶ 앞자리에 들어가기 위해 저는 기꺼이 밤새 줄을 서서 기다릴 거예요.

➡ _____

21 ▶ 두 번째로, 강아지를 입양하고 싶어요.

➡ _____

22 ▶ 저는 항상 강아지를 원해 왔어요.

➡ _____

23 ▶ 이제는 제가 애완동물을 돌볼 준비가 완벽히 되었다고 생각해요.

➡ _____

24 ▶ 제 마지막 목표는 좀 더 도전적이에요.

➡ _____

25 ▶ 저는 셜록 홈스 이야기들을 모두 읽고 싶어요.

➡ _____

26 ▶ 저는 작년에 이 탐정 시리즈의 열성 팬이 되었어요, 그래서 저는 단 하나도 놓치고 싶지 않아요.

➡ _____

※ 다음 우리말과 일치하도록 빈칸에 알맞은 밀을 쓰시오.

Work Together Step 3

1. This is the _____ _____ _____ _____.

2. First, I _____ I _____ meet my favorite _____.

3. _____, I hope I can _____ _____ _____ my role model.

4. _____, I hope I _____ _____ to _____ countries.

5. We _____ ninety dollars _____ _____ these items.

1. 이것은 우리가 산 버킷 리스트이다.
2. 첫째, 나는 내가 좋아하는 배우를 만나기를 바란다.
3. 둘째, 나는 역할 모델과 식사할 수 있기를 바란다.
4. 셋째, 나는 다른 나라를 여행할 수 있기를 바란다.
5. 이것들을 사기 위해 나는 90달러를 사용했다.

Writing Workshop

1. My "Bucket List" for _____ _____

2. _____ _____ my bucket list.

3. _____, I want to learn _____ _____ _____ cookies.

4. I _____ _____ make them _____ _____ my mom.

5. _____, I want _____ _____ a simple _____.

6. I will _____ _____ things _____ I do _____ _____.

7. The _____ _____ is _____ _____ online English _____ every day.

8. _____ _____ _____ of this year, I _____ _____ my problems with my _____ subject, English.

1. 올해의 나의 "버킷 리스트"
2. 여기에 나의 버킷 리스트가 있어.
3. 먼저, 나는 쿠키 만드는 법을 배우고 싶어.
4. 나는 엄마를 놀라게 하기 위해 그것들을 만들고 싶어.
5. 두 번째로, 나는 간소한 삶을 살고 싶어.
6. 나는 필요하지 않은 물건들을 버릴 거야.
7. 마지막 것은 매일 온라인으로 영어 공부를 하는 거야.
8. 올해 말에는 나는 가장 약한 과목인 영어에서의 문제를 극복할 거야.

Solve the Problem

1. Hi, _____ _____ Gijun.

2. I hope I _____ _____ _____ _____ this year, but I sleep too much.

3. Could you _____ me _____ _____?

4. _____ _____ _____ go to bed on time and _____ _____ early?

5. I think you need to _____ _____ _____ _____ and sleep on a regular schedule to _____ _____ _____.

1. 안녕, 나는 기준이야.
2. 나는 올해 좋은 성적을 받길 바라, 하지만 나는 너무 많이 자.
3. 나에게 조언을 좀 해주겠니?
4. 정해진 시간에 자고 일찍 일어나는 게 어떠니?
5. 나는 좋은 성적을 받기 위해서 네가 일찍 자고 규칙적으로 잘 필요가 있다고 생각해.

※ 다음 우리말을 영어로 쓰시오.

Work Together Step 3

1. 이것은 우리가 산 버킷 리스트이다.
   ➡ _____

2. 첫째, 나는 내가 좋아하는 배우를 만나기를 바란다.
   ➡ _____

3. 둘째, 나는 역할 모델과 식사할 수 있기를 바란다.
   ➡ _____

4. 셋째, 나는 다른 나라를 여행할 수 있기를 바란다.

5. 이것들을 사기 위해 나는 90달러를 사용했다.
   ➡ _____

Writing Workshop

1. 올해의 나의 "버킷 리스트"
   ➡ _____

2. 여기에 나의 버킷 리스트가 있어.
   ➡ _____

3. 먼저, 나는 쿠키 만드는 법을 배우고 싶어.
   ➡ _____

4. 나는 엄마를 놀라게 하기 위해 그것들을 만들고 싶어.
   ➡ _____

5. 두 번째로, 나는 간소한 삶을 살고 싶어.
   ➡ _____

6. 나는 필요하지 않은 물건들을 버릴 거야.
   ➡ _____

7. 마지막 것은 매일 온라인으로 영어 공부를 하는 거야.
   ➡ _____

8. 올해 말에는 나는 가장 약한 과목인 영어에서의 문제를 극복할 거야.
   ➡ _____

Solve the Problem

1. 안녕, 나는 기준이야.
   ➡ _____

2. 나는 올해 좋은 성적을 받길 바라, 하지만 나는 너무 많이 자.
   ➡ _____

3. 나에게 조언을 좀 해주겠니?
   ➡ _____

4. 정해진 시간에 자고 일찍 일어나는 게 어떠니?
   ➡ _____

5. 나는 좋은 성적을 받기 위해서 네가 일찍 자고 규칙적으로 잘 필요가 있다고 생각해.
   ➡ _____

※ 다음 영어를 우리말로 쓰시오.

01 pose	
02 bend	
03 pull	
04 hall	
05 advice	
06 blink	
07 avoid	
08 tip	
09 lean	
10 back	
11 deserted	
12 letter	
13 lower	
14 novel	
15 check	
16 protect	
17 service center	
18 text	
19 wrist	
20 reduce	
21 hold	

22 weather	
23 increase	
24 pain	
25 rule	
26 hurt	
27 upset	
28 pressure	
29 prevent	
30 historical	
31 break	
32 worse	
33 crack	
34 uncomfortable	
35 be good for	
36 cut down on	
37 right away	
38 get in touch with	
39 pay attention to	
40 from time to time	
41 keep A from B	
42 depend on	
43 keep in mind	

※ 다음 우리말을 영어로 쓰시오.

01 금, 깨진 틈 _____

02 초래하다, 야기하다 _____

03 떨어뜨리다 _____

04 규칙 _____

05 불편한 _____

06 ~ 아래에 _____

07 잡다 _____

08 증가하다 _____

09 역사적인 _____

10 나쁜 _____

11 휴식 _____

12 구명 조끼 _____

13 압력 _____

14 고통 _____

15 날씨 _____

16 줄이다, 감소시키다 _____

17 다치게 하다, 아프다 _____

18 화난 _____

19 예방하다, 막다 _____

20 (눈을) 깜빡이다 _____

21 손목 _____

22 피하다 _____

23 등 _____

24 보호하다 _____

25 당기다 _____

26 자세 _____

27 버려진 _____

28 복도 _____

29 조언, 비법 _____

30 확인하다 _____

31 기대다 _____

32 낮추다 _____

33 문자, 글자 _____

34 충고 _____

35 ~에 주의를 기울이다 _____

36 ~에 늦다 _____

37 ~에 의존하다 _____

38 ~와 연락[접촉]하다 _____

39 ~ 대신에 _____

40 ~을 줄이다 _____

41 적어도 _____

42 돌려주다 _____

43 산책하다 _____

※ 다음 영영풀이에 알맞은 단어를 <보기>에서 골라 쓴 후, 우리말 뜻을 쓰시오.

1 _____ : a helpful piece of advice: _____

2 _____ : to prevent something bad from happening: _____

3 _____ : empty and quiet because no people are there: _____

4 _____ : to fall suddenly onto the ground or into something: _____

5 _____ : to shut and open your eyes quickly: _____

6 _____ : to keep someone or something safe from harm, damage, or illness:
   _____

7 _____ : a long written story in which the characters and events are usually
   imaginary: _____

8 _____ : to move something down from higher up: _____

9 _____ : to make something smaller or less in size, amount, or price:
   _____

10 _____ : a period of time when you stop working in order to rest, eat, etc.:
   _____

11 _____ : to make something happen, especially something bad: _____

12 _____ : to send someone a written message on a mobile phone: _____

13 _____ : not feeling physically comfortable, or not making you feel comfortable:
   _____

14 _____ : the area just inside the door of a house or other building, that leads to
   other rooms: _____

15 _____ : to stop something from happening, or stop someone from doing
   something: _____

16 _____ : unhappy and worried because something unpleasant or disappointing has
   happened: _____

※ 다음 우리말과 일치하도록 빈칸에 알맞은 말을 쓰시오.

Listen & Speak 1 A

G: Oh, no! I have _____ _____ _____ my eyes.

M: You _____ _____ _____ _____ .

1. G: 오, 이런! 눈 밑에 다크서클이 있어요.
   M: 너는 잠을 더 자야 한단다.

Listen & Speak 1 B

1. G: I _____ Jenny's birthday!

   B: _____ she your _____ _____ ?

   G: _____ , she is. _____ _____ _____ _____ _____ ?

   B: _____ _____ _____ _____ _____ her you're very sorry.

2. B: I _____ _____ .

   G: Why? What's the _____ ?

   B: I _____ _____ 5 kg _____ winter. _____ _____ I do?

   G: I think you _____ _____ _____ _____ snacks.

1. G: 제니의 생일을 잊어버렸어!
   B: 그녀는 너의 가장 친한 친구 아니니?
   G: 응, 맞아. 어떻게 해야 할까?
   B: 나는 네가 그녀에게 정말 미안하다고 말해야 한다고 생각해.

2. B: 기분이 우울해.
   G: 왜? 무슨 일이니?
   B: 이번 겨울에 5kg이 늘었어. 어떻게 해야 할까?
   G: 나는 네가 간식을 줄여야 한다고 생각해.

Listen & Speak 1 C

1. A: I'm _____ _____ _____ school. What _____ _____ do?

   B: You _____ _____ _____ _____ _____ on your smartphone.

2. A: I _____ a _____ . _____ _____ _____ do?

   B: You _____ _____ _____ _____ .

3. A: My phone _____ _____ . _____ _____ _____ _____ ?

   B: You should _____ it to _____ _____ _____ .

1. A: 나는 항상 학교에 늦어. 어떻게 해야 할까?
   B: 너는 스마트폰 알람을 맞춰야 해.
2. A: 두통이 있어. 어떻게 해야 할까?
   B: 너는 좀 쉬어야 해.
3. A: 내 휴대 전화가 작동하지 않아. 어떻게 해야 할까?
   B: 너는 그것을 서비스 센터에 가져가야 해.

Listen & Speak 2 A

W: _____ _____ you are home _____ 12:00.

G: Okay, I _____ .

W: 반드시 12까지는 집에 있도록 하세요.
G: 알겠어요, 그럴게요.

Listen & Speak 2 B

1. **B:** Mom, may I _____ _____ _____ Jinsu's house?

   W: Did Jinsu's mom _____ it was _____?

   B: Yes. Jinsu _____ she _____ _____ pizza for us.

   W: Okay. _____ _____ _____ _____ me when you _____ _____ Jinsu's house.

2. **G:** Daniel, _____ are you _____?

   B: I'm _____ a novel _____ my smartphone.

   G: Make sure you _____ _____ _____ _____ _____.
   It's _____ _____ _____ your eyes.

   B: Okay. I'll _____ the light _____.

3. **B:** Oh, no! I _____ _____ my science book!

   G: Ms. Lee _____ be happy about that.

   B: I know. Umm, can I _____ your science book?

   G: Okay. Just _____ _____ you _____ _____ _____ _____ _____ you're _____.

1. **B:** 엄마, 신수네 집에서 자고 와도 돼요?
   W: 진수 엄마가 괜찮다고 하셨니?
   B: 네. 진수는 그녀가 우리를 위해 피자를 만들 것이라고 말했어요.
   W: 알겠어. 진수네 집에 도착하면 반드시 나에게 문자 하렴.
2. **G:** 다니엘, 뭐 하고 있니?
   B: 스마트폰에서 소설을 읽고 있어.
   G: 반드시 어두운 곳에서 읽지 않도록 해. 너의 눈에 좋지 않아.
   B: 알겠어. 불을 켤게.
3. **B:** 오, 이런! 과학 책을 가져오지 않았어!
   G: 이 선생님께서 좋아하지 않으실 거야.
   B: 알아. 음, 네 과학 책을 빌릴 수 있을까?
   G: 좋아. 다 사용하면 반드시 다시 돌려주도록 해.

Listen & Speak 2 C

1. **A:** _____ I _____ this pizza?

   B: Sure. Just _____ _____ _____ wash your hands _____.

2. **A:** _____ _____ use this computer?

   B: Sure. Just make sure you _____ _____ _____ _____ _____ _____ _____.

3. **A:** _____ _____ _____ _____ this boat?

   B: Sure. Just _____ _____ you _____ _____ _____ _____.

1. **A:** 이 피자를 먹어도 되나요?
   B: 물론이죠. 반드시 손을 먼저 씻도록 하세요.
2. **A:** 이 컴퓨터를 사용해도 되나요?
   B: 물론이죠. 사용 후에는 반드시 전원을 끄도록 하세요.
3. **A:** 이 보트를 타도 되나요?
   B: 물론이죠. 구명조끼를 반드시 입도록 하세요.

※ 다음 우리말에 맞도록 대화를 영어로 쓰시오.

Listen & Speak 1 A

G: _____

M: _____

1. G: 오, 이런! 눈 밑에 다크서클이 있어요.
   M: 너는 잠을 더 자야 한단다.

Listen & Speak 1 B

1. G: _____
   B: _____
   G: _____
   B: _____

2. B: _____
   G: _____
   B: _____
   G: _____

1. G: 제니의 생일을 잊어버렸어!
   B: 그녀는 너의 가장 친한 친구 아니니?
   G: 응, 맞아. 어떻게 해야 할까?
   B: 나는 네가 그녀에게 정말 미안하다고 말해야 한다고 생각해.

2. B: 기분이 우울해.
   G: 왜? 무슨 일이니?
   B: 이번 겨울에 5kg이 늘었어. 어떻게 해야 할까?
   G: 나는 네가 간식을 줄여야 한다고 생각해.

Listen & Speak 1 C

1. A: _____
   B: _____

2. A: _____
   B: _____

3. A: _____
   B: _____

1. A: 나는 항상 학교에 늦어. 어떻게 해야 할까?
   B: 너는 스마트폰 알람을 맞춰야 해.
2. A: 두통이 있어. 어떻게 해야 할까?
   B: 너는 좀 쉬어야 해.
3. A: 내 휴대 전화가 작동하지 않아. 어떻게 해야 할까?
   B: 너는 그것을 서비스 센터에 가져가야 해.

Listen & Speak 2 A

W: _____

G: _____

W: 반드시 12까지는 집에 있도록 하세요.
G: 알겠어요, 그럴게요.

Listen & Speak 2 B

1. B: _____
   W: _____
   B: _____
   W: _____

2. G: _____
   B: _____
   G: _____
   B: _____

3. B: _____
   G: _____
   B: _____
   G: _____

1. R: 엄마, 진수네 집에서 자고 와도 돼요?
   W: 진수 엄마가 괜찮다고 하셨니?
   B: 네. 진수는 그녀가 우리를 위해 피자를 만들 것이라고 말했어요.
   W: 알겠어. 진수네 집에 도착하면 반드시 나에게 문자 하렴.
2. G: 다니엘, 뭐 하고 있니?
   B: 스마트폰에서 소설을 읽고 있어.
   G: 반드시 어두운 곳에서 읽지 않도록 해. 너의 눈에 좋지 않아.
   B: 알겠어. 불을 켤게.
3. B: 오, 이런! 과학 책을 가져오지 않았어!
   G: 이 선생님께서 좋아하지 않으실 거야.
   B: 알아. 음, 네 과학 책을 빌릴 수 있을까?
   G: 좋아. 다 사용하면 반드시 다시 돌려주도록 해.

Listen & Speak 2 C

1. A: _____
   B: _____

2. A: _____
   B: _____

3. A: _____
   B: _____

1. A: 이 피자를 먹어도 되나요?
   B: 물론이죠. 반드시 손을 먼저 씻도록 하세요.
2. A: 이 컴퓨터를 사용해도 되나요?
   B: 물론이죠. 사용 후에는 반드시 전원을 끄도록 하세요.
3. A: 이 보트를 타도 되나요?
   B: 물론이죠. 구명조끼를 반드시 입도록 하세요.

※ 다음 우리말과 일치하도록 빈칸에 알맞은 것을 골라 쓰시오.

1 ＿＿＿＿＿ ＿＿＿＿＿ for Smartphone ＿＿＿＿＿

    A. Users   B. Tips   C. Health

2 Seongmin ＿＿＿＿ a ＿＿＿＿ of time ＿＿＿＿ his smartphone.

    A. using   B. lot   C. spends

3 He ＿＿＿＿ the ＿＿＿＿ and ＿＿＿＿.

    A. weather   B. checks   C. news

4 He ＿＿＿＿ smartphone ＿＿＿＿.

    A. games   B. plays

5 He ＿＿＿＿ ＿＿＿＿ friends.

    A. his   B. texts

6 He ＿＿＿＿ ＿＿＿＿ on the ＿＿＿＿.

    A. Internet   B. information   C. finds

7 He reads ＿＿＿＿ ＿＿＿＿ ＿＿＿＿.

    A. books   B. online   C. comic

8 He ＿＿＿＿ ＿＿＿＿.

    A. movies   B. watches

9 Seongmin cannot ＿＿＿＿ his hands ＿＿＿＿ his smartphone all day ＿＿＿＿.

    A. long   B. take   C. off

10 He does not know that ＿＿＿＿ a smartphone ＿＿＿＿ much can ＿＿＿＿ ＿＿＿＿ problems.

    A. health   B. using   C. too   D. cause

11 Are you a ＿＿＿＿ ＿＿＿＿ of your smartphone ＿＿＿＿ Seongmin?

    A. like   B. user   C. heavy

12 If ＿＿＿＿, here are some ＿＿＿＿ to ＿＿＿＿ your health.

    A. protect   B. so   C. tips

13 ＿＿＿＿ your ＿＿＿＿ and ＿＿＿＿.

    A. back   B. neck   C. watch

14 ＿＿＿＿ you ＿＿＿＿ on your smartphone, you ＿＿＿＿ ＿＿＿＿ your neck.

    A. bend   B. when   C. read   D. usually

15 This "＿＿＿＿ neck" pose ＿＿＿＿ the ＿＿＿＿ on your neck and ＿＿＿＿.

    A. back   B. text   C. increases   D. pressure

16 The best way to ＿＿＿＿ this pressure is to ＿＿＿＿ the phone ＿＿＿＿ ＿＿＿＿ the level of your eyes.

    A. to   B. prevent   C. bring   D. up

---

1 스마트폰 사용자들을 위한 건강 조언

2 성민이는 스마트폰을 사용하는 데 많은 시간을 보냅니다.

3 그는 뉴스와 날씨를 확인합니다.

4 그는 스마트폰 게임을 합니다.

5 그는 친구들에게 문자 메시지를 보냅니다.

6 그는 인터넷에서 정보를 찾습니다.

7 그는 온라인 만화책을 읽습니다.

8 그는 영화를 봅니다.

9 성민이는 하루 종일 스마트폰에서 손을 뗄 수가 없습니다.

10 그는 스마트폰을 너무 많이 사용하는 것이 건강 문제를 일으킬 수 있다는 것을 모릅니다.

11 여러분은 성민이와 같은 스마트폰 과다 사용자인가요?

12 그렇다면, 여기 여러분의 건강을 지켜 줄 몇 가지 조언이 있습니다.

13 여러분의 목과 척추를 조심하세요.

14 스마트폰을 볼 때, 여러분은 보통 목을 구부립니다.

15 이 "거북목" 자세는 여러분의 목과 척추에 가해지는 압력을 증가시킵니다.

16 이러한 압력을 예방하는 가장 좋은 방법은 휴대 전화를 여러분의 눈높이까지 올리는 것입니다.

17 _____ _____ is to lower your eyes _____ of _____ your neck.

A. bending   B. another   C. way   D. instead

18 _____ your _____ a _____ .

A. break   B. eyes   C. give

19 It _____ your eyes _____ tired and _____ to read small letters on a smartphone _____ a long time.

A. for   B. makes   C. feel   D. dry

20 _____ a smartphone in the dark or in a _____ car _____ this problem _____ .

A. worse   B. makes   C. moving   D. using

21 To _____ this, give your eyes a break _____ time time.

A. to   B. from   C. avoid

22 _____ the 20-20-20 rules: _____ 20 minutes, take a 20-second break and look at something at _____ 20 feet _____ .

A. away   B. follow   C. every   D. least

23 Also, _____ your eyes _____ .

A. often   B. blink

24 This will _____ your eyes _____ _____ dry.

A. becoming   B. from   C. keep

25 Do you _____ a _____ _____ your smartphone?

A. on   B. text   C. lot

26 _____ for a long time can _____ your fingers and _____ .

A. wrists   B. hurt   C. texting

27 _____ these _____ .

A. exercises   B. try

28 They will _____ _____ the _____ in your fingers and wrists.

A. pain   B. reduce   C. help

29 _____ _____ each finger of _____ hand.

A. each   B. on   C. pull

30 _____ the _____ of your hands together _____ your arms _____ in front of you.

A. out   B. with   C. backs   D. put

31 _____ _____ .

A. remember   B. but

32 The best _____ to _____ these health problems is to _____ your smartphone _____ .

A. less   B. tip   C. prevent   D. use

33 Give _____ some _____ _____ your smartphone.

A. from   B. rest   C. yourself

---

17 또 다른 방법은 여러분의 목을 구부리는 대신에 시선을 낮추는 것입니다.

18 눈을 쉬게 하세요.

19 오랫동안 스마트폰의 작은 글자를 읽는 것은 눈이 피곤해지고 건조하게 느끼도록 만듭니다.

20 어두운 곳이나 움직이는 차에서 스마트폰을 사용하는 것은 이러한 문제를 더욱 악화시킵니다.

21 이것을 피하려면, 눈을 때때로 쉬게 하세요.

22 20-20-20 규칙을 따르세요. 20분마다 20초의 휴식을 취하고 적어도 20피트 이상 떨어져 있는 사물을 바라보세요.

23 또한, 눈을 자주 깜박이세요.

24 이것은 여러분의 눈이 건조해지는 것을 막아 줄 것입니다.

25 스마트폰으로 문자 메시지를 많이 보내나요?

26 오랫동안 문자 메시지를 보내는 것은 여러분의 손가락과 손목을 상하게 할 수 있습니다.

27 이런 운동을 해 보세요.

28 그것은 여러분의 손가락과 손목의 통증을 줄이는 것을 도와줄 것입니다.

29 각 손의 각 손가락을 당기세요.

30 팔을 여러분 앞에서 벌린 채로 손등을 마주 놓으세요.

31 그러나 기억하세요.

32 이러한 건강 문제를 예방하는 가장 좋은 방법은 스마트폰을 덜 사용하는 것입니다.

33 여러분 자신에게 스마트폰으로부터 휴식을 주세요.

※ 다음 우리말과 일치하도록 빈칸에 알맞은 말을 쓰시오.

1 _____ _____ for Smartphone _____

2 Seongmin _____ a _____ of time _____ his smartphone.

3 He _____ the _____ and _____.

4 He _____ smartphone _____.

5 He _____ _____ _____.

6 He _____ _____ _____ the _____.

7 He _____ _____ _____ _____.

8 He _____ _____.

9 Seongmin cannot _____ his hands _____ his smartphone _____ _____ _____.

10 He does not know that _____ a smartphone _____ _____ can _____ _____ _____.

11 Are you _____ _____ _____ of your smartphone _____ Seongmin?

12 _____ _____, _____ _____ some tips _____ _____ your health.

13 _____ your _____ and _____.

14 _____ you read on your smartphone, you _____ _____ your neck.

15 This "_____ _____" _____ _____ the pressure on your neck and back.

16 The best way _____ _____ this pressure is _____ _____ the phone _____ _____ the level of your eyes.

---

1 스마트폰 사용자들을 위한 건강 조언

2 성민이는 스마트폰을 사용하는 데 많은 시간을 보냅니다.

3 그는 뉴스와 날씨를 확인합니다.

4 그는 스마트폰 게임을 합니다.

5 그는 친구들에게 문자 메시지를 보냅니다.

6 그는 인터넷에서 정보를 찾습니다.

7 그는 온라인 만화책을 읽습니다.

8 그는 영화를 봅니다.

9 성민이는 하루 종일 스마트폰에서 손을 뗄 수가 없습니다.

10 그는 스마트폰을 너무 많이 사용하는 것이 건강 문제를 일으킬 수 있다는 것을 모릅니다.

11 여러분은 성민이와 같은 스마트폰 과다 사용자인가요?

12 그렇다면, 여기 여러분의 건강을 지켜 줄 몇 가지 조언이 있습니다.

13 여러분의 목과 척추를 조심하세요.

14 스마트폰을 볼 때, 여러분은 보통 목을 구부립니다.

15 이 "거북목" 자세는 여러분의 목과 척추에 가해지는 압력을 증가시킵니다.

16 이러한 압력을 예방하는 가장 좋은 방법은 휴대 전화를 여러분의 눈높이까지 올리는 것입니다.

17 _____ _____ is _____ _____ your eyes _____ _____ _____ your neck.

18 _____ your eyes _____ _____.

19 It _____ your eyes _____ _____ and dry to read small letters on a smartphone _____ _____ _____ _____ _____.

20 _____ a smartphone _____ _____ _____ or in a moving car _____ this problem _____.

21 _____ _____ this, give your eyes a break _____ _____ _____ _____.

22 _____ the 20-20-20 rules: _____ 20 minutes, take _____ _____ _____ and look at something _____ _____ 20 _____ _____.

23 Also, _____ your eyes _____.

24 This will _____ your eyes _____ _____ dry.

25 Do you _____ a lot _____ _____ _____?

26 _____ for a long time can _____ your fingers and wrists.

27 _____ these _____.

28 They will _____ _____ the pain in your fingers and wrists.

29 _____ _____ each finger of _____ _____.

30 _____ the backs of your hands _____ _____ _____ _____ out _____ _____ _____ you.

31 But _____.

32 _____ _____ _____ _____ _____ _____ these health problems is _____ _____ your smartphone _____.

33 Give yourself _____ _____ _____ your smartphone.

17 또 다른 방법은 여러분의 목을 구부리는 대신에 시선을 낮추는 것입니다.

18 눈을 쉬게 하세요.

19 오랫동안 스마트폰의 작은 글자를 읽는 것은 눈이 피곤해지고 건조하게 느끼도록 만듭니다.

20 어두운 곳이나 움직이는 차에서 스마트폰을 사용하는 것은 이러한 문제를 더욱 악화시킵니다.

21 이것을 피하려면, 눈을 때때로 쉬게 하세요.

22 20-20-20 규칙을 따르세요. 20분마다 20초의 휴식을 취하고 적어도 20피트 이상 떨어져 있는 사물을 바라보세요.

23 또한, 눈을 자주 깜박이세요.

24 이것은 여러분의 눈이 건조해지는 것을 막아 줄 것입니다.

25 스마트폰으로 문자 메시지를 많이 보내나요?

26 오랫동안 문자 메시지를 보내는 것은 여러분의 손가락과 손목을 상하게 할 수 있습니다.

27 이런 운동을 해 보세요.

28 그것은 여러분의 손가락과 손목의 통증을 줄이는 것을 도와줄 것입니다.

29 각 손의 각 손가락을 당기세요.

30 팔을 여러분 앞에서 벌린 채로 손등을 마주 놓으세요.

31 그러나 기억하세요.

32 이러한 건강 문제를 예방하는 가장 좋은 방법은 스마트폰을 덜 사용하는 것입니다.

33 여러분 자신에게 스마트폰으로부터 휴식을 주세요.

※ 다음 문장을 우리말로 쓰시오.

1 ▷ Health Tips for Smartphone Users

➡ _____

2 ▷ Seongmin spends a lot of time using his smartphone.

➡ _____

3 ▷ He checks the news and weather.

➡ _____

4 ▷ He plays smartphone games.

➡ _____

5 ▷ He texts his friends.

➡ _____

6 ▷ He finds information on the Internet.

➡ _____

7 ▷ He reads online comic books.

➡ _____

8 ▷ He watches movies

➡ _____

9 ▷ Seongmin cannot take his hands off his smartphone all day long.

➡ _____

10 ▷ He does not know that using a smartphone too much can cause health problems.

➡ _____

11 ▷ Are you a heavy user of your smartphone like Seongmin?

➡ _____

12 ▷ If so, here are some tips to protect your health.

➡ _____

13 ▷ Watch your neck and back.

➡ _____

14 ▷ When you read on your smartphone, you usually bend your neck.

➡ _____

15 ▷ This "text neck" pose increases the pressure on your neck and back.

➡ _____

16 ▷ The best way to prevent this pressure is to bring the phone up to the level of your eyes.

➡ _____

17 Another way is to lower your eyes instead of bending your neck.

➡ _____

18 Give your eyes a break.

➡ _____

19 It makes your eyes feel tired and dry to read small letters on a smartphone for a long time.

➡ _____

20 Using a smartphone in the dark or in a moving car makes this problem worse.

➡ _____

21 To avoid this, give your eyes a break from time to time.

➡ _____

22 Follow the 20-20-20 rules: Every 20 minutes, take a 20-second break and look at something at least 20 feet away.

➡ _____

23 Also, blink your eyes often.

➡ _____

24 This will keep your eyes from becoming dry.

➡ _____

25 Do you text a lot on your smartphone?

➡ _____

26 Texting for a long time can hurt your fingers and wrists.

➡ _____

27 Try these exercises.

➡ _____

28 They will help reduce the pain in your fingers and wrists.

➡ _____

29 Pull on each finger of each hand.

➡ _____

30 Put the backs of your hands together with your arms out in front of you.

➡ _____

31 But remember.

➡ _____

32 The best tip to prevent these health problems is to use your smartphone less.

➡ _____

33 Give yourself some rest from your smartphone.

➡ _____

※ 다음 괄호 안의 단어들을 우리말에 맞도록 바르게 배열하시오.

1 (Tips / Health / Users / Smartphone / for)
➡ _____

2 (spends / Seongmin / lot / a / of / time / smartphone. / his / using)
➡ _____

3 (checks / he / news / the / weather. / and)
➡ _____

4 (plays / he / games. / smartphone)
➡ _____

5 (his / texts / friends. / he)
➡ _____

6 (finds / he / information / on / Internet. / the)
➡ _____

7 (reads / he / books. / comic / online)
➡ _____

8 (movies. / watches / he)
➡ _____

9 (cannot / Seongmin / take / hands / his / off / smartphone / his / long. / day / all)
➡ _____

10 (does / he / know / not / that / using / smartphone / a / much / too / cause / can / problems. / health)
➡ _____

11 (you / are / a / user / heavy / of / smartphone / your / Seongmin? / like)
➡ _____

12 (so, / if / are / here / some / to / tips / protect / health. / your)
➡ _____

13 (your / watch / back. / and / neck)
➡ _____

14 (you / when / read / your / on / smartphone, / usually / you / neck. / your / bend)
➡ _____

15 ("text / this / neck" / increases / pose / pressure / the / your / on / back. / and / neck)
➡ _____

16 (best / the / way / prevent / to / pressure / this / is / bring / to / phone / the / to / up / level / the / of / eyes. / your)
➡ _____

1 스마트폰 사용자들을 위한 건강 조언

2 성민이는 스마트폰을 사용하는 데 많은 시간을 보냅니다.

3 그는 뉴스와 날씨를 확인합니다.

4 그는 스마트폰 게임을 합니다.

5 그는 친구들에게 문자 메시지를 보냅니다.

6 그는 인터넷에서 정보를 찾습니다.

7 그는 온라인 만화책을 읽습니다.

8 그는 영화를 봅니다.

9 성민이는 하루 종일 스마트폰에서 손을 뗄 수가 없습니다.

10 그는 스마트폰을 너무 많이 사용하는 것이 건강 문제를 일으킬 수 있다는 것을 모릅니다.

11 여러분은 성민이와 같은 스마트폰 과다 사용자인가요?

12 그렇다면, 여기 여러분의 건강을 지켜 줄 몇 가지 조언이 있습니다.

13 여러분의 목과 척추를 조심하세요.

14 스마트폰을 볼 때, 여러분은 보통 목을 구부립니다.

15 이 "거북목" 자세는 여러분의 목과 척추에 가해지는 압력을 증가시킵니다.

16 이러한 압력을 예방하는 가장 좋은 방법은 휴대 전화를 여러분의 눈높이까지 올리는 것입니다.

17 (way / another / to / is / lower / eyes / your / of / instead / bending / neck. / your)
➡ _____

18 (eyes / give / your / break. / a)
➡ _____

19 (your / makes / it / feel / eyes / tired / and / to / dry / small / read / letters / on / smartphone / a / long / a / time. / for)
➡ _____

20 (a / using / in / smartphone / dark / the / or / a / in / moving / makes / car / worse. / problem / this)
➡ _____

21 (this, / avoid / to / your / give / eyes / break / a / time / from / time. / to)
➡ _____

22 (the / follow / rules: / 20-20-20 / minutes, / 20 / every / take / 20-second / a / break / and / at / look / something / least / at / away. / feet / 20)
➡ _____

23 (blink / also, / often. / eyes / your)
➡ _____

24 (will / this / keep / eyes / your / from / dry. / becoming)
➡ _____

25 (you / text / do / lot / a / on / smartphone? / your)
➡ _____

26 (for / texting / time / long / a / hurt / can / fingers / your / wrists. / and)
➡ _____

27 (try / exercises. / these)
➡ _____

28 (they / help / will / reduce / pain / the / in / fingers / your / wrists. / and)
➡ _____

29 (on / pull / finger / each / hand. / each / of)
➡ _____

30 (the / put / backs / your / of / hands / together / with / arms / your / in / out / you. / of / front)
➡ _____

31 (remember. / but)
➡ _____

32 (best / the / tip / prevent / to / health / these / problems / to / is / your / use / less. / smartphone)
➡ _____

33 (yourself / rest / give / some / smartphone. / your / from)
➡ _____

17 또 다른 방법은 여러분의 목을 구부리는 대신에 시선을 낮추는 것입니다.

18 눈을 쉬게 하세요.

19 오랫동안 스마트폰의 작은 글자를 읽는 것은 눈이 피곤해지고 건조하게 느끼도록 만듭니다.

20 어두운 곳이나 움직이는 차에서 스마트폰을 사용하는 것은 이러한 문제를 더욱 악화시킵니다.

21 이것을 피하려면, 눈을 때때로 쉬게 하세요.

22 20-20-20 규칙을 따르세요. 20분마다 20초의 휴식을 취하고 적어도 20피트 이상 떨어져 있는 사물을 바라보세요.

23 또한, 눈을 자주 깜박이세요.

24 이것은 여러분의 눈이 건조해지는 것을 막아 줄 것입니다.

25 스마트폰으로 문자 메시지를 많이 보내나요?

26 오랫동안 문자 메시지를 보내는 것은 여러분의 손가락과 손목을 상하게 할 수 있습니다.

27 이런 운동을 해 보세요.

28 그것은 여러분의 손가락과 손목의 통증을 줄이는 것을 도와줄 것입니다.

29 각 손의 각 손가락을 당기세요.

30 팔을 여러분 앞에서 벌린 채로 손등을 마주 놓으세요.

31 그러나 기억하세요.

32 이러한 건강 문제를 예방하는 가장 좋은 방법은 스마트폰을 덜 사용하는 것입니다.

33 여러분 자신에게 스마트폰으로부터 휴식을 주세요.

※ 다음 우리말을 영어로 쓰시오.

1 스마트폰 사용자들을 위한 건강 조언

➡ _____

2 성민이는 스마트폰을 사용하는 데 많은 시간을 보냅니다.

➡ _____

3 그는 뉴스와 날씨를 확인합니다.

➡ _____

4 그는 스마트폰 게임을 합니다.

➡ _____

5 그는 친구들에게 문자 메시지를 보냅니다.

➡ _____

6 그는 인터넷에서 정보를 찾습니다.

➡ _____

7 그는 온라인 만화책을 읽습니다.

➡ _____

8 그는 영화를 봅니다.

➡ _____

9 성민이는 하루 종일 스마트폰에서 손을 뗄 수가 없습니다.

➡ _____

10 그는 스마트폰을 너무 많이 사용하는 것이 건강 문제를 일으킬 수 있다는 것을 모릅니다.

➡ _____

11 여러분은 성민이와 같은 스마트폰 과다 사용자인가요?

➡ _____

12 그렇다면, 여기 여러분의 건강을 지켜 줄 몇 가지 조언이 있습니다.

➡ _____

13 여러분의 목과 척추를 조심하세요.

➡ _____

14 스마트폰을 볼 때, 여러분은 보통 목을 구부립니다.

➡ _____

15 이 "거북목" 자세는 여러분의 목과 척추에 가해지는 압력을 증가시킵니다.

➡ _____

16 이러한 압력을 예방하는 가장 좋은 방법은 휴대 전화를 여러분의 눈높이까지 올리는 것입니다.

➡ _____

17 또 다른 방법은 여러분의 목을 구부리는 대신에 시선을 낮추는 것입니다.

➡ _____

18 눈을 쉬게 하세요.

➡ _____

19 오랫동안 스마트폰의 작은 글자를 읽는 것은 눈이 피곤해지고 건조하게 느끼도록 만듭니다.

➡ _____

20 어두운 곳이나 움직이는 차에서 스마트폰을 사용하는 것은 이러한 문제를 더욱 악화시킵니다.

➡ _____

21 이것을 피하려면, 눈을 때때로 쉬게 하세요.

➡ _____

22 20-20-20 규칙을 따르세요. 20분마다 20초의 휴식을 취하고 적어도 20피트 이상 떨어져 있는 사물을 바라보세요.

➡ _____

23 또한, 눈을 자주 깜박이세요.

➡ _____

24 이것은 여러분의 눈이 건조해지는 것을 막아 줄 것입니다.

➡ _____

25 스마트폰으로 문자 메시지를 많이 보내나요?

➡ _____

26 오랫동안 문자 메시지를 보내는 것은 여러분의 손가락과 손목을 상하게 할 수 있습니다.

➡ _____

27 이런 운동을 해 보세요.

➡ _____

28 그것은 여러분의 손가락과 손목의 통증을 줄이는 것을 도와줄 것입니다.

➡ _____

29 각 손의 각 손가락을 당기세요.

➡ _____

30 팔을 여러분 앞에서 벌린 채로 손등을 마주 놓으세요.

➡ _____

31 그러나 기억하세요.

➡ _____

32 이러한 건강 문제를 예방하는 가장 좋은 방법은 스마트폰을 덜 사용하는 것입니다.

➡ _____

33 여러분 자신에게 스마트폰으로부터 휴식을 주세요.

➡ _____

※ 다음 우리말과 일치하도록 빈칸에 알맞은 말을 쓰시오.

Before You Read A

1. I use my smartphone _____ I _____ _____.

2. I use my smartphone _____ _____ _____.

3. I use my smartphone _____ _____ _____ _____.

4. I _____ _____ when I do _____ _____ my smartphone _____ me.

5. I use my smartphone _____ _____.

1. 나는 아침을 먹을 때 스마트폰을 사용한다.
2. 나는 차에서 스마트폰을 사용한다.
3. 나는 걸으면서 스마트폰을 사용한다.
4. 나는 수중에 스마트폰이 없으면 불편함을 느낀다.
5. 나는 잠자리에서 스마트폰을 사용한다.

Before You Read B

1. _____ _____!

2. Yesterday, Sejin _____ _____ a tree _____ _____ and _____ her head.

3. She needs to _____ _____ her phone _____ _____.

4. Also, she _____ _____ the time _____ _____ _____ it.

1. 조심해!
2. 어제, 세진이는 문자를 보내다가 나무에 부딪쳐서 머리를 다쳤다.
3. 그녀는 걷는 도중에 전화기를 사용하는 것을 피할 필요가 있다.
4. 또한, 그녀는 그것을 사용하는 데 보내는 시간을 줄여야 한다.

Writing Workshop

1. A _____ & _____

2. There _____ _____ good things _____ bad things about _____ a smartphone.

3. First, I can _____ _____ _____ _____ my friends _____ _____.

4. Also, I can easily get _____ _____ _____.

5. That is useful _____ I have a lot of homework _____ _____.

6. _____ _____ _____ _____, using a smartphone too much makes my eyes _____ _____ and _____.

7. Also, text messages and ads _____ me _____ _____ attention to my studies.

8. So I _____ _____ use my smartphone _____.

1. 스마트폰과 나
2. 스마트폰을 사용하는 것에 대해서 좋은 것과 나쁜 것 둘 다 있다.
3. 첫째, 내 친구들과 즉시 연락할 수 있다.
4. 또한, 나는 내가 필요한 정보를 쉽게 얻을 수 있다.
4. 그것은 내가 해야 할 숙제가 많을 때 유용하다.
6. 반면에, 스마트폰을 너무 많이 사용하는 것은 나의 눈을 건조하고 피곤하게 만든다.
7 또한 메시지를 보내는 것과 광고들은 공부에 집중하는 것을 막는다.
8. 그래서 나는 휴대 전화를 똑똑하게 사용할 필요가 있다.

※ 다음 우리말을 영어로 쓰시오.

Before You Read A

1. 나는 아침을 먹을 때 스마트폰을 사용한다.

   ➡ _____

2. 나는 차에서 스마트폰을 사용한다.

   ➡ _____

3. 나는 걸으면서 스마트폰을 사용한다.

   ➡ _____

4. 나는 수중에 스마트폰이 없으면 불편함을 느낀다.

   ➡ _____

5. 나는 잠자리에서 스마트폰을 사용한다.

   ➡ _____

Before You Read B

1. 조심해!

   ➡ _____

2. 어제, 세진이는 문자를 보내다가 나무에 부딪쳐서 머리를 다쳤다.

   ➡ _____

3. 그녀는 걷는 도중에 전화기를 사용하는 것을 피할 필요가 있다.

   ➡ _____

4. 또한, 그녀는 그것을 사용하는 데 보내는 시간을 줄여야 한다.

   ➡ _____

Writing Workshop

1. 스마트폰과 나

   ➡ _____

2. 스마트폰을 사용하는 것에 대해서 좋은 것과 나쁜 것 둘 다 있다.

   ➡ _____

3. 첫째, 내 친구들과 즉시 연락할 수 있다.

   ➡ _____

4. 또한, 나는 내가 필요한 정보를 쉽게 얻을 수 있다.

   ➡ _____

5. 그것은 내가 해야 할 숙제가 많을 때 유용하다.

   ➡ _____

6. 반면에, 스마트폰을 너무 많이 사용하는 것은 나의 눈을 건조하고 피곤하게 만든다.

   ➡ _____

7. 또한 메시지를 보내는 것과 광고들은 공부에 집중하는 것을 막는다.

   ➡ _____

8. 그래서 나는 휴대 전화를 똑똑하게 사용할 필요가 있다.

   ➡ _____

※ 다음 영어를 우리말로 쓰시오.

01 concert _____

02 grow _____

03 actually _____

04 bit _____

05 clothes _____

06 opportunity _____

07 bright _____

08 dolphin _____

09 elementary school _____

10 musical instrument _____

11 cook _____

12 free time _____

13 hold _____

14 join _____

15 easy _____

16 neighbor _____

17 main gate _____

18 orchestra _____

19 introduce _____

20 own _____

21 garden _____

22 vegetable _____

23 library _____

24 present _____

25 volunteer _____

26 experience _____

27 several _____

28 note _____

29 activity _____

30 leader _____

31 interest _____

32 practice _____

33 neighborhood _____

34 cooking _____

35 as a result _____

36 enjoy+동사ing _____

37 look for _____

38 would like to+동사원형 _____

39 participate in _____

40 change into _____

41 ask for help _____

42 be good at _____

43 how to+동사원형 _____

※ 다음 우리말을 영어로 쓰시오.

01	도넛	22	(사람 · 동물을) 걷게 하다
02	경험, 경력	23	실제로, 사실은
03	무인 비행기	24	기회
04	선물, 참석한	25	(모임 · 식 등을) 개최하다
05	연습; 연습하다	26	소개하다
06	활동	27	실제로, 사실은
07	요리, 음식	28	밝은
08	관심	29	옷, 의상
09	날게 하다	30	(동식물을) 기르다
10	봉사, 유익한 활동	31	(모임 · 식 등을) 개최하다
11	몇몇의	32	이웃
12	동네	33	정문
13	～을 사다, ～을 획득하다	34	채소
14	지도자, 대표	35	～로 변화시키다[바꾸다]
15	도서관	36	아주 조금
16	동아리	37	～에 빠지다
17	그러나, 하지만	38	결과적으로
18	봉사하다	39	～에 참여하다
19	음, 음표	40	(병 · 상황 등이) 나아지다
20	사업, 계획	41	～에 대해 감사하다
21	스페인어	42	도움을 청하다
		43	(～에 대해서) 조심하다

※ 다음 영영풀이에 알맞은 단어를 <보기>에서 골라 쓴 후, 우리말 뜻을 쓰시오.

1 _____ : strong and easy to see: _____

2 _____ : to develop or increase in size or length: _____

3 _____ : slightly or to a small degree(=a little): _____

4 _____ : to do something regularly in order to do it better: _____

5 _____ : to take a dog for a walk for exercise: _____

6 _____ : to cook something using dry heat, in an oven: _____

7 _____ : aircraft that does not have a pilot, but is operated by radio: _____

8 _____ : to become a member of an organization, society, or group: _____

9 _____ : someone who lives next to you or near you: _____

10 _____ : a part of the area next to a house, which has plants and flowers in it: _____

11 _____ : something that you use for playing music, such as a piano or guitar: _____

12 _____ : the person who directs or controls a group, organization, country, etc.: _____

13 _____ : a chance to do something or an occasion when it is easy for you to do something: _____

14 _____ : to have a meeting, party, election etc in a particular place or at a particular time: _____

15 _____ : a large group of musicians playing many different kinds of instruments and led by a conductor: _____

16 _____ : organization for people who share a particular interest or enjoy similar activities, or a group of people who meet together to do something they are interested in: _____

※ 다음 우리말과 일치하도록 빈칸에 알맞은 말을 쓰시오.

Listen & Speak 1 A

A: Do you _____ _____ _____ _____ a paper cat?

B: Of _____. It's _____.

Listen & Speak 1 B

1. **G:** I _____ _____ _____ _____ Yuna's violin concert yesterday. _____ was it?

   B: It was great. _____ _____ _____ _____ _____ the violin _____ _____ _____ .

   G: I didn't know you _____ _____ _____ _____ _____ _____ _____ .

   B: I can, but I'm _____ _____ _____ it _____ .

2. **G:** _____ _____ these pictures. I _____ these vegetables _____ . I have my _____ _____ .

   B: Cool! Do you know _____ _____ _____ the vegetables you _____ , _____ ?

   G: Yes, my grandmother _____ _____ .

1. G: 어제 유나의 바이올린 콘서트에 갔다고 들었어. 어땠니?
   B: 좋았어. 나도 언젠가 그녀처럼 바이올린을 연주할 수 있기를 바라.
   G: 나는 네가 바이올린 연주하는 법을 아는지 몰랐어.
   B: 할 수 있어, 그러나 아직 잘하지는 못해.
2. G: 이 사진들 좀 봐. 나는 이 채소를 직접 길렀어. 나는 내 자신의 정원이 있어.
   B: 멋지다! 네가 기르는 채소로 요리하는 법도 아니?
   G: 응, 할머니께서 내게 가르쳐 주셨어.

Listen & Speak 2 A

A: Do you enjoy _____ _____ the stars _____ _____ ?

G: Yes, I _____ _____ that.

Listen & Speak 2 B

1. **B:** _____ _____ _____ _____ books, Yumi?

   G: Yes, I _____ _____ science books. How _____ you?

   B: I love _____ books, _____ .

   G: Then, _____ _____ to _____ _____ after school today.

2. **G:** _____ _____ _____ _____ on the weekend, Minsu?

   B: I _____ _____ for my family.

   G: _____ _____ _____ _____ ?

   B: Yes, I'm a _____ _____ ! My family loves my _____ .

1. B: 유미야, 너는 책 읽는 것을 즐기니?
   G: 응, 나는 과학 책을 읽는 것을 좋아해. 너는 어때?
   B: 나도 책 읽는 것을 좋아해.
   G: 그럼 오늘 방과 후에 도서관 가자.
2. G: 민수야, 주말에 뭐 했니?
   B: 가족을 위해 아침을 만들었어.
   G: 너는 요리를 즐기니?
   B: 응, 나는 훌륭한 요리사야! 우리 가족은 내 요리를 좋아해.

3. **B:** Jiyun, that's a pretty backpack! _____ did you _____ it?

    G: My sister _____ _____ _____ _____.

    B: Wow! She's a _____ _____ _____.

    G: Yes, she is. And she _____ _____ _____, _____.

Real-Life Zone A

B: Hello, Kate. I'm Hamin, _____ _____ of the Nanum Orchestra. _____ you _____ _____ _____ in our club.

G: Hi. Nice _____ _____ you.

B: You play the violin? _____ _____ _____ _____ the violin?

G: I started learning _____ _____ _____ _____ _____ I was ten.

B: Do you have any _____ _____ in a group?

G: Yes. _____, I was a member of _____ _____ _____ I was in _____ _____.

B: Great. We also _____ _____ _____ children. _____ _____ _____ _____ _____?

G: I have no _____ teaching others. But I _____ _____ _____ people, so I'd _____ _____ _____.

B: Good. I think we'll _____ a great time _____ together. _____ _____ the Nanum Orchestra.

Wrap Up

B: These cookies _____ so _____. Did you make them?

G: Yes. I _____ _____ _____ yesterday. I enjoy _____. I'm _____ _____ make doughnuts _____ _____.

B: Oh, I _____ _____ _____ _____ _____ _____ doughnuts. _____ it _____?

G: Not _____ _____. You can come to my house and _____ _____ if you want.

B: Thanks, Bora. _____ _____ _____ I come?

G: _____ 2:00.

B: _____ good. _____ you _____.

3. **B:** 지윤아, 그거 예쁜 배낭이네! 어디서 샀어?
    G: 언니가 내게 만들어 준 거야.
    B: 와! 그녀는 정말 훌륭한 디자이너구나.
    G: 응, 그래. 그리고 그녀는 옷 만드는 것도 즐겨.

B: 안녕, 케이트. 나는 나눔 오케스트라의 대표 하민이야. 우리 동아리에 관심을 가져줘서 고마워.
G: 안녕. 만나서 반가워.
B: 너는 바이올린을 연주하니? 언제 바이올린 연주를 시작했니?
G: 10살 때 바이올린을 연주하는 법을 배우기 시작했어.
B: 그룹에서 연주해 본 경험이 있니?
G: 응. 사실 나는 초등학교 때 오케스트라 단원이었어.
B: 좋아. 우리는 자원봉사로 아이들도 가르쳐. 다른 사람들을 가르치는 것을 즐기니?
G: 나는 다른 사람들을 가르친 경험이 없어. 그러나 나는 사람들과 일하는 것을 즐겨, 그래서 나는 해보고 싶어.
B: 좋아. 나는 우리가 함께 연주하며 좋은 시간을 보낼 것이라고 생각해. 나눔 오케스트라에 온 걸 환영해.

B: 이 쿠키들은 정말 맛있어 보여. 네가 만들었니?
G: 응. 어제 내가 직접 만들었어. 나는 제빵을 즐겨. 이번 주 토요일에 도넛을 만들 예정이야.
B: 오, 나는 도넛 만드는 법을 배우고 싶어. 그건 어렵니?
G: 전혀 아니야. 네가 원한다면 우리 집에 와서 같이 해도 돼.
B: 고마워, 보라야. 내가 몇 시에 가야 해?
G: 2시에.
B: 좋아. 그때 보자.

※ 다음 우리말에 맞도록 대화를 영어로 쓰시오.

Listen & Speak 1 A

A: _____

B: _____

Listen & Speak 1 B

1. G: _____

   B: _____

   G: _____

   B: _____

2. G: _____

   B: _____

   G: _____

Listen & Speak 2 A

A: _____

G: _____

Listen & Speak 2 B

1. B: _____

   G: _____

   B: _____

   G: _____

2. G: _____

   B: _____

   G: _____

   B: _____

해석

G: 종이 고양이 만드는 법을 알고 있니?
B: 물론이지. 그건 쉬워.

1. G: 어제 유나의 바이올린 콘서트에 갔다고 들었어. 어땠니?
   B: 좋았어. 나도 언젠가 그녀처럼 바이올린을 연주할 수 있기를 바라.
   G: 나는 네가 바이올린 연주하는 법을 아는지 몰랐어.
   B: 할 수 있어, 그러나 아직 잘하지는 못해.
2. G: 이 사진들 좀 봐. 나는 이 채소를 직접 길렀어. 나는 내 자신의 정원이 있어.
   B: 멋지다! 네가 기르는 채소로 요리하는 법도 아니?
   G: 응, 할머니께서 내게 가르쳐 주셨어.

B: 너는 밤에 별을 보는 것을 즐기니?
G: 응, 나는 별을 보는 것을 아주 좋아해.

1. B: 유미야, 너는 책 읽는 것을 즐기니?
   G: 응, 나는 과학 책을 읽는 것을 좋아해. 너는 어때?
   B: 나도 책 읽는 것을 좋아해.
   G: 그럼 오늘 방과 후에 도서관 가자.
2. G: 민수야, 주말에 뭐 했니?
   B: 가족을 위해 아침을 만들었어.
   G: 너는 요리를 즐기니?
   B: 응, 나는 훌륭한 요리사야! 우리 가족은 내 요리를 좋아해.

3. B: _____

G: _____

B: _____

G: _____

Real-Life Zone A

B: _____

_____

G: _____

B: _____

G: _____

B: _____

G: _____

B: _____

G: _____

_____

B: _____

_____

Wrap Up

B: _____

G: _____

_____

B: _____

G: _____

B: _____

G: _____

B: _____

3. B: 지윤아, 그거 예쁜 배낭이네! 어디서 샀어?

G: 언니가 내게 만들어 준 거야.

B: 와! 그녀는 정말 훌륭한 디자이너구나.

G: 응, 그래. 그리고 그녀는 옷 만드는 것도 즐겨.

B: 안녕, 케이트. 나는 나눔 오케스트라의 대표 하민이야. 우리 동아리에 관심을 가져줘서 고마워.

G: 안녕. 만나서 반가워.

B: 너는 바이올린을 연주하니? 언제 바이올린 연주를 시작했니?

G: 10살 때 바이올린을 연주하는 법을 배우기 시작했어.

B: 그룹에서 연주해 본 경험이 있니?

G: 응. 사실 나는 초등학교 때 오케스트라 단원이었어.

B: 좋아. 우리는 자원봉사로 아이들도 가르쳐. 다른 사람들을 가르치는 것을 즐기니?

G: 나는 다른 사람들을 가르친 경험이 없어. 그러나 나는 사람들과 일하는 것을 즐겨, 그래서 나는 해보고 싶어.

B: 좋아. 나는 우리가 함께 연주하며 좋은 시간을 보낼 것이라고 생각해. 나눔 오케스트라에 온 걸 환영해.

B: 이 쿠키들은 정말 맛있어 보여. 네가 만들었니?

G: 응. 어제 내가 직접 만들었어. 나는 제빵을 즐겨. 이번 주 토요일에 도넛을 만들 예정이야.

B: 오, 나는 도넛 만드는 법을 배우고 싶어. 그건 어렵니?

G: 전혀 아니야. 네가 원한다면 우리 집에 와서 같이 해도 돼.

B: 고마워, 보라야. 내가 몇 시에 가야 해?

G: 2시에.

B: 좋아. 그때 보자.

※ 다음 우리말과 일치하도록 빈칸에 알맞은 것을 골라 쓰시오.

1 _____ _____ You _____ Our Club?

A. Join   B. Don't   C. Why

2 _____ in club activities is a great _____ to enjoy your school _____.

A. life   B. participating   C. way

3 _____ about _____ a club?

A. joining   B. how

4 Here _____ two club _____ _____ want students to _____ their clubs.

A. join   B. who   C. are   D. leaders

5 _____ listen _____ _____ they say.

A. what   B. to   C. let's

6 The Picasso _____ _____

A. Club   B. Art

7 Hi! I am Sora Kang _____ the Picasso _____ _____.

A. Club   B. from   C. Art

8 _____ you can _____ _____ the name of our club, we _____.

A. paint   B. as   C. guess   D. from

9 We also do _____ _____ from time _____ time.

A. to   B. work   C. volunteer

10 _____ summer, our club members _____ _____ the "_____ Our Neighborhood" project.

A. in   B. change   C. participated   D. last

11 On the _____ old walls of the buildings in our neighborhood, we painted birds _____ high in the sky and dolphins _____ over blue _____.

A. waves   B. dirty   C. flying   D. jumping

12 _____ a result, the old neighborhood changed _____ a _____ and beautiful _____.

A. bright   B. into   C. place   D. as

13 The _____ were happy _____ see our work and _____ us.

A. thanked   B. to   C. neighbors

14 You _____ _____ _____ be a good painter.

A. to   B. have   C. don't

15 _____ who likes to _____ can _____.

A. join   B. paint   C. anyone

1 우리 동아리에 가입하는 게 어때?

2 동아리 활동에 참여하는 것은 학교생활을 즐기는 좋은 방법이에요.

3 동아리에 가입하는 게 어떤가요?

4 여기 학생들이 그들의 동아리에 가입하기를 원하는 두 명의 동아리 대표가 있어요.

5 그들이 하는 말을 들어 봅시다.

6 피카소 미술 동아리

7 안녕하세요! 저는 피카소 미술 동아리의 강소라입니다.

8 우리 동아리의 이름에서 추측할 수 있듯이, 우리는 그림을 그립니다.

9 우리는 가끔 자원봉사도 합니다.

10 지난여름, 우리 동아리 회원들은 "우리 마을 바꾸기" 프로젝트에 참여했습니다.

11 우리 마을에 있는 건물의 더럽고 오래된 벽에 하늘 높이 나는 새들과 푸른 파도 위로 점프하는 돌고래들을 그렸습니다.

12 결과적으로. 오래된 마을은 밝고 아름다운 곳으로 바뀌었습니다.

13 이웃들은 우리의 작품을 보고 행복해 했고 고마워했습니다.

14 여러분은 그림을 잘 그릴 필요는 없습니다.

15 그림 그리는 것을 좋아하는 사람은 누구나 가입할 수 있습니다.

16 _____ and _____ a _____ of the Picasso Art Club.

    A. member   B. be   C. come

17 The _____ _____

    A. Orchestra   B. Boram

18 Hi! I am Minsu Jang, the _____ _____ the Boram _____.

    A. Orchestra   B. of   C. leader

19 Did you see _____ students _____ music at the _____ when you came to school today?

    A. gate   B. playing   C. main   D. several

20 We _____ _____ students.

    A. those   B. were

21 We _____ music _____ our friends _____ morning.

    A. every   B. for   C. play

22 You _____ to know _____ to play an instrument a _____ _____ to join our club.

    A. bit   B. how   C. need   D. little

23 But don't _____ _____ you don't _____ well.

    A. play   B. if   C. worry

24 We will _____ hard and _____ _____ together.

    A. better   B. get   C. practice

25 We also teach children how to play _____ _____ as a _____ to our _____.

    A. community   B. service   C. instruments   D. musical

26 I am _____ an _____ boy to _____ the violin.

    A. how   B. teaching   C. eleven-year-old

27 _____ first, he did not know _____ to read a _____.

    A. note   B. note   C. at

28 Now he _____ play a _____ _____.

    A. song   B. simple   C. can

29 _____ him _____ the violin _____ me very happy.

    A. makes   B. play   C. hearing

30 _____ _____ our club, you can have an _____ to help _____.

    A. joining   B. opportunity   C. others   D. by

31 _____ and _____ our _____.

    A. club   B. join   C. come

32 We are _____ _____ you.

    A. for   B. waiting

16 와서 피카소 미술 동아리의 회원이 되세요.

17 보람 오케스트라

18 안녕하세요! 저는 보람 오케스트라의 회장 장민수입니다.

19 오늘 학교에 왔을 때 정문에서 음악을 연주하는 몇 명의 학생들을 보았습니까?

20 우리가 그 학생들이었습니다.

21 우리는 매일 아침 친구들을 위해 음악을 연주합니다.

22 우리 동아리에 가입하기 위해서는 악기 연주하는 법을 조금 알아야 합니다.

23 그러나 여러분이 연주를 잘 못한다고 해서 걱정하지 마세요.

24 우리는 열심히 연습하고 함께 좋아질 것입니다.

25 우리는 지역 사회에 대한 봉사로 아이들에게 악기를 연주하는 법도 가르칩니다.

26 저는 열한 살 소년에게 바이올린을 가르치고 있습니다.

27 처음에 그는 음표를 읽는 법을 알지 못했습니다.

28 이제는 간단한 노래도 연주할 수 있습니다.

29 그가 바이올린을 연주하는 걸 듣는 것은 저를 매우 행복하게 합니다.

30 우리 동아리에 가입함으로써, 여러분은 다른 사람들을 도울 수 있는 기회를 가질 수 있습니다.

31 와서 우리 동아리에 가입하세요.

32 우리는 여러분을 기다리고 있습니다.

※ 다음 우리말과 일치하도록 빈칸에 알맞은 말을 쓰시오.

1 _____ _____ _____ _____ Our Club?

2 _____ _____ _____ _____ is a great way _____ _____ your school life.

3 _____ _____ _____ a club?

4 _____ _____ two club leaders _____ _____ students _____ _____ their clubs.

5 _____ listen _____ _____ they say.

6 The Picasso _____ _____

7 Hi! I am Sora Kang _____ the Picasso _____ _____ .

8 _____ you _____ _____ _____ the name of our club, we _____ .

9 We also _____ _____ _____ _____ _____ time _____ time.

10 _____ summer, our club members _____ _____ the "_____ Our _____" project.

11 _____ _____ _____ _____ _____ _____ of the buildings in our neighborhood, we _____ birds _____ high in the sky and dolphins _____ _____ _____ _____ .

12 _____ _____ _____ , the old neighborhood _____ _____ a bright and _____ _____ .

13 The neighbors _____ _____ _____ _____ _____ our work and _____ us.

14 You _____ _____ _____ be a good _____ .

15 _____ _____ _____ paint can _____ .

1 우리 동아리에 가입하는 게 어때?

2 동아리 활동에 참여하는 것은 학교생활을 즐기는 좋은 방법이에요.

3 동아리에 가입하는 게 어떤가요?

4 여기 학생들이 그들의 동아리에 가입하기를 원하는 두 명의 동아리 대표가 있어요.

5 그들이 하는 말을 들어 봅시다.

6 피카소 미술 동아리

7 안녕하세요! 저는 피카소 미술 동아리의 강소라입니다.

8 우리 동아리의 이름에서 추측할 수 있듯이, 우리는 그림을 그립니다.

9 우리는 가끔 자원봉사도 합니다.

10 지난여름, 우리 동아리 회원들은 "우리 마을 바꾸기" 프로젝트에 참여했습니다.

11 우리 마을에 있는 건물의 더럽고 오래된 벽에 하늘 높이 나는 새들과 푸른 파도 위로 점프하는 돌고래들을 그렸습니다.

12 결과적으로, 오래된 마을은 밝고 아름다운 곳으로 바뀌었습니다.

13 이웃들은 우리의 작품을 보고 행복해 했고 고마워했습니다.

14 여러분은 그림을 잘 그릴 필요는 없습니다.

15 그림 그리는 것을 좋아하는 사람은 누구나 가입할 수 있습니다.

16 _____ _____ _____ a member of the Picasso Art Club.

17 The Boram _____

18 Hi! I am Minsu Jang, _____ _____ _____ the Boram Orchestra.

19 Did you _____ several students _____ _____ at the _____ when you _____ _____ _____ today?

20 We _____ _____ students.

21 We _____ _____ _____ our friends every morning.

22 You need to know _____ _____ _____ an instrument _____ _____ _____ _____ our club.

23 But _____ _____ _____ you _____ play well.

24 We will _____ _____ and _____ _____ together.

25 We _____ _____ children _____ _____ play musical instruments _____ _____ _____ _____ our community.

26 I am _____ _____ _____ _____ _____ to play the violin.

27 _____ _____, he did not know _____ _____ _____ _____ _____.

28 Now he _____ _____ _____ _____ _____.

29 _____ _____ _____ the violin makes me very _____.

30 _____ _____ our club, you can _____ _____ _____ _____ _____ _____.

31 _____ _____ our club.

32 We are _____ _____ you.

16 와서 피카소 미술 동아리의 회원이 되세요.

17 보람 오케스트라

18 안녕하세요! 저는 보람 오케스트라의 회장 장민수입니다.

19 오늘 학교에 왔을 때 정문에서 음악을 연주하는 몇 명의 학생들을 보았습니까?

20 우리가 그 학생들이었습니다.

21 우리는 매일 아침 친구들을 위해 음악을 연주합니다.

22 우리 동아리에 가입하기 위해서는 악기 연주하는 법을 조금 알아야 합니다.

23 그러나 여러분이 연주를 잘 못한다고 해서 걱정하지 마세요.

24 우리는 열심히 연습하고 함께 좋아질 것입니다.

25 우리는 지역 사회에 대한 봉사로 아이들에게 악기를 연주하는 법도 가르칩니다.

26 저는 열한 살 소년에게 바이올린을 가르치고 있습니다.

27 처음에 그는 음표를 읽는 법을 알지 못했습니다.

28 이제는 간단한 노래도 연주할 수 있습니다.

29 그가 바이올린을 연주하는 걸 듣는 것은 저를 매우 행복하게 합니다.

30 우리 동아리에 가입함으로써, 여러분은 다른 사람들을 도울 수 있는 기회를 가질 수 있습니다.

31 와서 우리 동아리에 가입하세요.

32 우리는 여러분을 기다리고 있습니다.

※ 다음 문장을 우리말로 쓰시오.

1   Why Don't You Join Our Club?

➡ _____

2   Participating in club activities is a great way to enjoy your school life.

➡ _____

3   How about joining a club?

➡ _____

4   Here are two club leaders who want students to join their clubs.

➡ _____

5   Let's listen to what they say.

➡ _____

6   The Picasso Art Club

➡ _____

7   Hi! I am Sora Kang from the Picasso Art Club.

➡ _____

8   As you can guess from the name of our club, we paint.

➡ _____

9   We also do volunteer work from time to time.

➡ _____

10   Last summer, our club members participated in the "Change Our Neighborhood" project.

➡ _____

11   On the dirty old walls of the buildings in our neighborhood, we painted birds flying high in the sky and dolphins jumping over blue waves.

➡ _____

12   As a result, the old neighborhood changed into a bright and beautiful place.

➡ _____

13   The neighbors were happy to see our work and thanked us.

➡ _____

14   You don't have to be a good painter.

➡ _____

15   Anyone who likes to paint can join.

➡ _____

16   Come and be a member of the Picasso Art Club.

➡ _____

17 ⯈ The Boram Orchestra

➡ _____

18 ⯈ Hi! I am Minsu Jang, the leader of the Boram Orchestra.

➡ _____

19 ⯈ Did you see several students playing music at the main gate when you came to school today?

➡ _____

20 ⯈ We were those students.

➡ _____

21 ⯈ We play music for our friends every morning.

➡ _____

22 ⯈ You need to know how to play an instrument a little bit to join our club.

➡ _____

23 ⯈ But don't worry if you don't play well.

➡ _____

24 ⯈ We will practice hard and get better together.

➡ _____

25 ⯈ We also teach children how to play musical instruments as a service to our community.

➡ _____

26 ⯈ I am teaching an eleven-year-old boy to play the violin.

➡ _____

27 ⯈ At first, he did not know how to read a note.

➡ _____

28 ⯈ Now he can play a simple song.

➡ _____

29 ⯈ Hearing him play the violin makes me very happy.

➡ _____

30 ⯈ By joining our club, you can have an opportunity to help others.

➡ _____

31 ⯈ Come and join our club.

➡ _____

32 ⯈ We are waiting for you.

➡ _____

※ 다음 괄호 안의 단어들을 우리말에 맞도록 바르게 배열하시오.

1 (Don't / Why / Join / You / Club? / Our)
➡ _____

2 (in / participating / activities / club / is / great / a / to / way / enjoy / your / life. / school)
➡ _____

3 (about / how / club? / a / joining)
➡ _____

4 (are / here / two / leaders / club / who / students / want / clubs. / their / join / to)
➡ _____

5 (listen / let's / what / to / say. / they)
➡ _____

6 (Picasso / Club / The / Art)
➡ _____

7 (hi! // am / I / Kang / Sora / from / Picasso / Club. / Art / the)
➡ _____

8 (you / as / guess / can / from / name / the / of / club, / our / paint. / we)
➡ _____

9 (also / do / we / work / volunteer / to / time / from / time.)
➡ _____

10 (summer, / last / club / our / members / in / participated / the / Our / "Change / project. / Neighborhood")
➡ _____

11 (the / on / old / dirty / walls / the / of / buildings / our / in / neighborhood, / painted / we / flying / birds / high / the / in / sky / and / dolphins / over / jumping / waves. / blue)
➡ _____

12 (a / as / result, / old / the / neighborhood / into / changed / a / beautiful / and / place. / bright)
➡ _____

13 (neighbors / the / happy / were / see / to / work / our / and / us. / thanked)
➡ _____

14 (don't / have / you / be / to / painter. / good / a)
➡ _____

15 (who / anyone / likes / to / join. / can / paint)
➡ _____

16 (and / come / be / member / a / of / the / Club. / Art / Picasso)
➡ _____

1 우리 동아리에 가입하는 게 어때?

2 동아리 활동에 참여하는 것은 학교생활을 즐기는 좋은 방법이에요.

3 동아리에 가입하는 게 어떤가요?

4 여기 학생들이 그들의 동아리에 가입하기를 원하는 두 명의 동아리 대표가 있어요.

5 그들이 하는 말을 들어 봅시다.

6 피카소 미술 동아리

7 안녕하세요! 저는 피카소 미술 동아리의 강소라입니다.

8 우리 동아리의 이름에서 추측할 수 있듯이, 우리는 그림을 그립니다.

9 우리는 가끔 자원봉사도 합니다.

10 지난여름, 우리 동아리 회원들은 "우리 마을 바꾸기" 프로젝트에 참여했습니다.

11 우리 마을에 있는 건물의 더럽고 오래된 벽에 하늘 높이 나는 새들과 푸른 파도 위로 점프하는 돌고래들을 그렸습니다.

12 결과적으로, 오래된 마을은 밝고 아름다운 곳으로 바뀌었습니다.

13 이웃들은 우리의 작품을 보고 행복해 했고 고마워했습니다.

14 여러분은 그림을 잘 그릴 필요는 없습니다.

15 그림 그리는 것을 좋아하는 사람은 누구나 가입할 수 있습니다.

16 와서 피카소 미술 동아리의 회원이 되세요.

17 (Boram / The / Orchestra)
➡ _____

18 (hi! // am / I / Jang, / Minsu / leader / the / of / the / Orchestra. / Boram)
➡ _____

19 (you / did / several / see / students / playing / music / the / at / gate / main / when / you / to / came / today? / school)
➡ _____
_____

20 (were / students. / we / those)
➡ _____

21 (play / we / for / music / our / morning. / every / friends)
➡ _____

22 (need / you / know / to / how / play / to / an / instrument / little / a / bit / join / to / club. / our)
➡ _____

23 (don't / but / worry / you / if / play / well. / don't)
➡ _____

24 (will / practice / we / hard / and / together. / better / get)
➡ _____

25 (we / teach / also / children / to / how / play / instruments / musical / as / service / a / to / coummunity. / our)
➡ _____

26 (I / teaching / am / an / boy / eleven-year-old / play / violin. / the / to)
➡ _____

27 (first, / at / did / he / know / not / to / how / read / note. / a)
➡ _____

28 (he / now / play / can / song. / simple / a)
➡ _____

29 (him / hearing / play / violin / the / me / makes / happy. / very)
➡ _____

30 (joining / by / club, / our / can / you / have / opportunity / an / others. / help / to)
➡ _____

31 (join / and / come / club. / our)
➡ _____

32 (are / we / waiting / you. / for)
➡ _____

17 보람 오케스트라

18 안녕하세요! 저는 보람 오케스트라의 회장 장민수입니다.

19 오늘 학교에 왔을 때 정문에서 음악을 연주하는 몇 명의 학생들을 보았습니까?

20 우리가 그 학생들이었습니다.

21 우리는 매일 아침 친구들을 위해 음악을 연주합니다.

22 우리 동아리에 가입하기 위해서는 악기 연주하는 법을 조금 알아야 합니다.

23 그러나 여러분이 연주를 잘 못한다고 해서 걱정하지 마세요.

24 우리는 열심히 연습하고 함께 좋아질 것입니다.

25 우리는 지역 사회에 대한 봉사로 아이들에게 악기를 연주하는 법도 가르칩니다.

26 저는 열한 살 소년에게 바이올린을 가르치고 있습니다.

27 처음에 그는 음표를 읽는 법을 알지 못했습니다.

28 이제는 간단한 노래도 연주할 수 있습니다.

29 그가 바이올린을 연주하는 걸 듣는 것은 저를 매우 행복하게 합니다.

30 우리 동아리에 가입함으로써, 여러분은 다른 사람들을 도울 수 있는 기회를 가질 수 있습니다.

31 와서 우리 동아리에 가입하세요.

32 우리는 여러분을 기다리고 있습니다.

※ 다음 우리말을 영어로 쓰시오.

1 우리 동아리에 가입하는 게 어때?

➡ _____

2 동아리 활동에 참여하는 것은 학교생활을 즐기는 좋은 방법이에요.

➡ _____

3 동아리에 가입하는 게 어떤가요?

➡ _____

4 여기 학생들이 그들의 동아리에 가입하기를 원하는 두 명의 동아리 대표가 있어요.

➡ _____

5 그들이 하는 말을 들어 봅시다.

➡ _____

6 피카소 미술 동아리

➡ _____

7 안녕하세요! 저는 피카소 미술 동아리의 강소라입니다.

➡ _____

8 우리 동아리의 이름에서 추측할 수 있듯이, 우리는 그림을 그립니다.

➡ _____

9 우리는 가끔 자원봉사도 합니다.

➡ _____

10 지난여름, 우리 동아리 회원들은 "우리 마을 바꾸기" 프로젝트에 참여했습니다.

➡ _____

11 우리 마을에 있는 건물의 더럽고 오래된 벽에 하늘 높이 나는 새들과 푸른 파도 위로 점프하는 돌고래들을 그렸습니다.

➡ _____

_____

12 결과적으로, 오래된 마을은 밝고 아름다운 곳으로 바뀌었습니다.

➡ _____

13 이웃들은 우리의 작품을 보고 행복해 했고 고마워했습니다.

➡ _____

14 여러분은 그림을 잘 그릴 필요는 없습니다.

➡ _____

15 그림 그리는 것을 좋아하는 사람은 누구나 가입할 수 있습니다.

➡ _____

16 와서 피카소 미술 동아리의 회원이 되세요.

➡ _____

17 보람 오케스트라

➡ _____

18 안녕하세요! 저는 보람 오케스트라의 회장 장민수입니다.

➡ _____

19 오늘 학교에 왔을 때 정문에서 음악을 연주하는 몇 명의 학생들을 보았습니까?

➡ _____

20 우리가 그 학생들이었습니다.

➡ _____

21 우리는 매일 아침 친구들을 위해 음악을 연주합니다.

➡ _____

22 우리 동아리에 가입하기 위해서는 악기 연주하는 법을 조금 알아야 합니다.

➡ _____

23 그러나 여러분이 연주를 잘 못한다고 해서 걱정하지 마세요.

➡ _____

24 우리는 열심히 연습하고 함께 좋아질 것입니다.

➡ _____

25 우리는 지역 사회에 대한 봉사로 아이들에게 악기를 연주하는 법도 가르칩니다.

➡ _____

26 저는 열한 살 소년에게 바이올린을 가르치고 있습니다.

➡ _____

27 처음에 그는 음표를 읽는 법을 알지 못했습니다.

➡ _____

28 이제는 간단한 노래도 연주할 수 있습니다.

➡ _____

29 그가 바이올린을 연주하는 걸 듣는 것은 저를 매우 행복하게 합니다.

➡ _____

30 우리 동아리에 가입함으로써, 여러분은 다른 사람들을 도울 수 있는 기회를 가질 수 있습니다.

➡ _____

31 와서 우리 동아리에 가입하세요.

➡ _____

32 우리는 여러분을 기다리고 있습니다.

➡ _____

※ 다음 우리말과 일치하도록 빈칸에 알맞은 말을 쓰시오.

After You Read

1. Today, Minsu, the _____ of the Boram Orchestra, came to _____

   _____.

2. He _____ _____ me _____ _____ _____ the violin

   last month.

3. At first, I didn't know _____ _____ _____ _____ _____.

4. I _____ _____ _____ the Boram Orchestra and play the

   violin at the _____ _____ when I become a middle school

   student.

1. 오늘, 보람 오케스트라의 대표인 민수가 지역 주민회관에 왔다.
2. 그는 지난달에 바이올린을 연주하는 법을 나에게 가르쳐 주기 시작했다.
3. 처음에는 나는 하나의 음표도 읽는 법을 알지 못했다.
4. 나는 보람 오케스트라에 가입하여, 내가 중학생이 될 때 정문에서 바이올린을 연주하기를 희망한다.

Writing Workshop

1. Boram _____ _____ _____ Membership Form

2. • _____ of Club: FC Boram

3. • _____ _____: Sunho Park

4. • Why You Want _____ _____ the Club: I love soccer and

   _____ _____ _____ join FC Boram.

5. I am _____ _____ _____ the ball and _____ fast.

6. However, I don't know _____ _____ _____ the ball,

   _____ I want to learn how to do that.

7. I want to _____ a soccer player _____ can make wonderful

   heading goals.

8. • Your _____: If I _____ this club, I will _____ very

   _____ and become a good team player!

1. 보람중학교 동아리 지원서
2. 동아리 이름: FC Boram
3 학생 이름: 박순호
4. 가입을 원하는 이유: 나는 축구를 사랑하고 FC Boram에 가입하고 싶다.
5. 나는 공을 패스하는 것을 잘하고 빨리 달린다.
6. 그러나, 나는 공을 헤딩하는 법을 모르기 때문에 그것을 하는 법을 배우고 싶다.
7. 나는 멋진 헤딩 골을 만들 수 있는 축구 선수가 되기를 원한다.
8. 당신의 목표: 만약 내가 이 동아리에 가입하면, 나는 매우 열심히 연습해서 좋은 팀 플레이어가 될 것이다.

Real Life Zone

1. I _____ _____ to introduce our new orchestra member, Kate.

2. She knows _____ _____ _____ the violin.

3. She also has _____ _____ experience _____ in a group.

4. And she said she _____ _____ with people.

5. _____ all _____ her _____ the Nanum Orchestra.

1. 나는 우리의 새로운 오케스트라 회원인 케이트를 소개하고 싶어.
2. 그녀는 바이올린을 연주하는 법을 알아.
3. 그녀는 또한 그룹에서 연주해 본 경험이 많아.
4. 그리고 그녀는 사람들과 일하는 것을 즐긴다고 말했어.
5. 모두 그녀가 나눔 오케스트라에 온 걸 환영하자.

※ 다음 우리말을 영어로 쓰시오.

After You Read

1. 오늘, 보람 오케스트라의 대표인 민수가 지역 주민회관에 왔다.
   ➡ _____

2. 그는 지난달에 바이올린을 연주하는 법을 나에게 가르쳐 주기 시작했다.
   ➡ _____

3. 처음에는 나는 하나의 음표도 읽는 법을 알지 못했다.
   ➡ _____

4. 나는 보람 오케스트라에 가입하여, 내가 중학생이 될 때 정문에서 바이올린을 연주하기를 희망한다.
   ➡ _____
   _____

Writing Workshop

1. 보람중학교 동아리 지원서
   ➡ _____

2. 동아리 이름: FC Boram
   ➡ _____

3. 학생 이름: 박순호
   ➡ _____

4. 가입을 원하는 이유: 나는 축구를 사랑하고 FC Boram에 가입하고 싶다.
   ➡ _____

5. 나는 공을 패스하는 것을 잘하고 빨리 달린다.
   ➡ _____

6. 그러나, 나는 공을 헤딩하는 법을 모르기 때문에 그것을 하는 법을 배우고 싶다.
   ➡ _____

7. 나는 멋진 헤딩 골을 만들 수 있는 축구 선수가 되기를 원한다.
   ➡ _____

8. 당신의 목표: 만약 내가 이 동아리에 가입하면, 나는 매우 열심히 연습해서 좋은 팀 플레이어가 될 것이다.
   ➡ _____

Real Life Zone

1. 나는 우리의 새로운 오케스트라 회원인 케이트를 소개하고 싶어.
   ➡ _____

2. 그녀는 바이올린을 연주하는 법을 알아.
   ➡ _____

3. 그녀는 또한 그룹에서 연주해 본 경험이 많아.
   ➡ _____

4. 그리고 그녀는 사람들과 일하는 것을 즐긴다고 말했어.
   ➡ _____

5. 모두 그녀가 나눔 오케스트라에 온 걸 환영하자.
   ➡ _____

※ 다음 영어를 우리말로 쓰시오.

01	besides	22	separate
02	correct	23	review
03	reply	24	school cafeteria
04	ever	25	weather
05	character	26	cub
06	rule	27	disappointed
07	scene	28	nervous
08	friendly	29	foreigner
09	happiness	30	opinion
10	seagull	31	regret
11	item	32	scary
12	noisy	33	teenager
13	support	34	wide
14	title	35	be worried about
15	comfortable	36	get better
16	join	37	look good (on 사람)
17	such	38	take away
18	throne	39	be scared of
19	journey	40	look+like+명사
20	nearby	41	be good at
21	foreign	42	by the way
		43	What if+주어+동사 ~?

※ 다음 우리말을 영어로 쓰시오.

01	불안한	22	후회하다
02	대답하다	23	편안한
03	헤어지다	24	시끄러운
04	날씨	25	왕좌, 왕위
05	장면	26	지배하다
06	(곰, 사자 등의) 새끼	27	실망한, 기대에 어긋난
07	감상문, 논평	28	무서운
08	외국의	29	외국인
09	여행	30	학교 식당
10	너무나 ~한, 그러한	31	제목
11	십 대	32	넓은
12	지지; 지지하다	33	올바른
13	친절한	34	언제든, 한 번이라도
14	게다가	35	발발하다
15	행복	36	더 이상 ~않다
16	품목	37	그런데
17	등장인물	38	~하는 것을 노력하다
18	갈매기	39	~에 대해 걱정하다
19	함께 하다	40	~처럼 보이다
20	근처에	41	~을 두려워하다
21	의견	42	(병ㆍ상황 등이) 나아지다
		43	~에 들어가다

※ 다음 영영풀이에 알맞은 단어를 <보기>에서 골라 쓴 후, 우리말 뜻을 쓰시오.

1   _____ : to move apart: _____

2   _____ : a trip from one place to another: _____

3   _____ : the feeling of pleasure: _____

4   _____ : used to give an additional reason for something: _____

5   _____ : making a lot of loud noise: _____

6   _____ : a person in a film, book, or play: _____

7   _____ : to be in control of an area and its people: _____

8   _____ : the young of a bear, lion or other mammals: _____

9   _____ : from a country other than one's own: _____

10 _____ : to say or write something in response to something: _____

11 _____ : a person between the ages of thirteen and nineteen: _____

12 _____ : the name of a book, film, or other artistic work: _____

13 _____ : a bird with white or gray feathers that lives near the sea: _____

14 _____ : worried and anxious about something that is happening or might happen:
                _____

15 _____ : help, encouragement, or comfort given to someone during a difficult or
                unhappy time: _____

16 _____ : a critical comment in a newspaper that gives an opinion about a new
                book or film: _____

보기			
title	separate	reply	character
journey	cub	besides	happiness
review	rule	nervous	seagull
noisy	support	teenager	foreign

※ 다음 우리말과 일치하도록 빈칸에 알맞은 말을 쓰시오.

Listen & Speak 1 A

B: I'm _____ _____ the math test.

W: _____ _____ . You'll _____ _____ .

B: 저는 수학 시험이 걱정돼요.
W: 걱정하지 마. 넌 잘할 거야.

Listen & Speak 1 B

1. B: _____ _____ _____ any _____ _____ for tomorrow?

   G: I'm _____ _____ Jejudo in the morning. But I'm _____ _____ the weather.

   B: _____ _____ . It _____ _____ on Jejudo tomorrow.

   G: Oh, that's _____ _____ _____ .

2. B: Jina, _____ you _____ _____ your house first?

   G: Why? _____ _____ ?

   B: I'm _____ _____ your dog.

   G: Don't worry. He's a _____ dog. He _____ _____ _____ he's so big.

1. B: 내일 특별한 계획 있니?
   G: 아침에 제주도에 갈 거야. 그런데 날씨가 걱정돼.
   B: 걱정하지 마. 내일 제주도에는 비가 내리지 않을 거야.
   G: 오, 반가운 소리네.

2. B: 진아야, 네가 먼저 집에 들어갈 수 있어?
   G: 왜? 무슨 일 있니?
   B: 난 네 개가 무서워.
   G: 걱정하지 마. 친절한 개야. 너무 커서 무섭게 보일 뿐이야.

Listen & Speak 1 C

1. A: _____ _____ _____ your health.

   B: _____ _____ . I'm _____ _____ the doctor tomorrow.

2. A: _____ _____ _____ the speech contest.

   B: Don't _____ . _____ _____ _____ _____ .

3. A: _____ _____ _____ _____ _____ _____ .

   B: Don't _____ . You'll _____ _____ you _____ _____ _____ .

1. A: 나는 네 건강이 걱정돼.
   B: 걱정하지 마. 내일 진찰받으러 병원에 갈 거야.

2. A: 나는 말하기 대회가 걱정돼.
   B: 걱정하지 마. 넌 잘할 거야.

3. A: 나는 내 미래가 걱정돼.
   B: 걱정하지 마. 네가 하고 싶은 것을 발견할 거야.

Listen & Speak 2 A

B: _____ _____ _____ _____ _____ these sunglasses?

G: They're cool! You _____ _____ a movie star.

B: 이 선글라스에 대해 어떻게 생각해?
G: 멋져! 너는 영화배우 같아.

Listen & Speak 2 B

1. **G:** _____ you _____ the movie, *The Daughter*?

   B: Yes, I _____ it _____ _____.

   G: _____ _____ _____ _____ _____ _____?

   B: I was _____. It _____ very _____.

2. **B:** _____ _____ _____ _____ _____ our school cafeteria food?

   G: I _____ the cafeteria food is _____.

   B: _____ do you think is the _____ _____?

   G: I _____ the Gimbap _____ _____.

3. **G:** What _____ _____ _____ _____ this painting?

   B: It _____ _____. I like the colors.

   G: I'm _____ _____ you like it. I _____ it _____.

Listen & Speak 2 C

1. **A:** _____ do you _____ _____ my bike?

   B: It _____ _____ and _____.

2. **A:** _____ _____ _____ of these shoes?

   B: They _____ _____ _____ _____.

Real-Life Zone

G: I saw you with someone _____ _____ _____ a foreigner yesterday.

B: Yes. We _____ lunch together.

G: You _____ _____ you _____ _____ a good time.

B: We _____. We _____ _____ _____ _____ a month for lunch.

G: I _____ I _____ _____ more _____ talking with a foreigner.

B: I _____ _____ _____ _____ in English before, but not _____.

G: I _____ really _____ when I _____ _____ _____ in English.

B: Well, the first time is _____ _____. After that, it _____ _____ and _____.

G: _____ _____ _____ think _____ me joining _____ _____ you for lunch?

B: That's a _____ _____.

---

1. **G:** 너 영화 '딸' 봤니?

   B: 응, 지난 토요일에 봤어.

   G: 어떻게 생각했어?

   B: 나는 실망했어. 별로 좋지 않았어.

2. **B:** 학교 식당 음식에 대해 어떻게 생각해?

   G: 식당 음식이 맛있다고 생각해.

   B: 최고의 품목이 뭐라고 생각하니?

   G: 나는 김밥을 제일 좋아해.

3. **G:** 이 그림에 대해 어떻게 생각해?

   B: 아주 멋있어. 나는 색이 마음에 들어.

   G: 네가 좋아하니 기뻐. 내가 직접 그렸어.

1. **A:** 내 자전거에 대해 어떻게 생각해?

   B: 가볍고 빨라 보여.

2. **A:** 이 신발에 대해 어떻게 생각해?

   B: 너에게 잘 어울려.

G: 나는 어제 네가 외국인처럼 보이는 누군가와 있는 것을 봤어.

B: 응. 우리는 점심을 같이 먹었어.

G: 너희들은 좋은 시간을 보내고 있는 것처럼 보였어.

B: 그랬어. 우리는 한 달에 두 번 만나서 점심을 먹으려고 해.

G: 나는 외국인과 더 편하게 이야기할 수 있으면 좋을 텐데.

B: 나는 전에는 영어로 말하는 것에 대해 걱정했었지만, 더 이상은 아니야.

G: 영어로 말하려고 할 때 정말 불안해.

B: 음, 처음이 가장 힘들지. 그 후에 점점 쉬워져.

G: 내가 너희 둘과 함께 점심 먹는 거 어떻게 생각해?

B: 좋은 생각이야.

※ 다음 우리말에 맞도록 대화를 영어로 쓰시오.

Listen & Speak 1 A

B: _____

W: _____

해석

B: 저는 수학 시험이 걱정돼요.
W: 걱정하지 마. 넌 잘할 거야.

Listen & Speak 1 B

1. B: _____

   G: _____

   B: _____

   G: _____

2. B: _____

   G: _____

   B: _____

   G: _____

1. B: 내일 특별한 계획 있니?
   G: 아침에 제주도에 갈 거야. 그런데 날씨가 걱정돼.
   B: 걱정하지 마. 내일 제주도에는 비가 내리지 않을 거야.
   G: 오, 반가운 소리네.

2. B: 진아야, 네가 먼저 집에 들어갈 수 있어?
   G: 왜? 무슨 일 있니?
   B: 난 네 개가 무서워.
   G: 걱정하지 마. 친절한 개야. 너무 커서 무섭게 보일 뿐이야.

Listen & Speak 1 C

1. A: _____

   B: _____

2. A: _____

   B: _____

3. A: _____

   B: _____

1. A: 나는 네 건강이 걱정돼.
   B: 걱정하지 마. 내일 진찰받으러 병원에 갈 거야.

2. A: 나는 말하기 대회가 걱정돼.
   B: 걱정하지 마. 넌 잘할 거야.

3. A: 나는 내 미래가 걱정돼.
   B: 걱정하지 마. 네가 하고 싶은 것을 발견할 거야.

Listen & Speak 2 A

B: _____

G: _____

B: 이 선글라스에 대해 어떻게 생각해?
G: 멋져! 너는 영화배우 같아.

Listen & Speak 2 B

1. G: _____

   B: _____

   G: _____

   B: _____

2. B: _____

   G: _____

   B: _____

   G: _____

3. G: _____

   B: _____

   G: _____

Listen & Speak 2 C

1. A: _____

   B: _____

2. A: _____

   B: _____

Real-Life Zone

G: _____

B: _____

G: _____

B: _____

G: _____

B: _____

G: _____

B: _____

G: _____

B: _____

1. G: 너 영화 '딸' 봤니?
   B: 응, 지난 토요일에 봤어.
   G: 어떻게 생각했어?
   B: 나는 실망했어. 별로 좋지 않았어.

2. B: 학교 식당 음식에 대해 어떻게 생각해?
   G: 식당 음식이 맛있다고 생각해.
   B: 최고의 품목이 뭐라고 생각하니?
   G: 나는 김밥을 제일 좋아해.

3. G: 이 그림에 대해 어떻게 생각해?
   B: 아주 멋있어. 나는 색이 마음에 들어.
   G: 네가 좋아하니 기뻐. 내가 직접 그렸어.

1. A: 내 자전거에 대해 어떻게 생각해?
   B: 가볍고 빨라 보여.

2. A: 이 신발에 대해 어떻게 생각해?
   B: 너에게 잘 어울려.

G: 나는 어제 네가 외국인처럼 보이는 누군가와 있는 것을 봤어.
B: 응. 우리는 점심을 같이 먹었어.
G: 너희들은 좋은 시간을 보내고 있는 것처럼 보였어.
B: 그랬어. 우리는 한 달에 두 번 만나서 점심을 먹으려고 해.
G: 나는 외국인과 더 편하게 이야기할 수 있으면 좋을 텐데.
B: 나는 전에는 영어로 말하는 것에 대해 걱정했었지만, 더 이상은 아니야.
G: 영어로 말하려고 할 때 정말 불안해.
B: 음, 처음이 가장 힘들지. 그 후에 점점 쉬워져.
G: 내가 너희 둘과 함께 점심 먹는 거 어떻게 생각해?
B: 좋은 생각이야.

※ 다음 우리말과 일치하도록 빈칸에 알맞은 것을 골라 쓰시오.

1 The _____ _____
   A. Brothers   B. Two

2 Two brothers _____ _____ a _____.
   A. went   B. journey   C. on

3 They _____ a rock in _____ _____ a forest.
   A. front   B. found   C. of

4 It _____, "Go _____ the forest and swim _____ the river.
   A. said   B. across   C. into

5 There you will _____ a bear and _____ _____.
   A. her   B. find   C. cubs

6 _____ the bear cubs and _____ _____ the mountain.
   A. run   B. take   C. up

7 There you will _____ _____."
   A. happiness   B. find

8 The younger brother said, "Let's _____ and _____ happiness _____."
   A. find   B. go   C. together

9 "No," said the older brother, "_____ _____ we know this is _____?
   A. how   B. can   C. true

10 _____ _____ the river is too _____?
   A. if   B. wide   C. what

11 _____, will it be easy to take the cubs _____ _____ their mother?
   A. from   B. away   C. besides

12 _____ of _____ happiness, we can be _____!"
   A. finding   B. killed   C. Instead

13 The younger brother _____, "How can we know _____ we don't _____?"
   A. if   B. replied   C. try

14 They separated, and they both _____ their _____ _____.
   A. way   B. went   C. own

15 The younger brother _____ _____ the forest and _____ _____ the river.
   A. across   B. into   C. swam   D. went

16 _____ _____ the bear.
   A. was   B. there

1 두 형제

2 두 형제는 여정을 떠났다.

3 그들은 숲 앞에서 바위를 발견했다.

4 거기에 쓰여 있었다. "숲에 들어가 강을 헤엄쳐 건너시오.

5 당신은 거기에서 곰과 새끼들을 발견할 것입니다.

6 곰 새끼들을 데리고 산 위로 뛰어 올라가시오.

7 거기에서 당신은 행복을 찾을 수 있을 것입니다."

8 동생이 말했다. "함께 가서 행복을 찾자."

9 "싫어." 형은 말했다. "이것이 사실인지 우리가 어떻게 알 수 있어?

10 강이 너무 넓으면 어쩌지?

11 게다가, 곰 새끼들을 엄마에게서 빼앗는 것이 쉬울까?

12 행복을 찾는 대신에, 우리는 죽을 수 있어!"

13 동생은 대답했다. "우리가 시도하지 않으면 어떻게 알 수 있어?"

14 그들은 헤어졌고, 둘 다 자신의 길을 갔다.

15 동생은 숲에 들어가서 강을 헤엄쳐 건넜다.

16 곰이 있었다.

17 She _____ _____.

A. sleeping B. was

18 He _____ her cubs and _____ _____ the mountain.

A. ran B. took C. up

19 When he _____ the top, some people _____ him to their city and _____ him their king.

A. made B. took C. reached

20 There he _____ _____ a king _____ five years.

A. as B. for C. lived

21 Then a war _____ _____, and he _____ his throne.

A. out B. lost C. broke

22 He was _____ the _____ again.

A. on B. road

23 _____ day, the two brothers _____ again and talked about their lives _____ the _____ five years.

A. met B. last C. for D. one

24 The _____ brother said, "I was _____.

A. right B. older

25 I _____ _____ quietly and _____.

A. lived B. have C. well

26 You were _____ a king, but you have _____ a _____ of trouble."

A. had B. once C. lot

27 The _____ brother answered, "I don't _____ my _____.

A. regret B. choice C. younger

28 I may have _____ now, but I will always have _____ _____ _____."

A. something B. remember C. nothing D. to

17 그녀는 자고 있었다.

18 그는 새끼들을 데리고 산을 뛰어 올라갔다.

19 그가 정상에 도착했을 때, 어떤 사람들이 그를 자기들 도시로 데려가서 그들의 왕으로 만들었다.

20 그곳에서 그는 5년간 왕으로 살았다.

21 그런 다음 전쟁이 일어났고, 그는 왕좌를 잃었다.

22 그는 다시 길바닥에 나앉았다.

23 어느 날, 두 형제는 다시 만났고 지난 5년 동안의 그들의 삶에 대해 이야기했다.

24 형은 말했다. "내가 옳았어.

25 나는 조용히 잘 살았어.

26 너는 한때 왕이었지만 많은 어려움을 겪었지."

27 동생은 대답했다. "나는 내 선택을 후회하지 않아.

28 나는 지금 아무것도 없지만 언제까지나 기억할 어떤 것이 있어."

※ 다음 우리말과 일치하도록 빈칸에 알맞은 말을 쓰시오.

1 The _____ _____

2 Two brothers _____ _____ a _____.

3 They _____ a rock _____ _____ a forest.

4 It _____, "_____ _____ the forest and _____ _____ the river.

5 There you _____ _____ a bear and _____ _____.

6 _____ the bear cubs and _____ _____ the mountain.

7 There you _____ _____ _____."

8 The younger brother said, "_____ _____ _____ _____ _____ _____."

9 "No," said the _____ _____, "_____ _____ _____ this is _____?

10 _____ _____ the river is _____ _____?

11 _____, will it be _____ _____ the cubs _____ their mother?

12 _____ _____ _____ happiness, we can _____ _____!"

13 The younger brother _____, "_____ can we know _____ we _____ _____?"

14 They _____, and they _____ _____ _____.

15 The younger brother _____ _____ the forest and _____ _____ the river.

16 _____ _____ _____ the bear.

1 두 형제

2 두 형제는 여정을 떠났다.

3 그들은 숲 앞에서 바위를 발견했다.

4 거기에 쓰여 있었다. "숲에 들어가 강을 헤엄쳐 건너시오.

5 당신은 거기에서 곰과 새끼들을 발견할 것입니다.

6 곰 새끼들을 데리고 산 위로 뛰어 올라가시오.

7 거기에서 당신은 행복을 찾을 수 있을 것입니다."

8 동생이 말했다. "함께 가서 행복을 찾자."

9 "싫어." 형은 말했다. "이것이 사실인지 우리가 어떻게 알 수 있어?

10 강이 너무 넓으면 어쩌지?

11 게다가, 곰 새끼들을 엄마에게서 빼앗는 것이 쉬울까?

12 행복을 찾는 대신에, 우리는 죽을 수 있어!"

13 동생은 대답했다. "우리가 시도하지 않으면 어떻게 알 수 있어?"

14 그들은 헤어졌고, 둘 다 자신의 길을 갔다.

15 동생은 숲에 들어가서 강을 헤엄쳐 건넜다.

16 곰이 있었다.

17 She _____ _____.

18 He _____ _____ _____ and _____ _____ the mountain.

19 When he _____ _____ _____, some people _____ _____ _____ their city and _____ him their king.

20 There he _____ _____ _____ _____ _____ five years.

21 Then a war _____ _____, and he _____ _____ _____.

22 He _____ _____ _____ _____ again.

23 _____ _____, the two brothers met again and _____ _____ their _____ _____ _____ _____ five years.

24 The older brother said, " _____ _____ _____.

25 I _____ _____ _____ and _____.

26 You were _____ a king, but you _____ _____ _____ _____ _____ _____."

27 The _____ _____ answered, "I don't _____ _____ _____.

28 I may have _____ now, but I _____ _____ _____ _____ _____ _____."

17 그녀는 자고 있었다.

18 그는 새끼들을 데리고 산을 뛰어 올라갔다.

19 그가 정상에 도착했을 때, 어떤 사람들이 그를 자기들 도시로 데려가서 그들의 왕으로 만들었다.

20 그곳에서 그는 5년간 왕으로 살았다.

21 그런 다음 전쟁이 일어났고, 그는 왕좌를 잃었다.

22 그는 다시 길바닥에 나앉았다.

23 어느 날, 두 형제는 다시 만났고 지난 5년 동안의 그들의 삶에 대해 이야기했다.

24 형은 말했다. "내가 옳았어.

25 나는 조용히 잘 살았어.

26 너는 한때 왕이었지만 많은 어려움을 겪었지."

27 동생은 대답했다. "나는 내 선택을 후회하지 않아.

28 나는 지금 아무것도 없지만 언제까지나 기억할 어떤 것이 있어."

※ 다음 문장을 우리말로 쓰시오.

1 The Two Brothers

➡ _____

2 Two brothers went on a journey.

➡ _____

3 They found a rock in front of a forest.

➡ _____

4 It said, "Go into the forest and swim across the river.

➡ _____

5 There you will find a bear and her cubs.

➡ _____

6 Take the bear cubs and run up the mountain.

➡ _____

7 There you will find happiness."

➡ _____

8 The younger brother said, "Let's go and find happiness together."

➡ _____

9 "No," said the older brother, "How can we know this is true?

➡ _____

10 What if the river is too wide?

➡ _____

11 Besides, will it be easy to take the cubs away from their mother?

➡ _____

12 Instead of finding happiness, we can be killed!"

➡ _____

13 The younger brother replied, "How can we know if we don't try?"

➡ _____

14 They separated, and they both went their own way.

➡ _____

15 The younger brother went into the forest and swam across the river.

➡ _____

16 There was the bear.

➡ _____

17 She was sleeping.

➡ _____

18 He took her cubs and ran up the mountain.

➡ _____

19 When he reached the top, some people took him to their city and made him their king.

➡ _____

20 There he lived as a king for five years.

➡ _____

21 Then a war broke out, and he lost his throne.

➡ _____

22 He was on the road again.

➡ _____

23 One day, the two brothers met again and talked about their lives for the last five years.

➡ _____

24 The older brother said, "I was right.

➡ _____

25 I have lived quietly and well.

➡ _____

26 You were once a king, but you have had a lot of trouble."

➡ _____

27 The younger brother answered, "I don't regret my choice.

➡ _____

28 I may have nothing now, but I will always have something to remember."

➡ _____

※ 다음 괄호 안의 단어들을 우리말에 맞도록 바르게 배열하시오.

1 (Brothers / Two / The)
➡ _____

2 (brothers / two / on / a / journey. / went)
➡ _____

3 (found / they / rock / a / front / in / forest. / a / of)
➡ _____

4 (said, / it / into / "go / forest / the / and / across / swim / river. / the)
➡ _____

5 (you / there / find / will / bear / a / cubs. / her / and)
➡ _____

6 (the / take / cubs / bear / and / up / mountain. / run / the)
➡ _____

7 (you / will / there / happiness." / find)
➡ _____

8 (younger / the / said, /. brother / go / "let's / find / and / together." / happiness)
➡ _____

9 ("no," / the / said / brother, / older / "how / we / know / can / true? / is / this)
➡ _____

10 (if / what / river / the / wide? / too / is)
➡ _____

11 (besides, / it / will / easy / be / take / to / cubs / the / from / away / mother? / their)
➡ _____

12 (of / instead / happiness, / finding / can / we / killed!" / be)
➡ _____

13 (younger / the / replied, / brother / "how / we / can / if / know / we / try?" / don't)
➡ _____

14 (separated, / they / and / both / they / their / went / way. / own)
➡ _____

15 (younger / the / went / brother / into / forest / the / swam / and / river. / the / across)
➡ _____

16 (was / bear. / there / the)
➡ _____

1 두 형제

2 두 형제는 여정을 떠났다.

3 그들은 숲 앞에서 바위를 발견했다.

4 거기에 쓰여 있었다. "숲에 들어가 강을 헤엄쳐 건너시오.

5 당신은 거기에서 곰과 새끼들을 발견할 것입니다.

6 곰 새끼들을 데리고 산 위로 뛰어 올라가시오.

7 거기에서 당신은 행복을 찾을 수 있을 것입니다."

8 동생이 말했다. "함께 가서 행복을 찾자."

9 "싫어." 형은 말했다. "이것이 사실인지 우리가 어떻게 알 수 있어?

10 강이 너무 넓으면 어쩌지?

11 게다가, 곰 새끼들을 엄마에게서 빼앗는 것이 쉬울까?

12 행복을 찾는 대신에, 우리는 죽을 수 있어!"

13 동생은 대답했다. "우리가 시도하지 않으면 어떻게 알 수 있어?"

14 그들은 헤어졌고, 둘 다 자신의 길을 갔다.

15 동생은 숲에 들어가서 강을 헤엄쳐 건넜다.

16 곰이 있었다.

17 (was / she / sleeping.)

➡ _____

18 (took / he / cubs / her / and / up / ran / mountain. / the)

➡ _____

19 (he / when / reached / top, / the / people / some / him / took / their / to / city / and / made / king. / him / their)

➡ _____

_____

20 (he / there / lived / a / as / king / years. / five / for)

➡ _____

21 (a / then / broke / war / out, / and / lost / he / throne. / his)

➡ _____

22 (was / he / the / on / again. / road)

➡ _____

23 (day, / one / two / the / brothers / again / met / and / about / talked / lives / their / for / years. / five / the / last)

➡ _____

_____

24 (older / the / said, / brother / right. / was / "I)

➡ _____

25 (have / I / quietly / lived / well. / and)

➡ _____

26 (were / you / once / king, / a / but / have / you / had / trouble." / of / lot / a)

➡ _____

27 (younger / the / answered, / brother / don't / "I / choice. / my / regret)

➡ _____

28 (may / I / nothing / have / now, / but / will / I / always / something / have / remember." / to)

➡ _____

17 그녀는 자고 있었다.

18 그는 새끼들을 데리고 산을 뛰어 올라갔다.

19 그가 정상에 도착했을 때, 어떤 사람들이 그를 자기들 도시로 데려가서 그들의 왕으로 만들었다.

20 그곳에서 그는 5년간 왕으로 살았다.

21 그런 다음 전쟁이 일어났고, 그는 왕좌를 잃었다.

22 그는 다시 길바닥에 나앉았다.

23 어느 날, 두 형제는 다시 만났고 지난 5년 동안의 그들의 삶에 대해 이야기했다.

24 형은 말했다. "내가 옳았어.

25 나는 조용히 잘 살았어.

26 너는 한때 왕이었지만 많은 어려움을 겪었지."

27 동생은 대답했다. "나는 내 선택을 후회하지 않아.

28 나는 지금 아무것도 없지만 언제까지나 기억할 어떤 것이 있어."

※ 다음 우리말을 영어로 쓰시오.

1 두 형제

➡ _____

2 두 형제는 여정을 떠났다.

➡ _____

3 그들은 숲 앞에서 바위를 발견했다.

➡ _____

4 거기에 쓰여 있었다. "숲에 들어가 강을 헤엄쳐 건너시오.

➡ _____

5 당신은 거기에서 곰과 새끼들을 발견할 것입니다.

➡ _____

6 곰 새끼들을 데리고 산 위로 뛰어 올라가시오.

➡ _____

7 거기에서 당신은 행복을 찾을 수 있을 것입니다."

➡ _____

8 동생이 말했다. "함께 가서 행복을 찾자."

➡ _____

9 "싫어." 형은 말했다. "이것이 사실인지 우리가 어떻게 알 수 있어?

➡ _____

10 강이 너무 넓으면 어쩌지?

➡ _____

11 게다가, 곰 새끼들을 엄마에게서 빼앗는 것이 쉬울까?

➡ _____

12 행복을 찾는 대신에, 우리는 죽을 수 있어!"

➡ _____

13 동생은 대답했다. "우리가 시도하지 않으면 어떻게 알 수 있어?"

➡ _____

14 그들은 헤어졌고, 둘 다 자신의 길을 갔다.

➡ _____

15 동생은 숲에 들어가서 강을 헤엄쳐 건넜다.

➡ _____

16 곰이 있었다.

➡ _____

17 그녀는 자고 있었다.

➡ _____

18 그는 새끼들을 데리고 산을 뛰어 올라갔다.

➡ _____

19 그가 정상에 도착했을 때, 어떤 사람들이 그를 자기들 도시로 데려가서 그들의 왕으로 만들었다.

➡ _____

20 그곳에서 그는 5년간 왕으로 살았다.

➡ _____

21 그런 다음 전쟁이 일어났고, 그는 왕좌를 잃었다.

➡ _____

22 그는 다시 길바닥에 나앉았다.

➡ _____

23 어느 날, 두 형제는 다시 만났고 지난 5년 동안의 그들의 삶에 대해 이야기했다.

➡ _____

24 형은 말했다. "내가 옳았어.

➡ _____

25 나는 조용히 잘 살았어.

➡ _____

26 너는 한때 왕이었지만 많은 어려움을 겪었지."

➡ _____

27 동생은 대답했다. "나는 내 선택을 후회하지 않아.

➡ _____

28 나는 지금 아무것도 없지만 언제까지나 기억할 어떤 것이 있어."

➡ _____

※ 다음 우리말과 일치하도록 빈칸에 알맞은 말을 쓰시오.

Before You Read

1. A. _____ is a box _____ _____ gold behind a tree _____ the river.

2. But _____ _____! Dangerous animals _____ in the river.

3. B. Mr. Allen _____ to _____ _____ _____ to the city for his vacation.

4. _____ the city streets were _____ and _____.

5. A car even _____ _____ him.

6. He had _____ _____ _____ there.

7. _____ _____ _____ _____ _____ in the city, he _____ his choice and _____ _____ to his hometown.

1. A. 강 건너 나무 뒤에 황금으로 가득 찬 상자가 있다.
2. 하지만 조심해! 위험한 동물들이 강에 있어.
3. B. Allen씨는 휴가를 보내기 위해 도 시로 여행을 가기로 결정했다.
4. 슬프게도 도시의 거리는 더럽고 시끄 러웠다.
5. 심지어 차가 그를 칠 뻔 했다.
6. 그는 거기서 많은 어려움을 겪었다.
7. 도시에서의 며칠 후, 그는 그의 선택을 후회하고 고향으로 다시 돌아갔다.

Writing Workshop

1. A _____ _____

2. _____: *Jonathan Livingston Seagull*: a story

3. _____: Richard Bach

4. This story _____ _____ a seagull _____ Jonathan Livingston.

5. He dreams of _____ _____ _____ _____.

6. _____ _____ his goal, he works hard and _____ _____.

7. I like this story _____ it has _____ _____ _____ about the power of my own beliefs.

8. The book says _____ I can do _____ _____ I want if I do not _____ _____.

1. 독서 감상문
2. 제목: Jonathan Livingston Seagull(갈 매기의 꿈): 이야기
3. 작가: Richard Bach
4. 이 이야기는 Jonathan Livingston이 라는 이름의 갈매기에 대한 것이다.
5. 그는 다른 갈매기들보다 더 잘 나는 것을 꿈꾼다.
6. 그의 목표에 도달하기 위해 그는 열심 히 노력하고 비행을 연습한다.
7. 이 이야기가 내 자신의 믿음의 힘에 대해 배우도록 도와주었기 때문에 나 는 이 이야기를 좋아한다.
8. 이 책은 내가 포기하지 않으면 내가 원하는 어떤 것이라도 할 수 있다고 말한다.

Into the World

1. Happiness is _____ what you _____, what you _____, and what you do are _____ _____. - Mahatma Gandhi

2. _____ one door of happiness _____, _____ opens. - Helen Keller

3. Happiness is not _____ _____. It _____ _____ your own actions. - Dalai Lama XIV

1. 행복은 생각, 말, 행동이 조화를 이룰 때 찾아온다.– Mahatma Gandhi
2. 행복의 한쪽 문이 닫히면 다른 쪽 문 이 열리게 된다.
   – Helen Keller
3. 행복은 준비된 것이 아니다. 행복은 당신 자신의 행동에서 비롯된다.
   – Dalai Lama XIV

※ 다음 우리말을 영어로 쓰시오.

Before You Read

1. A. 강 건너 나무 뒤에 황금으로 가득 찬 상자가 있다.
➡ _____

2. 하지만 조심해! 위험한 동물들이 강에 있어.
➡ _____

3. B. Allen씨는 휴가를 보내기 위해 도시로 여행을 가기로 결정했다.
➡ _____

4. 슬프게도 도시의 거리는 더럽고 시끄러웠다.
➡ _____

5. 심지어 차가 그를 칠 뻔 했다.
➡ _____

6. 그는 거기서 많은 어려움을 겪었다.
➡ _____

7. 도시에서의 며칠 후, 그는 그의 선택을 후회하고 고향으로 다시 돌아갔다.
➡ _____

Writing Workshop

1. 독서 감상문
➡ _____

2. 제목: Jonathan Livingston Seagull(갈매기의 꿈): 이야기
➡ _____

3. 작가: Richard Bach
➡ _____

4. 이 이야기는 Jonathan Livingston이라는 이름의 갈매기에 대한 것이다.
➡ _____

5. 그는 다른 갈매기들보다 더 잘 나는 것을 꿈꾼다.
➡ _____

6. 그의 목표에 도달하기 위해 그는 열심히 노력하고 비행을 연습한다.
➡ _____

7. 이 이야기가 내 자신의 믿음의 힘에 대해 배우도록 도와주었기 때문에 나는 이 이야기를 좋아한다.
➡ _____

8. 이 책은 내가 포기하지 않으면 내가 원하는 어떤 것이라도 할 수 있다고 말한다.
➡ _____

Into the World

1. 행복은 생각, 말, 행동이 조화를 이룰 때 찾아온다.– Mahatma Gandhi
➡ _____

2. 행복의 한쪽 문이 닫히면 다른 쪽 문이 열리게 된다.– Helen Keller
➡ _____

3. 행복은 준비된 것이 아니다. 행복은 당신 자신의 행동에서 비롯된다. – Dalai Lama XIV
➡ _____

※ 다음 영어를 우리말로 쓰시오.

01 competition _____

02 fit _____

03 hide _____

04 crack _____

05 rule _____

06 miss _____

07 home team _____

08 anxious _____

09 shorts _____

10 determine _____

11 pitch _____

12 sometime _____

13 dirt _____

14 either _____

15 stadium _____

16 base _____

17 batter _____

18 international _____

19 decide _____

20 forget _____

21 pet _____

22 visiting team _____

23 better _____

24 ticket _____

25 match _____

26 order _____

27 then _____

28 vacation _____

29 mean _____

30 thunder _____

31 past _____

32 rock climbing _____

33 support _____

34 can't wait to 동사원형 _____

35 between A and B _____

36 wait for _____

37 be a big fan of _____

38 hurry up _____

39 look forward to (동)명사 _____

40 twice a week _____

41 be excited about _____

42 come back to _____

43 in a hurry _____

※ 다음 우리말을 영어로 쓰시오.

01 감추다, 숨기다

02 (부정문에서) ~도

03 티켓

04 휴가

05 경기장

06 (야구의) 루, 베이스

07 규칙

08 방문하다

09 타자

10 경기, 성냥

11 순서

12 결정하다

13 투구

14 암벽 등반

15 의미하다

16 천둥

17 찢어지는 듯한 소리

18 불안한

19 대회

20 맞다

21 애완동물

22 원정 팀

23 반바지

24 과거

25 잊다

26 국제적인

27 놓치다, 그리워하다

28 언젠가

29 먼지

30 획득하다, 사다

31 더 좋은, 더 나은

32 (특정 스포츠 팀을) 응원하다

33 그 뒤에, 그런 다음

34 막 ~하려고 하다

35 A와 B 사이에

36 서둘러 ~하다

37 ~의 열렬한 팬이다

38 ~을 몹시 기대하다

39 일주일에 두 번

40 서둘러

41 ~에 신나다, ~에 들뜨다

42 ~을 기대하다

43 ~을 기다리다

※ 다음 영영풀이에 알맞은 단어를 <보기>에서 골라 쓴 후, 우리말 뜻을 쓰시오.

1 _____ : to put something out of sight: _____

2 _____ : very nervous or worried about something: _____

3 _____ : to be the right size and shape for someone or something: _____

4 _____ : a sports team playing on its own ground: _____

5 _____ : the time before the moment of speaking or writing: _____

6 _____ : a throw of the ball for the batter to hit it: _____

7 _____ : relating to or involving different countries: _____

8 _____ : each corner of the square that makes a baseball diamond: _____

9 _____ : to decide or establish something conclusively: _____

10 _____ : a sports team playing on the competing team's field or court: _____

11 _____ : an event or contest in which people try to win something by defeating others: _____

12 _____ : the arrangement or disposition of people or things in a list from first to last: _____

13 _____ : the loud noise in the sky heard after a lightning flash during a storm: _____

14 _____ : used in a negative sentence to indicate a similarity with a statement just made: _____

15 _____ : the sudden loud explosive sound of something when it falls or bumps into itself or something else: _____

16 _____ : an athletic or sports ground used for playing and watching sports with rows of seats: _____

보기

anxious	determine	home team	pitch
base	either	international	stadium
competition	fit	order	thunder
crack	hide	past	visiting team

※ 다음 우리말과 일치하도록 빈칸에 알맞은 말을 쓰시오.

Listen & Speak 1 A

M: _____ _____ do you like? Soccer _____ basketball?

G: I like soccer _____. I play soccer _____ _____ _____.

Listen & Speak 1 B

1. G: What _____ you _____?

   B: _____ _____ _____ a world map.

   G: You _____ two countries. _____ _____ would you like _____ _____ first? The U.S. _____ Mexico?

   B: I want _____ _____ the U.S. I'd _____ _____ see a basketball game there.

2. G: _____ _____ about _____ a pet. Do you _____ a pet?

   B: Yes, I do. I have a dog and a cat.

   G: _____ _____ you _____? _____ pet is _____ _____ me? A cat _____ a dog?

   B: _____ _____ _____ _____ _____ _____ my house someday and _____ _____ my pets? Then you _____ _____.

Listen & Speak 2 A

G: _____ you get the tickets?

B: Yes! I _____ _____ _____ _____ the game.

Listen & Speak 2 B

1. G: Do you _____ _____ my new mountain bike?

   B: Sure. _____ _____ you get it?

   G: Yesterday my father _____ _____ _____ _____. Can you _____ _____ _____ _____ this afternoon?

   B: Of _____. I _____ _____ _____ _____ it.

M: 너는 어떤 운동을 좋아하니? 축구 아니면 농구?

G: 축구를 더 좋아해요. 저는 일주일에 두 번 축구를 해요.

1. G: 뭐 하고 있어?
   B: 세계 지도를 보고 있어.
   G: 두 나라에 표시를 했네. 어떤 나라를 먼저 방문하고 싶어? 미국 아니면 멕시코?
   B: 미국을 방문하고 싶어. 거기서 농구 경기를 보고 싶어.

2. G: 나는 애완동물을 기르는 것에 대해 생각 중이야. 넌 애완동물을 기르니?
   B: 응, 길러. 개와 고양이가 있어.
   G: 어떻게 생각해? 어떤 애완동물이 나에게 더 나아? 고양이 아니면 개?
   B: 어느 날 우리 집에 와서 내 애완동물과 놀아 보는 게 어때? 그런 다음 너는 결정할 수 있을 거야.

W: 너 티켓 구했니?
B: 응! 나는 경기를 빨리 보고 싶어.

G: 내 새 산악 자전거를 보고 싶니?
B: 물론이지. 언제 생긴 거야?
G: 어제 아빠가 나에게 사 주셨어. 오늘 오후에 우리 집에 올래?
B: 당연하지. 나는 그것을 빨리 보고 싶어.

2. B: _____ _____ _____ we're going _____ _____ this weekend!

   G: Don't _____ . I _____ _____ .

   B: I'm _____ _____ going. _____ _____ _____ .

3. G: Did you _____ _____ Jisu?

   B: What _____ her? She _____ _____ Canada.

   G: She _____ _____ to Korea last month. She _____ _____ _____ you.

   B: Oh, I _____ _____ _____ _____ her.

Real-Life Zone A

B1: Jiho, why are you in _____ _____ _____?

B2: Hi, Alex! I _____ _____ be home _____ 6:00. The game _____ the Thunders _____ the Cobras _____ at 6:00.

B1: Oh, are you a baseball fan? _____ _____ do you _____? The Cobras _____ the Thunders?

B2: The Cobras.

B1: Me, too! I don't want _____ _____ the game _____ .

B2: _____ _____ ! We only have thirty minutes _____ .

B1: Okay. _____ we can watch a game together _____ .

B2: That's a great idea! How _____ _____ _____ the next Cobras _____ _____ _____?

B1: Okay. They have a game next Saturday. We _____ _____ _____ _____ _____ _____ the game!

B2: That _____ great. _____ _____ _____ !

Wrap Up

B: Jimin, _____ _____ _____ _____ _____? Soccer _____ table tennis?

G: I love table tennis. _____ _____ you, Yunho?

B: I like soccer. I'm a _____ _____ _____ James Hood. He's a great soccer player.

G: Oh, really? There's a _____ _____ this weekend _____ Korea and Turkey. _____ you _____ _____ it?

B: Of course. I _____ _____ a ticket. _____ _____ _____ _____ the game on Saturday. I _____ _____ .

G: That's _____ .

2. B: 이번 주말에 암벽 등반하러 가기로 한 거 잊지 마.
  G: 걱정 마. 잊지 않을게.
  B: 등반하러 가는 거 너무 신난다. 너무 기다려져.

3. G: 너 지수에 대해 들었니?
  B: 그녀에 대한 거 뭐? 그녀는 캐나다에 살고 있잖아.
  G: 지난달에 그녀는 한국에 돌아왔어. 너를 보고 싶어해.
  B: 오, 그녀를 빨리 보고 싶어.

B1: 지호야, 너 왜 그렇게 서두르니?
B2: 안녕, 알렉스! 나는 6시 전에 집에 있어야 해. 천둥 대 코브라의 경기가 6시에 시작돼.
B1: 오, 너 야구 팬이니? 어느 팀을 응원해? 코브라 아니면 천둥?
B2: 코브라.
B1: 나도야! 나도 이 경기를 놓치고 싶지 않아.
B2: 서둘러! 우리는 30분밖에 안 남았어.
B1: 알겠어. 언젠가 함께 경기를 볼 수도 있겠다.
B2: 좋은 생각이야! 다음 코브라 홈 경기를 함께 보러 가지 않을래?
B1: 좋아. 다음 주 토요일에 경기가 있어. 우리는 경기를 보면서 프라이드 치킨을 먹을 수 있어!
B1: 굉장해. 너무 기다려져!

B: 지민아, 너는 어떤 운동을 좋아하니? 축구 아니면 탁구?
G: 탁구를 좋아해. 윤호야, 너는 어때?
B: 축구가 좋아. 나는 제임스 후드의 열렬한 팬이야. 그는 위대한 축구 선수야.
G: 오, 정말? 이번 주말에 한국 대 터키의 축구 경기가 있어. 그것에 대해 들었니?
B: 물론이지. 나는 이미 표가 있어. 토요일에 경기를 보러 갈 거야. 너무 기다려져.
G: 환상적이다.

※ 다음 우리말에 맞도록 대화를 영어로 쓰시오.

Listen & Speak 1 A

M: _____

G: _____

Listen & Speak 1 B

1. G: _____

   B: _____

   G: _____

   _____

   B: _____

2. G: _____

   B: _____

   G: _____

   B: _____

Listen & Speak 2 A

G: _____

B: _____

Listen & Speak 2 B

1. G: _____

   B: _____

   G: _____

   B: _____

M: 너는 어떤 운동을 좋아하니? 축구 아니면 농구?

G: 축구를 더 좋아해요. 저는 일주일에 두 번 축구를 해요.

1. G: 뭐 하고 있어?

   B: 세계 지도를 보고 있어.

   G: 두 나라에 표시를 했네. 어떤 나라를 먼저 방문하고 싶어? 미국 아니면 멕시코?

   B: 미국을 방문하고 싶어. 거기서 농구 경기를 보고 싶어.

2. G: 나는 애완동물을 기르는 것에 대해 생각 중이야. 넌 애완동물을 기르니?

   B: 응, 길러. 개와 고양이가 있어.

   G: 어떻게 생각해? 어떤 애완동물이 나에게 더 나아? 고양이 아니면 개?

   B: 어느 날 우리 집에 와서 내 애완동물과 놀아 보는 게 어때? 그런 다음 너는 결정할 수 있을 거야.

W: 너 티켓 받았니?

B: 응! 나는 경기를 빨리 보고 싶어.

G: 내 새 산악 자전거를 보고 싶니?

B: 물론이지. 언제 생긴 거야?

G: 어제 아빠가 나에게 사 주셨어. 오늘 오후에 우리 집에 올래?

B: 당연하지. 나는 그것을 빨리 보고 싶어.

2. B: _____

   G: _____

   B: _____

3. G: _____

   B: _____

   G: _____

   B: _____

Real-Life Zone A

B1: _____

B2: _____

     _____

B1: _____

     _____

B2: _____

B1: _____

B2: _____

B1: _____

B2: _____

B1: _____

     _____

B2: _____

Wrap Up

B: _____

G: _____

B: _____

G: _____

    _____

B: _____

G: _____

2. B: 이번 주말에 암벽 등반하러 가기로 한 거 잊지 마.
   G: 걱정 마. 잊지 않을게.
   B: 등반하러 가는 거 너무 신난다. 너무 기다려져.

3. G: 너 지수에 대해 들었니?
   B: 그녀에 대한 거 뭐? 그녀는 캐나다에 살고 있잖아.
   G: 지난 달에 그녀는 한국에 돌아왔어. 너를 보고 싶어해.
   B: 오, 그녀를 빨리 보고 싶어.

B1: 지호야, 너 왜 그렇게 서두르니?
B2: 안녕, 알렉스! 나는 6시 전에 집에 있어야 해. 천둥 대 코브라의 경기가 6시에 시작돼.
B1: 오, 너 야구 팬이니? 어느 팀을 응원해? 코브라 아니면 천둥?
B2: 코브라.
B1: 나도야! 나도 이 경기를 놓치고 싶지 않아.
B2: 서둘러! 우리는 30분밖에 안 남았어.
B1: 알겠어. 언젠가 함께 경기를 볼 수도 있겠다.
B2: 좋은 생각이야! 다음 코브라 홈 경기를 함께 보러 가지 않을래?
B1: 좋아. 다음 주 토요일에 경기가 있어. 우리는 경기를 보면서 프라이드 치킨을 먹을 수 있어!
D1: 굉장해. 너무 기다려져!

B: 지민아, 너는 어떤 운동을 좋아하니? 축구 아니면 탁구?
G: 탁구를 좋아해. 윤호야, 너는 어때?
B: 축구가 좋아. 나는 제임스 후드의 열렬한 팬이야. 그는 위대한 축구 선수야.
G: 오, 정말? 이번 주말에 한국 대 터키의 축구 경기가 있어. 그것에 대해 들었니?
B: 물론이지. 나는 이미 표가 있어. 토요일에 경기를 보러 갈 거야. 너무 기다려져.
G: 환상적이다.

※ 다음 우리말과 일치하도록 빈칸에 알맞은 것을 골라 쓰시오.

1　A _____ at the _____ _____
A. Day　　　　　B. Stadium　　　C. Baseball

2　Today the Thunders _____ the Cobras _____ a _____.
A. game　　　　B. have　　　　C. and

3　Jihun's family _____ _____ the baseball _____.
A. at　　　　　B. is　　　　　C. stadium

4　Jihun: Jian, this is _____ _____ time to come to the baseball stadium, _____ _____ ?
A. isn't　　　　B. first　　　　C. it　　　　D. your

5　Jian: Yes, I'm so _____. I _____ _____ _____ the game to start.
A. wait　　　　B. for　　　　C. excited　　　D. can't

6　Dad: Look, the players _____ _____ _____ now!
A. out　　　　　B. coming　　　C. are

7　Jian: _____ _____ is the Thunders?
A. team　　　　B. which

8　Jihun: _____ there, _____ _____ base.
A. third　　　　B. behind　　　C. over

9　They are _____ dark gray uniforms _____ they are the _____ team.
A. wearing　　　B. visiting　　　C. because

10　Jian: Does the visiting team _____ _____ a _____ color?
A. wear　　　　B. always　　　C. dark

11　Jihun: Yes, _____ 's the _____.
A. rule　　　　B. that

12　_____ teams have _____ uniforms and _____ teams have _____ uniforms.
A. dark　　　　B. bright　　　C. visiting　　　D. home

13　Jian: _____ is _____ ?
A. that　　　　B. why

14　Mom: _____ is an _____ story _____ that.
A. about　　　　B. interesting　　C. there

15　In the _____, visiting teams could not _____ their uniforms after _____ game.
A. every　　　　B. past　　　　C. wash

16　So they started _____ dark colors to _____ the _____.
A. hide　　　　B. dirt　　　　C. wearing

17　Jian: Hahaha! That _____ a _____ _____ !
A. idea　　　　B. was　　　　C. good

1　야구 경기장에서의 하루

2　오늘 천둥 대 코브라 게임이 있다.

3　지훈이네 가족은 야구 경기장에 있다.

4　지훈: 지안아, 네가 야구 경기장에 온 건 이번이 처음이야, 그렇지 않니?

5　지안: 응, 나 아주 흥분돼. 나는 경기가 빨리 시작했으면 좋겠어.

6　아빠: 봐, 선수들이 지금 나오고 있어!

7　지안: 어떤 팀이 천둥이야?

8　지훈: 저기, 3루 뒤.

9　그들은 원정 팀이기 때문에 어두운 회색 유니폼을 입고 있어.

10　지안: 원정 팀은 항상 어두운 색을 입어?

11　지훈: 응, 그게 규칙이야.

12　홈팀은 밝은 유니폼을 입고 원정팀은 어두운 유니폼을 입어.

13　지안: 왜?

14　엄마: 그것에 대한 흥미로운 이야기가 있단다.

15　과거에는 원정 팀이 매 경기 후 유니폼을 세탁할 수가 없었어.

16　그래서 그들은 때를 숨기기 위해 어두운 색을 입기 시작했지.

17　지안: 하하하! 좋은 생각이었네요!

18 The players are _____ _____.
    A. up   B. warming

19 Jian: Who's _____ _____ player?
    A. favorite   B. your

20 Jihun: _____ _____.
    A. 77   B. number

21 Jian: _____ _____ the number _____?
    A. what   B. mean   C. does

22 Jihun: Hmm…. Players _____ a number _____ _____.
    A. they   B. choose   C. like

23 Dad: You _____ _____?
    A. what   B. know

24 In the past, the numbers were _____ _____ the players' _____ _____.
    A. order   B. by   C. determined   D. batting

25 Jihun: That means _____ were _____ players _____ number 77!
    A. with   B. there   C. no

26 Now, Jihun's favorite player _____ _____ bat.
    A. about   B. is   C. to

27 Jihun _____ _____.
    A. anxious   B. looks

28 Jian: Your _____ player is _____ _____.
    A. favorite   B. bat   C. at

29 Jihun: Yes. He _____ _____ 21 home _____ _____ this year.
    A. already   B. hit   C. has   D. runs

30 If he _____ one _____ today, he will _____ the home run leader this _____.
    A. more   B. season   C. hits   D. be

31 The _____ _____ _____ balls.
    A. misses   B. several   C. batter

32 Now he _____ a _____ _____.
    A. count   B. full   C. has

33 He is _____ _____ the next _____.
    A. pitch   B. for   C. waiting

34 Jihun: HOME _____! _____ RUN!
    A. RUN   B. HOME

35 _____! The ball _____ _____.
    A. fast   B. flies   C. crack

36 It _____ _____, going, going, _____!
    A. gone   B. going   C. is

18 선수들이 몸을 풀고 있다.

19 지안: 가장 좋아하는 선수가 누구야?

20 지훈: 77번.

21 지안: 그 숫자는 무엇을 의미해?

22 지훈: 음... 선수들이 원하는 번호를 선택해.

23 아빠: 그거 알아?

24 과거에는 번호가 선수들의 타순에 의해 결정되었단다.

25 지훈: 77번 선수가 없었다는 뜻이네요!

26 이제 지훈이의 가장 좋아하는 선수가 막 공을 치려고 한다.

27 지훈이는 불안해 보인다.

28 지안: 오빠가 가장 좋아하는 선수가 타석에 서네.

29 지훈: 응. 그는 올해 이미 21개의 홈런을 쳤어.

30 그가 오늘 하나를 더 치면, 그는 이번 시즌 홈런 리더가 될 거야.

31 타자는 여러 개의 공을 놓친다.

32 이제 그는 풀카운트가 되었다.

33 그는 다음 투구를 기다리고 있다.

34 지훈: 홈런! 홈런!

35 땅! 공은 빠르게 날아간다.

36 그것은 가고, 가고, 가고, 사라져 버렸다!

Step2

※ 다음 우리말과 일치하도록 빈칸에 알맞은 말을 쓰시오.

1 _____ _____ at the _____ _____

2 Today the Thunders and the Cobras _____ _____ _____.

3 Jihun's family _____ _____ the _____ _____.

4 Jihun: Jian, this is _____ _____ _____ to come to the baseball stadium, _____ _____?

5 Jian: Yes, I'm so _____. I _____ _____ _____ the game _____ _____.

6 Dad: Look, the players _____ _____ _____ now!

7 Jian: _____ _____ is the Thunders?

8 Jihun: _____ _____, _____ _____ _____ _____.

9 They _____ _____ dark gray uniforms _____ they are the _____ _____.

10 Jian: Does the _____ _____ always _____ _____ _____ _____?

11 Jihun: Yes, that's the _____.

12 Home teams _____ _____ _____ and visiting teams have _____ _____.

13 Jian: _____ is that?

14 Mom: _____ is _____ _____ _____ about that.

15 _____ _____ _____, visiting teams could not _____ _____ _____ _____ _____ _____ _____.

16 So they _____ _____ dark colors _____ _____.

17 Jian: Hahaha! That was _____ _____ _____!

1 야구 경기장에서의 하루

2 오늘 천둥 대 코브라 게임이 있다.

3 지훈이네 가족은 야구 경기장에 있다.

4 지훈: 지안아, 네가 야구 경기장에 온 건 이번이 처음이야, 그렇지 않니?

5 지안: 응, 나 아주 흥분돼. 나는 경기가 빨리 시작했으면 좋겠어.

6 아빠: 봐, 선수들이 지금 나오고 있어!

7 지안: 어떤 팀이 천둥이야?

8 지훈: 저기, 3루 뒤.

9 그들은 원정 팀이기 때문에 어두운 회색 유니폼을 입고 있어.

10 지안: 원정 팀은 항상 어두운 색을 입어?

11 지훈: 응, 그게 규칙이야.

12 홈팀은 밝은 유니폼을 입고 원정팀은 어두운 유니폼을 입어.

13 지안: 왜?

14 엄마: 그것에 대한 흥미로운 이야기가 있단다.

15 과거에는 원정 팀이 매 경기 후 유니폼을 세탁할 수가 없었어.

16 그래서 그들은 때를 숨기기 위해 어두운 색을 입기 시작했지.

17 지안: 하하하! 좋은 생각이었네요!

18 The players _____ _____ _____.

19 Jian: Who's _____ _____ _____?

20 Jihun: _____ 77.

21 Jian: _____ _____ the _____ _____?

22 Jihun: Hmm…. Players _____ a number _____ _____.

23 Dad: _____ _____ _____?

24 In the past, the numbers _____ _____ _____ _____ _____ _____ _____.

25 Jihun: That means _____ _____ _____ players _____ number 77!

26 Now, Jihun's favorite player _____ _____ _____ bat.

27 Jihun _____ _____.

28 Jian: _____ _____ player is _____ _____.

29 Jihun: Yes. He _____ _____ 21 home runs already this year.

30 If he _____ _____ _____ today, he will be the home run leader _____ _____.

31 The batter _____ _____ _____.

32 Now he _____ _____ _____ _____.

33 He is _____ _____ the _____ _____.

34 Jihun: _____ _____! HOME RUN!

35 _____! The ball _____ _____.

36 It _____ _____, going, going, _____!

---

18 선수들이 몸을 풀고 있다.

19 지안: 가장 좋아하는 선수가 누구야?

20 지훈: 77번.

21 지안: 그 숫자는 무엇을 의미해?

22 지훈: 음... 선수들이 원하는 번호를 선택해.

23 아빠: 그거 알아?

24 과거에는 번호가 선수들의 타순에 의해 결정되었단다.

25 지훈: 77번 선수가 없었다는 뜻이네요!

26 이제 지훈이의 가장 좋아하는 선수가 막 공을 치려고 한다.

27 지훈이는 불안해 보인다.

28 지안: 오빠가 가장 좋아하는 선수가 타석에 서네.

29 지훈: 응. 그는 올해 이미 21개의 홈런을 쳤어.

30 그가 오늘 하나를 더 치면, 그는 이번 시즌 홈런 리더가 될 거야.

31 타자는 여러 개의 공을 놓친다.

32 이제 그는 풀카운트가 되었다.

33 그는 다음 투구를 기다리고 있다.

34 지훈: 홈런! 홈런!

35 땅! 공은 빠르게 날아간다.

36 그것은 가고, 가고, 가고, 사라져 버렸다!

※ 다음 문장을 우리말로 쓰시오.

1 A Day at the Baseball Stadium

➡ _____

2 Today the Thunders and the Cobras have a game.

➡ _____

3 Jihun's family is at the baseball stadium.

➡ _____

4 Jihun: Jian, this is your first time to come to the baseball stadium, isn't it?

➡ _____

5 Jian: Yes, I'm so excited. I can't wait for the game to start.

➡ _____

6 Dad: Look, the players are coming out now!

➡ _____

7 Jian: Which team is the Thunders?

➡ _____

8 Jihun: Over there, behind third base.

➡ _____

9 They are wearing dark gray uniforms because they are the visiting team.

➡ _____

10 Jian: Does the visiting team always wear a dark color?

➡ _____

11 Jihun: Yes, that's the rule.

➡ _____

12 Home teams have bright uniforms and visiting teams have dark uniforms.

➡ _____

13 Jian: Why is that?

➡ _____

14 Mom: There is an interesting story about that.

➡ _____

15 In the past, visiting teams could not wash their uniforms after every game.

➡ _____

16 So they started wearing dark colors to hide the dirt.

➡ _____

17 Jian: Hahaha! That was a good idea!

➡ _____

18 The players are warming up.
➡ _____

19 Jian: Who's your favorite player?
➡ _____

20 Jihun: Number 77.
➡ _____

21 Jian: What does the number mean?
➡ _____

22 Jihun: Hmm…. Players choose a number they like.
➡ _____

23 Dad: You know what?
➡ _____

24 In the past, the numbers were determined by the players' batting order.
➡ _____

25 Jihun: That means there were no players with number 77!
➡ _____

26 Now, Jihun's favorite player is about to bat.
➡ _____

27 Jihun looks anxious.
➡ _____

28 Jian: Your favorite player is at bat.
➡ _____

29 Jihun: Yes. He has hit 21 home runs already this year.
➡ _____

30 If he hits one more today, he will be the home run leader this season.
➡ _____

31 The batter misses several balls.
➡ _____

32 Now he has a full count.
➡ _____

33 He is waiting for the next pitch.
➡ _____

34 Jihun: HOME RUN! HOME RUN!
➡ _____

35 Crack! The ball flies fast.
➡ _____

36 It is going, going, going, gone!
➡ _____

※ 다음 괄호 안의 단어들을 우리말에 맞도록 바르게 배열하시오.

1 (Day / A / at / Baseball / the / Stadium)
➡ _____

2 (the / today / Thunders / and / Cobras / the / game. / a / have)
➡ _____

3 (family / Jihun's / at / is / baseball / stadium. / the)
➡ _____

4 (Jihun: / this / Jian, / is / first / your / to / time / come / to / baseball / the / it? / isn't / stadium,)
➡ _____

5 (Jian: / I'm / yes, / excited. / so // can't / I / for / wait / the / to / start. / game)
➡ _____

6 (Dad: / look, / players / the / coming / are / now! / out)
➡ _____

7 (Jian: / team / which / Thunders? / the / is)
➡ _____

8 (Jihun: / there, / over / base. / third / behind)
➡ _____

9 (are / they / dark / wearing / uniforms / gray / they / because / team. / visiting / the / are)
➡ _____

10 (Jian: / the / does / team / visiting / wear / always / color? / dark / a)
➡ _____

11 (Jihun: / that's / yes, / rule. / the)
➡ _____

12 (teams / home / bright / have / and / uniforms / teams / visiting / uniforms. / dark / have)
➡ _____

13 (Jian: / that? / is / why)
➡ _____

14 (Mom: / is / there / interesting / an / that. / about / story)
➡ _____

15 (the / in / past, / teams / visiting / not / could / wash / uniforms / their / game. / every / after)
➡ _____

16 (they / so / wearing / started / colors / dark / hide / dirt. / the / to)
➡ _____

17 (Jian: / hahaha! // was / that / idea! / good / a)
➡ _____

---

1 야구 경기장에서의 하루

2 오늘 천둥 대 코브라 게임이 있다.

3 지훈이네 가족은 야구 경기장에 있다.

4 지훈: 지안아, 네가 야구 경기장에 온 건 이번이 처음이야, 그렇지 않니?

5 지안: 응, 나 아주 흥분돼. 나는 경기가 빨리 시작했으면 좋겠어.

6 아빠: 봐, 선수들이 지금 나오고 있어!

7 지안: 어떤 팀이 천둥이야?

8 지훈: 저기, 3루 뒤.

9 그들은 원정 팀이기 때문에 어두운 회색 유니폼을 입고 있어.

10 지안: 원정 팀은 항상 어두운 색을 입어?

11 지훈: 응, 그게 규칙이야.

12 홈팀은 밝은 유니폼을 입고 원정팀은 어두운 유니폼을 입어.

13 지안: 왜?

14 엄마: 그것에 대한 흥미로운 이야기가 있단다.

15 과거에는 원정 팀이 매 경기 후 유니폼을 세탁할 수가 없었어.

16 그래서 그들은 때를 숨기기 위해 어두운 색을 입기 시작했지.

17 지안: 하하하! 좋은 생각이었네요!

18 (players / the / up. / warming / are)

➡ _____

19 (Jian: / your / who's / player? / favorite)

➡ _____

20 (Jihun: / 77. / number)

➡ _____

21 (Jian: / does / what / mean? / number / the)

➡ _____

22 (Jihun: / hmm.... // choose / players / number / a / like. / they)

➡ _____

23 (Dad: / what? / know / you)

➡ _____

24 (the / in / past, / numbers / the / determined / were / the / player's / by / order. / batting)

➡ _____

25 (Jihun: / means / that / were / there / players / no / 77! / number / with)

➡ _____

26 (now, / favorite / Jihun's / is / player / bat. / to / about)

➡ _____

27 (looks / Jihun / anxious.)

➡ _____

28 (Jian: / favorite / your / is / player / bat. / at)

➡ _____

29 (Jihun: / yes. // has / he / 21 / hit / home / already / runs / year. / this)

➡ _____

30 (he / if / hits / more / one / today, / will / he / the / be / run / home / season. / this / leader)

➡ _____

31 (batter / the / several / balls. / misses)

➡ _____

32 (he / now / a / has / count. / full)

➡ _____

33 (is / he / for / waiting / pitch. / next / the)

➡ _____

34 (Jihun: / RUN! / HOME / RUN! / HOME)

➡ _____

35 (crack! // ball / the / fast. / flies)

➡ _____

36 (is / it / going, / gone! / going, / going,)

➡ _____

18 선수들이 몸을 풀고 있다.

19 지안: 가장 좋아하는 선수가 누구야?

20 지훈: 77번.

21 지안: 그 숫자는 무엇을 의미해?

22 지훈: 음... 선수들이 원하는 번호를 선택해.

23 아빠: 그거 알아?

24 과거에는 번호가 선수들의 타순에 의해 결정되었단다.

25 지훈: 77번 선수가 없었다는 뜻이네요!

26 이제 지훈이의 가장 좋아하는 선수가 막 공을 치려고 한다.

27 지훈이는 불안해 보인다.

28 지안: 오빠가 가장 좋아하는 선수가 타석에 서네.

29 지훈: 응. 그는 올해 이미 21개의 홈런을 쳤어.

30 그가 오늘 하나를 더 치면, 그는 이번 시즌 홈런 리더가 될 거야.

31 타자는 여러 개의 공을 놓친다.

32 이제 그는 풀카운트가 되었다.

33 그는 다음 투구를 기다리고 있다.

34 지훈: 홈런! 홈런!

35 땅! 공은 빠르게 날아간다.

36 그것은 가고, 가고, 가고, 사라져 버렸다!

※ **다음 우리말을 영어로 쓰시오.**

1 야구 경기장에서의 하루

➡ _____

2 오늘 천둥 대 코브라 게임이 있다.

➡ _____

3 지훈이네 가족은 야구 경기장에 있다.

➡ _____

4 지훈: 지안아, 네가 야구 경기장에 온 건 이번이 처음이야, 그렇지 않니?

➡ _____

5 지안: 응, 나 아주 흥분돼. 나는 경기가 빨리 시작했으면 좋겠어.

➡ _____

6 아빠: 봐, 선수들이 지금 나오고 있어!

➡ _____

7 지안: 어떤 팀이 천둥이야?

➡ _____

8 지훈: 저기, 3루 뒤.

➡ _____

9 그들은 원정 팀이기 때문에 어두운 회색 유니폼을 입고 있어.

➡ _____

10 지안: 원정 팀은 항상 어두운 색을 입어?

➡ _____

11 지훈: 응, 그게 규칙이야.

➡ _____

12 홈팀은 밝은 유니폼을 입고 원정팀은 어두운 유니폼을 입어.

➡ _____

13 지안: 왜?

➡ _____

14 엄마: 그것에 대한 흥미로운 이야기가 있단다.

➡ _____

15 과거에는 원정 팀이 매 경기 후 유니폼을 세탁할 수가 없었어.

➡ _____

16 그래서 그들은 때를 숨기기 위해 어두운 색을 입기 시작했지.

➡ _____

17 지안: 하하하! 좋은 생각이었네요!

➡ _____

18 선수들이 몸을 풀고 있다.

➡ _____

19 지안: 가장 좋아하는 선수가 누구야?

➡ _____

20 지훈: 77번.

➡ _____

21 지안: 그 숫자는 무엇을 의미해?

➡ _____

22 지훈: 음... 선수들이 원하는 번호를 선택해.

➡ _____

23 아빠: 그거 알아?

➡ _____

24 과거에는 번호가 선수들의 타순에 의해 결정되었단다.

➡ _____

25 지훈: 77번 선수가 없었다는 뜻이네요!

➡ _____

26 이제 지훈이의 가장 좋아하는 선수가 막 공을 치려고 한다.

➡ _____

27 지훈이는 불안해 보인다.

➡ _____

28 지안: 오빠가 가장 좋아하는 선수가 타석에 서네.

➡ _____

29 지훈: 응. 그는 올해 이미 21개의 홈런을 쳤어.

➡ _____

30 그가 오늘 하나를 더 치면, 그는 이번 시즌 홈런 리더가 될 거야.

➡ _____

31 타자는 여러 개의 공을 놓친다.

➡ _____

32 이제 그는 풀카운트가 되었다.

➡ _____

33 그는 다음 투구를 기다리고 있다.

➡ _____

34 지훈: 홈런! 홈런!

➡ _____

35 땅! 공은 빠르게 날아간다.

➡ _____

36 그것은 가고, 가고, 가고, 사라져 버렸다!

➡ _____

※ 다음 우리말과 일치하도록 빈칸에 알맞은 말을 쓰시오.

Real-Life Zone B

1. A: _____ _____ do you _____? Basketball _____ soccer?

2. B: I like basketball. I'm _____ _____ play it _____ my friends _____ _____ . I _____ _____ .

1. A: 너는 어떤 운동을 좋아하니? 농구 아니면 축구?
2. B: 농구를 좋아해. 이번 주말에 친구들이랑 농구를 할 거야. 너무 기다려져.

Writing Workshop

1. Abebe Bikila _____ _____

2. _____: _____ 7, 1932

3. _____: Ethiopia

4. Speciality: He _____ _____ _____ a marathon winner at the Rome and Tokyo _____ _____ _____ .

5. When he was _____ _____ _____ _____ the marathon in Rome, he _____ _____ that his shoes _____ _____ _____ well, so he _____ _____ _____ the race _____ _____ .

6. He _____ _____ _____ the race, but he finished the race _____ _____ _____ .

7. He was _____ _____ the greatest runners in the world, _____ _____ ?

1. Abebe Bikila   마라톤 선수
2. 생일: 1932년 8월 7일
3. 국적: 에티오피아
4. 특별 사항: 그는 로마 국제 스포츠 대회와 도쿄 국제 스포츠 대회의 마라톤 우승자로 알려졌다.
5. 그가 로마에서 달리기를 준비하던 도중에 자신의 신발이 잘 맞지 않는다는 것을 알고 그는 신발을 신지 않고 달리기로 결심했다.
6. 그는 경주 도중에 통증을 느꼈지만 우승자로 경주를 끝마쳤다.
7. 그는 세계에서 가장 위대한 달리기 선수들 중의 한 명이었어, 그렇지 않니?

Wrap Up

1. Sarang _____ _____ _____ _____ _____

2. Sarang Middle School Sports Day _____ _____ _____ on the school playing field _____ _____ , _____ 15.

3. There _____ _____ _____ games _____ _____ baseball and soccer.

4. There _____ _____ be _____ .

5. It _____ _____ fun, _____ _____ ?

1. 사랑 중학교 운동회
2. 사랑 중학교 운동회가 학교 운동장에서 6월 15일 수요일에 열립니다.
3. 야구와 축구 같은 여러 가지 게임이 있을 것입니다.
4. 또한 탁구도 있을 것입니다.
5. 재미있게 들리지요, 그렇지 않나요?

※ 다음 우리말을 영어로 쓰시오.

Real-Life Zone B

1. 너는 어떤 운동을 좋아하니? 농구 아니면 축구?

　➡ _____

2. B: 농구를 좋아해. 이번 주말에 친구들이랑 농구를 할 거야. 너무 기다려져.

　➡ _____

Writing Workshop

1. Abebe Bikila　마라톤 선수

　➡ _____

2. 생일: 1932년 8월 7일

　➡ _____

3. 국적: 에티오피아

　➡ _____

4. 특별 사항: 그는 로마 국제 스포츠 대회와 도쿄 국제 스포츠 대회의 마라톤 우승자로 알려졌다.

　➡ _____

　　_____

5. 그가 로마에서 달리기를 준비하던 도중에 자신의 신발이 잘 맞지 않는다는 것을 알고 그는 신발을 신지 않고 달리기로 결심했다.

　➡ _____

　　_____

6. 그는 경주 도중에 통증을 느꼈지만 우승자로 경주를 끝마쳤다.

　➡ _____

7. 그는 세계에서 가장 위대한 달리기 선수들 중의 한 명이었어, 그렇지 않았니?

　➡ _____

Wrap Up

1. 사랑 중학교 운동회

　➡ _____

2. 사랑 중학교 운동회가 학교 운동장에서 6월 15일 수요일에 열립니다.

　➡ _____

3. 야구와 축구 같은 여러 가지 게임이 있을 것입니다.

　➡ _____

4. 또한 탁구도 있을 것입니다.

　➡ _____

5. 재미있게 들리지요, 그렇지 않나요?

　➡ _____

영어 기출 문제집

적중 100 plus
1학기·전과정

1학기

정답 및 해설

시사 | 송미정

중 2

영어 기출 문제집

적중 100

1학기

정답 및 해설

시사 | 송미정

중 2

My Bucket List

시험대비 실력평가   p.08

01 ①	02 ②	03 ④	04 (1) for
(2) in	05 ①	06 ④	07 (1) a

favor   (2) shared, with them

01 ① 입양하다 ② 맞추다, 조정하다 ③ 동반하다 ④ 인정하다 ⑤ 획득하다 / 그들은 개들을 애완동물 가게에서 사는 대신에 동물 보호소에서 입양하는 것을 추천받았다.

02 ② 중국의, 나머지 보기는 중국어의 뜻을 가진다. ① Mike는 중국어를 배우기를 원한다. ② 이 중국 음식은 치킨 수프와 잘 어울린다. ③ 중국어를 가르치는 학교의 숫자는 늘고 있다. ④ 그의 이름은 중국어로 '오렌지'의 의미이다. ⑤ 나는 밤낮으로 중국어를 공부한다.

03 ① introduce ② band ③ bucket list ④ adopted ⑤ overcome

04 (1) for a while: 잠깐 (2) stand in line: 줄을 서서 기다리다

05 ① right: 바로

06 aim: 목적, 목표 ① effort: 노력 ② turn: 차례 ③ cause: 원인 ④ goal: 목표 ⑤ result: 결과

07 (1) do a favor: 호의를 베풀다 (2) share A with B: A를 B와 나누다[공유하다]

서술형 시험대비   p.09

01 (1) make (2) taking (3) gets (4) ask

02 hope your, gets

03 (1) I fully accept what he says.

     (2) The house is right in front of you.

     (3) It was used only on special situations.

     (4) Poor light produces weak plants.

04 (f)reely

05 (c)hallenging

06 to

07 (1) exercise (2) experience

01 (1) make an effort: 노력하다 (2) take care of: ~을 돌보다 (3) get interested in: ~에 관심을 갖다 (4) ask for help: 도움을 청하다

02 hope: 희망하다, 바라다 get better: (병·상황 등이) 나아지다

03 (1) fully: 완전히 (2) right: 바로, in front of: ~의 앞에 (3) special: 특별한 (4) weak: 약한

04 freely: 자유롭게 / 어떤 것을 멈추거나 제한하는 사람 없이

05 challenging: 도전적인 / 흥미롭거나 재미있는 방식으로 어려운

06 be willing to 동사원형: 기꺼이 ~하다, be ready to 동사원형: ~할 준비가 되다

07 (1) exercise: 운동하다; 운동 (2) experience: 경험하다;경험

교과서 Conversation

핵심 Check   p.10~11

1 hope, I can read / I hope I get good grades this

2 I hope I can learn how to swim. / I hope that you finish it soon.

3 I'm planning to play games with friends.

4 Where are they planning to meet?

교과서 대화문 익히기

Check(√) True or False   p.12

(1) T   (2) T   (3) F   (4) F

교과서 확인학습   p.14~15

Listen & Speak 1 A

hope, get / worry

Listen & Speak 1 B

1 it's / What, want for / I hope I get

2 What / I'm making / the first / hope, make

3 How / It was, wrote, for / tell, yours / hope I, someday

Listen & Speak 1 C

1 hope I, this / sounds

2 sounds

3 hope I can learn, to

Everyday English 2. A Function Practice 2

What are you planning to / planning to get

Everyday English 2 – B Listening Activity

1 planning to do tomorrow / I'm planning, book fair with, like to / What time / At, in front of

2 are you planning / not / about going, with

3 Can, a favor / to buy, tomorrow, help, choose one

1 do at / to sell

2 are you planning to / to do a magic

3 What are you planning / to dance in a group

시험대비 기본평가   p.16

01 ④   02 ①   03 ③, ⑤   04 ②

01 be planning to 동사원형: ~할 계획이다

02 남자아이의 질문 다음에 새 컴퓨터를 받기를 바란다고 여자아이가 대답했으므로, 생일 선물로 무엇을 원하는지 질문하는 것이 어울린다.

03 ③ hope는 to부정사만을 목적어로 받을 수 있다. ⑤ '나는 네가 새로운 컴퓨터를 얻기를 원한다'의 의미로 밑줄 친 문장과 다른 뜻이다.

04 학교 축제에서 무엇을 할 계획인지 묻고 대답하는 표현이다. be planning to 동사원형: ~할 계획이다. festival: 축제

시험대비 실력평가   p.17~18

01 ③   02 ③   03 (1) making → to make / (that) I make   (2) lot of → a lot of / lots of / many

04 (B) → (C) → (D) → (A)   05 ①

06 ⑤ your → yours

07 I hope (that) I become a rock star someday.

08 ②   09 I'm planning to study one new Chinese word every day.

10 (B) what (C) studying   11 ④

12 두 번째: do 다섯 번째: for   13 ②, ③

01 이번 주 계획을 묻고 있는 말에, (B) 할머니 댁을 방문할 계획이라고 대답하며, 할머니가 편찮으시다는 말을 덧붙였다. (C) 이에 유감을 표하고, 그녀가 나아지길 바란다는 말에 (A) 고맙다고 대답하며 상대방의 계획을 묻는다.

02 (A) What are you doing?: '너 뭐 하는 중이니?'로 현재 하고 있는 것을 물어보는 표현으로 대답도 현재진행형(be동사의 현재형+동사ing)으로 하는 것이 어울린다. (B) sound는 2형식 동사로 보어(형용사)를 받을 수 있다.

03 (1) hope는 목적어로 that절이나 to부정사를 받을 수 있다. (2) a lot of+명사: 많은(= lots of+명사), friend는 셀 수 있는 명사로 many(많은)의 수식을 받는다.

04 (B) 내일의 계획에 대해 묻는 질문에 (C) 도서 박람회 Jimmy랑 같이 간다고 대답하며 같이 가자고 제안하자, (D) 상대방은 동의하고 언제 만날지 질문한다. (A) 이에 시간과 장소를 대답한다.

05 대답의 It이 가리키는 것이 질문에 나와야 한다. 과거시제로 대답했으므로 과거의 일을 질문하는 것이 어울린다. ① 영어 수업은 어땠니? ② 너는 무엇이 되고 싶니? ③ 너의 꿈을 적을 거니? ④ 너의 목록을 만들었니? ⑤ 영어 수업을 듣는 것은 어때?

06 your: 너의, yours: 너의 것 / 여기서 yours는 너의 꿈을 가리킨다.

07 hope: 희망하다, 바라다 become: ~이 되다 someday: 언젠가

08 주어진 말은 언제 중국어 공부를 시작했는지 묻고 있다. 이에 '겨우 지난달에.'라는 대답이 어울리므로 ②에 들어가는 것이 적절하다.

09 be planning to 동사원형: ~할 계획이다, Chinese: 중국의; 중국어, every day: 매일

10 (B) 그들이 말하고 있는 것의 뜻으로, what이 어울린다. (C) keep+동사ing: 계속 ~하다

11 과목마다 좋은 성적을 얻는 것으로 대답하였으므로, 금년 계획에 대해 묻는 ④번이 어울린다. ① 좋은 성적을 얻었니? ② 계획을 세울 거니? ③ 지난달의 계획이 무엇이었니? ④ 올해 계획이 무엇이니? ⑤ 너는 어디를 갈 계획이니?

12 What do you want for your birthday? / what: 무엇 want: 원하다

13 ① Hana의 생일은 오늘이다. ④ Hana의 생일이다. ⑤ 여자아이는 생일 선물로 새 컴퓨터를 받기를 바란다. ② 남자아이가 받기를 바라는 것은 무엇이니? ③ Hana의 생일 선물로 남자아이가 사려고 계획한 것은 무엇이니?

서술형 시험대비   p.19

01 (1) I'm planning to dance in a group

     (2) I hope I can travel to Europe this summer.

02 take pictures with your favorite singer

03 go → to go, concert → concerts

04 ② words → word

05 I didn't know you were interested in Chinese.

06 is planning, word, to study, last, now, herself in

01 (1) be planning to 동사원형: ~할 계획이다 dance: 춤추다 in a group: 그룹으로, 단체로

     (2) hope: 희망하다, 바라다 travel to: ~으로 여행가다 this summer: 이번 여름에

02 (A)가 가리키고 있는 것은 앞 문장의 'take pictures with my favorite singer'이다. my가 your로 바뀌는 것에 유의해야 한다.

03 be planning to 동사원형: ~할 계획이다, one of+복수명사: ~ 중의 하나

04 one(하나)의 수식을 받고 있으므로 word는 단수형을 쓰는 것이 적절하다

05 be interested in: ~에 관심을 갖다 Chinese: 중국어

06 be interested in: ~에 관심을 갖다, start to 동사원형: ~하는 것을 시작하다 last month: 지난달 introduce: 소개하다 in Chinese: 중국어로

핵심 Check
p.20~21

1 (1) the tallest (2) longest (3) the coolest

2 (1) to say (2) to do (3) to write

3 He studies science very hard to be a scientist.

시험대비 기본평가
p.22

01 (1) highest → the highest (2) most small → smallest
   (3) being → to be (4) to not → not to

02 (1) the thinnest/cheapest (2) the most boring
   (3) the cheapest/thinnest (4) to meet (5) in order
   to be

03 (1) Alice is the prettiest of the three sisters.
   (2) When is the busiest day of the year?
   (3) He studies Korean hard so as to watch Korean
   TV dramas.
   (4) I got up early in order not to miss the first train.

01 (1) 형용사의 최상급 앞에는 the를 붙인다. (2) small의 최상급
   은 smallest이다. (3) to be로 '목적'을 나타내는 것이 적절하
   다. (4) to부정사의 부정은 not을 to 앞에 붙인다.

시험대비 실력평가
p.23~25

01 ⑤   02 ④   03 ②

04 He is the fastest swimmer in my team.

05 (1) the most (2) in (3) to celebrate (4) to go
   (5) to be (6) to be   06 ①   07 ②

08 the prettiest   09 ②   10 the
   saddest 11 ①, ④   12 ②, ③

13 (1) I want to win first prize to surprise my mom.
   (2) Jack used a compass to find the right direction.
   (3) I visited the museum to see the works of Gogh.
   (4) Tom and Judy went to the restaurant so as to
   have lunch.

14 ③, ⑤   15 (1) to play basketball (2) opened,
   to study (3) turned on, to watch (4) the
   coldest (5) the cleverest (6) the worst of

16 ⑤   17 (1) to be a math teacher (2) to buy
   a dress (3) not to be late

18 most brightest → brightest

01 뒤에 of my blouses가 있으므로 최상급이 적절하다.

02 ④ most와 최상급을 겹쳐서 쓰지 않는다.

03 silly와 valuable의 최상급은 silliest와 most valuable이며
   형용사의 최상급 앞에는 the를 붙인다.

04 형용사의 최상급 앞에는 the를 붙인다.

05 (1) 형용사의 최상급 앞에는 the를 붙인다. (2) 최상급에서 보통
   'of+복수 명사', 'in+단수 명사'가 쓰인다. (3), (4) 부사적 용법
   의 '목적' (5), (6) 부사적 용법의 '결과'이다.

06 ①번은 time을 수식하는 형용사적 용법이지만 <보기>와 나머
   지는 모두 부사적 용법의 '목적'이다.

07 부사적 용법의 '목적'의 뜻을 보다 분명하게 하기 위하여 to부정
   사 앞에 in order나 so as를 쓰기도 한다.

08 that I've ever seen으로 보아 최상급이 적절하다.

09 부사적 용법의 '목적'을 이용한다.

10 in this village가 있으므로 최상급이 적절하다.

11 ① 형용사적 용법 ② 부사적 용법의 '목적' ③ 부사적 용법의
   '결과' ④ 명사적 용법(목적격 보어) ⑤ 부사적 용법의 '원인'

12 to부정사는 to 다음에 동사원형이 온다.

13 (1) 부사적 용법의 '목적'으로 쓰는 것이 적절하다. (2) 접속사
   없이 동사가 두 개 나올 수 없으므로 found를 '~하기 위하여'라
   는 뜻의 to부정사의 부사적 용법으로 고치는 것이 적절하다. (3)
   to부정사는 to 다음에 동사원형이 나온다. (4) 목적의 뜻을 보다
   분명하게 하기 위하여 to부정사 앞에 in order나 so as를 쓰기
   도 한다. *compass: 나침반

14 ① The biggest fruit in this shop is that watermelon. ②
   The light bulb is one of the most famous inventions of
   the 19th century. ④ The wisest man in the world was
   Gandhi.

15 (1), (2), (3) '~하기 위하여'라는 뜻의 to부정사의 부사적 용법
   (목적)을 이용한다. (4), (5), (6) 형용사의 최상급 앞에는 the
   를 붙인다. bad의 최상급은 worst이다.

16 flamingo가 키와 몸무게 모두 가장 작다.

17 '~하기 위하여'라는 뜻의 to부정사의 부사적 용법의 '목적'을 이
   용한다.

18 most와 최상급을 겹쳐 쓰지 않는다.

서술형 시험대비
p.26~27

01 heaviest → the lightest

02 (1) in order to
   (2) so as to
   (3) in order that, could[might]

03 (1) heavier than, bag
   (2) No, heavier than
   (3) No, as[so] heavy

04 (1) Arthur was pleased to get a good grade in
   science.
   (2) Sue went out at night to buy some water.

(3) Brenda went to Paris to study art.

05 (1) This is the largest room in my house.

(2) John is the tallest of the boys in his class.

(3) Marilyn studies English hard to get good grades.

(4) I want to use my computer to find the information on the Internet.

(5) The most famous scientist, Isaac Newton, lived to be 74.

06 (1) to buy (2) to have[eat] (3) not to be late

07 (1) Mom went to the store to buy my dress.

(2) She used a hairbrush to brush her daughter's hair.

(3) Tom was disappointed to find that she loved Mike.

(4) Solomon was one of the wisest men in the world.

(5) This book is the most useful of all the books that I have.

08 (1) wears the brightest

(2) the heaviest

(3) has the darkest

09 (1) the prettiest/nicest, to give

(2) the nicest, to make

(3) the longest, to get

10 (1) to study hard (2) to use the Internet better

01 문맥상 가벼운 신발이 적절하며 형용사의 최상급에는 the를 붙인다.

02 부사적 용법의 '목적'을 나타내는 to부정사는 (1) 'in order to부정사', (2) 'so as to부정사', (3) 'in order that 주어+can[may] ~'으로 바꿔 쓸 수 있다.

03 최상급 = 비교급 than+any other+단수 명사 = 부정 주어+비교급 than = 부정 주어+as[so] 원급 as

04 (1)은 to부정사의 부사적 용법의 '(감정의) 원인'을, (2)와 (3)은 '목적'을 나타내는 to부정사를 쓴다.

05 (1) most와 최상급을 겹쳐 쓰지 않는다. (2) 형용사의 최상급 앞에는 the를 붙인다. (3), (4) '~하기 위하여'라는 뜻의 to부정사의 부사적 용법의 '목적'을 이용한다. (5) to be 74가 동사 lived의 결과를 나타내는 to부정사의 부사적 용법의 '결과'를 이용한다.

06 부정사의 부사적 용법의 '목적'을 이용한다. 또한 부정사의 부정은 not을 to부정사 앞에 붙인다는 것에 유의한다.

07 (1), (2) 부정사의 부사적 용법의 '목적'을 이용한다. (3) 부사적 용법의 '감정의 원인'을 이용한다. (4) one of the+최상급+복수명사: 가장 ~한 …들 중의 하나 (5) '~ 중에서'는 'of+복수 명사'를 이용한다. the books that I have: 내가 갖고 있는 책들

08 형용사의 최상급 앞에는 the를 붙인다.

09 to부정사의 부사적 용법의 '목적'을 이용하고 형용사의 최상급 앞에는 the를 붙인다.

10 부정사의 부사적 용법의 목적으로 어법에 맞게 쓰면 정답임.

[교과서] Reading

확인문제   p.28

1 T 2 F 3 F 4 T

확인문제   p.29

1 T 2 F 3 T 4 F

확인문제   p.29

1 T 2 F 3 F 4 T

교과서 확인학습 A   p.30~31

01 for the New School Year   02 Hi

03 the first day   04 for this year   05 most

06 you want to do   07 make a bucket list, share, with

08 I'm

09 This is   10 go on a bike tour

11 I've been there before, on my bike

12 how to play   13 the most beautiful sound

14 on, by the end of   15 Finally

16 weakest subject overcome   17 put, into, to

18 My name is   19 right in front of

20 willing, stand in line   21 adopt a puppy

22 I've, wanted   23 I'm, ready to

24 a little more challenging   25 I'd like to

26 a big fan, a single one

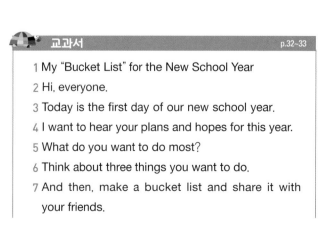

교과서   p.32~33

1 My "Bucket List" for the New School Year

2 Hi, everyone.

3 Today is the first day of our new school year.

4 I want to hear your plans and hopes for this year.

5 What do you want to do most?

6 Think about three things you want to do.

7 And then, make a bucket list and share it with your friends.

8 Hi! I'm Jinsu.

9 This is my bucket list for this year.

10 First, I want to go on a bike tour of Jejudo this summer.

11 I've been there before, but I want to experience the island more freely on my bike this time.

12 My second goal is to learn how to play the guitar.

13 I think the guitar has the most beautiful sound of all musical instruments.

14 I hope I can play my favorite song on my guitar by the end of this year.

15 Finally, I want to get a good grade in math.

16 Math is my weakest subject.

17 This year, I'll put more effort into studying math to overcome my weakness.

18 Hi! My name is Somi.

19 First, I want to see a concert of my favorite band right in front of the stage.

20 I'm willing to stand in line all night to enter the front area.

21 Second, I want to adopt a puppy.

22 I've always wanted a puppy.

23 I think I'm fully ready to take care of a pet now.

24 My last goal is a little more challenging.

25 I'd like to read all of the Sherlock Holmes stories.

26 I became a big fan of this detective series last year, so I don't want to miss a single one.

시험대비 실력평가
p.34~37

01 ④   02 ①, ③   03 a bucket list

04 ②, ⑤   05 (A) this   (B) weakest   (C) weakness

06 by the end of this year   07 ②   08 stand in line   09 ②   10 ⑤

11 (A) them (B) last   (C) every day   12 ④

13 ⑤   14 ①   15 ③, ⑤   16 ③

17 ①   18 willing   19 ③

20 (A) First   (B) Second (C) Third 또는 Finally나 Lastly

21 other   22 most famous   23 ③

24 ④   25 ②   26 What is the first thing on your list?

01 ④번 다음 문장의 then에 주목한다. 주어진 문장의 내용을 받고 있으므로 ④번이 적절하다.

02 ⓐ와 ②, ④, ⑤는 명사적 용법, ① 형용사적 용법, ③ 부사적 용법

03 '버킷 리스트'를 가리킨다.

04 ⓐ와 ②, ⑤는 경험 용법, ①과 ④ 계속 용법, ③ 결과 용법

05 (A) '올해의' 버킷 리스트라고 해야 하므로 this가 적절하다. last year: 작년, (B) 수학은 제가 '가장 약한' 과목이라고 해야 하므로 weakest가 적절하다. (C) '약점'을 극복하기 위해라고 해야 하므로 weakness가 적절하다.

06 by는 '완료'를 나타내는 전치사이다.

07 ② 진수는 전에 제주도에 가 본 적이 '있다.'

08 stand in line: 일렬로 서다

09 ⓑ와 ② 이미 나온 가산 명사의 반복을 피하여 씀. ① 하나의, ③ (강조의 의미로 쓰여) 유일한, ④ [another, the other와 대조적으로] 한쪽의, 한편의, ⑤ 사람, 세상 사람

10 위 글은 소미의 올해 버킷 리스트를 소개하는 글이므로, 제목으로는 ⑤ '소미가 올해 하고 싶어 하는 것'이 적절하다.

11 (A) 'cookies'를 가리키므로 them이 적절하다. (B) '마지막 것은'이라고 해야 하므로 last가 적절하다. latest: 최근의, 최신의, (C) '매일'이라고 해야 하므로 every day가 적절하다. everyday: 일상의

12 동족목적어를 가지는 동사는 have로 바꿔 쓸 수 있다.

13 ⑤는 접속사이고, ⓑ와 나머지는 다 관계대명사이다.

14 위 글은 진수의 올해 버킷 리스트를 소개하는 글이므로, 제목으로는 ① '진수의 올해 버킷 리스트'가 적절하다.

15 finally와 lastly: 순서상 '끝으로', '마지막으로', ① 결국, 마침내, ② 게다가, ④ 그러므로

16 ⓑ와 ②, ⑤는 부사적 용법(목적), ①과 ③ 형용사적 용법, ④ 명사적 용법

17 ⓐ와 ① 정확히, 바로(부사), ② 옳은, 올바른, ③ 맞는[알맞은], 제대로 된, ④ 권리(명사), ⑤ 오른쪽의

18 be willing to: 기꺼이 ~하다, 어떤 일을 강요받아서라기 보다는 자신이 하기를 원하기 때문에 꽤 열심히 하는

19 ③ 소미가 어떻게 애완동물을 돌볼 준비가 완벽히 될 수 있었는지는 대답할 수 없다. ① A concert of her favorite band. ② A puppy. ④ To read all of the Sherlock Holmes stories. ⑤ Last year.

20 순서를 표현할 때 First, Second, Third(Finally나 Lastly)로 쓰는 것이 적절하다.

21 another+단수명사, 뒤에 복수명사인 countries가 있으므로 other로 고치는 것이 적절하다.

22 famous는 규칙변화를 하는 형용사이며, 최상급은 most famous이다.

23 for: (이유·원인) ~ 때문에, ~으로 (인하여)

24 부사적 용법(목적)의 to부정사 = in order[so as] to 동사원형 = that[so that/in order that] ~ may[can]

25 ② 소미의 버킷 리스트가 실현될지는 알 수 없다. ① Yes, she did. ③ To see her favorite band in a concert, standing in front of the stage. ④ No, she doesn't. ⑤ It is a bike tour of Jejudo.

26 What about you?: 너는 어때?, 진수의 첫 번째 버킷 리스트가 무엇인지 물어보는 말이다.

01 Today is the first day of our new school year.

02 thinking about three things you want to do

03 bucket list

04 play guitar → play the guitar

05 I think the guitar has the most beautiful sound of all musical instruments.

06 (A) to get a good grade 또는 getting a good grade
(B) weakest subject

07 unwilling → willing

08 care for 또는 look after

09 one

10 I've been there before

11 I should

12 musical instrument

13 (A) night   (B) to take   (C) to read

14 she became a big fan of this detective series last year

15 (1) 가장 좋아하는 밴드의 공연을 무대 바로 앞에서 보기
(2) 강아지를 입양하기
(3) 셜록 홈스 이야기들을 모두 읽기

01 서수 first 앞에 the를 써야 한다. new school year: 새 학년

02 'And then(그러고 나서)'은 '여러분이 원하는 것 세 가지를 생각해 보고 나서'라는 뜻이다.

03 bucket list: 버킷 리스트, 사람들이 죽기 전에 경험하거나 성취하기를 원하는 것들의 목록, 'kick the bucket(죽다)'에서 유래하였다.

04 악기 이름 앞에는 the를 붙여야 한다.

05 형용사의 최상급 앞에 'the'를 보충하면 된다.

06 수학은 진수가 '가장 약한 과목'이기 때문에, 그의 마지막 목표는 수학에서 '좋은 점수를 받는 것'이다.

07 소미는 앞 자리에 들어가기 위해 '기꺼이' 밤새 줄을 서서 기다릴 것이다. unwilling: 꺼리는

08 take care of = care for = look after: ~을 돌보다

09 one은 이미 나온 가산 명사의 반복을 피할 때 쓰는 대명사이다.

10 have been to: ~에 가 본 적이 있다. / 부사인 there 앞에는 to를 쓰지 않는 것이 적절하다.

11 의문사+to부정사 = 의문사+주어+should+동사원형

12 '비교급 than any other 단수명사'로 최상급의 의미를 표현할 수 있다.

13 (A) all night: 밤새도록, 하룻밤 내내, (B) be ready to부정사: ~할 준비가 되다, (C) like는 목적어로 동명사와 to부정사를 둘 다 쓸 수 있지만, would like는 to부정사만 쓸 수 있다.
would like to부정사 = want to부정사

14 작년에 이 탐정 시리즈의 열성팬이 되었기 때문이다.

15 소미의 버킷 리스트는 '가장 좋아하는 밴드의 공연을 무대 바로 앞에서 보기', '강아지를 입양하기', '셜록 홈스 이야기들을 모두 읽기'이다.

01 weakness   02 ③   03 make

04 go   05 by   06 (1) goal (2) overcome

07 (1) The dogs can run more quickly to save people.
(2) This is my first visit to Europe.
(3) The bookstore is right next to my company.

08 ④   09 ④   10 planning

11 (1) happy → sorry   (B) got → gets[will get] 12 ④

13 I'm planning to go to the book fair with Jimmy.

14 to go, the book fair with, tomorrow, joining them, will, at, in front of   15 ②   16 ③

17 ⑤   18 ④   19 ③

20 (1) Brian was pleased to meet Scarlet yesterday.
(2) Emily went to bed early to take the first train.
(3) Audrey grew up to be an actress.
(4) Wendy went to Seoul never to return.

21 the most important

22 (1) Ann wants to go to Korea to learn the Korean language.
(2) Jane is planning to dance at the school festival to show her friends how well she dances.

23 ③   24 ①   25 (A) freely (B) how (C)studying   26 second   27 the most beautiful sound   28 ⑤   29 the Sherlock Holmes stories   30 ③   31 standing   32 first

33 ①, ④   34 No.

01 주어진 보기는 반의어의 관계이다. outside: 바깥쪽 inside: 안쪽 strength: 힘, 강점 weakness: 약함, 약점

02 ③ full → fully: 완전히 / 그 식당은 이번 주말에 완전히 예약되었다. ① challenging: 도전적인, 힘든, 간단하지 않은 / 어린 아이들을 가르치는 것은 도적적이며 보람된 일이다. ② missing: 없어진, 분실한 / 그들은 없어진 아이를 찾는 중이다. ④ complete: 완료하다, 완결하다 / 그 건물은 완성되는데 2년이 걸렸다. ⑤ bucket list: 버킷 리스트, 달성하고 싶은 목표 목록 / 나는 네가 정말 좋은 버킷 리스트를 만들었기를 바란다.

03 make a friend: 친구를 사귀다 make an effort: 노력하다

04 go back to ~: ~로 돌아가다 go on a tour: 여행을 가다

05 be p.p. by 행위자: …에 의해서 ~되다 by the end of ~: ~ 말까지는

06 (1) goal: 목표, 미래에 달성하기를 바라는 어떤 것 (2) overcome: 극복하다, 감정이나 문제를 성공적으로 통제하다

07 (1) save: 구하다, 살리다 (2) Europe: 유럽, 유럽 대륙 (3) right: 바로

08 좋은 성적을 얻기를 바란다는 말에 네가 좋은 성적을 받을 거니까 걱정하지 말라는 말이 어울린다. ① 그 말을 들으니 유감이야. ② 너는 어때? 너의 계획은 무엇이니? ③ 음, 나는 확실하지 않아. ⑤ 응, 뭔데?

7

09 Brian이 소민이의 계획을 먼저 묻고 이에 대답했다. 이어서 소민이가 Brian의 계획을 묻는 표현이 들어가야 한다. Brian이 자신의 계획은 개를 목욕시키는 것이라고 대답했으므로 ④가 적절하다.

10 Are you planning to 동사원형: ~할 계획이니?

11 (1) 할머니가 아프다는 말에 그 말을 들어 기쁘다는 표현은 어색하다. 그러므로 happy를 sorry로 바꾸는 것이 적절하다. I'm sorry to hear that: 유감이야. (2) 곧 나아지기를 바란다는 말이므로 과거형 got은 어울리지 않는다.

12 ④ 소민이는 이번 주말에 할머님을 방문할 것이다. this Friday → this weekend

13 be planning to 동사원형: ~할 계획이다 book fair: 도서 박람회

14 be planning to 동사원형: ~할 계획이다 suggest: 제안하다 join: 함께 하다, 합류하다 will+동사원형: ~할 것이다 at+시간: ~(시)에 in front of: ~ 앞에서

15 happy의 최상급은 happiest이다.

16 <보기>와 ③번은 부사적 용법의 '목적' ① 명사적 용법 ② 목적어로 쓰인 명사적 용법 ④ 보어로 쓰인 명사적 용법 ⑤ 형용사적 용법

17 뒤에서 in 이하로 한정되고 있으며 '~에서'를 의미하므로 최상급이 적절하고 형용사의 최상급 앞에는 the를 붙인다.

18 ① I want to get a good grade in math. ② I'll put more effort into studying math to overcome my weakness. ③ Arnold saved plenty of money to buy a car. ⑤ William Shakespeare lived to be fifty two.

19 ③ Emma is the kindest girl in her school.

20 (1) 부정사의 부사적 용법의 '감정의 원인'을, (2) 부사적 용법의 '목적'을, (3), (4) 부사적 용법의 '결과'를 이용한다. never to부정사: 결코 ~하지 못하다

21 부정 주어+비교급+than = 최상급

22 부정사의 부사적 용법의 '목적'을 이용한다.

23 '저는 여러분들의 올해 계획과 희망을 듣고 싶어요. 여러분이 가장 원하는 것은 무엇인가요?'라는 두 문장 사이의 '학생들이 더 높은 학년으로 올라가면, 그들은 훨씬 더 많은 시간을 공부하는 데 보낸다.'라는 ③번 문장은 전체 글의 흐름에서 벗어난다.

24 ⓐ for: (정해진 날짜나 시간을 나타내어) ~에[일자의], for this year: 올해의, ⓑ share A with B: B와 A를 공유하다

25 (A) 동사 experience를 수식하므로 부사 freely가 적절하다. (B) '기타 연주하는 법'이라고 해야 하므로 how가 적절하다. (C) 전치사 다음이므로 동명사 studying이 적절하다.

26 제 '두 번째' 목표라고 해야 하므로 second가 적절하다.

27 '부정주어 + 비교급 than'은 최상급의 의미를 지닌다.

28 ⓐ와 ⑤ 부사적 용법(형용사 수식), ① 부사적 용법(목적), ② 부사적 용법(원인), ③ 부사적 용법(결과), ④ 부사적 용법(판단의 근거)

29 '셜록 홈스 이야기'를 가리킨다.

30 ③ 소미는 이제는 애완동물을 돌볼 준비가 '완벽히 되었다'고 생각한다.

31 현재분사를 사용하여 동시동작을 나타내는 분사구문으로 고치는 것이 적절하다.

32 the first thing = the top thing

33 선행사가 사물이므로 관계대명사 which나 that이 적절하다.

34 글쓴이의 가장 약한 과목이 영어이므로, 글쓴이는 영어를 '잘하지 못한다.'

단원별 예상문제 p.46~49

01 (1) (c)omplete (2) (f)amous (3) (a)fter (4) (m)issing
02 ④   03 ④   04 ①
05 (D) → (C) → (A) → (B)   06 (A) → (C) → (B) → (D)
07 ⑤   08 (A) When did you start studying Chinese? (B) How did you get so into Chinese?
09 ③   10 I hope I can soon watch them in Chinese and understand what they are saying.
11 ②   12 ④   13 (1) healthiest (2) best
14 so as not to get wet   15 (1) He is the best student in my class. (2) Naomi is the smartest girl of them all.   16 (1) I used my smartphone to call Melanie. (2) Karen was glad to see him again tonight.
17 I want to go on a bike tour   18 ⑤
19 weakest   20 (A) willing (B) adopt (C) challenging
21 ④   22 ②   23 cookies
24 surprise   25 ③

01 (1) 시작하다 : 시작하다 = finish (끝내다) : complete (완료하다, 완결하다) (2) 처음의, 초기의 : 첫, 처음의 = well-known (유명한, 잘 알려진) : famous (유명한, 잘 알려진) (3) 안에 : 밖으로 = before (~ 전에) : after (~ 후에) (4) 똑똑한 : 똑똑한 = lost (잃은, 행방불명의) : missing (없어진, 분실한)

02 be willing to 동사원형: 기꺼이 ~하다 be ready to 동사원형: ~할 준비가 되다

03 선물로 무엇을 받기를 원하는지 묻는 질문에, 새로운 컴퓨터를 얻기를 바란다고 대답한다. ① 너는 그럴 거야. 걱정하지 마. ② 그거 좋겠다. ③ 나는 새 컴퓨터를 살 계획이다. ④ 나는 새 컴퓨터를 받기를 희망한다. ⑤ 나는 네가 새 컴퓨터를 받기를 희망해.

04 ① overcome: 극복하다 / 나는 네가 어려움들을 극복하길 바란다. ② learn: 배우다 / 언어를 배우는 최상의 방법이 무엇이니? ③ surprise: 놀라게 하다 / 그들이 말하고 있는 것은 나를 놀라게 하지 않는다. ④ ride: 타다 / 그는 결코 자전거 타는 것을 배운 적이 없다. ⑤ plan: 계획; 계획하다 / 우리는 시내 근처에 새로운 사무실을 열 계획이다.

05 (D) 부탁을 하는 말에, (C) 좋다고 대답하고. 부탁의 내용을 묻는다. (A) 새 자전거를 사는데 하나 골라 달라고 말하자 (B) 좋

다고 대답한다.

06 (A) 내일의 계획을 묻자 (C) 잘 모르겠다고 대답한다. (B) 그러면 영화 보러 가자고 제안하고 (D) 좋다고 대답한다.

07 새 학년을 위한 특별한 계획에 대해 얘기하는 중이다.

08 (A)의 답이 '지난달'이라는 시간의 정보이기 때문에 When으로 시작된 의문문이 어울린다. 중국어는 공부할 예정이 아니라 이미 공부하고 있기에 과거시제가 들어간 'When did you start studying Chinese?'이 어울린다. (B) It's because라고 답하고 있으므로 이유를 묻는 질문이 적절하다.

09 주어와 목적어가 같기 때문에 재귀대명사를 사용해야 한다. me 대신에 myself를 사용해야 적절하다.

10 I hope I can 동사원형 ~: 내가 ~할 수 있기를 바란다[희망한다] soon: 곧 in Chinese: 중국어로 understand: 이해하다

11 ① Sumi is the tallest in my class. ③ A rabbit is one of the fastest animals. ④ Bill is the hungriest boy in this restaurant. ⑤ Steve is the richest of the three gentlemen.

12 ④번은 부사적 용법의 '원인'이고 나머지는 '목적'이다.

13 (1), (2) 뒤에 in her class와 in his school이라는 비교 집단이 있고 앞에 the가 있으므로 최상급이 적절하다.

14 목적의 뜻을 보다 분명하게 하기 위하여 to부정사 앞에 so as를 쓰기도 한다.

15 (1) 비교급은 '비교급+than+비교 대상'으로 쓰지만 최상급은 'the+최상급'으로 쓴다. (2) most와 최상급을 겹쳐서 쓰지 않는다.

16 (1) 부정사의 부사적 용법의 '목적'을 이용한다. (2) 부정사의 부사적 용법의 '원인'을 이용한다.

17 want는 to부정사를 목적어로 가진다.

18 ⑤ subject는 (논의 등의) 주제[대상/화제], 과목, ⓑ와 나머지는 다 성취하고자 하는 '목표'를 나타낸다.

19 weak은 규칙변화를 하는 형용사이며, 최상급은 weakest이다.

20 (A) '기꺼이' 밤새 줄을 서서 기다릴 것이라고 해야 하므로 willing이 적절하다. unwilling: 꺼리는, (B) 강아지를 '입양하고' 싶다고 해야 하므로 adopt가 적절하다. adopt: 입양하다, adapt: 맞추다[조정하다], 적응하다, (C) 마지막 목표는 셜록 홈스 이야기를 다 읽는 것이라서 약간 '도전적'이라고 해야 하므로 challenging이 적절하다. challenging: 도전적인, 도전 의식을 북돋우는, relaxing: 마음을 느긋하게 해 주는, 편한

21 ④ 작년에 그녀가 셜록 홈스 이야기를 몇 권 읽었는지는 알 수 없다. ① Right in front of the stage. ② A puppy. ③ Yes, she is. ⑤ Because she became a big fan of this detective series last year.

22 ⓐ와 ② (못 보거나 못 듣고) 놓치다, (관심을 안 두고) 지나치다, ① 피하다, 면하다, ③ 그리워하다, ④ (있어야 할 것이) 없다는 것을 알다[눈치 채다], ⑤ 실수, 실패(명사), 조금이건 1마일이건 빗나간 것은 마찬가지다(오십보백보)

23 '쿠키'를 가리킨다.

24 엄마를 '놀라게' 하기 위해 쿠키를 만들고 싶어 한다.

25 ③ 필요하지 않은 물건들을 버릴 것이다.

서술형 실전문제 p.50~51

01 I will go to a movie with Toby. / I'm going to go to a movie with Toby.

02 (1) I hope I can travel to Japan next year.
(2) Next year, I hope I can become the winner.
(3) I'm planning to study all day to get good grades.

03 ① Its → It's, ② special anything → anything special, ⑤ How is your plan? → What's[What is] your plan?

04 (1) to play (2) to send

05 (1) bridge → bridges
(2) popularest → the most popular
(3) buying → to buy
(4) stayed → to stay

06 (1) higher than any other mountain
(2) No, more beautiful

07 learning

08 greet → overcome 또는 get over

09 (1) 이번 여름에 제주도로 자전거 여행을 가기
(2) 기타 치는 법을 배우기
(3) 수학에서 좋은 점수를 받기

10 challenged → challenging

11 to read

12 (A) second (B) ready

01 계획을 말할 때, I'm planning to 동사원형 ~.(나는 ~할 계획이야.) I'm going to 동사원형 ~.(나는 ~할 거야.) I'll 동사원형 ~.(나는 ~할 거야.)을 사용할 수 있다.

02 (1) I hope (that) 주어 can 동사원형 ~. 주어가 할 수 있기를 바란다. (2) next year: 내년(에) winner: 승자 (3) be planning to 동사원형: ~할 계획이다 all day: 하루 종일 grade: 성적

03 ① 요일을 나타내기 위해 비인칭 주어 it을 사용한다. ② -thing으로 끝나는 anything, nothing, something 등은 형용사가 뒤에 온다. (후치 수식) ⑤ 계획에 대해 남자아이가 대답하고 있으므로, What을 이용해 계획이 무엇인지 물어봐야 한다.

04 부정사의 부사적 용법의 '목적'을 이용한다.

05 (1) one of the+최상급+복수명사: 가장 ~한 …들 중의 하나 (2) popular의 최상급은 most popular이고 형용사의 최상급 앞에는 the를 붙인다. (3), (4) '~하기 위하여'라는 뜻의 to부정사의 부사적 용법을 이용하는 것이 적절하다.

06 최상급 = 비교급 than+any other+단수 명사 = 부정 주어+비교급 than = 부정 주어+as[so] 원급 as

07 보어로 쓰인 to부정사를 동명사로 바꿀 수 있다.

08 나의 약점을 '극복하기' 위해 나는 수학 공부에 더 많은 노력을 기울일 것이라고 하는 것이 적절하다. greet: 맞다, 환영하다,

overcome = get over: 극복하다

09 진수의 버킷 리스트는 '이번 여름에 제주도로 자전거 여행을 가기', '기타 치는 법을 배우기', '수학에서 좋은 점수를 받기'이다.

10 challenge의 형용사형 challenging이 알맞다.

11 like는 목적어로 동명사와 to부정사를 둘 다 쓸 수 있지만, would like는 to부정사만 쓸 수 있다. would like to부정사 = want to부정사

12 소미의 '두 번째' 버킷리스트는 강아지를 입양하는 것이다. 사실 그녀는 항상 강아지를 원해 왔고 이제 애완동물을 돌볼 '준비가 완전히 되어 있다'고 생각한다

창의사고력 서술형 문제   p.52

|모범답안|

01 (A) planning to do
(B) to visit the museum, What are you
(A) to go swimming

02 (1) I study math very hard to become a math teacher.
(2) I practice singing very hard to be a singer.

03 (A) bought (B) my favorite actor (C) my role model (D) can travel (E) to buy

단원별 모의고사   p.53~56

01 ③
02 (1) of (2) into (3) away (4) on
03 ②
04 (i)nstrument
05 (c)omplete 06 ⓑ to see ⓒ standing
07 The top thing on my list is a bike tour to Jejudo.
08 ④
09 do you have any special plans for the new school year?
10 ⓐ in ⓑ in ⓒ into 11 ③ 12 ①, ③
13 What are you planning to do this weekend?
14 ①, ④ 15 (f)avor 16 help you choose one
17 ② 18 ② 19 No, as[so] high
20 (1) Sarah took the subway to go to school.
(2) I sat under a tree to take a rest.
(3) Amy woke up to find her cellphone on the bed.
21 ③번, in → of 22 ② 23 get over 24 ④ 25 ③ 26 for
27 completed my bucket list for this year
28 How about you?

01 be planning to 동사원형: ~할 계획이다 get one's hair cut: ~의 머리를 자르다

02 (1) take care of: 돌보다 (2) put effort into: ~에 노력을 들이다, 힘들이다 (3) throw away: 버리다, 던지다 (4) go on a

---

tour: 관광하다, 여행을 떠나다

03 plan: 계획; 계획하다 / 그의 계획은 한 달에 두 권의 책을 읽는 것이다. 언제 유럽으로 갈 거니?

04 instrument: 기계, 기구 musical instrument: 악기

05 complete: 완료하다, 완결하다 / 특히 긴 시간이 걸릴 때 무엇인가를 하거나 만드는 행위를 끝내다

06 ⓑ want는 to부정사가 목적어로 올 수 있다. ⓒ standing은 접속사와 주어가 생략된 분사구문이다.

07 top: 꼭대기의, 위의 list: 목록 bike tour: 자전거 여행

08 ④ 소미가 좋아하는 밴드가 무엇인지는 나와 있지 않다. ① 소미는 좋아하는 밴드가 있다. ② 금년에 진수는 제주도에 자전거 여행을 가고 싶어 한다. ③ 그들은 금년의 버킷 리스트(하고 싶은 일)에 대해 얘기하는 중이다. ⑤ 소미는 콘서트에서 무대 앞에서 보기를 원한다.

09 special: 특별한 plan: 계획; 계획하다

10 ⓐ be interested in: ~에 관심을 갖다 ⓑ in Chinese: 중국어로 ⓒ get into: ~에 빠지게 되다

11 ③ not sure를 sure로 바꿔야 적절하다.

12 ① 맨 마지막 대화에, 보통 때처럼 과목마다 좋은 성적을 얻기를 원한다는 것으로 보아 남자아이는 보통 좋은 성적을 받는다. ② Kate는 중국어로 자신을 소개할 수 있다. ③ Kate는 중국어 공부를 지난달부터 시작했다. ④ Kate는 금년에 매일 새로운 중국어 단어를 외울 계획을 가지고 있다. ⑤ Kate가 중국 드라마의 열렬한 팬이다.

13 be planning to 동사원형: ~할 계획이다 this weekend: 이번 주말에

14 have[get]+목적어+p.p.: 목적어가 p.p.되도록 하다

15 favor: 친절, 호의

16 새로운 자전거를 찾는 것을 도와주려고 한다.

17 dirty와 wet의 최상급은 각각 dirtiest와 wettest이다.

18 Diana was at a restaurant to have lunch.

19 최상급 = 비교급 than+any other+단수 명사 = 부정 주어+비교급 than = 부정 주어+as[so] 원급 as

20 (1), (2) 부정사의 부사적 용법의 '목적'을 이용한다. (3) 부정사의 부사적 용법의 '결과'를 이용한다.

21 최상급 구문을 쓸 때 '~ 중에서'는 보통 'of+복수명사', 'in+단수 집합체'로 표현하는 것이 적절하다.

22 ⓐ와 ②는 과목, ① 지배를 받는, ③ 주제[대상/화제], ④ (그림•사진 등의) 대상[소재], ⑤ 연구[실험] 대상

23 overcome = get over: 극복하다

24 ④번 다음의 문장들이 주어진 문장의 내용을 설명하는 것이므로 ④번이 적절하다.

25 부사적 용법(목적)의 to부정사 = in order[so as] to동사원형 = that[so that/in order that] ~may[can]

26 be ready to부정사 = be ready for 동명사[명사]: ~할 준비가 되어 있다

27 '올해 나의 버킷 리스트를 완성했다.'

28 What about you? = How about you?: 너는 어때?

Let's Be Smart Smartphone Users

시험대비 실력평가   p.60

01 increase   02 ④   03 ②   04 ①
05 ②   06 ⑤   07 ⑤   08 ③
09 (p)revent

01 둘은 반의어 관계이다. pull: 당기다 push: 밀다 increase: 증가하다 decrease: 감소하다

02 in front of: ~ 앞에 instead of: ~ 대신에

03 crack: 금, 깨진 틈

04 advice: 충고

05 service center: 서비스 센터, 수리소

06 뉴욕 시는 5년 안에 최소한 20%까지 소금 섭취량을 줄일 것을 계획하고 있다. ⑤ 줄이다, 감소시키다

07 낡은 규칙이 새로운 규칙으로 바뀌었다 ⑤ rule: 규칙

08 ③ 등/등 부상을 피하기 위해서, 무거운 물체를 들 때, 항상 무릎을 구부려라. ① 그 소설은 그것의 역사적인 배경에서 보는 것이 중요하다. ② 아무 말도 하지 마, 너는 상황을 더 악화시킬 뿐이야. ④ 미스터리를 해결할 수 있는 첫 번째 법칙은 사실을 확인하는 것이다. ⑤ 10분 동안 휴식 시간을 갖자.

09 (p)revent: 예방하다, 막다.

서술형 시험대비   p.61

01 (1) worse   (2) behind
02 always late for
03 from
04 (1) leaning   (2) lower   (3) hurt   (4) Bend
05 (1) (g)et in touch   (2) give it back   (3) do warm up[warm-up] exercise   (4) paying attention to
06 (1) at / At   (2) on

01 주어진 보기는 반의어 관계이다. (1) better: 더 좋은 worse: 더 나쁜 (2) in front of: ~ 앞에 behind: ~ 뒤에

02 be late for: ~에 늦다

03 keep A from B: A를 B로부터 막다 / 연극이 너무 지루해서 나는 잠드는 것을 참을 수 없었다. from time to time: 가끔, 이따금 / 너는 가끔 휴식할 필요가 있다.

04 (1) lean: 기대다 (2) lower: 낮추다 (3) hurt: 다치게 하다,

아프다 (4) bend: 구부리다

05 (1) get in touch with: ~와 연락[접촉]하다 (2) give back: 돌려주다 (3) do warm up[warm-up] exercise: 준비운동을 하다 (4) pay attention to: ~에 주의를 기울이다

06 (1) at+시간: ~시에, at least: 적어도 (2) put on: ~을 늘리다, 더하다 have a ride on: ~을 타다

[교과서] Conversation

핵심 Check   p.62~63

1 (B) You should study tonight.
  (B) You'd better keep him warm.
2 (B) better eat
  (B) You'd better study
3 (B) Make sure you, for
  (A) Make sure you don't touch
  (B) I won't
4 (B) Make sure you drink a lot of warm water.

교과서 대화문 익히기

Check(√) True or False   p.64

(1) F   (2) T   (3) F   (4) T   (5) F   (6) T

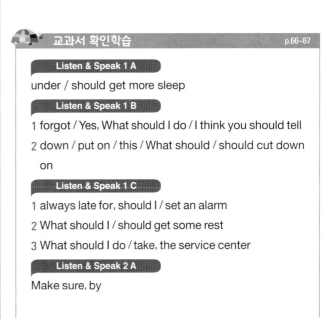

교과서 확인학습   p.66~67

Listen & Speak 1 A
under / should get more sleep

Listen & Speak 1 B
1 forgot / Yes, What should I do / I think you should tell
2 down / put on / this / What should / should cut down on

Listen & Speak 1 C
1 always late for, should I / set an alarm
2 What should I / should get some rest
3 What should I do / take, the service center

Listen & Speak 2 A
Make sure, by

Listen & Speak 2 B

1 sleep over at / make / Make sure you text, get to

2 what / reading / don't read in the dark, good for / turn, on

3 bring / won't / borrow / make sure / give it back

Listen & Speak 2 C

1 make sure you, first

2 Can I / turn it off after using it

3 Can I ride on, a life jacket

시험대비 기본평가 p.68

| 01 ② | 02 ④ | 03 (C) → (A) → (B) → (D) |
| 04 ③ | 05 ⑤ | |

01 'You should + 동사원형'을 사용해 충고하는 말을 할 수 있다.

02 'Make sure ~'에 대해서 응답을 할 때, 'Make sure ~' 다음에 대해 긍정이면 'OK. I will.'로 답하고, 부정이면 'OK. I won't.'로 답한다.

03 (C) 진수네 집에서 자는 것을 허락받기 위해서 질문을 하자, (A) 진수의 엄마가 허락을 했는지 물어본다. (B) 허락을 했고, 그녀가 피자를 만들어 줄 것이라고 대답하자, (D) 진수네 집에서 자는 것을 허락하고, 진수의 집에 도착하면 문자를 보내 연락할 것을 당부한다.

04 부정의문문의 질문에 대답할 때, 대답하는 내용이 긍정이면 Yes로 대답한다. No, she is. → Yes, she is.

05 ⑤ Jenny의 생일이 지난 것만 언급되어 있고, 정확히 언제 생일인지는 언급되지 않았다.

시험대비 실력평가 p.69~70

01 ③	02 ②	03 ②	04 ③
05 ①	06 make sure you take a walk for about 30 minutes		07 ②, ④
08 ④	09 Just make sure you give it back when you're done.	10 ③	11 crack
12 ④			

01 feel down: 우울하다 ① 실망한 ② 신난 ③ 우울한 ④ 불안한 ⑤ 당황스러운

02 put on: ~을 늘리다, 더하다 cut down on: ~을 줄이다

03 ② 과학책을 빌려줄 수 있느냐는 질문에, 안된다고 말하고 나서, 사용하고 나면 돌라달라는 말은 어색하다.

04 피자를 먹을 수 있는지 물어보는 질문에, 손을 먼저 씻으라는 당부를 하고 있다.

05 잠자기 전에 따뜻한 우유를 마시고, 30분 동안 걸으라는 것은 잠을 자지 못하는 사람에게 해 줄 수 있는 충고이다.

06 make sure ~.: 꼭 하도록 해. take a walk: 산책하다 about: 약

07 당부할 때 사용할 수 있는 표현은 Make sure ~.(꼭 하도록 해.), You had better ~. (~하는 것이 좋겠다.), Don't forget to ~. (~할 것을 잊지 마.), Remember to ~.(~할 것을 기억해라.) 등이 있다.

08 (A) 남자아이가 책을 안 가져와서 (B) 여자아이에게 책을 빌리는 대화이다. bring: 가져오다 borrow: 빌리다 lend: 빌려주다 rent: (땅·집 등을) 빌리다[빌려주다]

09 Make sure ~: 반드시 ~하도록 하다, ~을 확실히 하다 give back: 돌려주다 be done: 끝나다

10 'Did you drop it?(그것을 떨어뜨렸니?)라는 질문에 주어진 문장인 '여기 오는 길에 떨어뜨렸어.'라는 말이 어울리므로 ③이 적절하다.

11 crack 금, 깨진 틈 / 어떤 것이 깨졌지만 실제로 분리되지는 않았을 때 표면에 생긴 얇은 선

12 ④ Henry가 새로운 휴대 전화를 사용하는 방법을 모른다는 내용은 언급되어 있지 않다. ① 휴대 전화 케이스는 휴대 전를 보호해 준다. ② Henry는 그의 휴대 전화 화면이 깨져서 행복하지 않다. ③ Henry는 휴대 전화 케이스를 살 것이다. ⑤ Henry는 최근에 휴대 전화를 샀다.

서술형 시험대비 p.71

01 You should get some rest.

02 What should I keep in mind?

03 Make sure you don't lean on the door.

04 ⑤ turn the light off → turn the light on

05 (B) → (D) → (A) → (C)

06 (E) → (D) → (A) → (C) → (B)

07 less → more

01 should+동사원형: ~해야 한다(충고하기)

02 should+동사원형: ~해야 한다(충고하기) keep in mind: 명심하다

03 make sure: 반드시 ~하도록 하다, ~을 확실히 하다 lean on: ~에 기대다

04 휴대 전화로 소설을 읽고 있는 남자아이에게, 여자아이는 어두운 데서 읽지 말라고 당부하고 있으므로, 이 당부의 말에 '불을 끌 것이다.'는 어울리지 않는다. turn off: (불·라디오·텔레비전 등을) 끄다 turn on: (불·라디오·텔레비전 등을) 켜다

05 (B) 과학책을 가져오지 않았다는 말에, (D) 상대방은 선생님이 좋아하지 않을 것이라고 말한다. (A) 상대방에게 과학책을 빌려도 되는지 묻자 (C) 허락하며 꼭 돌려달라는 당부의 말을 한다.

06 무슨 일인지 묻는 질문에, (E) 휴대 전화를 보라고 얘기한다. (D) 휴대 전화 화면이 깨진 것을 보고, 떨어뜨렸는지 질문한다. (A) 여기 오는 길에 떨어뜨렸다고 답한다. (C) 이에 휴대 전화를 보호해 주는 휴대 전화 케이스에 대해 말하자, (B) 하나 살 것이라고 말한다.

07 눈 밑에 다크서클이 생겼다는 사람에게 좀 덜 자라는 충고가 아니라 좀 더 자라는 충고가 어울린다.

1 (1) to drink (2) to teach

  (3) to eat with (4) curious to ask

2 (1) laugh (2) repaired

  (3) to do (4) to paint

01 (1) write → write on (2) looking → look

  (3) play → to play (4) doing → (to) do

02 ④

03 (1) He made everyone work late.

  (2) Autumn is the season to harvest.

  (3) He helped me carry the heavy box.

  (4) I had a lot of work to do last night.

01 (1) to부정사가 형용사 역할을 할 때 수식받는 명사가 전치사의 목적어로 사용되었으면 전치사를 생략하면 안 된다. (2) 사역동사의 목적격보어로 동사원형이 적절하다. (3) to play로 time을 수식하는 것이 적절하다. (4) help는 준사역동사로 목적격보어로 동사원형이나 to부정사가 온다.

02 get은 to부정사가 목적격보어로 와야 한다.

03 사역동사는 목적격보어로 동사원형이 온다. (help는 to부정사도 가능) to부정사의 형용사적 용법을 이용하여 앞의 명사를 수식한다.

01 ⑤   02 ①   03 ⑤

04 to wear nice → nice to wear

05 (1) smile (2) painted (3) to find (4) to walk (5) to check (6) to take care of (7) wrong to correct

06 ②   07 ③, ④   08 ⑤   09 ②

10 ①   11 ③

12 (1) I want to make it happen during the school festival.

  (2) Is there anyone funny to bring to the party?

  (3) I'll have all the files copied for the meeting.

  (4) Dominick bought his daughter a doll to play with.

  (5) Amy got her sister to do her homework by herself.

13 ①   14 ⑤   15 ③

16 Susan wants a comfortable T-shirt to wear during the hiking.

17 I am looking for something nice to make me look

good.

18 (1) to become (2) do (3) to give, to make

  (4) finished (5) to talk with (6) to work

01 put on gloves와 같이 쓰므로 전치사 on이 있어야 하며 gloves를 수식해야 하므로 to부정사 형태가 적절하다.

02 사역동사는 목적격보어로 동사원형이 온다.

03 첫 문장에서는 사역동사의 목적격보어로 능동의 의미가 필요하므로 동사원형이 적절하다. 두 번째 문장에서는 something을 수식하는 형용사 역할을 하는 to부정사가 적절하다.

04 to부정사가 -thing, -body, -one으로 끝나는 부정대명사를 형용사와 함께 수식할 때는 '대명사+형용사+to부정사'의 어순이다.

05 (1) 사역동사는 목적격보어로 동사원형이 나온다. (2) 사역동사의 목적격보어로 수동의 의미가 필요하므로 과거분사가 적절하다. (3) help는 준사역동사로 목적격보어로 동사원형이나 to부정사가 나온다. (4) get은 to부정사가 목적격보어로 나와야 한다. (5) time을 수식하는 to check가 적절하다. (6) take care of two daughters와 같이 쓰므로 전치사 of가 있어야 한다. (7) to부정사가 -thing으로 끝나는 부정대명사를 형용사와 함께 수식할 때 '대명사+형용사+to부정사'의 어순이다.

06 ②번은 부사적 용법의 '결과'이지만 <보기>와 나머지는 모두 형용사적 용법이다.

07 ①, ②, ⑤ 형용사적 용법 ③ 부사적 용법의 '원인' ④ 명사적 용법(목적격보어) run into: ~을 우연히 만나다

08 사역동사 make의 목적격보어로 동사원형이 나와야 한다.

09 help는 목적격보어로 동사원형이나 to부정사가 나온다. emails를 수식하는 형용사 용법의 to부정사가 적절하다.

10 allowed는 목적격보어로 to부정사가 나와야 한다.

11 사역동사 let의 목적격보어로 동사원형이 적절하다.

12 (1) 사역동사의 목적격보어로 동사원형이 적절하다. (2) to부정사가 -one으로 끝나는 부정대명사를 형용사와 함께 수식할 때는 '대명사+형용사+to부정사'의 어순이다. (3) 사역동사의 목적격보어로 수동의 의미가 필요하므로 과거분사가 적절하다. (4) 인형을 노는 것이 아니라 인형을 갖고 노는 것이므로 with가 필요하다. play a doll (×) play with a doll (○) (5) get은 사역동사의 의미로 쓰일 수 있지만 목적격보어로 to부정사가 나와야 한다.

13 get은 목적격보어로 to부정사가 나와야 한다.

14 live in a house로 써야 하므로 in을 빠뜨리면 안 된다.

15 주어진 문장과 ③번의 make는 사역동사로 그 쓰임이 같다.

16 to를 보충하여 형용사적 용법으로 T-shirt를 수식하도록 한다.

17 '어떤 멋진 것'은 something nice로 쓰고 to make가 이것을 수식하도록 하고 사역동사 make의 목적격보어로 동사원형 look이 오도록 문장을 만든다.

18 (1) to become이 a chance를 수식하는 형용사적 용법으로 쓴다. (2) 사역동사 make의 목적격보어로 동사원형을 쓴다. (3) to give로 a present를 수식하게 하고 to make로 부사적 용

법(목적)으로 쓴다. (4) 사역동사의 목적격보어로 수동의 의미가 필요하므로 과거분사 finished가 적절하다. (5) to부정사가 -one으로 끝나는 부정대명사를 형용사와 함께 수식할 때는 '명사+형용사+to부정사'의 어순이다. with를 빠뜨리지 않도록 주의한다. (6) get은 사역동사의 의미로 쓰일 수 있지만 목적격보어로 to부정사인 to work가 나와야 한다.

01 achieving → to achieve

02 (1) Angie has twin sisters to take care of.

(2) Allen knows many silly jokes to make us laugh.

03 (1) Marilyn won't let her daughter sleep over at her friend's.

(2) I don't know how she got him to say yes.

(3) I asked him to have my computer repaired.

(4) He helped her (to) carry her things.

04 (1) I want to have the ability to speak English well.

(2) She took the chance to become an actress.

(3) Is there a way to solve the problem? 등 어법에 맞게 쓰면 정답

05 taken

06 (1) to decide

(2) to talk about

(3) to remember

07 to eat → eat, feeling → (to) feel

08 (1) to protecting → to protect

(2) look → look after

(3) write → write on

(4) important something to tell → something important to tell

09 (1) Our teacher made us hand in our report by tomorrow.

(2) The police officer made them leave immediately.

(3) My mom made me come home early today.

10 (1) Our teacher made us use only English in class.

(2) When he went to Paris, there was nobody to depend on.

(3) Simon had his computer checked.

(4) They needed a teacher to teach them English.

(5) I helped Mom to prepare dinner last night.

11 (1) to clean (2) repaired

01 goals를 수식하는 형용사적 용법의 to achieve가 적절하다.
02 형용사적 용법의 to부정사를 이용한다.
03 (1) 사역동사의 목적격보어로 동사원형이 적절하다. (2) get은 사

역동사의 의미로 쓰일 수 있지만 목적격보어로 to부정사가 나온다. (3) 사역동사의 목적격보어로 수동의 의미가 필요하므로 과거분사가 적절하다. (4) help는 목적격보어로 동사원형이나 to부정사가 나온다.

04 앞에 나오는 명사를 수식하는 형용사 용법의 to부정사를 이용한다.

05 사역동사의 목적격보어로 '개가 동물 병원으로 데려가지는' 수동의 의미가 필요하므로 과거분사가 적절하다.

06 앞에 나오는 명사를 수식하는 to부정사의 형용사적 용법을 이용한다. (2)번에서 talk topics가 아니라 talk about topics이므로 about을 빠뜨리면 안 된다.

07 사역동사의 목적격보어로 동사원형이 적절하며 help는 목적격보어로 동사원형이나 to부정사가 나온다.

08 (1) to protect가 tips를 수식하는 형용사적 용법이 적절하다. (2) look after는 두 단어가 하나의 타동사 역할을 하는 것이므로 after를 생략하면 안 된다. (3) to부정사가 형용사 역할을 할 때 수식받는 명사가 전치사의 목적어로 사용되었으면 전치사를 생략하면 안 된다. (4) to부정사가 -thing으로 끝나는 부정대명사를 형용사와 함께 수식할 때는 '대명사+형용사+to부정사'의 어순이다.

09 사역동사 make의 목적격보어로 동사원형이 적절하다.

10 (1) 사역동사의 목적격보어로 동사원형을 쓴다. (2) to부정사의 형용사적 용법을 이용한다. depend on의 on을 빠뜨리지 않도록 조심한다. (3) 컴퓨터가 검사를 받는 수동의 의미이므로 목적격보어로 과거분사를 써야 한다. (4) '가르칠 선생님'이므로 to teach가 a teacher를 수식하도록 한다. (5) help는 목적격보어로 동사원형이나 to부정사가 나온다. 단어 수에 맞춰 to부정사를 이용한다.

11 (1) get은 사역동사의 의미로 쓰일 수 있지만 목적격보어로 to부정사가 나와야 한다. (2) 자전거가 수리되는 것이므로 과거분사 repaired가 적절하다. mechanic: (기계) 수리공, 정비사

교과서
Reading

확인문제   p.80

1 T 2 F 3 F 4 T

확인문제   p.81

1 T 2 F 3 T 4 T 5 F

확인문제   p.81

1 T 2 F 3 F 4 T

01 Health Tips   02 spends, using

03 checks   04 plays, games   05 texts

06 finds information   07 online comic

books   08 watches   09 take, off

10 cause health problems   11 a heavy user

12 If so, to protect   13 Watch

14 usually bend   15 text neck pose

16 to prevent, up to   17 Another way,

instead of bending   18 a break

19 feel tired, for a long time   20 in the dark,

worse   21 To avoid, from time to time

22 Every, a 20-second break, feet away

23 blink, often   24 keep, from becoming

25 on your smartphone   26 Texting, hurt

27 Try   28 help reduce   29 Pull on

30 Put, together with your arms   31 remember

32 The best tip, to use, less

33 some rest from

1 Health Tips for Smartphone Users

2 Seongmin spends a lot of time using his smartphone.

3 He checks the news and weather.

4 He plays smartphone games.

5 He texts his friends.

6 He finds information on the Internet.

7 He reads online comic books.

8 He watches movies.

9 Seongmin cannot take his hands off his smartphone all day long.

10 He does not know that using a smartphone too much can cause health problems.

11 Are you a heavy user of your smartphone like Seongmin?

12 If so, here are some tips to protect your health.

13 Watch your neck and back.

14 When you read on your smartphone, you usually bend your neck.

15 This "text neck" pose increases the pressure on your neck and back.

16 The best way to prevent this pressure is to bring the phone up to the level of your eyes.

17 Another way is to lower your eyes instead of bending your neck.

18 Give your eyes a break.

19 It makes your eyes feel tired and dry to read small letters on a smartphone for a long time.

20 Using a smartphone in the dark or in a moving car makes this problem worse.

21 To avoid this, give your eyes a break from time to time.

22 Follow the 20-20-20 rules: Every 20 minutes, take a 20-second break and look at something at least 20 feet away

23 Also, blink your eyes often.

24 This will keep your eyes from becoming dry.

25 Do you text a lot on your smartphone?

26 Texting for a long time can hurt your fingers and wrists.

27 Try these exercises.

28 They will help reduce the pain in your fingers and wrists.

29 Pull on each finger of each hand.

30 Put the backs of your hands together with your arms out in front of you.

31 But remember.

32 The best tip to prevent these health problems is to use your smartphone less.

33 Give yourself some rest from your smartphone.

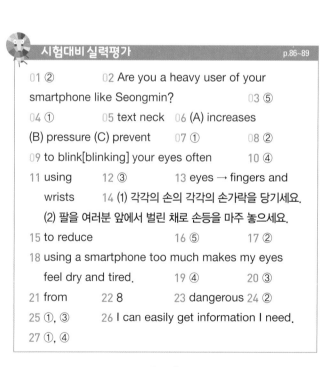

01 ②   02 Are you a heavy user of your smartphone like Seongmin?   03 ⑤

04 ①   05 text neck   06 (A) increases

(B) pressure (C) prevent   07 ①   08 ②

09 to blink[blinking] your eyes often   10 ④

11 using   12 ③   13 eyes → fingers and wrists   14 (1) 각각의 손의 각각의 손가락을 당기세요.

(2) 팔을 여러분 앞에서 벌린 채로 손등을 마주 놓으세요.

15 to reduce   16 ⑤   17 ②

18 using a smartphone too much makes my eyes feel dry and tired.   19 ④   20 ③

21 from   22 8   23 dangerous 24 ②

25 ①, ③   26 I can easily get information I need.

27 ①, ④

01 본문 끝에 여기 여러분의 '건강'을 지켜 줄 몇 가지 조언이 있습니다라는 말이 나오므로 빈칸에는 'health'가 적절하다. ④ posture: 자세, ⑤ grade: 성적

02 a heavy user: 과다 사용자

03 '여기 여러분의 건강을 지켜 줄 몇 가지 조언이 있다'는 말로 본문이 끝나므로, 뒤에는 '스마트폰 사용 시 여러분의 건강을 지켜 줄 몇 가지 조언'이 나온다고 하는 것이 적절하다.

04 read on your smartphone: 스마트폰을 보다, the pressure on: ~에 가해지는 압력

05 text neck: 거북목 증후군, 거북처럼 목이 앞으로 구부러진 자세, 손에 든 장치를 지나치게 보거나 문자를 보내는 것으로 인해서 목에 반복되는 스트레스, 부상 그리고 통증을 묘사하는 단어

06 (A) 압력을 '증가시킨다'고 해야 하므로 increases가 적절하다. decrease: 줄이다, 감소시키다, (B) '압력'을 증가시킨다고 해야 하므로 pressure가 적절하다. pressure: 압력, 압박, pleasure: 기쁨, 즐거움, (C) '예방'하는 가장 제일 좋은 방법이라고 해야 하므로 prevent가 적절하다. protect: 보호하다

07 ①번 다음 문장의 this problem이 주어진 문장의 내용을 받고 있으므로 ①번이 적절하다.

08 ② 드물게, ⓐ와 나머지는 다 '가끔'

09 '눈을 자주 깜빡이는 것'을 가리킨다.

10 many+복수명사, a lot of = lots of = plenty of: 수나 양이 많을 때 사용, ⑤ much = a great deal of: 양이 많을 때 사용

11 spend+시간+~ing: ~하는 데 시간을 보내다

12 스마트폰으로 친구들에게 '문자 메시지를 보낸다.'

13 오랫동안 문자 메시지를 보내는 것은 '손가락'과 '손목'을 상하게 할 수 있다. do harm to: ~에 해를 끼치다

14 본문의 마지막에 설명되어 있다.

15 help 다음에는 원형부정사와 to부정사 둘 다 올 수 있다.

16 위 글은 스마트폰 사용의 좋은 점들과 나쁜 점들에 관한 글이므로, 제목으로는 '스마트폰의 장점과 단점'이 적합하다.

17 앞에 나오는 내용과 상반되는 내용이 뒤에 이어지므로 ②번 On the other hand(한편, 반면)가 가장 적절하다. ① 게다가, ③ 그러므로, ④ 예를 들면, ⑤ 비슷하게

18 'using'을 보충하면 된다.

19 위 글은 스마트폰을 사용할 때의 눈 문제를 예방하는 법에 관한 글이다.

20 ⓐ와 ③ 가주어, ① 비인칭주어, ② 그것(앞에 이미 언급되었거나 현재 이야기되고 있는 사물·동물을 가리킴), ④ 사람의 신분을 나타낼 때 씀, ⑤ 가목적어

21 keep A from ~ing: ~가 …하는 것을 막다

22 1번 항목 2점 + 2번 항목 1점 + 3번 항목 1점 + 4번 항목 2점 + 5번 항목 2점 = 총 8점

23 7-10점이 'Danger!'인데, 글쓴이는 8점이므로 'dangerous'한 상황에 처해 있다고 할 수 있다.

24 차에서는 스마트폰을 '때때로' 사용한다.

25 ⓐ와 ②, ④, ⑤는 즉시, ① 잠시 동안, ③ 가끔

26 '내가 필요로 하는 정보를 쉽게 얻을 수 있다.'는 것을 가리킨다.

27 ②, ③은 언급되어 있지 않고, ⑤는 단점에 설명되어 있다.

서술형 시험대비 p.90~91

01 to use

02 If you are a heavy user of your smartphone like Seongmin

03 bend

04 "거북목 증후군" 자세 때문에 당신의 목과 척추에 증가된 압력

05 lift → lower

06 Give a break to your eyes

07 (A) tired (B) minutes (C) 20–second

08 20분마다 20초의 휴식을 취하고 적어도 20피트 이상 떨어져 있는 사물을 바라보는 것

09 wrist → finger

10 (A) backs (B) in front of

11 are → is

12 ⓐ pressure ⓑ up ⓒ bending

13 ⓐ eyes ⓑ break ⓒ blink

14 ⓐ fingers ⓑ wrists ⓒ with

01 주어 자리에 동명사와 to부정사를 쓸 수 있다.

02 '만약 여러분이 성민이와 같은 스마트폰 과다 사용자라면'이라는 뜻이다.

03 스마트폰을 볼 때, 여러분은 보통 목을 '구부린다.'

04 앞 문장의 내용을 가리킨다.

05 목을 구부리는 대신에 시선을 '낮추는' 것이라고 하는 것이 적절하다. lift: 들어 올리다

06 give는 'to'를 사용하여 3형식으로 고친다.

07 (A) 눈이 '피곤해진' 것이므로 tired가 적절하다. tiring: 피곤하게 만드는, (B) '20분마다'라고 해야 하므로 minutes가 적절하다. every+기수+복수명사: ~마다, (C) 'a'와 명사 'break' 사이에서 형용사 역할을 하고 있는데, 이런 경우에는 단수로 써야 하므로 20-second가 적절하다.

08 바로 뒤에 나오는 설명을 쓰면 된다.

09 '손목'이 아니라 '손가락'을 당기고 있다.

10 팔을 여러분 '앞에서' 벌린 채로 '손등'을 마주 놓으세요.

11 주어가 The best tip이므로 'is'로 고치는 것이 적절하다.

12 당신의 목을 구부린 것으로 인한 '압력'을 예방할 수 있는 제일 좋은 방법은 휴대 전화를 여러분의 눈높이까지 '올리고' 목을 '구부리는' 대신에 시선을 낮추는 것이다.

13 여러분의 '눈'이 피곤해지고 건조하게 느끼도록 만드는 것을 피하기 위해 20-20-20 규칙을 따르면서 눈을 때때로 '쉬게' 하고 눈을 자주 '깜빡여라.'

14 '손가락'과 '손목'의 통증을 줄이기 위해서 각 손의 각 손가락을 당기고 팔을 여러분 앞에서 벌린 채로 손등을 마주 놓으세요.

영역별 핵심문제 p.93~97

01 ③ 02 A) for (B) set 03 ①

04 ④ 05 keep 06 take 07 ①, ③

08 ②, ④, ⑤　　09 ②　　　10 ①　　　11 drop

12 ④　　　13 ⑤　　　14 (1) to sell (2) to see

15 ①　　　16 make, have, let 중의 하나를 쓰면 정답

17 (1) to write letters with　(2) to take pictures with

　　(3) to live in　　18 ④　　　19 ③

20 ②　　　21 ⑤　　　22 ④

23 (1) build, to produce　(2) turn down, to put

24 to talk about　　　25 ③

26 ⓑ와 같은 것: ②, ⑤　ⓒ와 같은 것: ①, ③, ④

27 Using a smartphone in the dark or in a moving car.

28 bending　　29 ④　　　30 ③

31 I can get in touch with my friends right away.

32 ②　　　33 (A) off (B) day (C) heavy　34 tips

---

01 ① dropped, drop: 떨어지다 ② reduce, reduce: 줄이다, 감소시키다 ③ cut, cut down on: ~을 줄이다 ④ pay, pay attention to: ~에 주의를 기울이다 ⑤ give, give back: 돌려주다

02 be late for: ~에 늦다 set an alarm: 자명종 시계를 맞추다

03 ① hall: 복도

04 대화에서는 text가 '(휴대 전화로) 문자를 보내다'의 의미로 쓰였다. ①가사/그 노래의 가사는 노래 부르기가 좋을 것이다. ② 본문, 글/이 책들은 삽화가 적고 글이 훨씬 많이 적혀 있다. ③ 문자/보낼 메시지 문자를 입력하세요. ④ (휴대 전화로) 문자를 보내다/내가 최종 득점을 네게 문자로 보내 줄게. ⑤ 문자/그녀는 어젯밤에 나한테 문자를 엄청 보냈어.

05 keep a diary: 일기를 쓰다 keep in mind: 명심하다

06 take: 가져가다 take a walk: 산책하다

07 reduce: 줄이다, 감소시키다 cut: 줄이다, 삭감하다 decrease: 감소하다

08 충고할 때 쓸 수 있는 표현은 'You'd better+동사원형', '(I think) You should 동사원형 ~.', 'Maybe you should 동사원형 ~.', 'Why don't you ~?' 등이 있다.

09 휴대 전화를 보라는 대답에 '네 휴대 전화 화면에 금이 갔어.'가 들어가는 것이 적절하다.

10 ① protect: 보호하다 ② prevent: 예방하다, 막다 ③ increase: 증가하다 ④ avoid: 피하다 ⑤ produce: 만들다, 생산하다

11 갑자기 땅이나 어떤 것에 떨어지다 / drop: 떨어지다

12 ④ 휴대 전화를 떨어뜨려서 휴대 전화 화면에 금이 갔다.

13 물놀이 활동에 대한 조언을 요청했는데 구명조끼를 입어서는 안 된다는 말은 어색하다.

14 (1) dresses와 (2) sights를 뒤에서 수식하는 형용사적 용법의 to부정사로 쓴다.

15 <보기>와 ①번은 형용사적 용법 ② 부사적 용법의 형용사 수식 ③ 보어로 쓰인 명사적 용법 ④ 부사적 용법의 '목적' ⑤ 부사적 용법의 '결과'

16 목적격보어로 동사원형이 나왔으므로 사역동사가 적절하다. 내용상 동사원형이 올 수 있는 help는 적절하지 않다.

17 to부정사의 형용사적 용법을 이용한다. 수식받는 명사가 전치사의 목적어로 사용되었으므로 전치사를 생략하면 안 된다.

18 ④번은 사역동사가 아니지만 나머지는 모두 사역동사로 쓰였다. ③ have[get]+목적어+과거분사: 목적어가 ~되도록 하다

19 사역동사의 목적격보어로 수동의 의미가 필요하므로 과거분사가 적절하다.

20 get은 사역동사의 의미로 쓰일 수 있지만 목적격보어로 to부정사가 나와야 한다.

21 ⑤ Linda doesn't have any patients to take care of.

22 ① My sister often helps me (to) do my homework. ② They had many options to choose about the experiment. ③ I'll have your health checked. ⑤ He spends a lot of time using his smartphone. option: 선택권, 옵션

23 사역동사의 목적격보어로 동사원형을 쓰고, to부정사의 형용사적 용법을 이용한다. put somebody to bed: 누군가를 재우다

24 to부정사의 형용사적 용법을 이용한다.

25 ⓐ와 ③ (작업 중의) 휴식 (시간), ① (법, 약속 등을) 어기다, ② ~에게 (안 좋은) 소식을 알리다, ④ 깨(트리)다, 부수다, ⑤ (파도가) 부서지다

26 ⓑ와 ②, ⑤는 동명사, ⓒ와 ①, ③, ④는 현재분사

27 눈이 더 피곤하고 더 건조하게 느끼도록 만드는 것(즉, 눈 문제를 악화시키는 것)은 '어두운 곳이나 움직이는 차에서 스마트폰을 사용하는 것'이다.

28 전치사 뒤에 '동명사'로 써야 한다.

29 ④ 이러한 압력을 예방하는 가장 좋은 방법은 휴대 전화를 여러분의 눈높이까지 올리는 것이다.

30 주어진 문장의 That에 주목한다. ③번 앞 문장의 내용을 받고 있으므로 ③번이 적절하다.

31 get in touch with: ~와 연락[접촉]하다, right away: 바로

32 ② 스마트폰을 사용하는 데에는 좋은 점들과 나쁜 점들이 둘 다 있기 때문에, 스마트폰을 '똑똑하게' 사용할 필요가 있다. ① 항상, ④ 즉시, ⑤ 되풀이하여

33 (A) 하루 종일 스마트폰에서 '손을 뗄 수가 없다.'고 해야 하므로 off가 적절하다. take one's hands off ~: ~에서 손 떼다, (B) all day long: 하루 종일, 온종일, (C) 스마트폰의 '과다' 사용자인가?라고 해야 하므로 heavy가 적절하다. proper: 적절한

34 tip: 조언, 유용한 충고, 동사 are에 맞춰 복수로 쓰는 것이 적절하다

단원별 예상문제　　　p.98~101

01 (1) depend on　(2) advice　　　02 ②

03 ④　　　04 (1) back, prevent him from playing

　　(2) should, watch out for　(3) I was late for

17

(4) instead of　　05 (C) → (B) → (A) → (D)

06 (B) → (D) → (C) → (A)　　07 ④　　08 ②, ⑤

09 ①　　　　10 I'm planning on doing it once a

month.　11 ①　　12 ④　　13 ②

14 (1) My dad didn't let me go camping.

(2) Emily had her new dress made last week.

(3) There's nothing wrong to correct in this report.

(4) I bought my parents a house to live in.

15 every → all 16 ④　　17 ②, ⑤　　18 ④

19 ③　　　　20 ⓐ minutes ⓑ break ⓒ away

21 ①, ④　　22 ①　　　　23 (A) a lot (B) less

(C) yourself　24 these exercises

01 보기의 단어는 동의어 관계이다. happen: 일어나다, 발생하다 occur: 발생하다 (1) rely on: ~에 의지[의존]하다 depend on: ~에 의존하다 (2) tip: 조언, 충고 advice: 조언, 충고

02 ① from, away from: ~에서 떨어져서 ② with, get in touch with: ~와 연락[접촉]하다 ③ for, be good for: ~에 좋다 ④ from, from time to time: 가끔, 이따금 ⑤ on, cut down on: ~을 줄이다

03 ④ break: 휴식

04 (1) back: 등 prevent 목적어 from Ving: 목적어가 ~하는 것을 막다 (2) watch out (for): (~에 대해서) 조심하다 (3) be late for: ~에 늦다 (4) instead of: ~ 대신에

05 (C) Jenny의 생일을 잊었다는 말에, (B) 상대방은 Jenny가 가장 친한 친구가 아니냐고 질문한다. (A) 맞다고 대답하고, 어떻게 해야 할지 충고를 부탁하는 말을 하자, (D) 정말 미안하다고 Jenny에게 말하라고 충고해준다.

06 (B) 기분이 우울하다는 말에, (D) 이유를 물어보니 (C) 겨울에 5킬로그램이 쪘다고 말한다. 어떻게 해야 하는지 질문을 하자, (A) 간식을 줄이라는 충고를 해준다.

07 ④ give back it → give it back 'give back'은 이어동사인데, '동사+부사'의 이어동사인 경우 목적어가 대명사이면 그 목적어를 반드시 동사와 부사 사이에 써야 한다.

08 ② 과학 수업을 얼마나 오래 하는지 나와 있지 않다. ⑤ 왜 남자아이가 과학책을 가져오지 않았는지는 언급되어 있지 않다.

09 티셔츠에 쓰여 있는 글을 설명하고 있다. 그러므로 티셔츠에 쓰여 있는 글의 내용을 묻는 질문 다음에 들어가야 적절하다.

10 be planning on ~ing: ~할 계획이다 once a month: 한 달에 한 번

11 24시간 동안 휴대 전화를 사용하지 않는 것을 생각해 보겠다고 했다.

12 ④ It's good for your eyes. → It's not good for your eyes.

13 ① The best way to prevent this pressure is to bring the phone up to the level of your eyes. ③ Some were really beautiful, but others made me feel scared. ④ I have

something important to tell you. ⑤ I'll get him to do the work.

14 (1) 사역동사의 목적격보어로 동사원형이 적절하다. (2) 사역동사의 목적격보어로 수동의 의미가 필요하므로 과거분사가 적절하다. (3) to부정사가 -thing, -body, -one으로 끝나는 부정대명사를 형용사와 함께 수식할 때는 '대명사+형용사+to부정사'의 어순이다. (4) to부정사가 형용사 역할을 할 때 수식받는 명사가 전치사의 목적어로 사용되었으면 전치사를 생략하면 안 된다.

15 all day long: 하루 종일

16 ⓐ와 ④ ~처럼, ①, ③, ⑤ 좋아하다, ② ~와 같은(such as)

17 ⓐ와 ②, ⑤는 형용사적 용법, ① 부사적 용법(원인), ③ 부사적 용법(결과), ④ 명사적 용법

18 목을 구부리는 '대신에'라고 해야 하므로 instead of가 적절하다. ① ~에도 불구하고, ② ~에 따르면, ③ ~ 때문에, ⑤ ~와 함께

19 ③ 위 글은 '스마트폰을 사용할 때 "거북목" 자세를 방지해야 한다'는 내용의 글이다.

20 20-20-20 규칙은 20'분'마다 20초의 '휴식'을 취하고 적어도 20피트 이상 '떨어져 있는' 사물을 바라보는 것이다. ⓑ rest도 break와 같은 뜻이지만, 일관성을 주기 위해 본문의 시작과 중간에서 사용한 break로 답하는 것이 적절하다.

21 keep[stop/prevent] … from ~ing: …이 ~하지 못하게 막다 [방해하다]

22 ① '머리'가 아니라 '눈'을 피곤해지고 건조하게 느끼도록 만든다.

23 (A) 문자 메시지를 '많이' 보내요?라고 해야 하므로 a lot이 적절하다. a lot of 뒤에는 명사가 나와야 한다. (B) 가장 좋은 방법은 스마트폰을 '덜' 사용하는 것이라고 해야 하므로 less가 적절하다. (C) 주어와 목적어가 같을 때는 재귀대명사를 써야 하므로 yourself가 적절하다.

24 '이런 운동들'을 가리킨다.

서술형 실전문제　　　　p.102~103

01 (1) You had better wash your hands first.

(2) Don't forget to wash your hands first.

(3) Remember to wash your hands first.

02 I think you should cut down on snacks.

03 ④What should I to do? → What should I do?

04 (1) Brian has a lot of homework to do today.

(2) Will you bring me a piece of paper to write names on?

(3) Is there anything valuable to keep separately?

(4) A delicious meal made his mouth water.

(5) They got him to sign a new contract.

05 (1) Julia made me do my homework.

(2) Her mom had Jenny prepare dinner.

(3) Sam helped me (to) repair my computer.

06 (A) neck   (B) back   07 up to

08 (1) 휴대 전화를 여러분의 눈높이까지 올리는 것.

   (2) 목을 구부리는 대신에 시선을 낮추는 것.

09 to feel → feel

10 (A) worse (B) Every (C) at least

11 This will keep your eyes from becoming dry.

01 당부할 때, Make sure ~. (꼭 ~하도록 해.), You had better ~. (~하는 것이 좋겠다.), Don't forget to ~. (~하는 것을 잊지 마.), Remember to ~.(~하는 것을 기억해라.)를 사용할 수 있다.

02 should+동사원형: ~해야 한다 cut down on: ~을 줄이다

03 should+동사원형: ~해야 한다

04 (1), (2), (3) 부정사의 형용사적 용법을 이용한다. 수식받는 명사가 전치사의 목적어로 사용되었으면 전치사를 생략하면 안 된다는 것과 -thing으로 끝나는 부정대명사를 형용사와 함께 수식할 때는 '대명사+형용사+to부정사'의 어순임에 유의한다. (4) made가 사역동사, water가 목적격 보어이다. (5) get은 사역동사의 의미로 쓰일 수 있지만 목적격보어로 to부정사가 나와야 한다.

05 사역동사의 목적격보어로 동사원형이 나오며 help는 목적격보어로 동사원형이나 to부정사가 나온다.

06 당신이 스마트폰을 볼 때 목을 구부리면, 이 자세 때문에 당신의 '목'과 '척추'에 압력이 증가한다.

07 압력을 예방하는 가장 좋은 방법은 휴대 전화를 여러분의 눈높이'까지' 올리는 것이다.

08 두 가지 방법은 다 목을 구부리지 않고 스마트폰을 볼 수 있는 방법이다.

09 사역동사 make+목적어+원형부정사

10 (A) 문제를 '악화'시킬 수 있다고 해야 하므로 worse가 적절하다. (B) 20분'마다'라고 해야 하므로 Every가 적절하다. every+기수+복수명사: ~마다, (C) '적어도' 20피트 이상 떨어져 있는 사물이라고 해야 하므로 at least가 적절하다. at least: 적어도, at last: 마침내

11 keep … from ~ing: …이 ~ 하는 것을 막다[방해하다]

|모범답안|

01 I think you should exercise every day. / You should eat more vegetables. / I think you should cut down on the fat in your diet.

02 (1) Mom made me prepare dinner.

   (2) Mom had me clean the room.

   (3) Mom let me go to the movies.

   (4) Mom let me play soccer.

03 (A) right away

   (B) information

   (C) dry and tired

(D) keep

(E) intelligently

01 should+동사원형: ~해야 한다 exercise: 운동하다
vegetables: 야채 cut down on: ~을 줄이다

01 ③   02 ④   03 ①   04 away

05 may I sleep over at Jinsu's house?

06 make / Make   07 Make sure you are
home by 12:00.   08 protect

09 get   10 ④   11 (A) for (B) depend on
(C) without   12 often

13 Make sure you keep up with it.   14 ④

15 ①

16 (1) It makes your eyes feel tired and dry to read small letters.

   (2) They had a big factory built at the top of the hill.

   (3) There was somebody important to meet there.

   (4) Olivia has few friends to play with.

   (5) Mike had his computer stolen.   17 ②

18 ⓐ off ⓑ of   19 If so

20 (A) eyes (B) neck   21 ②   22 ①

23 ④   24 ④ by → with   25 ③

01 turn off: ~을 끄다

02 pay attention to: ~에 주의를 기울이다

03 ride on: ~을 타다

04 away from: ~에서 떨어져서/나는 역에서 멀리 떨어진 곳에 산다. right away: 당장/나는 당장 그에게 전화할 것이다.

05 sleep over at: (남의 집에서) 자다

06 make: 만들다 make sure: 반드시 ~하도록 하다, ~을 확실히 하다

07 make sure: 반드시 ~하도록 하다, ~을 확실히 하다 by+시간: ~까지는

08 누군가 또는 무엇인가를 해, 손상, 질병으로부터 안전하게 유지하다/protect: 보호하다

09 get: 구하다, 사다

10 'Try it first.'는 '시험 삼아 먼저 해봐.'라는 의미로, 한 번 해보고, 얼마나 자주 할지는 그 이후에 결정하라는 말이 어울리므로 ④가 적절하다.

11 for+숫자+시간 단위: ~ 동안 during+기간 명사: ~ 동안 depend on: ~에 의존하다

12 how often: 얼마나 자주

13 make sure ~: 반드시 ~하도록 하다, ~을 확실히 하다 keep up with: ~을 따르다, ~에 뒤지지 않다

14 to부정사가 형용사 역할을 할 때 수식받는 명사가 전치사의 목적어로 사용되었으면 전치사를 생략하면 안 된다.

15 사역동사의 목적격보어로 동사원형이 적절하다.

16 (1) 사역동사의 목적격보어로 동사원형이 적절하다. (2) 공장이 세워지는 수동의 의미이므로 목적격보어로 과거분사가 적절하다. (3) to부정사가 -body로 끝나는 부정대명사를 형용사와 함께 수식할 때는 '대명사+형용사+to부정사'의 어순이다. (4) to부정사가 형용사 역할을 할 때 수식받는 명사가 전치사의 목적어로 사용되었으면 전치사를 생략하면 안 된다. (5) 컴퓨터가 훔치는 것이 아니라 도난당한 것으로 수동의 의미이므로 목적격보어로 과거분사가 적절하다.

17 ② There is a small pool to swim in. to부정사가 형용사 역할을 할 때 수식받는 명사가 전치사의 목적어로 사용되었으면 전치사를 생략하면 안 된다.

18 ⓐ 하루 종일 스마트폰에서 '손을 뗄 수가 없다.'고 해야 하므로 off가 적절하다. take one's hands off ~: ~에서 손 떼다, ⓑ of: (목적격 관계) ~을, ~의

19 '만약 여러분이 성민이와 같은 스마트폰 과다 사용자라면'이라는 뜻이다.

20 또 다른 방법은 '목'을 구부리는 대신에 '시선'을 낮추는 것이다.

21 ⓐ와 ①, ⑤는 명사적 용법, ② 형용사적 용법, ③ 부사적 용법(목적), ④ 부사적 용법(형용사 수식)

22 이 글은 '여러분의 눈에 휴식을 주라'는 내용의 글이므로, 제목으로는 '여러분의 눈을 쉬게 하는 게 어때?'가 적절하다.

23 ④번은 3형식 문장이고, ⓐ와 나머지는 다 5형식 문장이다.

24 with + 목적어 + 목적격보어: ~을 …한 채로

25 ③ '손바닥'이 아니라 '손등'을 마주 놓아야 한다.

The School Club Activity Day

시험대비 실력평가 p.112

01 ① 02 ① 03 ① 04 ①
05 (n)eighbor 06 leader 07 ⑤ 08 ④
09 who, can join

01 둘은 반의어 관계이다. increase: 증가하다 decrease: 감소하다 difficult: 어려운 easy: 쉬운

02 bake: (빵 등을) 굽다 oven: 오븐 / 나는 오븐에 빵을 굽고 있다.

03 grow: (동식물을) 기르다 vegetables: 채소 / 그들은 채소를 재배하는 데 있어 유기농 방식을 사용한다.

04 opportunity: 기회 chance: 가능성, 기회 / 그것은 부유한 사람들이 어떻게 사는지 보여주는 귀중한 기회였다.

05 neighbor: 이웃 / 당신의 옆이나 근처에 사는 어떤 사람

06 leader: 지도자, 대표 / 그녀는 유럽에서 가장 강력한 국가의 지도자이다.

07 hold: (모임·식 등을) 개최하다

08 ① 십대들에게 가장 인기 있는 여가 시간 활동이 무엇입니까? ② 나는 정말 너의 요리가 그립다. ③ 그녀는 밝은 색들을 좋아하지 않는다. ④ note: 음, 음표 / 그는 단 하나의 음표도 읽지 못하지만, 피아노를 완벽하게 연주한다. ⑤ 한국은 이미 몇 개의 메달을 획득했다.

09 join: 참여하다, 가입하다

서술형 시험대비 p.113

01 (1) (g)et (2) (p)resent
02 have / Have
03 How / how
04 (1) introduce (2) dolphins (3) doughnut (4) concert
05 (1) activity (2) neighborhood
06 (1) (c)lothes (2) introduce (3) interest (4) vegetables
07 If I join this club, I will practice very hard.

01 주어진 보기는 동의어 관계이다. happy: 행복한 pleased: 기쁜 (1) gain: 얻다, 입수하다 get: 얻다, 획득하다, 사다 (2) gift: 선물 present: 선물

02 have: 가지다 / 가지면 가질수록 더 갖고 싶다. have a great

time: 좋은 시간을 보내다 / 새 학기가 시작하기 전에 즐거운 시간을 보내라!

03 how: 어떻게 / 어떻게 제가 이 동아리에 가입할 수 있나요? how to+동사원형: ~하는 방법 / 나는 그것을 하는 방법을 배우고 싶다.

04 (1) introduce: 소개하다 (2) dolphin: 돌고래 (3) doughnut: 도넛 (4) concert: 연주회

05 (1) activity: 활동 / 어떤 종류의 동아리 활동을 좋아하세요? (2) neighborhood: 동네, (도시 내의 한 단위) 지역 / 이 근처 지역은 쇼핑하기에 아주 좋다.

06 (1) clothes: 옷, 의상 (2) introduce: 소개하다 (3) interest: 관심 (4) vegetables: 채소

07 join: 참여하다, 가입하다 club: 동아리 practice: 연습하다

교과서
Conversation

핵심 Check
p.114~115

1 how to use
2 I want to learn how to take good pictures.
3 What do you, doing, free time / I enjoy listening to music
4 I enjoy riding a bike

교과서 대화문 익히기

Check(√) True or False
p.116

(1) T (2) T (3) T (4) F (5) T (6) F

교과서 확인학습
p.118~119

Listen & Speak 1 A
know how to

Listen & Speak 1 B
1 heard you went to. How / I hope I can play / knew how to play the violin / good at
2 at, grew, myself, own / how to cook / taught

Listen & Speak 2 A
looking at, at night

Listen & Speak 2 B
1 Do you enjoy / love reading, about / reading / go,

the library
2 What did you do / made / Do you enjoy cooking / cook, cooking
3 Where, get / made it for me / designer / enjoys making clothes

Real-Life Zone A
the leader, interest / When did you start playing / how to play the violin when / experience playing / an orchestra when, elementary / volunteer to teach / Do you enjoy teaching / experience, enjoy working with / have

Wrap Up
look, delicious / made them myself, baking, going to / want to learn how to make / at / time / Sounds, See

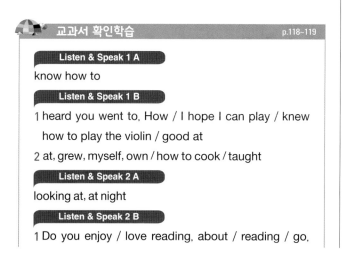
시험대비 기본평가
p.120

01 ④   02 ①   03 ④   04 ①

01 여가 시간에 무엇을 즐기는지 묻고 대답하고 있다. 'I enjoy 동명사 ~.'를 사용해서 자신이 좋아하는 것을 표현할 수 있다.
02 종이 고양이를 만들 수 있는지 여부를 묻고 대답하고 있다. how to+동사원형: ~하는 방법, 어떻게 ~하는지
03 'Do you know how to+동사원형~?'을 이용해 상대방의 능력이나 무언가를 하는 방법에 대해 물을 수 있다.
04 할머니에게서 배웠다는 내용이 나왔으므로, 여자아이는 요리를 하는 방법을 알고 있다.

시험대비 실력평가
p.121~122

01 ①   02 ③   03 ②   04 ①
05 ⑤   06 (A) looking (B) doing[to do]
07 ①   08 ⑤   09 ②   10 ③
11 (A) in a group (B) no experience
12 I started learning how to play the violin when I was ten.   13 ②

01 'How was it?'은 과거의 경험에 대한 느낌을 묻는 표현으로, 여기서는 유나의 바이올린 콘서트에 대한 느낌을 묻고 있고, 이에 대한 대답 'It was great.'으로 이어진다.
02 대화에서 (A)와 ③은 '~처럼'의 의미로 사용되었다. 이외의 보기는 '좋아하다'의 의미이다.
03 ② 남자아이는 자신이 바이올린을 잘 연주하지 못한다고 생각한다.
04 Do you know how to ~?: 어떻게 ~하는지 하니? how to+

동사원형: ~하는 방법, 어떻게 ~하는지. 스페인어를 하는 방법을 모른다는 말에, 상대방이 'Yes'라고 하고, 가르쳐 줄 수 있다고 말하므로, 상대방에게 스페인어를 말하는 법을 아느냐고 질문하는 것이 적절하다.

05 ⑤ Of course I am. → Of course I do.

06 enjoy는 동명사를 목적어로 취할 수 있고, love는 동명사와 to 부정사를 둘 다 목적어로 취할 수 있다.

07 get: ~을 사다, ~을 얻다. 주어진 말의 it이 a pretty backpack을 가리키므로 ①이 적절하다.

08 문장의 끝에 오는 too는 '또한'의 의미로, 내용상 그녀는 훌륭한 디자이너이고, 또한 옷 만드는 것을 즐긴다는 말이 나와야 하므로, 'Yes, she is (a really good designer).'의 의미를 가진 ⑤가 적절하다.

09 ② 지윤이 가방을 만드는 방법을 안다는 내용은 언급되지 않았다.

10 주어진 문장의 We는 나눔 오케스트라를 의미하며, 자원봉사로 아이들을 가르친다는 내용이 나온 후, 다른 사람들을 가르치는 것을 즐기는지 묻는 것이 어울린다.

11 (A)가 있는 질문의 대답이 오케스트라의 멤버였다고 말하고 있으므로, 그룹으로 연주한 경험이 있느냐고 질문해야 한다. (B)가 있는 문장 다음에 But이라는 접속사가 있으므로 뒤의 내용과 반대 또는 대조되는 내용이 나와야 어울린다.

12 start+동명사 또는 to부정사: ~하는 것을 시작하다 how to+동사원형: ~하는 방법, 어떻게 ~하는지

13 케이트는 지금이 아니라 초등학교 때 오케스트라의 구성원이었다.

서술형 시험대비   p.123

01 (C) → (A) → (B)

02 (A) → (C) → (B)

03 at

04 me → myself

05 Do you know how to cook the vegetables (that) you grow

06 enjoyed do → enjoy doing

07 I didn't know you knew how to play the violin.

08 I'm not good at it yet

---

01 요리하기를 즐기는지 묻는 질문에 (C) 가끔 요리하기를 즐기고, 피자 만드는 법을 알고 있다고 대답한다. (A) 이에 상대방이 요리 동아리에 가입하는 것을 권유하자 (B) 생각해 보겠다고 대답한다.

02 드론을 샀는지 질문하자 (A) 사지는 않았고, 선물로 받았다고 대답하면서 드론을 사용하는 방법을 모른다고 얘기하며 상대방이 방법을 아는지 질문하자 (C) 모르지만 지나가 알 것이라고 대답한다. (B) 그러면, 지나에게 물어보겠다고 말한다.

03 look at: ~을 보다

04 grow의 목적어로 these vegetables가 왔으므로 목적어의 자리

에 들어갈 수 있는 me는 어울리지 않는다. 여기서는 내가 했다는 것을 강조하는 재귀대명사가 어울린다.

05 how to+동사원형: ~하는 방법, 어떻게 ~하는지 cook: 요리하다 grow: 기르다

06 'Do you ~?'로 질문하고 있으므로 현재형의 동사를 사용해야 한다. 또한, enjoy는 동명사를 목적어로 취한다.

07 know 다음에 접속사 that이 생략되었다. play the 악기 이름: ~을 연주하다

08 be good at: ~을 잘하다

교과서

Grammar

핵심 Check   p.124~125

1 (1) what to / what I should
  (2) where to meet / where I should meet

2 (1) who[that] (2) which[that]

시험대비 기본평가   p.126

01 (1) eating → to eat   (2) go → to go
  (3) which → who[that]   (4) who → which[that]

02 ③, ④

03 (1) She didn't ask me what to do.
  (2) Mariel didn't know where to go.
  (3) Degas liked to paint dancers who were dancing.
  (4) He has the dog that barked at the girl yesterday.

---

01 (1), (2) '의문사+to부정사'가 문장 속에서 decide와 know의 목적어 역할을 하고 있다. (3) a man이 선행사이므로 which가 아니라 who나 that이 적절하다. (4) the movie가 선행사이므로 who가 아니라 which나 that이 적절하다.

02 ③ some pictures가 선행사이므로 who가 아니라 which나 that이 적절하다. ④ 'how to do'가 show의 목적어로 쓰여야 한다.

03 주격 관계대명사는 선행사가 사람이면 who나 that을 쓰고 사물이나 동물이면 which나 that을 쓴다.

시험대비 실력평가   p.127~129

01 ①   02 ②   03 ③   04 who →
which 또는 that   05 ⑤   06 ④
07 ⑤   08 (1) which (2) that (3) that (4) were

---

(5) who　　(6) who　　(7) which was

09 I can't decide what to wear. / I can't decide what I
　should wear.

10 (1) ③, who[that]　(2) ③, which[that]

11 (1) how　　(2) to spend　　(3) what　　(4) I should

(5) how to read　　　　12 ②　　　　13 ①, ⑤

14 ①　　　　　　15 (1) how they should[can] do

(2) where I should put　　(3) what I should do

16 ⑤　　　　17 ③　　　　18 ④

19 (1) where to buy　　(2) which[that] have

---

01 do it이 나와 있으므로 목적어로 쓰일 수 있는 것은 적절하지 않
　으며 'why+to부정사'는 쓰지 않는다.

02 사람을 선행사로 하는 주격 관계대명사로는 that이나 who를 쓴
　다.

03 첫 문장에서는 the problem이 solve의 목적어이므로 what
　이나 that은 적절하지 않다. 두 번째 문장에서는 the message
　from Kate가 선행사이므로 which나 that이 적절하다.

04 a party가 선행사이므로 who가 아니라 which나 that이 적절
　하다.

05 목적어 it이 있으므로 what이 아니라 how나 where 등이 나와
　야 한다.

06 주격 관계대명사는 선행사가 사람이면 who나 that을 쓰고 사물
　이나 동물이면 which나 that을 쓴다.

07 ① They went to the restaurant which[that] was
　famous for its traditional Korean food. ② I know
　a girl whose name is Karen. ③ Please let me know
　which way I should go. which가 way를 수식하도록 해
　야 한다. ④ Tom has a painting which was drawn by a
　famous artist.

08 (1) 선행사가 사물이므로 which가 적절하다. (2) 선행사가 '사
　람+동물[사물]'인 경우에는 반드시 관계대명사 that을 써야 한
　다. (3) 선행사가 사물이므로 that이 적절하다. (4) 주격 관계
　대명사의 선행사가 복수이므로 복수 동사가 적절하다. (5) a
　great novelist가 선행사로 사람이므로 who가 적절하다. (6)
　who를 목적격 whom 대신 쓸 수 있지만 whom을 who 대신
　쓰지는 않는다. (7) 주격 관계대명사는 생략할 수 없으나 뒤에
　분사나 부사구가 오는 경우 '주격 관계대명사+be동사'를 생략할
　수 있으므로 which was를 쓰거나 which was를 생략한 형태
　로 써야 한다.

09 의문사+to부정사 = 의문사+주어+should+동사원형, what to
　wear: 무엇을 입을지

10 주격 관계대명사는 다음에 동사가 나오며 선행사가 사람이면
　who나 that을, 사물이나 동물이면 which나 that을 쓴다.

11 (1) the machine이 목적어로 나와 있으므로 how가 적절하다.
　(2) '의문사+to부정사'가 적절하다. (3) why는 '의문사+to부
　정사'로 쓰이지 않는다. (4), (5) '의문사+to부정사'나 '의문사+

주어+should+동사원형'이 적절하다.

12 주어진 문장과 ②번은 주격 관계대명사로 그 쓰임이 같다. ④번
　은 목적격 관계대명사이다.

13 go는 자동사로 목적어가 필요 없으므로 what은 적절하지 않고
　'why+to부정사'는 쓰지 않는다.

14 주어진 문장과 ①번의 that은 주격 관계대명사이다. ② 접속사
　③ 지시대명사 ④ 지시형용사 ⑤ 지시부사

15 '의문사+to부정사'는 '의문사+주어+should/can+동사원형'으
　로 바꾸어 쓸 수 있다.

16 선행사가 사람이나 사물 또는 동물일 경우 모두 쓰일 수 있는 것
　은 that이다.

17 how to use: 어떻게 ~할지

18 an animal이 선행사이므로 which나 that을 써야 한다. ⑤번
　에서는 주격 관계대명사 that을 썼으므로 관계사절에서 주어로
　쓰인 it을 삭제해야 한다.

19 (1) where to buy: 어디에서 살지 (2) 선행사가 사물이므로
　which나 that을 쓴다.

서술형 시험대비　　　　　　　　p.130~131

01 which → who[that], taught → (to) teach, using →
　to use

02 (1) who → which[that]

(2) is running → (which[that] is) running

(3) whom → who

(4) is → are

(5) who she teaches → who teaches

03 (1) how you should swim

(2) Which movie we should watch

(3) whom I should thank

04 (1) Here are two club leaders who[that] want
　students to join their clubs.

(2) This is the tea which[that] is good for your
　health.

(3) The movie which[that] was directed by James
　Cameron was interesting.

(4) There are a boy and his dog that are running
　at the playground.

(5) Do you know the girl (who is) dancing on the
　stage?

05 (1) You need to know how to play an instrument to
　join our club.

(2) The old man didn't know how to use the
　smartphone.

(3) When I should visit London has to be decided.

(4) I don't know why I should go there.

06 (1) who is

23

(2) which were

07 (1) We must learn how to speak English.

(2) I don't know what to say to her.

(3) Tell me where to park the car. 등 어법에 맞게

쓰면 정답

08 who[that] is reading a book

09 how to play

10 (1) Can you tell me how I can write an email in
English?

(2) I do not know what to do first.

(3) Do you know that man who[that] is running
along the river?

01 선행사가 people이므로 who나 that이 되어야 하며 helped
의 목적격보어로 to부정사나 동사원형이 나와야 하고, '의문사
(how)+to부정사'가 문장 속에서 teach의 직접목적어 역할을
하도록 하는 것이 적절하다.

02 (1) 선행사가 사물이므로 which나 that이 적절하다. (2) 주격
관계대명사는 생략할 수 없으나 뒤에 분사나 부사구가 오는 경
우 '주격 관계대명사+be동사'를 생략할 수 있다. (3) 주격 관계
대명사가 나와야 하므로 who나 that이 적절하다 who를 목적
격 whom 대신 쓸 수 있지만 whom을 who 대신 쓰지는 않는
다. (4) 주격 관계대명사절의 동사는 선행사의 수에 일치시킨다.
(5) 관계대명사가 접속사와 대명사의 역할을 하므로 주어로 쓰인
she를 삭제해야 한다.

03 '의문사+to부정사'는 '의문사+주어+should/can+동사원형'으로
바꾸어 쓸 수 있다. 또한 의문사가 의문형용사로 쓰여 to부정사와
의 사이에 명사가 올 수 있다.

04 선행사가 사람이면 who나 that을, 사물이나 동물이면 which
나 that을, '사람+동물[사물]'이면 반드시 that을 쓴다. 주격 관
계대명사는 생략할 수 없으나 뒤에 분사나 부사구가 오는 경우
'주격 관계대명사+be동사'를 생략할 수 있다.

05 (1) '의문사+to부정사'가 적절하다. (2) the smartphone이
목적어로 나와 있으므로 how가 적절하다. (3) '의문사+주어
+should+동사원형'이 적절하다. (4) 'why+to부정사'는 쓰지
않는다.

06 주격 관계대명사는 생략할 수 없으나 뒤에 분사나 부사구가 오는
경우 '주격 관계대명사+be동사'를 생략할 수 있다.

07 '의문사+to부정사'는 문장 속에서 주어, 목적어, 보어 역할을 하
는 명사구로 사용되어 '~해야 할지, ~하는 것이 좋을지'라는 뜻
을 나타낸다.

08 the girl이 선행사이므로 who나 that을 이용한다.

09 피아노를 잘 친다는 대답으로 보아 'how to play the piano(피
아노 치는 법)'가 적절하다.

10 (1) how+to부정사: 어떻게 ~할지 (2) what + to부정사: 무
엇을 ~할지 (3) 주격 관계대명사는 선행사가 사람이면 who나
that을 쓴다.

Reading

확인문제   p.132

1 T   2 F   3 F   4 T   5 F   6 T

확인문제   p.133

1 T   2 F   3 T   4 T   5 T   6 F

교과서 확인학습 A   p.134~135

01 Why Don't You
in, to enjoy   03 How about
join   05 what
07 from   08 As, guess from
09 do volunteer work
11 On the dirty old walls, flying, jumping
12 As a result, into
thanked   14 don't have to
16 Come and be   17 Orchestra
19 playing music, came to school
21 play music for   22 how to play, a little bit
23 don't worry   24 practice hard, get better
25 also teach, as a service to
26 an eleven-year-old boy
27 At first, read a note
28 a simple song
29 Hearing him play, makes
30 By joining, have an opportunity
31 Come and join
32 for

02 Participating
04 who want, to
06 Art Club

10 participated in

13 to see,
15 Anyone who
18 the leader
20 those

교과서 확인학습 B   p.136~137

1 Why Don't You Join Our Club?

2 Participating in club activities is a great way to
enjoy your school life.

3 How about joining a club?

4 Here are two club leaders who want students to
join their clubs.

5 Let's listen to what they say.

6 The Picasso Art Club

7 Hi! I am Sora Kang from the Picasso Art Club.

8 As you can guess from the name of our club, we
paint.

9 We also do volunteer work from time to time.

10 Last summer, our club members participated in the "Change Our Neighborhood" project.

11 On the dirty old walls of the buildings in our neighborhood, we painted birds flying high in the sky and dolphins jumping over blue waves.

12 As a result, the old neighborhood changed into a bright and beautiful place.

13 The neighbors were happy to see our work and thanked us.

14 You don't have to be a good painter.

15 Anyone who likes to paint can join.

16 Come and be a member of the Picasso Art Club.

17 The Boram Orchestra

18 Hi! I am Minsu Jang, the leader of the Boram Orchestra.

19 Did you see several students playing music at the main gate when you came to school today?

20 We were those students.

21 We play music for our friends every morning.

22 You need to know how to play an instrument a little bit to join our club.

23 But don't worry if you don't play well.

24 We will practice hard and get better together.

25 We also teach children how to play musical instruments as a service to our community.

26 I am teaching an eleven-year-old boy to play the violin.

27 At first, he did not know how to read a note.

28 Now he can play a simple song.

29 Hearing him play the violin makes me very happy.

30 By joining our club, you can have an opportunity to help others.

31 Come and join our club.

32 We are waiting for you.

시험대비 실력평가
p.138~141

01 (A) is (B) want (C) to join 02 ①, ③ 03 two club leaders 04 ③ 05 ④
06 ⑤ 07 to play → playing 또는 play
08 ③ 09 준호 10 ②
11 잘하는 것: 공을 패스하는 것과 빨리 달리기
못하는 것: 공을 헤딩하는 것
12 will join → join 13 ②, ④

14 participating in 15 who 또는 that
16 ① 17 ④ 18 ③
19 how to play 또는 to play 20 ②
21 (1) 매일 아침 친구들을 위해 음악을 연주한다. (2) 지역 사회를 위해 아이들에게 악기를 연주하는 법을 가르친다.
22 ① joining → to join 23 ④ 24 ⓐ 득점, ⓑ 목표 25 ③ 26 They will introduce and sell books to people. 27 ③

01 (A) 동명사 'Participating'이 주어이므로 is가 적절하다. (B) 선행사가 'two club leaders'이므로 want가 적절하다. (C) want+목적어+to부정사이므로 to join이 적절하다.

02 How about ~ing? = What about ~ing? = Why don't you 동사원형?: ~하는 게 어때?

03 '두 명의 동아리 대표'를 가리킨다.

04 주어진 문장의 As a result에 주목한다. ③번 앞 문장의 결과를 가리키므로 ③번이 적절하다.

05 ⓐ와 ④번은 ~하다시피[~이듯이], ① 이유, ② (비례) ~함에 따라, ③ (자격 기능 등이) ~로(서), ⑤ (때) ~하고 있을 때, ~하면서

06 ⑤그림 그리는 것을 좋아하는 사람은 누구라도 피카소 미술 동아리의 회원이 될 수 있다.

07 지각동사 see의 목적격보어 자리에 to부정사를 쓸 수 없다.

08 동아리에 가입하려면 악기를 연주하는 '법'을 조금 알아야 한다고 하는 것이 적절하다.

09 보람 오케스트라 동아리에 가입하려면 악기를 연주하는 법을 조금 알아야 한다고 했기 때문에, '능숙한 피아니스트는 아니지만 열심히 피아노를 연습하는 준호'가 가입할 수 있다.

10 앞에 나오는 내용과 상반되는 내용이 뒤에 이어지므로 However가 가장 적절하다. ① 게다가, 더욱이, ③ 그러므로, ④ 비슷하게, ⑤ 예를 들어

11 '공을 패스하는 것'을 잘하고 '빨리 달린다.' 그러나, 나는 '공을 헤딩하는 법'을 모른다고 했다.

12 조건의 부사절에서는 현재시제가 미래시제를 대신한다.

13 ⓐ와 ①, ③, ⑤는 형용사적 용법, ② 부사적 용법, ④ 명사적 용법

14 participating만 쓰면 틀림. join = participate in: ~에 참석하다

15 선행사가 사람(two club leaders)이고 주어 자리이므로 주격 관계대명사 who 또는 that이 적절하다.

16 ⓐ from: (판단의 근거) ~로 (보아), ⓒ into: 상태의 변화를 나타냄

17 ④ 이웃 마을에 있는 건물들의 더럽고 오래된 벽에 그림을 그린 '결과', 오래된 마을이 밝고 아름다운 곳으로 바뀌었다고 하는 것이 적절하다. ② 게다가, ⑤ 즉, 다시 말해

18 ⓓ와 ②, ④, ⑤번은 부사적 용법, ① 명사적 용법, ③ 형용사적 용법

19 'teach+목적어+to부정사' 또는 'teach+목적어+의문사+to부정사'

20 ⓑ와 ②번은 음, 음표, strike a note on a piano: 피아노로 어

25

떤 음을 치다, ① (기억을 돕기 위한) 메모, 기록 ③ (격식을 차리지 않은 짧은) 편지, 쪽지, ④ 공책, ⑤ 주의하다, 유념하다, 주목하다

21 (1) 매일 아침 친구들을 위해 음악을 연주한다고 했다. (2) 민수가 열한 살 소년에게 바이올린을 가르치고 있는 것처럼, 지역 사회를 위해 아이들에게 악기를 연주하는 법을 가르친다

22 would like to부정사: ~하고 싶다

23 ④ 박 순호는 공을 헤딩하는 법을 모른다.

24 ⓐ make a goal: 득점하다, ⓑ goal(=aim, end, purpose): 목표

25 hold: 개최하다

26 사람들에게 책을 소개하고 팔 것이다.

27 ③ 전시회의 규모는 알 수 없다. ① 도서 전시회, ② 나눔중학교, ④ 5월 5일 ⑤ 책을 사랑하는 사람

서술형 시험대비 p.142~143

01 (A) volunteer work　(B) painting　(C) painting
02 ⓐ flying　ⓑ jumping
03 need not 또는 don't need to
04 (A) a little　(B) eleven-year-old　(C) happy
05 unless
06 We also teach children how to play musical instruments as a service to our community.
07 It changed into a bright and beautiful place.
08 must not → don't have to 또는 need not
09 Anyone who likes to paint can join.
10 악기를 연주하는 법을 조금 알아야 한다.
11 (A) worry　(B) get better
12 make → makes

01 피카소 미술 동아리는 미술 동아리이고 가끔 '자원봉사'도 한다. '그림 그리는 것'을 좋아하는 사람은 누구나 동아리에 가입할 수 있고 '그림을 잘 그릴' 필요는 없다.

02 각각 뒤에서 앞의 명사를 수식하는 현재분사로 고치는 것이 적절하다.

03 don't have to = need not = don't need to: ~할 필요가 없다

04 (A) a little: '양'이나 '정도'가 조금, a few: '수'가 조금, a bit: '정도'가 조금, (B) eleven-year-old가 boy를 수식하는 형용사 역할을 하기 때문에 year에 s를 붙이지 않는 것이 적절하다. (C) 목적격보어이므로 부사를 쓸 수 없고 형용사를 써야 한다.

05 if ~ not = unless

06 'as'를 보충하면 된다.

07 밝고 아름다운 곳으로 변했다.

08 여러분은 그림을 잘 그릴 '필요는 없다'고 해야 하므로 don't have to나 need not으로 고치는 것이 적절하다. must not은 '금지'를 나타낸다.

09 anyone who: ~인 사람은 누구나

10 우리 동아리에 가입하기 위해서는 '악기 연주하는 법을 조금 알

11 민수는 학생들에게 연주를 잘 못해도 그들이 열심히 연습하고 함께 '좋아질 것'이기 때문에 '걱정하지' 말라고 말한다.

12 동명사 Hearing이 주어이므로 단수 취급하여 makes로 고치는 것이 적절하다.

영역별 핵심문제 p.145~149

01 ②　02 ③　03 ④
04 for　05 (1) (A)ctually (2) Where, to cook
(3) (o)pportunity　06 ②　07 ①
08 ⑤　09 ⓐ cooking ⓑ cook ⓒ cooking
10 ⑤　11 ①　12 ③　13 looking
14 looking at the stars　15 ①, ⑤
16 where to put　17 ②　18 (1) I can get　(2) to take　(3) to look　(4) which, to wear
19 (1) who　(2) which　20 ⑤
21 (1) We are looking for volunteers.
　(2) They are good at English.
　(3) The friend lives in New Zealand.
　(4) Chuck gave the present to her on her birthday.
22 ④
23 (1) She wants to see a movie which is interesting.
　(2) Rose who works for a bank is Jake's best friend.
　(3) James bought a new computer which is really nice.
24 several students playing music at the main gate when you came to school today　25 ①, ④
26 ①　27 ②, ⑤　28 (A) Last summer
(B) high　(C) thanked　29 ③
30 sick children　31 magic　32 ②
33 ⑤

01 ②번은 반의어 관계이고 나머지는 동의어 관계이다. ① gift: 선물 present: 선물 ② dark: 어두운 bright: 밝은 ③ activity: 활동 action: 행동, 활동, 실행 ④ actually: 실제로, 사실은 really: 정말로, 실제로 ⑤ enter: ~에 들어가다 join: 참여하다, 가입하다

02 be good at: ~을 잘하다 look for: ~을 찾다 participate in: ~에 참여하다

03 그 사람들 결혼 선물로 뭘 사줘야 할까요? get: ~을 사다, ~을 획득하다

04 ask for help: 도움을 청하다 thank for: ~에 대해 감사하다

05 (1) actually: 실제로, 사실은 (2) cook: 요리하다 (3) opportunity: 기회

06 enjoy는 동명사를 목적어로 사용할 수 있고, love는 동명사와 to부정사 둘 다 목적어로 사용할 수 있다. ⓐ to read → reading ⓔ to go → go 제안하는 말을 할 때 'Let's 동사원형 ~.'을 사용한다.

07 ① 소년의 취미가 무엇인지는 언급되지 않았다. ② 유미는 무슨

종류의 책을 읽기를 좋아하니? ③ 방과 후에 그들은 어디에 갈 계획입니까? ④ 유미는 읽는 것을 좋아하니? ⑤ 남자아이는 읽는 것을 좋아하니?

08 질문에 대한 대답에 **made**를 사용하였으므로, 과거의 일을 물어보는 질문이 어울린다. breakfast: 아침식사

09 ⓐ enjoy는 동명사를 목적어로 취한다. ⓑ cook: 요리사,; 요리하다 ⓒ cooking: 요리, 음식

10 but은 '그러나', '하지만'이라는 뜻으로 반대 또는 대조되는 말이 나와야 한다. 사람들과 일하는 것을 즐기며, 해보고 싶다는 말이므로, ⑤번이 어울린다.

11 interest: 관심

12 ⓒ that → when 여기서 when은 접속사로 '~할 때'의 의미이다.

13 enjoy는 동명사를 목적어로 취한다.

15 사람을 선행사로 하는 주격 관계대명사는 that이나 who를 쓴다.

16 where to put: 어디에 두어야 할지

17 ②번은 명사절을 이끄는 접속사이고 나머지는 모두 주격 관계대명사이다.

18 (1)~(3) 의문사+to부정사 = 의문사+주어+should/can+동사원형 (4) 의문대명사 which가 의문형용사로 쓰여 to부정사와의 사이에 명사가 올 수 있다.

19 선행사가 사람이면 who, 사물이면 which를 쓴다.

20 ⑤ the story가 목적어로 나와 있으므로 what을 how나 when, where 등으로 고치거나 the story를 삭제해야 한다.

21 관계대명사는 두 문장의 공통되는 명사나 대명사와 접속사의 역할을 하는 것이므로 관계사절에 공통되는 (대)명사를 원래대로 써준다.

22 ④번은 부정사의 형용사적 용법이고 나머지는 모두 명사적 용법으로 '의문사+to 부정사'로 쓰였다.

23 주격 관계대명사는 선행사가 사람이면 who나 that을 쓰고 사물이나 동물이면 which나 that을 쓴다.

24 '여러분들이 오늘 학교에 왔을 때 정문에서 음악을 연주하고 있던 몇 명의 학생들'을 가리킨다.

25 ⓑ와 ②, ③, ⑤번은 동명사, ①, ④번은 현재분사

26 '매일 아침' 연주한다.

27 ⓐ와 ①, ③, ④: 가끔, ② 항상 ⑤: 거의 ~ 않다

28 (A) '여름에는' in summer라고 하지만, '지난여름에는' 전치사 in 없이 last summer라고 한다. (B) 하늘 '높이' 나는 새들이라고 해야 하므로 high가 적절하다. high: 높은; 높이, highly: 매우, 대단히, (C) were와 병렬구문을 이루도록 thanked라고 하는 것이 적절하다.

29 ③ Picasso Art Club은 그림 동아리이므로 '그림 그리는 것'을 좋아하는 사람은 누구나 가입할 수 있다고 하는 것이 적절하다.

30 '아픈 어린이들'을 가리킨다

31 Abracadabra 동아리는 '마술' 동아리이다. 5월 5일에 회원들이 한국 병원을 방문하여 아픈 어린이들에게 '마술'을 보여주고 '마술'하는 법을 가르쳐줄 것이다.

32 ⓐ와 ②번은 축제 마당, 풍물 장터, book fair: 도서 전시회, ① 공정한, ③ 금발의, ④ (수, 크기, 양이) 상당한, 제법 큰[많은], ⑤ (날씨가) 맑은 breezy: 산들바람이 부는

33 ⓑ look for: ~을 찾다, ⓒ sell은 'to'를 사용하여 3형식으로 고친다.

---

01 (p)ractice   02 ④   03 ④   04 What time   05 join   06 ③   07 to play

08 (1) As a result (2) At first, interested (3) change into (4) let us know how to

09 (B) → (C) → (A)   10 (B) → (A) → (C)

11 What do you enjoy doing when you have free time?

12 (1) Jisu asked her mother where to put the bag.
   (2) Do you know what we should do next?
   (3) I couldn't decide what to cook.
   (4) There are a few girls who[that] are playing basketball on the playground.
   (5) Janet loves books which[that] have many funny pictures.
   (6) Linda and her dog that were crossing the street were injured.   13 ③

14 (1) get → to get
   (2) what → how
   (3) What he to eat → What to eat 또는 What he should eat
   (4) which → who[that]
   (5) is standing → (who[that] is) standing
   (6) whom → who[that]
   (7) is → are
   (8) who he liked → who liked

15 ②, ⑤   16 to join   17 volunteer

18 we painted birds flying high in the sky and dolphins jumping over blue waves   19 ①   20 ②

21 ④   22 ②

---

01 주어진 단어는 동의어 관계이다. chief: 장, 우두머리 leader: 지도자, 대표 training: 훈련 practice: 연습

02 ① leader: 지도자, 대표 / 그는 음악 클럽의 지도자이다. ② interest: 관심 / 오페라에 관심 있어요? ③ garden: 정원 / 그 집은 나무와 꽃이 있는 정원이 있다. ④ a little bit: 아주 조금 / 너는 조금 더 늦게 와도 된다. ⑤ drone: 무인 비행기 / 무인비행기(드론)는 작은 원격 조정의 헬리콥터이다.

03 ⓐ, ⓑ, ⓒ는 cookies를 가리키며, ⓓ는 doughnuts를 가리킨다.

04 'At 2:00(2시에)'라는 시간 정보가 나왔으므로, What time(몇 시에)이 어울린다.

05 join: 참여하다, 가입하다 / 1. 조직, 사회, 그룹의 구성원이 되다 2. 다른 사람이 관련된 활동에 참여하기 시작하다. 위의 대화에서는 2번의 의미로 사용되었다.

06 ①, ④ 여자아이는 어제 쿠키를 만들었다. ② 그들은 이번 주 토요일에 여자아이 집에서 만날 것이다. ③ 남자아이가 무슨 음식을 만들 수 있는지는 언급되지 않았다. ⑤ 여자아이는 이번 주 토요일에 도넛을 만들 것이다.

07 would like to+동사원형: ~하고 싶다 how to+동사원형: ~하는 방법, 어떻게 ~하는지 play the 악기 이름: ~을 연주하다

27

08 (1) as a result: 결과적으로 (2) at first: 처음에 interested: 관심[흥미]이 있는 (3) change into: ~로 변화하다[바뀌다] (4) let+목적어+동사원형: …가 ~하게 하다

09 주말에 무엇을 했는지 질문하자, (B) 가족을 위해 아침식사를 만들었다고 대답한다. (C) 이어서 요리를 즐기는지 질문하자 (A) 요리를 즐기며, 자신은 좋은 요리사이고 가족들이 자신의 요리를 좋아한다고 대답한다.

10 예쁜 가방을 보고, 어디서 샀는지 질문하자 (B) 여동생이 만들어 주었다고 대답한다. (A) 여동생이 좋은 디자이너라고 칭찬하자, (C) 동의하며, 옷을 만드는 것도 즐긴다고 말한다.

11 enjoy+동명사: ~하는 것을 즐기다 free time: 여가 시간 when:(접) ~할 때

12 (1)~(3) '의문사+to부정사'는 문장 속에서 주어, 목적어, 보어 역할을 하는 명사구로 사용된다. (4)~(6) 주격 관계대명사는 선행사가 사람이면 who나 that을 쓰고 사물이나 동물이면 which나 that을 쓴다. 선행사가 '사람+동물[사물]'인 경우에는 반드시 관계대명사 that을 써야 한다.

13 ③ '의문사+to부정사'가 주어 역할을 하고 있다.

14 (1) '의문사+to부정사'가 적절하다. (2) weight가 목적어로 나와 있으므로 how가 적절하다. (3) '의문사+to부정사'나 '의문사+주어+should+동사원형'이 적절하다. (4) 선행사가 사람이므로 who나 that이 적절하다. (5) 주격 관계대명사는 생략할 수 없으나 뒤에 분사나 부사구가 오는 경우 '주격 관계대명사+be동사'를 생략할 수 있다. (6) 주격 관계대명사가 나와야 하므로 who나 that이 적절하다. who를 목적격 whom 대신 쓸 수 있지만 whom을 who 대신 쓰지는 않는다. (7) 주격 관계대명사절의 동사는 선행사(shoes)의 수에 일치시킨다. (8) 관계대명사가 접속사와 대명사의 역할을 하므로 주어로 쓰인 he를 삭제해야 한다.

15 ⓐ와 ②, ⑤번은 동명사, 나머지는 다 현재분사

16 want+목적어+to부정사

17 volunteer: 자원봉사자, 그 일을 하기 원하기 때문에 그 일에 대한 보수 없이 일을 하는 사람

18 'high'를 보충하면 된다.

19 ① anyone who = whoever: ~인 사람은 누구나

20 주어진 문장의 those students에 주목한다. ②번 앞 문장의 several students를 받고 있으므로 ②번이 적절하다.

21 ⓐ와 ④ ~으로, ~로서, ① ~이므로, ~이기 때문에, ② ~하는대로, ③ [보통 as … as ~로 형용사·부사 앞에서] ~와 같은 정도로, ⑤ ~함에 따라, ~할수록

22 ② '처음에' 그는 음표를 읽는 법을 몰랐지만 이제 그는 간단한 노래를 연주할 수 있다고 하는 것이 적절하다. ① ③ 마침내, ④ 그러므로, ⑤ 그 결과

서술형 실전문제   p.154~155

01 (D) → (A) → (B) → (C)

02 Can you make a paper cat?

03 Do you know how to?

04 I will ask her for help.

05 (1) how to get (2) how to make (3) when to wake

---

(4) where to stop (5) what to do (6) Whom to meet

06 (1) Kay lives in a house which has a beautiful garden.

  (2) Naomi who is standing over there is very beautiful.

07 They participated in the "Change Our Neighborhood" project.

08 As   09 that

10 (A) those (B) hard (C) play

11 they should

12 (A) leader (B) join

01 (D) 유미에게 책을 읽는 것을 즐기는지 질문하자, (A) 과학 책을 읽는 것을 좋아한다고 대답하면서 상대방은 어떤지 질문한다. (B) 상대방도 책을 읽는 것을 좋아한다고 대답하자 (C) 방과 후에 도서관에 가자고 제안한다.

02 'Do you know how to+동사원형 ~?' 또는 'Can you+동사원형 ~?'을 이용해 상대방의 능력이나 무언가를 하는 방법에 대해 물을 수 있다.

03 know: 알다 how to+동사원형: ~하는 방법, 어떻게 ~하는지 / 여기서 how to 뒤에 use it이 생략되어 있다.

04 will+동사원형: ~할 것이다 ask for help: 도움을 청하다

05 '의문사+to부정사'는 '의문사+주어+should/can+동사원형'으로 바꾸어 쓸 수 있다.

06 주격 관계대명사는 선행사가 사람이면 who나 that을 쓰고 사물이나 동물이면 which나 that을 쓴다.

07 피카소 미술 동아리 회원들은 지난여름 "우리 마을 바꾸기" 프로젝트에 참여했다.

08 as a result: 그 결과

09 주격 관계대명사 that이 적절하다.

10 (A) 뒤에 나오는 명사가 복수(students)이므로 지시형용사도 복수형인 those를 쓰는 것이 적절하다. (B) '열심히' 연습할 것이라고 해야 하므로 hard가 적절하다. hard: 열심히, hardly: 거의 ~않는, (C) 지각동사 hearing의 목적격보어 자리에 to부정사를 쓸 수 없으므로 play가 적절하다.

11 '의문사+to부정사'는 '의문사+주어+should+동사원형'으로 바꿔 쓸 수 있다. 아이들에게 악기를 연주하는 법을 가르치는 것이므로 they should로 고치는 것이 적절하다.

12 장 민수는 보람 오케스트라의 '회장'이고 동아리의 활동을 소개하면서 학생들에게 동아리에 '가입할' 것을 권한다.

창의사고력 서술형 문제   p.156

|모범답안|

01 (1) enjoy flying a drone

  (2) want to make a pizza

02 (A) Name (B) FC Boram (C) passing (D) running (E) heading (F) a good team player

03 (1) I don't know how to play the computer games.

  (2) What to say is important to you.

(3) I'd like to know when to start.

(4) Let me know where to go.

(5) Tell me whom to find.

01 (1) enjoy는 동명사를 목적어로 사용한다. fly: (항공기·우주선·인공위성을) 조종하다, 날게 하다 drone: 무인 비행기 (2) want는 to부정사를 목적어로 사용한다. make: 만들다

단원별 모의고사

01 ③　　　　02 ①　　　　03 (1) interest (2) join
(3) neighbors (4) own
04 (p)ractice (h)old (n)eighborhood
(1) held (2) neighborhood (3) practice　　05 ④
06 (A) them (B) I'm going (C) come　　07 ②, ④
08 ⑤　　　　09 drone　　　10 how to
11 ④ Of course not. → Of course.
12 (1) leader (2) orchestra　　13 Thank you for your interest in our club.
14 (A) When did you start playing the violin?
(B) Do you have any experience playing in a group?
(C) Do you enjoy teaching others?　　15 ①, ④
16 ②
17 (1) Tell me how to use this computer.
(2) He didn't know where[when/how] to go.
(3) Do you know how to swim? 또는 Do you know how you should swim?
(4) The doctors (who/[that] are) working in this hospital are very kind.
(5) Did you meet the girl that is wearing sunglasses?
(6) Mary has a cousin who[that] lives in Seoul.
(7) Melina took some pictures of her friends who were on a hiking trip.　　18 ①, ④
19 ④　　　　20 (A) to paint　(B) a good painter
21 ③　　　　22 ②, ④, ⑤
23 Hearing him play the violin makes me very happy.

01 walk: (사람·동물을) 걷게 하다
02 get: ~을 사다, ~을 획득하다.
03 (1) interest: 관심 (2) join: 참여하다, 가입하다 (3) neighbor: 이웃 one of 복수명사: ~ 중의 하나 (4) own: (소유격 다음에서 강조어로서) 자기 자신의, 직접 ~한
04 (1) hold: (모임·식 등을) 개최하다 / 회의, 파티, 선거 등을 특정한 장소 또는 특정한 시간에 갖다 / 그 회의가 이 호텔에서 개최될 것이다. (2) neighborhood: 동네, (도시 내의 한 단위) 지역 / 당신 주변의 지역이나 특정한 지역의 근처에 또는 거기에 사는 사람들 / 이 동네에 좋은 중국집이 있나요? (3) practice: 연습; 연습하다 / 더 잘하기 위해서 규칙적으로 무엇인가를 하다

/ 나는 기타 연주를 연습할 필요가 있다.

05 주어진 문장에서 '네가 원한다면 우리 집에 와서 같이 해도 돼.'라는 내용이 나왔으므로, 남자아이가 도넛을 만드는 방법을 배우고 싶다고 하는 말 다음에 주어진 문장이 오고, 이후 시간 약속을 하는 말이 나오는 것이 흐름상 적절하다.

06 (A) 복수명사 cookies를 받기 때문에 them을 사용해야 한다. (B) this Saturday는 미래에 관한 시간 정보이기 때문에 'be going to 동사원형(~할 예정이다)'을 사용해야 한다. (C) should+동사원형: ~해야 한다

07 ② went → will go ④ cookies → doughnuts로 바꿔야 대화의 내용과 일치한다.

08 주어진 문장에서 She는 지나를 의미하므로 '아마도 지나는 어떻게 하는지 알 거야.'라는 문장 다음에 나와야 적절하다.

09 drone: 무인 비행기 / 조종사가 없지만 무선으로 작동되는 비행기

10 how to+동사원형: ~하는 방법, 어떻게 ~하는지

11 종이 고양이를 만드는 방법이 쉽다고 말하고 있으므로, 종이 고양이를 만드는 법을 알고 있다고 대답해야 적절하다.

12 (1) leader: 지도자, 대표 / 그룹, 조직, 국가 등을 총괄하거나 통제하는 사람 (2) orchestra: 오케스트라, 교향악단 / 많은 다른 종류의 악기를 연주하는 음악가와 지휘자에 의해 지휘되는 큰 규모의 집단

13 thank for: ~에 대해 감사하다 interest: 흥미

14 (A) when: 언제 start: 시작하다 play the 악기 이름: ~을 연주하다 (B) experience: 경험, 경력 (C) enjoy: 즐기다 teach: 가르치다

15 ① do의 목적어 it이 있으므로 what을 쓸 수 없다. ④ 'why+to부정사'는 사용하지 않는다.

16 Where are the pictures that were taken by Gibson? 주격 관계대명사의 선행사가 복수이므로 복수 동사를 써야 하며 '접속사+(대)명사의 역할을 하므로 주어로 쓰인 it을 삭제해야 한다.

17 (1) '의문사+to부정사'가 적절하다. (2) go는 자동사이므로 what과는 어색하며 how나 where 또는 when 등이 적절하다. (3) '의문사+to부정사'나 '의문사+주어+should+동사원형'이 적절하다. (4) 주격 관계대명사는 생략할 수 없으나 뒤에 분사나 부사구가 오는 경우 '주격 관계대명사+be동사'를 생략할 수 있다. (5) 관계대명사가 접속사와 대명사의 역할을 하므로 주어로 쓰인 she를 삭제해야 한다. (6) 주격 관계대명사절의 선행사가 사람이므로 who나 that을 써야 하며 동사는 선행사(a cousin)의 수에 일치시킨다. (7) 주격 관계대명사가 나와야 하므로 who나 that이 적절하다. who를 목적격 whom 대신 쓸 수 있지만 whom을 who 대신 쓰지는 않는다.

18 ⓐ와 ①, ④: 참가했다, ② 계획을 짰다, ③ 준비했다, ⑤ 돌보았다

19 ⓑ와 ①번은 현재분사, 나머지는 다 동명사이다. ② 전치사의 목적어, ③ 주어, talk behind somebody's back 남의 험담을 하다, ④ 목적어, ⑤ 보어

20 만약 당신이 '그림 그리는 것'을 좋아한다면 피카소 미술 동아리의 회원이 될 수 있지만 '그림을 잘 그릴' 필요는 없다.

21 ⓐ as: ~으로, ~로서 ⓓ By ~ing: ~함으로써

22 ⓑ와 ①, ③은 명사적 용법, ② 형용사적 용법, ④ 부사적 용법(목적), ⑤ 부사적 용법(정도)

23 동명사 Hearing을 주어로 사용하여 영작하면 된다.

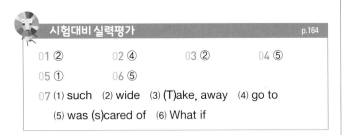

The Two Roads

01 ②   02 ④   03 ②   04 ⑤
05 ①   06 ⑤

07 (1) such (2) wide (3) (T)ake, away (4) go to
   (5) was (s)cared of (6) What if

01 silent(조용한)의 명사형은 silence이다. ① happy: 행복한 happiness: 행복 ③ sad: 슬픈 sadness: 슬픔 ④ kind:친절한 kindness: 친절 ⑤ dark: 어두운 darkness: 어두움

02 besides: 게다가 in addition: 더구나, 게다가 / 게다가 밖은 매우 춥다.

03 reply: 대답하다 answer: 답하다 / 나는 뭐라고 대답해야 할지 몰랐다.

04 look like+명사: ~처럼 보이다 / 그 옷을 입으니 완전히 다른 사람처럼 보여요.

05 break out: 발발하다 / 일부 사람들은 전쟁이 일어날 것을 우려하고 있다.

06 foreigner: 외국인 ① 그것은 긴 여행이었다. ② 그것에 대한 의견을 주시겠습니까? ③ 대부분의 십대들은 스트레스를 많이 받는다. ④ 갈매기들이 내 머리 위를 날고 있다. ⑤ 너의 삼촌은 외국인처럼 보인다.

07 (1) such: 너무나 ~한 (2) wide: 넓은 (3) take away: ~을 빼앗다 (4) go to the doctor: 병원에 가다 (5) be scared of: ~을 두려워하다 (6) What if 주어 동사 ~?: 만약 ~이라면 어떻게 될까?

01 (d)arkness   02 get
03 take
04 (c)ub, (o)pinion, (t)hrone
   (1) throne (2) cubs (3) opinion
05 (1) foreign (2) scared (3) worried (4) good
06 (1) Who is your favorite character in this movie?
   (2) Have you ever been to India before?
   (3) I liked the last scene in that drama.

01 beautiful: (형) 아름다운 beauty: (명) 아름다움 / 형용사인 dark는 뒤에 ness를 붙여 명사가 된다. dark(어두운): darkness(어두움)

02 get+형용사: ~하게 되다 / 나는 노래하기 위해 무대에 설 때마다 긴장된다. get better: (병·상황 등이) 좋아지다 / 오늘은 날씨가 더 좋아질 거라고 하던데요.

03 take ~ for a walk: ~을 산책하러 데리고 가다 / 그는 그의 개들과 해안가를 따라 산책하는 것을 좋아한다. take away: 빼앗다 / 그것들은 공기 중에서 나쁜 것들을 없애 준다.

04 cub: (곰, 사자 등의) 새끼 / 곰, 사자 또는 다른 포유류의 어린 새끼 opinion: 의견 / 어떤 것에 대한 생각이나 믿음 throne: 왕좌, 왕위 / 왕, 여왕 또는 황제가 앉는 장식용 의자 (1) 누가 왕위를 계승할 것인가? (2) 새끼 곰들은 사육사에 의해 보살핌을 받는다. (3) 우리는 고양이를 입양하는 것에 대해 다른 의견을 가지고 있다.

05 (1) foreign: 외국의 / 외국어를 배우는 가장 효과적인 방법은 무엇이냐? (2) be scared of: ~을 두려워하다 / 그 사람들도 치과의사를 무서워했다고 생각하니? (3) be worried about: ~에 대해 걱정하다 / 그의 가족들은 그의 나쁜 식습관 때문에 몹시 걱정했다. (4) be good at: ~을 잘하다 / 그는 어려운 수학 문제 푸는 것을 잘한다.

06 (1) character: 등장인물 (2) ever: 언제든, 한 번이라도 (3) scene: 장면

교과서
Conversation

1 I'm, about / worry, can pass
2 (C) → (B) → (A)
3 (1) you think of   (2) do you feel
4 (C) → (B) → (A) → (D)

교과서 대화문 익히기

(1) T (2) F (3) T (4) T (5) F (6) T

교과서 확인학습
p.170~171

Listen & Speak 1 A

(w)orried about / Don't

Listen & Speak 1 B

1. Do you have, plans / to, (w)orried about / worry, won't

2. go / wrong / scared of / (f)riendly, looks scary because

Listen & Speak 1 C

1. I'm worried about / Don't worry

2. I'm worried about / You'll do great

3. I'm worried about my future. / worry, find something

Listen & Speak 2 A

What do you, of / like

Listen & Speak 2 B

1. saw / What did you think of it / (d)isappointed

2. What do you think of / think, (d)elicious / What

3. do you think of / happy that, myself

Listen & Speak 2 C

1. think of / looks light

2. What do you think / good on you

Real-Life Zone

who looked like / (h)ad / looked / were, to meet / comfortable / was worried about speaking, anymore / the hardest / What do you, (a)bout

시험대비 기본평가
p.172

01 ④   02 ①   03 ①

04 (C) → (A) → (B) → (D)

01 Don't worry.: 걱정하지 마. 걱정하는 상대방을 안심시키고 있는 표현이다.

02 be worried about: ~에 대해 걱정하다 / 여자아이가 날씨에 대해서 걱정하고 있으니 남자아이가 내일 제주도에 비가 내리지 않을 거라고 여자아이를 안심시키고 있다.

03 'What do you think of+명사?'는 '~에 대해 어떻게 생각해?'의 의미로, 무언가에 대하여 상대방의 의견을 물을 때 사용할 수 있다.

04 (C) 영화 '딸'을 보았느냐는 질문에 (A) 봤다고 대답한다. (B) 영화에 대한 상대방의 의견을 묻고 (D) 별로 좋지 않았다고 대답한다.

시험대비 실력평가
p.173~174

01 ④   02 ③   03 ②   04 ④

05 ⑤   06 ③   07 ①, ⑤   08 like

09 (A) who   (B) but   (C) when   10 ③

11 ①   12 (A) for   (B) of[about]

01 스마트폰에 대해 걱정하고 있는 상대방에게 근처에 서비스 센터가 있다고 안심시켜 준다.

02 Do you have any special plans for tomorrow?: 내일 특별한 계획이 있니? / 내일 계획에 대해서 묻자, 아침에 제주도에 갈 거라고 대답한다.

03 weather: 날씨에 대해 걱정하니까, 상대방이 제주도에 비가 내리지 않을 거라고 대답했다.

04 ① 여자아이는 내일 아침에 할 계획을 가지고 있다. ② 여자아이는 제주도의 날씨에 대해 걱정하고 있다. ③ 남자아이는 내일 제주도에 비가 올지 안 올지에 대해 알고 있다. ④ 남자아이는 내일 아침에 제주도에 갈 것이다. ⑤ 내일 제주도에 비가 내리지 않을 것이다.

05 만화책에 대한 의견을 묻는 말에, '네가 멋지다고 생각해.'는 어색하다.

06 be worried about: ~에 대해 걱정하다

07 What do you think of[about]+명사?: ~에 대해 어떻게 생각해?

08 look like+명사: ~처럼 보이다

09 (A) 선행사 someone을 수식하는 주격 관계대명사이다. 선행사가 사람이므로 which가 아닌 who가 적절하다. (B) 예전에는 영어로 말하는 것에 걱정했다는 내용과 더 이상은 걱정하고 있지 않다는 역접의 접속사로 연결하는 것이 적절하다. (C) when: (접) ~할 때

10 ① 여자아이가 영어를 말할 때 어떻게 느끼는가? ② 남자아이는 외국인과 무엇을 했는가? ③ 현재 남자아이가 걱정하는 것은 무엇인가? ④ 언제 여자아이가 남자아이를 보았는가? ⑤ 얼마나 자주 남자아이가 외국인을 만나는가?

11 주어진 문장의 it은 the book that I borrowed from the library(도서관에서 빌린 책)를 의미한다. 책을 봤는지 물어보는 질문에 무슨 책을 찾는지 물으며, 거실에서 책을 본 것 같다는 말이 어울리므로 ①에 주어진 문장이 들어가는 것이 적절하다.

12 (A) look for: ~을 찾다 (B) What do you think of[about]+명사?: ~에 대해 어떻게 생각해?

서술형 시험대비
p.175

01 will rain → won't rain

02 It's cool! → They're cool!

03 it gets easier and easier.

04 What do you think about me joining both of you for lunch?

05 (B) → (A) → (C)   06 (A) → (C) → (B)

31

01 내일 아침에 제주도에 가기 때문에 날씨를 걱정하고 있는 여자아이에게 걱정하지 말라고 안심시키는 말과 내일 제주도에 비가 올 거라는 말은 어울리지 않는다.

02 These sunglasses는 복수 명사이므로 대명사 It이 아니라 They로 받는다.

03 get+형용사: ~하게 되다, 비교급 and 비교급: 점점 더 ~한[하게]

04 What do you think of[about]+명사?: ~에 대해 어떻게 생각해? join: 함께하다

05 학교 식당 음식에 대해 상대방의 의견을 묻자, (B) 식당 음식이 맛있다고 대답한다. (A) 이어서 최고의 품목이 무엇인지 질문하니까 (C) 김밥이라고 대답한다.

06 걱정스러워 보인다며 무슨 일이 있는지 질문하자, (A) 빌린 책을 찾을 수 없다며 본 적이 있는지 질문한다. (C) 어떤 책을 말하는지 질문하고, 거실에서 '갈매기의 꿈'을 본 것 같다고 말한다. (B) 그 책이 맞다고 얘기하며 감사를 표한다.

교과서
Grammar

핵심 Check
p.176~177

1 (1) has gone (2) has played (3) Have, watched

2 (1) If (2) leave[start], won't be (3) if[whether], will be

시험대비 기본평가
p.178

01 ③

02 (1) If school ends early
　(2) won't attend the party if she is not invited

03 (1) play → played
　(2) has met → met
　(3) Does he have → Has he
　(4) for → since
　(5) will rain → rains
　(6) don't turn → turn

01 ③ 'have gone to'는 '~에 가고 없다'는 결과를 나타내는 것으로 3인칭만 주어로 쓸 수 있다. We have been to Seoul.로 고쳐야 한다.

02 (1) if는 '만약 ~한다면'이라는 뜻의 접속사이다. (2) 조건의 부사절에서는 미래시제 대신에 현재시제를 쓴다.

03 (1) 현재완료는 'have[has]+과거분사'의 형태이다. (2) 현재완료는 과거를 나타내는 어구와 함께 쓸 수 없다. (3) 현재완

료의 의문문은 have를 주어 앞으로 보낸다. (4) 현재완료에서 'since+시간 명사', 'for+기간 명사'를 쓴다. (5) 조건의 부사절에서는 미래시제 대신에 현재시제를 쓴다. (6) unless는 'if ~ not'의 뜻이므로 don't를 삭제해야 한다.

시험대비 실력평가
p.179~181

01 ⑤　　02 ①　　03 ③　　04 ④
05 ②　　06 (1) has (2) visited (3) gone (4) went
　(5) if (6) call　　07 ⑤
08 You'll miss the bus unless you walk more quickly. / You'll miss the bus if you don't walk more quickly.
09 ①　　10 ②　　11 ④　　12 ③
13 ③, ⑤
14 (1) If my friend moves near my house, I can see her more often.
　(2) You will be late unless you hurry up. / You will be late if you don't hurry up.
　(3) Please let us know if you will come to the party tomorrow.
15 (1) Anna has loved Sam since she met him first.
　(2) Mariel has lived in Tallinn for seven years.
16 ②, ④　　17 ①　　18 ③　　19 ⑤

01 ⑤ 언제 컴퓨터를 샀는지 묻는 문장으로 특정한 과거의 한 시점을 묻는 것이므로 현재완료가 아니라 과거시제가 되어야 한다. 보통 when은 현재완료와 쓰이지 않는다.

02 조건의 부사절을 이끄는 if가 적절하다. unless는 'if ~ not'의 뜻으로 문맥상 적절하지 않다.

03 현재완료의 의문문은 'have+주어+과거분사 ~?'이다. 'have[has] been to'는 '~에 가 본 적이 있다'는 경험을 나타내고, 'have gone ~'은 '가버리고 없다'는 뜻이므로 gone이 적절하다.

04 ④ unless = if ~ not이므로 If가 아니라 Unless가 되어야 한다.

05 긍정문이므로 already가 적절하다.

06 (1) 주어가 3인칭 단수이므로 has가 적절하다. (2) 현재완료는 'have[has]+과거분사'의 형태이다. (3) have[has] gone to는 '~에 가고 없다'는 결과를 나타낸다. (4) 현재완료는 과거를 나타내는 어구와 함께 쓸 수 없다. (5) unless는 'if ~ not'이므로 if가 적절하다. (6) 조건의 부사절에서는 미래시제 대신에 현재시제를 쓴다.

07 ① Jenny raised a dog last year. ② Karen has been to Malaysia three times. ③ Susan and I have been to Paris. ④ Tom has studied English for ten years.

08 unless = if ~ not

09 현재완료형의 질문에 대한 답은 have 동사를 이용해 답한다.

10 ②번만 '~인지 아닌지'의 의미로 명사절을 이끄는 접속사로 쓰였다.

11 현재완료의 결과적 용법(…해서 (그 결과) 지금 ~하다)을 이용하여 과거에 우크라이나로 간 것이 아직도 거기에 있다는 현재의 결과를 나타내도록 한다.

12 조건의 부사절에서는 미래시제 대신에 현재시제를 쓰므로 앞에는 meet, 뒤에는 내용에 맞게 will give를 쓴다.

13 ③번은 계속 용법, ⑤번은 경험 용법, 나머지는 모두 완료 용법으로 쓰였다.

14 (1) 조건의 부사절에서는 미래시제 대신에 현재시제를 쓴다. (2) unless는 'if ~ not'의 뜻으로 보통 not과 함께 쓰이지 않는다. (3) if가 명사 역할을 하는 경우로 미래를 나타낼 때에는 미래 시제를 써야 한다.

15 (1) 처음 만났을 때 사랑에 빠져 지금도 사랑하고 있으므로 현재완료의 계속적 용법으로 나타낸다. (2) 7년 전에 살기 시작해서 아직도 살고 있으므로 현재완료의 계속적 용법으로 나타낸다.

16 의미상 ②, ④가 적절하다. unless = if ~ not, immediately: 즉시 take time: 천천히 하다

17 ①과 <보기>는 '경험' 용법이다. ②, ⑤ 결과 용법 ③ 계속 용법 ④ 완료 용법

18 조건의 부사절에서는 미래시제 대신에 현재시제를 쓰며 unless는 'if ~ not'의 뜻으로 not과 함께 쓰이지 않는다.

19 현재완료의 의문문은 'Have[Has]+주어+과거분사 ~?'로 나타낸다. 'have[has] been to'는 '~에 가 본 적이 있다'는 경험을 나타내고, 'have gone to ~'는 '~에 가고 (지금) 없다'는 결과를 나타낸다.

서술형 시험대비 p.182~183

01 (1) Have you read *Charlie and the Chocolate Factory* already?

(2) Jina has experienced a lot while traveling.

(3) Don't open a shop unless you know how to smile.

(4) Why don't you eat some snacks if you are hungry?

02 naming → named, help → helped, unless → if

03 (1) |예시답| I have cooked ramyeon many times.

(2) |예시답| I have never experienced skiing up to now.

04 (1) Sophia has lost her cap.

(2) I have visited Paris twice.

05 (1) then → 삭제, 또는 You had a lot of trouble then.

(2) since → for   (3) been → gone   (4) will go → go

(5) Unless → If

06 (1) Jason has eaten Korean food.

(2) Mankind has existed for thousands of years.

(3) If it rains, I will take an umbrella with me.

(4) Don't miss your classes unless it is really important.

07 (1) Stephanie hasn't used her computer for 3

years. / Has Stephanie used her computer for 3 years?

(2) You haven't seen it before. 또는 You have never seen it before. / Have you seen it before?

08 (1) If   (2) Unless

09 (1) has rained   (2) has gone   (3) has broken

01 (1) 현재완료의 '완료' 용법 (2) while 다음에 '주어+be동사'가 생략된 형태이다. (3) unless = if ~ not, how to smile: 웃는 법 (4) Why don't you ~?: ~하는 게 어때?

02 Louis라고 이름이 지어진 것이므로 named, 현재완료는 'have[has]+과거분사'의 형태, unless는 'if ~ not'이므로 의미상 if가 적절하다.

03 현재완료의 '경험' 용법을 이용하여 쓴다.

04 (1) 현재완료의 '결과' 용법을 이용한다. (2) 현재완료의 '경험' 용법을 이용한다.

05 (1) 현재완료는 과거를 나타내는 어구와 함께 쓸 수 없다. then은 '그때'라는 뜻으로 과거를 나타내는 말이다. (2) 현재완료에서 'since+시간 명사', 'for+기간 명사' (3) have[has] been to는 '~에 가 본 적이 있다'는 경험을 나타내고, have[has] gone to는 '~에 가고 없다'는 결과를 나타내므로 have gone to로 고쳐야 한다. (4) 조건의 부사절에서는 미래시제 대신에 현재시제를 쓴다. (5) unless는 'if ~ not'이므로 if가 적절하다.

06 (1) 현재완료의 '경험' 용법을 이용한다. (2) 현재완료의 '계속' 용법을 이용한다. (3) 조건의 부사절에서는 미래 시제 대신에 현재 시제를 쓴다. (4) unless는 'if ~ not'이므로 단어 수에 맞추어 unless를 쓴다. mankind: 인류

07 현재완료의 부정문은 'have[has]+not[never]+과거분사'로, 의문문은 'Have[Has]+주어+과거분사 ~?'로 나타낸다.

08 명령문, and ~: '~해라, 그러면'(= If ~), 명령문, or ~: '~해라, 그렇지 않으면'(= If not ~ = Unless ~)

09 (1) 현재완료의 '계속' 용법을 이용한다. (2), (3) 현재완료의 '결과' 용법을 이용한다.

교과서 Reading

확인문제 p.184

1 T   2 F   3 F   4 T   5 T   6 F

확인문제 p.185

1 T   2 F   3 F   4 T

02 went on   03 in front of
04 said, into, across   05 her cubs
06 Take, run up   07 find happiness
08 go and find   09 How can we know
10 What if   11 Besides, away from
12 Instead of   13 How, if
14 went their own way
15 went into, swam across   16 There was
17 sleeping   18 took her cubs
19 took him to, made   20 as a king
21 broke out, lost his throne   22 on the road
23 talked about, for the last   24 I was right
25 have lived   26 have had
27 regret my choice
28 nothing, something to remember

1 The Two Brothers
2 Two brothers went on a journey.
3 They found a rock in front of a forest.
4 It said, "Go into the forest and swim across the river.
5 There you will find a bear and her cubs.
6 Take the bear cubs and run up the mountain.
7 There you will find happiness."
8 The younger brother said, "Let's go and find happiness together."
9 "No," said the older brother, "How can we know this is true?
10 What if the river is too wide?
11 Besides, will it be easy to take the cubs away from their mother?
12 Instead of finding happiness, we can be killed!"
13 The younger brother replied, "How can we know if we don't try?"
14 They separated, and they both went their own way.
15 The younger brother went into the forest and swam across the river.
16 There was the bear.
17 She was sleeping.
18 He took her cubs and ran up the mountain.
19 When he reached the top, some people took him to their city and made him their king.

20 There he lived as a king for five years.
21 Then a war broke out, and he lost his throne.
22 He was on the road again.
23 One day, the two brothers met again and talked about their lives for the last five years.
24 The older brother said, "I was right.
25 I have lived quietly and well.
26 You were once a king, but you have had a lot of trouble."
27 The younger brother answered, "I don't regret my choice.
28 I may have nothing now, but I will always have something to remember."

01 ③   02 a rock   03 ④   04 ⑤
05 ④   06 ②   07 ③   08 ②, ③
09 ①   10 ②   11 ②, ④   12 ⑤
13 flying better than others   14 ①, ④ / ②, ③, ⑤
15 own beliefs
16 He was on the road again.   17 ②, ⑤
18 something → nothing, nothing → something
19 named   20 (A) others (B) hard (C) learn
21 ③   22 ③   23 ③, ⑤
24 In fact, As a matter of fact
25 You look like a traveler, not a king now.

01 ⓐ go on a journey: 여행을 떠나다, ⓑ swim across: ~을 헤엄쳐 건너다
02 '바위'를 가리킨다.
03 ④ '곰 새끼들'을 데리고 산 위로 뛰어 올라가라고 되어 있다.
04 주어진 문장의 replied에 주목한다. ⑤번 앞 문장의 형의 말에 대해 대답한 것이므로 ⑤번이 적절하다.
05 ⑤번은 현재분사이고 ⓐ와 나머지는 모두 동명사이다.
06 ② 동생은 "우리가 시도하지 않으면 어떻게 알 수 있어?"라고 말했다.
07 ③은 '형'을 가리키고, 나머지는 다 '동생'을 가리킨다.
08 ⓐ와 ①, ④, ⑤ 형용사적 용법, ② 부사적 용법, ③ 명사적 용법
09 ① 어떤 사람들이 왜 그를 그들의 왕으로 만들었는지는 대답할 수 없다. ② Because a war broke out. ③ He has lived quietly and well. ④ They talked about their lives for the last five years. ⑤ No.
10 동생은 "함께 가서 행복을 찾자. 우리가 시도하지 않으면 어떻게 알 수 있어?"라고 말했고, 형은 "싫어."라고 말했기 때문

에, 제목으로는 '행복을 향한 두 가지 선택들'이 적절하다. ④ doubtful: 확신이 없는, 의심[의문]을 품은, response: 반응, ⑤ put ~ into practice: 실천하다

11 ⓐ와 ①, ③, ⑤는 명사적 용법, ② 형용사적 용법, ④ 부사적 용법

12 ⑤ 도전적인, ① 부정적인, ② 이기적인, ③ 후한, 너그러운, ④ 수동적인, 소극적인

13 '남들(다른 갈매기들)보다 더 잘 나는 것'을 가리킨다.

14 ⓑ와 ①, ④번은 명사절을 이끄는 접속사, ⓒ와 ②, ③, ⑤번은 관계대명사

15 위의 독서 감상문을 쓴 사람이 이 책을 좋아하는 이유는 이 책이 '자기 자신의 믿음'의 힘에 대해 배우도록 도와주었기 때문이다.

16 on the road: 여행 중인, (살 수 있는 집이 없이) 이리저리 옮겨 다니는

17 ⓑ와 ②, ⑤번은 계속 용법, ① 완료 용법, ③ 결과 용법, ④ 경험 용법

18 나는 지금 '아무것도' 없지만 언제까지나 기억할 '어떤 것'이 있다고 하는 것이 적절하다.

19 A named[called] B: B라고 일컫는[불리는] A

20 (A) '남들(다른 갈매기들)보다'라고 해야 하므로 others가 적절하다. the other: 둘 중 나머지 하나, (B) '열심히' 일한다고 해야 하므로 hard가 적절하다. hardly: 거의 ~ 않는, (C) help+목적어+원형(혹은 to부정사)이기 때문에 learn이 적절하다.

21 위 글은 '독서 감상문'이다. ① 수필, ② 전기, ④ 일기, ⑤ (신문·잡지의) 글, 기사

22 ⓐ와 ④, ⑤번은 계속 용법, ① 완료 용법, ② 경험 용법, ③ 결과 용법

23 ⓑ와 ①, ②, ④: (오랜만에 만났을 때) 어떻게 지내셨어요? How have you been? = What have you been up to? = What have you been doing? = How have you been getting along? ③ 처음 뵙겠습니다. ⑤ 컨디션이 어때요?

24 Actually: 실제로, In fact, As a matter of fact를 쓰면 된다.

25 앞 문장에서 형이 한 말을 가리킨다.

---

(4) 행복을 찾는 대신에, 자신들이 죽을 수 있기 때문이다.

08 unless we try

09 for

10 I may have nothing now, but I will always have something to remember.

11 (A) quietly and well   (B) as a king

12 flying

13 anything

---

01 What if: ~이라면 어찌 되는가?, ~이라면 어쩌지?

02 '형'은 동생과 함께 가지 '않는' 것을 선택했고, '동생'은 혼자 숲에 들어가서 강을 헤엄쳐 건너 새끼 곰들을 데리고 산을 '뛰어 올라갔다.'

03 그들은 '헤어졌고' 둘 다 자신의 길을 갔다라고 해야 하므로 separated로 고쳐야 한다. separate: 갈라지다, 헤어지다, unite: (다른 사람들과) 연합하다

04 (A) reach는 타동사로 전치사 없이 바로 목적어를 써야 하므로 reached가 적절하다. (B) 전쟁이 '일어났다'고 해야 하므로 broke가 적절하다. break out: 발발[발생]하다, (C) 동사 (lived)를 꾸며주므로 부사 quietly가 적절하다.

05 그는 '왕좌'를 잃었다, throne: 왕위, 왕좌, 왕

06 우리는 '죽을 수 있어'라고 해야 하므로 수동태로 쓰는 것이 적절하다.

07 "No," 다음에 형이 한 말을 쓰면 된다.

08 unless = if ~ not

09 지난 5년 '동안'이라고 해야 하므로 for가 적절하다. for+숫자, during+특정 기간

10 'nothing'을 보충하면 된다.

11 지난 5년 동안 형은 '조용히 잘' 살아 왔고, 동생은 '왕으로' 살았다.

12 practice는 목적어로 동명사를 취한다.

13 이 책에 따르면, 만약 내가 포기하지 않으면 내가 원하는 '어떤 것'이라도 할 수 있다. give up = stop trying to do something

---

서술형 시험대비   p.194~195

01 What if

02 (A) older   (B) not   (C) younger   (D) ran

03 united → separated

04 (A) reached   (B) broke   (C) quietly

05 throne

06 kill → be killed

07 (1) 이것이(앞에 나온 내용이) 사실인지 알 수 없기 때문이다.
   (2) 강이 너무 넓을 수도 있기 때문이다.
   (3) 곰 새끼들을 엄마에게서 빼앗는 것이 쉽지 않을 수도 있기 때문이다.

영역별 핵심문제   p.197~201

01 (1) unfriendly   (2) happiness   02 ③

03 ①

04 (1) The king ruled his country for a long time.
   (2) Thank you for your support.

05 ④   06 ④   07 ①

08 (A) great (B) that

09 about the painting, painted herself, the colors

10 (A) What   (B) What   11 ④

12 I was worried about speaking in English before, but not anymore.   13 ①

14 If you are Spring people   15 ⑤   16 ①

35

17 ④	18 ③	19 ⑤
20 founded → found		21 cubs
22 On the mountain		23 In addition 24 ②
25 25	26 ①	27 ④ 28 ②
29 ⑤	30 ②	31 ④

01 (1) 반의어 관계이다. noisy: 시끄러운 quiet: 조용한 friendly: 친절한 unfriendly: 불친절한, 쌀쌀맞은 (2) 형용사와 명사의 관계이다. popular: 인기 있는 popularity: 인기 happy: 행복한 happiness: 행복

02 character는 '성격'이라는 뜻도 있지만, ③에서는 '등장인물'의 의미로 사용되었다. ① 이 상점의 전 품목이 세일이에요! ② 나는 그 신문에서 그의 작품을 논평했다. ③ 처음에 그녀는 가장 중요한 인물인 신데렐라의 배역을 원했다. ④ 베스트셀러의 제목이 뭔가요? ⑤ 그들은 지난달에 헤어졌다.

03 correct: 올바른 / 잘못을 가지고 있지 않은

04 (1) rule: 지배하다 (2) support: 지지; 지지하다

05 'What do you think of/about ~?', 'What's your opinion of/about/on ~?', 'What's your view on ~?', 'How do you feel about ~?', 'How do you like ~?' 등은 의견을 묻는 말이다. ④ 너는 무엇을 하고 싶니?

06 많이 가지면 가질수록 더 많이 원한다는 말에, 상대방이 걱정된다는 말은 어색하다.

07 역사 수업에 대한 의견을 묻는 말에, 나한테는 어렵다고 대답한다. ① 나에게 어려워. ② 너에게 잘 어울려. ③ 네가 좋아하니 기뻐. ④ 좋은 생각이야. ⑤ 가볍고 빨라 보여.

08 (A) look+형용사: ~하게 보이다 (B) happy 다음에 '주어+동사'가 있으므로 접속사인 that을 사용해야 한다.

09 그들은 여자아이가 직접 그린 그림에 대해 이야기하고 있다. 남자아이는 그 그림의 색을 좋아한다. talk about: ~에 대해 이야기하다 painting: 그림 color: 색깔

10 (A) What do you think of/about+명사?: ~에 대해 어떻게 생각해? (B) what: 무엇 / 최고의 품목이 뭐라고 생각하니?

11 외국인처럼 보이는 사람과 같이 있는 것을 보았다는 말에, (C) 그렇다고 대답하며, 외국인과 점심을 같이 먹었다고 대답한다. (B) 좋은 시간을 보내고 있었던 것처럼 보인다는 말에 (A) 그렇다고 말하며, 한 달에 두 번 만나서 점심을 먹는다고 대답한다. (D) 여자아이는 외국인과 좀 더 편하게 이야기하고 싶은 자신의 소망을 말한다.

12 be worried about: ~에 대해 걱정하다 not anymore: 더 이상 않는

13 since(~한 이래로)는 보통 현재완료와 함께 많이 쓰인다. 이때 since절에는 과거 시제가 많이 쓰인다.

14 그림의 내용에 맞게 if를 이용하여 조건절을 쓴다.

15 ⑤번은 '결과' 용법이지만 나머지는 '계속' 용법이다.

16 '~한다면'이라는 조건과 '~인지 아닌지'를 나타낼 수 있는 if가 적절하다.

17 ⓐ have met → met ⓓ have gone to → have been to

18 ③번은 명사절을 이끌어 '~인지 아닌지'의 뜻으로 쓰였고 나머

지는 모두 부사절을 이끌어 '만약 ~한다면'으로 쓰였다.

19 현재완료는 과거를 나타내는 어구와 함께 쓸 수 없다.

20 바위를 '발견했다'라고 해야 하므로 find의 과거형인 found로 고쳐야 한다. found - founded: 설립하다

21 cub: (곰·늑대·사자 등의) 새끼, the young: 새끼들(the+형용사 = 복수 보통명사)

22 '산에서'를 가리킨다.

23 besides = in addition: 게다가

24 ② 모험하지 않으면 얻는 것도 없다. "우리가 시도하지 않으면 어떻게 알 수 있어?"라는 말은 행동으로 옮겨 실천할 것을 뜻한다. ① 돌다리도 두드려 보고 건너라. ③ 엎질러진 우유를 놓고 울어봐야 소용없다. ④ 말하기는 쉬워도 실천하기는 어렵다. ⑤ 쥐구멍에도 볕들 날이 있다.

25 총 20명의 학생들 중에서 5명의 학생들이 친구와 이야기할 때 행복하다고 했으므로 '25'퍼센트에 해당한다.

26 ①은 의문부사(언제), 나머지는 모두 접속사(때)

27 맛있는 음식을 먹을 때 행복한 학생은 3명이고 수학에서 좋은 점수를 받을 때 행복한 학생은 2명이므로, 맛있는 음식을 먹을 때 행복한 학생의 수가 더 '많다.'

28 ⓐ와 ②, ③은 부사적 용법, ①, ⑤ 명사적 용법, ④ 형용사적 용법

29 ⑤ Jonathan이 언제 나는 연습을 하는지는 대답할 수 없다. ① *Jonathan Livingston Seagull* ② Richard Bach. ③ A seagull named Jonathan Livingston. ④ Flying better than others.

30 그는 그곳에서 많은 문제를 겪었다고 했으므로 자신의 선택을 '후회했다'고 하는 것이 적절하다. ① 받아 주다, 수락하다, ③ 개선하다, 향상시키다, ④ 달성하다, 성취하다, ⑤ 거절하다

31 여행가기로 결정할 때는 '기대에 찬' 심경이었다가 '실망하게' 되었다. disappointed: 실망한, expectant; 기대에 찬, frightened: 겁먹은, 무서워하는

단원별 예상문제 p.202~205

01 ① 02 look, on 03 about / are, at

04 (1) bigger and bigger (2) (H)appiness

05 ② 06 (C) → (D) → (A) → (B) 07 ③

08 ⑤ 09 character 10 ④ 11 ③

12 What do you think of our school cafeteria food?

13 (1) They have sold all the books.

(2) Mina has been to the flea market once.

(3) I have lived in Paris since I was born.

(4) The train has already departed from the station.

(5) If it is sunny tomorrow, we will go to the beach.

(6) I wonder if the dress will look good on you.

14 (1) gone → been (2) has → did (3) for → since

01 ① have, have a good time: 좋은 시간을 보내다 / 휴가 잘 보내셨어요? ② ruled, rule: 지배하다 / 로마는 500년 이상 동안 세계를 지배했다. ③ reply, reply: 대답하다 / 그녀에게 직업을 물어봤지만 그녀는 대답하지 않았다. ④ support, support: 지지; 지지하다 / 너는 그녀의 선택을 존중하고 지지해야 한다. ⑤ regret, regret: 후회하다 / 나는 그렇게 부주의했던 것이 후회스럽다.

02 look good (on 사람): (~에게) 잘 어울리다

03 be worried about: ~에 대해 걱정하다 be good at: ~을 잘하다

04 (1) 비교급 and 비교급: 점점 더 ~한[하게] (2) happiness: 행복

05 'I think I should study harder to get good grades.'는 '나는 좋은 성적을 얻기 위해 더 열심히 공부해야 한다고 생각한다.'의 의미로 수학에 대한 걱정을 해결하기 위해 할 수 있는 일이다.

06 (C) 내일의 계획을 물어보고 (D) 아침에 제주도에 갈 거라고 대답하며 날씨를 걱정하자, (A) 내일 제주도에는 비가 내리지 않는다고 걱정하지 말라고 안심시킨다. (B) 비가 오지 않는다는 말에 좋아한다.

07 ⓐ first ⓑ wrong ⓒ friendly ⓓ scary ⓔ big / 남자아이는 개를 무서워해 여자아이가 먼저 들어가기를 원했다.

08 주어진 문장은 '이미 두 번 읽었어요.'란 의미로 책을 읽어 봤는지 물어보는 질문의 대답으로 어울린다.

09 character: 등장인물 / 영화, 책 또는 연극에 있는 인물

10 by the way: 그런데(대화에서 화제를 바꿀 때 씀)

11 ① 여자아이는 '갈매기의 꿈'을 몇 번 읽었는가? ② 그들은 무슨 관계인가? ③ 여자는 '갈매기의 꿈'에서 어떤 등장인물을 좋아하는가? ④ 처음에, 왜 여자아이가 걱정스러워 보였는가? ⑤ 여자아이는 도서관에서 무슨 책을 빌렸는가?

12 What do you think of/about+명사?: ~에 대해 어떻게 생각해?

13 (1) 현재완료의 '결과' 용법을 이용한다. (2) 'have[has] been to'는 '~에 가 본적이 있다'는 경험을 나타낸다. (3) 현재완료의 '계속' 용법을 이용한다. (4) 현재완료의 '완료' 용법을 이용한다. (5) 조건의 부사절에서는 미래시제 대신에 현재시제를 쓴다. (6) if절이 명사 역할을 하는 경우도 있으며, 미래를 나타낼 때 미래시제를 써야 한다. look good on: ~에게 잘 어울리다

14 (1) have[has] been to는 '~에 가 본 적이 있다'는 경험을 나타내고, have[has] gone to는 '~에 가고 없다'는 결과를 나타내므로 have been to로 고쳐야 한다. (2) '시장에서 기술이 활용 가능한 때는 언제였습니까?'라는 질문으로 when이 과거

의 어느 시점인지를 묻는 의문사로 쓰여 현재완료와는 쓸 수 없다. (3) 현재완료에서 'since+시간 명사', 'for+기간 명사' (4) until now로 보아 현재완료가 적절하다. (5) 조건의 부사절에 시는 미래시제 대신에 현재시제를 쓴다.

15 가주어 'it'을 보충하면 된다.

16 ④ 행복을 찾는 '대신에', 우리는 죽을 수 있어! ① ~ 외에도, ② ~와 함께, ③ ~ 때문에, ⑤ ~에 더하여

17 ① ~인지(ask, know, find out, wonder 등의 동사 뒤에 쓰여 두 가지 이상의 가능성 중 하나를 도입할 때 씀). ⓒ와 나머지는 모두 '만약'의 뜻으로 조건절을 이끈다.

18 주어진 문장은 "너는 한때 왕이었지만 많은 어려움을 겪었다."는 형의 말에 대한 동생의 대답이므로 The younger brother answered 다음인 ⑤번이 적절하다.

19 ⓐ와 ③, ⑤ ~에 도착하다, ① start from: ~를 떠나다, ② leave for: ~로 떠나다, ④ contact: 접촉하다, 연락을 취하다

20 이 글에서 형은 '자신의 선택이 옳았다 '고 말하고 동생은 '자신의 선택을 후회하지 않는다'고 말하므로, 제목으로는 '나는 내 선택에 만족해!'가 적절하다. ③ get along with: ~와 잘 지내다, ④ quarrel: 다툼, ⑤ harmonious relations: 의좋은 사이

21 break out: 발발[발생]하다

22 ⓑ와 ④번은 (추측을 나타내어) ~일지[할지]도 모르다, 아마 ~ 일[할] 것이다, ①과 ⑤ (허락을 나타내어) ~해도 되다[좋다], ② ~하기 위하여, ③ (기원을 나타내어) ~이기를 (빌다)

23 ③ 만족한, ① 지루한, ② 후회하는, ④ 실망한, ⑤ 불안해하는, 염려하는

24 understands의 목적어에 해당하므로 간접의문문의 순서(의문사+주어+동사)로 고치는 것이 적절하다.

25 Why don't you 원형? = How about ~ing?: ~하는 게 어때?

서술형 실전문제   p.206~207

01 ⑤ excited → disappointed

02 ① think with → think of[about] ⑤ painted it mine → painted it myself

03 (1) I'm (a)nxious   (2) I'm (c)oncerned

04 (1) for   (2) before   (3) since

05 (1) has lived   (2) has gone to
   (3) have visited, three times

06 (1) If you finish your report by 6, you can play the computer games.
   (2) If you don't work hard, you won't overcome your weakness. (또는 Unless you work hard, you won't overcome your weakness.)

07 ② If I meet Suji, I will give her this letter.

01 영화가 어땠는지 의견을 묻는 질문에 별로 좋지 않았다는 내용과 영화를 재미있게 봤다는 내용은 일치하지 않으므로 어울리지 않는다.

02 ① What do you think of/about+명사?: ~에 대해 어떻게 생각해? ⑤ 주어가 직접 했다는 사실을 강조하기 위해 재귀대명사를 사용한다.

03 'be worried about ~.', 'be anxious about ~.', 'be concerned about ~.' 모두 걱정을 표현하는 말이다.

04 (1) 현재완료에서 'since+시간 명사', 'for+기간 명사' (2) ago는 현재완료와 함께 사용할 수 없으나 before는 사용할 수 있다. (3) since(~이래로)는 보통 현재완료와 함께 많이 쓰인다. 이때 since절에는 과거시제가 많이 쓰인다.

05 (1) 현재완료의 '계속' 용법을 이용한다. (2) 현재완료의 '결과' 용법을 이용한다. (3) 현재완료의 '경험' 용법을 이용한다.

06 명령문, + and ~: '~해라, 그러면'(= If ~), 명령문, + or ~: '~해라, 그렇지 않으면'(= If not ~ = Unless ~)

07 조건의 부사절에서는 미래시제 대신에 현재시제를 쓴다.

08 왕좌를 잃고 다시 길바닥에 나앉은 사람은 '형'이 아니라 '동생'이다.

09 앞에 소유격이 있으므로 명사로 쓰는 것이 적절하다.

10 형의 생각: "나는 조용히 잘 살았어."라고 말하면서 자신이 옳았다고 했다. 동생의 생각: "나는 지금 아무것도 없지만 언제까지나 기억할 것이 있어."라고 말하면서 자신의 선택을 후회하지 않는다고 했다.

11 (A) '어떻게' 알 수 있어?라고 해야 하므로 How가 적절하다. (B) '게다가'라고 해야 하므로 Besides가 적절하다. beside: ~ 옆에, (C) '우리가 시도하지 않으면'이라고 해야 하므로 if가 적절하다.

12 Instead of 뒤에 동명사로 써야 하고, 수동태(be killed)를 사용하는 것이 적절하다.

13 ⓑ는 '곰'을, ⓒ는 '동생'을 가리킨다.

창의사고력 서술형 문제   p.208

|모범답안|

01 I'm worried that I can't finish reading these books.

02 (1) If it is sunny tomorrow, I will go hiking.

(2) If I go to Jejudo, I'll swim in the sea.

(3) If you know the result, please let me know.

(4) If you exercise hard, you will become healthy.

03 (A) who   (B) character   (C) how   (D) such

(E) Why don't you

01 be worried about: ~에 대해 걱정하다 finish: 끝내다 do great: 잘하다

단원별 모의고사   p.209~212

01 ①   02 about, to, for, at   03 ③

04 ④   05 ⑤

06 What do you think of this painting?   07 worried

08 ④   09 I'm scared of your dog.   10 ⑤

11 ⑤   12 nervous   13 ③   14 ③

15 ②

16 (1) have you started → did you start

(2) was → have been

(3) since → for

(4) will sleep → sleep

(5) Unless she doesn't wear → Unless she wears

(또는 Unless → If)

17 (1) Judy has been in her friend's house for two hours.

(2) Someone has taken away my umbrella.

18 ②   19 ③   20 ⑤   21 ④

22 ②   23 remember   24 ①

01 ①은 반의어 관계이다. 이외의 보기는 동의어 관계이다. ① separate: 헤어지다 unite: 통합하다 ② disappointed: 실망한, 기대에 어긋난 discouraged: 낙담한 ③ character: 등장인물 role: 배역 ④ happiness: 행복 pleasure: 즐거움, 기쁨 ⑤ correct: 올바른 right: 바른, 옳은

02 be worried about: ~에 대해 걱정하다 have to 동사원형: ~해야 한다 take ~ for a walk: ~을 산책하러 데리고 가다 at night: 밤에

03 ① scary: 무서운 / 이 큰 집에서 혼자 있는 것은 무섭다. ② nervous: 불안한 / 나는 시험 전에 정말 불안하다. ③ correct: 올바른 / 올바른 날짜와 시간을 선택하세요. ④ noisy: 시끄러운 / 나는 시끄러운 곳에서는 일에 집중할 수 없다. ⑤ comfortable: 편안한 / 그것은 사람들을 더 행복하고 더 편안하게 해줍니다.

04 ④는 never에 대한 영영풀이다 ever: 언제든, 한 번이라도 (at any time 언제든지) ① support: 지지 / 어렵거나 불행한 시기 동안 누군가에게 주어지는 도움, 격려 또는 위로 ② reply: 대답하다 / 어떤 것에 응답하여 무언가를 말하거나 쓰다 ③ teenager: 십대 / 13살에서 19살 사이의 사람 ⑤ separate: 헤어지다 / 따로 이동하다

05 'You'll find something you like to do. (네가 하고 싶은 것을 발견할 거야)'는 미래에 대해 걱정하고 있을 때 위로로 할 수 있는 말이다.

06 What do you think of/about+명사?: ~에 대해 어떻게 생각해?

07 be worried about: ~에 대해 걱정하다

08 (B) 아침에 제주도에 가기 때문에 날씨를 걱정하고 있는 여자아이에게 남자아이는 비가 안 온다고 안심시키는 것이 적절하다. (C) That's good to hear.: 그거 반가운 소리다.

09 be scared of: ~을 두려워하다

10 개가 커서 무섭게 보인다는 말이므로 이유를 나타내는 because가 어울린다.

11 주어진 문장에서 that은 the first time을 의미한다. 처음이 지나고 점점 쉬워진다는 것이므로 ⑤가 적절하다.

12 nervous: 불안한 / 일어나고 있는 일 또는 일어날 수도 있는 일에 대해서 걱정하고 염려하는

13 ⓐ look worried ⓑ that I borrowed ⓒ Have you seen ⓓ have you read ⓔ What did you think

14 주어진 문장과 ③번은 부사절을 이끌고 있으나 나머지는 명사절을 이끌고 있다.

15 ② 현재완료는 과거를 나타내는 어구와 함께 쓸 수 없다.

16 (1) 현재완료는 과거의 특정 시점을 나타내는 when과는 함께 쓰이지 않는다. (2) 7월 1일에 도착해서 7월 10일인 오늘까지 있으므로 현재완료의 '계속' 용법으로 나타내는 것이 적절하다. (3) 현재완료에서 'since+시간 명사', 'for+기간 명사' (4) 조건의 부사절에서는 미래시제 대신에 현재시제를 쓴다. (5) unless = if ~ not

17 (1) 현재완료의 '계속', (2) '결과' 용법을 이용한다.

18 동생의 말에 "싫어,"라며 여러 이유를 말하고 있으므로 '의심이 많다'고 하는 것이 적절하다. doubtful: 확신이 없는, 의심[의문]을 품은, ① 긍정적인, ③ 활동적인, ④ 자신감 있는, ⑤ 근면한, 성실한

19 추가하는 내용이 뒤에 이어지므로 Besides(게다가)가 가장 적절하다. ① 그러나, ② 그러므로, ④ 예를 들어, ⑤ 다시 말해

20 ⓑ와 ⑤번은 가주어, ① 그것(앞에 이미 언급되었거나 현재 이야기되고 있는 사물·동물을 가리킴), ②와 ④ 비인칭 주어, ③ 가목적어

21 ⓐ take 사람 to 장소: ~을 …로 데리고 가다, ⓒ talk about ~: ~에 대해 이야기하다

22 ⓑ와 ②번은 '~으로, ~로서(전치사)', ① (비례) ~함에 따라, ~할수록, ③ ~이므로, ~이기 때문에, ④ ~와 같이, ~하는 대로, ⑤ (보통 as ... as ~로 형용사·부사 앞에서) ~와 같을 정도로 statesman: 정치가

23 그 당시에는 그가 아무것도 없을지 모르지만, 언제까지나 '기억할' 거리가 있을 것이기 때문이다.

24 ① 동생이 '정상'에 도착했을 때, 어떤 사람들이 그를 자기들 도시로 데려가서 그들의 왕으로 만들었다.

Lesson 5

We Love Baseball

01 ⑤   02 I was about to call you when you called me.   03 ①   04 support, (1) 응원하다 (2) 지원하다 (3) 지원, 후원   05 ④   06 ③ 07 ④

01 ⑤를 제외한 나머지는 동사와 동사의 행위를 하는 사람이다. 반면에 'cook'은 '요리하다'이나 'cooker'는 '요리 기구'라는 뜻이며, 요리사는 'cook'이다.

02 be about to: 막 ~하려는 참이다

03 order: 순서 / 그 문제들을 다른 순서로 살펴보자. ② class: 학급, 반 ③ lesson: 수업, 강의 ⑤ nature: 자연

05 in a hurry: 서둘러 / 이 일이 급하지 않기 때문에 서둘러 하지 않아도 된다. in the past: 과거에 / 과거에 의사들은 그 이유를 몰랐었습니다.

06 <보기>의 miss는 '놓치다'의 의미로 사용했다. ③은 '그리워하다'의 의미로 사용되었고 나머지는 '놓치다'의 의미로 사용되었다. ① 나는 영화의 시작 부분을 놓치는 걸 싫어한다. ② 내년에는 이 신나는 축제를 놓치지 마세요. ③ 저는 여러분이 학창시절(학교 생활)을 그리워할 것이라고 확신합니다. ④ 과학을 배우고 경험할 수 있는 이번 기회를 놓치지 마세요! ⑤ 그 경기를 놓치다니 애석합니다.

07 thunder: 천둥 / 폭풍우 동안 번개가 번쩍인 후에 들리는 하늘에서 나는 큰 소리

01 (1) batter (2) writer   02 can't wait 03 (1) stadium (2) home team (3) thunder (4) match 04 Why   05 come   6 up 07 (1) a big fan of (2) at bat (3) is about to (4) over there (5) twice a week (6) like to

01 주어진 보기는 동작과 동작의 행위자의 관계이다. act: 연기하다 actor: 배우 (1) bat: 공을 치다 batter: 타자 (2) write: 쓰다 writer: 작가

02 be looking forward to ~: ~을 기대하다, can't wait for ~: ~을 몹시 기대하다

39

03 (1) stadium: 경기장 / 이 경기장은 정말 거대해, 그렇지 않니?
(2) home team: 홈팀 / 홈팀은 3대 0으로 원정 팀을 이겼다. (3) thunder: 천둥 / 경보음이 천둥 소리와 같다. (4) match: 경기 / 스페인 팀이 축구 경기에서 이기고 있어.

04 Why don't we ~?: ~하는 게 어때?(제안, 권유) Why not?: 좋아.

05 come back to: ~으로 돌아오다, come out: 나오다

06 hurry up: 서두르다 / 서둘러 줄 수 있나요? 시간이 별로 없어요. warm up: (스포츠나 활동 전에) 몸을 천천히 풀다, 준비 운동을 하다 / 무거운 역기를 들기 전에 준비운동을 해라.

07 (1) be a big fan of: ~의 열렬한 팬이다 (2) at bat: 타석에 서서 (3) be about to 동사원형: 막 ~하려고 하다 (4) over there: 저기 (5) twice a week: 일주일에 두 번 (6) would like to 동사원형: ~하고 싶다

교과서
Conversation

핵심 Check
p.218~219

1 Which, or fish / meat
2 Which do you like better, dogs or cats
3 (B) → (D) → (A) → (C)
4 I can't wait for the trip. / I can't wait to take the trip.
5 can't, to

교과서 대화문 익히기

Check(√) True or False
p.220

1 F   2 T   3 F   4 T

교과서 확인학습
p.222~223

Listen and Speak 1 A
Which sport, or / more, twice, week

Listen and Speak 1 B
1 doing / I'm, at / Which country, or / to visit, like to
2 I'm thinking, getting, have / What, Which, better, or / Why don't, play with, can decide

Listen and Speak 2 A
Did / can't wait to watch

Listen and Speak 2 B
1 want to see / When did / bought it for me, come / can't wait to see
2 forget that / won't forget / excited, I can't wait
3 about, in / came, wants to see / can't wait to see

Real-Life Zone A
such / before, between, starts / Which team, support / miss, either / Hurry, left / sometime / about going to / while watching / I can't wait

Wrap Up
which sport do you like, or / about / big fan of / between, Have / I'm going to see, can't wait / fantastic

시험대비 기본평가
p.224

01 ③   02 ②   03 ②, ④   04 ④

01 I can't wait.: 너무 기다려져.(희망, 기대 표현하기)

02 빈칸 다음에 일주일에 두 번 축구를 한다는 말로 보아 농구보다 축구를 더 좋아하는 것을 유추할 수 있다.

03 피터팬 아니면 마지막 잎새라는 말과 피터팬을 좋아한다는 말로 보아, 둘 중에 어느 것을 좋아하는지를 묻는다는 것을 유추할 수 있다. Which do you prefer?: 어느 것을 더 선호하니? Which story book do you like?: 너는 어떤 이야기책을 좋아하니?

04 '더 좋아하는 것에 대해 말할 때는 'I like A.', 'I like A better[more] (than B).'로 말할 수 있다.

시험대비 실력평가
p.225~226

01 ②   02 ④   03 ③   04 ④
05 ④   06 ④   07 I can't wait to see it.
08 ②   09 ①   10 I'm going to go surfing.

01 주어진 문장은 개와 고양이가 있다는 의미인데, 이것은 'Do you have a pet?(넌 애완동물을 기르니?)'의 대답이 될 수 있다. 그러므로 ②의 위치가 적절하다.

02 ④의 문장은 '너의 애완동물과 놀 것이 매우 기다려져.'라는 기대의 말인데, 남자아이가 자신의 집에 와서 애완동물과 놀아 보는 것을 제안하기 전에 여자아이가 미리 말한 것이므로 어색하다.

03 ③ 여자아이가 개와 고양이 중 어떤 동물을 더 좋아하는지는 대화에 서 언급되어 있지 않다. ① 남자아이는 애완동물을 기르는 가? ② 왜 남자아이는 여자아이에게 자신의 집에 오라고 제안을 하는가? ③ 어떤 동물을 여자 아이가 더 좋아하는가? 개 아니면

고양이? ④ 얼마나 많은 개를 남자아이는 기르고 있는가? ⑤ 어떤 종류의 애완동물을 남자아이는 가지고 있는가?

04 무엇을 하고 있는지 묻는 질문에 (C) 지도를 보고 있다고 대답한다. (A) 두 나라에 표시한 것을 얘기하면서, 어느 나라를 먼저 방문하고 싶은지 묻자, (B) 미국을 방문하고 싶다고 대답하고 미국에서 농구 경기를 보고 싶다는 말을 한다.

05 선호에 대해 묻고 있는 질문에, 어느 것을 더 좋아한다는 답이 아닌 'Of course I do.(물론 나도 그래.)'는 어울리지 않는다.

06 '주어진 문장은 '오늘 오후에 우리 집에 올래?'라고 제안하는 말이다. 이에 대해 상대방이 거절이나 수락하는 것이 어울리므로, 'Of course.(당연하지.)'의 수락의 답과 연결될 수 있는 ④의 위치가 적절하다.

07 I can't wait: 너무 기다려져 'I can't wait.' 뒤에는 'for+ 명사'나 'to+동사원형'을 덧붙여 어떤 것을 기대하는지 쓸 수 있다.

08 지호에게 왜 그렇게 서두르는지 질문하자 (B) 천둥 대 코브라 경기 가 6시에 시작한다며 6시 전에 집에 있어야 한다고 대답한다. (C) 코브라와 천둥 팀 중 어느 팀을 응원하는지 질문하자 (A) 코브라라고 대답한다. (D) 상대방도 코브라 팀을 응원한다고 말하며, 자신도 그 경기를 놓치고 싶지 않다고 말한다.

09 ① 다음 코브라 홈 경기가 몇 시에 시작하는가? ② 경기를 보면서 그들은 무엇을 먹을 수 있는가? ③ 다음 코브라 홈 경기가 언제 있는가? ④ 그들은 어느 팀을 더 좋아하는가, 코브라 아니면 천둥? ⑤ 지금은 몇 시인가?

10 be going to 동사원형: ~할 것이다. 빈칸 다음에 서핑을 하러 가는 것이 기다려진다는 말을 했으므로 방학에 서핑을 하러 갈 것이다.

01 (A) 다음에 주어와 동사가 나와 있으므로 접속사인 that이 어울린다. (B) be excited about: ~에 신나다, ~에 들뜨다

02 대화의 흐름상 이번 주말에 암벽 등반하러 가기로 한 것을 잊지 않겠다고 말하는 것이 어울린다.

03 be looking forward to (동)명사: ~을 기대하다 can't wait to 동사원형: ~을 기대하다

04 지수에 대해서 들었는지 물어보는 질문에 (C) 그녀에 대한 뭐를 얘 기하는 것인지 질문하며 그녀가 캐나다에 살고 있다고 말한다. (A) 그녀가 한국에 돌아왔으며, 그녀가 상대방을 보고싶어 한다는 것을 전해 준다. (B) 이에, 그녀를 빨리 보고 싶다고 기

대를 표현하는 말을 한다.

05 테니스와 야구 중 어떤 운동을 하는 것을 좋아하는지 질문하자 (A) 테니스 치는 것을 좋아한다고 대답한다. (C) 오늘 오후에 같이 테니스를 칠 것을 제안하자. (B) 수락의 대답을 한다.

06 Have you heard about ~?: ~에 대해 들어본 적 있니? (현재완료의 경험적 용법) have: 가지다

07 'I can't wait.' 뒤에는 'to+동사원형'을 덧붙여 어떤 것을 기대하는지 쓸 수 있다.

01 능동태를 수동태로 만들 때는 수동태 문장의 주어 자리에는 능동태 문장의 목적어가 오고, 동사를 'be+pp'로 바꾸고 by 다음에는 능동태 문장의 주어를 목적격으로 쓴다.

02 앞 문장에 일반동사가 사용되고 현재시제이므로 do를 사용하며, 앞 문장이 긍정이므로 부정으로 쓰고, 인칭대명사 주어 they를 써야 하며, 축약형으로 쓴다.

03 (1) 수동태는 'be+pp'의 형태이다. (2) 책 이름은 단수로 취급한다. (3), (4) 부가의문문은 앞의 문 장이 긍정이면 부정으로 하고 부정이면 긍정으로 한다. be동사나 조동사가 있으면 그 be동사나 조동사를 이용하고 일반동사일 경우는 do/does/did를 이용한다. 반드시 축약형을 사용해야 하고 주어는 인칭대명사로 바꿔 주어야 한다는 것에 주의해야 한다.

04 (1) 다리가 건설되는 것이므로 수동태가 적절하다. (2) 부가의 문문에서 주어는 인칭대명사로 바꿔 주어야 한다는 것에 주의해야 한다.

01 ⑤   02 ②

03 (1) to   (2) for   (3) of   (4) doesn't   (5) isn't   04 ④

05 ③   06 ①   07 ④   08 ⑤

09 ③   10 ②   11 ①   12 ②

13 (1) Was this letter delivered by David?

  (2) My uncle's house was destroyed by the flood.

  (3) The table is made of wood.

  (4) The teenagers will travel to Europe, won't they?

  (5) Let's go to play tennis, shall we?

14 (1) doesn't she   (2) didn't you   (3) can she

  (4) was he   (5) will[won't] you   (6) shall we

15 (1) chosen to → chosen for

  (2) is reduced → reduces

  (3) be appeared → appear

  (4) didn't Mina → didn't she

  (5) will you → won't you

  (6) does she → is she

16 ②   17 will be held

01 The dirt가 숨겨지는 것이므로 수동태가 적절하다.

02 부가의문문은 앞의 문장이 긍정이면 부정으로 하고 부정이 면 긍정으로 한다. be동사나 조동사가 있으면 그 be동사나 조동사를 이용하고 일반동사일 경우는 do/does/did를 이용한다. 반드시 축약형을 사용해야 하고 주어는 인칭대명사로 바꿔 주어야 한다는 것에 주의해야 한다.

03 직접목적어를 주어로 한 수동태에서 간접목적어 앞에 (1) give는 전치사 to를, (2) make는 전치사 for를, (3) ask는 전치사 of를 쓴다. (4), (5) 부가의문문은 앞의 문장이 긍정이면 부정으로, be동사나 조동사가 있으면 그 be동사나 조동사를 이용하고 일반 동사일 경우는 do/does/did를 이용한다.

04 ④ A nice pen was given to me by Emily. ③ 능동태의 주어가 명확하지 않을 경우 생략할 수 있다.

05 ① isn't she ② isn't she ④ wasn't she ⑤ didn't she

06 4형식의 직접목적어를 주어로 하는 수동태에서 make는 간접목적어 앞에 for를 쓰는 동사이다. 또한 make, buy, read, write 등은 직접목적어를 주어로 하는 수동태만 가능하다

07 have가 일반동사 '먹다'의 뜻으로 쓰였으므로 do로 받는다. 앞이 과거이고 긍정이므로 didn't가 적절하다.

08 능동태의 목적어로 쓰인 the numbers를 주어로 하고 동사를 'be+pp' 형태인 'were determined'로 한 후 일반주어인 they를 'by them'으로 쓰거나 생략한다. by the players' batting order는 부사구로 쓰인 것이므로 그대로 둔다.

09 일반동사 긍정이므로 do를 이용하여 부정으로하고 대명사 주어 she를 쓴다.

10 ② 수동태는 'be+과거분사'이다.

11 ①번은 be동사가 쓰였으므로 wasn't he를 쓰지만, 나머지는 일반동사의 과거형이므로 didn't he를 써야 한다.

12 be filled with: ~로 가득 차다, be pleased with: ~로 기뻐하다

13 (1), (2) 편지가 배달되고 집이 무너지는 것이므로 수동태가 적절하다. (3) be made of: ~로 만들어지다(물리적 변화) (4) 조동사 will이 있으므로 won't를 쓰고 주어로 대명사 they를 쓴다. (5) Let's의 부가의문문은 shall we이다.

14 부가의문문은 앞의 문장이 긍정이면 부정으로 하고 부정이면 긍정으로 한다. be동사나 조동사가 있으면 그 be동사나 조동사를 이용하고 일반동사일 경우는 do/does/did 를 이용한다. 축약형을 사용해야 하고 주어는 인칭대명사로 바꿔 주어야 준다. 또한 명령문의 부가의문문은 will you? 나 won't you?를 쓰고 권유문(Let's ~)의 경우에는 shall we?를 쓴다.

15 (1) choose는 직접목적어를 주어로 한 수동태에서 간접목적어 앞에 for를 쓴다. (2) my stress가 목적어이므로 능동태가 적절하다. (3) appear는 자동사이므로 수동태로 쓰이지 않는다. (4), (5), (6) 부가의문문은 앞의 문장이 긍정이면 부정으로 하고 부정이면 긍정으로 한다. be동사나 조동사가 있으면 그 be동사나 조동사를 이용하고 일반동사일 경우는 do/does/did를 이용 한다. 축약형을 사용해야 하고 주어는 인칭대명사로 바꿔 주어야 준다.

16 그가 준비하는 것이므로 능동태 'was preparing'이 적절하다.

17 시제가 미래(next week)이므로 'will be+pp' 형태가 적절하다.

01 (1) The big house is cleaned by Tino on Sundays.

  (2) They will hold Sarang Middle School Sports Day on the school playing field on Wednesday, June 15.

  (3) Delicious spaghetti was made for Judy by Jonathan.

  (4) Are you satisfied with your job as a tour guide?

  (5) By whom was Water Lilies painted in 1906?

  (6) He will be made to take part in the science camp by Cathy.

  (7) The animals are being looked after by them.

02 didn't he

03 (1) aren't they   (2) can he   (3) did he   (4) is she

  (5) doesn't it   (6) will[won't] you   (7) shall we

04 (1) was repaired   (2) was bought for

  (3) are made   (4) was made to

05 doesn't she   06 was painted

07 (1) The pens were bought by the boy. 또는 The boy bought the pens.

  (2) Soy sauce is made from soy beans and salt.

(3) Jack wrote Cloe a letter. 또는 A letter was written to Cloe by Jack.

(4) Vivian was heard to open the window by her son.

(5) *Samgyupsal* will be cooked for Emma by her husband next weekend.

(6) By whom was this table made?

08 (1) My bike was stolen last Friday.

(2) These cookies were made by my mom.

(3) His house is filled with books.

(4) Jenny wasn't at the party last night, was she?

(5) Let's talk about our favorite sport, shall we?

01 (1) 수동태는 능동태의 목적어를 주어로 하고 동사는 'be+pp'로 바꾸고 능동태의 주어를 'by+목적격'으로 바꾸어 쓴다. (2) 미래 시제의 수동태는 'will be+과거분사'이다. (3) make는 직접목적어를 주어로 하는 수동태만 가능하며 수동태에서 간접목적어 앞에 for를 쓴다. (4) be satisfied with: ~에 만족하다 (5) 의문대명사 who가 whom으로 바뀌는 것에 주의한다. 전치사 by를 문장 뒤로 보내 Who[Whom] was Water Lilies painted in 1906 by?로 바꿔 쓸 수도 있다. (6) 목적격보어가 원형부정사인 경우, 수동태 문장에서는 to부정사로 바뀐다. (7) 구동사의 수동태는 구동사를 하나의 동사처럼 취급한다. after나 by를 빠뜨리지 않도록 주의한다.

02 과거시제이며 일반동사 긍정이므로 didn't를 쓰고 인칭대명사 he가 적절하다.

03 부가의문문은 앞의 문장이 긍정이면 부정으로 하고 부정이면 긍정으로 한다. be동사나 조동사가 있으면 그 be동사나 조동사를 이용하고 일반동사일 경우는 do/does/did 를 이용한다. 반드시 축약형을 사용해야 하고 주어는 인칭대 명사로 바꿔 주어야 준다. 또한 명령문의 부가의문문은 will you?나 won't you?를 쓰고 권유문(Let's ~)의 경우에는 shall we?를 쓴다.

04 (1), (2), (3) 컴퓨터나 스마트폰이 만들어지고 책이 구매되어지는 것이므로 수동태가 적절하다. buy는 간접목적어 앞에 전치사 for를 쓴다. (4) 목적격보어가 원형부정사인 경우, 수동태 문장에서는 to부정사로 바뀐다.

05 앞 문장이 긍정이고 현재이며 일반동사가 사용되었으므로 doesn't she가 적절하다.

06 샤갈의 '나와 마을'이란 작품이 샤갈에 의해 그려진 것이므로 수동태가 적절하다.

07 (1) The pens를 주어로 하면 수동태가, The boy를 주어로 하면 능동태가 적절하다. (2) be made of: ~로 만들어지다(물리적 변화), be made from: ~로 만들어지다(화학적 변화) (3) write는 직접목적어를 주어로 하는 수동태만 가능하다. (4) 목적격보어가 원형부정사인 경우, 수동태 문장에서는 to부정사로 바뀐다. (5) cook은 직접목적어를 주어로 한 수동태에서는 간

접목적어 앞에 for를 쓰며 next weekend가 있으므로 미래서체인 'will be+과거분사'로 써야 한다. (6) 수동태에서 능동태의 주체가 'by+목적격'이 되므로 'By whom'으로 시작되는 의문문이 적절하다.

08 (1), (2) 수동태는 '주어+be동사+동사의 과거분사+by+행위자'의 형식이다. 행위자가 중요치 않거나 확실하지 않은 경우 'by+행위자'는 생략한다. (3) be filled with: ~로 가득 차다 (4) wasn't가 있고 주어가 Jenny이므로 was she?를 쓴다. (5) 권유문(Let's ~)의 부가의문문은 shall we?이다.

교과서
Reading

확인문제   p.236

1 T   2 F   3 T   4 F   5 T   6 F

확인문제   p.237

1 T   2 F   3 T   4 F   5 T   6 F

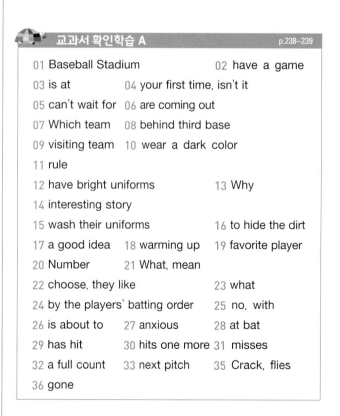

교과서 확인학습 A   p.238~239

01 Baseball Stadium   02 have a game
03 is at   04 your first time, isn't it
05 can't wait for   06 are coming out
07 Which team   08 behind third base
09 visiting team   10 wear a dark color
11 rule
12 have bright uniforms   13 Why
14 interesting story
15 wash their uniforms   16 to hide the dirt
17 a good idea   18 warming up   19 favorite player
20 Number   21 What, mean
22 choose, they like   23 what
24 by the players' batting order   25 no, with
26 is about to   27 anxious   28 at bat
29 has hit   30 hits one more   31 misses
32 a full count   33 next pitch   35 Crack, flies
36 gone

교과서 확인학습 B   p.240~241

1 A Day at the Baseball Stadium
2 Today the Thunders and the Cobras have a game.

3 Jihun's family is at the baseball stadium.

4 Jihun: Jian, this is your first time to come to the baseball stadium, isn't it?

5 Jian: Yes, I'm so excited. I can't wait for the game to start.

6 Dad: Look, the players are coming out now!

7 Jian: Which team is the Thunders?

8 Jihun: Over there, behind third base.

9 They are wearing dark gray uniforms because they are the visiting team.

10 Jian: Does the visiting team always wear a dark color?

11 Jihun: Yes, that's the rule.

12 Home teams have bright uniforms and visiting teams have dark uniforms.

13 Jian: Why is that?

14 Mom: There is an interesting story about that.

15 In the past, visiting teams could not wash their uniforms after every game.

16 So they started wearing dark colors to hide the dirt.

17 Jian: Hahaha! That was a good idea!

18 The players are warming up.

19 Jian: Who's your favorite player?

20 Jihun: Number 77.

21 Jian: What does the number mean?

22 Jihun: Hmm.... Players choose a number they like.

23 Dad: You know what?

24 In the past, the numbers were determined by the players' batting order.

25 Jihun: That means there were no players with number 77!

26 Now, Jihun's favorite player is about to bat.

27 Jihun looks anxious.

28 Jian: Your favorite player is at bat.

29 Jihun: Yes. He has hit 21 home runs already this year.

30 If he hits one more today, he will be the home run leader this season.

31 The batter misses several balls.

32 Now he has a full count.

33 He is waiting for the next pitch.

34 Jihun: HOME RUN! HOME RUN!

35 Crack! The ball flies fast.

36 It is going, going, going, gone!

시험대비 실력평가 p.242~245

01 ④　　　02 ②, ⑤　　　03 ③　　　04 bright

05 Home teams have bright uniforms and visiting teams have dark uniforms.

06 ②　　　07 ①　　　08 without

09 (A) to run　(B) to run　(C) during

10 ④　　　11 ⑤

12 The players are warming up.

13 과거: 선수의 타순이 7번째였다.
　　현재: 선수가 좋아하는 숫자인 7을 등번호로 선택한 것이다.

14 ②　　　15 home run leader　　　16 ④

17 ③　　　18 wasn't she　　　19 ②

20 ②　　　21 Who do you think will win?

22 22nd　　　23 do　　　24 ②　　　25 ⑤

26 How → What

27 In the past, catchers stood about one meter behind home base and stopped the ball.

01 동의를 구하거나 사실을 확인하기 위해 '~해. 그렇지?'라고 되묻는 부가의문문 문장은 앞 문장이 긍정이면 부정으로 만든다. This는 it으로 바꾸는 것이 적절하다.

02 ⓐ와 ②, ⑤번: 형용사적 용법, ①, ④: 명사적 용법, ③: 부사적 용법

03 지안이가 야구 경기장에 온 건 이번이 처음이다.

04 dark의 반의어가 알맞다

05 '홈팀은 밝은 유니폼을 입고 원정 팀은 어두운 유니폼을 입는 것'을 가리킨다.

06 '때'를 숨기기 위해 어두운 색을 입기 시작했다고 하는 것이 적절하다. ① (정형화된) 양식, 패턴, 무늬

07 ⓐ be known as: ~로 알려져 있다, ⓒ as the winner: 우승자로서

08 신발이 잘 맞지 않아서 '신발을 신지 않고(신발 없이)' 달리기로 결정했다고 하는 것이 적절하다.

09 (A) prepare는 목적어로 to부정사를 취하므로 to run이 적절하다. (B) decide는 목적어로 to부정사를 취하므로 to run이 적절하다. (C) 'during+기간을 나타내는 명사', 'while+주어+동사'이므로 during이 적절하다.

10 '도쿄'가 아니라 '로마'에서 신발을 신지 않고 달렸다.

11 ⓐ by: [척도·표준을 나타내어] …에 의거하여, …에 따라, by the batting order: 타순에 의해, ⓑ with number 77: 77번을 가진

12 warm up: (스포츠나 활동 전에) 몸을 천천히 풀다[준비 운동을 하다]

13 현재는 선수들이 좋아하는[원하는] 번호를 선택하지만, 과거에는 번호가 선수들의 타순에 의해 결정되었다.

14 ⓐ와 ①, ②, ④번은 완료 용법, ③ 계속 용법, ⑤ 결과 용법

15 지훈이의 가장 좋아하는 선수가 마침내 홈런을 쳤기 때문에 그

는 이번 시즌 '홈런 리더'가 될 것 같다.

16 ④ 지훈이의 가장 좋아하는 선수가 오늘 몇 개의 파울 볼을 쳤는지는 대답할 수 없다. ① Jihun's favorite player. ② 21 home runs. ③ Yes. ⑤ Yes. / inning: (야구에서 9 =회 중의 한) 회

17 (A) 어렸을 때 학교 최고의 '아마추어' 골프 선수였다. (B) 1996년에 '프로' 골프 선수가 되었다. ② mature: 성숙한, immature: 미숙한, ④ expert: 전문가

18 부가의문문은 앞 문장이 긍정이면 부정으로 만든다.

19 골프를 시작한 나이는 알 수 없다. ① 프로 골프선수, ③ 1996년, ④ 1998년부터 2016년까지, ⑤ 2007년 11월

20 ⓐ와 ②번: 차례, ① 돌다, ③ (어떤 것이 다른 방향을 향하도록) 돌리다, 뒤집다, ④ (차량의) 방향 전환, ⑤ (…한 상태로) 변하다

21 Who를 맨 앞에 쓰는 것이 적절하다.

22 그는 올해 이미 21개의 홈런을 쳤다고 했으므로, 22번째 홈런을 친 것이다. twenty-second도 가능하다.

23 play를 받는 대동사 'do'를 쓰는 것이 적절하다.

24 A: newscaster(뉴스 프로 진행자) - B: 스포츠 기자의 관계이다.

25 위 글은 '스포츠 뉴스 대본'이다. ① 요약, 개요, ② (신문, 잡지의) 글, 기사, ③ 수필, ④ (책, 연극, 영화 등에 대한) 논평 [비평], 감상문

26 think의 목적어로 'What'을 쓰는 것이 적절하다.

27 앞 문장의 내용을 가리킨다. 과거에 포수들은 홈 베이스의 약 1미터 뒤에 서서 공을 잡았다.

서술형 시험대비
p.246~247

01 (1) wait (2) dying

02 They are wearing dark gray uniforms because they are the visiting team.

03 (A) never (B) excited

04 원정 팀은 항상 어두운 유니폼을 입는 것

05 in order / so as / in order that, might[could] / so that might[could]

06 take a shower → wash their uniforms

07 Players choose a number that[which] they like.

08 4

09 과거에는 번호가 선수들의 타순에 의해 결정되었는데, 한 팀의 야구선수는 9명이기 때문이다.

10 (A) has hit (B) hits

11 Your favorite player is at bat.

12 Jihun's favorite player

---

01 I can't wait: 기다리기 힘들 정도로, 무엇인가를 너무나 하고 싶을 때 쓸 수 있는 표현, I'm dying to 부정사(for 명사): 몹시 …하고 싶어 하는, …하고 싶어 못 견디는

02 'visiting'을 보충하면 된다.

03 지안이는 전에 야구 경기장에 온 적이 '결코' 없어서 그녀는 아주 '흥분된다.'

04 바로 다음 문장의 내용을 쓰면 된다.

05 목적(~하기 위하여)을 나타내는 부사적 용법의 to부정사는 in order to, so as to, in order that ~ may[can], so that ~ may[can]로 바꿀 수 있다.

06 과거에는 원정 팀이 매 경기 후 '유니폼을 세탁할 수' 없었기 때문에 그들은 때를 숨기기 위해 어두운 색을 입기 시작했다. take a shower: 샤워를 하다

07 목적격 관계대명사 that[which]이 생략되어 있다.

08 과거에는 번호가 선수들의 타순에 의해 결정되었다고 했기 때문에 '4'번이라고 하는 것이 적절하다.

09 한 팀의 야구선수는 9명이므로, 등번호도 9번까지만 있었을 것이다.

10 (A) already가 있으므로 현재완료가 적절하다. (B) 조건의 부사절에서는 현재가 미래를 나타낸다.

11 at bat 타석에 서서

12 '지훈이의 가장 좋아하는 선수'를 가리킨다.

영역별 핵심문제
p.249~253

01 ④   02 ④   03 miss

04 ④   05 ②

06 Which sport do you like? Soccer or table tennis?

07 ticket   08 ④

09 Which baseball player do you like?

10 more than Daniel Parker 11 ③

12 I'm looking forward to seeing it.

13 ④   14 ③

15 (1) At last the thief was caught by the police last Saturday.

(2) We don't know exactly when the accident happened.

(3) Delicious galbitang is being made for him by Anna.

(4) Your love can be shown to your partner by saying "I love you."

(5) Mariel was seen to go out with her friend by Andy.

(6) The festival was put off by the city on account of the bad weather.

(7) She didn't say good-bye, did she?

(8) She can play soccer very well, can't she?

(9) Tino is wearing a blue shirt, isn't he?

(10) The hotel where we stayed was near the city hall, wasn't it?

16 (1) Tino likes eating ice cream, doesn't he?

(2) It was an interesting movie, wasn't it?

17 ②

18 (1) Where was your dog found yesterday?

(2) French is spoken in many countries in Africa.

(3) Mr. Park goes shopping every Sunday, doesn't he?

19 (A) can't (B) is (C) visiting　　20 ②

21 the Thunders　　22 ③　　23 ②

24 ⑤　　25 ②　　26 ③　　27 ⑤

28 gone　　29 batting

30 it falls to the ground → it flies fast (and is gone)

---

01 ④ order: 순서 / 술을 섞을 때는 순서를 지키는 것이 중요합니다.

02 anxious: 불안한 ① excited: 신난, 흥분한 ② pleased: 기쁜 ③ bored: 지루한 ④ nervous: 불안한 ⑤ interested: 관심 있는, 흥미 있는

03 miss: 놓치다 / 타자는 여러 개의 공을 놓쳤다. 나는 이 경기를 놓치고 싶지 않아.

04 while+동사ing: ~하는 동안

05 축구와 탁구 중에 어떤 것을 좋아하는지 묻는 질문에 여자아이는 탁구를 좋아한다고 대답하고, 상대방은 어떤지 물어보는 질문이 들어가야 남자아이가 축구를 좋아한다고 대답할 수 있으므로 주어진 문장의 위치는 ②가 적절하다.

06 Which 명사 do you like? A or B?: 어떤 ~을 좋아하니? A 아니면 B?

07 ticket: 티켓 / 어느 장소에 들어가기 위해 또는 어떤 것을 하기 위해 당신이 돈을 지불했다는 것을 보여 주는 공식적인 종이나 카드

08 ⓐ I looked at → I'm looking at ⓑ What country → Which country ⓒ would you like to visiting → would you like to visit ⓔ I'd like to seeing → I'd like to see

09 Which 명사 do you like?: 어느 ~을 좋아하니?

10 더 좋아하는 것에 대해 말할 때는 'I like A.', 'I like A better[more] than B.' 또는 'I prefer A to B.'로 표현한다. 이때 비교대상이 되는 'than B'나 'to B'는 생략할 수 있다.

11 남자아이가 'When did you get it?(언제 생긴 거야?)'으로 물었으므로 때에 대한 정보를 대답해야 한다. ⓒYesterday my father bought it for me.

12 can't wait to 동사원형: ~하기를 기대하다, be looking forward to 동명사: ~하기를 기대하다

13 ① James teaches math, doesn't he? ② She was great, wasn't she? ③ The door was opened by Tom. ⑤ The wall will be painted by the painters tomorrow.

14 첫 문장은 집이 청소하는 것이 아니라 청소되는 것이므로 수동태로 쓰인 is cleaned가, 두 번째 문장은 앞에 일반동사가 쓰였고 현재시제이며 긍정이므로 doesn't를 쓰고 주어가 Jejudo이므로 주어를 대명사 it으로 받는 것이 적절하다.

15 (1) 도둑이 경찰에 잡힌 것이므로 수동태 (2) happen은 자동사이므로 수 동태로 쓰이지 않는다. (3) 직접목적어를 주어로 한 수동태에서 make는 간접목적어 앞에 for를 쓴다. (4) 조동사가 있는 문장의 수동태는 '조동사 (7)~(10) 부가의문문은 앞의 문장이 긍정이면 부정으로 하고 부정이면 긍정 으로 한다. be동사나 조동사가 있으면 그 be동사나 조동사를 이용하고 일반 동사일 경우는 do/does/did를 이용한다. 반드시 축약형을 사용해야 하고 주어는 대명사로 바꿔 주어야 한다.

16 부가의문문은 '평서문(긍정문 또는 부정문)+반대 상황의 의문문'의 형태를 갖는다.

17 be interested in: ~에 흥미가 있다 be covered with: ~로 덮여 있다 be satisfied with: ~에 만족하다 be pleased with: ~로 기뻐하다 be filled with: ~로 가득 차다

18 (1), (2) 개가 발견되고 프랑스어가 말해지는 것이므로 수동태로 쓴다. (3) Mr. Park이 주어이므로 대명사 he로 받고 일반동사, 현재시제, 긍정이므로 doesn't를 쓴다.

19 (A) I can't wait: 기다리기 힘들 정도로, 무엇인가를 너무나 하고 싶을 때 쓸 수 있는 표현, (B) 'Which team'이 주어이므로 is가 적절하다. (C) visiting team: 원정 팀

20 ⓐ와 ②번: 형용사적 용법, ①, ④: 부사적 용법, ⑤ 명사적 용법

21 '천둥 팀'을 가리킨다.

22 과거에는 원정 팀이 매 경기 후 유니폼을 세탁할 수가 없었기 때문에 때를 숨기기 위해 어두운 색을 입기 시작했다는 말이 뒤에 나오므로, 홈팀은 '밝은' 유니폼을 입고 원정 팀은 '어두운' 유니폼을 입는다고 하는 것이 적절하다.

23 ⓒ와 ①, ④번은 동명사, 나머지는 다 현재분사

24 ⑤ 지안이는 그것이 '좋은' 생각이라고 말한다.

25 ⓐ와 ②번: 순서, ① (상품의) 주문, ③ 명령[지시]하다, ④ 정돈[정리](된 상태), ⑤ 주문하다

26 ③ 지훈이가 그 선수를 왜 좋아하는지는 대답할 수 없다., ① They are warming up. ② Number 77. ④ It means that the player likes the number 77. ⑤ They were determined by the players' batting order.

27 (A) at bat 타석에 서서, (B) wait for: ~을 기다리다

28 공이 '사라져 버렸다'고 해야 홈런을 치는 것이 된다.

29 be about to 동사원형 = be on the point of ~ing: 막 ~하려는 참이다

30 공이 땅에 떨어지는 것이 아니라, 빠르게 날아가서 사라진다.

01 ③

02 (1) first base (2) competition (3) either (4) orders

03 (A) to take (B) wait   04 ③, ⑤   05 ④

06 ③   07 ②   08 ⓐ in ⓑ and ⓒ up

09 Which country would you like to visit first? The U.S. or Mexico?   10 ②

11 There's a soccer match this weekend between Korea and Turkey.

12 ③   13 ①

14 (1) will be read to his son by Simon tonight

(2) was fixed by Peter this morning

15 (1) didn't she (2) can't they (3) was it 16 isn't it

17 (A) excited (B) to start (C) third base 18 ⑤

19 ②   20 wash their uniforms, to hide

21 ②, ③, ④ 22 It is 77. 23 ①, ④   24 ②

01 at bat: 타석에 서서 / 내가 아주 좋아하는 선수가 타석에서 있다. be about to 동사원형: 막 ~하려고 하다 / 영화가 막 시작하려 하고 있다. twice a week: 일주일에 두 번 / 그는 또한 일주일에 두 번 영어 수업을 듣는다.

02 (1) base: (야구의) 루, 베이스 (2) competition: 대회 (3) either: (부정문에서) ~도 (4) order: 순서

03 (A) take a boat ride: 보트를 타다 be going to 동사원형: ~할 것이다 (B) can't wait to 동사원형: ~을 기대하다

04 ① hide: 감추다, 숨기다 / 딸이 반지를 침대 밑에 숨겼다. ② fit: 맞다 / 헬멧이 잘 맞는지 확인하는 것을 잊지 마세요. ③ either: (부정문에서) ~도 / 그는 못 가고, 나도 못 간다. ④ decide: 결정하다 / 무엇을 먹을지 결정하는 것은 쉽지 않다. ⑤ support: (특정 스포츠 팀을) 응원하다 / 당신은 어느 팀을 응원하나요?

05 ④번은 visiting team(원정 팀: 경쟁하는 팀의 경기장이나 코트에서 경기를 하는 스포츠 팀)에 대한 설명이다.

06 주어진 문장에서 the game은 천둥 대 코브라의 경기를 의미한다. 지호가 그 경기를 보러 서둘러 집에 가고 있는 상황에서 알렉스가 놓치고 싶지 않다고 얘기하고 있다.

07 support: (특정 스포츠 팀을) 응원하다

08 ⓐ in a hurry: 서둘러 ⓑ between A and B: A와 B 사이에 ⓒ hurry up: 서두르다

09 would like to 동사원형: ~하고 싶다 visit: 방문하다

10 ② 남자아이는 멕시코에서 무엇을 하고 싶은가?

11 there is 단수명사: ~가 있다 between A and B: A와 B 사이에

12 ③ 윤호는 이번 주말의 축구 경기에 대해 들었다.

13 수동태 문장에서 행위자가 중요치 않거나 확실하지 않은 경우 'by+행위자'는 생략한다.

14 능동태의 목적어가 주어 자리에 있으므로 수동태로 쓴다.

15 부가의문문은 몰라서 질문하는 것이 아니고 상대방의 동의를 구

하거나 사실을 확인하기 위해 사용된다.

16 동의를 구하거나 사실을 확인하기 위해 '~해, 그렇지?'라고 되묻는 부가의문문은 앞 문장이 긍정이면 부정으로 만든다. This는 it으로 바꾸는 것이 직질하다.

17 (A) 감정을 나타내는 동사는 수식받는 명사가 감정을 느끼게 되는 경우에 과거분사를 써야 하므로 excited가 적절하다. (B) to start가 wait의 목적어이고, for the game은 to start의 의미상의 주어이다. (C) '3루' 뒤라고 해야 하므로 third base가 적절하다. three bases: 세 개의 루

18 원정 팀의 선수들이 어두운 회색 유니폼을 입고 있는 이유는 대답할 수 없다. ① The Thunders and the Cobras do. ② At the baseball stadium. ③ No. ④ She feels so excited.

19 이 글은 '원정 팀이 어두운 유니폼을 입게 된' 이유에 관한 글이다. strong points: 강점, weak points: 약점

20 과거에는 원정 팀이 매 경기 후 '유니폼을 세탁할 수'가 없었기 때문에 그들은 때를 '숨기기 위해' 어두운 색을 입기 시작했다.

21 ⓐ와 ①, ⑤: 부사적 용법(목적), ②, ④: 명사적 용법, ③ 형용사적 용법

22 ③ 'Players choose a number they like.'라고 했기 때문에, 지훈이가 가장 좋아하는 77번 선수가 좋아하는 숫자는 '77'이다.

23 ⓐ와 ①, ④: (이야기 첫 머리에서) 재미있거나 놀라운 의견·소식 등을 말하려 할 때 씀. '저 있잖아, 내 이야기 들어봐'라는 뜻. ②, ⑤: 그것에 대해 어떻게 생각해? ③ 어떻게 (요리 를) 해드릴까요?

24 '지훈'이가 가장 좋아하는 선수가 77번 선수이다.

01 will → won't   02 can → can't

03 I'm looking forward to watching the game.

04 (1) What was cooked for her family by her last night?

(2) Kimdaesung built Dabotap in the eighth century.

(3) Kevin waters the plants every morning.

(4) Some flowers were given (to) me by my friend two days ago. 또는 I was given some flowers by my friend two days ago.

05 (1) The light bulb was invented by Edison. 또는 Edison invented the light bulb.

(2) A dress was made for Sue by her mom.

(3) You aren't paying attention, are you?

(4) You forgot to bring your umbrella, didn't you?

06 (A) excited (B) wearing

07 I can't wait for the game to start.

08 they are the visiting team

09 has come → has never come

10 (A) warming (B) Who's (C) what

11 A number they like is chosen by players. 또는 A number players like is chosen by them.

12 they determined the numbers by the players' batting order.

13 In the past, the numbers were determined by the players' batting order.

---

01 암벽 등반하러 가기로 한 것을 잊지 말라는 말에 걱정하지 말라며 잊을 거라고 말하는 것은 어색하고 잊지 않을 것이라고 말하는 것이 어울린다. won't = will not: ~하지 않을 것이다

02 볼링과 야구 중 어떤 운동을 좋아하는지 묻는 질문에, 야구를 좋아한다며 이번 주말에 친구들이랑 야구를 하러 간다는 대답을 했는데 'I can wait.(나는 기다릴 수 있어.)'라는 말은 어색하다. I can't wait.: 너무 기다려져.

03 I can't wait to 동사원형.: ~하는 것이 너무 기다려져 = I'm looking forward to 동명사.

04 (1) 의문문의 수동태는 능동태의 의문문을 평서문으로 바꾼 후 이것을 수동태로 고치고, 다시 의문문으로 바꾸면 쉽다. (4) 4형식 문장의 수동태는 간접목적어와 직접목적어 각각을 주어로 하는 수동태가 가능하며 직접목적어를 주어로 한 수동태에서 give 동사는 간접목적어 앞에 전치사 to를 쓴다. 이 때의 to는 생략하기도 한다.

05 (1) 전구가 무엇을 발명할 수는 없으므로 수동태로 쓰거나 목적어로 쓰여야 한다. (2) make는 간접목적어를 주어로 하는 수동태로 쓰이지 않는다. 수동태에서 간접목적어 앞에 for을 쓰며 능동태(Her mom made Sue a dress.)로 고쳐도 좋다. (3) be동사가 쓰이고 있으므로 are you가 되어야 한다. (4) 일반동사의 과거시제가 쓰이고 있으므로 did를 써야 하고, 긍정이므로 부정으로 써야 하며 반드시 축약형 didn't로 써야 함에 유의한다.

06 (A) 지안이가 흥분을 느끼는 것이므로 과거분사 excited가 적절하다. (B) 선수들이 유니폼을 입고 있는 것이므로 현재 분사가 적절하다.

07 I can't wait: 기다리기 힘들 정도로, 무엇인가를 너무나 하고 싶을 때 쓸 수 있는 표현.

08 '그들은 원정 팀이기' 때문에 어두운 회색 유니폼을 입고 있다. the Thunders가 팀 선수들을 가리키고 있기 때문에 복수로 취급하는 것이 적절하다.

09 지안이가 야구 경기장에 온 건 이번이 처음이라고 했기 때문에 has 'never' come으로 고쳐야 한다.

10 (A) warm up: (스포츠나 활동 전에) 몸을 천천히 풀다, 준비운동을 하다, 현재진행형으로 써야 하므로 warming이 적절하다.

(B) 가장 좋아하는 선수가 '누구야?'라고 해야 하므로 Who's가

적절하다. whose: 누구의, (C) You know what?: (이야기 첫머리에서) 재미있거나 놀라운 의견·소식 등을 말하려 할 때 씀.

11 능동태의 목적어인 a number they like를 주어로 하여 수동태로 바꾼다.

12 by the players' batting order가 행위자를 나타내는 것이 아니고 야구팀의 감독이나 팀 관계자들이 선수들의 타순에 의거하여 선수들의 번호를 결정한 것이므로 they를 주어로 하여 고쳐야 한다.

13 앞 문장의 내용을 가리킨다.

|모범답안|

01 (1) The dress was chosen for her by her mom.

(2) Lots of money is donated to charity by me.

(3) Lights should be turned off when you leave the room.

(4) Chicken soup was made for him by her.

(5) *Romeo and Juliet* was written by Shakespeare.

02 (A) amateur (B) professional
(C) LPGA Tours (D) World Golf Hall of Fame

01 ①

02 (c)ompetition, (c)rack, (p)ast, (h)ide
(1) hide (2) cracks (3) competition (4) past

03 (1) over there (2) in a hurry
(3) come out (4) waiting for

04 ④　　　05 more[better] than the red ones

06 I prefer the green ones to the red ones.

07 ⑤　　　08 ②　　　09 (A) starts (B) either
(C) left　　10 team　　11 ②

12 more → better　　13 ④　　　14 ③

15 (1) from → of
(2) William was bought a new computer
　 → A new computer was bought for William
(3) are taken place → take place
(4) don't → aren't
(5) can't → will 또는 won't

16 ②

17 (1) don't you (2) isn't she (3) wasn't he
(4) doesn't he (5) won't you (6) didn't you
(7) will[won't] you (8) shall we

18 ③　　　19 The Cobras.

20 wearing dark colors to hide the dirt　　21 ④

22 the numbers were determined by the players' batting order

23 (A) players (B) like

01 decide: 결정하다 determine: 결정하다 / 가격은 수요와 공급에 의해 결정된다.

02 (1) hide: 감추다, 숨기다 / 보이지 않는 곳에 무언가를 두다 / 그 개는 어제 뼈다귀를 땅속에 숨겼다. (2) crack: 찢어지는 듯한[날카로운] 소리 / 어떤 것이 떨어지거나 자체로 또는 다른 것과 부딪칠 때 나는 갑작스러운 큰 폭발음 / 밤새 큰 천둥 소리가 울렸다. (3) competition: 대회 / 사람들이 다른 사람들을 물리침으로써 어떤 것을 얻으려고 하는 행사나 경기 / 경쟁이 심해지고 있다. (4) in the past: 과거에 past: 과거 / 말하거나 쓰는 순간 이전의 시간 / 과거에 사람들은 말을 타고 여행을 다녔다.

03 (1) over there: 저기 (2) in a hurry: 서둘러 (3) come out: 나오다 (4) wait for: ~를 기다리다

04 go+동사ing: ~하러 가다 go surfing: 서핑하러 가다 go swimming: 수영하러 가다 play+운동 이름: ~하다 play soccer: 축구를 하다 play tennis: 테니스를 치다

05 더 좋아하는 것에 대해 말할 때는 'I like A.', 'I like A better[more] than B.' 이때 비교 대상이 되는 'than B'는 생략할 수 있다.

06 prefer A (to B): B보다 A를 더 좋아하다

07 다음 코브라 홈 경기를 함께 보자고 제안하고 있으므로 'Okay. (좋아.)'라고 수락하는 것이 어울린다.

08 어느 팀을 응원하는지 선호를 묻는 문장이 나와야 하므로 의문사 'Which'로 질문해야 한다. support: (특정 스포츠 팀을) 응원하다

09 (A) The game이 문장의 주어로 3인칭 단수이기 때문에 동사에 s를 붙여야 한다. (B) either는 부정문에서 '~도'의 의미로 사용된다. (C) thirty minutes를 수식하므로 수동의 의미로 '남겨진'의 의미인 left가 어울린다.

10 team: 팀 / 다른 모임의 사람들에 대항해서 운동이나 경기를 함께 하는 사람들의 모임

11 ② watched → will watch 대화의 내용상 그들은 다음 코브라 홈 경기를 함께 보러 갈 것이다.

12 어떤 동물이 나에게 더 나은지 질문하고 있으므로, more(더 많은)보다 good의 비교급인 better(더 좋은)가 내용상 어울린다.

13 ① Cheesecake is baked for Scott every day. ② Mr. Lee wrote a letter. ③ My computer was fixed by my brother. ⑤ You have a pen, don't you?

14 ③ The plan was given up because of the heavy costs (by them). give up을 한 단어처럼 취급해야 한다.

15 (1) be made of: ~로 만들어지다(물리적 변화) be made from: ~로 만들어지다(화학적 변화) (2) buy는 간접목적어를 주어로 수동태를 만들 수 없으며 수동태로 바뀔 때 간접목적어 앞에 for를 쓴다. (3) take place는 자동사로 쓰이므로 수동태로 쓰이지 않는다. (4) 긍정의 현재시제 be동사가 쓰이고 있으므로 'be동사+n't'로 부가의문문을 만들어야 한다. (5) 명령문이므로 부가의문문은 'will you?'나 'won't you?'로 써야 한다.

16 ②번은 과거 동사로 쓰였고 나머지는 과거분사로 수동태를 만들고 있다.

17 부가의문문은 앞의 문장이 긍정이면 부정으로 하고 부정이면 긍정으로 한다. be동사나 조동사가 있으면 그 be동사나 조동사를 이용하고 일반동사일 경우는 do/does/did를 이용한다. 반드시 축약형을 사용해야 하고 주어는 대명사로 바꿔 주어야 준다. 또한 명령문의 부가의문문은 will you?나 won't you?를 쓰고 권유문(Let's ~)의 경우에는 shall we?를 쓴다.

18 ⓐ와 ①, ④번은 현재분사, 나머지는 다 동명사

19 '코브라'가 홈팀이다.

20 '때를 숨기기 위해 어두운 색을 입기 시작한 것'을 가리킨다.

21 어떤 팀이 처음으로 어두운 유니폼을 입기 시작했는지는 대답할 수 없다.

22 'by'를 보충하면 된다. by: [척도·표준을 나타내어] …에 의거하여, …에 따라

23 요즘은 '선수들' 자신에 의해 번호가 선택되는데, 그것은 그들이 '좋아하는' 숫자이다.

교과서 파헤치기

Lesson 1

1 fully, 완전히   2 right, 바로   3 challenging, 도전적인

4 band, 밴드   5 freely, 자유롭게   6 goal, 목표

7 most, 가장   8 overcome, 극복하다

9 spend, 쓰다, 소비하다   10 draw, 그리다

11 book fair, 도서 박람회   12 save, 구하다, 살리다

13 someday, 언젠가   14 complete, 완료하다, 완결하다

15 favor, 호의. 친절   16 detective, 탐정

01 호의, 친절	02 극복하다	03 탐정, 형사
04 약한	05 완료하다, 완결하다	
06 걱정하다	07 유럽, 유럽 대륙	08 경험하다; 경험
09 시작하다	10 ~까지(는)	11 머무르다, 지내다
12 바로	13 입양하다	14 자유롭게
15 만화	16 작가	17 목표
18 희망하다, 바라다; 희망		19 소개하다
20 도전적인, 힘든, 간단하지 않은		21 그리다
22 씻다	23 놀라게 하다	24 구하다, 아끼다
25 도서 박람회	26 중국어; 중국의	
27 걷게 하다, 데리고 가다		28 약점
29 없어진, 분실한	30 언젠가	31 기쁜
32 완전히	33 마지막으로	34 쓰다, 소비하다
35 ~을 돌보다	36 기꺼이 ~하다	37 잠깐
38 A를 B와 나누다[공유하다]		39 도움을 청하다
40 ~에 흥미를 갖게 되다		41 ~할 준비가 되다
42 노력하다	43 ~을 버리다, ~을 던지다	

Listen & Speak 1 A

hope, get good grades / Don't worry

Listen & Speak 1 B

1 it's your birthday / What, want for / I hope I get /

2 What, doing / I'm making, wish list / cool, the first /
hope, make a lot of

3 How, English class / It was, wrote down, for / you,
tell, yours / hope I, someday

Listen & Speak 1 C

1 hope I can travel, this / sounds

2 hope, can see / sounds

3 hope I can learn, to / sounds great

Everyday English 2. A Function Practice 2

What are you planning to / planning to get, cut

Everyday English 2. B Listening Activity

1 planning to do tomorrow / I'm planning, book fair
with / like to join / What time, going to meet / At,
in front of

2 are you planning / not sure / how about going,
with / sounds

3 Can, a favor / what / to buy, tomorrow, help,
choose one / love to

Listen & Speak 2 C

1 do at / planning to sell

2 are you planning to / planning to do a magic

3 What are you planning / to dance in a group

01 national	02 concert	03 bucket list
04 drama	05 musical instrument	
06 save	07 surprise	08 wash
09 detective	10 challenging	11 favorite
12 spend	13 band	14 weakness
15 festival	16 fully	17 subject
18 someday	19 special	20 missing
21 plan	22 pleased	23 ride
24 finally	25 sell	26 talk
27 adopt	28 worry	29 favor
30 stay	31 overcome	32 experience
33 weak	34 complete	35 by the end of ~
36 get better	37 be ready to 동사원형	
38 throw away	39 ask for help	40 make an effort
41 for a while	42 be willing to 동사원형	
43 make a friend		

Listen & Speak 1 A

G: I hope I get good grades this year.

B: You will. Don't worry.

Listen & Speak 1 B

1 B: Hana, it's your birthday today. Happy birthday!

   G: Thank you.

B: What do you want for your birthday?

G: I hope I get a new computer.

2 G: What are you doing?

B: I'm making my wish list for the new school year.

G: That sounds cool! What's the first thing on your list?

B: I hope I make a lot of new friends.

3 G: How was your English class?

B: It was fun! We wrote down our dreams for the future.

G: Oh, did you? So tell me. What's yours?

B: Well, first, I hope I become a rock star someday.

Listen & Speak 1 C

1 A: I hope I can travel to Europe this summer.

B: That sounds great.

2 A: I hope I can see my grandmother.

B: That sounds great.

3 A: I hope I can learn how to swim.

B: That sounds great.

Everyday English 2. A Function Practice 2

G: What are you planning to do tomorrow?

B: I'm planning to get my hair cut.

Everyday English 2. B Listening Activity

1 B: What are you planning to do tomorrow?

G: I'm planning to go to the book fair with Jimmy. Would you like to join us?

B: Sure. What time are you going to meet?

G: At 3:00 in front of the school cafeteria.

2 G: What are you planning to do tomorrow?

B: Well, I'm not sure.

G: Then how about going to a movie with me?

B: That sounds wonderful. 3

3 G: Jack! Can you do me a favor?

B: Yes, what is it?

G: I'm planning to buy a new bike tomorrow. Can you help me choose one?

B: Sure, I'd love to.

Listen & Speak 2 C

1 A: What are you planning to do at the school festival?

B: I'm planning to sell snacks.

2 A: What are you planning to do at the school festival?

B: I'm planning to do a magic show.

3 A: What are you planning to do at the school festival?

B: I'm planning to dance in a group.

본문 TEST Step 1   p.09~10

01 My, School Year   02 Hi, everyone

03 first, our, year 04 hear, plans, this

05 What, want, most

06 Think about, things

07 then, make, share, with   08 I'm Jinsu

09 my, list, this year   10 First, on, tour

11 been, experience, freely on

12 second, to, how

13 think, most, sound, instruments

14 play, on, by, end

15 Finally, get, grade in

16 weakest subject

17 put, into, overcome, weakness   18 My name is

19 favorite, right, front, stage

20 willing, line, enter

21 Second, adopt, puppy

22 always wanted

23 fully ready, care

24 last, little, challenging

25 like, all, stories

26 big, detective, so, miss

본문 TEST Step 2   p.11~12

01 for the New School Year   02 Hi, everyone

03 the first day, new school year

04 want to hear, for this year

05 What, want, most

06 Think about, you want to do

07 make a bucket list, share, with 08 I'm

09 This is, this year

10 go on a bike tour, this summer

11 I've been there before, freely on my bike

12 second goal, how to play

13 the most beautiful sound, musical instruments

14 hope, can play, on, by the end of

15 Finally, get a good grade

16 weakest subject

17 put, into, to overcome my weakness

18 My name is   19 want to see, right in front of

20 willing, stand in line, front area

21 Second, adopt a puppy

22 I've, wanted   23 I'm, ready to take care of

24 last goal, a little more challenging

25 I'd like to, all of

26 a big fan, detective series, miss a single one

1 나의 새 학년 버킷 리스트

2 모두들, 안녕.

3 오늘은 우리 새 학년의 첫날이에요.

4 저는 여러분들의 올해 계획과 희망을 듣고 싶어요.

5 여러분이 가장 원하는 것은 무엇인가요?

6 여러분이 원하는 것 세 가지를 생각해 보세요.

7 그러고 나서 버킷 리스트를 만들어 친구들과 공유해 봐요.

8 안녕하세요! 저는 진수예요.

9 이것은 올해 제 버킷 리스트예요.

10 우선, 저는 이번 여름에 제주도로 자전거 여행을 가고 싶어요.

11 저는 그곳을 전에 가 본 적이 있지만 이번에는 제 자전거를 타고 좀 더 자유롭게 그 섬을 경험해 보고 싶어요.

12 제 두 번째 목표는 기타 연주하는 법을 배우는 거예요.

13 저는 기타가 모든 악기 중에 가장 아름다운 소리를 낸다고 생각해요.

14 올해 말쯤에는 제가 가장 좋아하는 곡을 제 기타로 연주할 수 있으면 좋겠어요.

15 마지막으로 수학에서 좋은 점수를 받고 싶어요.

16 수학은 제가 가장 약한 과목이에요.

17 올해는 제 약점을 극복하기 위해 수학 공부에 좀 더 노력을 기울일 거예요.

18 안녕하세요! 제 이름은 소미예요.

19 우선, 저는 제가 가장 좋아하는 밴드의 공연을 무대 바로 앞에서 보고 싶어요.

20 앞자리에 들어가기 위해 저는 기꺼이 밤새 줄을 서서 기다릴 거예요.

21 두 번째로, 강아지를 입양하고 싶어요.

22 저는 항상 강아지를 원해 왔어요.

23 이제는 제가 애완동물을 돌볼 준비가 완벽히 되었다고 생각해요.

24 제 마지막 목표는 좀 더 도전적이에요.

25 저는 셜록 홈스 이야기들을 모두 읽고 싶어요.

26 저는 작년에 이 탐정 시리즈의 열성 팬이 되었어요, 그래서 저는 단 하나도 놓치고 싶지 않아요.

1 My "Bucket List" for the New School Year

2 Hi, everyone.

3 Today is the first day of our new school year.

4 I want to hear your plans and hopes for this year.

5 What do you want to do most?

6 Think about three things you want to do.

7 And then, make a bucket list and share it with your friends.

8 Hi! I'm Jinsu.

9 This is my bucket list for this year.

10 First, I want to go on a bike tour of Jejudo this summer.

11 I've been there before, but I want to experience the island more freely on my bike this time.

12 My second goal is to learn how to play the guitar.

13 I think the guitar has the most beautiful sound of all musical instruments.

14 I hope I can play my favorite song on my guitar by the end of this year.

15 Finally, I want to get a good grade in math.

16 Math is my weakest subject.

17 This year, I'll put more effort into studying math to overcome my weakness.

18 Hi! My name is Somi.

19 First, I want to see a concert of my favorite band right in front of the stage.

20 I'm willing to stand in line all night to enter the front area.

21 Second, I want to adopt a puppy.

22 I've always wanted a puppy.

23 I think I'm fully ready to take care of a pet now.

24 My last goal is a little more challenging.

25 I'd like to read all of the Sherlock Holmes stories.

26 I became a big fan of this detective series last year, so I don't want to miss a single one.

Work Together Step 3

1. bucket list we bought

2. hope, can, actor

3. Second, have dinner with

4. Third, can travel, other

5. spent, to buy

My Writing Portfolio

1. This Year

2. Here is

3. First, how to make

4. want to, to surprise

5. Second, to live, life

6. throw away, that, not need

7. last thing, to study, lessons

8. At the end, will overcome, weakest

Culture Link

1. I am

2. get good grades

3. give, some advice

4. Why don't you, wake up

5. go to bed early, get better grades

구석구석지문 TEST Step 2   p.20

Work Together Step 3

1. This is the bucket list we bought.

2. First, I hope I can meet my favorite actor.

3. Second, I hope I can have dinner with my role model.

4. Third, I hope I can travel to other countries.

5. We spent ninety dollars to buy these items.

My Writing Portfolio

1. My "Bucket List" for This Year

2. Here is my bucket list.

3. First, I want to learn how to make cookies.

4. I want to make them to surprise my mom.

5. Second, I want to live a simple life.

6. I will throw away things that I do not need.

7. The last thing is to study online English lessons every day.

8. At the end of this year, I will overcome my problems with my weakest subject, English.

Culture Link

1. Hi, I am Gijun.

2. I hope I get good grades this year, but I sleep too much.

3. Could you give me some advice?

4. Why don't you go to bed on time and wake up early?

5. I think you need to go to bed early and sleep on a regular schedule to get better grades.

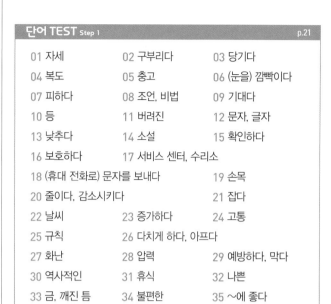

단어 TEST Step 1   p.21

01 자세	02 구부리다	03 당기다
04 복도	05 충고	06 (눈을) 깜빡이다
07 피하다	08 조언, 비법	09 기대다
10 등	11 버려진	12 문자, 글자
13 낮추다	14 소설	15 확인하다
16 보호하다	17 서비스 센터, 수리소	
18 (휴대 전화로) 문자를 보내다		19 손목
20 줄이다, 감소시키다		21 잡다
22 날씨	23 증가하다	24 고통
25 규칙	26 다치게 하다, 아프다	
27 화난	28 압력	29 예방하다, 막다
30 역사적인	31 휴식	32 나쁜
33 금, 깨진 틈	34 불편한	35 ~에 좋다
36 ~을 줄이다	37 당장	
38 ~와 연락[접촉]하다		
39 ~에 주의를 기울이다		40 가끔, 이따금
41 A를 B로부터 막다		42 ~에 의존하다
43 명심하다		

단어 TEST Step 2   p.22

01 crack	02 cause	03 drop
04 rule	05 uncomfortable	06 under
07 hold	08 increase	09 historical
10 worse	11 break	12 life jacket
13 pressure	14 pain	15 weather
16 reduce	17 hurt	18 upset
19 prevent	20 blink	21 wrist
22 avoid	23 back	24 protect
25 pull	26 pose	27 deserted
28 hall	29 tip	30 check
31 lean	32 lower	33 letter
34 advice	35 pay attention to	
36 be late for	37 depend on	
38 get in touch with		39 instead of
40 cut down on	41 at least	42 give back
43 take a walk		

단어 TEST Step 3   p.23

1 tip, 조언, 비법   2 avoid, 피하다   3 deserted, 버려진

4 drop, 떨어지다   5 blink, (눈을) 깜빡이다

6 protect, 보호하다　7 novel, 소설

8 lower, 낮추다　9 reduce, 줄이다, 감소시키다

10 break, 휴식　11 cause, 초래하다, 야기하다

12 text, (휴대 전화로) 문자를 보내다

13 uncomfortable, 불편한　14 hall, 복도

15 prevent, 예방하다, 막다　16 upset, 화난

대화문 TEST Step 1　p.24~25

Listen & Speak 1 A

dark circles under / should get more sleep

Listen & Speak 1 B

1 forgot / Isn't, best friend / Yes, What should I do / I think you should tell

2 feel down / matter / put on, this, What should / should cut down on

Listen & Speak 1 C

1 always late for, should I / should set an alarm

2 have, headache. What should I / should get some rest

3 doesn't work, What should I do / take, the service center

Listen & Speak 2 A

Make sure, by / will

Listen & Speak 2 B

1 sleep over at / say, okay / said, would make / Make sure you text , get to

2 what, doing / reading, on / don't read in the dark, not good for / turn, on

3 didn't bring / won't / borrow / make sure, give it back when, done

Listen & Speak 2 C

1 Can, eat / make sure you, first

2 Can I / turn it off after using it

3 Can I ride on / make sure, wear a life jacket

대화문 TEST Step 2　p.26~27

Listen & Speak 1 A

G: Oh, no! I have dark circles under my eyes.

M: You should get more sleep.

Listen & Speak 1 B

1 G: I forgot Jenny's birthday!

B: Isn't she your best friend?

G: Yes, she is. What should I do?

B: I think you should tell her you're very sorry.

2 B: I feel down.

G: Why? What's the matter?

B: I put on 5kg this winter. What should I do?

G: I think you should cut down on snacks.

Listen & Speak 1 C

1 A: I'm always late for school. What should I do?

B: You should set an alarm on your smartphone.

2 A: I have a headache. What should I do?

B: You should get some rest.

3 A: My phone doesn't work. What should I do?

B: You should take it to the service center.

Listen & Speak 2 A

W: Make sure you are home by 12:00.

G: Okay, I will.

Listen & Speak 2 B

1 B: Mom, may I sleep over at Jinsu's house?

W: Did Jinsu's mom say it was okay?

B: Yes. Jinsu said she would make pizza for us.

W: Okay. Make sure you text me when you get to Jinsu's house.

2 G: Daniel, what are you doing?

B: I'm reading a novel on my smartphone.

G: Make sure you don't read in the dark. It's not good for your eyes.

B: Okay. I'll turn the light on.

3 B: Oh, no! I didn't bring my science book!

G: Ms. Lee won't be happy about that.

B: I know. Umm, can I borrow your science book?

G: Okay. Just make sure you give it back when you're done.

Listen & Speak 2 C

1 A: Can I eat this pizza?

B: Sure. Just make sure you wash your hands first.

2 A: Can I use this computer?

B: Sure. Just make sure you turn it off after using it.

3 A: Can I ride on this boat?

B: Sure. Just make sure you wear a life jacket.

본문 TEST Step 1　p.28~29

01 Health Tips, Users

02 spends, lot, using

03 checks, news, weather　04 plays, games

05 texts his　06 finds information, Internet

07 online comic books

08 watches movies　09 take, off, long

10 using, too, cause health

11 heavy user, like 12 so, tips, protect

13 Watch, neck, back

14 When, read, usually bend

15 text, increases, pressure, back

16 prevent, bring, up to

17 Another way, instead, bending

18 Give, eyes, break

19 makes, feel, dry, for

20 Using, moving, makes, worse 21 avoid, from, to

22 Follow, Every, least, away 23 blink, often

24 keep, from becoming 25 text, lot on

26 Texting, hurt, wrists 27 Try, exercises

28 help reduce, pain 29 Pull on, each

30 Put, backs, with, out 31 But remember

32 tip, prevent, use, less

33 yourself, rest from

01 Health Tips, Users

02 spends, lot, using

03 checks, news, weather 04 plays, games

05 texts his friends

06 finds information on, Internet

07 reads online comic books

08 watches movies

09 take, off, all day long

10 using, too much, cause health problems

11 a heavy user, like

12 If so, here are, to protect

13 Watch, neck, back

14 When, usually bend

15 text neck, pose increases

16 to prevent, to bring, up to

17 Another way, to lower, instead of bending

18 Give, a break

19 makes, feel tired, for a long time

20 Using, in the dark, makes, worse

21 To avoid, from time to time

22 Follow, Every, a 20-second break, at least, feet
away 23 blink, often

24 keep, from becoming

25 text, on your smartphone 26 Texting, hurt

27 Try, exercises 28 help reduce

29 Pull on, each hand

30 Put, together with your arms, in front of

31 remember

32 The best tip to prevent, to use, less

33 some rest from

1 스마트폰 사용자들을 위한 건강 조언

2 성민이는 스마트폰을 사용하는 데 많은 시간을 보냅니다.

3 그는 뉴스와 날씨를 확인합니다.

4 그는 스마트폰 게임을 합니다.

5 그는 친구들에게 문자 메시지를 보냅니다.

6 그는 인터넷에서 정보를 찾습니다.

7 그는 온라인 만화책을 읽습니다.

8 그는 영화를 봅니다.

9 성민이는 하루 종일 스마트폰에서 손을 뗄 수가 없습니다.

10 그는 스마트폰을 너무 많이 사용하는 것이 건강 문제를
일으킬 수 있다는 것을 모릅니다.

11 여러분은 성민이와 같은 스마트폰 과다 사용자인가요?

12 그렇다면, 여기 여러분의 건강을 지켜 줄 몇 가지 조언이 있습니다.

13 여러분의 목과 척추를 조심하세요.

14 스마트폰을 볼 때, 여러분은 보통 목을 구부립니다

15 이 "거북목" 자세는 여러분의 목과 척추에 가해지는 압력을
증가시킵니다.

16 이러한 압력을 예방하는 가장 좋은 방법은 휴대 전화를
여러분의 눈높이까지 올리는 것입니다.

17 또 다른 방법은 여러분의 목을 구부리는 대신에 시선을
낮추는 것입니다.

18 눈을 쉬게 하세요.

19 오랫동안 스마트폰의 작은 글자를 읽는 것은 눈이
피곤해지고 건조하게 느끼도록 만듭니다.

20 어두운 곳이나 움직이는 차에서 스마트폰을 사용하는 것은
이러한 문제를 더욱 악화시킵니다.

21 이것을 피하려면, 눈을 때때로 쉬게 하세요.

22 20-20-20 규칙을 따르세요. 20분마다 20초의 휴식을 취하고
적어도 20피트 이상 떨어져 있는 사물을 바라보세요.

23 또한, 눈을 자주 깜박이세요.

24 이것은 여러분의 눈이 건조해지는 것을 막아 줄 것입니다.

25 스마트폰으로 문자 메시지를 많이 보내나요?

26 오랫동안 문자 메시지를 보내는 것은 여러분의 손가락과
손목을 상하게 할 수 있습니다.

27 이런 운동을 해 보세요.

28 그것은 여러분의 손가락과 손목의 통증을 줄이는 것을 도와줄 것입니다.

29 각 손의 각 손가락을 당기세요.

30 팔을 여러분 앞에서 벌린 채로 손등을 마주 놓으세요.

31 그러나 기억하세요.

32 이러한 건강 문제를 예방하는 가장 좋은 방법은 스마트폰을 덜
사용하는 것입니다.

33 여러분 자신에게 스마트폰으로부터 휴식을 주세요.

1 Health Tips for Smartphone Users.

2 Seongmin spends a lot of time using his smartphone.

3 He checks the news and weather.

4 He plays smartphone games.

5 He texts his friends.

6 He finds information on the Internet.

7 He reads online comic books.

8 He watches movies.

9 Seongmin cannot take his hands off his smartphone all day long.

10 He does not know that using a smartphone too much can cause health problems.

11 Are you a heavy user of your smartphone like Seongmin?

12 If so, here are some tips to protect your health.

13 Watch your neck and back.

14 When you read on your smartphone, you usually bend your neck.

15 This "text neck" pose increases the pressure on your neck and back.

16 The best way to prevent this pressure is to bring the phone up to the level of your eyes.

17 Another way is to lower your eyes instead of bending your neck.

18 Give your eyes a break.

19 It makes your eyes feel tired and dry to read small letters on a smartphone for a long time.

20 Using a smartphone in the dark or in a moving car makes this problem worse.

21 To avoid this, give your eyes a break from time to time.

22 Follow the 20-20-20 rules: Every 20 minutes, take a 20-second break and look at something at least 20 feet away.

23 Also, blink your eyes often.

24 This will keep your eyes from becoming dry.

25 Do you text a lot on your smartphone?

26 Texting for a long time can hurt your fingers and wrists.

27 Try these exercises.

28 They will help reduce the pain in your fingers and wrists.

29 Pull on each finger of each hand.

30 Put the backs of your hands together with your arms out in front of you.

31 But remember.

32 The best tip to prevent these health problems is to use your smartphone less.

33 Give yourself some rest from your smartphone.

Before You Read A

1. when, eat breakfast

2. in a car

3. when I am walking

4. feel uncomfortable, not have, with

5. in bed

Before You Read B

1. Watch Out

2. walked into, while texting, hurt

3. avoid using, while walking

4. should reduce, she spends using

Writing Workshop

1. Smartphone, Me

2. are both, and, using

3. get in touch with, right away

4. information I need

5. when, to do

6. On the other hand, feel dry, tired

7. keep, from paying

8. need to, intelligently

Before You Read A

1. I use my smartphone when I eat breakfast.

2. I use my smartphone in a car.

3. I use my smartphone when I am walking.

4. I feel uncomfortable when I do not have my smartphone with me.

5. I use my smartphone in bed.

Before You Read B

1. Watch Out!

2. Yesterday, Sejin walked into a tree while texting and hurt her head.

3. She needs to avoid using her phone while walking.

4. Also, she should reduce the time she spends using it.

Writing Workshop

1. A Smartphone & Me

2. There are both good things and bad things about using a smartphone.

3. First, I can get in touch with my friends right away.

4. Also, I can easily get information I need.

5. That is useful when I have a lot of homework to do.

6. On the other hand, using a smartphone too much makes my eyes feel dry and tired.

7. Also, text messages and ads keep me from paying attention to my studies.

8. So I need to use my smartphone intelligently.

단어 TEST Step 1   p.40

01 연주회   02 (동식물을) 기르다, 자라다
03 실제로, 사실은   04 조금, 한 조각(가지), 부분
05 옷, 의상   06 기회   07 밝은, 똑똑한
08 돌고래   09 초등학교   10 악기
11 요리하다; 요리사 12 여가 시간
13 (모임 · 식 등을) 개최하다   14 참여하다, 가입하다
15 쉬운   16 이웃   17 정문
18 오케스트라, 교향악단   19 소개하다
20 자기 자신의   21 정원   22 채소
23 도서관   24 선물; 참석한   25 봉사하다
26 경험, 경력   27 몇몇의   28 음, 음표
29 활동   30 지도자, 대표
31 관심; ~의 관심[흥미]을 끌다   32 연습; 연습하다
32 동네, (도시 내의 한 단위) 지역   33 요리, 음식
34 결과적으로   35 ~하는 것을 즐기다
36 ~을 찾다   37 ~하고 싶다   38 ~에 참여하다
39 ~로 변화시키다[바꾸다]   40 도움을 청하다
41 ~을 잘하다   42 ~하는 방법

단어 TEST Step 2   p.41

01 doughnut   02 experience   03 drone
04 present   05 practice   06 activity
07 cooking   08 interest   09 fly
10 service   11 several   12 neighborhood
13 get   14 leader   15 library
16 club   17 however   18 volunteer
19 note   20 project   21 Spanish
22 walk   23 actually   24 opportunity
25 hold   26 introduce   27 actually
28 bright   29 clothes   30 grow
31 hold   32 neighbor   33 main gate
34 vegetable   35 change into   36 a little bit
37 fall into   38 as a result   39 participate in
40 get better   41 thank for   42 ask for help
43 watch out (for)

단어 TEST Step 3   p.42

1 bright, 밝은   2 grow, 자라다   3 a bit, 조금, 약간
4 practice, 연습하다   5 walk, (동물을) 걷게 하다

6 bake, (빵 등을) 굽다   7 drone, 무인 비행기
8 join, 가입하다   9 neighbor, 이웃   10 garden, 정원
11 musical instrument, 악기   12 leader, 지도자, 대표
13 opportunity, 기회   14 hold, (모임 · 식 등을) 개최하나
15 orchestra, 오케스트라, 교향악단   16 club, 동아리

대화문 TEST Step 1   p.43~44

Listen & Speak 1 A

know how to make / course, easy

Listen & Speak 1 B

1 heard you went to, How / I hope I can play, like her someday / knew how to play the violin / not good at, yet
2 Look at, grew, myself, own garden / how to cook, grow, too / taught me

Listen & Speak 2 A

looking at, at night / love doing

Listen & Speak 2 B

1 Do you enjoy reading / love reading, about / reading, too / let's go, the library
2 What did you do / made breakfast / Do you enjoy cooking / good cook, cooking
3 Where, get / made it for me / really good designer / enjoys making clothes, too

Real-Life Zone A

the leader, Thank, for your interest / to meet / When did you start playing / how to play the violin when / experience playing / Actually, an orchestra when, elementary school / volunteer to teach, Do you enjoy teaching others / experience, enjoy working with, like to try / have, playing, Welcome to

Wrap Up

look, delicious / made them myself, baking, going to, this Saturday / want to learn how to make, Is, difficult / at all, join me / What time should / At / Sounds, See, then

대화문 TEST Step 2   p.45~46

Listen & Speak 1 A

A: Do you know how to make a paper cat?
B: Of course. It's easy.

Listen & Speak 1 B

1 G: I heard you went to Yuna's violin concert yesterday. How was it?

B: It was great. I hope I can play the violin like her someday.

G: I didn't know you knew how to play the violin

B: I can, but I'm not good at it yet.

2 G: Look at these pictures. I grew these vegetables myself. I have my own garden.

B: Cool! Do you know how to cook the vegetables you grow, too?

G: Yes, my grandmother taught me.

Listen & Speak 2 A

A: Do you enjoy looking at the stars at night?

G: Yes, I love doing that.

Listen & Speak 2 B

1 B: Do you enjoy reading books, Yumi?

G: Yes, I love reading science books. How about you?

B: I love reading books, too.

G: Then, let's go to the library after school today.

2 G: What did you do on the weekend, Minsu?

B: I made breakfast for my family.

G: Do you enjoy cooking?

B: Yes, I'm a good cook! My family loves my cooking.

3 B: Jiyun, that's a pretty backpack! Where did you get it?

G: My sister made it for me.

B: Wow! She's a really good designer.

G: Yes, she is. And she enjoys making clothes, too.

Real-Life Zone A

B: Hello, Kate. I'm Hamin, the leader of the Nanum Orchestra. Thank you for your interest in our club.

G: Hi. Nice to meet you.

B: You play the violin? When did you start playing the violin?

G: I started learning how to play the violin when I was ten.

B: Do you have any experience playing in a group?

G: Yes. Actually, I was a member of an orchestra when I was in elementary school.

B: Great. We also volunteer to teach children. Do you enjoy teaching others?

G: I have no experience teaching others. But I enjoy working with people, so I'd like to try.

B: Good. I think we'll have a great time playing together. Welcome to the Nanum Orchestra.

Wrap Up

B: These cookies look so delicious. Did you make them?

G: Yes. I made them myself yesterday. I enjoy baking. I'm going to make doughnuts this Saturday.

B: Oh, I want to learn how to make doughnuts. Is it difficult?

G: Not at all. You can come to my house and join me if you want.

B: Thanks, Bora. What time should I come?

G: At 2:00.

B: Sounds good. See you then.

본문 TEST Step 1 p.47~48

01 Why Don't, Join

02 Participating, way, life   03 How, joining

04 are, leaders who, join   05 Let's, to what

06 Art Club   07 from, Art Club

08 As, guess from, paint

09 volunteer work, to

10 Last, participated in, Change

11 dirty, flying, jumping, waves

12 As, into, bright, place

13 neighbors, to, thanked   14 don't have to

15 Anyone, paint, join

16 Come, be, member

17 Boram Orchestra

18 leader of, Orchestra

19 several, playing, main gate   20 were those

21 play, for, every

22 need, how, little bit   23 worry if, play

24 practice, get better

25 musical instruments, service, community

26 teaching, eleven-year-old, play 27 At, how, note

28 can, simple song

29 Hearing, play, makes

30 By joining, opportunity, others

31 Come, join, club   32 waiting for

본문 TEST Step 2 p.49~50

01 Why Don't You Join

02 Participating in club activities, to enjoy

03 How about joining

04 Here are, who want, to join   05 Let's, to what

06 Art Club   07 from, Art Club

08 As, can guess from, paint

09 do volunteer work from, to

10 Last, participated in, Change, Neighborhood

11 On the dirty old walls, painted, flying, jumping over blue waves

12 As a result, changed into, beautiful place

13 were happy to see, thanked

14 don't have to, painter

15 Anyone who likes to, join

16 Come and be   17 Orchestra

18 the leader of

19 see, playing music, main gate, came to school

20 were those   21 play music for

22 how to play, a little bit to join

23 don't worry if, don't

24 practice hard, get better

25 also teach, how to, as a service to

26 teaching an eleven-year-old boy

27 At first, how to read a note

28 can play a simple song

29 Hearing him play, happy

30 By joining, have an opportunity, to help others

31 Come and join   32 waiting for

---

17 보람 오케스트라

18 안녕하세요! 저는 보람 오케스트라의 회장 장민수입니다.

19 오늘 학교에 왔을 때 정문에서 음악을 연주하는 몇 명의 학생들을 보았습니까?

20 우리가 그 학생들이었습니다.

21 우리는 매일 아침 친구들을 위해 음악을 연주합니다.

22 우리 동아리에 가입하기 위해서는 악기 연주하는 법을 조금 알아야 합니다.

23 그러나 여러분이 연주를 잘 못한다고 해서 걱정하지 마세요.

24 우리는 열심히 연습하고 함께 좋아질 것입니다.

25 우리는 지역 사회에 대한 봉사로 아이들에게 악기를 연주하는 법도 가르칩니다.

26 저는 열한 살 소년에게 바이올린을 가르치고 있습니다.

27 처음에 그는 음표를 읽는 법을 알지 못했습니다.

28 이제는 간단한 노래도 연주할 수 있습니다.

29 그가 바이올린을 연주하는 걸 듣는 것은 저를 매우 행복하게 합니다.

30 우리 동아리에 가입함으로써, 여러분은 다른 사람들을 도울 수 있는 기회를 가질 수 있습니다.

31 와서 우리 동아리에 가입하세요.

32 우리는 여러분을 기다리고 있습니다.

---

1 우리 동아리에 가입하는 게 어때?

2 동아리 활동에 참여하는 것은 학교생활을 즐기는 좋은 방법이에요.

3 동아리에 가입하는 게 어떤가요?

4 여기 학생들이 그들의 동아리에 가입하기를 원하는 두 명의 동아리 대표가 있어요.

5 그들이 하는 말을 들어 봅시다.

6 피카소 미술 동아리

7 안녕하세요! 저는 피카소 미술 동아리의 강소라입니다.

8 우리 동아리의 이름에서 추측할 수 있듯이, 우리는 그림을 그립니다.

9 우리는 가끔 자원봉사도 합니다.

10 지난여름, 우리 동아리 회원들은 "우리 마을 바꾸기" 프로젝트에 참여했습니다.

11 우리 마을에 있는 건물의 더럽고 오래된 벽에 하늘 높이 나는 새들과 푸른 파도 위로 점프하는 돌고래들을 그렸습니다.

12 결과적으로, 오래된 마을은 밝고 아름다운 곳으로 바뀌었습니다.

13 이웃들은 우리의 작품을 보고 행복해 했고 고마워했습니다.

14 여러분은 그림을 잘 그릴 필요는 없습니다.

15 그림 그리는 것을 좋아하는 사람은 누구나 가입할 수 있습니다.

16 와서 피카소 미술 동아리의 회원이 되세요.

---

1 Why Don't You Join Our Club?

2 Participating in club activities is a great way to enjoy your school life.

3 How about joining a club?

4 Here are two club leaders who want students to join their clubs.

5 Let's listen to what they say.

6 The Picasso Art Club

7 Hi! I am Sora Kang from the Picasso Art Club.

8 As you can guess from the name of our club, we paint.

9 We also do volunteer work from time to time.

10 Last summer, our club members participated in the "Change Our Neighborhood" project.

11 On the dirty old walls of the buildings in our neighborhood, we painted birds flying high in the sky and dolphins jumping over blue waves.

12 As a result, the old neighborhood changed into a bright and beautiful place.

13 The neighbors were happy to see our work and thanked us.

14 You don't have to be a good painter.

15 Anyone who likes to paint can join.

16 Come and be a member of the Picasso Art Club.

17 The Boram Orchestra

18 Hi! I am Minsu Jang, the leader of the Boram Orchestra.

19 Did you see several students playing music at the main gate when you came to school today?

20 We were those students.

21 We play music for our friends every morning.

22 You need to know how to play an instrument a little bit to join our club.

23 But don't worry if you don't play well.

24 We will practice hard and get better together.

25 We also teach children how to play musical instruments as a service to our community.

26 I am teaching an eleven-year-old boy to play the violin.

27 At first, he did not know how to read a note.

28 Now he can play a simple song.

29 Hearing him play the violin makes me very happy.

30 By joining our club, you can have an opportunity to help others.

31 Come and join our club.

32 We are waiting for you.

After You Read

1. leader, community center

2. started teaching, how to play

3. how to read a note

4. hope to join, main gate

Writing Workshop

1. Middle School Club

2. Name

3. Student Name

4. to Join, would like to

5. good at passing, running

6. how to head, so

7. become, who

8. Goals, join, practice, hard

Real Life Zone

1. would like

2. how to play

3. lots of, playing

4. enjoys working

5. Let's, welcome, to

After You Read

1. Today, Minsu, the leader of the Boram Orchestra, came to community center.

2. He started teaching me how to play the violin last month.

3. At first, I didn't know how to read a note.

4. I hope to join the Boram Orchestra and play the violin at the main gate when I become a middle school student.

Writing Workshop

1. Boram Middle School Club Membership Form

2. • Name of Club: FC Boram

3. • Student Name: Sunho Park

4. • Why You Want to Join the Club: I love soccer and would like to join FC Boram.

5. I am good at passing the ball and running fast.

6. However, I don't know how to head the ball, so I want to learn how to do that.

7. I want to become a soccer player who can make wonderful heading goals.

8. • Your Goals: If I join this club, I will practice very hard and become a good team player!

Real Life Zone

1. I would like to introduce our new orchestra member, Kate.

2. She knows how to play the violin.

3. She also has lots of experience playing in a group.

4. And she said she enjoys working with people.

5. Let's all welcome her to the Nanum Orchestra.

단어 TEST Step 1 — p.59

01 게다가
02 올바른
03 대답하다
04 언제든, 한 번이라도
05 등장인물
06 지배하다
07 장면
08 친절한
09 행복
10 갈매기
11 품목
12 시끄러운
13 지지; 지지하다
14 제목
15 편안한
16 함께 하다
17 그러한, 너무나 ~한
18 왕좌, 왕위
19 여행
20 근처에
21 외국의
22 헤어지다
23 감상문, 논평
24 학교 식당
25 날씨
26 (곰, 사자 등의) 새끼
27 실망한, 기대에 어긋난
28 불안한
29 외국인
30 의견
31 후회하다
32 무서운
33 십 대
34 넓은
35 ~에 대해 걱정하다
36 (병·상황 등이) 나아지다
37 (~에게) 잘 어울리다
38 ~을 빼앗다
39 ~을 두려워하다
40 ~처럼 보이다
41 ~을 잘하다
42 그런데
43 만약 ~이라면 어떻게 될까?

단어 TEST Step 2 — p.60

01 nervous
02 reply
03 separate
04 weather
05 scene
06 cub
07 review
08 foreign
09 journey
10 such
11 teenager
12 support
13 friendly
14 besides
15 happiness
16 item
17 character
18 seagull
19 join
20 nearby
21 opinion
22 regret
23 comfortable
24 noisy
25 throne
26 rule
27 disappointed
28 scary
29 foreigner
30 school cafeteria
31 title
32 wide
33 correct
34 ever
35 break out
36 not anymore
37 by the way
38 try to+동사원형
39 be worried about
40 look like+명사
41 be scared of
42 get better
43 go into

단어 TEST Step 3 — p.61

1 separate, 헤어지다 2 journey, 여행 3 happiness, 행복
4 besides, 게다가 5 noisy, 시끄러운 6 character, 등장인물
7 rule, 지배하다 8 cub, (곰, 사자 등의) 새끼
9 foreign, 외국의 10 reply, 대답하다 11 teenager, 십대

12 title, 제목 13 seagull, 갈매기 14 nervous, 불안한
15 support, 지지. 후원 16 review, 감상문, 논평

대화문 TEST Step 1 — p.62~63

Listen & Speak 1 A

worried about / Don't worry, do fine

Listen & Speak 1 B

1 Do you have, special plans / going to, worried about / Don't worry, won't rain

2 can, go into / What's wrong / scared of / friendly, just looks scary because

Listen & Speak 1 C

1 I'm worried about / Don't worry, going to

2 I'm worried about / worry, You'll do great

3 I'm worried about my future / worry, find something, like to do

Listen & Speak 2 A

What do you think of / look like

Listen & Speak 2 B

1 Did, watch / saw, last Saturday / What did you think of it / disappointed, wasn't, good

2 What do you think of / think, delicious / What, best item / like, the best

3 do you think of / looks great / happy that, painted, myself

Listen & Speak 2 C

1 What, think of / looks light, fast

2 What do you think / look good on you

Real-Life Zone

who looked like / had / looked like, were having / were, try to meet twice / wish, could feel, comfortable / was worried about speaking, anymore / get, nervous, try to speak / the hardest, gets easier, easier / What do you, about, both of / great idea

대화문 TEST Step 2 — p.64~65

Listen & Speak 1 A

B: I'm worried about the math test.
W: Don't worry. You'll do fine.

Listen & Speak 1 B

1 B: Do you have any special plans for tomorrow?
  G: I'm going to Jejudo in the morning. But I'm worried about the weather.
  B: Don't worry. It won't rain on Jejudo tomorrow.
  G: Oh, that's good to hear.

2 B: Jina, can you go into your house first?
  G: Why? What's wrong?

B: I'm scared of your dog.

G: Don't worry. He's a friendly dog. He just looks scary because he's so big.

Listen & Speak 1 C

1 A: I'm worried about your health.

　B: Don't worry. I'm going to the doctor tomorrow.

2 A: I'm worried about the speech contest.

　B: Don't worry. You'll do great.

3 A: I'm worried about my future.

　B: Don't worry. You'll find something you like to do.

Listen & Speak 2 A

B: What do you think of these sunglasses?

G: They're cool! You look like a movie star.

Listen & Speak 2 B

1 G: Did you watch the movie, *The Daughter*?

　B: Yes, I saw it last Saturday.

　G: What did you think of it?

　B: I was disappointed. It wasn't very good.

2 B: What do you think of our school cafeteria food?

　G: I think the cafeteria food is delicious.

　B: What do you think is the best item?

　G: I like the Gimbap the best.

3 G: What do you think of this painting?

　B: It looks great. I like the colors.

　G: I'm happy that you like it. I painted it myself.

Listen & Speak 2 C

1 A: What do you think of my bike?

　B: It looks light and fast.

2 A: What do you think of these shoes?

　B: They look good on you.

Real-Life Zone

G: I saw you with someone who looked like a foreigner yesterday.

B: Yes. We had lunch together.

G: You looked like you were having a good time.

B: We were. We try to meet twice a month for lunch.

G: I wish I could feel more comfortable talking with a foreigner.

B: I was worried about speaking in English before, but not anymore.

G: I get really nervous when I try to speak in English.

B: Well, the first time is the hardest. After that, it gets easier and easier.

G: What do you think about me joining both of you for lunch?

B: That's a great idea.

본문 TEST Step 1　　　　　　　　p.66~67

01 Two Brothers　02 went on, journey

03 found, front of　04 said, into, across

05 find, her cubs　06 Take, run up　07 find happiness

08 go, find, together　　　09 How can, true

10 What if, wide　11 Besides, away from

12 Instead, finding, killed　　13 replied, if, try

14 went, own way

15 went into, swam across　16 There was

17 was sleeping　18 took, ran up

19 reached, took, made　20 lived as, for

21 broke out, lost　22 on, road

23 One, met, for, last　24 older, right

25 have lived, well　26 once, had, lot

27 younger, regret, choice

28 nothing, something to remember

본문 TEST Step 2　　　　　　　　p.68~69

01 Two Brothers　02 went on, journey

03 found, in front of

04 said, Go into, swim across

05 will find, her cubs　　　06 Take, run up

07 will find happiness

08 Let's go and find happiness together

09 older brother, How can we know, true

10 What if, too wide

11 Besides, easy to take, away from

12 Instead of finding, be killed

13 replied, How, if, don't try

14 separated, both went their own way

15 went into, swam across　16 There was

17 was sleeping　18 took her cubs, ran up

19 reached the top, took him to, made

20 lived as a king for

21 broke out, lost his throne

22 was on the road

23 One day, talked about, lives for the last

24 I was right　25 have lived quietly, well

26 once, have had a lot of trouble

27 younger brother, regret my choice

28 nothing, will always have something to remember

본문 TEST Step 3　　　　　　　　p.70~71

1 두 형제

2 두 형제는 여정을 떠났다.

3 그들은 숲 앞에서 바위를 발견했다.

4 거기에 쓰여 있었다. "숲에 들어가 강을 헤엄쳐 건너시오.

5 당신은 거기에서 곰과 새끼들을 발견할 것입니다.

6 섬 새끼들을 데리고 산 위로 뛰어 올라가시오.

7 거기에서 당신은 행복을 찾을 수 있을 것입니다."

8 동생이 말했다. "함께 가서 행복을 찾자."

9 "싫어." 형은 말했다. "이것이 사실인지 우리가 어떻게 알 수 있어?

10 강이 너무 넓으면 어쩌지?

11 게다가, 곰 새끼들을 엄마에게서 빼앗는 것이 쉬울까?

12 행복을 찾는 대신에, 우리는 죽을 수 있어!"

13 동생은 대답했다. "우리가 시도하지 않으면 어떻게 알 수 있어?"

14 그들은 헤어졌고, 둘 다 자신의 길을 갔다.

15 동생은 숲에 들어가서 강을 헤엄쳐 건넜다.

16 곰이 있었다.

17 그녀는 자고 있었다.

18 그는 새끼들을 데리고 산을 뛰어 올라갔다.

19 그가 정상에 도착했을 때, 어떤 사람들이 그를 자기들 도시로 데려가서 그들의 왕으로 만들었다.

20 그곳에서 그는 5년간 왕으로 살았다.

21 그런 다음 전쟁이 일어났고, 그는 왕좌를 잃었다.

22 그는 다시 길바닥에 나앉았다.

23 어느 날, 두 형제는 다시 만났고 지난 5년 동안의 그들의 삶에 대해 이야기했다.

24 형은 말했다. "내가 옳았어.

25 나는 조용히 잘 살았어.

26 너는 한때 왕이었지만 많은 어려움을 겪었지."

27 동생은 대답했다. "나는 내 선택을 후회하지 않아.

28 나는 지금 아무것도 없지만 언제까지나 기억할 어떤 것이 있어."

from their mother?

12 Instead of finding happiness, we can be killed!"

13 The younger brother replied, "How can we know if we don't try?"

14 They separated, and they both went their own way.

15 The younger brother went into the forest and swam across the river.

16 There was the bear.

17 She was sleeping.

18 He took her cubs and ran up the mountain.

19 When he reached the top, some people took him to their city and made him their king.

20 There he lived as a king for five years.

21 Then a war broke out, and he lost his throne.

22 He was on the road again.

23 One day, the two brothers met again and talked about their lives for the last five years.

24 The older brother said, "I was right.

25 I have lived quietly and well.

26 You were once a king, but you have had a lot of trouble."

27 The younger brother answered, "I don't regret my choice.

28 I may have nothing now, but I will always have something to remember."

본문 TEST Step 4 - Step 5   p.72~75

1 The Two Brothers

2 Two brothers went on a journey.

3 They found a rock in front of a forest.

4 It said, "Go into the forest and swim across the river.

5 There you will find a bear and her cubs.

6 Take the bear cubs and run up the mountain.

7 There you will find happiness."

8 The younger brother said, "Let's go and find happiness together."

9 "No," said the older brother, "How can we know this is true?

10 What if the river is too wide?

11 Besides, will it be easy to take the cubs away

구석구석지문 TEST Step 1   p.76

Before You Read

1. There, filled with, across

2. watch out, are

3. chose, go on journey

4. Sadly, dirty, noisy

5. almost hit

6. lots of trouble

7. After a few days, regretted, went back

Writing Workshop

1. Book Review

2. Title

3. Writer

4. is about, named

5. flying better than others

6. To reach, practices flying

7. because, helped me learn

8. that, anything that, give up

Into the World

1. when, think, say, in harmony

2. When, closes, another

3. something ready-made, comes from

구석구석지문 TEST Step 2   p.77

Before You Read

1. A. There is a box filled with gold behind a tree across the river.

2. But watch out! Dangerous animals are in the river.

3. B. Mr. Allen chose to go on journey to the city for his vacation.

4. Sadly the city streets were dirty and noisy.

5. A car even almost hit him.

6. He had lots of trouble there.

7. After a few days in the city, he regretted his choice and went back to his hometown.

Writing Workshop

1. A Book Review

2. Title : *Jonathan Livingston Seagull*: a story

3. Writer : Richard Bach

4. This story is about a seagull named Jonathan Livingston.

5. He dreams of flying better than others .

6. To reach his goal, he works hard and practices flying.

7. I like this story because it has helped me learn about the power of my own beliefs.

8. The book says that I can do anything that I want if I do not give up.

Into the World

1. Happiness is when what you think , what you say , and what you do are in harmony.
   - Mahatma Gandhi

2. When one door of happiness closes, another opens. - Helen Keller

3. Happiness is not something ready-made. It comes from your own actions. - Dalai Lama XIV

단어 TEST Step 1   p.78

01 대회	02 맞다	03 감추다, 숨기다
04 찢어지는 듯한[날카로운] 소리		05 규칙
06 놓치다, 그리워하다		07 홈팀
08 불안한	09 반바지	10 결정하다
11 투구	12 언젠가	13 먼지, 때
14 (부정문에서) ~도	15 경기장	16 (야구의) 루, 베이스
17 타자	18 국제적인	19 결정하다
20 잊다	21 애완동물	22 원정 팀
23 (good의 비교급) 더 좋은, 더 나은		24 티켓
25 경기, 성냥	26 순서, 명령	27 그 뒤에, 그런 다음
28 휴가	29 의미하다	30 천둥
31 과거	32 암벽 등반	
33 (특정 스포츠 팀을) 응원하다, 지원하다		34 ~을 몹시 기대하다
35 A와 B 사이에	36 ~을 기다리다	37 ~의 열렬한 팬이다
38 서둘러 ~하다	39 ~을 기대하다	40 일주일에 두 번
41 ~에 신나다, ~에 들뜨다		42 ~로 돌아오다
43 서둘러		

단어 TEST Step 2   p.79

01 hide	02 either	03 ticket
04 vacation	05 stadium	06 base
07 rule	08 visit	09 batter
10 match	11 order	
12 determine, decide		13 pitch
14 rock climbing	15 mean	16 thunder
17 crack	18 anxious	19 competition
20 fit	21 pet	22 visiting team
23 shorts	24 past	25 forget
26 international	27 miss	28 sometime
29 dirt	30 get	31 better
32 support	33 then	
34 be about to 동사원형		
35 between A and B		36 hurry up
37 be a big fan of	38 can't wait to 동사원형	
39 twice a week	40 in a hurry	41 be excited about
42 look forward to (동)명사		43 wait for

단어 TEST Step 3   p.80

1 hide, 감추다, 숨기다   2 anxious, 불안한   3 fit, 맞다

4 home team, 홈팀   5 past, 과거   6 pitch, 투구

7 international, 국제적인   8 base, (야구의) 루, 베이스
9 determine, 결정하다   10 visiting team, 원정 팀
11 competition, 대회   12 order, 순서   13 thunder, 천둥
14 either, (부정문에서) ~도   15 crack, 찢어지는 듯한[날카로운] 소리   16 stadium, 경기장

Listen & Speak 1 A

Which sport, or / more, twice a week

Listen & Speak 1 B

1 are, doing / I'm looking at / checked, Which country, to visit, or / to visit, like to

2 I'm thinking, getting, have / What do, think, Which, better for, or / Why don't you come to, play with, can decide

Listen & Speak 2 A

Did / can't wait to watch

Listen & Speak 2 B

1 want to see / When did / bought it for me, come to my house / course, can't wait to see

2 Don't forget that, rock climbing / worry, won't forget / excited about, I can't wait

3 hear about / about, lives in / came back, wants to see / can't wait to see

Real-Life Zone A

such a worry / have to, before, between, and, starts / Which team, support, or / to miss, either / Hurry up, left / Maybe, sometime / about going to, home game together / can eat fried chicken while watching, sounds, I can't wait

Wrap Up

which sport do you like, or / How about / big fan of / soccer match, between, Have, heard about / already have, I'm going to see, can't wait / fantastic

Listen & Speak 1 A

M: Which sport do you like? Soccer or basketball?
G: I like soccer more. I play soccer twice a week.

Listen & Speak 1 B

1 G: What are you doing?
  B: I'm looking at a world map.
  G: You checked two countries. Which country would you like to visit first? The U.S. or Mexico?
  B: I want to visit the U.S. I'd like to see a basketball

game there.

2 G: I'm thinking about getting a pet. Do you have a pet?
  B: Yes, I do. I have a dog and a cat.
  G: What do you think? Which pet is better for me? A cat or a dog?
  B: Why don't you come to my house someday and play with my pets? Then you can decide.

Listen & Speak 2 A

G: Did you get the tickets?
B: Yes! I can't wait to watch the game.

Listen & Speak 2 B

1 G: Do you want to see my new mountain bike?
  B: Sure. When did you get it?
  G: Yesterday my father bought it for me. Can you come to my house this afternoon?
  B: Of course. I can't wait to see it.

2 B: Don't forget that we're going rock climbing this weekend!
  G: Don't worry. I won't forget.
  B: I'm excited about going. I can't wait.

3 G: Did you hear about Jisu?
  B: What about her? She lives in Canada.
  G: She came back to Korea last month. She wants to see you.
  B: Oh, I can't wait to see her.

Real-Life Zone A

B1: Jiho, why are you in such a hurry?
B2: Hi, Alex! I have to be home before 6:00. The game between the Thunders and the Cobras starts at 6:00.
B1: Oh, are you a baseball fan? Which team do you support? The Cobras or the Thunders?
B2: The Cobras.
B1: Me, too! I don't want to miss the game either.
B2: Hurry up! We only have thirty minutes left.
B1: Okay. Maybe we can watch a game together sometime.
B2: That's a great idea! How about going to the next Cobras home game together?
B1: Okay. They have a game next Saturday. We can eat fried chicken while watching the game!
B2: That sounds great. I can't wait!

Wrap Up

B: Jimin, which sport do you like? Soccer or table tennis?
G: I love table tennis. How about you, Yunho?
B: I like soccer. I'm a big fan of James Hood. He's a

great soccer player.

G: Oh, really? There's a soccer match this weekend between Korea and Turkey. Have you heard about it?

B: Of course. I already have a ticket. I'm going to see the game on Saturday. I can't wait.

G: That's fantastic.

01 Day, Baseball Stadium

02 and, have,game   03 is at, stadium

04 your first, isn't it

05 excited, can't wait for   06 are coming out

07 Which team   08 Over, behind third

09 wearing, because, visiting

10 always wear, dark   11 that, rule

12 Home, bright, visiting, dark   13 Why, that

14 There, interesting, about

15 past, wash, every

16 wearing, hide, dirt   17 was, good idea

18 warming up   19 your favorite   20 Number 77

21 What does, mean

22 choose, they like   23 know what

24 determined by, batting order   25 there, no, with

26 is about to   27 looks anxious

28 favorite, at bat

29 has hit, runs already

30 hits, more, be, season

31 batter misses several   32 has, full count

33 waiting for, pitch   34 RUN, HOME

35 Crack, flies fast   36 is going, gone

01 A Day, Baseball Stadium

02 have a game   03 is at, baseball stadium

04 your first time, isn't it

05 excited, can't wait for, to start   06 are coming out

07 Which team   08 Over there, behind third base

09 are wearing, because, visiting team

10 visiting team, wear a dark color 11 rule

12 have bright uniforms, dark uniforms

13 Why   14 There, an interesting story

15 In the past, wash their uniforms after every game

16 started wearing, to hide the dirt

17 a good idea

18 are warming up

19 your favorite player   20 Number

21 What does, number mean

22 choose, they like   23 You know what

24 were determined by the players' batting order

25 there were no, with   26 is about to

27 looks anxious 28 Your favorite, at bat

29 has hit   30 hits one more, this season

31 misses several balls

32 has a full count

33 waiting for, next pitch   34 HOME RUN

35 Crack, flies fast   36 is going, gone

1 야구 경기장에서의 하루

2 오늘 천둥 대 코브라 게임이 있다.

3 지훈이네 가족은 야구 경기장에 있다.

4 지훈: 지안아, 네가 야구 경기장에 온 건 이번이 처음이야, 그렇지 않니?

5 지안: 응, 나 아주 흥분돼. 나는 경기가 빨리 시작했으면 좋겠어.

6 아빠: 봐, 선수들이 지금 나오고 있어!

7 지안: 어떤 팀이 천둥이야?

8 지훈: 저기, 3루 뒤

9 그들은 원정 팀이기 때문에 어두운 회색 유니폼을 입고 있어.

10 지안: 원정 팀은 항상 어두운 색을 입어?

11 지훈: 응, 그게 규칙이야.

12 홈팀은 밝은 유니폼을 입고 원정팀은 어두운 유니폼을 입어.

13 지안: 왜?

14 엄마: 그것에 대한 흥미로운 이야기가 있단다.

15 과거에는 원정 팀이 매 경기 후 유니폼을 세탁할 수가 없었어.

16 그래서 그들은 때를 숨기기 위해 어두운 색을 입기 시작했지.

17 지안: 하하해 좋은 생각이었네요!

18 선수들이 몸을 풀고 있다.

19 지안: 가장 좋아하는 선수가 누구야?

20 지훈: 77번.

21 지안: 그 숫자는 무엇을 의미해?

22 지훈: 음... 선수들이 원하는 번호를 선택해.

23 아빠: 그거 알아?

24 과거에는 번호가 선수들의 타순에 의해 결정되었단다.

25 지훈: 77번 선수가 없었다는 뜻이네요!

26 이제 지훈이의 가장 좋아하는 선수가 막 공을 치려고 한다.

27 지훈이는 불안해 보인다.

28 지안: 오빠가 가장 좋아하는 선수가 타석에 서네.

29 지훈: 응. 그는 올해 이미 21개의 홈런을 쳤어.

30 그가 오늘 하나를 더 치면, 그는 이번 시즌 홈런 리더가 될 거야.

31 타자는 여러 개의 공을 놓친다.

32 이제 그는 풀카운트가 되었다.

33 그는 다음 투구를 기다리고 있다.

34 지훈: 홈런! 홈런!

35 땅! 공은 빠르게 날아간다.

36 그것은 가고, 가고, 가고, 사라져 버렸다!

1 A Day at the Baseball Stadium

2 Today the Thunders and the Cobras have a game.

3 Jihun's family is at the baseball stadium.

4 Jihun: Jian, this is your first time to come to the baseball stadium, isn't it?

5 Jian: Yes, I'm so excited. I can't wait for the game to start.

6 Dad: Look, the players are coming out now!

7 Jian: Which team is the Thunders?

8 Jihun: Over there, behind third base.

9 They are wearing dark gray uniforms because they are the visiting team.

10 Jian: Does the visiting team always wear a dark color?

11 Jihun: Yes, that's the rule.

12 Home teams have bright uniforms and visiting teams have dark uniforms.

13 Jian: Why is that?

14 Mom: There is an interesting story about that.

15 In the past, visiting teams could not wash their uniforms after every game.

16 So they started wearing dark colors to hide the dirt.

17 Jian: Hahaha! That was a good idea!

18 The players are warming up.

19 Jian: Who's your favorite player?

20 Jihun: Number 77.

21 Jian: What does the number mean?

22 Jihun: Hmm.... Players choose a number they like.

23 Dad: You know what?

24 In the past, the numbers were determined by the players' batting order.

25 Jihun: That means there were no players with number 77!

26 Now, Jihun's favorite player is about to bat.

27 Jihun looks anxious.

28 Jian: Your favorite player is at bat.

29 Jihun: Yes. He has hit 21 home runs already this year.

30 If he hits one more today, he will be the home run leader this season.

31 The batter misses several balls.

32 Now he has a full count.

33 He is waiting for the next pitch.

34 Jihun: HOME RUN! HOME RUN!

35 Crack! The ball flies fast.

36 It is going, going, going, gone!

Real-Life Zone B

1. Which sport, like, or

2. going to, with, this weekend, can't wait

Writing Workshop

1. Marathon Runner

2. Born, August

3. Nationality

4. was known as, international sports competitions

5. preparing to run, found out, did not fit, decided to run, without shoes

6. felt pain during, as the winner

7. one of, wasn't he

Wrap Up

1. Middle School Sports Day

2. will be held, on Wednesday, June

3. will be various, such as

4. wil also, table tennis

5. sounds like, doesn't it

Real-Life Zone B

1. A: Which sport do you like? Basketball or soccer?

2. B: I like basketball. I'm going to play it with my friends this weekend. I can't wait.

Writing Workshop

1. Abebe Bikila Marathon Runner

2. Born : August 7, 1932

3. Nationality: Ethiopia

4. Speciality: He was known as a marathon winner at the Rome and Tokyo international sports competitions.

5. When he was preparing to run the marathon in Rome, he found out that his shoes did not fit well, so he decided to run the race without shoes .

6. He felt pain during the race, but he finished the race as the winner.

7. He was one of the greatest runners in the world, wasn't he?

1. Sarang Middle School Sports Day
2. Sarang Middle School Sports Day will be held on the school playing field on Wednesday, June 15.
3. There will be various games such as baseball and soccer.
4. There wil also be table tennis.
5. It sounds like fun, doesn't it?

적중100 plus

1학기 전과정

영어 기출 문제집

정답 및 해설

시사 | 송미정

적중 **100** + 특별부록

Plan B

우리학교
최신기출

시사 · 송미정 교과서를 배우는

학교 시험문제 분석 · 모음 · 해설집

전국단위 학교 시험문제 수집 및 분석
출제 빈도가 높은 문제 위주로 선별
문제 풀이에 필요한 상세한 해설

중2-1
영어

시사 · 송미정

2학년 영어 1학기 중간고사(1과) 1회

반		점수
이름		

문항수 : 선택형(23문항) 서술형(4문항)   20 . . .

◎ 선택형 문항의 답안은 컴퓨터용 수정 씨인펜을 사용하여 OMR 답안지에 바르게 표기하시오.
◎ 서술형 문제는 답을 답안지에 반드시 검정 볼펜으로 쓰시오.
◎ 총 27문항 100점 만점입니다. 문항별 배점은 각 문항에 표시되어 있습니다.

[양천구 ㅇㅇ중]

1. 다음 빈칸에 공통으로 들어갈 단어로 가장 적절한 것은? (3점)

• Do you know the _____ animal of England is a lion?
• Ryan's family played taekwondo, a _____ Korean martial art, last weekend.

*martial art: 무예

① arrival   ② musical   ③ removal
④ physical   ⑤ national

[동작구 ㅇㅇ중]

2. 다음 중 〈보기〉에 있는 문장이 들어가기에 어색한 대화는? (5점)

보기

• I hope I make a lot of new friends.
• You will. Don't worry.
• That sounds great.
• What are you planning to do this weekend?

① G: I hope I get good grades this year.
  B: _____
② B: _____
  G: Sure. I can do that.
③ G: What's the first thing on your list?
  B: _____
④ G: _____
  B: I'm planning to get my hair cut.
⑤ G: I hope I can travel to Europe this summer.
  B: _____

[울산 ㅇㅇ중]

3. 다음 문장을 완성할 때 필요 없는 단어는? (3점)

• Can you do me a _____?
• Susan _____ has breakfast at eight.
• Your song is so _____.
• I eat out with my family _____ a week.

① until   ② favor   ③ once
④ usually   ⑤ amazing

[동작구 ㅇㅇ중]

4. 다음 대화의 빈칸 (A)에 들어가기에 알맞은 문장을 쓰시오. 〈보기〉의 단어를 사용하시오. (4점)

G: Hi, Brian.
B: Hi, Somin. It's Friday. Are you planning to do anything special this weekend?
G: Well, I'm planning to visit my grandmother. She is sick.
B: Oh, (A)_____ that. I hope she gets better soon.
G: Thank you. What about you? What's your plan?
B: I'm planning to wash my dog.

조건

• 반드시 주어와 동사가 포함된 문장을 쓰시오.
• 반드시 〈보기〉의 단어를 포함해서 문장을 만드시오.

보기

sorry / hear

→ _____

– 1 –

[5~6] 다음 대화를 읽고, 물음에 답하시오.

> B: Kate. Do you have any special plans for the new school year?
> G: I'm planning to study one new Chinese word every day.
> B: I didn't know you were interested in Chinese. When did you start studying Chinese?
> G: Only last month. But now I can introduce myself in Chinese.
> B: That's amazing! How did you get so into Chinese?
> G: It's because I'm a big fan of Chinese dramas. I hope I can soon watch them in Chinese and understand what they're saying.
> B: Well, keep studying hard, and I'm sure you'll be able to do it someday.
> G: I hope so. What about you? What are your plans for this year?
> B: Let me think. Hmm.... Getting a good grade in every subject? As usual.
> G: Hahaha.

5. 위 대화의 밑줄 친 it이 의미하는 것은? (3점)

① To watch Chinese dramas and understand them
② Having special plans for the new school year
③ To get a good grade in every subject
④ Being a big fan of Chinese dramas
⑤ To introduce herself in Chinese

6. 위 대화의 내용과 일치하는 것은? (4점)

① Kate has studied Chinese since last year.
② The boy is interested in Chinese dramas.
③ Now Kate can talk about herself in Chinese.
④ The boy wants to get a good grade only in math.
⑤ Kate doesn't have any special plans for the new school year.

7. 다음 대화가 자연스럽게 이어지도록 (A)~(E) 문장의 순서를 올바르게 배열한 것은? (5점)

> David: ⓐ_____
> Jack: ⓑ_____
> David: ⓒ_____
>   ⓓ_____
> Jack: ⓔ_____

> (A) Jack! Can you do me a favor?
> (B) Sure, I'd love to.
> (C) Yes, what is it?
> (D) Can you help me choose one?
> (E) I'm planning to buy a new bike tomorrow.

① (A)-(B)-(C)-(D)-(E)
② (A)-(C)-(E)-(D)-(B)
③ (A)-(C)-(D)-(B)-(E)
④ (E)-(A)-(B)-(D)-(C)
⑤ (E)-(A)-(C)-(D)-(B)

8. 다음 대화의 빈칸에 가장 적절한 것은? (3점)

> A: What are you going to do on Monday evening?
> B: _____

① I hope I can travel to Europe this summer.
② You're going to go on a bike tour.
③ I'm free. What about you?
④ I think you are busy.
⑤ That sounds great.

[9~11] 다음 대화를 읽고 물음에 답하시오.

> Boy: ⓐKate, do you had any special plans for the new school year?
>
> Girl: ⓑI'm planning to study one new Chinese words every day.
>
> Boy: ⓒI didn't know you were interested in Chinese. ⓓWhen will you start studying Chinese?
>
> Girl: ⓔOnly last month. But now I can introduce myself in Chinese.
>
> Boy: That's amazing! How did you get so into Chinese?
>
> Girl: It's because I'm a big fan of Chinese dramas. I hope I can soon watch them in Chinese and (A)_____ what they're saying.
>
> Boy: Well, keep studying hard, and I'm sure you'll be able to do it someday.
>
> Girl: I hope so. What about you? What (B)_____ your plans for this year?
>
> Boy: Let me think. Hmm.... Getting a good grade in every subject? As usual.
>
> Girl: Hahaha.
>
> *Boy: Jiho, Girl: Kate

9. 위 대화의 밑줄 친 부분 중 어법상 어색한 것의 개수는? (4점)

① 1개 ② 2개 ③ 3개 ④ 4개 ⑤ 5개

10. 위 대화의 내용과 일치하지 않는 것은? (3점)

① 지호는 케이트의 새 학기의 특별한 계획이 궁금하다.

② 케이트는 이제는 중국어로 자신의 소개를 할 수 있다.

③ 케이트는 중국 드라마를 많이 좋아한다.

④ 지호의 올해 계획은 모든 과목에서 좋은 성적을 받는 것이다.

⑤ 케이트는 이미 중국어 드라마를 모두 이해할 수 있다.

11. 위 대화의 빈칸 (A), (B)에 들어갈 말로 알맞게 연결된 것은? (3점)

	(A)	(B)
①	understand	are
②	understands	is
③	understand	is
④	understands	are
⑤	understood	are

12. 다음 문장의 밑줄 친 부분의 용법이 나머지 넷과 다른 것은? (4점)

① I went to the hospital to meet my friend.

② I was at a fast food restaurant to have lunch.

③ My second goal is to learn how to play the guitar.

④ I went shopping to buy sunglasses.

⑤ I'm willing to stand in line all night to enter the front area.

13. Which one sounds differently? (3점)

① Chinese ② watch ③ church
④ charge ⑤ headache

14. 다음 문장을 〈보기〉와 같이 형용사의 최상급을 사용하여 다시 쓰시오. (4점)

> • No other boy in this town is taller than you.
> = You are the tallest boy in this town.

• No other student in my class is shorter than I.

= _____

[15~16] 다음 글을 읽고, 물음에 답하시오.

Hi! I'm Jinsu. This is my bucket list for this year. First, I want to go on a bike tour of Jejudo this summer. I ⓐhave been there before, but I want to experience the island more ⓑfreely on my bike this time. My second goal is ⓒto learn how to play the guitar. I think the guitar has ⓓthe beautifulest sound of all musical instruments. I hope I can play my favorite song on my guitar by the end of this year. Finally, I want to get a good grade in math. Math is my weakest subject. This year, I'll put more effort into studying math ⓔto overcome my weakness.

15. 위 글의 밑줄 친 ⓐ~ⓔ 중 어법상 <u>어색한</u> 것은?
(3점)

① ⓐ   ② ⓑ   ③ ⓒ   ④ ⓓ   ⑤ ⓔ

16. 위 글을 읽고, 답할 수 있는 질문은? (4점)

① What does Jinsu hope to do when he can play the violin?
② What will Jinsu do to overcome his weakness?
③ Where does Jinsu want to go this winter?
④ What is the title of Jinsu's favorite song?
⑤ What is Jinsu's fourth goal?

17. 다음 주어진 단어를 알맞게 배열하여 '우리는 지구를 구하기 위해 에너지를 덜 쓰는 데 많은 노력을 들일 필요가 있다.'의 뜻이 되도록 문장을 완성하시오. (5점)

we, less, save, to, put, lot, into, using, a, to, the, effort, energy, need, of, earth

→ _____

[18~19] 다음 글을 읽고 물음에 답하시오.

Hi! I'm Jinsu. This is my bucket list for this year. First, I want to ⓐ_____ a bike tour of Jejudo this summer. I've been there before, but I want to experience the island more freely on my bike this time. My second goal is to learn ⓑ_____ play the guitar. I think the guitar has the most beautiful sound of all musical instruments. I hope I can play my favorite song on my guitar (가)_____ this year. Finally, I want to get a good grade in math. Math is my weakest subject. This year, I'll put more effort into studying math to ⓒ_____ my weakness.

18. 위 글의 내용과 어법을 고려할 때 ⓐ~ⓒ에 들어갈 말로 적절하게 짝지어진 것은? (4점)

	ⓐ	ⓑ	ⓒ
①	go on	how to	overcome
②	going on	how to	overcome
③	go on	how to	come over
④	going on	what to	come over
⑤	go on	what to	come over

19. 위 글의 흐름을 고려할 때 빈칸 (가)에 들어가기에 가장 알맞은 표현은? (3점)

① a lot of
② a kind of
③ by the end of
④ in front of
⑤ instead of

[20~22] 다음 글을 읽고 물음에 답하시오.

Hi, everyone. Today is the first day of our new school year. (A) I want to hear your plans and hopes for this year. What do you want to do most? Think about ⓐunderline{three thing} you want to do. And then, make a bucket list and ⓑunderline{shares them} with your friends. (B)

(Jinsu)

Hi! I'm Jinsu. This is my bucket list for this year. (C) I've ⓒunderline{been there} before, but I want to experience the island more freely on my bike this time. My second goal is to learn how to play the guitar. I think the guitar has the most beautiful sound of all ⓓunderline{musical instruments}. (D) I hope I can play my favorite song on my guitar by the end of this year. Finally, I want to get a good grade in math. Math is my weakest subject. (E) This year, I'll put more effort into ⓔunderline{studying math} to overcome my weakness.

20. 위 글의 흐름으로 보아 주어진 문장이 들어가기에 가장 적절한 곳은? (4점)

First, I want to go on a bike tour of Jejudo this summer.

① (A)　② (B)　③ (C)　④ (D)　⑤ (E)

21. 위 글을 읽고 답할 수 **없는** 질문은? (3점)

① What are the students going to do in today's class?

② What does the teacher want to hear?

③ Where does Jinsu want to go on a bike tour?

④ What is Jinsu's strongest subject?

⑤ What does Jinsu hope to do on his guitar?

22. 위 글의 밑줄 친 부분 중 의미나 어법상 **어색한** 것을 모두 고르면? (정답 2개) (3점)

① ⓐ　② ⓑ　③ ⓒ　④ ⓓ　⑤ ⓔ

23. 다음 글의 내용을 표로 요약할 때 빈칸에 알맞은 문장을 쓰시오. (6점)

Hi! My name is Somi. First, I want to see a concert of my favorite band right in front of the stage. I'm willing to stand in line all night to enter the front area. Second, I want to adopt a puppy. I've always wanted a puppy. I think I'm fully ready to take care of a pet now. My last goal is a little more challenging. I'd like to read all of the Sherlock Holmes stories. I was fascinated by this detective series last year.

	Bucket List	Reason
(1)	I want to see a concert of my favorite band.	I've never been to their concert.
(2)	(2-1)_____ _____	I've always wanted a puppy. Also, I am able to take care of a pet.
(3)	I want to read all of the Sherlock Holmes stories.	(2-2)_____ _____

(2-1) _____

(2-2) _____

[24~26] 다음 글을 읽고 물음에 답하시오.

Hi! I'm Jinsu. This is my bucket list for this year. First, I want to go on a bike tour of Jejudo this summer. I've been there before, but I want to experience the island (A)freely on my bike this time. My second goal is to learn how to ⓐplaying the guitar. I think the guitar has (B)beautiful sound of all musical instruments. I hope I can play my favorite song on my guitar by the end of this year. Finally, I want to get a good grade in math. Math is my (C)weak subject. This year, I'll put more effort into ⓑstudy math to overcome my weakness.

Hi! My name is Somi. First, I want to see a concert of my favorite band right in front of the stage. I'm ⓒwill to stand in line all night to enter the front area. Second, I want to adopt a puppy. I've always ⓓwanted a puppy. I think I'm fully ready to take care of a pet now. My last goal is a little more challenging. I'd like to read all of the Sherlock Holmes stories. I became a big fan of this detective series last year, so I don't want to ⓔmisses a single one.

24. 위 글의 밑줄 친 ⓐ~ⓔ 중 올바른 것은? (3점)

① ⓐ ② ⓑ ③ ⓒ ④ ⓓ ⑤ ⓔ

25. 위 글의 밑줄 친 (A), (B), (C)를 바꿔 쓴 것으로 올바르게 짝지은 것은? (4점)

	(A)	(B)	(C)
①	freelier —	beautifulest —	weakest
②	more freely —	most beautiful —	most weak
③	more freely —	the most beautiful —	weakest
④	freelier —	most beautiful —	the weakest
⑤	more freely —	the most beautiful —	the most weak

26. 위 글의 내용과 일치하는 것은? (3점)

① 진수는 제주도에 가본 적이 없다.

② 소미는 전부터 강아지를 입양하고 싶어했다.

③ 소미는 셜록홈즈 시리즈를 이미 한 권도 빼놓지 않고 읽었다.

④ 진수는 바이올린이 가장 아름다운 소리를 가졌다고 생각한다.

⑤ 진수는 좋아하는 과목이 수학이어서 높은 점수를 받기를 희망한다.

27. 다음 글에 이어질 내용으로 가장 적절한 것은? (4점)

Hi, everyone. Today is the first day of our new school year. I want to hear your plans and hopes for this year. What do you want to do most? Think about three things you want to do. And then, make a bucket list and share it with your friends.

① tips to be a good friend

② things on students' bucket lists

③ how to make the perfect first day

④ ways to make a plan of the school life

⑤ what to do on the first day of new school year

◎ 선택형 문항의 답안은 컴퓨더용 수정 싸인펜을
　사용하여 OMR 답안지에 바르게 표기하시오.
◎ 서술형 문제는 답을 답안지에 반드시 검정
　볼펜으로 쓰시오.
◎ 총 27문항 100점 만점입니다. 문항별 배점
　은 각 문항에 표시되어 있습니다.

[동작구 ○○중]

1. 다음 중 〈보기〉에 있는 단어를 빈칸에 넣어 문장을 완성
할 수 없는 것은?　　　　　　　　　　(4점)

보기

willing to / by the end of / natural / national

① We need to put a lot of _____ into
using less energy to save the earth.

② You don't look _____ in this photo.

③ Mr. Smith was pleased that Ms. Parker was
_____ meet him.

④ Do you know the _____ animal of
England is a lion?

⑤ A new library will open in the city
_____ this month.

[동작구 ○○중]

2. 다음 대화 중 바르게 짝지어진 것은?　　　(3점)

① A: Would you like to join us?
　B: You will. Don't worry.

② A: How about going to a movie with me?
　B: That sounds wonderful.

③ A: I hope I get good grades this year.
　B: What? Who said that?

④ A: What time are you going to meet?
　B: My plan is to meet Jim to eat pizza.

⑤ A: Can you do me a favor?
　B: Sure. I'm planning to get my hair cut.

[대전 ○○중]

3. 다음 대화의 내용과 일치하지 않는 것은?　　(3섬)

B: Hi, Somin. It's Friday! Are you planning
to do anything special this weekend?

G: Well, I'm planning to visit my uncle in
the hospital. He is sick.

B: Oh, I'm sorry to hear that. I hope he gets
better soon.

G: Thank you. What about you? What's
your plan?

B: I'm planning to wash my dog. Then why
don't we meet next weekend? Let's go
swimming.

G: Okay. See you next week.

G: Girl B: Boy

① 소녀는 이번 주말에 병원을 방문할 예정이다.

② 소년은 소녀에게 금요일 일정을 물어보았다.

③ 소년은 소녀의 삼촌이 어서 회복하기를 바란다.

④ 소녀와 소년은 다음 주말에 수영하러 갈 것이다.

⑤ 소년은 이번 주말에 자신의 개를 씻길 계획이다.

[동작구 ○○중]

4. 다음 〈보기〉에 있는 단어(형용사) 중 하나를 선택하시
오. 그리고 선택한 단어의 최상급을 포함해서 한 문장을
만드시오.　　　　　　　　　　　　　(5점)

보기

old / tall / big / dark / short / light / bright

조건

• 반드시 주어와 동사가 포함된 한 개의 문장을 쓰시
오.

• 반드시 최상급을 포함해서 문장을 만드시오.

→ _____

[5~6] 다음 대화를 읽고 물음에 답하시오.

> B: Kate, do you have any special plans for the new school year?
>
> G: I'm planning to study one new Chinese word every day.
>
> B: I didn't know you were interested (A)_____ Chinese. When did you start studying Chinese?
>
> G: Only last month. But now I can introduce myself in Chinese.
>
> B: That's (B)_____! How did you get so into Chinese?
>
> G: It's because I'm a big fan of Chinese dramas. I hope I can soon watch them in Chinese and understand what they're saying.
>
> B: Well, keep studying hard, and I'm sure you'll be able to do (C)it someday.

5. 위 대화의 빈칸 (A), (B)에 들어갈 낱말로 적절한 것은?
(3점)

	(A)	(B)
①	in	amaze
②	in	amazed
③	in	amazing
④	on	amazing
⑤	on	amazed

6. 위 대화의 밑줄 친 (C)가 의미하는 것으로 적절한 것은?
(4점)

① introducing herself in Chinese

② making a bucket list for this year

③ to be a big fan of Chinese dramas

④ getting a good grade in every subject

⑤ to watch Chinese dramas and understand them

7. 다음 대화에서 어법상 어색한 부분을 찾아 바르게 고쳐 쓰시오.
(5점)

> G: Kate, do you have any special plans for the new school year?
>
> K: I'm planning to study one new Chinese word every day.
>
> G: I didn't know you were interested to Chinese. When did you start studying Chinese?
>
> K: Only last month. But now I can introduce myself in Chinese.
>
> G: That's surprising! How did you get so into Chinese?
>
> K: It's because I really like to watch Chinese dramas. I hope I can soon watch them in Chinese and understand what are they saying.
>
> G: Well, keep studying hard, and I'm sure you'll be able to do it someday.
>
> K: I hope so. What about you? What are your plans for this year?
>
> G: Let me think. Hmm... Getting a good grade in every subject? As usual.
>
> K: Hahaha.

(어색한 부분)		(바르게 고치기)
(1) _____	→	_____
(2) _____	→	_____

8. 다음 〈보기〉의 밑줄 친 부분과 쓰임이 다른 것은?
(3점)

보기
• I will put more effort into studying math to overcome my weakness.

① I came here to meet you.

② He went there to help his mom.

③ She studies hard to become a doctor.

④ Please give the dog some water to drink.

⑤ He went to the library to return the books.

9. Which dialogue is correct? (4점)

① A: I hope I can see my grandmother this winter.

  B: I'm afraid I don't want to join her.

② A: What are you going to do next Saturday?

  B: I am planning to walk my dog in the park.

③ A: What are you planning to do after school?

  B: You will. Don't worry.

④ A: Do you have a special plan for this summer?

  B: Why don't you do some volunteer work?

⑤ A: What is the first thing on your bucket list?

  B: I bought that bucket in the market. I love it.

10. 다음 밑줄 친 부분과 같은 용법으로 쓰인 것은? (3점)

> • I was at the French restaurant to have lunch with my uncle.

① It seems that she needs some food to have.

② One of my wishes is to have lunch with the boy.

③ Their family went out to have spaghetti for dinner.

④ To have breakfast every day is good for your health.

⑤ To have lots of money is not significant in your life.

11. Which one is TRUE? (4점)

> B: Kate, what are your plans for the new school year?
>
> G: I am planning to spend more time studying Chinese.
>
> B: I didn't know you were interested in Chinese. When did you start studying Chinese?
>
> G: Only three months ago. But now I can speak a little Chinese.
>
> B: That's awesome! How did you get so into Chinese?
>
> G: It's because I like Chinese dramas a lot. I hope I can soon watch them in Chinese and understand what they're saying.
>
> B: Well, I believe you'll be able to do it soon.
>
> G: I hope so. How about you, Danny? What do you want to do this year?
>
> B: Hmm.... I am still planning what to do.

① Kate doesn't have any special plans for this year.

② Kate is interested in studying Chinese history.

③ Kate is a big fan of Chinese dramas.

④ Kate is able to watch Chinese dramas in Chinese and understand them.

⑤ The boy thinks that Kate should try to speak Chinese very well.

12. 주어진 단어를 이용하여 우리말을 영어로 옮기시오. (5점)

> (1) 나는 이번 주말까지 책 한 권을 반납할 필요가 있다. (need / return / a / by / end / week, 9단어)
>
> (2) 그것은 내 인생 최고의 순간이었다. (it / moment / life, 8단어)

→ (1) _____

  (2) _____

[13~14] 다음 글을 읽고 물음에 답하시오.

Hi! I'm Jinsu. This is my bucket list for this year. (A) My first goal is ⓐto go on a bike tour of Jejudo this summer. I ⓑhave been there before, but I want to experience the island more freely on my bike this time. (B) Secondly, I want to learn how to play the guitar. I think the guitar has ⓒmore beautiful sound of all musical instruments. (C) I hope I can play my favorite song on my guitar ⓓby the end of this year. (D) I am really poor at math. This year, I'll put more effort ⓔinto studying math to overcome my weakness. (E)

13. Which is the best place for the following sentence? **(4점)**

Finally, I want to get a good grade in math.

① (A) ② (B) ③ (C) ④ (D) ⑤ (E)

14. Which is NOT correct? **(3점)**
① ⓐ ② ⓑ ③ ⓒ ④ ⓓ ⑤ ⓔ

15. Which is NOT correct when you make a noun into an adjective? **(4점)**
① economy → economycal
② music → musical
③ person → personal
④ tradition → traditional
⑤ nature → natural

[16~17] 다음 글을 읽고, 물음에 답하시오.

Hi! My name is Somi. First, I want to see a concert of my favorite band right in front of the stage. (A) I'm willing to stand in line all night to enter the front area. Second, I want to adopt a puppy. (B) I've always wanted a puppy. (C) I think I'm fully ready to take care of a pet now. (D) My last goal is a little more challenging. (E) I became a big fan of this detective series last year, so I don't want to miss a single one.

16. 위 글의 밑줄 친 right와 문맥상 같은 의미로 쓰인 것은? **(3점)**
① That's not right.
② You've no right to be here.
③ He waited for Jina right here.
④ Could you raise your right hand?
⑤ Please go straight and turn right.

17. 위 글의 (A)~(E) 중 다음 문장이 들어가기에 적절한 곳은? **(4점)**

I'd like to read all of the Sherlock Holmes stories.

① (A) ② (B) ③ (C) ④ (D) ⑤ (E)

18. 다음 (A)~(D)를 순서대로 배열한 것은? **(4점)**

(A) Finally, he found it!
(B) A woman adopted two cats.
(C) He made every effort to find her missing cat.
(D) One cat was missing. She asked a detective for help.

① (A)-(B)-(C)-(D)　　② (B)-(A)-(C)-(D)
③ (B)-(D)-(C)-(A)　　④ (C)-(A)-(B)-(D)
⑤ (D)-(B)-(A)-(C)

19. 주어진 글 다음에 이어질 글의 순서로 가장 적절한 것은? (4점)

Hi! My name is Somi. First, I want to see a concert of my favorite band right in front of the stage.

(A) I'd like to read all of the Sherlock Holmes stories. I became a big fan of this detective series last year, so I don't want to miss a single one.

(B) I've always wanted a puppy. I think I'm fully ready to take care of a pet now. My last goal is a little more challenging.

(C) I'm willing to stand in line all night to enter the front area. Second, I want to adopt a puppy.

① (A)-(B)-(C)
② (A)-(C)-(B)
③ (C)-(A)-(B)
④ (B)-(C)-(A)
⑤ (C)-(B)-(A)

20. 다음 글의 밑줄 친 ⓐ~ⓔ 중 문맥상 낱말의 쓰임이 어색한 것은? (4점)

Today is the first day of your new school year. I want to hear your plans for this year. What do you want to do most? Think about three things you want to do. And then, make a bucket list and ⓐshare it with your friends.

Let me tell you my bucket list first. First of all, I want to learn how to make cookies. I want to make them to ⓑannoy my mom because she likes them a lot. Second, I want to live a ⓒeco-friendly life. I won't use paper cups or plasfic bags. The last thing is to study ⓓonline English lessons every day. I'm planning to study English using a smartphone. At the end of this year, I will ⓔovercome my problems with my weakness, English.

① ⓐ   ② ⓑ   ③ ⓒ   ④ ⓓ   ⑤ ⓔ

[21~22] 다음 글을 읽고 물음에 답하시오.

Hi! My name is Somi. First, I want to see a concert of my favorite band right in front of the stage. I'm willing to stand in line all night ⓐto enter the front area. Second, I want to adopt a puppy. I've always wanted a puppy. I think I'm fully ready to take care of a pet now. (ㄱ)My last goal is a little more (_____). I'd like to read all of the Sherlock Holmes stories. I became a big fan of this detective series last year, so I don't want to miss a single one

21. 밑줄 친 부분이 ⓐ와 같이 '~하기 위해서'로 해석되는 것은? (3점)

① I went to the new market.
② Her hobby is to read books.
③ I want to be a great baseball player.
④ She went to the mall to buy a new jacket.
⑤ He ran fast to his room, but he couldn't see her.

22. 밑줄 친 (ㄱ)이 '나의 마지막 목표는 조금 더 도전적이다.'의 뜻이 되도록 할 때, 빈칸에 들어갈 한 단어를 쓰시오. (4점)

→ _____

[23~25] 다음 글을 읽고 물음에 답하시오.

Hi! My name is Somi. First, I want to see a concert of my favorite band right in front of the stage. I'm willing (A)[standing / to stand] in line all night ⓐto enter the front area. Second, I want to adopt a puppy. I've always wanted a puppy. I think I'm fully ready to take care of a pet now. My last goal is a little (B)[more / most] challenging. I'd like to read all of the Sherlock Holmes stories. I became a big fan of this detective series last year, (C)[but / so] I don't want to miss a single one.

23. 위 글의 어법상 (A), (B), (C)에 들어갈 알맞은 단어를 고르면? (4점)

	(A)	(B)	(C)
①	to stand	most	so
②	standing	more	so
③	to stand	most	but
④	standing	most	but
⑤	to stand	more	so

24. 위 글의 밑줄 친 ⓐ와 쓰임이 같은 것은? (3점)

① I have no time to talk to him.
② My dream is to become a pianist.
③ They left for Africa to help people in need.
④ We decided to go to the amusement park.
⑤ I have nothing to wear to the party.

25. 위 글의 내용과 일치하지 않는 것은? (3점)

① 소미는 강아지를 입양하고 싶어 한다.
② 소미는 3가지의 버킷 리스트가 있다.
③ 소미는 좋아하는 밴드의 콘서트를 무대 바로 앞에서 보고 싶어 한다.
④ 소미는 셜록 홈즈 시리즈의 팬이다.
⑤ 소미에게 셜록 홈즈 전 시리즈를 읽는 것은 도전적인 일이 아니다.

[26~27] 다음 글을 읽고 물음에 답하시오.

Hi, everyone. I'm your new English teacher. Today is the first day of our new school year. I want to hear your plans and hopes for this year. What do you want to do most? Think about three things you want to do. And then, make a bucket list and share it with your friends.

Hi! I'm Jinsu. This is my bucket list for this year. First, I want to go on a bike tour of Jejudo this summer. ⓐI've been there before, but I want to experience the island ⓑmore freely on my bike this time. My second goal is to learn ⓒhow to play the guitar. I think the guitar has ⓓthe beautifulest sound of all musical instruments. Finally, I want to get a good grade in math. Math is my ⓔweakest subject. This year, I'll put more effort into studying math to overcome my weakness.

26. 위 글의 밑줄 친 ⓐ~ⓔ 중 어법상 옳지 않은 것은? (3점)

① ⓐ   ② ⓑ   ③ ⓒ   ④ ⓓ   ⑤ ⓔ

27. 위 글의 내용으로 옳지 않은 것은? (4점)

① Jinsu has three plans for this year.
② Jinsu finally got a good grade in math.
③ Jinsu hopes to take a cycling tour in Jejudo.
④ The teacher wants to know the students' plans for this year.
⑤ The students are going to make a bucket list for this year.

◎ 선택형 문항의 답안은 컴퓨터용 수정 싸인펜을 사용하여 OMR 답안지에 바르게 표기하시오.
◎ 서술형 문제는 답을 답안지에 반드시 검정 볼펜으로 쓰시오.
◎ 총 26문항 100점 만점입니다. 문항별 배점은 각 문항에 표시되어 있습니다.

[동작구 ㅇㅇ중]

1. 다음 중 빈칸에 들어갈 수 <u>없는</u> 단어는? (4점)

• Ms. Smith gets bored _____ when she reads a historical novel.
• Daniel _____ passed the test after he failed it five times.
• The students sat _____ while the teacher was checking their homework.
• I _____ get up early. But I got up late this morning because I watched a movie until late at night.

① usually ② easily ③ finally
④ careful ⑤ quietly

[동작구 ㅇㅇ중]

2. 다음 대화의 빈칸 (A)에 들어가기에 알맞은 것은? (3점)

G: What's the matter, Henry?
B: Look at my new cellphone.
G: Oh, your phone screen has a crack. (A)_____?
B: Yes. I dropped it on the way here. I'm so upset.
G: I think you should get a phone case. It will protect your phone.
B: Okay, I'll get one.

① Do you dropped it
② Did you drop it
③ Did you dropped it
④ Do I drop it
⑤ Did I dropped it

[양천구 ㅇㅇ중]

3. 다음 대화의 빈칸 (A)와 (B)에 들어갈 수 있는 문장으로 적절하지 <u>않은</u> 것은? (3점)

B: I feel down.
G: Why? What's the matter?
B: I put on 5kg this winter. (A)_____?
G: (B)_____
B: Yeah. You're right.

① What should I do?
② You should exercise every day.
③ You should cut down on snakes.
④ Why do you think I should do it?
⑤ Can you give me some advice for me?

[울산 ㅇㅇ중]

4. 다음 중 짝지어진 대화가 자연스러운 것은? (4점)

ⓐ A: I am going to go swimming today.
  B: Make sure you don't warm up exercises before swimming.
ⓑ A: What does your shirt say?
  B: It says "Never Give Up."
ⓒ A: I put on 3kg last winter. I want to lose weight.
  B: Oh, I think you should get more snack.
ⓓ A: I have a problem with Lou. What should I do?
  B: They don't talk anymore.
ⓔ A: Can I borrow your music book?
  B: Of course not. Just make sure you give it back.

① ⓐ ② ⓑ ③ ⓒ ④ ⓓ ⑤ ⓔ

[5~6] 다음 대화를 읽고, 물음에 답하시오.

> G: What does your shirt say?
> B: Oh, this? It says "No Cellphone for 24 Hours."
> G: No cellphone? Why?
> B: People depend on our phones too much these days.
> G: That's true. How often will you do this?
> B: I'm planning on doing it once a month, but I'm not sure.
> G: Try it first. Then, decide how often you should do it.
> B: Okay. I'm going to keep a diary of what I did without my phone for 24 hours. You should try it, too.
> G: I'll think about it. _____
> B: I will. After I do it, I'll talk about my experience in class.
>
> G: Girl B: Boy

5. 위 대화의 빈칸에 들어갈 말로 가장 적절한 것은?

(3점)

① Why don't we hang out?
② Never give up and go for it.
③ When are you going to do it?
④ Make sure your phone works well.
⑤ Let me know if you need my phone.

6. 위 대화의 내용을 읽고 유추할 수 없는 것은? (3점)

① 소녀는 후에 소년의 계획에 동참할 수도 있다.
② 소년은 24시간 동안 핸드폰 없이 생활해 볼 것이다.
③ 소년은 사람들이 핸드폰에 지나치게 의존한다고 생각한다.
④ 소년은 자신의 실행에 대해 기록한 후 친구들에게 발표할 것이다.
⑤ 소녀는 핸드폰 없이 지내는 날을 지금 정확히 결정할 것을 조언했다.

7. 다음 대화의 의미가 자연스럽도록 ⓐ~ⓔ를 바르게 배열한 것은? (4점)

> ⓐ Did Henny's mom say it was okay?
> ⓑ Thank you so much. I love you.
> ⓒ Mom, may I sleep over at Henny's house?
> ⓓ Yes. Henny said she would make pizza for us.
> ⓔ Okay. Make sure you text me when you get to Henny's house.

① ⓐ - ⓓ - ⓒ - ⓔ - ⓑ
② ⓑ - ⓐ - ⓔ - ⓒ - ⓓ
③ ⓑ - ⓒ - ⓐ - ⓓ - ⓔ
④ ⓒ - ⓐ - ⓑ - ⓓ - ⓔ
⑤ ⓒ - ⓐ - ⓓ - ⓔ - ⓑ

8. 다음 대화의 밑줄 친 부분 중 문맥상 어색한 것은?

(4점)

> G: What does your shirt say?
> B: Oh, this? ⓐIt says "No Cellphone for 24 Hours".
> G: No cellphone? Why?
> B: ⓑWe rely on our phones too much these days.
> G: That's true. How often will you do this?
> B: ⓒI am planning on doing it once a month, but I'm not sure.
> G: Try it first. Then, decide how often you should do it.
> B: Okay. ⓓI am going to write what I did with my phone for 24 hours. You should try it, too.
> G: ⓔI'll think about it.

① ⓐ   ② ⓑ   ③ ⓒ   ④ ⓓ   ⑤ ⓔ

- 14 -

[9~10] 다음 대화를 읽고 물음에 답하시오.

> G: What does your shirt say?
>
> B: Oh, this? ⓐIt says "No Cellphone for 24 Hours."
>
> G: No cellphone? What for?
>
> B: We depend on our phones too much these days.
>
> G: You can say that again. How often will you do this?
>
> B: I'm planning on doing ⓑit once a month, but I'm not sure.
>
> G: Try it first. Then, decide how often you should do ⓒit.
>
> B: Okay, I will. I'm going to keep a diary of what I did without my phone for 24 hours. You should try ⓓit, too.
>
> G: I'll think about it. Make sure (A)_____ _____.
>
> B: I plan to. After I do ⓔit, I'll talk about my experience in class.

9. Which is the best for (A)? (3점)

① you put up with it

② you give it up soon

③ you keep up with it

④ you clean it up after using

⑤ you get rid of it before leaving

10. 위 대화의 ⓐ~ⓔ 중 가리키는 것이 <u>다른</u> 하나는? (4점)

① ⓐ   ② ⓑ   ③ ⓒ   ④ ⓓ   ⑤ ⓔ

11. 다음 문장 중 어법상 옳은 문장의 총 개수는? (4점)

> ⓐ She made us bake cookies.
>
> ⓑ Mom had me cook dinner.
>
> ⓒ Danny let her write a letter.
>
> ⓓ I helped him to buy some food.
>
> ⓔ He helped you bring his car from the garage.

① 1개   ② 2개   ③ 3개   ④ 4개   ⑤ 5개

12. 다음 중 올바른 문장을 고르면? (3점)

① Cindy made her children to do their homework.

② Mr. Smith let us taking a break for 30 minutes.

③ Mom had my brother walked the dog.

④ Tom let me using his new laptop.

⑤ My teacher let me go home early.

13. 우리말과 일치하도록 주어진 낱말을 한 번씩만 사용하여 배열하시오. (6점)

> (1) 쓸 펜이 필요하세요?
> (a, do, to, pen, you, need, with, write)

→ _____?

> (2) 그는 우리에게 앉을 의자를 몇 개 가져다 주었다.
> (he, on, to, us, sit, some, chairs, brought)

→ _____.

[14~15] 다음 글을 읽고 물음에 답하시오.

(A)
Like this Seongmin cannot take his hands off his smartphone all day long. He does not know that using a smartphone too much can increase health problems. Are you a heavy user of your smartphone like Seongmin? If so, _____.

(B)
After class, he texts his friends while walking. He finds information on the Internet to do his homework. He reads online comic books to have some fun. He watches movies before he goes to the bed.

(C)
Seongmin spends a lot of time using his smartphone. He checks the news and weather every morning. When he goes to school, he plays smartphone games in the bus.

14. 위 글의 (A)~(C)를 흐름에 맞게 순서대로 바르게 배열한 것은? (4점)

① (A)-(B)-(C) ② (A)-(C)-(B)

③ (B)-(A)-(C) ④ (C)-(A)-(B)

⑤ (C)-(B)-(A)

15. 위 글의 빈칸에 들어갈 말로 가장 적절한 것은? (3점)

① you'd better watch out

② you should keep up with it

③ think about serious cyber attacks

④ you can search information easily

⑤ it is useful to follow his daily life

[16~17] 다음 글을 읽고 물음에 답하시오.

Watch your neck and back. When you read on your smartphone, you usually bend your neck. ㉠This "text neck" pose (_____) the pressure on your neck and back. The best way to prevent this pressure is to bring the phone up to the level of your eyes. (A)또 다른 방법은 여러분의 목을 구부리는 대신에 시선을 낮추는 것입니다.

16. ㉠이 '이 "거북목" 자세는 여러분의 목과 척추에 가해지는 압력을 증가시킵니다.'의 의미가 되도록 할 때 빈칸에 들어갈 한 단어를 쓰시오. (3점)

→ _____

17. 밑줄 친 (A)의 우리말 의미가 되도록 아래 제시된 단어를 모두 포함하여 문장을 쓰시오. (4점)

lower, another, bending, instead, way

→ _____

18. 다음 글의 밑줄 친 ⓐ~ⓔ 중 가리키는 대상이 다른 것을 고르면? (4점)

Yesterday, Sejin walked into a tree while texting and hurt ⓐher head and toe. It was so badly painful that ⓑshe couldn't talk and move. Fortunately, her friend, Sumi, found ⓒher cry and helped to go to the hospital. ⓓShe told her to avoid using her phone while walking. Also, her mom said that she should reduce the time ⓔshe spends using it.

① ⓐ ② ⓑ ③ ⓒ ④ ⓓ ⑤ ⓔ

[19~20] 다음 글을 읽고 물음에 답하시오.

Give your eyes a break. ⓐ<u>It makes your eyes feel tired and dry to reading small letters on a smartphone for a long time.</u> ⓑ<u>Using a smartphone in the dark or in a moving car make this problem worse.</u> To avoid this, give your eyes a break from time to time. Follow the 20-20-20 rule: Every 20 minutes, take a 20-second break and ⓒ<u>look at something at most 20 feet away.</u> Also, ⓓ<u>blinks your eyes often.</u> ⓔ<u>This will keep your eyes from becoming dry.</u>

19. 위 글의 밑줄 친 부분 중 의미나 어법상 알맞은 것은? (3점)

① ⓐ ② ⓑ ③ ⓒ ④ ⓓ ⑤ ⓔ

20. 위 글의 내용과 일치하는 것은? (3점)

① 눈은 사용할수록 시력이 좋아진다.
② 움직이는 차에서 스마트폰 사용은 눈을 건조하게 만들지 않는다.
③ 20분 핸드폰 사용, 20분 휴식은 눈 상태 악화를 예방할 수 있다.
④ 어두운 곳에서 스마트폰의 큰 글자를 읽는 것은 눈이 쉽게 피곤해지지 않는다.
⑤ 눈을 자주 깜빡이면 눈이 건조해지는 것을 막아줄 수 있다.

21. 다음 글의 내용과 일치하지 <u>않는</u> 것은? (4점)

Do you text a lot on your smartphone? Texting for a long time can hurt your fingers and wrists. Try these exercises. They will help reduce the pain in your fingers and wrists.

- Pull on each finger of each hand.
- Put the backs of your hands together with your arms out in front of you.

But remember. The best tip to prevent these health problems is to use your smartphone less. Give yourself some rest from your smartphone.

① 오랫동안 문자 메시지를 보내는 것은 손가락과 손목을 상하게 할 수 있다.
② 각 손의 각 손가락을 당기면 통증을 줄일 수 있다.
③ 통증을 줄이는 하나의 방법으로 팔을 앞으로 벌린 채로 손바닥을 마주 보게 한다.
④ 스마트폰을 덜 사용하는 것이 건강 문제를 예방하는 가장 좋은 방법이다.
⑤ 너 자신에게 스마트폰으로부터 휴식을 주세요.

22. 다음 글의 빈칸 (A), (B)에 들어갈 말로 가장 적절한 것은? (4점)

There are both good things and bad things about using a smartphone. First, I can get in touch with my friends right away. Also, I can easily get information I need. That is useful when I have a lot of homework to do. (A)_____, using a smartphone too much has my eyes feel dry and tired. Also, text messages and ads stop me from paying attention to my studies. (B)_____ I need to use my smartphone intelligently.

	(A)	(B)
①	However	Therefore
②	Therefore	On the contrary
③	In addition	So
④	Besides	However
⑤	On the other hand	Besides

[23~25] 다음 글을 읽고 물음에 답하시오.

Watch your neck and back. When you use your smartphone, you usually bend your neck. This "text neck" pose increases the pressure on your neck and back. ⓐThe best way to prevent this pressure is to bring the phone up to the level of your eyes. ⓑ Another way is to lower your eyes instead of bending your neck.

Give your eyes a break. (A) ⓒIt makes your eyes to feel tired and dry to read small letters on a smartphone for a long time. (B) Using a smartphone in the dark or in a moving car makes this problem worse. (C) Follow the 20-20-20 rule: Every 20 minutes, take a 20-second break and look at something at least 20 feet away. (D) Also, blink your eyes often. (E) ⓓThis will keep your eyes from becoming dry.

Do you text a lot on your smartphone? Texting for a long time can hurt your fingers and wrists. Try these exercises. ⓔThey will help reduce the pain in your fingers and wrists.

23. 위 글의 밑줄 친 ⓐ~ⓔ 중 어법상 어색한 것을 고르면? (3점)

① ⓐ ② ⓑ ③ ⓒ ④ ⓓ ⑤ ⓔ

24. 위 글에서 다음 문장이 들어가기에 적절한 곳은? (4점)

To avoid this, give your eyes a break from time to time.

① (A) ② (B) ③ (C) ④ (D) ⑤ (E)

25. 위 글의 내용과 일치하지 <u>않는</u> 것을 고르면? (3점)

① 스마트폰 사용시 당신은 보통 목을 구부린다.

② 먼 곳에 있는 물체를 보면 눈이 더 건조해진다.

③ 거북목 포즈는 당신의 목과 등에 압력을 증가시킨다.

④ 움직이는 차 안에서의 스마트폰 사용은 눈을 건조하게 한다.

⑤ 눈을 자주 깜빡이는 것은 눈이 건조해지는 것을 막아준다.

26. 다음 중 밑줄 친 부분을 바르게 고쳐 쓰시오. (10점)

A Smartphone & Me
There are both good things and bad things about using a smartphone. First, I can get in touch with my friends right away. Also, I can ⓐeasy get information I need. That is useful when I have a lot of homework ⓑdoing. On the other hand, using a smartphone too much ⓒmake my eyes feel dry and tired. Also, text messages and ads keep me from ⓓpay attention to my studies. So I have to use my smartphone ⓔintelligent.

ⓐ _____ → _____

ⓑ _____ → _____

ⓒ _____ → _____

ⓓ _____ → _____

ⓔ _____ → _____

2학년 영어 1학기 중간고사(2과) 2회

반		점수
이름		

문항수 : 선택형(26문항) 서술형(2문항)   20 . . .

◎ 선택형 문항의 답안은 컴퓨터용 수정 싸인펜을 사용하여 OMR 답안지에 바르게 표기하시오.
◎ 서술형 문제는 답을 답안지에 반드시 검정 볼펜으로 쓰시오.
◎ 총 28문항 100점 만점입니다. 문항별 배점은 각 문항에 표시되어 있습니다.

[울산 ○○중]

1. 다음 빈칸에 공통으로 들어갈 말은? (3점)

- Using a smartphone too much can _____ health problems.
- Lots of stress may _____ heart disease.

① cause   ② decrease   ③ prepare
④ prevent   ⑤ suggest

[양천구 ○○중]

2. 다음 대화의 Henry가 언짢아하는 이유로 가장 알맞은 것은? (3점)

G: What's the matter, Henry? You look upset.
B: Look at my new cellphone.
G: Oh, your phone screen has a crack. Did you drop it?
B: Yes, I dropped it on the way home. I'm so upset!
G: I think you should get a phone case. It will protect your phone.
B: Okay. I'll get one.

① He lost his new cellphone.
② His friend used his new cellphone.
③ His new cellphone screen has a crack.
④ He dropped his cellphone in water.
⑤ His friend dropped his new cellphone on the way home.

[경기 ○○중]

3. Complete the following dialogue by using the given phrase. (4점)

A: I am always late for school. What should I do?
B: _____
(set an alarm, your smartphone)

→ _____

[대전 ○○중]

4. 다음 대화 중 어색하게 짝지어진 것은? (3점)

① A: I have dark circles under my eyes.
   B: You should get more sleep.
② A: What's the matter?
   B: I put on 5kg this winter. What should I do?
③ A: Mom, may I sleep over at Jinsu's house?
   B: Did his mom say it was okay?
④ A: Can I borrow your science book?
   B: Sure. Make sure you give it back when you're done.
⑤ A: Make sure you don't read in the dark. It's not good for your eyes.
   B: Okay. I'll turn the light off.

[경기 ○○중]

5. What is the relationship between the two speakers? (4점)

A: I heard that you were sick yesterday. Do you feel better now?
B: Yes. I feel nice today. Thanks for caring about me.
A: Oh, no! I forgot to bring my English book.
B: Ms. Yu won't be happy about that.
A: I know. May I borrow your English book?
B: Why not? Just give it back to me when you are done.

① teacher - student   ② mom - son
③ doctor - patient   ④ librarian - visitor
⑤ friend - friend

[6~7] 다음 대화를 읽고 물음에 답하시오.

G: What does your shirt say?
B: Oh, this? It says "No Cellphone for 24 Hours."
G: No cellphone? Why?
B: We (A)_____ our phones too much these days.
G: That's true. How often will you do this?
B: I'm planning on doing it once a month, but I'm not sure.
G: Try it first. Then, decide how often you should do it.
B: Okay. I'm going to keep a diary of what I did without my phone for 24 hours. You should try it, too.
G: I'll think about it. Make sure you keep up with it.
B: I plan to. After I do it, I'll talk about my experience in class.

G: 소녀, B: 소년

6. 위 대화의 (A)에 들어가기에 적절한 말을 고르면?

(3점)

① buy   ② go to
③ don't use   ④ depend on
⑤ are not dependent on

7. 위 대화의 내용과 일치하는 것은?   (4점)

① 소년은 휴대전화 없이 하루를 살아보기로 했다.
② 소년은 자신의 경험을 가족과 공유할 것이다.
③ 우리는 요즘 휴대전화를 적당히 사용하고 있다.
④ 소년은 48시간 동안의 경험을 일기로 쓸 예정이다.
⑤ 소년은 자신의 셔츠 위에 쓰인 글과 반대로 행동할 것이다.

[8~9] 다음 대화를 읽고 물음에 답하시오.

G: What does your shirt say?
B: Oh, this? It ⓐsays "No Cellphone for 24 Hours."
G: No cellphone? Why?
B: We depend on our phones too much these days.
G: That's true. ⓑ얼마나 자주 이것을 할 거니?
B: I'm planning on doing ⓒit once a month, but I'm not sure.
G: Try it first. Then, decide how often you should do it.
B: Okay. I'm going to keep a diary of what I did ___(가)___ my phone for 24 hours. ⓓYou should try it, too.
G: I'll think about it. ⓔMake sure you keep up with it.
B: I plan to. After I do it, I'll talk about my experience in class.

8. 위 대화의 밑줄 친 ⓐ~ⓔ에 대한 설명으로 적절하지 않은 것은?   (4점)

① ⓐ는 문맥상 '~라고 쓰여 있다'의 의미이다.
② ⓑ는 'How often will you do this?'로 영작할 수 있다.
③ ⓒ는 대화의 흐름상 '휴대전화 없이 24시간 지내기'를 가리킨다.
④ ⓓ는 B가 A에게 하는 충고나 제안의 표현으로 이해할 수 있다.
⑤ ⓔ는 대화의 흐름상 '그 사람과 계속 연락하고 지내야 하는 것을 명심해.'라는 의미이다.

9. 위 대화의 내용을 고려할 때 빈칸 (가)에 들어갈 말로 적절한 한 단어를 쓰시오.   (3점)

→ _____

10. 다음 대화의 주어진 우리말의 의미가 되도록 빈칸을 완성할 때 빈칸 (A)에 들어갈 단어로 적절한 것은? (4점)

> B: Oh, no! I didn't bring my English book!
> G: Ms. Kim won't be happy about that.
> B: I know. Umm, can I borrow your English book?
> G: Okay. Just make _____ you _____ (A)_____ _____ _____ you're done. (다 사용하면 꼭 돌려줘야 해.)

① it   ② back   ③ give
④ sure   ⑤ when

11. 다음 짝지어진 대화가 <u>어색한</u> 것은? (3점)

① A: I forgot Jenny's birthday! What should I do?
　 B: I think you should tell her you're very sorry.

② A: Oh, no! I have dark circles under my eyes.
　 B: You should get more sleep.

③ A: What should I keep in mind?
　 B: I don't think so.

④ A: Make sure you are home by 12:00.
　 B: Okay, I will.

⑤ A: Can I eat this pizza?
　 B: Sure. Just make sure you wash your hands first.

12. 다음 밑줄 친 부분의 용법이 나머지 넷과 <u>다른</u> 것은? (3점)

① I have something <u>to read</u>.
② There is no pen <u>to write</u> with.
③ Everybody needs someone <u>to lean</u> on.
④ A kind man brought me a chair <u>to sit</u> on.
⑤ I worked hard <u>to succeed</u> in this business.

13. Which is the best for that blank? (3점)

> Watch Out!
> Yesterday, Sejin walked into a tree while texting and hurt her head. She needs to _____ using her phone while walking. Also, she should reduce the time she spends using it.

① avoid   ② remember   ③ enjoy
④ try   ⑤ practice

14. 다음 ⓐ~ⓔ에 들어갈 단어로 올바른 것은? (4점)

> • Logan cannot take his eyes ⓐ_____ the box.
> • My mom enjoys shopping ⓑ_____ time ⓒ_____ time.
> • Why don't you have some fruit instead ⓓ_____ sweets?
> • I respect her ⓔ_____ a doctor.

① ⓐ: of   ② ⓑ: to
③ ⓒ: from   ④ ⓓ: off
⑤ ⓔ: as

15. 다음 〈보기〉의 빈칸 (A), (B)에 들어갈 전치사를 바르게 짝지은 것은? (4점)

> **보기**
> • The boy needs a friend to play (A)_____
> • My teacher gave me some paper to write (B)_____.

① on – with   ② with – on
③ in – with   ④ with – in
⑤ in – on

[16~18] 다음 글을 읽고 물음에 답하시오.

Give your eyes a break. (ㄱ)It makes your eyes feel tired and dry to read small letters on a smartphone for a long time. Using a smartphone in the dark or in a moving car ⓐmakes this problem worse. To avoid this, give your eyes a break ⓑfrom time to time. Follow the 20-20-20 rule: Every 20 minutes, take a 20-second break and look at something at least 20 feet away. Also, blink your eyes often. This will ⓒkeep your eyes of becoming dry.

Do you text a lot on your smartphone? Texting for a long time can hurt your fingers and wrists. Try these exercises. They will ⓓhelp reduce the pain in your fingers and wrists.

- (ㄴ)Pull on each finger of each hand.
- (ㄷ)Put the backs of your hands together with your arms out in front of you.

But remember. The best tip to prevent these health problems ⓔis to use your smartphone less. Give yourself some rest from your smartphone.

16. 위 글의 주제로 가장 알맞은 것은? (4점)

① Useful advice for healthy foods
② Health tips for smartphone users
③ Health advice for women of all ages
④ A list of our favortie apps on smartphone
⑤ How to download 'youtube' video on our smartphone

17. 위 글의 밑줄 친 ⓐ~ⓔ 중 어법상 옳지 않은 것은? (3점)

① ⓐ   ② ⓑ   ③ ⓒ   ④ ⓓ   ⑤ ⓔ

18. 다음은 위 글을 읽고 질문에 답한 학생의 답안지를 나타낸 것이다. 한 문제에 1점이라면 학생이 받을 점수로 옳은 것은? (4점)

Quiz #2

1. 밑줄 친 (ㄱ)이 가리키는 것을 우리말로 쓰시오.
→ 눈을 쉬게 하는 것

2. 'this 20-20-20- rule'은 무엇인가?
→ 스마트폰을 사용할 때 20분마다 20초의 휴식을 취하고 적어도 20피트 이상 떨어져 있는 사물을 바라보는 것

3~4. (ㄴ)~(ㄷ)을 그림으로 표현하시오.

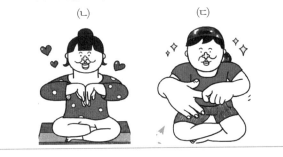

(ㄴ)   (ㄷ)

① 0점   ② 1점   ③ 2점   ④ 3점   ⑤ 4점

19. 다음 글의 밑줄 친 부분 중 알맞게 고치지 않은 것을 고르면? (정답 2개) (4점)

My dad studies living things on islands. I went to a ⓐdesert island last weekend with him. I wanted to swim while I was on the island, but my dad wouldn't let me ⓑswam. He had me ⓒto help him. There were so many small animals ⓓlive there. Some were really beautiful, but others made me ⓔfeeling scared.

① ⓐ desert island → desserted island
② ⓑ swam → swims
③ ⓒ to help → help
④ ⓓ live → living
⑤ ⓔ feeling → feel

[20~21] 나음 글을 읽고 물음에 답하시오.

Watch your neck and back. When you read on your smartphone, you usually bend your neck. This "text neck" pose ⓐ<u>increases</u> the pressure on your neck and back. The best way to prevent this pressure is to bring the phone ⓑ<u>up</u> to the level of your eyes. Another way is to lower your eyes instead of bending your neck.

Do you text a lot on your smartphone? Texting for a long time can ⓒ<u>relax</u> your fingers and wrists. Try these exercises. They will help ⓓ<u>reduce</u> the pain in your fingers and wrists.

• Pull on each finger of each hand.
• Put the backs of your hands together with your arms out in front of you.

The best tip to prevent these health problems is to use your smartphone ⓔ<u>less</u>. Give yourself some rest from your smartphone.

20. 위 글의 밑줄 친 ⓐ~ⓔ 중 문맥상 낱말의 쓰임이 <u>어색</u>한 것은? (3점)

① ⓐ   ② ⓑ   ③ ⓒ   ④ ⓓ   ⑤ ⓔ

21. 위 글의 내용을 한 문장으로 요약했을 때, 빈칸 (A), (B)에 들어갈 말로 가장 적절한 것은? (4점)

Using a smartphone for a long time can (A)_____ health problems, so we need to follow some (B)_____ to improve bad posture.

	(A)	(B)
①	cause	advice
②	avoid	tips
③	avoid	challenges
④	cause	mistakes
⑤	lessen	exercise

[22~23] 다음 글을 읽고 물음에 답하시오.

You need to give your eyes a break. Reading small letters on a smartphone for a long time makes your eyes tired and dry. If you use a smartphone in the dark or in a moving car, you would make this problem ⓐ<u>badder</u>. You'd better give your eyes a break ⓑ<u>from times to times</u> in order to protect them. Follow the 20-20-20 rule. Every 20 minutes, take a 20-second break and look at something at least 20 feet away. Also, blink your eyes often. This will keep your eyes ⓒ<u>from become</u> dry.

Do you text a lot on your smartphone? Texting for a long time can hurt your fingers and wrists. Try these exercises. They will help ⓓ<u>to reduce</u> the pain in your fingers and wrists.

- Pull on each finger of each hand.
- Put the backs of your hands together with your arms out in front of you.

But remember. The best tip to prevent these health problems ⓔ<u>are</u> to use your smartphone less. Give yourself some rest from your smartphone.

22. Which one is correct? (3점)

① ⓐ   ② ⓑ   ③ ⓒ   ④ ⓓ   ⑤ ⓔ

23. 위 글의 내용과 일치하지 <u>않는</u> 것은? (4점)

① 스마트폰의 작은 글씨를 오래 읽는 것은 눈을 피로하고 건조하게 만든다.

② 어두운 곳이나 움직이는 차에서 스마트폰을 사용하는 것은 눈에 좋지 않다.

③ 스마트폰 사용시, 20분마다 20초 정도의 휴식을 취하는 것이 눈을 위해 좋다.

④ 팔을 앞으로 한 채로 손등을 마주하는 것은 손목의 고통을 완화시켜 준다.

⑤ 눈의 건강을 위해서 스마트폰을 사용하지 않는 것이 좋다.

[24~25] 다음 글을 읽고 물음에 답하시오.

Give your eyes a break. It makes your eyes feel tired and dry ⓐto read small letters on a smartphone for a long time. Using a smartphone in a dark or in a moving car ⓑmake this problem ⓒbetter. (A)이것을 피하기 위해서는, 눈을 때때로 쉬게 하세요. Follow the 20-20-20 rule. Every 20 minutes, take a 20-second break and look at something at least 20 feet away. Also, blink your eyes often. This will keep your eyes from becoming dry.

Do you text a lot on your smartphone? Texting for a long time can hurt your fingers and wrists. Try these exercises. They will help you ⓓincrease the pain in your fingers and wrists.

• Pull on each finger of each hand.
• Put the backs of your hands together with your arms out in front of you.

But remember. The best tip to prevent these health problem is to use your smartphone ⓔmore. Give yourself some rest from your smartphone.

24. 위 글의 밑줄 친 (A)의 의미가 되도록 영작한 것으로 가장 적절한 것은? (4점)

① To avoid this, give your eyes a break sometimes.
② To enjoy this, give your eyes a break sometimes.
③ To protect this, give your eyes a break sometimes.
④ To support this, give your eye a break sometimes.
⑤ To practice this, give your eyes a break sometimes.

25. 위 글의 밑줄 친 ⓐ~ⓔ 중 문맥상 또는 어법상 어색한 낱말의 개수는? (4점)

① 1개   ② 2개   ③ 3개   ④ 4개   ⑤ 5개

26. 다음 글의 흐름상 어색한 것은? (3점)

I am a ⓐheavy user of my smartphone. I use it when I eat and even ⓑwhile I walk. I can't ⓒtake my hands off my smartphone all day long. So I feel ⓓcomfortable when I don't have it with me. I need some ⓔtips to be a smart smartphone user.

① ⓐ   ② ⓑ   ③ ⓒ   ④ ⓓ   ⑤ ⓔ

27. 다음 글의 분위기로 가장 적절한 것은? (4점)

My dad studies living things on islands. I went to a deserted island last weekend with him. I was so excited and enjoyed swimming all day long while I was on the island. There were so many small animals living on the island. Some were really beautiful, but others looked scared. I climbed the mountain and found the perfect place with the great sea view. I saw dolphins swimming. It was one of the best moments in my life.

① noisy and confusing
② dangerous and lonely
③ mysterious and gloomy
④ adventures and horrible
⑤ interesting and peaceful

28. 다음 글의 (A)에 들어갈 단어를 본문 중에서 찾아 알맞은 형태로 고쳐 쓰시오. (4점)

When you read on your smartphone, you usually (A)_____ your neck. This "text neck" pose increases the pressure on your neck and back. The best way to prevent this pressure is to bring the phone up to the level of your eyes. Another way is to lower your eyes instead of bending your neck.

→ _____

◎ 선택형 문항의 답안은 컴퓨터용 수정 싸인펜을 사용하여 OMR 답안지에 바르게 표기하시오.

◎ 서술형 문제는 답을 답안지에 반드시 검정 볼펜으로 쓰시오.

◎ 총 27문항 100점 만점입니다. 문항별 배점음 각 문항에 표시되어 있습니다.

[충남 ○○중]

1. 다음 중 짝지어진 단어의 관계가 <u>어색한</u> 것은? (3점)

① get - getful
② help - helpful
③ care - careful
④ hope - hopeful
⑤ delight - delightful

[양천구 ○○중]

2. 다음 영어 문장과 우리말이 일치하도록 제시된 철자로 시작하여 빈칸을 알맞은 단어로 채우시오. (4점)

> • Minho dreams of p_____ i_____ a music festival in Germany. (민호는 독일에서 음악 축제에 참가할 것을 꿈꾼다.)

[양천구 ○○중]

3. 다음 주어진 말에 이어질 대화의 순서로 가장 알맞은 것은? (4점)

> B: Jiyun, that's a pretty backpack!
>
> G: _____
>
> B: Wow! _____
>
> G: Yes, she is. _____

↓

(A) Where did you get it?
(B) My sister made it for me.
(C) She's a really good designer.
(D) And she enjoys making clothes, too.

① (A)-(B)-(C)-(D)   ② (A)-(C)-(B)-(D)
③ (B)-(C)-(D)-(A)   ④ (C)-(D)-(A)-(B)
⑤ (D)-(A)-(B)-(C)

[경기 ○○중]

4. What is the purpose of the following dialogue? (4점)

> B: Hello, Kate. I'm Hamin, the leader of the Nanum Orchestra. Thank you for your interest in our club.
>
> G: Hi. Nice to meet you.
>
> B: You play the violin? When did you start playing the violin?
>
> G: I started to play the violin when I was 10.
>
> B: Do you have any experience playing in a group?
>
> G: Yes. Actually, I was a member of an orchestra when I was in elementary school.
>
> B: Great. We also volunteer to teach children. Do you enjoy teaching others?
>
> G: I have no experience teaching others. But I enjoy working with people, so I'd like to try.
>
> B: Good. I think we'll have a great time playing together. Welcome to the Nanum Orchestra.

① to join the violin club
② to practice playing the violin
③ to volunteer for teaching children
④ to interview a new member of the club
⑤ to ask questions of Hamin for the project

[충남 ○○중]

5. 다음 문장의 빈칸에 들어갈 적절한 말을 고르면? (3점)

> • Minho dreams of _____ a music festival in Germany.

① get better   ② changes into
③ participating in   ④ broke out
⑤ what if

[6~7] 다음 대화를 읽고 물음에 답하시오.

B: Hello, Kate. I'm Hamin, the leader of the Nanum Orchestra. Thank you for your interest in our club.
G: Hi. Nice to meet you.
B: You play the violin? When did you start playing the violin?
G: I started to play the violin when I was ten.
B: Do you have any experience playing in a group?
G: Yes. Actually, I was a member of an orchestra when I was in elementary school.
B: Great. We also volunteer to teach children. (A)_____
G: I have no experience teaching others. But I enjoy working with people, so I'd like to try.
B: Good. I think we'll have a great time playing together. Welcome to the Nanum Orchestra.

6. Which sentence is proper in the blank (A)?

(3점)

① What do you want to have?
② Do you enjoy teaching children?
③ Do you want to be a violinist?
④ Do you want to be a music teacher?
⑤ Do you have any interest in instruments?

7. 위 대화를 읽고 Kate와 관련된 사실이 아닌 것은?

(4점)

ⓐShe is a new orchestra member in the Nanum Orchestra. ⓑShe started to learn violin when she was ten years old. ⓒShe knows how to play the violin. ⓓShe also volunteered to teach children. ⓔAnd she says she enjoys working with people. Let's all welcome her to the Nanum Orchestra.

① ⓐ　　② ⓑ　　③ ⓒ　　④ ⓓ　　⑤ ⓔ

8. 다음 주어진 단어를 한 번씩만 사용하여 대화를 완성하시오.

(4점)

A: Mina, do you enjoy cooking?
B: Sometimes. _____.
　 (how / I / make / know / pizza / to)
A: Then, let's join the cooking club!
B: Hmm, I'll think about it.

→ _____

9. 다음 대화를 읽고 G가 할 수 있는 일을 고르면?

(3점)

G: Look at these pictures. I grew these vegetables myself. I have my own garden.
B: Cool! Do you know how to cook the vegetables you grow, too?
G: Yes, my grandmother taught me.

10. 다음 대화의 문맥상 빈칸 (A)에 들어가기에 알맞은 말은? (4점)

> B: Hello, Kate. I'm Hamin, the leader of the Nanum Orchestra. Thank you for your interest in our club.
> G: Hi. Nice to meet you.
> B: You play the violin? When did you start playing the violin?
> G: I started learning how to play the violin when I was ten.
> B: Do you have any experience playing in a group?
> G: Yes. Actually, I was a member of an orchestra when I was in elementary school.
> B: Great. We also volunteer to teach children. Do you enjoy teaching others?
> G: (A)_____ But I enjoy working with people, so I'd like to try.
> B: Good. I think we'll have a great time playing together. Welcome to the Nanum Orchestra.

① Yes, I love children.
② Do you really think so?
③ I have no experience teaching others.
④ People say that I am a great violinist.
⑤ I like playing games on a smartphone.

11. Which dialogue is correct? (4점)

① A: Why don't you come to my house someday and play with my pets?
　B: Oh, I can't wait for that. I love to do.
② A: Did you get the tickets?
　B: It looks great! I like the colors.
③ A: Have you read the book? What did you think of it?
　B: Thank you, Mom. I like this dress.
④ A: I am thinking about getting a pet. Do you have a pet?
　B: I'm excited about going to the concert.
⑤ A: Did you buy that drone?
　B: Not at all. You can come to my house.

12. 다음 문장의 의미에 맞게 영작할 때 사용하기에 <u>어색한 것은?</u> (3점)

> • 그녀는 어떻게 이 노래를 잘 부르는지 안다.

① She　　② how to　　③ knows
④ sings　　⑤ this song

13. 제시된 두 문장을 관계대명사를 사용하여 한 문장으로 쓰시오. (4점)

> • Pippi is stronger than the man.
> • The man has the biggest arms in town.
>
> → _____

14. 다음 중 밑줄 친 부분이 어법상 <u>어색한 것은?</u> (3점)

① Tell the driver <u>where to stop</u>.
② I don't know <u>what to do</u> first.
③ Do you know <u>when to start</u> for London?
④ Jiho asked her <u>why to buy</u> used books.
⑤ Can you tell me <u>how to make</u> a kite?

[15~19] 다음 글을 읽고 물음에 답하시오.

(A) The Picasso Club

Hi! I am Sora Kang from the Picasso Art Club. As you can guess from the name of our ⓐclub, we paint. We also do ⓑvolunteer work sometimes. Last summer, our club members ©participated in the "Change Our Neighborhood" project. On the dirty old walls of the buildings in our ⓓneighborhood, we painted birds flying high in the sky and dolphins jumping over blue waves. (가)_____, the old neighborhood changed into a bright and beautiful place. The neighbors were happy to see our work and thanked us. You don't have to be a good painter. Anyone who likes to paint can ⓔjoin. Come and be a member of the Picasso Art Club.

(B) The Boram Orchestra

Hi! I am Minsu Jang, the leader of the Boram Orchestra. Did you see several ㉠students playing music at the main gate when you came to school today? We were ㉡those students. We play music for our friends every morning. You need to know how to play an instrument a little bit ㉢to join our club. But don't worry if you don't play well. We will practice hard and get better together. We also teach children how to play musical instruments as a service to our community. I am teaching an eleven-year-old boy to play the violin. (나)_____, he did not know how to read a note. Now he can play a simple song. Hearing him play the violin ㉣makes me very happy. By joining our club, you can have an opportunity ㉤to help others. Come and join our club. We are waiting for you.

15. 위 글을 읽고 답할 수 <u>없는</u> 질문은?　　(4점)

① Who can join the Picasso Art Club?

② How many students are there in each club?

③ What did the club members paint on the walls?

④ What musical instrument does Minsu teach the boy?

⑤ Where do several Boram Orchestra members play music every morning?

16. 위 글의 흐름상 (가), (나)에 들어갈 말로 가장 적절한 것은?　　(4점)

	(가)	(나)
①	For example	At first
②	As a result	At first
③	For example	At last
④	As a result	At last
⑤	Furthermore	At last

17. 다음은 위 글 (A)의 내용의 요지를 표로 정리한 것이다. 위 글의 내용과 일치하는 문장의 총 개수는?　(4점)

The Picasso Art Club
Summary
(A) Our club name was named after Van Gogh.
(B) Last winter, we joined an art project.
(C) The name of the project was "Change Our Community".
(D) We painted birds and horses on the walls of the buildings.
(E) Come and join our club. You don't have to be a good painter.

① 1개　② 2개　③ 3개　④ 4개　⑤ 5개

18. 위 글 (B)의 내용, 어법, 표현 등에 대한 설명으로 옳지 않은 것은? (4점)

① ㉠ 'students'와 'playing' 사이에 'who were'가 생략되어 있다.

② ㉡은 정문에서 연주하던 학생들을 가리킨다.

③ ㉢은 감정의 원인을 나타내는 'to부정사의 부사적 용법'으로 '~해서 (감정을) 느끼다'라고 해석한다.

④ ㉣은 문장의 주어가 동명사 'Hearing'이므로 makes가 알맞다.

⑤ ㉤은 앞의 명사 'opportunity'를 수식하는 'to부정사의 형용사적 용법'이다.

19. 위 글의 밑줄 친 ⓐ~ⓔ의 영영 풀이로 옳지 않은 것은? (4점)

① ⓐ: a group for people who share a particular interest

② ⓑ: a person who offers to do something without expecting a reward

③ ⓒ: to prevent something bad from happening

④ ⓓ: the people who live in the same area, town, etc.

⑤ ⓔ: to become a member of a group or an organization

[동작구 ○○중]

[20~21] 다음 글을 읽고 물음에 답하시오.

We play music for our friends every morning. You need to know (A)＿＿＿＿ to play an instrument a little bit to join our club. But don't worry (B)＿＿＿＿ you don't play well. We will practice hard and get better together. We also teach children (C)＿＿＿＿ to play musical instruments as a service to our community. ⓐI am teaching a eleven-year-old boy to play the violin. ⓑAt first, he did not know how to read a note. ⓒNow he can't play a simple song. (D)＿＿＿＿ the violin makes me very happy. (E)＿＿＿＿ our club, ⓓI can have an opportunity to help others. Come and join our club. ⓔWe are wait for you.

20. 위 글의 빈칸 (A)~(C)에 들어갈 말로 알맞은 것을 모두 고르면? (정답 2개) (4점)

① (A): when

② (B): while

③ (C): how

④ (D): Hear him play

⑤ (E): By joining

21. 위 글의 밑줄 친 부분 중 의미나 어법상 알맞은 것은? (4점)

① ⓐ　② ⓑ　③ ⓒ　④ ⓓ　⑤ ⓔ

[동작구 ○○중]

22. 다음 글의 내용과 일치하는 것은? (3점)

April 30

Hi! My name is Chris. Today, Minsu, the leader of the Boram Orchestra, came to our community. He started teaching me how to play the violin last month. At first, I didn't know how to read a note. I hope to join the Boram Orchestra and play the violin at the main gate when I become a middle school student.

① Minsu started to learn how to play the violin.

② Chris knew how to read a note before he met Minsu.

③ Minsu told Chris how to join the Boram Orchestra.

④ Chris taught Minsu how to play violin.

⑤ Chris is an elementary school student.

[23~24] 다음 글을 읽고 물음에 답하시오.

Did you see several students ⓐplayed music at the main gate? We were those students. We play music for our friends every morning. You need to know how to play an instrument a little bit to join our club. But don't worry ⓑand you don't play well. We will practice hard and get better together. We also teach children how to play musical instruments ⓒafter a service to our community. I am teaching an eleven-year-old boy to play the violin. At first, he did not know how to read a note. Now he can play a simple song. Hearing him play the violin ⓓmake me very happy. By ⓔjoining our club, you can have an opportunity to help others. Come and join our club. We are waiting for you.

23. 위 글에서 악기 연주 이외에 동아리 학생들이 하는 일은? (4점)

① They teach their neighbors how to play the guitar.

② They have an opportunity to help others.

③ They learn how to write notes.

④ They participate in various projects.

⑤ They make simple songs.

24. 위 글에서 밑줄 친 부분 중 올바른 것은? (4점)

① ⓐ   ② ⓑ   ③ ⓒ   ④ ⓓ   ⑤ ⓔ

[25~26] 다음 글을 읽고 물음에 답하시오.

Participating in club activities (A)[is / are] a great way to enjoy your school life. How about joining a club? Here are two club leaders (B)[who / which] want students to join their clubs. Let's listen to (C)[which / what] they say.

25. 위 글의 괄호 (A), (B), (C) 안에 들어갈 낱말로 가장 적절한 것은? (3점)

	(A)	(B)	(C)
①	is	who	what
②	is	which	what
③	are	who	what
④	are	which	which
⑤	are	who	which

26. 위 글 다음에 이어질 내용으로 가장 적절한 것은? (4점)

① Health tips for smartphone users.

② The best ways to be a club leader

③ Two bucket lists of the club leaders

④ Good points of becoming a club leader

⑤ Some information of school clubs and their activities

27. 다음 글을 읽고 알 수 없는 것은? (4점)

Last spring, our club members took part in the "Change Our Neighborhood" project. On the dirty old walls of the buildings in our neighborhood, we painted birds flying high in the sky and dolphins jumping over blue waves. As a result, the old neighborhood changed into a bright and beautiful place. The neighbors were happy to see our work and thanked us. You don't have to be a good painter. Anyone who likes to paint can join. Come and be a member of the Picasso Art Club.

① Who can join the club?

② When was the project happened?

③ How often does the club do the volunteer work?

④ What did the club members paint on the walls?

⑤ How did the neighbors feel about the painting?

◎ 선택형 문항의 답안은 컴퓨터용 수정 싸인펜을
   사용하여 OMR 답안지에 바르게 표기하시오.
◎ 서술형 문제는 답을 답안지에 반드시 검정
   볼펜으로 쓰시오.
◎ 총 31문항 100점 만점입니다. 문항별 배점
   은 각 문항에 표시되어 있습니다.

[양천구 ○○중]

1. 다음 밑줄 친 어휘의 쓰임이 바르지 않은 것은?(3점)

① He lent me a very <u>useful</u> book.

② Be <u>carefully</u>! My painting is not dry yet.

③ Look at the <u>colorful</u> umbrellas on the street!

④ Eating regular meals is also <u>helpful</u> to stay healthy.

⑤ The designer is famous for making <u>beautiful</u> clothes.

[울산 ○○중]

2. 다음 ⓐ~ⓓ 중 단어의 관계가 〈보기〉와 같은 것을 모두 고르면? (2점)

> **보기**
> play – player

ⓐ teach – teacher	ⓑ sing – singer
ⓒ cook – cooker	ⓓ lead – leader

① ⓐ, ⓒ

② ⓑ, ⓓ

③ ⓐ, ⓑ, ⓒ

④ ⓐ, ⓑ, ⓓ

⑤ ⓑ, ⓒ, ⓓ

[경기 ○○중]

3. How does A feel in this dialogue? (3점)

> A: Look at these pictures. I grew these vegetables myself. I have my own garden.
> B: Cool! Can you cook the vegetables you grow, too?
> A: Yes, my grandmother taught me.

① proud　　② nervous　　③ regretful

④ surprised　　⑤ disappointed

[양천구 ○○중]

4. 다음 대화의 내용으로 알 수 없는 것은? (3점)

> G: I heard you went to Yuna's violin concert yesterday. How was it?
> B: It was great. I hope I can play the violin like her someday.
> G: I didn't know you knew how to play the violin.
> B: I can, but I'm not good at it yet.

① B는 어제 Yuna의 바이올린 콘서트에 갔다.

② B는 언젠가 Yuna처럼 바이올린을 연주할 수 있기를 소망한다.

③ G는 B가 바이올린을 연주할 수 있다는 사실을 몰랐다.

④ G는 바이올린을 잘 연주할 수 있다.

⑤ B는 바이올린을 아직 잘 연주하지는 못한다.

[동작구 ○○중]

5. 다음 짝지어진 대화 중 어색한 것은? (3점)

① A: Do you know how to use this computer?
　 B: I'm sorry. I don't know it, either.

② A: Could you give me some advice? I want to lose some weight.
　 B: I think you should eat lots of fast food every day.

③ A: Why don't you join the tennis club?
　 B: Hmm, let me think about it.

④ A: Can my children ride on this boat?
　 B: Of course. Just make sure they wear life jackets.

⑤ A: What does she enjoy doing when she has free time?
　 B: She enjoys walking her dog.

6. 다음 대화의 밑줄 친 말의 의도로 알맞은 것은?

(3점)

> A: <u>Which sport do you like?</u> Baseball or basketball?
> B: I like baseball more. I play baseball twice a week.

① 동의 묻기　　　　② 선호 묻기
③ 계획 묻기　　　　④ 충고 구하기
⑤ 소망 묻기

7. 다음 중 짝지어진 대화가 <u>어색한</u> 것은?　　(3점)

① A: What are you doing?
　B: I'm looking at a world map.

② A: Do you have a pet?
　B: Yes, I do. I have a cat.

③ A: Did you get the tickets?
　B: Yes! I can't wait to watch the game.

④ A: What did you do on the weekend?
　B: Don't worry. I won't forget.

⑤ A: What are you going to do on your vacation?
　B: I'm going to go surfing.

8. 다음 빈칸에 들어갈 표현으로 알맞은 것은?　(3점)

> • We will practice hard and _____ together.
> (우리는 열심히 연습해서 함께 나아질 것이다.)

① get better　　　　② jump into
③ participate in　　④ put on
⑤ take off

[9~11] 다음 대화를 읽고 물음에 답하시오.

> B: Hello, Kate. I'm Hamin, the leader of the Nanum Orchestra. Thank you for your interest in our club. (A)
> G: Hi. Nice to meet you.
> B: You play the violin? When did you start ⓐ<u>playing</u> the violin? (B)
> G: I started learning how to ⓑ<u>play</u> the violin when I was ten.
> B: Do you have any experience playing in a group?
> G: Yes. Actually, I was a member of an orchestra when I was in elementary school. (C)
> B: Great. We also volunteer to ⓒ<u>teaching</u> children. (D)
> G: I have no experience teaching others. But I enjoy ⓓ<u>working</u> with people, so I'd like to ⓔ<u>try</u>. (E)
> B: Good. I think we'll have a great time playing together. Welcome to the Nanum Orchestra.

9. 위 대화의 빈칸 (A)~(E) 중 주어진 문장이 들어가기에 가장 적절한 곳은?　　(3점)

> Do you enjoy teaching others?

① (A)　② (B)　③ (C)　④ (D)　⑤ (E)

10. 위 대화의 밑줄 친 ⓐ~ⓔ 중 어법상 옳지 <u>않은</u> 것은?

(4점)

① ⓐ　② ⓑ　③ ⓒ　④ ⓓ　⑤ ⓔ

11. 위 대화의 내용과 일치하지 <u>않는</u> 것은? (3점)

① The leader of the Nanum Orchestra is Hamin.

② Kate is interested in joining the Nanum Orchestra.

③ Kate has no experience playing in a group.

④ Kate has no experience teaching others.

⑤ Hamin is welcoming Kate as a new member of the Nanum Orchestra.

12. 다음 우리말과 같은 뜻이 되도록 〈보기〉의 단어들과 〈조건〉을 참고하여 영작하시오. (4점)

• 세 권의 책들을 가지고 있는 그 여자애는 나의 여동생이다.

보기
the girl / my / books / is / sister / three

조건
• 관계대명사 사용하기.
• 필요시 영어 단어 추가하기.
• 주어와 동사가 포함된 한 개의 문장을 쓰시오.
• 반드시 <보기>의 단어들을 모두 사용하시오.

→ _____

13. 다음 빈칸에 들어갈 말이 알맞게 짝지어진 것은? (3점)

• Kate has a dog (A)_____ likes to hide in boxes.
• Look at the people (B)_____ are standing in line.

	(A)	(B)
①	who	which
②	whose	that
③	that	which
④	which	who
⑤	which	what

14. 다음 중 올바른 문장을 고르면? (3점)

① My father told me why to use the machine.

② Jisu asks her mother where can put she the bag.

③ Do you know when to start the performance?

④ Tell the driver where he should stops.

⑤ I do not know what to doing first.

15. 다음 우리말과 일치하도록 주어진 단어와 관계대명사를 이용하여 문장을 완성하시오. (4점)

(A) I have a friend _____.
(나는 항상 큰 부츠를 신는 친구가 있습니다.)
(boots, wear / I have a friend 포함 총 9단어)

(B) She is stronger than the man _____
_____. (그녀는 가장 큰 팔을 가진 남자보다 힘이 셉니다.) (arms, the / She is stronger that the man 포함 총 11단어)

16. 다음 중 어법상 옳지 <u>않은</u> 문장은? (3점)

① I want to learn how to make a paper plane.

② He knows a woman who is taller than Tom.

③ I have a friend who always plays the guitar.

④ The man who have the biggest arms is running.

⑤ There are a lot of people who can sing well in my club.

[17~20] 다음 글을 읽고 물음에 답하시오.

The Picasso Art Club
Hi! I am Sora Kang from the Picasso Art Club. As you can guess from the name of our club, we paint. We also do volunteer work ⓐfrom time to time. Last summer, our club members participated in the "Change Our Neighborhood" project. On the dirty old walls of the buildings in our neighborhood, we painted ⓑbirds flying high in the sky and dolphins jumping over blue waves. As a result, the old neighborhood changed into a bright and beautiful place. The neighbors were happy to see our work and thanked us. You don't have to be a good painter. Anyone (A)_____ likes to paint can join. Come and ⓒbe a member of the Picasso Art Club.

The Boram Orchestra
Hi! I am Minsu Jang, the leader of the Boram Orchestra. Did you see ⓓseveral students playing music at the main gate when you came to school today? We were those students. We play music for our friends every morning. You need to know how to play an instrument a little bit (B)_____ our club. But don't worry if you don't play well. We will practice hard and ⓔget better together. We also teach children how to play musical instruments as a service to our community. I am teaching an eleven-year-old boy to play the violin. At first, he did not know how to read a note. Now he can play a simple song. Hearing him play the violin (C)_____ me very happy. Ⓐ우리 동아리에 가입함으로써, 당신은 다른 사람들을 도울 기회를 가질 수 있다. Come and join our club. We are waiting for you.

17. 위 글의 내용과 흐름을 고려할 때, (A)~(C)에 들어가기에 알맞은 표현으로 바르게 짝지어진 것은? (3점)

	(A)	(B)	(C)
①	who	to join	make
②	who	to join	makes
③	who	to joining	make
④	which	to joining	makes
⑤	which	joining	make

18. 위 글의 내용과 흐름을 고려할 때, 밑줄 친 ⓐ~ⓔ를 우리말로 해석한 것으로 옳지 않은 것은? (3점)

① ⓐ: 가끔
② ⓑ: 하늘을 높이 나는 새들
③ ⓒ: Picasso Art Club의 회원이 되어라
④ ⓓ: 정문에서 음악을 연주하는 학생 몇 명
⑤ ⓔ: 함께 모이다

19. 위 글의 밑줄 친 Ⓐ의 의미가 되도록 문장을 쓴 것으로 가장 적절한 것은? (4점)

① By joining our club, you will others help having opportunity.
② By our club joining, you can have an opportunity help others.
③ By our club joining, you can have an opportunities to help other.
④ By joining our club, you will have help others opportunity.
⑤ By joining our club, you can have an opportunity to help others.

20. 위 글의 내용과 일치하지 않는 것은? (3점)

① 'The Piccaso Art Club'은 그림 그리는 동아리이다.
② Sora가 속한 동아리는 마을의 오래된 벽에 그림을 그렸다.
③ 그림 그리기를 좋아하면 누구나 'The Piccaso Art Club'에 가입 가능하다.
④ 'The Boram Orchestra'에 가입하기 위해서는 반드시 악기를 잘 다루어야 한다.
⑤ Minsu는 열 한 살된 소년에게 바이올린을 가르치고 있다.

[21~23] 다음 글을 읽고 물음에 답하시오.

> The Picasso Art Club
> Hi! I am Sora Kang from the Picasso Art Club. As you can guess from the name of our club, we paint. We also do volunteer work from time to time. Last summer, our club members participated in the "Change Our Neighborhood" project. (A) On the dirty old walls of the buildings in our neighborhood, we painted birds flying high in the sky and dolphins jumping over blue waves. (B) The neighbors were happy to see our work and thanked us. (C) You don't have to be a good painter. (D) Anyone who likes to paint can join. (E) Come and be a member of the Picasso Art Club.

21. 위 글의 (A)~(E) 중 주어진 문장이 들어가기에 가장 알맞은 곳은? (4점)

> As a result, the old neighborhood changed into a bright and beautiful place.

① (A)   ② (B)   ③ (C)   ④ (D)   ⑤ (E)

22. Which statement is correct according to the passage? (3점)

① The art club name was named after Van Gogh.

② Only a great painter can be a group member.

③ Last spring, club members joined an art project.

④ The name of the project was "Change Our Community."

⑤ Club members painted birds and dolphins on the dirty walls of the buildings.

23. 위 글에서 주어진 영영 풀이에 맞는 어휘를 찾아 한 단어로 쓰시오. (3점)

> form an opinion when someone does not know exactly

→ _____

[24~25] 다음 글을 읽고 물음에 답하시오.

> Hi! I am Minsu Jang, the ⓐ_____ of the Boram Orchestra. Did you see several students (A)_____ playing music at the main gate when you came to school today? We were those students. We play music for our friends every morning. You need to know how to play an instrument ⓑ_____ to join our club. But don't ⓒ_____. We will practice hard and ⓓ_____ together. We also teach children how to play musical instruments as a ⓔ_____ to our community.

24. 위 글의 빈칸 ⓐ~ⓔ에 들어갈 말로 알맞지 <u>않은</u> 것은? (4점)

① ⓐ leader   ② ⓑ a little bit

③ ⓒ worry   ④ ⓓ get better

⑤ ⓔ serve

25. 위 글의 흐름에 맞게 빈칸 (A)에 들어갈 두 단어를 쓰시오. (3점)

→ _____ _____

[26~28] 다음 글을 읽고 물음에 답하시오.

Hello! I am Minsu Jang, the leader of the Boram Orchestra. (A) Did you see a few students playing music at the gate when you came to school today? (B) We play music for our friends every morning. (C) You should know how to play an instrument a little bit to join our club. But you don't have to worry if you don't play well. (D) We will practice hard and get better together. (E) We also teach children to play musical instruments as a service to our community. I am teaching an eleven-year-old boy from my neighborhood to play the violin. At first, he did not know how to read a note. Now he can play simple children's songs. It makes me happy to hear him play the violin. By joining our club, you can have an opportunity to help others. Come and join our club. We are waiting for you.

26. 위 글에서, 민수가 가르치는 소년에 대해 알 수 없는 것은? (4점)

① How old is he?
② Where does he live?
③ What instrument is he learning?
④ What kind of song can he play now?
⑤ How does he feel when he plays an instrument?

27. Which is the best place for the following sentence? (3점)

We were those students.

① (A) ② (B) ③ (C) ④ (D) ⑤ (E)

28. What is the purpose of the text? (3점)
① to apply for the Boram Orchestra
② to report his work during this year
③ to introduce his club for a new member
④ to invite friends to his violin performance
⑤ to volunteer to help children in his community

[29~31] 다음 글을 읽고 물음에 답하시오.

Last summer, ⓐour club members participated in the "Change Our Neighborhood" project. ⓑOn the dirty old walls of the buildings in our neighborhood, ⓒwe painted birds flying high in the sky and dolphins jump over blue waves. (A)_____, ⓓthe old neighborhood changed into a bright and beautiful place. (가)이웃들은 우리의 작품을 보고 행복해했고 고마워했다. ⓔYou don't have to be a good painter. Anyone who likes to paint can join our club.

29. 위 글의 밑줄 친 부분 중 어법상 어색한 것은? (3점)
① ⓐ   ② ⓑ   ③ ⓒ   ④ ⓓ   ⑤ ⓔ

30. 위 글의 빈칸 (A)에 들어갈 말로 가장 알맞은 것은? (3점)
① As a result   ② As we told them
③ Carefully   ④ Uncomfortably
⑤ Quietly

31. 밑줄 친 (가)의 우리말과 의미가 같도록 <보기>의 단어들을 배열하여 영작하시오. (4점)

보기
thanked / our work / were / to / the neighbors / us / see / happy / and

조건
• 반드시 주어와 동사가 포함된 한 개의 문장을 쓰시오.
• 반드시 <보기>의 단어들을 모두 사용하시오.

→ _____

◎ 선택형 문항의 답안은 컴퓨터용 수정 싸인펜을 사용하여 OMR 답안지에 바르게 표기하시오.
◎ 서술형 문제는 답을 답안지에 반드시 검정 볼펜으로 쓰시오.
◎ 총 31문항 100점 만점입니다. 문항별 배점은 각 문항에 표시되어 있습니다.

[충남 ○○중]
1. 다음 문장의 빈칸에 적절한 것은? (2점)

• If you _____ the button, the bell will ring.

① rain
② meet
③ pull
④ push
⑤ help

[경기 ○○중]
2. 다음과 같이 명사형 접미사 '-ness'를 사용하여 형용사에서 파생된 명사를 4개 쓰시오. (3점)

kind → kindness

→ (1) _____ (2) _____
  (3) _____ (4) _____

[동작구 ○○중]
3. 주어진 문장 다음에 이어질 순서로 가장 적절한 것은? (3점)

Do you have any special plans for tomorrow?

(A) Don't worry. It won't rain on Jejudo tomorrow.
(B) I'm going to Jejudo in the morning. But I'm worried about the weather.
(C) Oh, that's good to hear.

① (C)-(A)-(B)
② (B)-(A)-(C)
③ (A)-(C)-(B)
④ (B)-(C)-(A)
⑤ (C)-(B)-(A)

[동작구 ○○중]
4. 다음 대화 중 의미상 어색한 것끼리 모아 놓은 것은? (3점)

ⓐ B: Jina, can you go into your house first?
   G: Why? What's wrong?
   B: I'm scared of your dog.
   G: Don't worry. He's a scary dog. He just looks scary because he's so big.
ⓑ G: Did you watch the movie, *The Daughter*?
   B: Yes, I saw them last Saturday.
   G: What did you think of it?
   B: I was disappointed. It wasn't very good.
ⓒ B: What do you think of our school cafeteria food?
   G: I think the cafeteria food is delicious.
   B: What do you think is the best item?
   G: I like the Gimbap the best.
ⓓ G: What do you think of this painting?
   B: They look great. I like the colors.
   G: I'm happy that you like it. I painted it myself.

① ⓐ, ⓑ, ⓓ
② ⓑ, ⓓ
③ ⓑ, ⓒ, ⓓ
④ ⓐ, ⓑ, ⓒ
⑤ ⓐ, ⓒ

[동작구 ○○중]
5. 다음 밑줄 친 (A)의 의도로 알맞은 것은? (3점)

A: (A)What do you think of our school cafeteria food?
G: I think the cafeteria food is fantastic.
B: What do you think is the best item?
G: I like the Gimbap the best.

① 의견 묻기
② 걱정하기
③ 충고하기
④ 안심시키기
⑤ 능력 여부 묻기

[6~7] 다음 대화를 읽고 물음에 답하시오.

G: ⓐI saw you with someone who looked like a foreigner yesterday.

B: Yes. We had lunch together.

G: You looked like you were having a good time.

B: ⓑWe were. We try to meet twice a month for lunch.

G: I wish I could feel more comfortable talking with a foreigner.

B: ⓒI was not worried about speaking in English before, but not anymore.

G: I get really nervous when I try to speak in English.

B: Well, the first time is the hardest. ⓓAfter that, it gets easier and easier.

G: ⓔWhat do you think about me join both of you for lunch?

B: That's a great idea.

*B: Jiho, G: Sujin

6. 위 대화의 밑줄 친 부분 중 어색한 것의 개수는? (3점)

① 1개 ② 2개 ③ 3개 ④ 4개 ⑤ 5개

7. 위 대화의 내용으로 알맞지 않은 것은? (3점)

① Sujin은 Jiho 그리고 그의 외국인 친구와 함께 점심을 먹으려고 한다.

② Jiho는 그의 외국인 친구와 함께 점심을 먹었었다.

③ Sujin은 지난주에 Jiho가 외국인으로 보이는 사람과 함께 있는 것을 보았다.

④ Sujin은 외국인과 좀 더 편하게 대화하기를 원한다.

⑤ Jiho는 Sujin에게 처음이 힘들다고 얘기해 주고 있다.

8. 다음 대화의 흐름상 빈칸에 들어갈 문장으로 알맞지 않은 것은? (3점)

A: What do you think of our school cafeteria food?

B: I think the cafeteria food is delicious.

A: What do you think is the best item?

B: _____

① I like Gimbap the best.

② I like Gimbap the most.

③ I suppose Gimbap is the worst.

④ I guess the best item is Gimbap.

⑤ My favorite food is Gimbap there.

9. Which is correct? (3점)

① If you finish your homework by three, you can go out.

② If it will be sunny tomorrow, Jim will go hiking.

③ Jin easily felt tired if she does not eat well.

④ You will get wet if you will go out now.

⑤ If I met Suji, I will give her this letter.

10. 다음 중 어법상 올바른 것은? (3점)

① I have just finish my homework.

② Jina has experienced a lot while traveling.

③ Judy have been at the bookstore for two hours.

④ Mr. Lee never has heard his son sing before.

⑤ I have knew Minho since he moved to our village.

[11~12] 다음 대화를 읽고 물음에 답하시오.

> G: @I saw you with someone which looked like a foreigner yesterday.
>
> B: Yes. We had lunch together.
>
> G: ⓑYou looked like you were having a good time.
>
> B: We were. We try to meet twice a month for lunch.
>
> G: ©I wish I could feel more comfortable talking with a foreigner.
>
> B: I was worried about speaking in English before, but not anymore.
>
> G: I get really nervous when I try to speak in English.
>
> B: Well, ⓓthe first time is the hardest. After that, it gets easier and easier.
>
> G: ⓔWhat do you think about me joining both of you for lunch?
>
> B: That's a great idea.
>
> G: Girl, B: Boy

11. 위 대화의 내용과 일치하면 T, 일치하지 않으면 F로 표시할 때 옳지 <u>않은</u> 것은? (3점)

① The boy wants to meet the foreigner twice a month for lunch. - (T)

② The boy was not worried about speaking in English at all in the past. - (F)

③ The girl wants to join the lunch with the boy and the foreigner. - (T)

④ The boy doesn't like the girl to join his meeting with a foreigner. - (T)

⑤ The girl wants to feel more comfortable while talking with a foreigner. - (T)

12. 위 대화의 @~ⓔ 중 어법상 옳지 <u>않은</u> 문장은? (3점)

① @　　② ⓑ　　③ ©　　④ ⓓ　　⑤ ⓔ

13. 다음 두 문장의 해석을 각각 쓰고 의미의 차이를 설명하시오. (5점)

> Ⓐ I lost my cat.
>
> Ⓑ I have lost my cat.

→ (1) Ⓐ의 해석: ＿＿＿＿＿＿＿＿＿＿＿＿

(2) Ⓑ의 해석: ＿＿＿＿＿＿＿＿＿＿＿＿

(3) 의미의 차이: ＿＿＿＿＿＿＿＿＿＿＿

14. 다음 중 어법상 올바른 문장은 몇 개인가? (3점)

> • You get wet if you go out now.
> • I have visited Busan three years ago.
> • If you are interested, please let us know.
> • The Second World War broke out in 1939.
> • I will always have remember to something.
> • There is a box filled with gold behind a tree.
> • I am teaching an eleven-years-old boy.

① 1개　② 2개　③ 3개　④ 4개　⑤ 5개

15. 다음 중 어법상 <u>어색한</u> 것은? (3점)

① If I meet Suji, I will give her this letter.

② If you have any problems, I will help you.

③ If it will be sunny tomorrow, Jim will go hiking.

④ If you push the button, the bell will ring.

⑤ If you don't get up now, you will be late for school.

[16~19] 다음 글을 읽고 물음에 답하시오.

> Two brothers went on a journey. They ⓐ found a rock in front of a forest.

(A) The younger brother ⓑreplied, "How can we know (가)if we don't try?" They separated, and they both went their own way.

(B) It said, "Go into the forest and swim across the river. There you will find a bear and ⓒtheir cubs. Take the bear cubs and run up the mountain. There you will find happiness."

(C) The younger brother said, "Let's go and find happiness together." "No," said the older brother, "How can we know this is true? What if the river ⓓis too wide? Besides, will it ⓔbe easy to take the cubs away from their mother? Instead of finding happiness, we can be killed!"

16. 주어진 글 다음에 이어질 글의 순서로 가장 적절한 것은? (3점)

① (A)-(B)-(C) ② (A)-(C)-(B)
③ (C)-(A)-(B) ④ (B)-(C)-(A)
⑤ (B)-(A)-(C)

17. 위 글의 밑줄 친 (가)if를 포함한 영어 문장을 만드시오. (4점)

조건
• 밑줄 친 (가)if와 의미 그리고 어법상 쓰임이 같도록 영어 문장을 만드시오.
• If로 시작하는 문장을 만드시오.
• 시험지에 있는 If가 포함된 문장을 그대로 쓰면 0점.

→ _____

18. 위 글을 읽고 답할 수 없는 질문은? (3점)

① Why didn't the older brother follow his younger brother?
② What did the two brothers find in front of a forest?
③ Why did the younger brother regret his choice?
④ What did the two brothers see on a rock?
⑤ Who went on a journey?

19. 위 글의 밑줄 친 부분 중 어법상 어색한 것은? (3점)

① ⓐ ② ⓑ ③ ⓒ ④ ⓓ ⑤ ⓔ

20. 다음 빈칸 (A), (B), (C)에 들어갈 알맞은 것끼리 짝지어진 것은? (3점)

> The younger brother said, "Let's go and find happiness together." "No," said the older brother, "How can we know this is true? (A)_____ if the river is too wide? Besides, will it be easy to take the cubs away from their mother? Instead of (B)_____ happiness, we can be killed!" The younger brother replied, "How can we know if we don't (C)_____?" They separated, and they both went their own way.

	(A)	(B)	(C)
①	What	to find	trying
②	How	find	trying
③	What	finding	try
④	How	to find	try
⑤	What	finding	trying

[21~24] 다음 글을 읽고 물음에 답하시오.

(A) The younger brother went into the forest and swam across the river. There were the bear. She was sleeping. He took her cubs and run up the mountain. (B)
When he reached the top, some people took him to their city and made him their king. (C) Then a war broke out, and he lost his throne. He was on the road again. (D)
One day, the two brothers met again and talk about their lives for the last five years. (E)
The older brother said, "I was right. I have lived quietly and well. You are once a king, but you have had a lot of trouble."

21. 위 글의 흐름으로 보아 주어진 문장이 들어가기에 가장 적절한 곳은? (3점)

There he lived as a king for five years.

① (A)　② (B)　③ (C)　④ (D)　⑤ (E)

22. 위 글에서 의미나 어법상 어색한 것의 개수는? (5점)

① 1개　② 2개　③ 3개　④ 4개　⑤ 5개

23. 위 글에 관한 내용으로 어색한 것은? (3점)

① 동생은 강을 헤엄쳐 건넜다.
② 동생은 전쟁으로 인해 왕좌를 잃었다.
③ 두 형제는 다시 만나 그동안의 삶에 대해서 얘기했다.
④ 형은 자신의 판단이 옳았다고 말했다.
⑤ 동생은 곰의 새끼들을 데리고 산을 뛰어 내려갔다.

24. 위 글을 읽고 주어진 질문에 알맞은 답을 쓰시오. (4점)

What happened to the younger brother when he reached the top?

<u>조건</u>
• 주어와 동사가 포함된 문장을 쓰시오.
• make, take를 동사로 사용해서 문장을 쓰시오.
• 필요시 make, take의 형태를 바꾸어 쓰시오.

→ _____

25. 다음 글에서 형이 걱정한 것이 아닌 것은? (4점)

Two brothers went on a journey. They found a rock in front of a forest. It said, "Go into the forest and swim across the river. There you will find a bear and her cubs. Take the bear cubs and run up the mountain. There you will find happiness."
The younger brother said, "Let's go and find happiness together." "No," said the older brother, "How can we know this is true? What if the river is too wide? Besides, will it be easy to take the cubs away from their mother? Instead of finding happiness, we can be killed!" The younger brother replied, "How can we know if we don't try?" They separated, and they both went their own way.
The younger brother went into the forest and swam across the river. There was the bear. She was sleeping. He took her cubs and ran up the mountain.
When he reached the top, some people took him to their city and made him their king. There he lived as a king for five years. Then a war broke out, and he lost his throne. He was on the road again.

① 새끼곰을 어미곰에게서 빼앗는 것이 쉽지 않을 것이다.
② 돌에 쓰인 내용이 거짓일 수 있다.
③ 행복을 찾기 전에 죽을 수 있다.
④ 동생이 행운을 찾을 수 있을 것이다.
⑤ 강이 너무 넓을지도 모른다.

[26~29] 다음 글을 읽고 물음에 답하시오.

The Two Brothers

Two brothers went (A)_____ a journey. They found a rock in front of a forest. It said, "Go into the forest and swim across the river. There you will find a bear and her cubs. Take the bear cubs and run up the mountain. There you will find happiness."
The younger brother said, "Let's go and find happiness together." "No," said the older brother, "How can we know this is true? (B)만약 강이 너무 넓으면 어떡하지? (C)게다가, will it be easy to take the cubs away from their mother? Instead of finding happiness, we can be killed!" The younger brother replied, "How can we know if we don't try?" They separated, and they both went (D)their own way.

26. 위 글의 빈칸 (A)에 들어갈 말로 가장 적절한 것은? (3점)

① to   ② from   ③ over

④ on   ⑤ in

27. 위 글의 밑줄 친 (B)의 뜻에 맞도록 〈보기〉의 단어를 순서대로 배열한 것은? (3점)

<보기>

if / what / is / wide / too / river / the

① If the river what wide is too?

② If what the river is too wide?

③ What is the river too wide if?

④ What if is the river too wide?

⑤ What if the river is too wide?

28. 위 글의 (C)에 들어갈 말을 한 단어로 쓰시오. (3점)

→ _____

29. 위 글의 밑줄 친 (D)를 참조하여 〈보기〉의 뜻에 맞도록 영작한 것은? (3점)

<보기>

그녀 자신의 집

① her house itself   ② the house herself

③ her house of   ④ her own house

⑤ her used house

[30~31] 다음 글을 읽고 물음에 답하시오.

One day, the two brothers met again and talked about their lives for the last five years. The older brother said, "I was right. I (A)live quietly and well. You were once a king, but you (B)have a lot of trouble." The younger brother answered, "I don't regret my choice. I may have nothing now, but I will always have something to remember."

30. 위 글의 (A), (B)에 들어갈 동사의 형태를 바르게 짝지은 것은? (4점)

	(A)	(B)
①	have live	have
②	have lived	have had
③	lives	had
④	was living	having
⑤	living	was having

31. 위 글의 밑줄 친 부분의 의미로 가장 적절한 것은? (3점)

① 나는 나의 선택을 후회한다.

② 나는 항상 추억할 것이 있다.

③ 나는 조용하게 사는 삶을 싫어한다.

④ 형의 말을 따랐다면 좋았을 것 같다.

⑤ 나에게는 지금 아무것도 남아 있지 않다.

◎ 선택형 문항의 답안은 컴퓨터용 수정 싸인펜을 사용하여 OMR 답안지에 바르게 표기하시오.
◎ 서술형 문제는 답을 답안지에 반드시 검정 볼펜으로 쓰시오.
◎ 총 27문항 100점 만점입니다. 문항별 배점은 각 문항에 표시되어 있습니다.

[동작구 ㅇㅇ중]

1. 다음 중 영영 풀이에 해당하는 단어로 알맞게 짝지어진 것은? (4점)

(A) do again and again to learn to do something well
(B) a small piece; a small amount

	(A)	(B)
①	join	pleasure
②	result	character
③	regret	noise
④	practice	bit
⑤	reply	wide

[울산 ㅇㅇ중]

2. 다음 빈칸에 공통으로 들어갈 말로 알맞은 것은? (3점)

- If you miss it, you'll _____ it.
- She is trying not to _____ what she did.

① contest
② concern
③ separate
④ regret
⑤ worry

[양천구 ㅇㅇ중]

3. 다음 짝지어진 대화 중 어색한 것은? (4점)

① A: What is your opinion of this painting?
　B: It looks great. I like the colors.

② A: I'm scared of your dog.
　B: He just looks scary but he is actually friendly.

③ A: I'm worried about your health.
　B: There's nothing to worry about.

④ A: I'm concerned about the weather.
　B: There will be no rain tomorrow, so don't worry.

⑤ A: What do you think of these sunglasses?
　B: It will be sunny tomorrow.

[양천구 ㅇㅇ중]

4. 다음 대화의 빈칸 (A)~(C)에 들어갈 낱말로 알맞은 것은? (4점)

A: (A)_____ you watch the movie, *The Daughter*?
B: Yes. I saw it last Saturday.
A: How did you (B)_____ about it?
B: I was (C)_____. It wasn't very good.

	(A)	(B)	(C)
①	Have	feel	disappointing
②	Have	think	disappointed
③	Did	feel	disappointing
④	Did	think	disappointing
⑤	Did	feel	disappointed

[경기 ㅇㅇ중]

5. Which is NOT good for the blank? (3점)

A: I am concerned about the speech contest.
B: _____
A: Thank you so much.

① Cheer up!
② It makes me uneasy.
③ Everything will be okay.
④ Don't worry. You'll do fine.
⑤ There's nothing to worry about.

[6~7] 다음 대화를 읽고 물음에 답하시오.

Sujin: (A)I saw you with someone that looked like a foreigner yesterday.

Jiho: Yes. We had lunch together.

Sujin: You looked like you were having a good time.

Jiho: (B)We were. We try to meet twice a month for lunch.

Sujin: (C)I wish I could feel more comfortable talking with a foreigner.

Jiho: (D)I was worried about speaking in English before, but anymore.

Sujin: I feel really nervous when I try to speak in English.

Jiho: (E)Well, the first time is the hardest. (F)After that, it gets easy and easier.

Sujin: What do you think about me joining both of you for lunch?

Jiho: That's a great idea.

6. 위 대화의 밑줄 친 (A)~(F) 중 어법상 어색한 것은?

(4점)

① (A), (C) 　　② (B), (C)
③ (D), (E) 　　④ (D), (F)
⑤ (E), (F)

7. 위 대화의 내용과 일치하지 <u>않는</u> 것은? (3점)

① Jiho was worried about speaking in English before.

② Sujin wants to join the lunch with Jiho and the foreigner.

③ Jiho tries to meet the foreigner twice a month for lunch.

④ Jiho was not worried about speaking in English at all in the past.

⑤ Sujin wishes she could feel more comfortable talking with a foreigner.

8. 다음 두 사람의 대화가 자연스럽도록 (A)~(D)를 바르게 배열한 것은? (4점)

(A) I like Gimbap the best.
(B) What do you think is the best item?
(C) I think the cafeteria food is delicious.
(D) What do you think of our school cafeteria?

① (B) - (A) - (C) - (D)
② (B) - (C) - (D) - (A)
③ (C) - (B) - (A) - (D)
④ (D) - (A) - (B) - (C)
⑤ (D) - (C) - (B) - (A)

9. 다음 대화의 빈칸 (A)에 들어갈 말로 가장 적절한 것은? (4점)

W: Jimin, you look worried. What's wrong?

G: Mom, I can't find the book that I borrowed from the library. Have you seen it?

W: What book are you looking for? *Jonathan Livingston Seagull*? I think I saw it in the living room.

G: Yes, that's it. Thank you, Mom.

W: By the way, (A)_____? What did you think of it?

G: I've read it two times already. It was really interesting. I loved the character of Jonathan a lot.

① have you read the books
② have you read the book
③ has he read the books
④ has you read the book
⑤ have I read the book

[10~11] 다음 대화를 읽고 물음에 답하시오.

Yuna: I saw you with a foreigner yesterday.
Siwon: Yes. We ate lunch together.
Yuna: You looked like you were having a good time.
Siwon: We were. We try to meet once a month for lunch.
Yuna: I wish I could feel (A)_____ talking with a foreigner.
Siwon: I was worried about speaking in English before, but not anymore.
Yuna: I get really nervous when I try to speak in English.
Siwon: Well, the first time is (B)_____. After that, it gets (C)_____.
Yuna: What do you think about me joining both of you for lunch?
Siwon: That's a great idea.

10. Which one is true? (4점)

① Yuna met a foreigner yesterday.

② Siwon and Yuna try to meet as often as possible.

③ Siwon gets nervous when he speaks with a stranger.

④ Yuna wants to join Siwon and his friend for lunch.

⑤ Yuna and Siwon are going to have lunch together next week.

11. 위 대화의 (A)~(C)에 알맞은 형태를 바르게 짝지은 것은? (4점)

        (A)   (B)   (C)

① more comfortable – harder – easier and easier

② more comfortable – the hardest – easier and easier

③ more comfortable – harder – easiest and easiest

④ less comfortable – harder – easiest and easiest

⑤ less comfortable – the hardest – easier and easier

12. 다음 주어진 문장과 현재완료의 쓰임이 같은 것은? (4점)

• I have lived well for the last five years.

① I have already had lunch.

② My friend has lost his cellphone.

③ Some of them have eaten Korean food before.

④ They have missed each other since they broke up.

⑤ I have been to the British Museum several times.

13. 다음 <보기>의 문장 중 빈칸에 since가 들어갈 문장을 모두 고르면? (3점)

보기
(A) I have _____ had lunch.
(B) I have lived in Paris _____ I was born.
(C) Judy has been in her friend's house _____ two hours.
(D) I have never seen Minho _____ he moved to a new neighborhood.

① (A), (B)   ② (A), (C)

③ (B), (C)   ④ (B), (D)

⑤ (C), (D)

[14~15] 다음 글을 읽고 물음에 답하시오.

Two brothers @went on a journey. They found a rock in front of a forest. It said, "Go into the forest and swim across the river. There you will find a bear and her cubs. Take the bear cubs and run up the mountain. There you will find happiness."
The younger brother said, "Let's go and find happiness together." "No," said the older brother, "How can we know this is true? ⓑWhat if the river is too wide? Besides, will it be easy to take the cubs away from their mother? ⓒInstead of find happiness, we can ⓓget killed!" The younger brother replied, "How can we know if we don't try?" They separated, and they both went their own way. The younger brother went into the forest and swam across the river. There was the bear. She ⓔwas sleeping. He took her cubs and ran up the mountain.

14. 위 글을 읽고 학생들이 자신의 생각을 발표한 것으로 옳지 않은 것은? (4점)

① Amy: The brothers had different opinions about the message on the rock.

② Jeff: The rock said the brothers could find happiness when they complete the mission.

③ Kate: I think the older brother was more cautious than the younger brother.

④ Danny: The older brother insisted that it would not be easy to take the cubs away from their mother.

⑤ Issac: The older brother seemed to love his brother since he wanted to go together.

15. Which is NOT correct? (3점)

① ⓐ ② ⓑ ③ ⓒ ④ ⓓ ⑤ ⓔ

[16~18] 다음 글을 읽고 물음에 답하시오.

(A)_____ the younger brother arrived at the top, some people took him to their city and (B)그들의 왕으로 만들었다. There he lived (A)_____ a king for five years. Then a war broke out, and he lost his throne. He was on the road again.
ⓐOne day, the two brothers met again and talked about their lives since the last five years. The older brother said, "I was right. ⓑI have lived quietly and well. You were once a king, ⓒbut you had have much trouble." The younger brother answered, "ⓓI don't regretted my choice. I may have nothing now, but ⓔI will always have something to remembering."

16. 위 글의 빈칸 (A)에 공통으로 들어갈 단어로 알맞은 것은? (대 · 소문자 무시) (4점)

① as ② if ③ when

④ what ⑤ because

17. 위 글의 밑줄 친 (B)를 바르게 영작한 것은? (3점)

① they made him his king

② they made him their king

③ they made them his king

④ he made them his king

⑤ he made them their king

18. 위 글의 밑줄 친 ⓐ~ⓔ 중 어법상 옳은 것은? (4점)

① ⓐ ② ⓑ ③ ⓒ ④ ⓓ ⑤ ⓔ

[19~21] 다음 글을 읽고 물음에 답하시오.

Two brothers went on a ⓐjourney. (A) They found a rock in front of a forest. It said, (B) "Go into the forest and swim across the river. (C) There you will find a bear and her ⓑcubs. (D) There you will find happiness." (E)

The younger brother said, "Let's go and find ⓒhappiness together." "No," said the older brother, "How can we know this is true? What if the river is too wide? ㉠[Beside / Besides], will it be easy to take the cubs away from their mother? Instead of finding happiness, someone can ㉡[kill us / be killed]!" The younger brother ⓓreplied, "How can we know ㉢[if / how] we do not try?" They ⓔseparated, and they both went their own way.

19. 위 글의 (A)~(E) 중 다음 문장이 들어갈 알맞은 곳은? (3점)

Take the bear cubs and run up the mountain.

① (A) ② (B) ③ (C) ④ (D) ⑤ (E)

20. 위 글의 ㉠, ㉡, ㉢ 괄호 안에서 문맥에 맞는 낱말로 적절한 것은? (4점)

	㉠	㉡	㉢
①	Beside	kill us	if
②	Beside	be killed	how
③	Besides	kill us	if
④	Besides	kill us	how
⑤	Besides	be killed	if

21. 위 글의 밑줄 친 ⓐ~ⓔ의 영영 풀이 중 적절하지 않은 것은? (4점)

① ⓐ: a trip from one place to another

② ⓑ: the young of a bear, lion or other mammals

③ ⓒ: the feeling of pleasure

④ ⓓ: to feel sadness or disappointment

⑤ ⓔ: to move apart

22. Which is the best order for the following? (3점)

When John reached the top, some people took him to their city.
ⓐ Then a war broke out.
ⓑ He lost his throne.
ⓒ They made him their king.
ⓓ There he lived as a king for five years.
He was on the road again.

① ⓐ-ⓑ-ⓒ-ⓓ ② ⓑ-ⓐ-ⓓ-ⓒ
③ ⓒ-ⓐ-ⓓ-ⓑ ④ ⓒ-ⓓ-ⓐ-ⓑ
⑤ ⓓ-ⓐ-ⓑ-ⓒ

23. 다음 글의 마지막 문장이 주는 교훈으로 가장 알맞은 것은? (4점)

One day, the two brothers met again and talked about their lives for the last five years. The older brother said, "I was right. My life was peaceful. You were once a king, but you have nothing now. Moreover, your life has been rough." The younger brother answered, "I don't regret my choice. I may have nothing now, but I will always have something to remember."

① No pain, no gain.

② Honesty is the best policy.

③ Blood is thicker than water.

④ A little knowledge is dangerous.

⑤ A friend in need is a friend indeed.

[24~26] 다음 글을 읽고 물음에 답하시오.

ⓐTwo brothers went on a journey. They found a rock in front of a forest. It said, "Go into the forest and swim across the river. There you will find a bear and her cubs. Take the bear cubs and run up the mountain. There you will find happiness."
The younger brother said, "ⓑLet's go and find happiness together." "No," said the older brother, "How can we know this is true? ⓒHow if the river is too wide? Besides, ⓓwill it be easy to take the cubs away from their mother? Instead of finding happiness, we can be killed!" The younger brother replied, "(A)만약 우리가 시도하지 않으면 어떻게 알 수 있어?" They separated, and they both went their own way. The younger brother went into the forest and swam across the river. There was the bear. She was sleeping. ⓔHe took her cubs and ran up the mountain.

24. 위 글의 밑줄 친 ⓐ~ⓔ 중 어법상 <u>어색한</u> 것은?

(4점)

① ⓐ   ② ⓑ   ③ ⓒ   ④ ⓓ   ⑤ ⓔ

25. 위 글을 읽고 알 수 있는 것만 있는 대로 고른 것은?

(4점)

a. One day, the two brothers met again.
b. Two brothers found a bear in front of a forest.
c. The younger brother went to the forest to achieve love.
d. Finding the bear, the older brother took the bear cubs and ran up the hill.
e. Two brothers had different opinions about what the rock said, so they went their own way.
f. The older brother thought that he could be killed instead of finding happiness.

① a, d, f   ② b, c, f   ③ b, d, e, f
④ c, d, f   ⑤ e, f

26. 위 글의 밑줄 친 (A)의 우리말을 참고하여 주어진 조건에 맞게 문장을 완성하시오.   (4점)

(A) "만약 우리가 시도하지 않으면 어떻게 알 수 있어?"
→ How can we know _____?

조건

• 조건문으로 완성할 것.
• How can we know 포함 총 8단어.

27. 다음 글의 밑줄 친 부분 중 어법상 <u>어색한</u> 것의 개수는?   (4점)

A Book Review
Title: *Jonathan Livingston Seagull*: a story
Writer: Richard Bach

This story is about a seagull named Jonathan Livingston. He ⓐdreamed of flying better than ⓑthe other. To reach his goal, he works hard and ⓒpractices to fly. I like this story because it ⓓhave helped me learn about the power of my own beliefs. The book says that I can do ⓔanything who I want if I do not give up.

① 1개   ② 2개   ③ 3개   ④ 4개   ⑤ 5개

2학년 영어 1학기 기말고사(5과) 1회

반		점수
이		
름		

문항수 : 선택형(23문항)   서술형(4문항)   20 . . .

◎ 선택형 문항의 답안은 컴퓨터용 수정 싸인펜을
 사용하여 OMR 답안지에 바르게 표기하시오.
◎ 서술형 문제는 답을 답안지에 반드시 검정
 볼펜으로 쓰시오.
◎ 총 27문항 100점 만점입니다. 문항별 배점
 은 각 문항에 표시되어 있습니다.

[동작구 ○○중]

1. Which of these words is NOT explained?   (4점)

- to put something out of sight
- a throw of the ball for the batter to hit it
- the test in which people try to win something by defeating others
- an athletic or sports ground used for playing and watching sports with rows of seats
- the sudden loud sound of something when it falls or bumps into itself or something else

① show   ② pitch   ③ crack
④ competition   ⑤ stadium

[전북 ○○중]

2. 다음 대화를 읽고 알 수 없는 것은?   (4점)

Mingyu: Jiheon, which sport do you like? Soccer or table tennis?
Jiheon: I love table tennis. How about you, Mingyu?
Mingyu: I like soccer. I'm a big fan of James Hood. He's a great soccer player.
Jiheon: Oh, really? There's a soccer match this weekend between Korea and Turkey. Have you heard about it?
Mingyu: Of course. I already have a ticket. I'm going to see the game on Saturday. I can't wait.
Jiheon: That's fantastic.

① Which sport does Jiheon like?
② Which sport does Mingyu like?
③ What will Jiheon do this weekend?
④ What will Mingyu do this weekend?
⑤ Who is Mingyu's favorite soccer player?

[동작구 ○○중]

3. 다음 중 밑줄 친 부분의 어법 또는 의미가 바르지 않은 것은?   (3점)

① The Second World War broke into in 1939. (발생했다)
② What if the room is too small? (~하면 어쩌지?)
③ He is at bat. (타석에 서서)
④ It might be hard to take his computer away from him. (빼앗다)
⑤ The dancers are coming out on the stage now. (나오는 중이다)

[양천구 ○○중]

4. 다음 대화의 내용과 일치하는 것은?   (3점)

Yura: I'm thinking about getting a pet. Do you have a pet?
Minu: Yes, I do. I have a dog and a cat.
Yura: What do you think? Which pet is better for me? A cat or a dog?
Minu: Why don't you come to my house someday and play with my pets? Then you can decide.

① Yura doesn't have a pet yet.
② Yura prefers a dog to a cat.
③ Minu wants to have a new pet.
④ They have played with their pets.
⑤ Yura came to Minu's house to adopt a pet.

[5~6] 다음 대화를 읽고 물음에 답하시오.

Alex: Jiho, why are you in such a hurry?

Jiho: Hi, Alex! I have to be home before 6:00. The game between the Thunders and the Cobras starts at 6:00

Alex: Oh, are you a baseball fan? Which team do you (A)_____? The Cobras or the Thunders?

Jiho: The Cobras.

Alex: Me, too! I don't want to miss the game, either.

Jiho: Hurry up! We only have thirty minutes left.

Alex: Okay. Maybe we can watch a game together sometime.

Jiho: That's a great idea! How about going to the next Cobras home game together?

Alex: Okay. They have a game next Saturday. We can eat fried chicken while watching the game!

Jiho: That sounds great. I can't wait!

5. Which is NOT true?　　　　　　　(4점)

① Alex should be home by six o'clock.

② Both Alex and Jiho are baseball fans.

③ It is 5:30 now.

④ Alex and Jiho are going to the baseball game next Saturday.

⑤ Jiho's favorite food is fried chicken.

6. Which is the best for the blank (A)?　　(3점)

① support　　② try　　③ lead

④ keep　　　⑤ practice

7. Which one is NOT used in the blank?　　(4점)

A: The batter with number 77 is my favorite player. He has _____ 21 home runs this year.

B: He is _____. The Thunders' fans look very _____.

A: Home run! Home run!

B: He will be the home run _____ this year!

① pitch　　　　　　② leader

③ hit　　　　　　　④ anxious

⑤ at bat

8. 다음 밑줄 친 부분을 어법상 바르게 고쳐 쓰시오.

(6점)

(A) The letters wrote by Jenny last night.

→ _____

(B) Where did your bag found yesterday?

→ _____

(C) Let's take a walk, won't you?

→ _____

9. 다음 주어진 문장을 수동태로 바르게 변형한 것은?

(3점)

• My mom made these cakes.

① These cakes is made by my mom.

② These cakes are made by my mom.

③ These cakes were made by my mom.

④ These cakes was maked by my mom.

⑤ These cakes were maked by my mom.

[10~12] 다음 대화를 읽고, 물음에 답하시오.

> Alex: Jiho, why are you in such a hurry?
>
> Jiho: Hi, Alex! I have to be home before 6:00. The game between the Thunders and the Cobras starts at 6:00.
>
> Alex: Oh, are you a baseball fan? (A)_____ _____ The Cobras or the Thunders?
>
> Jiho: The Cobras.
>
> Alex: Me, too! I don't want to miss the game either.
>
> Jiho: Hurry up! We only have thirty minutes left.
>
> Alex: Okay. Maybe we can watch a game together sometime.
>
> Jiho: That's a great idea! How about going to the next Cobras home game together?
>
> Alex: Okay. They have a game next Saturday. We can eat fried chicken while watching the game!
>
> Jiho: That sounds great. (B)너무 기다려져!

10. 위 대화의 (A)에 들어갈 알맞은 표현은? (4점)

① What time does the game start?

② Which team do you support?

③ Where is the baseball stadium?

④ Where can we watch the game?

⑤ What do you want to eat while watching TV?

11. 위 대화의 (B) 우리말을 영어로 알맞게 표현한 것은? (3점)

① I can wait!　　② I can't wait!

③ I can't tell!　　④ I can't help it!

⑤ I'm sorry but I can't!

12. 위 대화를 아래와 같이 바꿔 쓸 경우 빈칸에 들어갈 수 없는 것은? (3점)

> I met Jiho on the street. He was _____ home to watch the _____. He also _____ the Cobras like me! So we are going to watch the game together _____ and eat _____.

① supports　　② on the way

③ fried chicken　　④ next Saturday

⑤ basketball game

13. 다음 문장들의 부가의문문을 쓰시오. (8점)

> (1) Jenny is tired, _____?
> (2) You will go there, _____?
> (3) Let's take a walk, _____?
> (4) Wash your hands, _____?

→ (1) _____?

　(2) _____?

　(3) _____?

　(4) _____?

14. 다음 중 어법상 올바른 문장은? (3점)

① Where are you born?

② I was broken the window.

③ This school built 100 years ago.

④ Soccer is played in many countries.

⑤ How many languages are speaking in China?

[15~17] 다음 대화를 읽고 물음에 답하시오.

> Jian: Does the visiting team always wear a dark color?
>
> Jihun: Yes, that's the rule. Home teams have bright uniforms and visiting teams have dark uniforms.
>
> Jian: Why is that?
>
> Mom: There is an interesting story about that. ⓐIn the past, visiting teams could not wash their uniforms after every games. ⓑSo they started wearing dark colors hide the dirt.
>
> Jian: Hahaha! That was a good idea!
>
> *The players are warming up.*
>
> Jian: Who's your favorite player?
>
> Jihun: Number 77.
>
> Jian: What does the number mean?
>
> Jihun: Hmm.... ⓒPlayers choose a number which is they like.
>
> Dad: (A)_____ ⓓIn the past, the numbers determined by the players' batting order.
>
> Jihun: ⓔThat meants there were no players with number 77!

15. Which question CANNOT be answered? (4점)

① Why did visiting teams start wearing dark colors in the past?

② Which teams wear bright uniforms?

③ What is Jian's favorite player's number?

④ What determined the players' numbers in the past?

⑤ Was there a player with number 77 in the past?

16. Which one is proper for the blank (A)? (3점)

① No problem.　② How about you?

③ Is that all right?　④ You know what?

⑤ What do you think of that?

17. Which one is grammatically correct among ⓐ~ⓔ? (3점)

① ⓐ　② ⓑ　③ ⓒ　④ ⓓ　⑤ ⓔ

[18~19] 다음 글을 읽고 물음에 답하시오.

> Today my friend Sein and I are at the racing park.
>
> a. We are cheering for the driver in the red car.
> b. Now, the drivers are coming out onto the track.
> c. There are so many people at the park waiting to see the races.
> d. The drivers are moving their cars to the starting line.
> e. They are all in colorful uniforms.
>
> They are warming up their cars.
> The race (A)_____ _____ _____ start. (경기가 이제 막 시작되려고 한다.)

18. 위 글의 흐름에 맞게 자연스러운 글이 되도록 a~e를 바르게 배열한 것은? (3점)

① a-d-b-c-e　　② b-a-d-c-e

③ b-c-e-d-a　　④ c-b-e-a-d

⑤ c-e-d-a-b

19. 위 글의 빈칸 (A)에 들어갈 알맞은 말을 쓰시오.
(4점)

> • The race _____ _____ _____ start.

[20~22] 다음 글을 읽고 물음에 답하시오.

> Jian: Which team is the Thunders?
> Jihun: (A) Over there, behind third base. They are wearing dark gray uniforms ⓐ_____ they are the visiting team. (B)
> Jian: Does the visiting team always wear a dark color?
> Jihun: Yes, that's the rule. Home teams have bright uniforms and visiting teams have dark uniforms. (C)
> Jian: Why is that?
> Mom: (D) In the past, visiting teams could not wash their uniforms after every game. ⓑ_____ they started wearing dark colors to hide the dirt. (E)
> Jian: Hahaha! That was a good idea!
>
> The players are warming up.
>
> Jian: Who's your favorite player?
> Jihun: Number 77.
> Jian: What does the number mean?
> Jihun: Hmm.... Players choose a number they like.

20. 위 글의 (A)~(E) 중 다음 문장이 들어갈 가장 알맞은 곳은? (3점)

> There is an interesting story about that.

① (A) ② (B) ③ (C) ④ (D) ⑤ (E)

21. 위 글의 내용과 일치하지 <u>않는</u> 것은? (4점)

① the Thunders는 원정팀이다.
② 원정팀은 어두운 색의 유니폼을 입는다.
③ 과거에 어두운 색의 유니폼을 입은 이유는 더러움을 감추기 위함이었다.
④ 지훈이가 좋아하는 선수는 Number 77이다.
⑤ 선수의 번호는 선수가 직접 정할 수 없다.

22. 위 글의 빈칸 ⓐ, ⓑ에 들어갈 말로 알맞게 짝지어진 것은? (3점)

	ⓐ	ⓑ
①	because	So
②	because	But
③	however	So
④	however	But
⑤	because of	So

[23~24] 다음 글을 읽고 물음에 답하시오.

> Today my friend Sein and I are at the racing park. ⓐThere are so many people at the park waiting to see the race. Now, the drivers ⓑare coming out onto the track. They are all in (A)colorful uniforms. We ⓒare cheering for the drivers in the red car. The drivers are moving their cars to the starting line. They ⓓare warming up their cars. The race ⓔis about to start.

23. 위 글의 밑줄 친 부분의 해석이 <u>어색한</u> 것은? (4점)

① There are: ~ (들이) 있다
② are coming out: 나오고 있다
③ are cheering for: ~을 응원하고 있다
④ are warming up: 준비 운동을 하고 있다
⑤ is about to: ~에 관해서이다

24. 위 글의 밑줄 친 (A)와 단어의 변화형이 <u>다른</u> 것은? (3점)

① beauty ② care ③ hope
④ join ⑤ power

[25~26] 다음 글을 읽고 물음에 답하시오.

The players are warming up.

Jian: Who's your favorite player?

Jihun: Number 77.

Jian: What does the number mean?

Jihun: Hmm.... Players choose a number they like.

Dad: You know what? In the past, the numbers were determined by the players' batting order.

Jihun: That means there were no players with number 77!

Now, Jihun's favorite player ⓐis about to bat. Jihun ⓑlooks anxious.

Jian: Your favorite player is at bat.

Jihun: Yes. (A)그는 올해 이미 21개의 홈런을 쳤다. If he hits one more today, he will be the home run leader this season.

The batter ⓒmisses several balls. Now he was a ⓓfull count. He is waiting for the next pitch.

Jihun: HOME RUN! HOME RUN!

Crack!

The ball ⓔflies fast. It is going, going, going, gone!

25. 위 글의 밑줄 친 ⓐ~ⓔ 중 의미가 바르지 않은 것은?
(3점)

① ⓐ: 막 ~하려고 한다

② ⓑ: 불안해 보인다

③ ⓒ: 여러 개의 볼을 놓친다

④ ⓓ: 야구에서 스트라이크 1, 볼 4인 상태

⑤ ⓔ: 빠르게 날아간다

26. 위 글의 밑줄 친 (A)의 우리말 의미와 같도록 〈보기〉의 단어들을 배열하여 영작하시오.
(4점)

조건

• 〈보기〉의 단어들을 모두 사용하시오.

• 주어와 동사가 포함된 한 개의 문장으로 쓰시오.

• 필요시 어형을 바꾸시오.

보기

this / runs / he / 21 / hit / already / home / have / year

→ _____

27. 다음 글을 읽고 Abebe Bikila에 대해 답할 수 없는 질문은?
(4점)

Abebe Bikila

Born: August 7, 1932

Nationality: Ethiopia

He was known as a marathon winner at the Rome and Tokyo international sports competition. When he was preparing to run the marathon in Rome, he found out that his shoes did not fit well, so he decided to run the race without shoes. He felt pain during the race, but he finished the race as the winner. He was one of the greatest runners in the world, wasn't he?

① When is his birthday?

② Where did he run the marathon?

③ What did he feel when he ran the race without shoes?

④ What was wrong about his shoes?

⑤ What was his record when he finished the race as the winner?

2학년 영어 1학기 기말고사(5과) 2회

문항수 : 선택형(23문항) 서술형(3문항)

반 이 름

점수

20 . . .

◎ 선택형 문항의 답안은 김퓨터용 수정 싸인펜을 사용하여 OMR 답안지에 바르게 표기하시오.
◎ 서술형 문제는 답을 답안지에 반드시 검정 볼펜으로 쓰시오.
◎ 총 26문항 100점 만점입니다. 문항별 배점은 각 문항에 표시되어 있습니다.

[양천구 ㅇㅇ중]

1. 다음 영영 풀이에 해당하는 단어로 알맞은 것은? (4점)

the arrangement or disposition of people or things in a list from first to last.

① pitch   ② crack   ③ ticket
④ opinion   ⑤ order

[경기 ㅇㅇ중]

2. 다음 (1), (2)의 대화가 같은 의미를 가지도록 5 단어를 사용하여 빈칸을 완성하시오. (4점)

(1) A: Which sport do you like? Soccer or basketball?
    B: I like soccer more.
(2) A: Which sport do you prefer, soccer or basketball?
    B: _____.

→ _____.

[동작구 ㅇㅇ중]

3. 다음 대화를 읽고 답할 수 <u>없는</u> 질문은? (4점)

Mike: Chris, why are you in such a hurry?
Chris: Hi, Mike! I have to be home before 6:00. The game between the Thunders and the Cobras starts at 6:00.
Mike: Oh, are you a baseball fan? Which team do you support? The Cobras or the Thunders?
Chris: The Thunders.
Mike: Me, too. I don't want to miss the game, either.

Chris: Hurry up! We only have thirty minutes left.
Mike: Okay. Maybe we can watch a game together sometime.
Chris: That's a great idea! How about going to the next Thunders home game together?
Mike: Okay. They have a game next Saturday. We can eat fried chicken while watching the game!
Chris: That sounds great. I can't wait.

① Is Chris in such a hurry?
② How much time do the boys have before the game starts?
③ Which team does Mike support?
④ Which team won the game between the Thunders and the Cobras?
⑤ What are Mike and Chris going to do next Saturday?

[동작구 ㅇㅇ중]

4. 다음 밑줄 친 부분 중 바르게 쓰인 것은? (3점)

① The last <u>runner</u> is finally coming into the stadium.
② The <u>drive</u> is moving his car to the starting line.
③ My father is the <u>lead</u> of the bowling team.
④ Jay was the best <u>play</u> of the year in 2020.
⑤ <u>Happyness</u> is not something ready-made.

[양천구 ㅇㅇ중]

5. 다음 밑줄 친 부분 중 어법상 옳지 <u>않은</u> 것은? (4점)

① It is really delicious, <u>is it</u>?
② He doesn't eat fish, <u>does he</u>?
③ Jinsu is your brother, <u>isn't he</u>?
④ She walked her bag, <u>didn't she</u>?
⑤ Mike and Lisa are happy, <u>aren't they</u>?

[6~9] 다음 대화를 읽고 물음에 답하시오.

Jiyeon: Oh, I can't believe it's still Wednesday.

Yeongji: I know, I know. There isn't any holiday this week.

Jiyeon: You know what? I have a new bike. This gives me some energy.

Yeongji: Wow. When did you get it?

Jiyeon: Yesterday my father bought it for me. Do you want to see my new mountain bike?

Yeongji: Sure.

Jiyeon: Can you come to my house this afternoon?

Yeongji: Of course. Plus, don't forget that we're going rock climbing this weekend!

Jiyeon: Don't worry. I won't forget.

Yeongji: Anyway, did you hear about Solmi?

Jiyeon: What about her? (A)She lives in Canada,_____?

Yeongji: No, she came back to Korea last month. She wants to see you.

Jiyeon: Oh, I can't wait (B)_____ see her.

---

6. 위 대화에서 영지가 지연의 집으로 오기로 한 시간을 주어진 일정표에서 고르면? (4점)

	Wed	Thur	Fri	Sat	Sun
morning	ⓐ			ⓑ	
afternoon	ⓒ			ⓓ	
evening				ⓔ	

① ⓐ   ② ⓑ   ③ ⓒ   ④ ⓓ   ⑤ ⓔ

7. 위 대화의 내용과 일치하는 것은? (3점)

① 오늘은 금요일이다.

② 이번 주에는 쉬는 날이 많다.

③ 솔미는 지금 캐나다에 있다.

④ 솔미는 지난달에 한국에 돌아왔다.

⑤ 지연이는 지난주에 새 자전거를 샀다.

8. 위 대화의 밑줄 친 (A)의 주어와 동사에 주의하여 부가의문문을 만드시오. (4점)

→ _____

9. 위 대화의 빈칸 (B)에 들어갈 말로 가장 적절한 것은? (4점)

① to   ② on   ③ in

④ for   ⑤ from

10. Which dialogue is correct? (4점)

① A: Did you hear about Jisu?

   B: I'm excited about going there.

② A: Do you want to see my new mountain bike?

   B: Of course. I can't expect to see it.

③ A: When did you get a new mountain bike?

   B: Yesterday my father bought it for me. Can you come to my house this afternoon?

④ A: I'm going to Jejudo in the morning. But I'm worried about the weather.

   B: Don't worry. You'll do fine.

⑤ A: What do you think? Which pet is better for me? A cat or a dog?

   B: Why don't you come to my house someday and play with me?

[11～12] 다음 대화를 읽고 물음에 답하시오.

Alex: Jiho, why are you in such a hurry?

Jiho: Hi, Alex! I have to be home before 6:00. The game between the Thunders and the Cobras starts at 6:00.

Alex: Oh, are you a baseball fan? Which team do you support? The Cobras or the Thunders?

Jiho: The Cobras.

Alex: Me, too! I don't want to miss the game, (A)_____.

Jiho: Hurry up! We only have thirty minutes (B)_____.

Alex: Okay. Maybe we can watch a game together sometime.

Jiho: That's a great idea! How about going to the next Cobras home game together?

Alex: Okay. They have a game next Saturday. We can eat fried chicken while watching the game!

Jiho: That sounds great. I can't wait!

11. 위 대화의 빈칸 (A), (B)에 들어갈 낱말로 알맞은 것은? (4점)

	(A)	(B)
①	either	left
②	either	leaving
③	either	leave
④	neither	left
⑤	neither	to leave

12. 위 대화를 읽고 답을 찾을 수 없는 질문은? (4점)

① Why is Jiho in a hurry?

② Which team do they support?

③ What time is the dialog taking place?

④ Where does the Cobras have a home game?

⑤ When are they going to watch a game together?

13. 다음 〈보기〉의 빈칸과 똑같은 부가의문문이 필요한 문장은? (4점)

> **보기**
>
> • You forgot to bring your umbrella, _____?

① Mr. Park goes shopping every Sunday, _____?

② The teenagers will travel to Europe, _____?

③ Jenny wasn't at the party last night, _____?

④ You had a pen, _____?

⑤ Emily is tired, _____?

14. 다음 중 어법상 올바른 문장은? (4점)

① The house cleaned by Tim every Sunday.

② My uncle's house destroyed by the flood.

③ Where did your dog found yesterday?

④ Was the letter delivered by David?

⑤ These cookies made by my mom.

15. 다음 문장 중 어법상 어색한 것은? (4점)

① I don't like candies, either.

② James teaches math, doesn't he?

③ Was the letter written by Jane?

④ Where have you found the dog yesterday?

⑤ You can speak Japanese very well, can't you?

[16~19] 다음 글을 읽고, 물음에 답하시오.

[A]

Today the Thunders and the Cobras have a game. Jihun's family is at the baseball stadium.

Jihun: Jian, this is your first time to come to the baseball stadium, isn't it?

Jian: Yes. I'm so excited. I can't wait for the game to start.

Dad: Look, the players are coming out now!

Jian: Which team is the Thunders?

Jihun: Over there, behind third base. They are wearing dark gray uniforms because they are the visiting team.

Jian: Does the visiting team always wear a dark color?

Jihun: Yes, that's the rule. Home teams have bright uniforms and visiting teams have dark uniforms.

Jian: Why is that?

Mom: There is an interesting story about that. In the past, visiting teams could not wash their uniforms after every game. So they started wearing dark colors to hide the dirt.

Jian: Hahaha! That was a good idea!

[B]

The players are warming ⓐ_____.

Jian: Who's your favorite player?

Jihun: Number 77.

Jian: What does the number mean?

Jihun: Hmm... Players choose a number they like.

Dad: You know what? In the past, the numbers were determined ⓑ_____ the players' batting order.

Jihun: That means there were no players with number 77!

[C]

(A) Now, Jihun's favorite player is about to bat. Jihun looks anxious.

Jian: (B) Your favorite player is at bat.

Jihun: Yes. (C) If he hits one more today, he will be the home run leader this season. (D)

The batter misses several balls. Now he has a full count. He is waiting for the next pitch. (E)

Jihun: HOME RUN! HOME RUN!

Crack!

The ball flies fast. It is going, going, going, gone!

16. 위 글 [B]의 빈칸 ⓐ, ⓑ에 들어갈 단어가 알맞게 연결된 것은? (4점)

① up – by
② up – to
③ to – by
④ to – in
⑤ at – of

17. 위 글 [C]의 (A)~(E) 중 주어진 문장이 들어가기에 가장 적절한 곳은? (4점)

He has hit 21 home runs already this year.

① (A)　② (B)　③ (C)　④ (D)　⑤ (E)

18. 위 글 [A]~[C]를 읽고 내용이 맞으면 T, 틀리면 F에 표시하였다. 맞게 표시한 것을 고르면? (4점)

① The Thunders are wearing bright uniforms.
② Jian has visited the baseball stadium several times.
③ Jihun's favorite player's uniform number is 77.
④ In the past, players used to choose a number they liked.
⑤ Jihun looks anxious when his favorite player is about to bat.

① T　② T　③ F　④ F　⑤ F

19. 위 글 [A]~[C]를 읽고, 답을 찾을 수 없는 질문은?

(4점)

① What is Jihun's family doing?

② How many members are there in Jihun's family?

③ What color uniform are the Thunders wearing?

④ Why did the visiting team start wearing dark colors?

⑤ How many home runs have the Thunders' players hit?

20. 위 글의 내용과 일치하는 것은?

(4점)

① In the past, visiting teams could wash their uniforms after every game.

② This is Jihun's first time to come to the baseball stadium.

③ Thunders are wearing dark black uniforms.

④ Home teams wear bright uniforms.

⑤ Jian is very nervous now.

[충북 ○○중]

[20~21] 다음 글을 읽고, 물음에 답하시오.

Today the Thunders and the Cobras have a game. Jihun's family is at the baseball stadium.

Jihun: Jian, this is your first time to come to the baseball stadium, isn't it?

Jian: Yes, I'm so excited. I can't wait for the game to start.

Dad: Look, the players are coming out now!

Jian: Which team is the Thunders?

Jihun: Over there, behind third base. They are ⓐwear dark gray uniforms because they are the visiting team.

Jian: Does the visiting team always ⓑwear a dark color?

Jihun: Yes, that's the rule. Home teams have bright uniforms and visiting teams have dark uniforms.

Jian: Why is that?

Mom: There is an interesting story about that. In the past, visiting teams could not wash their uniforms after every game. So they started ⓒwear dark colors to hide the dirt.

Jian: Hahaha! That was a good idea!

21. 위 글의 밑줄 친 ⓐ, ⓑ, ⓒ에 wear의 형태를 바르게 짝지은 것은?

(4점)

	ⓐ	ⓑ	ⓒ
①	wear	wearing	wear
②	wear	wearing	wearing
③	wearing	wear	wearing
④	wearing	wear	wear
⑤	to wear	wear	to wear

[동작구 ○○중]

22. 다음 글의 빈칸 (A), (B)에 들어갈 말로 알맞은 것은?

(4점)

Seho is about to bat with a full count. He is waiting for the (A)_____. Yongmin is wearing a dark blue uniform and has 27 on his back. He is now on first (B)_____. Minu is about to throw the ball.

	(A)	(B)
①	pitch	back
②	pitcher	hit
③	catcher	base
④	base	back
⑤	pitch	base

[23~24] 다음 글을 읽고 물음에 답하시오.

The players ⓐare warming up.

Jian: Who's your favorite player?
Jihun: Number 77.
Jian: What does the number mean?
Jihun: Hmm... Players choose a number they like.
Dad: ⓑYou know what? In the past, the numbers (A)determine by the players' batting order.
Jihun: That means there were no players with number 77!

Now, Jihun's favorite player ⓒis about to bat. Jihun looks anxious.

Jian: Your favorite player is at bat.
Jihun: Yes. He has hit 21 home runs already this year. I hope that he hits one more today and becomes the home run leader this season.

The batter misses several balls. Now he has ⓓa full count. He is waiting for the next pitch.

Jihun: HOME RUN! HOME RUN!

Crack!
The ball flies fast. It is ⓔgoing, going, going, gone!

---

23. Which is NOT a correct meaning for ⓐ~ⓔ?
(3점)

① ⓐare warming up: 준비 운동을 하다

② ⓑYou know what?: 그거 알아?

③ ⓒis about to: ~에 대해서 준비하다

④ ⓓa full count: 스트라이크가 둘이고 볼이 셋

⑤ ⓔgoing, going, going, gone!: 가고, 가고, 가고, 사라졌다!

---

24. Which is the correct form of (A)? (4점)

① determined

② were determining

③ was determined

④ were determined

⑤ have been determined

[25~26] 다음 대화를 읽고 물음에 답하시오.

Jihun: Hmm... Players choose a number they like.
Dad: You know what? In the past, (A)the players' batting order determined the numbers.
Jihun: That means there were no players with number 77!
Now, Jihun's favorite player (B)막 배트를 휘두르려고 한다. Jihun looks anxious.
Jian: Your favorite player is at bat.
Jihun: Yes. He has hit 21 home runs already this year. If he hits one more today, he will be the home run leader this season.

---

25. 위 대화의 밑줄 친 (A)를 주어진 〈조건〉에 맞추어 바꾸어 쓰시오. (4점)

조건
• be동사+과거분사의 형태인 수동태 문장으로 바꾼다.
• 주어와 목적어를 적절한 위치로 옮겨 쓴다.

→ _____

26. 위 대화의 밑줄 친 (B)를 영작한 것으로 가장 적절한 것은? (3점)

① is full of bats

② is about to bat

③ is running the bat

④ is coming out to bat

⑤ is interested in batting

정답 및 해설

'your plans'로 복수이므로 are가 적절하다.

Lesson 1 (중간) **1회**

01 ⑤ 02 ② 03 ① 04 I am[I'm] sorry to hear
05 ① 06 ③ 07 ② 08 ③ 09 ③ 10 ⑤ 11 ①
12 ③ 13 ⑤
14 I am the shortest student in my class.
15 ④ 16 ②
17 We need to put a lot of effort into using less energy to save the earth.
18 ① 19 ③ 20 ③ 21 ④ 22 ①, ②
23 (2-1) I want to adopt a puppy.
　　(2-2) I was fascinated by this detective series last year.
24 ④ 25 ③ 26 ② 27 ②

01 national: 국가의
02 ②번에서 G가 'Sure. I can do that.'이라고 답하고 있으므로 'can'을 이용해서 묻는 질문이 적절하다.
　① You will. Don't worry.
　③ I hope I make a lot of new friends.
　④ What are you planning to do this weekend?
　⑤ That sounds great.
03 순서대로 favor, usually, amazing, once가 들어간다.
04 할머님이 편찮으시다고 했으므로 '유감'을 나타내는 'I am sorry to hear that.'이 적절하다.
05 밑줄 친 it은 바로 앞에서 언급한 'I hope I can soon watch them in Chinese and understand what they're saying.'을 의미한다.
06 'now I can introduce myself in Chinese'라고 했다.
07 (A)에서 Jack에게 부탁이 있다고 하자 (C)에서 무엇인지 묻고 (E)에서 자전거를 살 계획을 말하고 (D)에서 자전거를 고르는 걸 도와줄 수 있는지 묻자 (B)에서 좋다고 하는 순서가 적절하다.
08 월요일 저녁에 무얼 할지 묻자 한가하다고 답하는 ③번이 적절하다.
09 ⓐ had → have ⓑ words → word ⓓ will → did
10 'I hope I can soon watch them in Chinese and understand what they're saying.'이라고 했다.
11 (A) 동사가 필요한 자리이므로 understand (B) 주어가

12 ③은 명사적 용법이지만 나머지는 모두 부사적 용법의 목적이다.
13 모두 [tʃ] 발음인데 ⑤번은 [hédèik]로 'k' 발음이다.
14 최상급을 '부정주어+비교급 than'으로 쓸 수도 있다.
15 ⓓ beautiful의 최상급은 ⓓ the most beautiful이다.
16 'I'll put more effort into studying math to overcome my weakness.'라고 했다.
17 put effort into: 노력을 기울이다 a lot of: 많은. into의 목적어로 동명사 using을 쓰고 using의 목적어로 less energy를 쓴 후 부사적 용법의 목적을 이용하여 '지구를 구하기 위해'를 'to save the earth'를 쓴다.
18 ⓐ want의 목적어로 to부정사가 와야 하므로 go on ⓑ '~하는 법'에 해당하는 how to ⓒ overcome: 극복하다
19 by the end of: ~ 말 무렵에
20 (C) 다음에서 'I've been there before, but I want to experience the island more freely on my bike this time.'이라고 했으므로 (C)가 적절하다.
21 Jinsu의 weakest subject가 수학이라고 했으나 strongest subject는 언급하지 않았다.
22 ⓐ three things ⓑ share it
23 (2-1) 'Second, I want to adopt a puppy.'라고 했다.
　　(2-2) 'I was fascinated by this detective series last year.'라고 했다.
24 각각 ⓐ play ⓑ studying ⓒ willing ⓔ miss가 적절하다.
25 (A) freely의 비교급 more freely (B) beautiful의 최상급 the most beautiful (C) weak의 최상급으로 앞에 my가 있으므로 weakest만 쓴다.
26 'I want to adopt a puppy. I've always wanted a puppy.'라고 했다.
27 글의 마지막에 'make a bucket list and share it with your friends'라고 했으므로 친구들의 bucket list가 이어질 것으로 생각할 수 있다.

Lesson 1 (중간) **2회**

01 ① 02 ② 03 ②
04 She is the shortest girl in our class. 05 ③ 06 ⑤
07 (1) interested to → interested in
　　(2) what are they saying → what they are saying
08 ④ 09 ② 10 ① 11 ③

12 (1) I need to return a book by this weekend.
　　(2) It was the best moment in my life.
13 ④　**14** ③　**15** ①　**16** ③　**17** ⑤　**18** ③　**19** ⑤
20 ②　**21** ④
22 challenging **23** ⑤　**24** ③　**25** ⑤　**26** ④　**27** ②

01 각각 ① effort ② natural ③ willing to ④ national ⑤ by the end of가 들어가는 것이 적절하다.

02 ②번은 '나와 영화 보러 가는 게 어떠니?'라고 묻자 '좋다'고 답하는 자연스러운 대화이다.

03 'Are you planning to do anything special this weekend?'라고 했다.

04 형용사의 최상급은 보통 '-est'를 붙이고 앞에 the를 쓴다.

05 (A)에는 'be interested in', (B)에는 감정을 불러일으키는 경우 현재분사를 쓰므로 'amazing'이 적절하다.

06 바로 앞에서 언급한 'I hope I can soon watch them in Chinese and understand what they're saying.'을 의미한다.

07 (1) be interested in: ~에 관심[흥미]이 있다
　　(2) understand의 목적어로 쓰인 간접의문문으로 '의문사+주어+동사'의 어순이 적절하다.

08 ④: 형용사적 용법, <보기>와 나머지: 부사적 용법의 목적.

09 ②번은 다음 주 토요일 계획을 묻자 개를 산책시킬 것이라고 올바르게 답하고 있다.

10 밑줄 친 부분과 ③: 부사적 용법 ①: 형용사적 용법 ②, ④, ⑤: 명사적 용법

11 'I like Chinese drama a lot'이라고 했다.

12 (1) by this weekend: 이번 주말까지
　　(2) good의 최상급으로 the best를 쓴다.

13 'Finally'는 '마지막으로'라는 의미이고, (D) 다음부터 math에 대한 이야기가 나오기 시작하므로 (D)가 적절하다.

14 ⓒ는 최상급으로 the most beautiful이 되어야 한다.

15 접미사 'al'을 붙여 형용사로 만드는 단어들이다. 'economical'이 올바르다.

16 밑줄 친 right와 ③: 바로 ①: 옳은 ②: 권리 ④: 오른쪽의 ⑤: 오른쪽으로

17 마지막 목표는 약간 도전적이라고 한 후 주어진 문장에서 '셜록 홈스 이야기들을 모두 읽는 것'이라고 언급한 후 (E) 다음에 그 이유를 설명하는 것이 자연스럽다. 그러므로 (E)가 적절하다.

18 (B)에서 고양이 두 마리를 입양하고 (D)에서 하나를 잃어버려서 탐정에게 도움을 요청하고 (C)에서 그가 모든 노력을 다해서 (A)에서 마침내 찾는 순서가 적절하다.

19 가장 좋아하는 밴드의 공연을 무대 바로 앞에서 보고 싶다는 글에 이어 (C)에서 앞자리에 들어가기 위해 기꺼이 밤새 줄을 서서 기다릴 거라고 하고 (B)에서 강아지를 입양하고 싶다고 한 후 마지막 목표가 도전적이라고 언급하고 (A)에서 셜록 홈스 이야기들을 모두 읽고 싶다고 하는 순서가 적절하다.

20 ⓑ의 annoy는 '괴롭히다, 귀찮게[성가시게] 굴다, 속태우다'라는 뜻이므로 surprise나 다른 긍정적인 의미의 단어가 적절하다.

21 ①, ⑤ ~으로 ②, ③ 명사적 용법 ④ 부사적 용법(목적)

22 challenging: 도전적인

23 (A) be willing to: 기꺼이 ~하다
　　(B) most를 쓰려면 the가 앞에 있어야 한다.
　　(C) 결과를 이끄는 so가 적절하다.

24 밑줄 친 ⓐ와 ③: 부사적 용법의 목적 ①, ⑤: 형용사적 용법 ②, ④: 명사적 용법

25 'My last goal is a little more challenging.'이라고 했다.

26 ⓓ는 the most beautiful이 되어야 한다.

27 'I want to get a good grade in math.'라고 했을 뿐이다.

Lesson 2 (중간)
1회

01 ④　**02** ②　**03** ④　**04** ②　**05** ②　**06** ⑤　**07** ⑤
08 ④　**09** ③　**10** ①　**11** ⑤　**12** ⑤
13 (1) Do you need a pen to write with?
　　(2) He brought us some chairs to sit on.
14 ⑤　**15** ①　**16** increases
17 Another way is to lower your eyes instead of bending your neck.
18 ④　**19** ⑤　**20** ⑤　**21** ③　**22** ①　**23** ③　**24** ③
25 ②
26 ⓐ easy → easily ⓑ doing → to do
　　ⓒ make → makes ⓓ pay → paying
　　ⓔ intelligent → intelligently

01 순서대로 · easily · finally · quietly · usually가 들어간다.

02 뒤에서 'Yes. I dropped it on the way here.'라고 했으므로 떨어뜨렸는지를 묻는 ②번이 적절하다.

03 (A) What should I do? 또는 Can you give me some advice for me? (B) You should exercise every day. 또는 You should cut down on snakes.

04 ⓑ는 셔츠에 쓰여 있는 것을 묻자 '절대 포기하지 마'라고 쓰여 있다고 답하는 자연스러운 대화이다.

05 뒤에서 'I will.'이라고 했으므로 ②번이 적절하다.

06 'Try it first. Then, decide how often you should do it.'이라고 했다.

07 ⓒ에서 Henny네 집에서 자도 되는지 묻고 ⓐ에서 Henny 엄마가 괜찮다고 했는지 되묻고 ⓓ에서 그렇다고 답하자 ⓔ에서 알았다며 도착하면 문자하라고 하고 ⓑ에서 고맙다고 하는 순서가 적절하다.

08 'No Cellphone for 24 Hours'라고 했으므로 ⓓ는 with를 without으로 써야 한다.

09 'I plan to.'라고 답하고 있으므로 ③번이 적절하다. put up with: 참다, give it up: 포기하다, keep up with: 계속하다, clean it up: 치우다[청소하다], get rid of: 제거하다

10 ⓐ는 your shirt를 가리키고, 나머지는 'No Cellphone for 24 Hours.'를 가리킨다.

11 ⓐ ⓑ ⓒ: 사역동사 뒤에 목적격 보어로 동사원형이 제대로 쓰이고 있다. ⓓ, ⓔ help는 목적격 보어로 동사원형이나 to부정사가 올 수 있다.

12 ① to do → do ② taking → take ③ walked → walk ④ using → use

13 (1) 'to write with'가 뒤에서 'a pen'을 수식하도록 쓴다.
(2) 'to sit on'이 뒤에서 'some chairs'를 수식하도록 쓴다.

14 (C)에서 성민이가 스마트폰을 사용하는 데 많은 시간을 보낸다고 하면서 아침에 스마트폰을 사용하는 내용이 나온 후 (B)에서 오후와 저녁에 스마트폰을 사용하는 내용이 나오고 (A)에서 스마트폰을 너무 많이 사용하는 것이 건강 문제를 일으킬 수 있다는 언급으로 이어지는 것이 자연스럽다.

15 앞에서 스마트폰을 너무 많이 사용하는 것이 건강 문제를 일으킬 수 있다고 했으므로 조심하는 게 좋다고 언급하는 것이 적절하다.

16 increase: 증가시키다

17 또 다른 방법: another way
여러분의 목을 구부리는 대신에: instead of bending your neck
시선을 낮추는 것: to lower your eyes

18 ⓓ는 Sumi이고 나머지는 모두 Sejin이다.

19 ⓐ reading → read ⓑ make → makes
ⓒ most → least ⓓ blinks → blink

20 'blink your eyes often. This will keep your eyes from becoming dry.'라고 했다.

21 'Put the backs of your hands together with your arms out in front of you.'라고 했다.

22 (A) 서로 상반되는 내용이 이어지므로 However나 On the other hand (B) 결과에 해당하는 내용이 이어지므로 Therefore나 So가 적절하다.

23 ⓒ에서 makes의 목적격 보어로 to feel이 아니라 feel이 되어야 한다.

24 주어진 문장의 this가 (C) 앞 문장의 내용을 가리키므로 (C)가 적절하다.

25 '먼 곳에 있는 물체를 보면 눈이 더 건조해진다.'라는 언급은 없으며 'look at something at least 20 feet away'라고 했을 뿐이다.

26 ⓐ get을 수식하는 부사 easily ⓑ homework를 수식하는 부정사 to do ⓒ using이 주어이므로 makes ⓓ from의 목적어로 paying ⓔ use를 수식하는 부사 intelligently가 적절하다.

Lesson 2 (중간)

2회

> **01** ① **02** ③
> **03** You should set an alarm on your smartphone.
> **04** ⑤ **05** ⑤ **06** ④ **07** ① **08** ⑤ **09** without
> **10** ① **11** ③ **12** ⑤ **13** ① **14** ⑤ **15** ② **16** ②
> **17** ③ **18** ② **19** ①, ② **20** ③ **21** ① **22** ④
> **23** ⑤ **24** ① **25** ④ **26** ④ **27** ⑤ **28** bend

01 cause: ~을 야기하다

02 소녀가 Oh, your phone screen has a crack.이라고 했다.

03 'You should ~'를 이용하여 충고의 말을 쓴다.

04 어둠 속에서 읽지 말라고 했는데 알았다며 불을 끄겠다는 것은 어색하다.

05 영어 책을 안 가져와서 빌리고 있으므로 친구 사이라고 할 수 있다.

06 depend on: ~에 의지하다

07 'I'm planning on doing it once a month'라고 했다.

08 keep up with: ~을 계속하다

09 휴대폰 없이 지내는 것이므로 without이 적절하다.

10 'Just make sure you give it back when you're

done.'이 주어진 의미가 되도록 영작한 것이다. make sure: 반드시 (~하도록) 하다[(~을) 확실히 하다] give it back: 돌려주다

11 'What should I ~?'를 이용하여 충고를 구하고 있는데 '나는 그렇게 생각하지 않는다'라는 말은 어색하다.

12 ⑤번은 부사적 용법이고 나머지는 모두 형용사적 용법이다.

13 수진이는 문자를 하다가 나무에 부딪혀서 다쳤으므로 걸을 때 휴대폰 사용을 피해야 할 필요가 있다. avoid: 피하다

14 ⓐ off, ⓑ from, ⓒ to, ⓓ of, ⓔ as

15 (A) 함께 놀 친구이므로 with (B) 종이 위에 쓰는 것이므로 on이 적절하다.

16 스마트폰 사용자들을 위한 건강에 대한 조언을 한 글이다.

17 ⓒ는 keep your eyes from becoming dry가 되어야 한다.

18 2. 올바른 답이다. 1. (ㄱ)은 가주어로 'to read ~ time'을 가리킨다. 3. (ㄷ) 4. (ㄴ)

19 ⓐ deserted island가 맞음 ⓑ let의 목적격 보어로 swim이 적절하다.

20 ⓒ는 relax가 아니라 hurt가 적절하다.

21 (A) 스마트폰을 오래 사용하면 건강 문제를 일으킬 (cause) 수 있다. (B) 나쁜 자세를 향상시킬 조언 (advice)을 따를 필요가 있다.

22 ⓐ worse ⓑ from time to time ⓒ from becoming ⓔ is

23 'The best tip to prevent these health problems is to use your smartphone less.'라고 했을 뿐이다.

24 avoid: 피하다, 이것을 피하기 위해서: To avoid this

25 ⓑ makes ⓒ worse ⓓ reduce ⓔ less가 적절하다.

26 ⓓ uncomfortable로 쓰는 것이 적절하다.

27 'excited and enjoyed', 'beautiful', 'perfect place', 'best moments' 등에서 ⑤번을 유추할 수 있다.

28 '스마트폰을 볼 때, 여러분은 보통 목을 구부린다'

Lesson 3 (기말)

1회

01 ① 02 participating in 03 ① 04 ④ 05 ③
06 ② 07 ④ 08 I know how to make pizza.
09 ① 10 ③ 11 ① 12 ④
13 Pippi is stronger than the man who[that] has the biggest arms in town.
14 ④ 15 ② 16 ② 17 ① 18 ③ 19 ③
20 ③, ⑤ 21 ② 22 ⑤ 23 ② 24 ⑤ 25 ①
26 ⑤ 27 ③

01 get은 동사이므로 ful을 붙여서 형용사로 쓰이지 않는다.

02 of의 목적어로 동명사를 써야 한다. participate in: ~에 참가하다

03 배낭이 예쁘다며, 어디서 샀는지 묻고(A), 여동생이 만들어 줬다고 답하자(B), 훌륭한 디자이너라고 칭찬하자(C), 그렇다고 하며 옷 만드는 것도 즐긴다(D)는 순서가 자연스럽다.

04 새로운 동아리 회원을 인터뷰하고 있다.

05 participate in: ~에 참여하다

06 답으로 'I have no experience teaching others.'라고 했으므로 ②번이 적절하다.

07 Kate가 자원한 것은 아니다.

08 'I know' 다음에 '의문사+to부정사' 구문을 목적어로 쓴다.

09 채소를 기르고 요리를 할 수 있으므로 ①번이 적절하다.

10 앞에서 질문이 'We also volunteer to teach children. Do you enjoy teaching others?'이고 (A) 뒤에서 'But I enjoy working with people, so I'd like to try.'라고 이어지므로 ③번이 적절하다.

11 ①번은 자기 집으로 와서 애완동물들과 놀아 보라는 말에 그러고 싶다는 기대를 표현하고 있는 자연스러운 대화이다.

12 '의문사+to부정사' 구문을 이용하여 쓰면 'She knows how to sing this song.'이다.

13 Pippi is stronger than the man을 쓰고, 'the man'을 선행사로 하여 주격 관계대명사 who나 that을 쓰고 'has the biggest arms in town'으로 관계사절을 쓴다.

14 why to부정사는 사용하지 않는다.

15 각 동아리에 얼마나 많은 학생들이 있는지는 알 수 없다.

16 (가) 앞 내용의 결과가 이어지므로 As a result, (나) 처음의 상황을 말하고 있으므로 At first가 적절하다.

17 (A) False (B) False (C) False (D) False (E) True. 'You don't have to be a good painter.'라고 했다.

18 ⓒ은 목적을 나타내는 'to부정사의 부사적 용법'으로 ~하기 위해서'라고 해석한다.

19 participate: to take part in an activity or event with others

20 (A): how (B): if (D): Hearing him play

21 ⓐ a → an ⓒ can't → can ⓓ I → you ⓔ wait → waiting

22 'when I become a middle school student'라고 했다.

23 'By joining our club, you can have an opportunity to help others.'라고 했다.

24 ⓐ play[playing] ⓑ if ⓒ as ⓓ makes

25 (A) Participating이 주어이므로 is (B) leaders가 주어이므로 who (C) to와 say의 목적어가 필요하므로 what이 적절하다.

26 글의 마지막에 'Let's listen to what they say.'라고 했으므로 ⑤번이 적절하다.

27 얼마나 자주 자원봉사 일을 하는지는 알 수 없다.

Lesson 3 (기말)

01 ② **02** ④ **03** ① **04** ④ **05** ② **06** ② **07** ④
08 ① **09** ④ **10** ③ **11** ③
12 The girl who has three books is my sister.
13 ④ **14** ③
15 (A) who always wears big boots
　　 (B) who has the biggest arms
16 ④ **17** ② **18** ⑤ **19** ⑤ **20** ④ **21** ② **22** ⑤
23 guess　　**24** ⑤ **25** who were　**26** ⑤ **27** ②
28 ③ **29** ③ **30** ①
31 The neighbors were happy to see our work and thanked us.

01 동사 Be의 보어로 형용사 careful이 와야 한다.

02 <보기>는 동사에 '-er'을 붙여서 '~하는 사람'이라는 명사가 된 것으로 ⓐ, ⓑ, ⓓ가 이에 해당한다. cook은 요리사이고 cooker는 요리 기구를 뜻한다.

03 자신의 정원이 있고 야채를 키우고 요리까지 할 수 있다는 것으로 보아 'proud(자랑스러워하는)'가 적절하다.

04 G가 바이올린을 잘 연주할 수 있는지는 언급되지 않았다.

05 살이 좀 빠지게 조언 좀 해달라는 말에 패스트 푸드를 많이 먹으라는 것은 어색하다.

06 'Which sport do you like?'는 선호하는 것을 묻는 것이다.

07 주말에 무엇을 했는지 물었는데 걱정 말라며 잊지 않겠다고 답하는 것은 어색하다.

08 get better: 좋아지다, 나아지다

09 (D) 뒤에서 'I have no experience teaching others.'라고 했으므로 (D)가 적절하다.

10 ⓒ는 to teach가 적절하다.

11 Kate는 'I was a member of an orchestra when I was in elementary school.'이라고 했다.

12 the girl을 주어로 하고 주격 관계대명사 who나 that을 쓴 후 'has three books'로 관계사절을 쓰고 'is my

sister'로 마무리한다.

13 (A) a dog이 선행사이므로 which나 that, (B) the people이 선행사이므로 who나 that이 적절하다.

14 ① why to use → how to use
② where can put she → where she can put
④ stops → stop ⑤ doing → do

15 (A) a friend를 선행사로 하여 관계대명사 who나 that을 쓰고 'always wears big boots'를 관계절로 쓴다. (B) the man을 선행사로 하여 관계대명사 who나 that을 쓰고 'has the biggest arms'를 관계절로 쓴다.

16 The man who has the biggest arms is running.

17 (A) Anyone이 선행사이므로 who (B) 목적을 나타내는 to join (C) Hearing이 주어이므로 makes가 적절하다.

18 get better: 좋아지다

19 우리 동아리에 가입함으로써: By joining our club, 당신은 가질 수 있다: you can have, 다른 사람들을 도울 기회: an opportunity to help others

20 'You need to know how to play an instrument a little bit to join our club.'이라고 했다.

21 주어진 문장의 'As a result'로 (B) 앞 문장의 내용에 대한 결과를 말하고 있으므로 (B)가 적절하다.

22 'On the dirty old walls of the buildings in our neighborhood, we painted birds flying high in the sky and dolphins jumping over blue waves.'라고 했다.

23 '정확히 알지 못할 때 의견을 형성하다'는 'guess(추측하다)'이다.

24 ⓔ는 명사형 service가 되어야 한다.

25 '주격 관계대명사+be동사(were)'가 생략되어 있는 형태이다.

26 그가 악기를 연주할 때 어떻게 느끼는지는 알 수 없다.

27 주어진 문장의 'those students'가 (B) 앞에 나온 'a few students playing music at the gate'이므로 (B)가 적절하다.

28 글의 마지막에 'Come and join our club. We are waiting for you.'라고 하고 있으므로 ③번이 적절하다.

29 'flying'에 맞게 현재분사 'jumping'이 적절하다.

30 앞의 내용에 대한 결과가 이어지므로 ①번이 적절하다.

31 'to see'가 'happy'를 수식하도록 쓴다.

Lesson 4 (기말)

01 ④
02 (1) happiness (2) darkness (3) sadness
(4) loneliness
03 ② 04 ① 05 ① 06 ② 07 ③ 08 ③ 09 ①
10 ② 11 ④ 12 ①
13 (1) 나는 나의 고양이를 잃어버렸다.
(2) 나는 나의 고양이를 잃어버려서 지금도 못 찾고 있다.
(3) (1)은 잃어버린 고양이를 찾았는지 못 찾았는지 알
수 없지만, (2)는 아직 못 찾았다는 의미이다.
14 ③ 15 ③ 16 ④
17 If I study hard, I will pass the test.
18 ③ 19 ③ 20 ③ 21 ③ 22 ④ 23 ⑤
24 Some people took him to their city and made him
their king.
25 ④ 26 ④ 27 ⑤ 28 Besides 29 ④ 30 ②
31 ②

01 버튼을 누르면 벨이 울릴 것이다.
02 '형용사+~ness'로 명사를 만들 수 있다.
03 내일 특별한 계획이 있는지 묻자 (B)에서 제주도에 갈 건
데 날씨가 걱정이라고 하자 (A)에서 걱정하지 말라며 비
가 안 올 것이라고 하자 (C)에서 반가운 소리라고 하는 순
서가 자연스럽다.
04 ⓐ 개가 무섭다고 했는데 걱정하지 말라며 무서운 개라고
하고 있다. ⓑ I saw it이 되어야 한다. ⓓ They look을
It looks로 써야 한다.
05 'What do you think of ~?'는 '의견 묻기'에 쓰인다.
06 ⓒ was not → was ⓔ join → joining
07 'I saw you with someone who looked like a
foreigner yesterday.'라고 했다.
08 ③번은 김밥이 가장 나쁘다는 것이고 나머지는 모두 가장
좋다는 것이다.
09 ② will be → is ③ felt → feels ④ will go → go
⑤ met → meet
10 ① I have just finished my homework.
③ Judy has been at the bookstore for two hours.
④ Mr. Lee has never heard his son sing before.
⑤ I have known Minho since he moved to our
village.
11 G의 'What do you think about me joining both of
you for lunch?'라는 말에 B는 'That's a great idea.'
라고 했다.

12 ⓐ에서 someone이 주어이므로 관계대명사로 which가
아니라 who를 써야 한다.
13 과거 시제는 단순히 과거의 일만을 말하지만 현재완료는
과거의 일이 현재까지 미치는 영향을 의미한다.
14 순서대로 get → will get, I have visited → visited,
맞음, 맞음, remember to something → something
to remember, 맞음, eleven-years-old boy →
eleven-year-old boy
15 If it is sunny tomorrow, Jim will go hiking.
16 두 형제가 여정을 떠나고 (B)의 It이 주어진 글의 'a
rock'을 가리키므로 바로 다음에 이어지고, (A)의 'The
younger brother replied'에서 그 앞에 질문이 있었음
을 알 수 있고 그 질문이 (C)에 있으므로 (C) 다음에 (A)
가 이어진다. 그러므로 (B)-(C)-(A)의 순서가 적절하다.
17 밑줄 친 (가)의 if는 조건절을 이끄는 접속사로 '~한다면'
이라는 의미이다. 의미에 맞게 쓴다.
18 왜 동생이 그의 선택을 후회했는지는 언급되지 않았다.
19 앞에서 'a bear'라고 했으므로 ⓒ는 its가 되어야 한다.
20 (A) What if ~?: ~하면 어쩌지[어떻게 되지]? (B) of의
목적어로 동명사 finding, (C) 앞에 조동사 don't가 있으
므로 try가 적절하다.
21 주어진 문장의 There가 (C) 앞 문장의 'their city'를 가
리키므로 (C)가 적절하다.
22 There were → There was, run up → ran up,
talk about → talked about, are once → were once
23 'He took her cubs and ran up the mountain.'이라고
했다.
24 'When he reached the top, some people took him
to their city and made him their king.'이라고 했다.
25 '동생이 행운을 찾을 수 있을 것이다.'는 말은 나오지 않는
다.
26 go on a journey: 여행을 떠나다
27 What if ~?: ~하면 어쩌지[어떻게 되지]?
28 besides: 게다가, beside: ~의 곁[옆]에
29 one's own: 자기만의 ~
30 5년 동안의 삶에 대해 말하는 것이므로 현재완료형이 적절
하다. (A) have lived (B) have had
31 'but I will always have something to remember.'
라고 했다.

01 ④	02 ④	03 ⑤	04 ⑤	05 ②	06 ④	07 ④
08 ⑤	09 ②	10 ④	11 ②	12 ④	13 ④	14 ⑤
15 ③	16 ①	17 ②	18 ②	19 ④	20 ③	21 ④
22 ④	23 ①	24 ③	25 ⑤	26 if we don't try		
27 ⑤						

01 (A) '어떤 것을 잘하도록 배우기 위해 계속해서 하다'는 'practice(연습하다)'이다.
(B) '작은 조각, 작은 양'을 뜻하는 것은 'bit'이다.

02 • 놓치면 '후회할' 것이다.
• 한 것을 '후회하지' 않기 위해 노력한다.

03 선글라스가 어떤지 물었는데 내일 맑을 것이라는 답은 어색하다.

04 (A) watch로 보아 Did
(B) How did you feel ~?: 소감이 어땠어요?
(C) 주어가 감정을 느끼는 것이므로 disappointed가 적절하다.

05 걱정된다는 말에 '나를 불안하게 한다'라는 것은 어색하다.

06 (D) anymore → not anymore
(F) easy and easier → easier and easier

07 지호는 'I was worried about speaking in English before'라고 했다.

08 (D)에서 학교 식당 음식에 대해 어떻게 생각하는지 묻고 (C)에서 맛있다고 생각한다고 답하자 (B)에서 최고의 품목을 묻고 (A)에서 김밥이라고 답하는 순서가 자연스럽다.

09 책 한 권이므로 단수이고 주어가 you이므로 'Have you ~'로 현재완료 의문문을 쓴다.

10 Yuna가 'What do you think about me joining both of you for lunch?'라고 했다.

11 (A) 더 편하게 이야기하기를 바라므로 more comfortable
(B) 처음이 가장 힘들다는 것이 자연스러우므로 the hardest
(C) 비교급 and 비교급: 점점 더 ~한

12 주어진 문장과 ④: 계속 용법 ①: 완료 용법 ②: 결과 용법 ③, ⑤: 경험 용법

13 since는 보통 계속 용법에 자주 쓰인다. (A) never나 already 등 (B)와 (D) '~한 이래로'를 의미하며 절이 이어지므로 적절하다. (C) 숫자가 있는 기간이 나오므로 for가 적절하다.

14 'They separated, and they both went their own way'라고 했다.

15 ⓒ는 of의 목적어로 동명사 finding이 되어야 한다.

16 as는 접속사로 '~할 때'를 나타낼 수 있고, 전치사로 '~으로'를 나타낼 수도 있다.

17 '주어+make+목적어+목적격 보어'의 5형식 문형으로 쓴다.

18 ⓐ since → for
ⓒ had have → have had
ⓓ regretted → regret
ⓔ remembering → remember

19 주어진 문장의 the bear cubs가 (D) 앞의 her cubs이므로 (D)가 가장 적절하다.

20 ㉠ besides: 게다가, beside: ~의 곁[옆]에 ㉡ someone이 주어이므로 kill us, ㉢ '~하지 않는다면'이라는 뜻이 자연스러우므로 if가 적절하다.

21 reply: to say, write, or do something as an answer or response

22 어떤 사람들이 그를 도시로 데려가고 ⓒ에서 그들이 그를 왕으로 삼고 ⓓ에서 거기서 5년간 왕으로 살고 ⓐ에서 전쟁이 일어나고, 다시 길바닥에 나앉는 순서가 적절하다.

23 'I may have nothing now'이 'pain'에 해당한다면 'but I will always have something to remember'는 'gain'에 해당한다.

24 ⓒ What if ~?: ~하면 어쩌지[어떻게 되지]?

25 a. 두 형제가 다시 만났는지는 알 수 없다. b. 강 건너편에 곰이 있었다. c. 행복을 찾기 위해 갔다. d. 동생이 새끼들을 데리고 산을 뛰어 올라갔다.

26 '만약 ~하지 않으면'을 'If+주어+don't ~'로 나타내고 '우리가 시도하다'를 'we try'로 쓴다.

27 ⓐ dreamed → dreams ⓑ the other→ others
ⓒ to fly → flying ⓓ have → has
ⓔ anything who → anything that

01 ①	02 ③	03 ①	04 ①	05 ⑤	06 ①	07 ①

08 (A) were written (B) was (C) shall we **09** ③

10 ② **11** ② **12** ⑤

13 (1) isn't she? (2) won't you? (3) shall we?
(4) will[won't] you?

14 ④ **15** ④ **16** ④ **17** ⑤ **18** ④ **19** is about to

20 ④ **21** ⑤ **22** ① **23** ⑤ **24** ④ **25** ④

26 He has already hit 21 home runs this year.

27 ⑤

01 순서대로 hide, pitch, competition, stadium, crack 이다.

02 Jiheon이 이번 주말에 무엇을 할지는 알 수 없다.

03 break out: 발생하다 break into: 침입하다

04 Yura는 'I'm thinking about getting a pet.'라고 했다.

05 Jiho의 좋아하는 음식은 언급되지 않았다.

06 어느 팀을 응원하는지 묻는 'support'가 적절하다.

07 순서대로 hit, at bat, anxious, leader가 들어간다.

08 (A) The letters가 주어이므로 수동태로 써야 한다.
(B) your bag이 주어이므로 수동태로 써야 한다.
(C) 'Let's'로 시작하는 문장의 부가의문은 'shall we?'이다.

09 능동태의 목적어를 수동태의 주어로 쓰고 동사를 'be+과거분사'로 바꾼 후 주어를 'by+목적격'으로 바꿔 쓴다.

10 뒤에 나오는 'The Cobras or the Thunders?'로 보아 어느 팀을 응원하는지 묻는 ②번이 적절하다.

11 I can't wait!: 너무 기다려져!

12 순서대로 on the way, baseball game, supports, next Saturday, fried chicken이 들어간다.

13 부가의문문은 긍정이면 부정으로 쓰고 부정이면 긍정으로 쓴다. 또 주어는 인칭대명사로 쓰며 be동사나 조동사가 있으면 be동사나 조동사를 이용하여 축약형으로 써야 한다.

14 ① are → were ② was broken → broke
③ built → was built ⑤ speaking → spoken

15 Jian이 가장 좋아하는 선수의 번호는 알 수 없다.

16 You know what?: 그거 알아?

17 ⓐ every game ⓑ to hide ⓒ is 삭제
ⓓ were determined

18 c에서 많은 사람들이 있고 b에서 이제 운전사들이 나오고 e에서 그들이 다채로운 유니폼을 입고 있다고 한 후 a에서 빨간색 차의 운전사를 응원하고 d에서 운전사들이 출발선으로 차를 옮겨가는 순서가 적절하다.

19 is about to: 막 ~하려고 하다

20 Jian이 'Why is that?'이라고 묻자 (D) 앞에서 주어진 문장의 that을 언급하며 (D) 다음부터 설명하고 있으므로 (D)가 적절하다.

21 'Players choose a number they like.'라고 했다.

22 ⓐ 이유가 나오며 절이 이어지므로 because ⓑ 앞의 내용의 결과가 이어지므로 So가 적절하다.

23 is about to: 막 ~하려고 하다

24 명사 color에 ful을 붙인 것이다. ① beautiful ② careful ③ hopeful ⑤ powerful ④ join은 동사로 ful

25 ⓓ: 야구에서 스트라이크 2, 볼 3인 상태

26 he가 주어이므로 have를 has로 바꾸고 현재완료형으로 쓴다.

27 우승자로서 경주를 마쳤을 때 그의 기록은 알 수 없다.

Lesson 5 (기말)

> **01** ⑤ **02** I prefer soccer to basketball. **03** ④
> **04** ① **05** ① **06** ③ **07** ④ **08** dosen't she?
> **09** ① **10** ③ **11** ① **12** ④ **13** ④ **14** ① **15** ④
> **16** ① **17** ③ **18** ④ **19** ⑤ **20** ④ **21** ③ **22** ⑤
> **23** ③ **24** ④
> **25** The numbers were determined by the players' batting order.
> **26** ②

01 '처음부터 마지막까지 목록에 있는 사람들이나 물건들의 배열이나 배치'를 가리키는 말은 'order(순서)'이다.

02 'like soccer more'를 선호한다는 prefer를 써서 'prefer soccer to'로 쓸 수 있다.

03 어느 팀이 이겼는지는 알 수 없다.

04 ② driver ③ leader ④ player ⑤ Happiness

05 부가의문문에서는 반드시 축약형을 써야 한다. isn't it? 이 맞다.

06 오늘은 수요일인데 오늘 오후에 올 수 있는지 물었으므로 ⓒ가 적절하다.

07 'she came back to Korea last month.'라고 했다.

08 She가 주어이고 lives라는 일반동사의 현재형이 쓰였으므로 does를 이용하여 'dosen't she?'라고 쓴다.

09 can't wait to 동사원형: 너무 ~하고 싶다

10 새 산악 자전거를 언제 샀는지 묻자 어제 아빠가 사주셨다며 오후에 집으로 올 수 있는지 묻고 있다.

11 (A) 'don't'가 있으므로 either, (B) have 동사가 쓰였고 남겨진 시간이므로 left가 적절하다.

12 the Cobras가 홈경기를 어디에서 하는지는 알 수 없다.

13 <보기>와 ④: didn't you ① doesn't he ② won't they ③ was she ⑤ isn't she

14 ① cleaned → was cleaned
② destroyed → was destroyed ③ did → was
⑤ made → were made

15 ④ Where did you find the dog yesterday?

16 ⓐ warm up: (스포츠나 활동 전에) 몸을 천천히 풀다[준

비 운동을 하다] ⓑ 수동태의 행위자를 나타내는 by가 적절하다.

17 주어진 문장의 He가 (C) 앞에서 Jian이 말한 Your favorite player이므로 (C)에 들어가는 것이 적절하다.

18 ① F ② F ③ T ⑤ T

19 Thunders 선수들이 몇 개의 홈런을 쳤는지는 알 수 없다.

20 'Home teams have bright uniforms and visiting teams have dark uniforms.'라고 했다.

21 ⓐ 현재진행형이므로 wearing, ⓑ 의문문에서 Does가 앞에 있으므로 동사원형 wear, ⓒ started의 목적어로 동명사 wearing이 적절하다.

22 Yongmin이가 1루에 있고 Minu가 풀카운트에서 공을 던지려고 하고 있다. (A) pitch: 투구 (B) base: [야구] 베이스, 누(壘)

23 is about to: 막 ~하려고 하다

24 the numbers가 주어이므로 수동태로 were determined 가 적절하다.

25 목적어를 주어로 하고 동사를 'be+과거분사'로 바꾼 후 주어를 'by+목적격'으로 쓴다.

26 is about to(막 ~하려고 하다)를 이용한다.

MEMO

MEMO